T0166803

Langenscheidt
Universal Dictionary

Italian

Italian – English
English – Italian

Langenscheidt

Based on Langenscheidt's Pocket Dictionary Italian
compiled by LEXUS

1. Auflage 2017 (1,02 - 2021)
© PONS GmbH, Stöckachstraße 11, 70190 Stuttgart 2017
All Rights Reserved.

www.langenscheidt.com

Print: Druckerei C. H. Beck, Nördlingen
Printed in Germany

ISBN 978-3-12-514037-0

Contents
Indice

Abbreviations / Abbreviazioni........................ 4

Pronuncia delle parole inglesi 8

Italian pronunciation................................. 11

Italian – English / Italiano – Inglese 13

English – Italian / Inglese – Italiano 281

Verbi irregolari inglesi 633

Numbers / Numerali 637

Abbreviations / Abbreviazioni

vedi	☞	see
marchio registrato	®	registered trademark
aggettivo	*adj*	adjective
avverbio	*adv*	adverb
aggettivo	*agg*	adjective
agricoltura	AGR	agriculture
inglese americano	*Am*	American English
anatomia	ANAT	anatomy
architettura	ARCHI	architecture
articolo	*art*	article
astronomia	AST	astronomy
astrologia	ASTR	astrology
uso attributivo	*attr*	attributive usage
automobilismo	AUTO	motoring
aviazione	AVIA	civil aviation
avverbio	*avv*	adverb
biologia	BIO	biology
botanica	BOT	botany
inglese britannico	*Br*	British English
chimica	CHEM	chemistry
chimica	CHIM	chemistry
commercio	COM	commerce, business
informatica	COMPUT	computers, IT term
congiunzione	*cong*	conjunction
congiunzione	*conj*	conjunction
diritto	DIR	law
eccetera	*ecc*	et cetera
educazione	EDU	education

elettricità, elettronica	EL	electricity, electronics
elettricità, elettronica	ELEC	electricity, electronics
specialmente	*esp*	especially
eccetera	*etc*	et cetera
eufemismo	*euph*	euphemistic
familiare	**F**	familiar, colloquial
femminile	*f*	feminine
sostantivo femminile e aggettivo	*f/agg*	feminine noun and adjective
ferrovia	FERR	railways
figurato	*fig*	figurative
finanze	FIN	financial
fisica	FIS	physics
uso formale	*fml*	formal usage
fotografia	FOT	photography
femminile plurale	*fpl*	feminine plural
femminile singolare	*fsg*	feminine singular
gastronomia	GASTR	cooking
generalmente	*gen*	generally
geografia	GEOG	geography
geologia	GEOL	geology
grammatica	GRAM	grammatical
informatica	INFOR	IT term
interiezione	*int*	interjection
invariabile	*inv*	invariable
diritto	LAW	law
maschile	*m*	masculine
sostantivo maschile e aggettivo	*m/agg*	masculine noun and adjective
marineria, navigazione	MAR	nautical

matematica	MAT	mathematics
matematica	MATH	mathematics
medicina	MED	medicine
maschile e femminile	*m/f*	masculine and feminine
militare	MIL	military
mineralogia	MIN	mineralogy
automobilismo	MOT	motoring
maschile plurale	*mpl*	masculine plural
maschile singolare	*msg*	masculine singular
musica	MUS	music
sostantivo	*n*	noun
marineria, navigazione	NAUT	nautical
sostantivo plurale	*npl*	plural noun
sostantivo singolare	*nsg*	singular noun
sé, se stesso	o.s.	oneself
popolare	P	popular, slang
spregiativo	*pej*	pejorative
fotografia	PHOT	photography
fisica	PHYS	physics
pittura	PITT	painting
plurale	*pl*	plural
politica	POL	politics
participio passato	*pp*	past participle
preposizione	*prep*	preposition
pronome	*pron*	pronoun
preposizione	*prp*	preposition
psicologia	PSI	psychology
psicologia	PSYCH	psychology
qualcosa	qc	something

qualcuno	qu	someone
radio	RAD	radio
ferrovia	RAIL	railways
religione	REL	religion
sci	SCI	skiing
singolare	*sg*	singular
qualcuno	s.o.	someone
sport	SP	sports
uso spiritoso	*spir*	humorous
uso spregiativo	*spreg*	pejorative
qualcosa	sth	something
congiuntivo	*subj*	subjunctive
teatro	TEA	theatre
tecnica	TEC	technology
tecnica	TECH	technology
telecomunicazioni	TELEC	telecommunications
teatro	THEA	theatre
tipografia	TIP	typography, typesetting
televisione	TV	television
università	UNIV	university
volgare	V	vulgar
verbo ausiliario	*v/aus*	auxiliary verb
verbo ausiliario	*v/aux*	auxiliary verb
verbo intransitivo	*v/i*	intransitive verb
verbo transitivo	*v/t*	transitive verb
zoologia	ZO	zoology

Pronuncia delle parole inglesi

Vocali e dittonghi

[ɑː]	*a* molto lunga, più che in *mare*: *far* [fɑː(r)]
[ʌ]	simile alla seconda *a* in *mamma* non accentata: *mother* ['mʌðə(r)]
[æ]	simile alla prima *a* in *mamma*: *man* [mæn]
[ɛə]	dittongo composto da una *e* molto aperta e lunga e da [ə]: *care* [kɛə(r)]
[aɪ]	dittongo composto da [a] e [ɪ]: *time* [taɪm]
[aʊ]	dittongo composto da [a] e [ʊ]: *cloud* [klaʊd]
[e]	*e* aperta e breve, più che in *bello*: *get* [get]
[eɪ]	dittongo composto da una *e* lunga, seguita da un leggero suono di *i*: *name* [neɪm]
[ə]	suono atono simile alla *e* nell'articolo francese *le*: *about* [ə'baʊt]
[ɜː]	forma più prolungata del suono anteriore: *bird* [bɜːd]
[ɪ]	suono molto breve tra la *i* di *fitto* e la *e* di *fetta*: *city* ['sɪtɪ]
[iː]	*i* molto lunga, più che in *vino*: *tea* [tiː]
[ɪə]	dittongo composto da [ɪ] e [ə]: *here* [hɪə(r)]
[ɒ]	simile alla *o* di *lotta*: *not* [nɒt]
[ɔː]	*o* aperta e lunga, più che in *noto*: *ball* [bɔːl]
[ɔɪ]	dittongo composto da [ɔ] e [ɪ]: *boy* [bɔɪ]
[əʊ]	dittongo composto da una *o* lunga, seguita da un leggero suono di *u*: *boat* [bəʊt]
[ʊ]	suono molto breve tra la *u* di *tutto* e la *o* di *rotto*: *book* [bʊk]

[uː]   *u* lunga, più che in *fiume*: *fruit* [fruːt]

[ʊə]   dittongo composto da [ʊ] e [ə]: *sure* [ʃʊə(r)]

Consonanti

*Le consonanti si pronunciano nella maggior parte dei casi
quasi come in italiano. Le doppie si pronunciano come se
fossero semplici.*

[b]   come la *b* in *burro*: *bag* [bæg]

[d]   come la *d* in *dare*: *dear* [dɪə(r)]

[f]   come la *f* in *forte*: *coffee* ['kɒfɪ]

[g]   come la *g* in *gatto*: *give* [gɪv]

[h]   suono aspirato simile a quello della *c* di *casa* dei
fiorentini: *head* [hed]

[j]   come la *i* in *ieri*: *yes* [jes], *use* [juːz]

[k]   ome la *c* in *casa*: *come* [kʌm]

[l]   come la *l* in *lungo*: *land* [lænd]

[m]   come la *m* i *madre*: *summer* ['sʌmə(r)]

[n]   come la *n* in *no*: *night* [naɪt]

[p]   come la *p* in *pane*: *top* [tɒp]

[r]   una *r* gutturale che si pronuncia soltanto
quando precede una vocale: *right* [raɪt], *carol*
['kærəl]

[s]   *s* aspra come in *sono*: *cycle* ['saɪkl], *sun* [sʌn]

[t]   come la *t* in *torre*: *take* [teɪk]

[v]   come la *v* in *valore*: *vain* [veɪn]

[w]   come la *u* in *uomo*: *wait* [weɪt], *quaint*
[kweɪnt]

[z]   *s* dolce come in *rosa*: *rose* [rəʊz]

[ŋ]   come la *n* in *banca*: *bring* [brɪŋ]

[ʃ] come *sce* in *scena*: *she* [ʃiː]

[tʃ] come *ce* in *cento*: *chair* [tʃeə(r)], *rich* [rɪtʃ]

[dʒ] come *ge* in *gente*: *join* [dʒɔɪn], *range* [reɪndʒ]

[ʒ] non esiste in italiano, simile alla *j* francese in *je*: *leisure* ['leʒə(r)], *usual* ['juːʒʊəl]

[θ] lingua tra i denti: *think* [θɪŋk]

[ð] lingua dietro l'arcata superiore dei denti: *the* [ðə], *lather* ['lɑːðə(r)]

' il segno dell'accento viene sempre collocato prima della sillaba accentata, es. *ability* [ə'bɪlətɪ]

Italian pronunciation

Vowels

a	mare	as in father but shorter
e	bello	as in bed
	neve	like the *e* sound in they
i	vino	as in machine
o	lotta	as in pot
	nome	like the *o* sound in blow
u	fiume	as *oo* in cool but shorter

Consonants

b, d, f, l, m, n, p, t and **v** are pronounced as in English.
When a word has double consonants, each consonant is
pronounced separately: contat-to.

c	certo	before *e* and *i* as in ch in church
	canto	before *a, o, u* (almost) as in cake
ch	chiamare	before *e* and *i* to make *c* hard as in cat
g	gelo	before *e* and *i* as in general
	gatto	before *a, o, u* as in gate
gh	laghi	before *e* and *i* to make *g* hard as in got
gl	biglietto	like English *lli* in million
gn	ogni	like English *ni* in onion
h	hanno	not pronounced
r	rotto	with the tongue against the upper teeth
s	sole	unvoiced as in case
	rosa	voiced as in cheese
sc	uscire	before *e* and *i* like *sh* in ship
z	prezzo	unvoiced as *ts* in hats
	mezzo	voiced as *ds* in maids
j, k, w,		these letters do not belong to the
x, y		Italian alphabet and are found only in
		foreign words

Italian-English
Italiano-Inglese

A

A (= *autostrada*) M (= motorway), *Am* I (= interstate)

a ◇ *stato in luogo* at; ~ *Roma* in Rome; ~ *casa* at home ◇ *moto a luogo* to; **andare** ~ *Roma* go to Rome ◇ *tempo*: **alle quattro** at four o'clock; ~ *Natale* at Christmas; ~ *maggio* in May; ~ *vent'anni* at the age of twenty; ~ *due* ~ *due* two at a time ◇ *modo*: ~ **piedi** on foot ◇ *mezzo*: **ricamato** ~ **mano** embroidered by hand ◇ *prezzo, misura*: ~ **che prezzo** at what price; **al metro** by the metre; **100 km all'ora** 100 km an hour

abate *m* abbot

abbacchio *m* GASTR young lamb

abbagliante 1 *agg* dazzling **2** *m gen pl* **-i** AUTO full beam; **abbagliare** dazzle

abbaiare bark

abbandonare abandon; **abbandono** *m* abandon; (*rinuncia*) abandonment

abbassare lower; *radio* turn down; **abbassarsi** (*chinarsi*) bend down; *di prezzo* come down; *fig* ~ **a** stoop to; **ab-**basso: ~ *la scuola!* down with school!

abbastanza enough; (*alquanto*) quite

abbattere knock down; *casa* demolish; *albero* cut down; *aereo* shoot down; *fig* dishearten; **abbattersi** fall; *fig* become disheartened; **abbattuto** disheartened

abbazia *f* abbey

abbellire embellish

abbi, abbia ☞ *avere*

abbigliamento *m* clothing; ~ **sportivo** sportswear

abbinare match; (*combinare*) combine

abboccare *di pesce* bite; *fig* swallow the bait

abbonamento *m a giornale,* TEA subscription; *a treno, bus* season ticket; **abbonare** take out a subscription for; (*condonare*) deduct; **abbonarsi** subscribe; **abbonato** *m* subscriber; TELEC **elenco** *m degli* **-i** telephone directory, phone book

abbondante abundant; *porzione* generous; *vestito* loose; *nevicata* heavy

abbordabile *persona* approachable; *prezzo* reasonable; **abbordare 1** *v/t persona* approach; F *persona dell'altro sesso* chat up F, Am come on to; *argomento* tackle **2** *v/t* MAR board

abbottonare button up

abbozzo *m* sketch

abbracciare embrace, hug; *fig* take up; **abbracciarsi** embrace, hug; **abbraccio** *m* embrace, hug; **un ~** *a fine lettera* love

abbreviare abbreviate; **abbreviazione** *f* abbreviation

abbronzante *m* sun-tan lotion; **lettino** *m* ~ sunbed; **abbronzare** *pelle* tan; **abbronzarsi** get a tan; **abbronzato** tanned; **abbronzatura** *f* tan

abbrustolire roast

abbuffarsi stuff o.s. (**di** with)

abdicare abdicate

abete *m* fir

abile good (**in** at); fit (**a** for); **abilità** *f inv* ability

abilitazione *f* qualification

abisso *m* abyss

abitacolo *m* AUTO passenger compartment

abitante *m/f* inhabitant; **abitare 1** *v/t* live in **2** *v/i* live; **abitato 1** *agg* inhabited **2** *m* built-up area; **abitazione** *f* house

abiti *mpl* clothes; **abito** *m* dress; *da uomo* suit; **~ da sera** evening dress

abituale usual; **abituarsi ~ a**

get used to; **abitudinario 1** *agg* of fixed habits **2** *m* creature of habit; **abitudine** *f* habit

abolire abolish; **abolizione** *f* abolition

abominevole abominable

aborigeno *m/agg* aboriginal

abortire MED miscarry; *volontariamente* have an abortion; *fig* fail; **aborto** *m* MED miscarriage; *provocato* abortion

abrogare repeal

abusare: ~ di abuse; (*approfittare*) take advantage of; **~ nel bere** drink to excess; **abusivo** illegal; **abuso** *m* abuse

a.C. (= *avanti Cristo*) BC (= before Christ)

accademia *f* academy; **~ di belle arti** art college; **accademico** academic

accadere happen; **accaduto** *m*: **raccontami l'~** tell me what happened

accaldato overheated

accampamento *m* camp; **accampare 1** *v/t*: **~ scuse** come up with excuses **2** *v/i e* **accamparsi** camp

accanimento *m* (*tenacia*) tenacity; (*furia*) rage; **accanirsi** (*ostinarsi*) persist; **~ contro qu** rage against s.o.; **accanito** *odio* fierce; *fumatore* inveterate

accanto 1 *prp* **~ a** next to **2** *avv* near, nearby; **abitare** next door

accantonare put aside

accappatoio m bathrobe; *da mare* beachrobe

accarezzare caress; *speranza* cherish; *animale* stroke

accasciarsi flop down

accattone m beggar

accavallare cross; **accavallarsi** fig overlap

accecare 1 v/t blind **2** v/i be blinding

accedere: ~ *a* enter

accelerare speed up; AUTO accelerate; **acceleratore** m AUTO accelerator, Am gas pedal; **accelerazione** f acceleration

accendere light; RAD, TV turn on; **accendersi** light up; *apparecchio* come on; **accendino** m, **accendisigari** m inv (cigarette) lighter

accennare indicate; *con parole* mention; ~ *a fare qc* show signs of doing sth; **accenno** m (cenno) gesture; (indizio) sign; (allusione) hint

accensione f ignition

accento m accent; **accentuare** accentuate

accertare check; **accertarsi**: ~ *di qc* check sth

acceso colore bright; *motore* running; *TV, luce* on

accessibile accessible; *prezzo* reasonable; **accesso** m access; fig e MED fit; **divieto d'** ~ no entry

accessori mpl accessories; **accessoriato** AUTO complete with accessories

accetta f axe, Am ax

accettabile acceptable; **accettare** accept; **accettazione** f acceptance; *di albergo* reception; ~ **bagagli** check-in

acchiappare catch

acciaio m steel; ~ **inossidabile** stainless steel

accidentale accidental

accidentato terreno rough

accidenti F damn! F; *di sorpresa* wow!

accigliato frowning

accingersi: ~ *a fare qc* be about to do sth

acciottolato m cobbles

acciuffare grab

acciuga f anchovy

acclimatarsi get acclimatized

accludere enclose; **accluso** enclosed; *qui* ~ enclosed

accogliente welcoming; **accogliere** welcome; *richiesta* grant

accollarsi take on

accollato abito high-necked

accoltellare knife

accolto pp ☞ **accogliere**

accomodante accommodating; **accomodare** (*riparare*) mend; *lite* resolve; **accomodarsi** make o.s. at home; *si accomodi!* come in!; (*sedersi*) have a seat!

accompagnare accompany; **accompagnatore** m, **-trice** f escort; MUS accompanist

acconciatura f hairdo

acconsentire consent (*a* to)

accontentare satisfy; **accontentarsi** be happy (*di* with)

acconto *m* deposit

accorciare shorten; **accorciarsi** get shorter

accordare grant; MUS tune; (*armonizzare*) harmonize; **accordarsi** agree; *di colori* match; **accordo** *m* agreement; (*armonia*) harmony; MUS chord; **essere d'~** agree; **mettersi d'~** reach an agreement; **d'~!** OK!

accorgersi: ~ *di* notice

accorrere hurry; ~ *in aiuto di qu* rush to help s.o.

accortezza *f* forethought

accorto 1 *pp* ↗ **accorgersi 2** *agg* shrewd

accostare approach; *porta* leave ajar; **accostarsi** get close

accreditare confirm; FIN credit; **accredito** *m* credit

accrescere increase; **accrescersi** grow bigger

accudire 1 *v/t* look after **2** *v/i*: ~ *a qc* attend to sth

accumulare accumulate; **accumulatore** *m* battery

accuratezza *f* care; **accurato** careful

accusa *f* accusation; DIR charge; **accusare** accuse; DIR charge; **accusato** *m*, **-a** *f* accused

acerbo unripe

acero *m* maple

aceto *m* vinegar

acetone *m* nail varnish remover

ACI *m* (= *Automobile Club d'Italia*) Automobile Club of Italy

acidità *f* acidity; ~ *di stomaco* heartburn; **acido 1** *agg* acid; *fig* sour **2** *m* acid

acne *f* acne

acqua *f* water; ~ *minerale* mineral water; ~ *potabile* drinking water; ~ *di rubinetto* tap water; ~ *ossigenata* hydrogen peroxide; **-e** *pl* **territoriali** territorial waters; *fig* **in cattive -e** in deep water

acquaforte *f* etching

acquaio *m* sink

acquario *m* aquarium; ASTR **Acquario** Aquarius

acquascivolo *m* water slide

acquatico aquatic

acquavite *f* brandy

acquazzone *m* downpour

acquedotto *m* aqueduct

acqueo: *vapore m* ~ water vapour *o Am* vapor

acquerello *m* watercolour, *Am* watercolor

acquirente *m/f* purchaser; **acquisizione** *f* acquisition; **acquistare 1** *v/t* buy; *fig* gain **2** *v/i* improve; **acquisto** *m* purchase

acquolina *f*: *mi viene l'~ in bocca* my mouth's watering

acre sour; *voce* harsh

acrilico acrylic

acrobata *m/f* acrobat

adrenalina

acustica f acoustics; **acusti-co** acoustic

acuto 1 agg intense; *nota, dolore* sharp; *suono, voce* shrill; MED acute **2** m MUS high note

ad ☞ **a** (before vowels)

adagiarsi lie down; **adagio 1** avv slowly; *con cautela* cautiously **2** m MUS adagio

adattamento m adaptation; (*rielaborazione*) reworking; **adattare** adapt; **adattarsi** (*adeguarsi*) adapt (**a** to); (*adirsi*) be suitable (**a** for); **adattatore** m adaptor; **adat-to** right (**a** for)

addebitare FIN ~ **qc a qu** debit s.o. with sth; fig ascribe sth to s.o.; **addebito** m FIN debit; **nota f di** ~ debit note

addensarsi thicken

addestramento m training; **addestrare** train

addetto 1 agg assigned (**a** to) **2** m, -a f person responsible; **vietato l'ingresso ai non** ~ authorized personnel only

addio 1 int goodbye **2** m goodbye, farewell

addirittura (*assolutamente*) absolutely; (*perfino*) even

additivo m additive; **addizionare** add; **addizione** f addition

addobbare decorate; **addob-bo** m decoration

addolcire sweeten; fig soften

addolorare grieve

addome m abdomen

addomesticare tame

addominale abdominal

addormentarsi fall asleep; **addormentato** asleep; (*assonnato*) sleepy

addossare (*appoggiare*) lean (**a** on); fig colpa put, lay (**a** on); **addossarsi** lean (**a** on); fig shoulder; **addosso 1** prp on; *vicino* next to **2** avv: **avere** ~ **vestiti** have on; **avere** ~ **qu** have s.o. breathing down one's neck

adeguarsi conform; **adegua-to** adequate

adempiere: ~ **a** dovere carry out, do

aderente 1 agg vestito tight **2** m/f follower; **aderire**: ~ **a** adhere to; *partito* support; *richiesta* agree to; **adesione** f adhesion; (*consenso*) agreement; **adesivo 1** agg adhesive **2** m sticker

adesso now; **da** ~ **in poi** from now on; **fino a** ~ up to now; **per** ~ for the moment

adiacente adjacent; ~ **a** next to, adjacent to

adirato angry

adolescente m/f adolescent, teenager; **adolescenza** f adolescence, teens

adoperare use

adorare adore

adottare adopt; **adottivo** *genitori* adoptive; *figlio* adopted; **adozione** f adoption

adrenalina f adrenalin

adriatico Adriatic; *mare m* **Adriatico** Adriatic Sea

adulare flatter

adulterio *m* adultery; **adulto 1** *agg* adult 2 *m*, **-a** *f* adult

adunare assemble

aereo air; **aereo 1** *agg* air *attr*, *fotografia* aerial; *compagnia f* **-a** airline; *posta f* **-a** airmail **2** *m* plane

aerobica *f* aerobics *sg*

aerodinamico aerodynamic

aeronautica *f*: **~ militare** Air Force

aeroplano *m* plane, aeroplane, *Am* airplane

aeroporto *m* airport

aerosol *m inv contenitore* aerosol; MED inhaler

aerostazione *f* air terminal

afa *f* closeness, mugginess

affabile affable

affaccendarsi busy o.s. (*in* with); **affaccendato** busy

affacciarsi appear

affamato starving

affannato breathless; **affanno** *m* breathlessness; *fig* anxiety

affare *m* matter, business; FIN transaction; **-i** *pl* business; *non sono* **-i tuoi** it's none of your business; *uomo m d'* **-i** businessman

affascinante fascinating; **affascinare** fascinate

affaticarsi tire o.s. out

affatto completely; *non ...* **~** not ... at all

affermare state; **affermarsi** become established; **affermazione** *f* assertion; (*successo*) achievement

afferrare seize, grab; (*comprendere*) grasp; **afferrarsi** cling (*a* to)

affettare (*tagliare*) slice

affettato¹ *m* sliced meat

affettato² *agg* affected

affetto *m* affection; **affettuoso** affectionate; **affezionarsi**: **~ a qu** become fond of s.o.; **affezionato**: **~ a qu** fond of s.o.

affibbiare: **~ qc a qu** saddle s.o. with sth

affidabilità *f* dependability; **affidamento** *m* trust; *fare* **~ su** rely on; **affidare** entrust; **affidarsi**: **~ a** rely on

affiggere *avviso* put up

affilare sharpen; *fig* make thinner; **affilato** sharp; *naso* thin

affiliato *m*, **-a** *f* member

affinché so that

affine similar

affinità *f inv* affinity

affiorare *dall'acqua* emerge; *fig* (*mostrarsi*) appear

affissione *f* bill-posting; **affisso 1** *pp* ☞ **affiggere 2** *m* bill

affittacamere *m/f* landlord; *donna* landlady; **affittare** rent; **affittasi** to rent; **affitto** *m* rent; *dare in* **~** rent (out); *prendere in* **~** rent

affliggere distress; *di malattia* trouble, plague; **afflitto** distressed

affluente *m* tributary; **affluenza** *f fig* influx

affogare drown

affollare, affollarsi crowd; **affollato** crowded

affondare sink

affrancare free; *posta* frank; **affrancatura** *f* franking; (*tassa di spedizione*) postage

affresco *m* fresco

affrettarsi hurry

affrontare face, confront; *spese* meet

affumicare *stanza* fill with smoke; *alimenti* smoke; **affumicato** smoked

afoso sultry

Africa *f* Africa; **africano 1** *agg* African **2** *m*, -**a** *f* African

afroamericano 1 *agg* African-American **2** *m*, -**a** *f* African-American

afrodisiaco *m/agg* aphrodisiac

agenda *f* diary

agente *m/f* agent; ~ **immobiliare** estate agent, *Am* realtor; ~ **di pubblica sicurezza** police officer

agenzia *f* agency; ~ **di cambio** bureau de change; ~ **immobiliare** estate agency, *Am* real estate office,; ~ **di viaggi** travel agency

agevolare make easier; **agevolazione** *f* FIN special term

agganciare hook; *cintura, collana* fasten

aggeggio *m* gadget

aggettivo *m* adjective

agghiacciante spine-chilling

aggiornamento *m* updating; (*rinvio*) postponement; **corso m d'~** refresher course; **aggiornare** (*mettere al corrente*) update; (*rinviare*) postpone; **aggiornarsi** keep up to date

aggirare surround; *fig ostacolo* get around

aggirarsi hang around; FIN be in the region of

aggiudicare award; *all'asta* knock down

aggiungere add; **aggiunta** *f* addition

aggiustare (*riparare*) repair; (*sistemare*) settle

agglomerato *m*: ~ **urbano** built-up area

aggrapparsi cling, hold on (**a** to)

aggravare *punizione* increase; (*peggiorare*) make worse; **aggravarsi** worsen, deteriorate

aggraziato graceful

aggredire attack; **aggressione** *f* aggression; (*attacco*) attack; **aggressività** *f* aggressiveness; **aggressivo** aggressive; **aggressore** *m* attacker; MIL aggressor

agguato *m* ambush

agguerrito hardened

agiato comfortable, well-off; (*comodo*) comfortable

agibile fit for human habitation

agile agile; **agilità** *f* agility; *fig* liveliness

agio *m* ease; **sentirsi a proprio ~** feel at ease

agire act; *di medicina* take effect

agitare shake; *fazzoletto* wave; *fig (turbare)* upset, agitate; **agitato** agitated; *mare* rough; **agitazione** *f* agitation

agli = *a* and *art* **gli**

aglio *m* garlic

agnello *m* lamb

agnolotti *mpl* type of ravioli

ago *m* needle

agonia *f* agony

agonistico competitive

agopuntura *f* acupuncture

agorafobia *f* agoraphobia

agosto *m* August

agricolo agricultural; **agricoltore** *m* farmer; **agricoltura** *f* agriculture

agrifoglio *m* holly

agriturismo *m* farm holidays

agrodolce bittersweet; GASTR sweet and sour

agrumi *mpl* citrus fruit

aguzzare sharpen; **~ la vista** keep one's eyes peeled; **aguzzo** pointed

ahi! ouch!

ai = *a* and *art* **i**

Aids *m o f* Aids

airbag *m inv* airbag

airone *m* heron

aiuola *f* flower bed

aiutante *m/f* assistant; **aiutare** help; **aiuto** *m* help, assist-ance; *persona* assistant

aizzare incite

al = *a* and *art* **il**

ala *f* wing

alabastro *m* alabaster

alano *m* Great Dane

alba *f* dawn; **all'~** at dawn

albanese *agg*, *m/f* Albanian; **Albania** *f* Albania

alberato tree-lined

alberghiero hotel *attr*; **albergo** *m* hotel

albero *m* tree; MAR mast; AUTO shaft; **~ genealogico** family tree; **~ di Natale** Christmas tree

albicocca *f* apricot; **albicocco** *m* apricot (tree)

albo *m* notice board, *Am* bulletin board; *(registro)* register; **radiare dall'~** strike off

album *m inv* album

alcol *m* alcohol; **alcolico 1** *agg* alcoholic **2** *m* alcoholic drink; **alcolismo** *m* alcoholism; **alcolizzato** *m*, **-a** *f* alcoholic; **alcoltest** *m inv* Breathalyzer®

alcuno 1 *agg* any; **non ~** no, not any **2** *pron* any; **-i** *pl* some, a few

aldilà *m*: **l'~** the next world

aletta *f* fin

alfabetico alphabetical; **alfabeto** *m* alphabet

alfiere *m scacchi* bishop

alga *f* seaweed

algebra *f* algebra

Algeria *f* Algeria; **algerino 1** *agg* Algerian **2** *m*, **-a** *f* Alge-

rian
aliante *m* glider
alice *f* anchovy
alienato 1 *agg* alienated **2** *m*, **-a** *f* madman; *donna* madwoman; **alienazione** *f* alienation; **~ mentale** madness
alimentare 1 *v/t* feed **2** *agg* food *attr*, **generi** *mpl* **-i** foodstuffs; **alimentazione** *f* feeding; **alimento** *m* food; **-i** *pl* DIR alimony
aliquota *f* share; **~ d'imposta** rate of taxation
aliscafo *m* hydrofoil
alito *m* breath
all. (= **allegato**) enc(l). (= enclosed)
all', alla = **a** and *art* **l', la**
allacciamento *m* TEC connection; **allacciare** fasten; TEC connect
allagamento *m* flooding; **allagare** flood
allargare widen; *vestito* let out; *braccia* open; **allargarsi** widen
allarmare alarm; **allarmarsi** become alarmed; **allarme** *m* alarm; **dare l'~** raise the alarm
allattare *bambino* feed
alle = **a** and *art* **le**
alleanza *f* alliance; **allearsi** ally o.s.; **alleato 1** *agg* allied **2** *m*, **-a** *f* ally
allegare *documento* enclose; INFOR attach; **allegato** *m* enclosure; INFOR attachment; **qui ~** enclosed

alleggerire lighten; *fig: dolore* ease
allegria *f* cheerfulness; **allegro 1** *agg* cheerful; *colore* bright **2** *m* MUS allegro
allenamento *m* training; **allenare, allenarsi** train (**per** for; **a** in); **allenatore** *m*, **-trice** *f* trainer
allentare 1 *v/t* loosen **2** *v/i* e **allentarsi** loosen
allergia *f* allergy; **allergico** allergic (**a** to)
allertare alert
allestimento *m* preparation; MAR fitting out; TEA **~ scenico** sets, scenery; **allestire** prepare; MAR fit out
allevamento *m* BOT, ZO breeding; **allevare** BOT, ZO breed; *bambini* bring up, raise; **allevatore** *m*, **-trice** *f* breeder
alleviare alleviate
allievo *m*, **-a** *f* pupil, student
alligatore *m* alligator
allineare line up; FIN adjust; TIP align
allo = **a** and *art* **lo**
allodola *f* skylark
alloggiare 1 *v/t* put up **2** *v/i* stay, put up; **alloggio** *m* accommodation, *Am* accommodations; **vitto e ~** bed and board
allontanarsi go away; *fig* grow apart
allora then; **da ~ in poi** from then on; **fin d'~** since then
alloro *m* laurel; GASTR bay

alluce m big toe

allucinante F incredible, mind-blowing F; **allucinazione** f hallucination

alludere allude (**a** to)

alluminio m aluminium, Am aluminum

allungare lengthen; (diluire) dilute; mano put out; **allungarsi** di giorni get longer; di persona stretch out, lie down

allusione f allusion

alluvione f flood

almeno at least

alogena f halogen

Alpi fpl Alps; **alpinismo** m mountaineering; **alpinista** m/f mountain climber; **alpino** Alpine

alquanto 1 agg some 2 avv a little, somewhat

alt stop

altalena f swing

altare m altar

alterare, alterarsi (guastarsi) go bad o off; (irritarsi) get angry

alternare, alternarsi alternate; **alternativa** f alternative; **alternativo** alternative; **alternato**: **corrente** f **-a** alternating current; **alterno**: **a giorni** pl **-i** on alternate days

altezza f height; titolo Highness

alticcio tipsy

altitudine f altitude

alto 1 agg high; persona tall; **a voce -a** in a loud voice; leg-gere aloud; **in ~** at the top; moto up 2 m top

altoatesino 1 agg South Tyrolean 2 m, **-a** f South Tyrolean

altoparlante m loudspeaker

altopiano m plateau

altrettanto as much; **-i** pl as many

altrimenti (in modo diverso) differently; (in caso contrario) otherwise

altro 1 agg other; **un ~** another; **l'altr'anno** last year; **l'~ ieri** the day before yesterday 2 pron other; **l'un l'~** one another; **gli altri** other people; **tra l'~** what's more, moreover; **desidera ~?** anything else?; **tutt'~ che** anything but; **qualcun'~** someone o somebody else

altronde: **d'~** on the other hand

altrove elsewhere

altruismo m altruism

altura f hill

alunno m, **-a** f pupil, student

alzacristallo m inv AUTO window winder

alzare raise; **alzarsi** stand up, rise; da letto get up; di sole rise

amaca f hammock

amalgamare amalgamate

amante m/f lover; **amare** love; amico be fond of

amareggiato embittered

amarena f sour black cherry

amarezza f bitterness; **amaro**

1 *agg* bitter **2** *m liquore* bitters

ambasciata *f* embassy; **ambasciatore** *m*, **-trice** *f* ambassador

ambedue both

ambientale environmental; **ambientalista 1** *agg* environmental **2** *m/f* environmentalist; **ambientarsi** become acclimatized; **ambiente** *m* environment

ambiguità *f inv* ambiguity; **ambiguo** ambiguous

ambito *m* sphere

ambizione *f* ambition; **ambizioso** ambitious

ambo 1 *agg* both **2** *m lotteria* double

ambulante 1 *agg* travelling, *Am* traveling **2** *m/f* pedlar; **ambulanza** *f* ambulance; **ambulatorio** *m* MED outpatients

America *f* America; **americano 1** *agg* American **2** *m*, **-a** *f* American **3** *m* American English

ametista *f* amethyst

amianto *m* asbestos

amichevole friendly; **amicizia** *f* friendship; **amico 1** *agg* friendly **2** *m*, **-a** *f* friend

amido *m* starch

ammaccare dent; *frutta* bruise; **ammaccatura** *f* dent; *su frutta* bruise

ammaestrare teach; *animali* train

ammalarsi fall sick; **ammala-to 1** *agg* sick **2** *m*, **-a** *f* sick person

ammarare *di aereo* put down in the water; *di navetta spaziale* splash down

ammassare, **ammassarsi** mass; **ammasso** *m* pile; GEOL mass

ammazzare kill; *animali* slaughter; **ammazzarsi** (*suicidarsi*) kill o.s.

ammenda *f* (*multa*) fine

ammesso *pp* ◁ **ammettere**; **ammettere** admit; (*supporre*) suppose; (*riconoscere*) acknowledge; **ammesso che** ... supposing (that) ...

amministrare administer; *azienda* manage, run; **amministrativo** administrative; **amministratore** *m*, **-trice** *f* administrator; *di azienda* manager; **amministrazione** *f* administration

ammirare admire; **ammiratore** *m*, **-trice** *f* admirer; **ammirazione** *f* admiration; **ammirevole** admirable

ammobiliare furnish; **ammobiliato** furnished

ammollo: **in ~** soaking

ammonimento *m* reprimand, admonishment; (*consiglio*) warning; **ammonire** reprimand, admonish; (*avvertire*) warn; DIR caution; **ammonizione** *f* reprimand, admonishment; SP warning; DIR caution

ammontare: **~ a** amount to

ammorbidire soften

ammortizzare FIN pay off; **ammortizzatore** m AUTO shock absorber

ammucchiare pile up

ammuffire go mouldy, Am go moldy; fig moulder away, Am molder away

ammutolire be struck dumb

amnesia f amnesia

amnistia f amnesty

amo m hook; fig bait

amore m; **fare l'~ con qu** make love to s.o.; **amoroso** loving; sguardo amorous; lettera, poesia love attr

ampiezza f di stanza spaciousness; di gonna fullness; fig di cultura breadth; fig **~ di vedute** broadmindedness; **ampio** stanza spacious, large; abito roomy; gonna full

ampliamento m broadening, widening; di edificio extension; **ampliare** broaden, widen; edificio extend

amplificare TEC suono amplify; **amplificatore** m amplifier

amputare amputate

amuleto m amulet

anabbagliante dipped, Am low-beam

anacronistico anachronistic

anagrafe f ufficio registry office

analcolico 1 agg non-alcoholic **2** m non-alcoholic drink

anale anal

analfabeta m/f illiterate person, person who cannot read or write; **analfabetismo** m illiteracy

analgesico m/agg analgesic

analisi f inv analysis; **~ del sangue** blood test; **analista** m/f analyst; **~ programmatore** systems analyst

analizzare analyse, Am analyze

analogia f analogy; **analogo** analogous

ananas m inv pineapple

anarchia f anarchy; **anarchico 1** agg anarchic **2** m, **-a** f anarchist

anatomia f anatomy; **anatomico** anatomical

anatra f duck

anca f hip

anche too, also; (perfino) even; **~ se** even if

ancora[1] avv still; di nuovo again; di più (some) more; **non ~** not yet; **~ una volta** once more; **dammene ~ un po'** give me a bit more

ancora[2] f anchor

andamento m di vendite performance

andare 1 v/i go; (funzionare) work; **~ via** (partire) leave; di macchia come out; **~ bene** suit; taglia fit; **~ a male** go off; **come va?** how are you?; **non mi va** di vestito it doesn't fit me; **non mi va di venire** I don't feel like coming **2** *m*: *a lungo~* in the long run; **andarsene** go away; **andata** *f* outward journey; *(biglietto m di)* ~ single (ticket), *Am* oneway ticket, *(biglietto m di)* ~ *e ritorno* return (ticket), *Am* round-trip ticket; **andatura** *f* walk; SP pace

androne *m* hallway

aneddoto *m* anecdote

anello *m* ring

anemia *f* anaemia, *Am* anemia; **anemico** anaemic, *Am* anemic

anestesia *f* *sostanza* anaesthetic, *Am* anesthetic; **anestetico** *m* anaesthetic, *Am* anesthetic

anfibio 1 *agg* ambibious **2** *m* ZO amphibian; MIL amphibious vehicle

anfiteatro *m* amphitheatre, *Am* amphitheater

anfora *f* amphora

angelo *m* angel

anglicano 1 *agg* Anglican **2** *m*, **-a** *f* Anglican

angolo *m* corner; MAT angle; ~ *cottura* kitchenette; MAT ~ *retto* right angle

angoscia *f* anguish; **angoscioso** anguished; *che da angoscia* heart-rending

anguilla *f* eel

anguria *f* water melon

angusto narrow

anice *m* aniseed

anidride *f*: ~ *carbonica* carbon dioxide

anima *f* soul

animale *m* animal; ~ *domestico* pet

animare give life to; *conversazione* liven up; *(promuovere)* promote; *animato strada* busy; *conversazione, persona* animated; **animatore** *m*, **-trice** *f* di gruppo leader; **animazione** *f* animation; INFOR ~ *al computer* computer animation

animo *m* nature; *(coraggio)* heart; **perdersi d'~** lose heart

anitra *f* duck

annaffiare water; **annaffiatoio** *m* watering can

annata *f* vintage; *(anno)* year; *importo* annual amount

annegare 1 *v/t* drown **2** *v/i* e **annegarsi** drown

annerire, **annerirsi** turn black, blacken

annessione *f* POL annexation

annidarsi nest

anniversario *m* anniversary

anno *m* year; **buon ~!** Happy New Year!; *quanti -i hai?* how old are you?; **ho 33 -i** I'm 33 (years old)

annodare tie (together); *cravatta* tie, knot

annoiare bore; *(dare fastidio a)* annoy; **annoiarsi** get bored; **annoiato** bored

annotare make a note of; *testo* annotate; **annotazione** *f* note; *in testo* annotation

annuale annual, yearly; *di un*

anno year-long

annuire *(assentire)* assent (*a* to)

annullamento *m* cancellation; *di matrimonio* annulment; **annullare** cancel; *matrimonio* annul; *gol* disallow; *(vanificare)* cancel out

annunciare announce; **annunciatore** *m*, **-trice** *f* RAD, TV announcer; **Annunciazione** *f* REL Annunciation; **annuncio** *m* announcement; *in giornale* advertisement; **-i** *pl economici* classifieds

annuo annual, yearly

annusare sniff; *fig* smell

anomalo anomalous

anonimo anonymous

anoressia *f* anorexia; **anoressico** anorexic

anormale abnormal

ansia *f* anxiety

ansimare wheeze

ansioso anxious

antagonismo *m* antagonism; **antagonista** *m/f* antagonist

antartico Antarctic *attr*

antecedente 1 *agg* preceding **2** *m* precedent

antenato *m*, **-a** *f* ancestor

antenna *f* RAD, TV aerial, *Am* antenna; ZO antenna; **~ parabolica** satellite dish

anteprima *f* preview

anteriore front; *precedente* previous

anti ... anti ...

antibiotico *m/agg* antibiotic

anticamente in ancient times; **antichità** *f inv* antiquity

anticiclone *m* anticyclone

anticipato: *pagamento m* **~** advance payment; **anticipare** anticipate; *denaro* pay in advance; *partenza, riunione ecc* bring forward; **anticipo** *m* advance; *(caparra)* deposit; *in* **~** ahead of time, early

antico ancient; *mobile* antique

anticoncezionale *m/agg* contraceptive

anticonformista *m/f* nonconformist

anticostituzionale unconstitutional

antidoto *m* antidote

antifurto 1 *agg* antitheft **2** *m* anti-theft device

antigas *inv* gas *attr*

antincendio *inv* fire *attr*

antinebbia *m inv* foglamp

antiorario: *in senso* **~** anticlockwise, *Am* counterclockwise

antipasto *m* starter

antipatia *f* antipathy; **antipatico** disagreeable

antiquariato *m* antique business; *negozio m di* **~** antique shop; **antiquario** *m*, **-a** *f* antique dealer; **antiquato** antiquated

antiriflesso *m* anti-glare

antiruggine *m* rust inhibitor

antisemitismo *m* anti-Semitism

antisettico *m/agg* antiseptic

antisismico earthquake-proof

antologia *f* anthology

anulare *m* ring finger

anzi in fact; (*o meglio*) (or) better still

anzianità fold age; **~ di servizio** seniority; **anziano 1** *agg* elderly; *per servizio* (most) senior **2** *m*, **-a** *f* old man; *-donna* old woman; **gli -i** *pl* the elderly *pl*

anziché rather than

anzitutto first of all

aorta *f* aorta

apatia *f* apathy; **apatico** apathetic

ape *f* bee

aperitivo *m* aperitif

aperto 1 *pp* **~ aprire 2** *agg* open; **all'~** *piscina* open-air; **mangiare all'~** eat in the open air, eat outside; **apertura** *f* opening; FOT aperture

apice *m* apex; *fig* height

apicoltura *f* bee-keeping

apnea *f* SP free diving

apostolo *m* apostle

apostrofo *m* apostrophe

app *f* INFOR app

appagare satisfy

appalto *m* (*contratto*) contract; **dare in ~** contract out; **prendere in ~** win the contract for

appannarsi *di vetro* mist up; *di vista* grow dim

apparato *m* apparatus; **~ di-**

gerente digestive system

apparecchiare *tavola* set; (*preparare*) prepare; **apparecchio** *m* TEC device; AVIA F plane; *per denti* brace

apparenza *f* appearance; **apparire** appear; **appariscente** striking

appartamento *m* flat, *Am* apartment

appartarsi withdraw

appartenere belong

appassionare excite; (*commuovere*) move; **appassionarsi** become excited (**a** by); **appassionato** passionate

appassire wither

appellarsi appeal (**a** to; **contro** against); **appello** *m* appeal; **fare ~ a qu** appeal to s.o

appena 1 *avv* just **2** *cong* as soon as

appendere hang

appendiabiti *m* hatstand

appendice *f* appendix; **appendicite** *f* appendicitis

Appennini *mpl* Apennines

appesantire make heavier

appeso *pp* **~ appendere**

appetito *m* appetite; **buon ~!** enjoy (your meal)!; **appetitoso** appetizing

appiattire flatten

appiccicare stick; **appiccicarsi** stick; **appiccicoso** sticky; *fig* clingy

appiglio *m* *per mani* fingerhold; *per piedi* toehold; *fig* excuse

applaudire applaud; **applauso** *m* applause

applicare *etichetta* attach; *regolamento* apply; **applicazione** *f* application

appoggiare lean (*a* against); (*posare*) put; *fig* support, back; **appoggiarsi**: ~ *a* lean on; *fig* rely on; **appoggiatesta** *m inv* headrest; **appoggio** *m* support

apporre put; ~ *la firma su qc* put one's signature to sth

apportare bring; *fig* (*causare*) cause

apposito appropriate

apposta deliberately, on purpose; (*specialmente*) specifically

apprendere learn; *notizia* hear

apprendistato *m* apprenticeship

apprensione *f* apprehension; **apprensivo** apprehensive

appreso *pp* ☞ **apprendere**

appresso 1 *prp* close, near; (*dietro*) behind. **2** *avv* near, close by; **portarsi qc ~** bring sth (with one)

apprezzare appreciate

approccio *m* approach

approdare land; *di barca* moor

approdo *m* landing; *luogo* landing stage

approfittare: ~ *di qc* take advantage of sth

approfondire deepen; *fig*

study in depth

appropriarsi: ~ *di qc* appropriate sth; **appropriato** appropriate

approvare approve of; *legge* approve; **approvazione** *f* approval

appuntamento *m* appointment

appuntito pointed; *matita* sharp

appunto 1 *m* note; **prendere -i** take notes **2** *avv*: (**per l'**) ~ exactly

apribottiglie *m inv* bottle opener

aprile *m* April

aprire open; *rubinetto* turn on; **aprirsi** open; **apriscatole** *m inv* can-opener, *Br anche* tin-opener

aquila *f* eagle

aquilone *m* kite

arabesco *m* arabesque; *spir* scrawl, scribble

Arabia Saudita *f* Saudi (Arabia)

arabo 1 *agg* Arab **2** *m*, **-a** *f* Arab **3** *m* Arabic

arachide *f* peanut

aragosta *f* lobster

arancia *f* orange; **aranciata** *f* orangeade

arancio 1 *agg inv* orange **2** *m albero* orange tree; *colore* orange; **arancione** *m/agg* orange

arare plough, *Am* plow; **aratro** *m* plough, *Am* plow

arazzo *m* tapestry

arbitrario arbitrary

arbitro *m* arbiter; SP referee

arbusto *m* shrub

arcaico *m* archaic

arcata *f* arch

archeologia *f* archaeology, *Am* archeology; **archeologo** *m*, **-a** *f* archaeologist, *Am* archeologist

archetto *m* MUS bow

architetto *m* architect; **architettonico** architectural

archiviare file; **archivio** *m* archives

arcipelago *m* archipelago

arcivescovo *m* archbishop

arco *m* bow; ARCHI arch; **~ di tempo** period of time; **arcobaleno** *m* rainbow

ardere burn

area *f* surface; *zona* area; **~ di servizio** service area

arena *f* arena

arenarsi run aground; *fig* come to a halt

areo ... ☞ **aereo ...**

argano *m* winch

argentato silver-plated; **argenteria** *f* silver(ware)

Argentina *f* Argentina; **argentino 1** *agg* Argentinian **2** *m*, **-a** *f* Argentinian

argento *m* silver

argilla *f* clay; **argilloso** clayey

arginare embank; **argine** *m* embankment

argomento *m* argument; *(contenuto)* subject

arguto witty; *(perspicace)* shrewd

aria *f* air; *(aspetto)* appearance; MUS tune; *di opera* aria; **~ condizionata** air conditioning; **all'~ aperta** in the fresh air; **mandare all'~** *qc* ruin sth; **aver l'~ stanca** look tired; **darsi delle -e** give o.s. airs

arido dry, arid

arieggiare *stanza* air

ariete *m* ZO ram; ASTR *Ariete* Aries

aringa *f* herring

arista *f* GASTR chine of pork

aristocratico 1 *agg* aristocratic **2** *m*, **-a** *f* aristocrat

aritmetica *f* arithmetic

arma *f* weapon; **~ da fuoco** firearm; **chiamare alle -i** call up; *fig* **essere alle prime -i** be a beginner

armadio *m* cupboard; **~ a muro** fitted cupboard

armamento *m* armament; **armarsi** arm o.s. *(di* with*)*; **armato** armed

armatura *f* armour, *Am* armor; *(struttura)* framework

armistizio *m* armistice

armonia *f* harmony

armonica *f* harmonica; **~ a bocca** mouth organ, harmonica

armonioso harmonious

arnese *m* tool

arnia *f* beehive

aroma *m* aroma; **aromaterapia** *f* aromatherapy; **aromatico** aromatic

aromatizzare flavour, *Am*

arpa 30

flavor
arpa f harp
arpione m harpoon
arrabattarsi do everything one can
arrabbiarsi get angry; **arrabbiato** angry; *(idrofobo)* rabid
arrampicarsi climb; **arrampicata** f climb
arrangiarsi *(accordarsi)* agree (**su** on); *(destreggiarsi)* manage
arrecare bring; *fig* cause
arredamento m décor; *mobili* furniture; *arte* interior design; **arredare** furnish; **arredatore** m, **-trice** f interior designer
arrendersi surrender; *fig* give up; **arrendevole** soft, yielding
arrestare stop; DIR arrest; **arrestarsi** stop; **arresto** m coming to a stop; DIR arrest
arretrato 1 *agg* in arrears; *paese* underdeveloped **2 -i** *mpl* arrears
arricchire *fig* enrich; **arricchirsi** get rich
arricciare *capelli* curl; **~ il naso** turn up one's nose
arringa f DIR closing speech for the defence *o Am* defense
arrivare arrive, come; **~ a** reach, get to; **~ a fare qc** manage to do sth
arrivederci, arrivederla goodbye
arrivista m/f social climber

arrivo m arrival; SP finish line
arrogante arrogant; **arroganza** f arrogance
arrossire blush
arrosto m roast
arrotolare roll up
arrotondare round off; *stipendio* supplement
arroventato red-hot
arruffato ruffled
arrugginire 1 *v/t* rust **2** *v/i* e **arrugginirsi** rust; *fig* get rusty
arruolarsi enlist
arsenale m arsenal; MAR dockyard
arso 1 *pp* v *ardere* **2** *agg* burnt; *(secco)* dried-up
arte f art; *(abilità)* gift
artefice m/f *fig* author, architect
arteria f artery; **arterioso** arterial
artico Arctic
articolazione f ANAT joint
articolo m item, article; GRAM **~ determinativo** definite article; GRAM **~ indeterminativo** indefinite article
artificiale artificial; **artificio** m artifice; **artificioso** *maniere* artificial
artigianale handmade; **artigianato** m craftsmanship; **artigiano** m, **-a** f craftsman; *donna* craftswoman
artiglieria f artillery
artiglio m claw
artista m/f artist; **artistico** ar-

assedio

tistic
arto *m* limb
artrite *f* arthritis
artrosi *f* rheumatism
ascella *f* armpit
ascendente 1 *agg* ascending;
strada sloping upwards; *mo-*
vimento upwards **2 m** ASTR
ascendant; *fig* influence;
ascensione *f* ascent; REL
Ascension; **ascensore** *m*
lift, *Am* elevator; **ascesa** *f*
ascent
ascesso *m* abscess
ascia *f* axe, *Am* ax
asciugacapelli *m* hairdryer;
asciugamano *m* towel;
asciugare dry; **asciugarsi**
dry o.s.; **~ i capelli** dry one's
hair; **asciugatrice** *f* tumble
dryer; **asciutto** dry
ascoltare listen to; **ascolta-**
tore *m*, **-trice** *f* listener;
ascolto *m* listening; **dare ~**
listen (**a** to)
asettico aseptic
asfaltare asphalt; **asfalto** *m*
asphalt
asfissiare asphyxiate
Asia *f* Asia; **asiatico 1** *agg*
Asian **2** *m*, **-a** *f* Asian
asilo *m* shelter; **~ politico** political asylum; **~ nido** day
nursery, *Am* day care center
asimmetrico asymmetrical
asino *m* ass (*anche fig*)
asma *f* asthma
asociale antisocial
asola *f* buttonhole
asparago *m* spear of aspara-

gus; **-gi** asparagus
aspettare wait for; **~ un bam-**
bino be expecting a baby;
aspettarsi expect; **aspetta-**
tiva *f* expectation; **da lavoro**
unpaid leave
aspetto[1] *m* look, appearance;
di problema aspect
aspetto[2]: **sala f d'~** waiting
room
aspirapolvere *m* vacuum
cleaner
aspirare 1 *v/t* inhale; TEC suck
up **2** *v/i:* **~ a qc** aspire to sth
aspirina *f* aspirin
asportare take away
aspro sour; (*duro*) harsh; *liti-*
gio bitter
assaggiare taste; **assaggio**
m taste, sample
assai 1 *agg* a lot of **2** *avv con*
verbo a lot; *con aggettivo*
very; (*abbastanza*) enough
assalire attack
assaltare attack; **assalto** *m*
attack; *fig* **prendere d'~**
storm
assassinare murder; POL assassinate; **assassinio** *m*
murder; POL assassination;
assassino 1 *agg* murderous
2 *m*, **-a** *f* murderer; POL assassin
asse[1] *f* board; **~ da stiro** ironing board
asse[2] *m* TEC axle; MAT axis
assecondare support; (*esau-*
dire) satisfy
assediare besiege; **assedio**
m siege

assegnare *premio* award; (*destinare*) assign; **assegno** *m* cheque; *Am* check; **~ in bianco** blank cheque; **~ turistico** traveller's cheque, *Am* traveler's cheque; **contro ~** cash on delivery, *Am* collect on delivery; **-i familiari** child benefit; **emettere un ~** write a cheque

assemblea *f* meeting

assentarsi go away, leave; **assente** absent, away; *fig* absent-minded; **assenza** *f* absence; **~ di qc** lack of sth

assessore *m* councillor, *Am* councilor; **~ comunale** local councillor

assicurare insure; (*legare*) secure; *lettera, pacco* register; **assicurarsi** make sure, ensure; **assicurata** *f* registered letter; **assicurato 1** *agg* insured; *lettera, pacco* registered **2** *m,* **-a** *f* person with insurance, insured party; **assicurazione** *f* insurance

assideramento *m* exposure

assieme together

assillante nagging; **assillare** pester; **assillo** *m fig: persona* pest F, nuisance; (*preoccupazione*) nagging thought

assistente *m/f* assistant; **~ sociale** social worker; **~ di volo** flight attendant; **assistenza** *f* assistance; **~ medica** medical care; **assistere 1** *v/t* assist, help; (*curare*) nurse **2** *v/i* (*essere presente*) be pre-

sent (**a** at)

asso *m* ace

associare take into partnership; *fig* **~ qu a qc** associate s.o. with sth; **associarsi** enter into partnership (**a** with); (*unirsi*) join forces; (*iscriversi*) subscribe (**a** to); (*prendere parte*) join (**a** sth); **associazione** *f* association

assolo *m inv* MUS solo

assolto *pp* ☞ **assolvere**

assolutamente absolutely; **assoluto** absolute; **assoluzione** *f* DIR acquittal; REL absolution; **assolvere** DIR acquit; *da un obbligo* release; *compito* carry out; REL absolve, give absolution to

assomigliare: ~ a qu be like s.o., resemble s.o.; **assomigliarsi** be like *o* resemble each other

assonnato sleepy

assorbente 1 *agg* absorbent **2** *m:* **~ igienico** sanitary towel, *Am* sanitary napkin; **assorbire** absorb

assordante deafening; **assordare 1** *v/t* deafen **2** *v/i* go deaf

assortimento *m* assortment

assorto engrossed

assuefatto *pp* ☞ **assuefare**; **assuefazione** *f* resistance, tolerance; **agli alcolici, alla droga** addiction

assumere *impiegato, incarico* take on

assunzione f di impiegato employment; REL **Assunzione** Assumption

assurdità f inv absurdity; **assurdo** absurd

asta f pole; FIN auction; **mettere all'~** sell at auction

astemio 1 agg abstemious 2 m, -a f abstemious person; **astenersi: ~ da** abstain from

asterisco m asterisk

astigmatico astigmatic; **astigmatismo** m astigmatism

astinenza f abstinence

astio m rancour, Am rancor

astratto abstract

astringente m/agg MED astringent

astro m star; **astrologia** f astrology; **astronauta** m/f astronaut; **astronave** f spaceship; **astronomia** f astronomy; **astronomico** astronomical

astuccio m case

astuto astute

ateo m, -a f atheist

atlante m atlas

atlantico Atlantic; **Oceano ~ Atlantico** Atlantic Ocean

atleta m/f athlete; **atletica** f athletics; **~ leggera** track and field (events); **atletico** athletic

atmosfera f atmosphere; **atmosferico** atmospheric

atomico atomic; **atomo** m atom

atrio m foyer, Am lobby

atroce atrocious; **atrocità** f inv atrocity

attaccabrighe m o f inv F troublemaker; **attaccante** m SP forward; **attaccapanni** m inv clothes hook; a stelo clothes hanger; **attaccare** 1 v/t attach; (incollare) stick; (appendere) hang; (assalire) attack 2 v/i stick; **attaccarsi** stick; (aggrapparsi) hold on (a to); **attacco** m attack; (punto di unione) junction; SCI binding; MED fit

atteggiamento m attitude; **atteggiarsi: ~ a** pose as

attendere 1 v/t wait for 2 v/i: ~ **a** attend to

attendibile reliable

attenersi stick (a to)

attentare: ~ a attack; ~ **alla vita di qu** make an attempt on s.o.'s life; **attentato** m attempted assassination

attento 1 agg attentive; **stare ~ a** be careful of 2 int ~! look out!, (be) careful!

attenuante f extenuating circumstance; **attenuare** reduce; colpo cushion; **attenuarsi** lessen

attenzione f attention; ~! look out!, (be) careful!; **far ~ a qc** mind o watch sth

atterraggio m landing; **atterrare** 1 v/t avversario knock down 2 v/i land

attesa f waiting; (tempo d'attesa) wait; (aspettativa) expectation

atteso *pp* ☞ **attendere**

attestato *m* certificate

attico *m* attic

attimo *m* moment; *un ~!* just a moment!

attirare attract

attitudine *f* attitude; *avere ~ per qc* have an aptitude for sth

attivare activate; **attività** *f inv* activity; *pl* FIN assets; **attivo** **1** *agg* active **2** *m* FIN assets; GRAM active (voice)

atto *m* act; *(gesto)* gesture; *documento* deed; *mettere in ~* carry out; *prendere ~ di* note

attorcigliare, **attorcigliarsi** twist

attore *m*, **-trice** *f* actor; *donna anche* actress

attorno: *~ a qc* around sth; *qui ~* around here

attraccare MAR berth, dock

attraente attractive; **attrarre** attract; **attrattiva** *f* attraction; **attratto** *pp* ☞ **attrarre**

attraversare *strada, confine* cross; *un momento difficile* be going through a bad patch; **attraverso** across

attrazione *f* attraction

attrezzare equip; **attrezzarsi** get o.s. kitted out; **attrezzato** equipped; **attrezzatura** *f* equipment, gear F; **attrezzo** *m* piece of equipment

attribuire attribute

attrice *f* actress

attuale current; **attualità** *f inv* news *sg*; *d'~* topical; **attuare** put into effect; **attuazione** *f* putting into effect

audace bold

audioleso **1** *agg* hearing-impaired **2** *m*, **-a** *f* person who is hearing-impaired

audiovisivo audiovisual

audizione *f* audition

augurare wish; **augurio** *m* wish; *tanti -ri!* all the best!

aula *f di scuola* class room; *di università* lecture room

aumentare increase; **aumento** *m* increase

aureola *f* halo

auricolare *m* earphone

aurora *f* dawn

ausiliare *m/agg* auxiliary

australe southern

Australia *f* Australia; **australiano** **1** *agg* Australian **2** *m*, **-a** *f* Australian

Austria *f* Austria; **austriaco** **1** *agg* Austrian **2** *m*, **-a** *f* Austrian

autenticare authenticate; **autentico** authentic

autista *m/f* driver

auto *f inv* ☞ **automobile**

autoadesivo **1** *agg* self-adhesive **2** *m* sticker

autoambulanza *f* ambulance

autobiografia *f* autobiography

autobomba *f* car bomb

autobus *m* bus; *~ di linea* city bus

autocarro *m* truck, *Br anche* lorry

autocisterna f tanker
autocontrollo m self-control
autodidatta m/f self-taught person
autodifesa f self-defence, Am self-defense
autodromo m motor racing circuit
autogol m inv own goal
autografo m autograph
autogrill m inv roadside café
autolavaggio m car-wash
automa m robot
automatico 1 agg automatic **2** m bottone press-stud, Am snap fastener
automezzo m motor vehicle
automobile f car, Am anche automobile; **automobilismo** m driving; SP motor racing; **automobilista** m/f driver
autonoleggio m car rental; azienda car-rental firm
autonomia f autonomy; TEC battery life; **autonomo** autonomous
autoradio f inv car radio
autore m, **-trice** f author; DIR perpetrator; **autorevole** authoritative
autorimessa f garage
autorità f inv authority; **autoritario** authoritarian; **autorizzare** authorize; **autorizzazione** f authorization
autoscuola f driving school
autostop m: **fare l'~** hitch-hike; **autostoppista** m/f hitchhiker

autostrada f motorway, Am highway
autovettura f motor vehicle
autrice f ► **autore**
autunno m autumn, Am fall
avambraccio m forearm
avanguardia f avant-garde; azienda leading-edge
avanti 1 avv in front, ahead; **d'ora in poi** from now on; **andare** ~ di orologio be fast; **essere** ~ **nel programma** be ahead of schedule **2** int ~! come in!
avanzare 1 v/i advance; fig make progress; (rimanere) be left over **2** v/t put forward
avanzo m remainder; FIN surplus; **gli** -**i** pl the leftovers
avaria f failure; **avariato** damaged; cibi spoiled
avarizia f avarice; **avaro 1** agg miserly **2** m, -**a** f miser
avena f oats
avere 1 v/t have; ~ **20 anni** be 20 (years old); ~ **fame** / **sonno** be hungry / sleepy; ~ **caldo** / **freddo** be hot / cold; **avercela con qu** have it in for s.o **2** v/aus have; **hai visto Tony?** have you seen Tony?; **hai visto Tony ieri?** did you see Tony yesterday? **3** m FIN credit; -**i** mpl wealth
avi mpl ancestors
aviazione f aviation; MIL Air Force
avidità f avidness; **avido** avid
avocado m avocado

avorio

36

avorio *m* ivory

avvalersi: ~ *di qc* avail o.s. of sth

avvantaggiare favour, *Am* favor; **avvantaggiarsi:** ~ *di qc* take advantage of sth

avveduto astute

avvelenamento *m* poisoning; **avvelenare** poison; **avvelenarsi** poison o.s.

avvenimento *m* event; **avvenire 1** *v/i (accadere)* happen **2** *m* future

Avvento *m* Advent

avventura *f* adventure; **avventurarsi** venture; **avventuriero** *m*, **-a** *f* adventurer; *donna* adventuress; **avventuroso** adventurous

avvenuto *pp* ☞ **avvenire**

avverarsi come true

avverbio *m* adverb

avversario 1 *agg* opposing **2** *m*, **-a** *f* opponent, adversary

avversione *f* aversion (*per* to)

avvertenza *f (ammonimento)* warning; *(premessa)* foreword; **-e** *pl (istruzioni per l'uso)* instructions

avvertimento *m* warning; **avvertire** warn; *(percepire)* catch

avviamento *m* introduction; TEC, AUTO start-up; **avviare** start; **avviarsi** set out, head off; **avviato** established

avvicendarsi alternate

avvicinare approach; ~ *qc a*

qc move sth closer to sth; **avvicinarsi** approach, near (*a* sth)

avvilire depress; *(mortificare)* humiliate; **avvilirsi** demean o.s.; *(scoraggiarsi)* get depressed; **avvilito** *(scoraggiato)* depressed

avvio *m*: **dare l'~** *a qc* get sth under way

avvisare inform, advise; *(mettere in guardia)* warn; **avviso** *m* notice; **a mio** ~ in my opinion

avvitare screw in; *fissare* screw

avvocato *m* lawyer

avvolgere wrap; **avvolgibile** *m* roller blind; **avvolto** *pp* ☞ **avvolgere**

avvoltoio *m* vulture

azienda *f* business; **aziendale** company *attr*

azionare activate; *allarme* set off; **azionario** share *attr*; **azione** *f* action; *(effetto)* influence; FIN share; **azionista** *m/f* stockholder, shareholder

azoto *m* nitrogen

azzannare bite into

azzardarsi dare; **azzardo** *m* hazard; **gioco** *m* **d'~** game of chance

azzerare TEC reset

azzuffarsi come to blows

azzurro 1 *agg* blue **2** *m* blue; SP **gli -i** *pl* the Italian national team

B

babbo *m* F dad F, pop F; **Babbo Natale** Santa (Claus), *Br anche* Father Christmas

babordo *m* MAR port (side)

baby-sitter *m/f inv* baby-sitter

bacato wormeaten

bacca *f* berry

baccalà *m inv* dried salt cod

baccano *m* din

bacchetta *f* rod; MUS *del direttore d'orchestra* baton; *per suonare il tamburo* (drum) stick; ~ **magica** magic wand

bacheca *f* notice board, *Am* bulletin board; *di museo* showcase

baciare kiss; **baciarsi** kiss (each other)

bacillo *m* bacillus

bacinella *f* basin; FOT tray

bacino *m* basin; ANAT pelvis; MAR port

bacio *m* kiss

baco *m* worm; ~ **da seta** silkworm

bada: **tenere a ~** *qu* keep s.o. at bay; **badare**: ~ **a** look after; *(fare attenzione a)* look out for, mind

baffo *m*: **-i** *pl* moustache, *Am* mustache; *di animali* whiskers

bagagliaio *m* FERR luggage van, *Am* baggage car; AUTO boot, *Am* trunk; **bagaglio** *m* luggage, baggage; **fare i -i** pack

bagliore *m* glare; *di speranza* glimmer

bagnante *m/f* bather; **bagnare** wet; *(immergere)* dip; *(inzuppare)* soak; *(annaffiare)* water; *di fiume* flow through; **bagnarsi** get wet; **bagnato** wet; **bagnino** *m*, **-a** *f* lifeguard; **bagno** *m* bath, *Am* (bath)tub; *stanza* bathroom; *gabinetto* toilet; **fare il ~** have a bath; **mettere a ~** soak; **bagnomaria** *m inv* double boiler, bain marie

baia *f* bay

baita *f* mountain chalet, *Am* mountain lodge

balaustra *f* balustrade

balbettare stammer; *di bambino* babble; **balbettio** *m* stammering; *di bambino* babble, prattle

balbuzie *f* stutter; **balbuziente** *m/f* stutterer

balconata *f* TEA dress circle, *Am* balcony; **balcone** *m* balcony

baldoria *f* revelry; **fare ~** have a riotous time

balena *f* whale

balenare *fig* **gli è balenata un'idea** an idea flashed through his mind; **baleno** *m* lightning; **in un ~** in a flash

balia f: **in ~ di** at the mercy of

balla f bale; fig F (frottola) fib F

ballare dance

ballata f MUS ballad

ballerina f dancer; di balletto ballet dancer; di rivista chorus girl; scarpa ballet shoe; **ballerino** m dancer; di balletto ballet dancer

balletto m ballet

ballo m dance; (il ballare) dancing; (festa) ball; **essere in ~** persona be involved; (essere in gioco) be at stake; **tirare in ~ qc** bring sth up

balneare centro seaside attr

balordo 1 agg ragionamento shaky; idea stupid; tempo, consiglio unreliable 2 m (teppista) lout

balsamico aceto balsamic; aria balmy; **balsamo** m per i capelli hair conditioner

balzare jump, leap; **balzo** m jump, leap; fig **cogliere la palla al ~** jump at the chance

bambinaia f nanny; **bambino** m, -a f child; in fasce baby

bambola f doll; **bambolotto** m baby boy doll

bambù m bamboo

banale banal; **banalità** f inv banality

banana f banana

banca f bank; INFOR **~ dati** data bank

bancarella f stall

bancario 1 agg istituto, segreto

banking attr, deposito, estratto conto bank attr **2** m, -a f bank employee

bancarotta f bankruptcy

banchetto m banquet

banchiere m banker

banchina f FERR platform; MAR quay; di strada verge

banchisa f ice floe

banco m FIN bank; di scuola desk; di bar bar; di chiesa pew; di negozio counter; **bancomat®** m inv (distributore) ATM; carta cash card, debit card

bancone m (work)bench

banconota f banknote, Am bill

banda f band; di delinquenti gang; **banda** f **larga** broadband

banderuola f weathercock (anche fig)

bandiera f flag

bandire proclaim; concorso announce; (esiliare) banish; fig (abolire) dispense with; **bandito** m bandit; **bando** m proclamation; (esilio) banishment

bar m inv bar

bara f coffin

baracca f hut; spreg hovel; **baraccopoli** f inv shanty town

barare cheat

baratro m abyss

barattare barter

barattolo m can, Br anche tin; di vetro jar

barba f beard; **farsi la ~** shave; fig **che ~!** what a pain! F

barbabietola f beetroot, Am red beet; **~ da zucchero** sugar beet

barbarico barbaric; **barbaro 1** agg barbarous **2** m barbarian

barbecue m inv barbecue

barbiere m barber

barboncino m (miniature) poodle

barbone[1] m cane poodle

barbone[2] m, **-a** f (vagabondo) tramp, Am hobo

barca f boat; **~ a remi** rowing boat, Am rowboat; **~ a vela** sailing boat, Am sail boat

barcaiolo m boatman

barcollare stagger

barcone m barge

barella f stretcher

barile m barrel

barista m/f barman; donna barmaid; Am bartender; proprietario bar owner

baritono m baritone

barocco m/agg Baroque

barometro m barometer

barone m, **-essa** f baron; donna baroness

barra f bar

barricata f barricade

barriera f barrier (anche fig)

barzelletta f joke

basare base; **basarsi** be based (**su** on)

basco m (berretto) beret

base f base; fig basis; **in ~ a** on the basis of

basette fpl sideburns

basilica f basilica

basilico m basil

basso 1 agg low; di statura short; MUS bass; fig despicable **2** avv: **in ~** stato down below; **da ~** in una casa downstairs **3** m MUS bass; **basso-piano** m GEOG lowland; **bassorilievo** m bas-relief; **bassotto** m dachshund

basta → **bastare**

bastardo m, **-a** f cane mongrel; fig bastard

bastare be enough; (durare) last; **basta!** that's enough; **basta che** (purché) as long as

bastonare beat; **bastone** m stick; di pane baguette, French stick

battaglia f battle (anche fig)

battello m boat

battente m di porta wing; di finestra shutter

battere 1 v/i (bussare, dare colpi) knock **2** v/t beat; record break; **~ le mani** clap (one's hands); **~ al computer** key

batteri mpl bacteria

batteria f battery; MUS drums; **batterista** m/f drummer

battersela run off; **battersi** fight

battesimo m christening, baptism; **battezzare** christen, baptize

battibecco m argument; **batticuore** m palpitations; fig **con un gran ~** with great anxiety; **battipanni** *m inv* carpet beater

battistero *m* baptistry

battistrada *m inv* AUTO tread

battito *m* beating, beat; **~ cardiaco** heartbeat

battuta *f* beat; *in dattilografia* keystroke; MUS bar; TEA cue; *nel tennis* service; **~ (di spirito)** wisecrack

baule *m* trunk, AUTO boot, *Am* trunk

bavaglino *m* bib

bavaglio *m* gag

bavero *m* collar

bazzecola *f* trifle

bazzicare 1 *v/t un posto* haunt; *persone* associate with **2** *v/i* hang about

beatificare beatify; **beato** happy; REL blessed; **~ te!** lucky you!

beauty-case *m inv* toilet bag

bebè *m inv* baby

beccare peck; F *fig (cogliere sul fatto)* nab F; F *fig: malattia* catch, pick up F; **beccarsi** F *malattia* catch, pick up F

becchino *m* grave digger

becco *m* beak; *di teiera ecc* spout

befana *f* kind old witch who brings presents to children on Twelfth Night; REL Twelfth Night; *fig* old witch

beffa *f* hoax; **farsi -e di qu** make a fool of s.o.; **beffardo** scornful; **beffare** mock; **beffarsi: ~ di** mock

bega *f (litigio)* fight, argu-

ment; *(problema)* can of worms

begli ☞ **bello**

bei ☞ **bello**

belare bleat

belga *agg, m/f* Belgian; **Belgio** *m* Belgium

bellezza *f* beauty

bellico *(di guerra)* war *attr*; *(del tempo di guerra)* wartime *attr*

bello 1 *agg* beautiful; *uomo* handsome; *tempo* fine, nice, beautiful; **questa è -a!** that's a good one!; **nel bel mezzo** right in the middle **2** *m* beauty; **sul più ~** at the worst possible moment

belva *f* wild beast

belvedere *m* viewpoint

bemolle *m inv* MUS flat

benché although

benda *f* bandage; *per occhi* blindfold; **bendare** MED bandage

bene 1 *avv* well; **~!** good!; **per ~** properly; **stare ~** *di salute* be well; *di vestito* suit; **ben ti sta!** serves you right!; **va ~!** OK!; **andare ~ a qu** *di abito* fit s.o.; *di orario, appuntamento* suit s.o.; **sentirsi ~** feel well **2** *m* good; **fare ~ alla salute** be good for you; **per il tuo ~** for your own good; **voler ~ a qu** love s.o.; *(amare)* love s.o.; **-i** *pl* assets, property; **-i** *pl* **immobili** real estate

benedetto 1 *pp* ☞ **benedire 2** *agg* blessed; REL **acqua** *f* **-a**

holy water; **benedire** bless;
benedizione f blessing
beneducato well-mannered
beneficenza f charity; ***spettacolo*** m **di ~** benefit (performance)
beneficio m benefit; ***a ~ di*** for the benefit of; **benefico** beneficial; *organizzazione, istituto* charitable; *spettacolo* charity *attr*
benessere m well-being; *(agiatezza)* affluence; **benestante 1** *agg* well-off **2** m/f person with money
benigno MED benign
beninteso of course; **~ che** provided that
benone splendid
benpensante m/f moderate; *spreg* conformist
bensì but rather
benvenuto 1 *agg* welcome **2** m welcome; ***dare il ~ a qu*** welcome s.o.
benvolere: ***farsi ~ da qu*** win s.o. over
benzina f petrol, *Am* gas; ***fare ~*** get petrol; **benzinaio** m, ***-a*** f petrol o *Am* gas station attendant
bere drink; *fig* swallow
berlina f AUTO saloon, *Am* sedan
bermuda *mpl* Bermuda shorts
bernoccolo m bump
berretto m cap
berrò ☞ **bere**
bersaglio m target; *fig: di*

scherzi butt
bestemmia f swear-word; **bestemmiare 1** *v/i* swear *(contro* at) **2** *v/t* curse
bestia f animal; *fig* **andare in ~** fly into a rage; **bestiale** bestial; F *(molto intenso)* terrible; **bestiame** m livestock
bettola f *spreg* dive
betulla f birch
bevanda f drink
beve f *beve*
biancheria f linen; **~ intima** underwear
bianco 1 *agg* white; *foglio* blank **2** m white; **~ d'uovo** egg white; **mangiare in ~** avoid rich food; **in ~ e nero** *film* black and white
biasimare blame; **biasimo** m blame
bibbia f bible
biberon m *inv* baby's bottle
bibita f soft drink
bibliografia f bibliography
biblioteca f library; *mobile* book-case; **bibliotecario** m, **-a** f librarian
bicamerale POL two-chamber
bicarbonato m: **~ (di sodio)** bicarbonate of soda
bicchiere m glass
bicentenario m bicentenary, *Am* bicentennial
bici f *inv* F bike F; **~ elettrica** e-bike; **bicicletta** f bike, bicycle; **andare in ~** go by bike, *Br anche* cycle
bidè m *inv* bidet

bidone *m* drum; *della spazza-tura* (dust)bin, *Am* garbage can; F (*imbroglio*) swindle

biennale biennial; (*che dura due anni*) two-year; **biennio** *m* two-year period

bietola *f* beet

biforcarsi fork; **biforcazione** *f* fork

bigamo *m*, **-a** *f* bigamist

bigiotteria *f* costume jewellery *o Am* jewelry; *negozio* jeweller's, *Am* jewelry store

bigliettaio *m*, **-a** *f* ticket seller; *sul treno*, *tram* conductor, *Am* guard; **biglietteria** *f* ticket office; *di cinema*, *teatro* box office; **biglietto** *m* ticket; **~ d'auguri** (greetings) card; **~ da visita** business card; **un ~ da 10 dollari** a ten-dollar bill; **fare il ~** buy the ticket

bigodino *m* roller

bigotto 1 *agg* bigoted **2** *m*, **-a** *f* bigot

bikini *m inv* bikini

bilancia *f* scales; ASTR *Bilancia* Libra; **bilanciare** balance; (*pareggiare*) equal; *fig* weigh up; FIN **~ un conto** balance an account; **bilanciarsi** balance; **bilancio** *m* balance; (*rendiconto*) balance sheet; **~ preventivo** budget; **fare il ~** draw up a balance sheet; *fig* take stock

bile *f* bile; *fig* rage

biliardo *m* billiards *sg*, *Am* pool

bilico *m*: **essere in ~** be precariously balanced; *fig* be undecided

bilingue bilingual

bilocale *m* two-room flat *o Am* apartment

bimbo *m*, **-a** *f* child

bimotore *m* twin-engine plane

binario 1 *agg* binary **2** *m* track; (*marciapiede*) platform

binocolo *m* binoculars

biochimica *f* biochemistry

biodegradabile biodegradable

biografia *f* biography; **biografico** biographical; **biografo** *m*, **-a** *f* biographer

biologia *f* biology; **biologico** biological; *alimento* organic; **biologo** *m*, **-a** *f* biologist

biondo blonde

biossido *m* dioxide

birbante *m* rascal

birichino 1 *agg* naughty **2** *m*, **-a** *f* little devil

birillo *m* skittle

biro® *f inv* ballpoint (pen), *Br anche* biro

birra *f* beer; **~ alla spina** draught *o Am* draft beer; **birreria** *f* pub that sells only beer; *fabbrica* brewery

bis *m inv* encore

bisbetico bad-tempered

bisbigliare whisper

bisca *f* gambling den

biscia *f* grass snake

biscotto *m* biscuit, *Am* cook-

43

boicottare

ie
bisessuale bisexual
bisestile: *anno* m ~ leap year
bisnonno m, **-a** f great-grand-
father; *donna* great-grand-
mother
bisognare: *bisogna farlo* it
must be done, it needs to
be done; *non bisogna farlo*
it doesn't have to be done,
there's no need to do it; **bisogno** m need; *(mancanza)*
lack; *(fabbisogno)* requirements; *avere ~ di qc* need
sth; **bisognoso** needy
bisonte m ZO bison
bistecca f steak
bisticciare quarrel; **bisticcio**
m quarrel
bisturi m inv MED scalpel
bitter m inv aperitif
bivio m junction; *fig* crossroads sg
bizantino Byzantine
bizzarro bizarre
bizzeffe: *a ~* galore
blando mild, gentle
blatta f cockroach
blindato armoured, Am ar-
mored
blitz m inv blitz
bloccare block; MIL block-
ade; *(isolare)* cut off; *prezzi,
conto* freeze; **bloccarsi** di
ascensore, persona get stuck;
di freni, porta jam; **bloccaruota** m AUTO wheel clamp,
Am Denver boot; *mettere il
~ a* clamp; **bloccasterzo** m
AUTO steering lock

blocchetto m per appunti
notebook
blocco m block; *di carta* pad;
~ *stradale* road block
bloc-notes m inv writing pad
blu blue
blusa f blouse
boa[1] m inv ZO boa constrictor
boa[2] f MAR buoy
boato m rumble
bob m inv SP bobsleigh, bob-
sled; **bobbista** m/f bobsled-
der
bobina f spool
bocca f mouth; *(apertura)*
opening; *in ~ al lupo!* good
luck!; **boccaccia** f *(smorfia)*
grimace; **boccaglio** m di
maschera per il nuoto mouthpiece
boccale m jug; da birra tank-
ard
boccetta f small bottle
boccheggiare gasp
bocchino m per sigarette cigarette holder; MUS, di pipa
mouthpiece
boccia f *(palla)* bowl; **boccia-
re** *(respingere)* reject, vote
down; EDU fail; *boccia* hit,
strike; **bocciatura** f failure
bocciolo m bud
bocconcino m morsel; **boccone** m mouthful
bocconi face down
body m inv body(suit)
boia m inv executioner; F *fa
un freddo ~* it's freezing
boicottaggio m boycott; **boicottare** boycott

bolide m meteor; **come un ~** like greased lightning

bolla[1] f bubble; MED blister

bolla[2] f documento note, docket; **~ di consegna** delivery note

bollare stamp; fig brand

bollente boiling hot

bolletta f bill; **~ della luce** electricity bill

bollettino m: **~ meteorologico** weather forecast

bollire boil; **bollito 1** agg boiled **2** m boiled meat; **bollitore** m kettle

bollo m stamp

bomba f bomb; **bombardamento** m shelling, bombardment; (attacco aereo) air raid; fig bombardment; **bombardare** bomb; fig bombard

bombola f cylinder

bomboniera f wedding keepsake

bonaccia f MAR calm

bonaccione m, -a f kindhearted person

bonario kind-hearted

bonificare FIN (scontare) discount; (accreditare) credit; AGR reclaim; (prosciugare) drain; **bonifico** m (trasferimento) (money) transfer

bontà f inv goodness; (gentilezza) kindness

bora f bora (a cold north wind)

borbottare mumble

bordello m brothel; fig F bedlam F; (disordine) mess

bordo m (orlo) edge; **a ~** on board

boreale northern; **aurora** f **~** northern lights

borgata f village; (rione popolare) suburb

borghese middle-class; **in ~** in civilian clothes; **borghesia** f middle classes pl

borgo m village

borraccia f flask

borsa f bag; (borsetta) handbag, Am purse; per documenti briefcase; FIN Stock Market; **~ di studio** scholarship; **borsaiolo** m, -a f pickpocket; **borsellino** m purse, Am coin purse; **borsetta** f handbag, Am purse

borsista m/f speculatore speculator; studente scholarship holder

boscaiolo m woodcutter; **bosco** m wood

bossolo m di proiettili (shell) case

botanico 1 agg botanical **2** m, -a f botanist

botola f trapdoor

botta f blow; (rumore) bang; **fare a -e** come to blows

botte f barrel

bottega f shop; (laboratorio) workshop; **bottegaio** m, -a f shopkeeper; **botteghino** m box office; (del lotto) sales outlet for lottery tickets

bottiglia f bottle

bottino m loot

botto *m* (*rumore*) bang

bottone *m* button; **~ automatico** press-stud, *Am* snap fastener

bovino 1 *agg* bovine **2** *m*: **-i** *pl* cattle *pl*

box *m inv* per auto lock-up (garage); *per bambini* playpen; *per cavalli* loose box

boxe *f* boxing

bozza *f* draft; TIP proof; **bozzetto** *m* sketch

bozzolo *m* cocoon

braccetto: a ~ arm in arm

bracciale *m* bracelet; (*fascia*) armband; *di orologio* watch strap; **braccialetto** *m* bracelet; **bracciante** *m/f* day labourer, *Am* day laborer

bracciata *f* nel nuoto stroke; **braccio** *m* arm; **portare in ~ qu** carry s.o.; **bracciolo** *m* arm(rest)

bracconiere *m* poacher

brace *f* embers; **alla ~** char-grilled, *Am* char-broiled

braciola *f* GASTR chop

branca *f* branch (*anche fig*)

branchia *f* gill

branco *m* di cani, lupi pack; *di pecore, uccelli* flock; *fig spreg* gang

brancolare grope

branda *f* camp-bed, *Am* cot

brandello *m* shred, scrap; **a -i** in shreds *o* tatters

brano *m* di testo, musica passage

brasato *m* di manzo braised beef

Brasile *m* Brazil; **brasiliano 1** *agg* Brazilian **2** *m*, **-a** *f* Brazilian

bravata *f* boasting; *azione* bravado

bravo good; (*abile*) clever, good; **~!** well done!; **bravura** *f* skill

bretella *f* (*raccordo*) slip road, *Am* ramp; **-e** *pl* braces, *Am* suspenders

breve short; **in ~** briefly, in short

brevettare patent; **brevetto** *m* patent; *di pilota* licence, *Am* license

brezza *f* breeze

bricco *m* jug, *Am* pitcher

briciola *f* crumb; **briciolo** *m* fig grain, scrap

bricolage *m* do-it-yourself, DIY, *Am* home improvement

briga *f*: **darsi la ~ di fare qc** take the trouble to do sth; **attaccar~ con qu** pick a quarrel with s.o.

brigadiere *m* MIL sergeant

brigante *m* bandit

briglia *f* rein

brillante 1 *agg* sparkling; *colore* bright; *fig* brilliant **2** *m* diamond; **brillare** shine

brillo tipsy

brina *f* hoar-frost

brindare drink a toast (**a** to); **~ alla salute di qu** drink to s.o.'s health; **brindisi** *m inv* toast

brioche *f inv* brioche

britannico 1 *agg* British **2** *m*, **-a** *f* Briton, Brit F

brivido *m di freddo, spavento* shiver; *di emozione* thrill

brizzolato *capelli* greying, *Am* graying

brocca *f* jug, *Am* pitcher

broccato *m* brocade

broccoli *mpl* broccoli *sg*

brodo *m* (clear) soup; *di polo, di manzo, di verdura* stock; **brodoso** watery, thin

bronchite *f* bronchitis

broncio *m*: **avere il ~** sulk

broncopolmonite *f* bronchial pneumonia

brontolare grumble; *di stomaco* rumble; **brontolio** *m* grumble; *di stomaco* rumble; **brontolone 1** *agg* grumbling **2** *m*, **-a** *f* grumbler

bronzo *m* bronze

bruciapelo. a ~ point-blank; **bruciare 1** *v/t* burn; *(incendiare)* set fire to **2** *v/i* burn; *fig: di occhi* sting; **bruciarsi** burn o.s.; **bruciato** burnt; *dal sole* scorched, parched; **bruciatura** *f* burn; **bruciore** *m* burning sensation; **~ di stomaco** heartburn

bruco *m* grub; *(verme)* worm

brufolo *m* spot

brulicare swarm

brullo bare

bruno brown; *capelli* dark

bruschetta *f* GASTR bruschetta *(toasted bread with garlic and olive oil, Naples variant with chopped tomatoes)*

brusco sharp; *persona, modi* brusque, abrupt; *(improvviso)* sudden

brutale brutal; **brutalità** *f inv* brutality

brutta *f*: *(copia f)* ~ rough copy; **bruttezza** *f* ugliness; **brutto** ugly; *(cattivo)* bad; *tempo, tipo, affare* nasty

Bruxelles *f* Brussels

buca *f* hole; *(avvallamento)* hollow; *del biliardo* pocket; **~ delle lettere** letter-box, *Am* mailbox; **bucare** make a hole in; *(pungere)* prick; *biglietto* punch; **~ una gomma** have a flat (tyre)

bucato *m* washing, laundry; **fare il ~** do the washing

buccia *f* peel

bucherellare make holes in; **bucherellato dai tarli** riddled with woodworm

buco *m* hole

budello *m* gut; *(vicolo)* alley

budget *m inv* budget

budino *m* pudding

bue *m* ox; *carne* beef

bufalo *m* buffalo

bufera *f* storm

buffet *m inv* buffet; *mobile* sideboard, *Am* buffet

buffo funny; **buffone** *m*, **-a** *f* buffoon, fool; *di corte* fool, jester

bugia *f* *(menzogna)* lie; **bugiardo 1** *agg* lying **2** *m*, **-a** *f* liar

buio 1 *agg* dark **2** *m* darkness; **al ~** in the dark

cacciarsi

bulbo *m* BOT bulb
Bulgaria *f* Bulgaria; **bulgaro**
1 *agg* Bulgarian **2** *m*, **-a** *f* Bulgarian
bullone *m* bolt
buoi ☞ **bue**
buon ☞ **buono**
buonafede *f*: **in ~** in good faith
buonanotte good night
buonasera good evening
buongiorno good morning, hello
buongustaio *m*, **-a** *f* gourmet; **buongusto** *m* good taste; **di ~** in good taste
buono 1 *agg* good; *momento* right; **alla -a** informal, casual **2** *m* good; FIN bond; (*tagliando*) voucher; **~ regalo** gift voucher, *Am* gift certificate; **~ sconto** discount voucher
buonsenso *m* common sense
burattino *m* puppet
burbero gruff, surly
burla *f* practical joke, trick; **burlarsi**: **~ di qu** make fun

of s.o.; **burlone** *m*, **-a** *f* joker
burocratico bureaucratic; **burocrazia** *f* bureaucracy
burrasca *f* storm; **burrascoso** stormy
burro *m* butter
burrone *m* ravine
bussare knock
bussola *f* compass
busta *f* per *lettera* envelope; *per documenti* folder; (*astuccio*) case; **~ paga** pay packet
bustarella *f* bribe
bustina *f*: **~ di tè** tea bag
busto *m* ANAT torso; *scultura* bust; (*corsetto*) girdle
buttafuori *m inv* TEA callboy; *di locale notturno* bouncer; **buttare 1** *v/i* BOT sprout **2** *v/t* throw; **~ via** throw away; *fig* waste; **~ giù** knock down; *lettera* scribble down; *boccone* gulp down; F **~ la pasta** put the pasta on; **buttarsi** throw o.s.; *fig* have a go (**in** at)
by-pass *m inv* by-pass
byte *m inv* INFOR byte

C

ca (= *circa*) ca (= circa)
c.a. (= *corrente alternata*) AC (= alternating current)
cabina *f di nave, aereo* cabin; *di ascensore, funivia* cage; **~ telefonica** phone box, *Am* pay phone
cabriolè, cabriolet *m inv* con-

vertible
cacao *m* cocoa
caccia *f* hunting; **cacciagione** *f* GASTR game; **cacciare** hunt; (*scacciare*) drive out; (*ficcare*) shove; **~ via** chase away; **cacciarsi**: *dove ti eri cacciato?* where did you

cacciatora 48

get to?; **cacciatora** f: *alla ~* stewed; **cacciatore** m, **-trice** f hunter; **cacciavite** m inv screwdriver

cachemire m inv cashmere
cactus m inv cactus
cadavere m corpse
cadente: *stella f ~* falling star; **cadere** fall; *di edificio* fall down; *di capelli, denti* fall out; *di aereo* crash; **caduta** f fall
caffè m inv coffee; *locale* café; *~ corretto* espresso with a shot of alcohol; *~ macchiato* espresso with a splash of milk; **caffeina** f caffeine; *senza ~* caffeine-free; **caffelatte** m inv latte (*hot milk with a small amount of coffee*); **caffettiera** f (*bricco*) coffee pot; (*macchinetta*) coffee maker
cafone m boor
cagna f bitch
calabrese agg, m/f Calabrian
calabrone m hornet
calamari mpl squid
calamità f inv calamity; *~ naturale* natural disaster
calamita f magnet
calante: *luna f ~* waning moon; **calare** v/t lower **2** v/i di vento drop; *di prezzi, sipario* fall; *di sole* set, go down
calca f throng
calcagno m heel
calcare[1] (*pigiare*) press down; *con i piedi* tread; *parole* emphasize

calcare[2] m limestone
calcareo chalky
calce f lime
calcestruzzo m concrete
calciatore m football o soccer player
calcina f (*malta*) mortar; **calcinaccio** m (*intonaco*) bit of plaster; *di muro* bit of rubble
calcio[1] m kick; *attività* football, soccer; MIL butt; *~ di rigore* penalty kick
calcio[2] m CHIM calcium
calco m mould, *Am* mould
calcolare calculate; (*valutare*) weigh up; **calcolatore** m calculator; *fig* calculating person; *elettronico* computer; **calcolatrice** f calculator; **calcolo** m calculation
caldaia f boiler
caldarrosta f roast chestnut
caldo 1 agg warm; (*molto caldo*) hot **2** m warmth; *molto caldo* heat; *ho ~* I'm warm; I'm hot
calendario m calendar
calibro m calibre, *Am* caliber; TEC callipers
calice m goblet; REL chalice
calle f a *Venezia* lane
calligrafia f calligraphy
callo m corn
calma f calm; *prendersela con ~* take it easy; **calmante** m sedative; **calmare** calm; *dolore* soothe; **calmarsi** di *dolore* ease (off); **calmo** calm
calo m di *peso* loss; *dei prezzi*

drop, fall

calore *m* warmth; *intenso* heat

caloria *f* calorie

caloroso *fig* warm

calpestare walk on or *fig* trample over

calunnia *f* slander

calvario *m* REL Calvary; *fig* ordeal

calvizie *f* baldness; **calvo** bald

calza *f da donna* stocking; *da uomo* sock; **calzamaglia** *f* tights, *Am* pantyhose; *da ginnastica* leotard; **calzare** **1** *v/t scarpe* put on; *(indossare)* wear **2** *v/i fig* fit; **calzascarpe** *m* shoehorn; **calzatoio** *m* shoehorn; **calzature** *fpl* footwear; **calzettone** *m* knee sock; **calzino** *m* sock; **calzolaio** *m* shoemaker

calzoncini *mpl* shorts; **~ da bagno** (swimming) trunks

calzone *m* GASTR *folded-over pizza*

calzoni *mpl* trousers, *Am* pants

camaleonte *m* chameleon

cambiale *f* bill (of exchange)

cambiamento *m* change; **cambiare 1** *v/t* change; *(scambiare)* exchange **2** *v/i e* **cambiarsi** change; **cambio** *m* change; FIN, *(scambio)* exchange; AUTO, TEC gear; *in ~* in exchange (*di* for)

camera *f* room; **~ da letto** bedroom; **~ singola** single

room; **~ matrimoniale** double room; **Camera dei Deputati** House of Commons, *Am* House of Representatives; **~ d'aria** inner tube; **~ dell'industria e del commercio** chamber of commerce; **camerata** *f* stanza dormitory; *in ospedale* ward

cameriera *f* waitress; *(domestica)* maid; **cameriere** *m* waiter

camerino *m* dressing room

camice *m di medico* white coat; *di chirurgo* gown; **camicetta** *f* blouse; **camicia** *f* shirt; **~ da notte** nightdress

caminetto *m* fireplace; **camino** *m* chimney; *(focolare)* fireplace

camion *m inv* truck, *Br anche* lorry; **camioncino** *m* van; **camionista** *m* lorry driver, *Am* truck driver

cammello *m* camel; *stoffa* camel hair

camminare walk; *(funzionare)* work, go; **camminata** *f* walk; **cammino** *m*: *un'ora di ~* an hour's walk; *mettersi in ~* set out

camomilla *f* camomile; *(infuso)* camomile tea

camoscio *m* chamois; **scarpe** *fpl di ~* suede shoes

campagna *f* country; *fig*, POL campaign

campana *f* bell; **campanello** *m* bell; *della porta* doorbell; **campanile** *m* bell tower

campare 50

campare live
campeggiatore *m* camper;
campeggio *m* camping; *posto* camp site; camper *m inv*
camper van; camping *m*
camp site
campionario *m* samples
campionato *m* championship
campione *m* sample; (*esemplare*) specimen; SP champion
campo *m* field; ~ *da golf* golf
course; ~ *da calcio* football
o soccer pitch; ~ *da tennis*
tennis court; ~ *profughi* refugee camp; camposanto *m*
cemetery
Canada *m* Canada; canadese 1 *agg* Canadian 2 *m/f* Canadian 3 *f* half-litre bottle of
beer
canale *m* channel; *artificiale*
canal
canapa *f* hemp
canarino *m* canary
cancellare cross out; *con
gomma* erase; INFOR delete;
appuntamento cancel
cancellata *f* railings
cancelleria *f*: *articoli mpl di* ~
stationery
cancelliere *m* chancellor; DIR
clerk of the court
cancello *m* gate
cancerogeno carcinogenic
cancrena *f* gangrene
cancro *m* MED cancer; ASTR
Cancro Cancer
candeggina *f* bleach

candela *f* candle; candelabro
m candelabra; candeliere *m*
candlestick
candidarsi stand (for election), *Am* run; candidato
m, -a *f* candidate; candidatura *f* candidacy, candidature
candido pure white; (*sincero*)
frank; (*innocente*) innocent,
pure; (*ingenuo*) naive
canditi *mpl* candied fruit
cane *m* dog
canestro *m* basket
canguro *m* kangaroo
canile *m* (*casotto*) kennel; *luogo* kennels
canino 1 *agg* dog *attr* 2 *m*
(*dente*) canine (tooth)
canna *f* reed; (*bastone*) stick;
P joint P; ~ *da pesca* fishing
rod
cannella *f* GASTR cinnamon
cannelloni *mpl* cannelloni *sg*
cannibale *m* cannibal
cannocchiale *m* telescope
cannone *m* MIL gun, cannon;
(*asso*) ace
cannuccia *f* straw
canoa *f* canoe
canone *m* FIN rental (fee);
RAD, TV licence (fee); (*norma*) standard
canottaggio *m* a pagaie canoeing; *a remi* rowing
canottiera *f* vest, *Am* undershirt
canotto *m* rowing boat, *Am*
rowboat; ~ *pneumatico* rubber dinghy

cantante *m/f* singer; **cantare** sing; **cantautore** *m*, **-trice** *f* singer-songwriter

cantiere *m* building site; MAR shipyard

cantina *f* cellar; *locale* wine-shop

canto[1] *m* song; (*il cantare*) singing

canto[2] *m*: **d'altro ~** on the other hand

cantone *m* POL canton

canzonare tease

canzone *f* song

caos *m* chaos; **caotico** chaot-ic

C.A.P. *m* (= *Codice di Avviamento Postale*) postcode, *Am* zip code

capace (*abile*) capable; (*ampio*) large; **~ di fare qc** capable of doing sth; **capacità** *f inv* ability; (*capienza*) capacity

capanna *f* hut; **capannone** *m* shed; AVIA hangar

caparra *f* FIN deposit

capello *m* hair; **-i** *pl* hair

capezzolo *m* nipple

capiente large, capacious; **capienza** *f* capacity

capigliatura *f* hair

capillare MED capillary

capire understand; **capisco** I see; **ho capito** I see

capitale 1 *agg* capital; *fig* major **2** *f* città capital **3** *m* FIN capital; **capitalismo** *m* capitalism; **capitalista** *agg, m/f* capitalist

capitaneria *f*: **~ di porto** port authorities

capitano *m* captain

capitare *di avvenimento* happen; *di persona* find o.s.; **~ a proposito** come along at the right time

capitolo *m* chapter

capo *m* head; *persona* head, chief, boss; GEOG cape; **~ di vestiario** item of clothing; **da ~** from the beginning; **andare a ~** start a new paragraph; **capodanno** *m* New Year's Day; **capofamiglia** *m/f* head of the family; **capofitto**: **a ~** headlong; **capogiro** *m* dizzy spell; **capogruppo** *m/f* group leader; POL leader; **capolavoro** *m* masterpiece; **capolinea** *m* terminus; **capoluogo** *m* principal town; **caporeparto** *m/f di fabbrica* foreman; *donna* forewoman; *di ufficio* superintendent; **caposala** *m/f in ospedale* ward sister; *uomo* charge nurse; **capostazione** *m/f* station master; **capostipite** *m/f* founder; **capotavola**: **a ~** at the head of the table; **capotreno** *m/f* guard, *Am* conductor; **capoufficio** *m/f* supervisor; **capoverso** *m* paragraph; TIP indent; **capovolgere** turn upside down; *piani* upset; *situazione* reverse; **capovolgersi** turn upside down; *di barca* capsize; **capovolgimento**

m complete change; **capovolto** *pp* ☞ **capovolgere**

cappa *f* (*mantello*) cloak; *di cucina* hood; **~ del camino** cowl

cappella *f* chapel

cappelletti *mpl* pasta, *shaped like little hats, with meat, cheese and egg filling;* **cappello** *m* hat

cappero *m* caper

cappio *m* noose

cappone *m* capon

cappotto *m* coat

cappuccino *m bevanda* cappuccino

cappuccio *m* hood; *di penna* top, cap

capra *f* (nanny)goat; (*cavalletto*) trestle; **capretto** *m* kid

capriccio *m* whim; *di bambini* tantrum; **fare i -i** have tantrums; **capriccioso** capricious; *bambino* naughty; *tempo* changeable

Capricorno ASTR Capricorn

capriola *f* somersault

capriolo *m* roe deer; GASTR venison; **capro** *m* billy goat; **~ espiatorio** scapegoat

capsula *f* capsule; *di dente* crown

captare RAD pick up

carabiniere *m* police officer

caraffa *f* carafe

caramella *f* sweet

caramello *m* caramel

carato *m* carat

carattere *m* character; (*caratteristica*) characteristic; **-i** *pl*

TIP font; **caratteristica** *f* characteristic; **caratteristico** characteristic; **caratterizzare** characterize

caravan *m inv* caravan

carboidrato *m* carbohydrate

carbone *m* coal; **carbonella** *f* charcoal

carburante *m* fuel

carburatore *m* carburettor, *Am* carburetor

carcassa *f* carcass; TEC (*intelaiatura*) frame; MAR wreck

carcerato *m*, **-a** *f* prisoner; **carcerazione** *f* imprisonment; **~ preventiva** preventive detention; **carcere** *m* jail, prison

carciofo *m* artichoke

cardiaco cardiac, heart *attr*

cardinale *m/agg* cardinal

cardiologo *m*, **-a** *f* heart specialist, cardiologist

cardo *m* thistle

carena *f* MAR keel

carenza *f* lack (**di** of)

carestia *f* shortage

carezza *f* caress; **carezzare** caress

cariato: **dente** *m* **~** decayed tooth

carica *f* (*incarico*) office; (*slancio, energia*) drive; TEC load; MIL (*attacco*) charge; SP tackle; **caricabatteria** *m* TEL charger

caricare load; MIL charge; *orologio* wind up; **caricarsi** overload o.s. (**di** with)

caricatura *f* caricature

cartellone

carico 1 *agg* loaded; EL charged **2** *m* load; MAR cargo

carie *f inv* tooth decay

carino (*grazioso*) pretty; (*gentile*) nice

carisma *m* charisma

carità *f* charity

carnagione *f* complexion

carne *f* flesh; GASTR meat; **~ di maiale / manzo** pork / beef; **~ tritata** mince, *Am* ground beef; **carneficina** *f* slaughter

carnevale *m* carnival

carnivoro *m* carnivore

caro 1 *agg* dear; (*costoso*) dear, expensive **2** *avv* a lot; **costare ~** be very expensive; *fig* have a high price

carogna *f* carrion; F swine

carota *f* carrot

carotide *f* carotid artery

carovana *f* caravan

carovita *m* high cost of living; **indennità *f di ~*** cost of living allowance

carpa *f* carp

carpire: **~ qc a qu** get sth out of s.o.

carponi on all fours

carrabile ✎ **carraio**

carraio: **passo** *m* **~** driveway

carreggiata *f* roadway

carrello *m* trolley, *Am* cart; AVIA undercarriage

carretto *m* cart

carriera *f* career

carriola *f* wheelbarrow

carro *m* cart; AST Bear; **~ armato** tank; **~ attrezzi** tow car; *Am* wrecker

carrozza *f* FERR carriage, *Am* car; **~ con cuccette** sleeping car; **~ ristorante** restaurant car

carrozzella *f per bambini* pram, *Am* baby carriage; *per invalidi* wheelchair

carrozzeria *f* bodywork, coachwork; **carrozziere** *m* AUTO (*progettista*) (car) designer; (*costruttore*) coachbuilder; *chi fa riparazioni* panel beater; **carrozzina** *f* pram, *Am* baby carriage

carta *f* paper; (*menù*) menu; **~ geografica** map; **~ da gioco** (playing) card; **~ da parati** wallpaper ~ **~ di credito** credit card; **~ d'identità** identity card; **~ d'imbarco** boarding card; **~ igienica** toilet paper; **~ stagnola** silver paper; GASTR tinfoil; **~ telefonica** phone card; **cartamodello** *m* pattern; **cartapesta** *f* papier-mâché; **cartastraccia** *f* waste paper

cartella *f* (*borsa*) briefcase; *di alunno* schoolbag; *per documenti* folder, file; **cartellino** *m* (*etichetta*) label; *con prezzo* price tag; (*scheda*) card

cartello *m* sign; *nelle dimostrazioni* placard; FIN cartel; **~ stradale** road sign

cartellone *m pubblicitario* hoarding, *Am* billboard; TEA bill

cartiera f paper mill

cartilagine f cartilage

cartina f GEOG map; (*bustina*) packet; *per sigarette* cigarette paper

cartoccio m paper bag; *a cono* paper cone; GASTR *al ~* baked in tinfoil

cartoleria f stationer's, *Am* stationery store

cartolina f postcard

cartoncino m (thin) cardboard; (*biglietto*) card

cartone m cardboard; *-i pl animati* cartoons

cartuccia f cartridge

casa f edificio house; (*abitazione*) home; *~ di cura* nursing home; *~ editrice* publishing house; *cambiare ~* move (house); *fatto in ~* homemade; *andare a ~* go home; *essere a ~* be at home; SP *giocare in* / *fuori ~* play at home / away; *casalinga* f housewife; *casalingo* domestic; (*fatto in casa*) home-made; *persona* home-loving; *-ghi mpl* household goods

cascare fall (down); *fig cascarci* fall for it; *cascata* f waterfall

cascina f (*casa colonica*) farmhouse; (*caseificio*) dairy farm

casco m helmet; *dal parrucchiere* hair dryer

caseggiato m (*edificio*) block of flats, *Am* apartment block

caseificio m dairy

casella f *di schedario* pigeonhole; (*quadratino*) square; *~ postale* post office box; *casellario* m pigeon holes; *~ giudiziario* criminal records (office); *casello* m autostradale toll booth, pay station

casereccio homemade

caserma f barracks

casinò m inv casino

casino m P brothel; (*rumore*) din, racket; (*disordine*) mess

caso m case; (*destino*) chance; (*occasione*) opportunity; *~ d'emergenza* emergency; *per ~* by chance; *a ~* at random; *in ~ contrario* should that not be the case; *in ogni ~* in any case, anyway; *in nessun ~* under no circumstances

casolare m farmhouse

caspita! good heavens!

cassa f case; *di legno* crate; *di negozio* till; *sportello* cash desk; (*banca*) bank; *~ toracica* ribcage; *cassaforte* f safe; *cassapanca* f chest

casseruola f (sauce)pan

cassetta f box; *per frutta, verdura* crate; (*musicassetta*) cassette; *~ delle lettere* (*buca*) post box, *Am* mailbox; (*casella*) letterbox, *Am* mailbox

cassetto m drawer; **cassettone** m chest of drawers

cassiere m, *-a* f cashier; *di*

banca teller; *di supermercato* checkout assistant
cassonetto *m* dustbin, *Am* garbage can
casta *f* caste
castagna *f* chestnut; **castagno** *m* chestnut (tree)
castano *capelli* chestnut; *occhi* brown
castello *m* castle
castigo *m* punishment
castità *f* chastity
castoro *m* beaver
castrare castrate; *gatto* neuter; *femmina di animale* spay
casual 1 *agg* casual **2** *m* casual clothes, casual wear; **casuale** chance *attr*, casual
cataclisma *m* disaster
catacomba *f* catacomb
catalizzatore *m* catalyst; AUTO catalytic converter
catalogare catalogue, *Am* catalog; **catalogo** *m* catalogue, *Am* catalog
catapecchia *f* shack
catarifrangente *m* reflector; *lungo la strada* cat's eye, *Am* reflector
catarro *m* catarrh
catasto *m* land register
catastrofe *f* catastrophe; **catastrofico** catastrophic
categoria *f* category; *di albergo* class; **categorico** categoric(al)
catena *f* chain; **-e** *pl* **da neve** snow chains; **~ montuosa** mountain range, chain of mountains

cateratta *f* sluice(gate); (*cascata*) falls
catino *m* basin
catrame *m* tar
cattedra *f* (*scrivania*) desk
cattedrale *f* cathedral
cattiveria *f* wickedness; *di bambini* naughtiness; *azione* nasty thing to do; *parole crudeli* nasty thing to say; **cattivo** bad; *bambino* naughty, bad
cattolicesimo *m* (Roman) Catholicism; **cattolico 1** *agg* (Roman) Catholic **2** *m*, **-a** *f* (Roman) Catholic
cattura *f* capture; (*arresto*) arrest; **catturare** capture; (*arrestare*) arrest
caucciù *m* rubber
causa *f* cause; (*motivo*) reason; DIR lawsuit; **a ~ di** because of; **causare** cause
cautela *f* caution; (*precauzione*) precaution; **cauto** cautious; **cauzione** *f* (*deposito*) security; *per la libertà provvisoria* bail
cava *f* quarry
cavalcare ride; **cavalcavia** *m inv* flyover, *Am* overpass; **cavalcioni: a ~** astride; **cavaliere** *m* rider; *accompagnatore* escort; *al ballo* partner
cavalla *f* mare; **cavalletta** *f* grasshopper; **cavalletto** *m* trestle; FOT tripod; *da pittore* easel; **cavallo** *m* horse; *scacchi* knight; *dei pantaloni* crotch; **andare a ~** go riding;

cavallone *m* breaker; **cavalluccio** *m*: **~ marino** sea horse

cavare take out; **cavarsela** manage, get by; **cavarsi**: **~ da un impiccio** get out of trouble; **cavatappi** *m inv* corkscrew

caverna *f* cave

cavia *f* guinea pig (*anche fig*)

caviale *m* caviar

caviglia *f* ANAT ankle

cavillo *m* quibble

cavità *f inv* cavity

cavo 1 *agg* hollow **2** *m* cable; (*fune*) rope

cavolfiore *m* cauliflower

cavolo *m* cabbage; **~ di Bruxelles** Brussels sprout

cazzo *m* V prick V; **~!** fuck! V

CC (= **Carabinieri**) Italian police force

cc (= **centimetri cubici**) cc (= cubic centimetres)

c.c. (= **corrente continua**) DC (= direct current)

c/c (= **conto corrente**) current account, *Am* checking account

CD *m inv* CD; **lettore** *m* **~** CD player; **CD-Rom** *m inv* CD-Rom; **drive** *m* **per ~** CD-Rom drive

ce = **ci** (*before* **lo, la, li, le, ne**)

c'è there is

cecchino *m* sniper

cece *m* chickpea

ceco 1 *agg* Czech **2** *m*, **-a** *f* Czech

cedere 1 *v/t* (*dare*) hand over, give up; (*vendere*) sell; **~ il posto** give up one's seat **2** *v/i* give in, surrender (**a** to); *muro, terreno* collapse, give way; **non ~!** don't give in!

cedola *f* coupon

cedro *m del Libano* cedar

ceffone *m* slap

celebrare celebrate; **celebrazione** *f* celebration; **celebre** famous; **celebrità** *f inv* fame; *persona* celebrity

celeste sky blue; (*divino*) heavenly (*anche fig*)

celibato *m* celibacy; **celibe 1** *agg* single, unmarried **2** *m* bachelor

cella *f* cell

cellula *f* cell; **cellulare 1** *agg* cell *attr*; **telefono** *m* **~** mobile (phone), *Am* cell(ular) phone **2** *m* prison van; *telefono* mobile, *Am* cell (phone); **~ con fotocamera** camera phone

cellulite *f* cellulite

cemento *m* cement; **~ armato** reinforced concrete

cena *f* supper, evening meal; *importante, con ospiti* dinner; **cenacolo** *m* PITT Last Supper; **cenare** have supper; *formalmente* dine

cencio *m* rag; *per spolverare* duster; **bianco come un ~** white as a sheet

cenere *f* ash; **le Ceneri** *fpl* Ash Wednesday

cenno *m* sign; *della mano*

cervello

wave; *del capo* nod; *con gli occhi* wink; (*breve notizia*) mention; (*allusione*) hint

cenone *m* feast, banquet

censimento *m* census

censura *f* censorship; **censurare** censor

centenario 1 *agg* hundred-year-old **2** *m persona* centenarian; *anniversario* centenary, *Am* centennial; **centesimo 1** *agg* hundredth **2** *m* FIN cent

centigrado *m* centigrade; **centimetro** *m* centimetre, *Am* centimeter; ~ *cubo* cubic centimetre; ~ *quadrato* square centimetre; **centinaio** *m* hundred; *un* ~ *di* about a hundred; **cento** hundred; *per* ~ per cent

centrale 1 *agg* central **2** *f* station, plant; **centralinista** *m/f* switchboard operator; **centralino** *m* switchboard; **centrare** centre, *Am* center; ~ *il bersaglio* hit the bull's eye

centrifuga 1 *agg* centrifugal **2** *f* spin-dryer; TEC centrifuge; **centrifugare** spin-dry; TEC centrifuge

centro *m* centre, *Am* center; *di bersaglio* bull's eye; ~ *commerciale* shopping centre, *Am* downtown; ~ *storico* old (part of) town

ceppo *m*: ~ *bloccaruota* wheel clamp, *Am* Denver boot

cera *f* wax; *per lucidare* polish

ceramica *f* ceramics *sg*; *oggetto* piece of pottery

cerata *f* oilskins

cerca *f*: *in* ~ *di* ... in search of ...; **cercare 1** *v/t* look for **2** *v/i*: ~ *di fare* try to do

cerchio *m* circle; **cerchione** *m* TEC rim

cereale 1 *agg* grain *attr* **2** -**i** *mpl* grain, cereals

cerebrale: **commozione** *f* ~ concussion

cerimonia *f* ceremony; REL service; -**e** *pl* (*convenevoli*) pleasantries

cerino *m* (wax) match

cernia *f* grouper

cerniera *f* hinge; ~ *lampo* zip (fastener), *Am* zipper

cernita *f* selection, choice

cero *m* (large) candle

cerotto *m* (sticking) plaster, *Am* Bandaid®

certezza *f* certainty

certificare certify; **certificato** *m* certificate

certo 1 *agg* (*sicuro*) certain, sure; *un* ~ *signor Federici* a (certain) Mr Federici; *ci vuole un* ~ *coraggio* it takes (some) courage; *di una* -**a** *età* of a certain age; -**i** some **2** *avv* (*certamente*) certainly; (*naturalmente*) of course; *che* ... surely ... **3** *pron*: -**i**, -**e** some, some people

certosa *f* Carthusian monastery

cervello *m* brain; GASTR brains

cervo m deer; *carne* venison

cesareo: taglio m ~ Caesarean, *Am* Cesarean

cesoie fpl shears

cespuglio m bush, shrub

cessare stop, cease; **cessate il fuoco** m ceasefire; **cessazione** f *di contratto* termination

cessione f transfer, handover

cesso m P bog P, *Am* john F

cesta f basket

cestinare throw away, bin F; **cestino** m little basket; *per la carta* wastepaper basket, *Am* waste basket; **cesto** m basket

ceto m (social) class; ~ **medio** middle class

cetriolino m gherkin; **cetriolo** m cucumber

che 1 agg what; **a ~ cosa serve?** what is that for?; ~ **brutta giornata!** what a filthy day! **2** pron persona: soggetto who; *persona:* oggetto who, that, *fml* whom; *cosa* that, which; *ciò* ~ what; **non c'e di** ~ don't mention it, you're welcome **3** cong dopo il comparativo than

check-in m inv check-in

chemioterapia f chemotherapy, chemo F

chi who; **di** ~ **è il libro?** whose book is this? **a** ~ **ha venduto la casa?** who did he sell the house to?; **c'è** ~ **dice che** some people say that; ~ ... ~ some ... others

chiacchiera f chat; (*maldicenza*) gossip; (*notizia infondata*) rumour, *Am* rumor; **chiacchierare** chat, chatter; *spreg* gossip; **chiacchierata** f chat; **chiacchierone 1** agg talkative, chatty; (*pettegolo*) gossipy **2** m, -a f chatterbox; (*pettegolo*) gossip

chiamare call; **andare a** ~ **qu** go and get s.o., fetch s.o.; **chiamarsi** be called; **come ti chiami?** what's your name?; **mi chiamo ...** my name is ...; **chiamata** f call; TELEC (telephone) call, (phone)call

chiara f egg white; **chiarezza** f clarity; **chiarimento** m clarification; **chiarire** clarify; **chiarirsi** become clear; **chiaro** clear; *colore* light, pale; (*luminoso*) bright; ~! obviously!; **chiaroscuro** m chiaroscuro

chiasso m din, racket; **fare** ~ make a din o racket; **chiassoso** noisy

chiatta f barge; **ponte** m **di -e** pontoon bridge

chiave 1 agg inv key **2** f key; MUS clef; ~ **inglese** spanner, *Am* monkey wrench; **chiavistello** m bolt

chiazza f (*macchia*) stain; *sulla pelle, di colore* patch

chic inv chic, stylish

chicco m grain; *di caffè* bean; ~ **d'uva** grape

chiedere *per sapere* ask (*di*

cibo

about); *per avere* ask for; *(esigere)* demand, require; **~ qc a qu** ask s.o. sth; **~ di qu** *(chiedere notizie di)* ask about s.o.; *per parlargli* ask for s.o; **~ un piacere a qu** ask s.o. a favour; **~ scusa a qu** apologize to s.o.; **chiedersi** wonder (**se** whether)

chiesa *f* church

chiesto *pp* ☞ **chiedere**

chiglia *f* MAR keel

chilo *m* kilo; **chilogrammo** *m* kilogram; **chilometraggio** *m* AUTO *mileage*; **chilometro** *m* kilometre, *Am* kilometer; **-i** *pl* **all'ora** kilometres per hour

chilowatt *m inv* kilowatt

chimica *f* chemistry; **chimico 1** *agg* chemical **2** *m*, **-a** *f* chemist

chinare *testa* bend; *occhi* lower; **chinarsi** stoop, bend down

chincaglierie *fpl* knick-knacks

chioccia *f fig* mother hen

chiocciola *f* snail; *in indirizzo e-mail* at; **scala** *f* **a ~** spiral staircase

chiodato: SP **scarpe** *fpl* **-e** spikes

chiodo *m* nail

chioma *f* mane; *di cometa* tail

chiosco *m* kiosk

chiostro *m* cloister

chiromante *m/f* palmist

chirurgia *f* surgery; **chirurgo** *m* surgeon

chissà who knows; *(forse)* maybe

chitarra *f* guitar; **chitarrista** *m/f* guitarist

chiudere close, shut; *a chiave* lock; *strada* close off; *gas, luce* turn off; *fabbrica, negozio* *per sempre* shut down; **chiudersi** *di porta, ombrello* close, shut; *di ferita* heal up

chiunque anyone; *relativo* whoever; **~ lo vede** whoever sees it

chiuso 1 *pp* ☞ **chiudere 2** *agg* closed, shut; *a chiave* locked; *persona* reserved; **chiusura** *f* closing, shutting

choc *m inv* shock

ci 1 *pron* ◇ us; **non ~ ha parlato** he didn't speak to us, **~ siamo divertiti molto** we had a great time; **~ vogliamo bene** we love each other ◇: **~ penso** I'm thinking about it **2** *avv* here; *(lì)* there; **c'è ...** there is ...; **~ sono ...** there are ...

ciabatta *f* slipper

cialda *f* wafer

ciambella *f* GASTR *type of cake, baked in a ring-shaped mould*; *(salvagente)* lifebelt

cianfrusaglia *f* knick-knack

ciao! hi!; *nel congedarsi* bye!

ciarpame *m* junk

ciascuno 1 *agg* each; *(ogni)* every **2** *pron* everyone

ciber... cyber...

cibo *m* food; **-i** *pl* foodstuffs, foods; **~ pronto** fast food

cicala f insetto cicada

cicalino m buzzer, bleeper

cicatrice f scar; **cicatrizzare, cicatrizzarsi** heal

cicca f (mozzicone) stub, butt; (gomma da masticare) (chewing) gum

ciccia f (grasso) flab; **ciccione** m, **-a** f fatty

ciclamino m cyclamen

ciclismo m cycling; **ciclista** m/f cyclist; **ciclistico** bike attr, cycle attr; **ciclo** m cycle; **ciclomotore** m moped

ciclone m cyclone

cicloturismo m cycling holidays

cicogna f stork

cicoria f chicory

cieco 1 agg blind; **vicolo m ~** dead end, blind alley **2** m, **-a** f blind man; **donna blind woman**

cielo m sky; REL heaven; **grazie al ~** thank heavens

cifra f figure; (monogramma) monogram; (somma) amount, sum; (codice) cipher, code

ciglio m ANAT eyelash; (bordo) edge

cigno m swan

cigolare squeak; **cigolio** m squeak

Cile m Chile

cilecca f: **far ~** di arma da fuoco misfire

cileno 1 agg Chilean **2** m, **-a** f Chilean

ciliegia f cherry; **ciliegio** m cherry (tree)

cilindro m cylinder; **cappello** top hat

cima f top; **in ~ a** on top of; **da ~ a fondo** from top to bottom; **fig** from beginning to end

cimentarsi: **~ in** embark on

ciminiera f smokestack

cimitero m cemetery

cin cin! F cheers!

Cina f China

cineforum m inv film followed by a discussion; **club** film club

cinema m inv cinema, luogo cinema, **Am** movie theater; **cinematografico** film attr, movie attr

cinepresa f cine-camera

cinese agg, m/f Chinese

cinghia f strap; (cintura) belt

cinghiale m wild boar

cinguettare twitter

cinico 1 agg cynical **2** m -a f cynic; **cinismo** m cynicism

cinquanta fifty; **cinquantenne** m/f 50-year-old; **cinquantesimo** fiftieth; **cinquantina** f: **una ~ di** about 50; **cinque** five; **cinquecento 1** agg five hundred **2** m: **il Cinquecento** the sixteenth century; **cinquemila** five thousand

cintura f belt; (vita) waist; **~ di sicurezza** seatbelt; **cinturino** m strap

ciò (questo) this; (quello) that; **~ che** what; **~ nonostante**

nevertheless

ciocca *f di capelli* lock

cioccolata *f* chocolate; **cioccolatino** *m* chocolate; **cioccolato** *m* chocolate

cioè that is, i.e.

ciondolo *m* pendant

ciotola *f* bowl

ciottolo *m* pebble

cipolla *f* onion; *di pianta* bulb; **cipollina** *f* small onion

cipresso *m* cypress (tree)

cipria *f* (face) powder

circa about

circo *m* circus

circolare 1 *v/i* circulate; *di persone* move along **2** *agg* circular **3** *f lettera* circular; **circolazione** *f* traffic; MED circulation; *mettere in ∼ voci* spread

circolo *m* circle; *(club)* club

circondare surround

conferenza *f* circumference

circonvallazione *f* ring road, *Am* beltway

circoscrizione *f* area, district; *∼ elettorale* constituency

circostante surrounding; **circostanza** *f* circumstance; *(occasione)* occasion

circuito *m* SP *(percorso)* track; EL circuit; EL *corto ∼* short circuit

cisterna *f* cistern; *(serbatoio)* tank; *nave f ∼* tanker

cisti *f* cyst; **cistifellea** *f* gall bladder; **cistite** *f* cystitis

citofono *m* entry phone; *in uffici* intercom

città *f inv* town; *grande* city; *Città del Vaticano* Vatican City; **cittadina** *f* (small) town; **cittadinanza** *f* citizenship; *(popolazione)* citizens; **cittadino 1** *agg* town *attr*, city *attr* **2** *m*, *-a f* citizen; *(abitante di città)* city dweller

ciuccio *m* F *(succhiotto)* dummy, *Am* pacifier

ciuffo *m* tuft

civetta *f* ZO (little) owl; *fig far la ∼* flirt

civico *della città* municipal, town *attr*; *delle persone* civic

civile 1 *agg* civil; *civilizzato* civilized; *(non militare)* civilian **2** *m* civilian; **civiltà** *f inv* civilization

clacson *m inv* horn

clamoroso *fig* sensational

clandestino 1 *agg* clandestine; *(illegale)* illegal **2** *m*, *-a f* stowaway

clarinetto *m* clarinet

classe *f* class; *(aula)* classroom

classico 1 *agg* classical; *(tipico)* classic **2** *m* classic

classifica *f* classification; *(elenco)* list; *sportiva* league standings, league table; *musicale* charts; **classificare**

classify; **classificatore** *m* (*cartella*) folder; *mobile* filing cabinet, *Am* file cabinet

classismo *m* class consciousness

clausola *f* clause; (*riserva*) proviso

claustrofobia *f* claustrophobia

clavicola *f* collar-bone

clero *m* clergy

clessidra *f* hourglass

cliccare INFOR click (**su** on); **~ due volte** double-click

cliché *m inv* fig cliché

cliente *m/f* customer; *di professionista* client; *di albergo* guest; MED patient; **clientela** *f* customers, clientele; *di professionista* clients; *di medico* patients

clima *m* climate; **climatico** climate *adj* fig, climatic; **stazione** *f* **climatica** health resort

clinica *f* (*ospedale*) clinic; (*casa di cura*) nursing home; **clinico 1** *agg* clinical **2** *m* clinician

clip *m inv* clip

clonare BIO clone; **clonazione** *f* cloning; **clone** *m* clone

cloro *m* chlorine

clorofilla *f* chlorophyll

cloroformio *m* chloroform

club *m inv* club

coabitare share a flat *o Am* an apartment

coagularsi *di sangue* coagulate, clot; *di latte* curdle; **coalizione** *f* coalition; **governo** *m* **di** ~ coalition government; **coalizzarsi** join forces; POL form a coalition

cobra *m inv* cobra

cocaina *f* cocaine

coccinella *f* ladybird, *Am* ladybug

coccio *m* earthenware; *frammento* fragment (of pottery); **cocciuto** stubborn, obstinate

cocco *m* *albero* coconut palm

coccodrillo *m* crocodile

coccolare F cuddle; (*viziare*) spoil

cocktail *m inv* cocktail; *festa* cocktail party

cocomero *m* water melon

coda *f* tail; (*fila*) queue, *Am* line; *di veicolo, treno* rear; MUS coda; **fare la** ~ queue (up), *Am* stand in line

codardo 1 *agg* cowardly **2** *m*, **-a** *f* coward

codice *m* code; **~ di avviamento postale** postcode, *Am* zip code; **~ fiscale** tax code; **~ segreto** PIN; **codificare** *dati* encode; DIR codify

codino *m* pigtail, plait, *Am* braid

coerente coherent; fig consistent; **coerenza** *f* coherence; fig consistency

coetaneo 1 *agg* the same age (**di** as) **2** *m*, **-a** *f* contemporary

cofanetto *m* casket

cofano *m* AUTO bonnet, *Am* hood

cogliere pick; (*raccogliere*) gather; (*afferrare*) seize; *occasione* take, seize; (*capire*) grasp

cognac *m inv* cognac

cognato *m*, **-a** *f* brother-in-law; *donna* sister-in-law

cognizione *f* knowledge; *filosofia* cognition; **parla con ~ di causa** he knows what he's talking about

cognome *m* surname, family name

coi = **con** and *art* **i**

coincidenza *f* coincidence; FERR connection; **coincidere** coincide

coinquilino *m*, **-a** *f* in *condominio* fellow tenant; *in appartamento* flatmate, *Am* roommate

coinvolgere involve; **coinvolto** *pp* ☞ **coinvolgere**

col = **con** and *art* **il**

colapasta *m inv* colander

colare 1 *v/t* strain; *pasta* drain **2** *v/i* drip; (*perdere*) leak; *di naso* run; *di cera* melt; **~ a fondo** *o* **a picco** sink, go down; **colazione** *f prima* breakfast; *di mezzogiorno* lunch; **far ~** have breakfast

colei *pron f* the one; **~ che** the one that

colera *m* cholera

colesterolo *m* cholesterol

colica *f* colic

colino *m* strainer

colla *f* glue; *di farina* paste

collaborare co-operate, collaborate; *con giornale* contribute; **collaboratore** *m*, **-trice** *f* collaborator; *di giornale* contributor; **collaborazione** *f* co-operation, collaboration

collana *f* necklace; *di libri* series *sg*

collant *m inv* tights, *Am* pantyhose

collare *m* collar

collasso *m* collapse

collaudare test; *fig* put to the test; **collaudo** *m* test

colle *m* hill; (*valico*) pass

collega *m/f* colleague, co-worker

collegamento *m* connection; MIL liaison; RAD, TV link; **collegare** connect, link; **collegarsi** RAD, TV link up

collegio *m* boarding school

collera *f* anger; **essere in ~ con qu** be angry with s.o.

colletta *f* collection; **collettività** *f* community; **collettivo** *m/agg* collective

colletto *m* collar

collezionare collect; **collezione** *f* collection; **fare ~ di qc** collect sth; **collezionista** *m/f* collector; **~ di francobolli** stamp collector

collina *f* hill

collirio *m* eyewash

collisione *f* collision

collo *m* neck; (*bagaglio*) piece of luggage; (*pacco*) package

collocamento *m* placing; (*impiego*) employment;

agenzia f **di ~** employment agency; **collocare** place, put

colloquiale colloquial

colloquio m talk, conversation; *ufficiale* interview; *(esame)* oral (exam)

colluttazione f scuffle

colmare fill (**di** with); *fig: di gentilezze* overwhelm (**di** with); **colmo** full (**di** of)

colomba f ZO, *fig* dove

colombo m pigeon

colon m colon

colonia f colony; *per bambini* holiday camp, *Am* summer camp; **colonizzare** colonize

colonna f column; **~ vertebrale** spinal column; **colonnato** m colonnade

colonnello m colonel

colorante m dye; **senza -i** with no artificial colouring o *Am* coloring; **colorare** colour, *Am* color; *disegno* colour in; **colorato** coloured, *Am* colored; **colore** m colour, *Am* color; *carte* suit; **a -i** *film, televisione* colour *attr*; **colorito 1** *agg volto* rosycheeked; *fig (vivace)* colourful, *Am* colorful **2** m complexion

coloro *pron pl* the ones; **~ che** those who

colossale colossal

colpa f fault; REL sin; **dare a qu la ~ di qc** blame s.o. for sth; **per ~ tua** because of you; **colpevole 1** *agg* guilty **2** m/f culprit, guilty party

colpire hit, strike; *fig* impress; **colpo** m blow; *di pistola* shot; MED stroke; *di telefono* phonecall; **di ~** suddenly

coltellata f *ferita* stab wound; **coltello** m knife

coltivare AGR, *fig* cultivate; **coltivazione** f cultivation; *di prodotti agricoli e piante* growing; *campi coltivati* crops

colto[1] cultured, learned

colto[2] *pp* ☞ **cogliere**

coltura f growing; *piante* crop

colui *pron* m the one; **~ che** the one that

coma m coma

comandante m commander; AVIA, MAR captain; **comandare** *v/t (ordinare)* order, command; *esercito* command; *nave* captain, be captain of; TEC control **2** *v/i* be in charge; **comando** m order, command; TEC control

combaciare fit together; *fig* correspond

combattere fight; **combattimento** m fight

combinare combine; *(organizzare)* arrange; **~ un guaio** make a mess; **combinazione** f combination; *(coincidenza)* coincidence; **per ~** by chance

combustibile 1 *agg* combustible **2** m fuel

come 1 *avv* as; *(in modo simile o uguale)* like; *interrogativo, esclamativo* how; *(prego?)*

pardon?, *Am* pardon me?; **fa' ~ ti ho detto** do as I told you; **~ me** like me; **un cappello ~ il mio** a hat like mine; **~ sta?** how are you?; **~ mai?** how come?, why?; **~ se** as if **2** *cong* (*come se*) as if, as though; (*appena, quando*) as (soon as)

cometa *f* comet

comfort *m inv* comfort; **dotato di tutti i ~ moderni** with all mod cons

comico 1 *agg* funny, comical; **genere comic 2** *m*, **-a** *f* comedian; *donna* comedienne

comignolo *m* chimney pot

cominciare start, begin (**a** to)

comitato *m* committee; **~ direttivo** steering committee; **comitiva** *f* group, party

comizio *m* meeting

commedia *f* comedy; *fig* play-acting; **commediografo** *m*, **-a** *f* playwright

commemorare commemorate; **commemorazione** *f* commemoration

commentare comment on; **commento** *m* comment

commerciale commercial; *relazioni, trattative* attr; *lettera* business attr; **commercialista** *m/f* accountant; **commercializzare** market; **commerciante** *m/f* merchant; (*negoziante*) shopkeeper, *Am* storekeeper; **commercio** *m* trade, business; *di droga* traffic; **essere**

in ~ be available

commesso *m*, **-a** *f* shop assistant, *Am* sales clerk

commestibile 1 *agg* edible **2** **-i** *mpl* foodstuffs

commettere commit; *errore* make

commiserare feel sorry for

commissariato *m*: **~ (di pubblica sicurezza)** police station; **commissario** *m di polizia* police superintendent, *Am* police chief; *membro di commissione* commissioner

commissione *f* commission; (*incarico*) errand; **-i** *pl* shopping

commosso 1 *pp* ☞ **commuovere 2** *agg* *fig* moved, touched

commovente moving, touching; **commozione** *f* emotion; **~ cerebrale** concussion; **commuovere** move, touch; **commuoversi** be moved *o* touched

comò *m inv* chest of drawers; **comodino** *m* bedside table

comodità *f inv* comfort; (*vantaggio*) convenience

comodo 1 *agg* comfortable; (*facilmente raggiungibile*) easy to get to; (*utile*) useful, handy; F *persona* laidback F; **stia ~!** don't get up! **2** *m* comfort; **con ~** at one's convenience; **far ~ di denaro** come in useful; **le fa ~ così** she finds it easier that way;

fare il propio ~ do as one pleases

compagnia f company; *(gruppo)* group; ~ *aerea* airline; *far ~ a qu* keep s.o. company

compagno *m*, **-a** f companion; *(convivente)* partner; POL comrade; ~ *di scuola* schoolfriend

comparativo *m/agg* comparative

comparire appear; *(far figura)* stand out; **comparizione** *f*: DIR *mandato m di* ~ summons *sg*; **comparsa** f appearance; TEA person with a walk-on part; *in film* extra; **comparso** *pp* ~ *comparire*

compartimento *m* compartment

compassione f compassion, pity; *provare* ~ *per qu* feel sorry for s.o.

compasso *m* compass

compatibile compatible; **compatibilità** f compatibility

compatire: ~ *qu* feel sorry for s.o.

compatto compact; *folla* dense; *fig* united

compensare *(controbilanciare)* compensate for, make up for; *(ricompensare)* reward; *(risarcire)* pay compensation to; **compenso** *m* *(ricompensa, risarcimento)* compensation; *(retribuzione)*

fee; *in* ~ *(d'altra parte)* on the other hand

compera f purchase; *fare le* **-e** go shopping

competente competent; *(responsabile)* appropriate; **competenza** f *(esperienza)* competence; *essere di* ~ *di qu* be s.o.'s responsibility

competere *(gareggiare)* compete; **competitivo** competitive; **competizione** f competition

compiacere please; **compiacersi** *(provare piacere)* be pleased *(di* with); **compiaciuto** *pp* ~ *compiacere*

compiangere pity; *per lutto* mourn; **compianto** *pp* ~ *compiangere*

compiere *(finire)* complete, finish; *(eseguire)* carry out; ~ *gli anni* have one's birthday

compilare compile; *modulo* complete

compito *m* task; EDU *i* **-i** *pl* homework

compiuto *lavoro, opera* completed, finished; *ha 10 anni* **-i** he's 10

compleanno *m* birthday; *buon* ~! happy birthday!

complementare complementary; **complemento** *m* complement; GRAM object

complessato full of complexes, uptight F; **complessivo** all-in; **complesso 1** *agg* complex **2** *m* complex;

MUS group; *di circostanze* set, combination; *in o nel ~* on the whole

completare complete; **completo 1** *agg* complete; (*pieno*) full; TEA sold out **2** *m* set; (*vestito*) suit; *al ~* (*pieno*) full (up); TEA sold out

complicare complicate; **complicarsi** get complicated; **complicato** complicated; **complicazione** *f* complication

complice *m/f* DIR accomplice **complimentarsi**: *~ con qu* congratulate s.o. (*per* on); **complimento** *m* compliment; *-i!* (congratulations!; *non fare -i!* help yourself!

componente 1 *m* component **2** *m/f* (*persona*) member; **componibile** modular; *cucina* fitted; **comporre** (*mettere in ordine*) arrange; MUS compose; *~ un numero* dial a number

comportamento *m* behaviour, *Am* behavior; **comportare** involve; **comportarsi** behave

compositore *m*, **-trice** *f* composer; **composizione** *f* composition; *di fiori* arrangement; DIR settlement

composto 1 *pp* ☞ **comporre 2** *agg* compound; *abiti, capelli* tidy, neat; *~ da* made up of **3** *m* compound

comprare buy, purchase; (*corrompere*) bribe, buy off;

compratore *m*, **-trice** *f* buyer, purchaser; **compravendita** *f* buying and selling

comprendere (*includere*) comprise, include; (*capire*) understand; **comprensibile** understandable, comprehensible; **comprensione** *f* understanding; **comprensivo** (*tollerante*) understanding; *~ di* inclusive of; **compreso 1** *pp* ☞ **comprendere 2** *agg* inclusive; (*capito*) understood; *tutto ~* all in; *~ te* including you

compressa *f* (*pastiglia*) tablet; *di garza* compress

compresso *pp* ☞ **comprimere**; **comprimere** press; (*reprimere*) repress; FIS compress

compromesso *pp* ☞ **compromettere 2** *m* compromise; **compromettere** compromise; **compromettersi** compromise o.s.

computer *m inv* computer; *~ portatile* laptop

comunale *del comune* municipal, town *attr*; **comune 1** *agg* common; *amico* mutual; (*ordinario*) ordinary, common; *in ~* in common; *fuori del ~* out of the ordinary **2** *m* municipality; **comunemente** commonly

comunicare 1 *v/t notizia* pass on, communicate; *contagio* pass on; REL give Communion to **2** *v/i* (*esprimersi*) communicate; *di persone* keep in touch, communicate; **comunicato** *m* announcement; ~ **stampa** press release; **comunicazione** *f* communication; (*annuncio*) announcement; TELEC (*collegamento*) connection

comunione *f* REL communion; *di idee* sharing

comunismo *m* Communism; **comunista** *m/f* Communist

comunità *f inv* community; **comunitario** community *attr, dell'Ue* Community *attr*

comunque 1 *cong* however, no matter how **2** *avv* (*in ogni modo*) in any case, anyhow; (*in qualche modo*) somehow; (*tuttavia*) however

con with; (*mezzo*) by

conato *m*: ~ **di vomito** retching

concedere grant; *premio* award; **concedersi**: ~ **qc** treat o.s. to sth

concentramento *m* concentration; **concentrare, concentrarsi** concentrate; **concentrazione** *f* concentration

concentrico concentric

concepibile conceivable; **concepimento** *m* conception; **concepimento** *m* conception; **concepire** conceive

concernere concern

concerto *m* concert; *composizione* concerto

concessionario *m* agent

concesso *pp* ☞ **concedere**

concetto *m* concept; (*giudizio*) opinion

conchiglia *f* shell

conciare *pelle* tan; (*sistemare*) arrange; **come ti sei conciato!** what a state you're in!; ~ **qu per le feste** tan s.o.'s hide

conciliare reconcile; *multa* pay, settle

concimare *pianta* feed; **concime** *m* manure

conciso concise

concittadino *m,* **-a** *f* fellow citizen

concludere conclude; (*portare a termine*) achieve, carry off; ~ **un affare** clinch a deal; **concludersi** end, close; **conclusione** *f* conclusion; **in** ~ in short; **conclusivo** conclusive; **concluso** *pp* ☞ **concludere**

concordare 1 *v/t* agree (on); GRAM make agree **2** *v/i* agree; (*coincidere*) tally; **concorde** in agreement; (*unanime*) unanimous

concorrente 1 *agg* (*rivale*) competing, rival *attr* **2** *m/f in una gara, gioco* competitor, contestant; FIN competitor; **concorrenza** *f* competition; **concorrere** (*contribuire*) concur; (*competere*) compete (**a** for); *di strade* converge; **concorso** *m* (*competizione*) competition, contest

concreto concrete; (*pratico*) practical

condanna *f* DIR sentence;

condannare condemn (*a* to); DIR sentence (*a* to)

condensare, **condensarsi** condense

condimento *m* seasoning; *di insalata* dressing; **condire** season; *insalata* dress; **condito** seasoned

condividere share; **condiviso** *pp* ☞ **condividere**

condizionale 1 *m/agg* conditional **2** *f* suspended sentence; **condizionamento** *m* PSI conditioning; **~ dell'aria** air conditioning; **condizionare** PSI condition; **condizionato: con aria -a** air-conditioned; **condizionatore** *m* air conditioner; **condizione** *f* condition; **a ~ che** on condition that

condoglianze *fpl* condolences; **fare le ~ a qu** express one's condolences to s.o.

condominio *m* (*comproprietà*) joint ownership; *edificio* block of flats, *Am* condo(-minium); **condomino** *m* owner-occupier, *Am* condo owner

condono *m* remission; **~ fiscale** conditional amnesty for tax evaders

condotta *f* (*comportamento*) behaviour, *Am* behavior, conduct; (*canale*) piping; **condotto 1** *pp* ☞ **condurre 2** *m* pipe; ANAT duct

conducente *m/f* driver; **condurre** lead; (*accompagnare*)

take; *veicolo* drive; **conduttore** *m*, **-trice** *f* RAD, TV presenter; **conduttura** *f* (*condotto*) pipe

confederazione *f* confederation

conferenza *f* conference; **~ stampa** press conference; **conferire 1** *v/t* (*dare*) confer; *premio* award **2** *v/i*: **~ con qu** confer with s.o.

conferma *f* confirmation; **confermare** confirm

confessare, **confessarsi** confess; **confessione** *f* confession

confetto *m* GASTR sugared almond; MED pill

confettura *f* jam, *Am* jelly

confezione *f* wrapping, packaging; *di abiti* making, **~ regalo** gift wrap; **-i** *pl* (*abiti*) garments

conficcare hammer, drive

confidare 1 *v/t* confide **2** *v/i*: **~ in** trust in, rely on; **confidarsi: ~ con** confide in; **confidenza** *f* (*familiarità*) familiarity, trust; **avere ~ con qu** be familiar with s.o.; **prendere ~ con qc** familiarize o.s. with sth; **confidenziale** (*riservato*) confidential

configurazione *f* configuration

confinante neighbouring, *Am* neighboring

confinare border (**con** sth); *fig* confine; **confine** *m* border; *fra terreni, fig* boundary

confisca f seizure; **confiscare** confiscate

conflitto m conflict

confluire merge

confondere confuse, mix up; (*imbarazzare*) embarrass; **confondersi** get mixed up

conformarsi: ~ *a* conform to; (*adattarsi*) adapt to; **conforme** (*simile*) similar; ~ *a* in accordance with; **conformismo** m conformity; **conformista** m/f conformist; **conformità** f conformity; **in** ~ *a* in accordance with

confortare comfort; **confortevole** comfortable; **conforto** m comfort

confrontare compare; **confronto** m confrontation; (*comparazione*) comparison; *a* ~ *di*, **in** ~ *a* compared with; **nei** -*i di* towards

confusione f confusion; (*disordine*) muddle, mess; (*baccano*) noise; (*imbarazzo*) embarrassment; **confuso 1** pp ☞ **confondere 2** agg (*non chiaro*) confused, muddled; (*imbarazzato*) embarrassed

congedare dismiss; MIL discharge; **congedarsi** take leave (**da** of); **congedo** m (*permesso*) leave; MIL ~ *assoluto* discharge

congelare 1 v/t freeze **2** v/i e **congelarsi** freeze; **congelato** frozen; **congelatore** m freezer

congenito congenital

congestionato congested; *volto* flushed; **congestione** f congestion

congettura f conjecture

congiungere join; **congiungersi** join (up)

congiuntivite f conjunctivitis

congiuntivo m GRAM subjunctive; **congiunto 1** pp ☞ **congiungere 2** m, -*a* f relative, relation; **congiunzione** f GRAM conjunction

congiura f conspiracy, plot

congratularsi: ~ *con qu* congratulate s.o. (**per** on); **congratulazioni** fpl: **fare le proprie** ~ *a qu* congratulate s.o.; -*i!* congratulations!

congressista m/f convention participant, Am conventioneer; **congresso** m convention

conguaglio m balance

coniare mint; *fig* coin

coniglio m rabbit

coniugare conjugate; **coniugato** married; **coniugazione** f conjugation; **coniuge** m/f spouse; -*i pl* husband and wife; *i -i Rossi* Mr and Mrs Rossi

connazionale m/f compatriot

connessione f connection

connotati mpl features

cono m cone; ~ *gelato* ice-cream cone

conoscente m/f acquaintance; **conoscenza** f knowledge; *persona* acquaintance;

(sensi) consciousness; ***perdere* ~** lose consciousness, faint; **conoscere** know; *(fare la conoscenza di)* meet; **conosciuto** well-known

conquista *f* conquest; **conquistare** conquer; *fig* win

consacrare consecrate; *(sacerdote)* ordain; *(dedicare)* dedicate

consanguineo *m*, **-a** *f* blood relative

consapevole: ~ di conscious of, aware of; **consapevolezza** *f* consciousness, awareness; **conscio** conscious, aware

consecutivo consecutive; **tre giorni -i** three consecutive days, three days in a row

consegna *f di lavoro, documento* handing in; *di prigioniero, ostaggio* handover; **~ bagagli** left luggage, *Am* baggage checkroom; **consegnare** *lavoro, documento* hand in; *prigioniero, ostaggio* hand over; *merci, posta* deliver

conseguenza *f* consequence; **di ~** consequently; **conseguire 1** *v/t* achieve; *laurea* obtain **2** *v/i* follow

consenso *m (permesso)* consent, permission; **consentire 1** *v/i (accondiscendere)* consent **2** *v/t* allow

conserva *f* preserve; **~ di pomodoro** tomato purée; **~ di frutta** jam, *Am* jelly; **conservante** *m* preservative; **conservare** keep; GASTR preserve; **conservarsi** keep; *in salute* keep well; **conservatore** *m*, **-trice** *f* conservative; **conservatorio** *m* music school, conservatoire

considerare consider; **considerazione** *f* consideration; *(osservazione)* remark, comment; ***prendere in* ~** take into consideration; **considerevole** considerable

consigliare advise; *(raccomandare)* recommend; **consigliarsi** seek advice; **consigliere** *m* adviser; **~ municipale** town councillor, *Am* councilman; **consiglio** *m* piece of advice; *(organo amministrativo)* council; **~ d'amministrazione** board (of directors); **~ dei ministri** Cabinet; **consigli** *pl* advice

consistente substantial; *(denso)* thick; **consistenza** *f (densità)* consistency, thickness; *di materiale* texture; *di argomento* basis; **consistere** consist (**~, in, di** of)

consolare¹ *v/t* console, comfort

consolare² *agg* consular

consolarsi console o.s.

consolato *m* consulate

consolazione *f* consolation

console *m diplomatico* consul

consolidare consolidate; **consolidarsi** stabilize

consonante 72

consonante f consonant

consorte m/f spouse; **principe** m ~ prince consort

consorzio m di imprese consortium

constatare ascertain, determine; (notare) note; **constatazione** f statement

consueto usual

consulente m/f consultant; ~ **legale** legal adviser; ~ **tributario** tax consultant; **consulenza** f consultancy; **consultare** consult; **consultarsi ~ con qu** consult (with) s.o.; **consultazione** f consultation; **consultorio** m family planning clinic

consumare acqua, gas use, consume; (logorare) wear out; (mangiare) eat, consume; (bere) drink; **consumarsi** wear out; **consumatore** m, **-trice** f consumer; **consumazione** f food; (bevanda) drink; **consumismo** m consumerism; **consumo** m consumption; (usura) wear

contabile m/f book-keeper; **contabilità** f FIN disciplina accounting; ufficio accounts department; **tenere la ~** keep the books

contachilometri m inv mileometer; Am odometer

contadino 1 agg rural, country attr 2 m, **-a** f farmer; (bracciante) farm labourer o Am laborer

contagiare infect; **contagio** m infection; **per contatto diretto** contagion; (epidemia) outbreak; **contagioso** infectious; **per contatto** contagious

contagiri m inv rev(olution) counter; **contagocce** m inv dropper

container m inv container

contaminare contaminate, pollute; **contaminazione** f contamination, pollution

contante m cash; **in -i** cash

contare 1 v/t count 2 v/i count; ~ **di fare qc** plan on doing sth; **contascatti** m inv time meter on phone; **contatore** m meter

contatto m contact

conte m count

contemplare contemplate

contemporaneamente at the same time; **contemporaneo** 1 agg contemporary (di with); movimenti simultaneous 2 m, **-a** f contemporary

contendersi contend for, compete for

contenere contain, hold; (reprimere) repress; (limitare) limit; **contenersi** contain o.s.; **contenitore** m container

contentezza f happiness; **contento** pleased (di with); (lieto) glad, happy

contenuto m contents

contesa f dispute

conteso *pp* ☞ **contendere**
contessa *f* countess
contestare protest; DIR serve; **contestazione** *f* protest
contesto *m* context
contiene ☞ **contenere**
continentale continental; **continente** *m* continent
continuare 1 *v/t* continue **2** *v/i* continue, carry on (**a fare** doing); **continuazione** *f* continuation; *di film* sequel; **in ~** over and over again; (*ininterrottamente*) non stop; **continuità** *f* continuity; **continuo** (*ininterrotto*) continuous; (*molto frequente*) continual; **di ~** (*ininterrottamente*) continuously; (*molto spesso*) continually
conto *m* (*calcolo*) calculation; FIN account; *in ristorante* bill, *Am* check; **~ corrente** current account, *Am* checking account; **rendere ~ di qc** account for sth; **rendersi ~ di qc** realize sth; **tenere ~ di qc** take sth into account; **~ alla rovescia** countdown; **in fin dei -i** when all's said and done, after all
contorcersi: ~ dal dolore / dalle risate roll about in pain / laughing
contorno *m* outline, contour; GASTR accompaniment
contorto twisted
contrabbandare smuggle; **contrabbandiere** *m* smug-

gler; **contrabbando** *m* contraband
contrabbasso *m* MUS double bass
contraccambiare return
contraccettivo *m* contraceptive
contraccolpo *m* rebound; *di arma da fuoco* recoil
contraddire contradict; **contraddizione** *f* contradiction
contraffare (*falsificare*) forge; (*imitare*) imitate; **contraffatto** forged; *voce* imitated; **contraffazione** *f* (*imitazione*) imitation; (*falsificazione*) forgery
contralto *m* MUS contralto
contrappeso *m* counterbalance
contrapporre set against; **contrapposizione** *f* opposition; **mettere in ~** contrast; **contrapposto** *pp* ☞ **contrapporre**
contrariamente: ~ a contrary to
contrariare *piani* thwart, oppose; *persona* irritate, annoy; **contrariato** irritated, annoyed
contrarietà *fpl* difficulties
contrario 1 *agg* contrary; *direzione* opposite; *vento* adverse; **essere ~** be against (**a** sth) **2** *m* contrary, opposite; **al ~** on the contrary
contrarre contract; **contrarsi** contract
contrassegnare mark;

contrassegno *m* mark; FIN (*in*) ~ cash on delivery, *Am* collect on delivery

contrastante contrasting; **contrasto** *m* contrast; (*litigio, discordia*) dispute

contrattacco *m* counter-attack

contrattare negotiate; *persona* hire

contrattempo *m* hitch

contratto 1 *pp* ☞ **contrarre 2** *m* contract

contravvenire contravene; **contravvenzione** *f* contravention; (*multa*) fine

contrazione *f* contraction; (*riduzione*) reduction

contribuente *m/f* taxpayer; **contribuire** contribute; **contributo** *m* contribution

contro against

controbattere (*replicare*) answer back; (*confutare*) rebut

controcorrente 1 *agg* nonconformist **2** *avv* against the current; *in fiume* upstream

controffensiva counter-offensive

controfigura *f* in *film* stand-in

controindicazione *f* MED contraindication

controllare control; (*verificare*) check; **controllo** *m* control; (*verifica*) check; MED check-up; ~ (*dei*) *passaporti* passport control; **controllore** *m* controller; *di bus, treno* ticket inspector

controluce *f:* *in* ~ against the light

contromano: *andare a* ~ be going the wrong way

controproducente counter-productive

contrordine *m* counterorder

controsenso *m* contradiction in terms; (*assurdità*) nonsense

controversia *f* controversy, dispute; DIR litigation; **controverso** controversial

controvoglia unwillingly

contusione *f* bruise; **contuso** bruised

convalescente 1 *agg* convalescent **2** *m/f* person who is convalescent; **convalescenza** *f* convalescence; *essere in* ~ be convalescing

convalidare validate

convegno *m* convention; *luogo* meeting place

convenevoli *mpl* pleasantries

conveniente (*vantaggioso*) good; (*opportuno*) appropriate; **convenienza** *f di prezzo, offerta* good value; *di gesto* appropriateness; *fare qc per* ~ do sth out of self-interest

convenire 1 *v/i* gather, meet; (*concordare*) agree; (*essere opportuno*) be advisable, be better **2** *v/t* (*stabilire*) stipulate

convento *m di monache* con-

vent; *di monaci* monastery
convenuto *pp* ☞ **convenire**
convenzionale conventional; **convenzione** *f* convention; (*accordo*) agreement, convention
convergere converge
conversare talk, make conversation; **conversazione** *f* conversation
conversione *f* conversion; AUTO U-turn; **convertirsi** be converted
convincere convince; **convinto** *pp* ☞ **convincere**; **convinzione** *f* conviction
convivente *m/f* common-law husband; *donna* common-law wife; **convivenza** *f* living together, cohabitation; **convivere** live together
convocare call, convene
convoglio *m* MIL, MAR convoy; FERR train
cooperare co-operate (*a* in); (*contribuire*) contribute (*a* to); **cooperativa** *f*: (*società f*) ~ co-operative; **cooperazione** *f* cooperation
coordinamento *m* co-ordination; **coordinare** co-ordinate; **coordinatore** *m*, **-trice** *f* co-ordinator; **coordinazione** *f* co-ordination
coperchio *m* lid, top
coperta *f* blanket; MAR deck; **copertina** *f* cover; **coperto 1** *pp* ☞ **coprire 2** *agg* covered (*di* with); *cielo* overcast, cloudy **3** *m* cover, shelter;

piatti e posate place; *prezzo* cover charge; **essere al ~** be under cover, be sheltered
copertone *m* AUTO tyre, *Am* tire
copia *f* copy; **copiare** copy
copione *m per attore* script
copisteria *f* copy centre *o Am* center
coppa *f* cup; (*calice*) glass; ~ (*di*) **gelato** dish of ice-cream; **coppetta** *f di gelato* tub
coppia *f* couple, pair
copricapo *m inv* head covering; **copricostume** *m inv* beachrobe; **coprifuoco** *m* curfew; **copriletto** *m inv* bedspread; **coprire** cover; *errore, suono* cover up; **coprirsi** (*vestirsi*) put something on; (*rannuvolarsi*) become overcast
coraggio *m* courage; (*sfacciataggine*) nerve; **coraggioso** brave, courageous
corallo *m* coral
Corano *m* Koran
corda *f* cord; (*fune*) rope; (*cordicella*), MUS string; **essere giù di ~** feel down; **tagliare la ~** cut and run
cordiale 1 *agg* cordial; **-i saluti** *mpl* kind regards **2** *m* cordial
cordoglio *m* (*dolore*) grief; (*condoglianze*) condolences
cordone *m* cord; *di marciapiedi* kerb, *Am* curb; (*sbarramento*) cordon; **~ ombelica-**

coreografo 76

le umbilical cord

coreografo *m*, **-a** *f* choreographer

coriandolo *m* BOT coriander; **-i** *mpl* confetti *sg*

coricarsi lie down

cornacchia *f* crow

cornamusa *f* bagpipes

cornea *f* cornea

cornetta *f* del telefono receiver

cornetto *m* (*brioche*) croissant; (*gelato*) cone, cornet

cornice *f* frame

cornicione *m* ARCHI cornice

corno *m* horn; *ramificate* antlers; *fig* F **fare le -a a qu** cheat on s.o.; **facciamoci le -a!** touch wood!; **cornuto** F cheated, betrayed

coro *m* chorus; *cantori* choir; **in ~** (*insieme*) all together

corona *f* crown; (*rosario*) rosary

corpo *m* body; MIL corps; (*a*) **~ a ~** hand-to-hand; **corporatura** *f* build

corpulento stout, corpulent

corredo *m* equipment; *da sposa* trousseau; *da neonato* layette

correggere correct; **correggersi** correct o.s.

correlazione *f* correlation

corrente 1 *agg* current; *acqua* running; *lingua* fluent; **2** *m*: **essere al ~** know (*di* sth); **tenere qu al ~** keep s.o. up to date, keep s.o. informed **3** *f* current; *fig*: *di opinione*

trend; *fazione* faction; **~ d'aria** draught, *Am* draft

correre 1 *v/t* run; **~ il pericolo** run the risk **2** *v/i* run; (*affrettarsi*) hurry; *di veicolo* speed; *di tempo* fly; **lascia ~!** let it go!; **corre voce** it is rumoured *o Am* rumored

correttezza *f* correctness; (*onestà*) honesty; **corretto 1** *pp* **correggere 2** *agg* correct; **correzione** *f* correction

corridoio *m* corridor; *in aereo, teatro* aisle

corridore *m* in *auto* racing driver; *a piedi* runner

corriera *f* bus

corriere *m* courier

corrispondente 1 *agg* corresponding **2** *m/f* correspondent; **corrispondenza** *f* correspondence; (*posta*) mail; **corrispondere 1** *v/t* (*pagare*) pay; (*ricambiare*) reciprocate **2** *v/i* correspond; (*coincidere*) coincide; (*equivalere*) be equivalent; **corrisposto 1** *pp* **corrispondere 2** *agg* reciprocated

corrodere, corrodersi corrode, rust

corrompere corrupt; *con denaro* bribe; **corroso** *pp* **corrodere**; **corrotto 1** *pp* **corrompere 2** *agg* corrupt

corrugare wrinkle; **~ la fronte** frown

corruzione *f* corruption; *con denaro* bribery

77

costo

corsa f run; *attività* running; *di autobus* trip, journey; *(gara)* race; **di ~** at a run; *in fretta* in a rush; **fare una ~** rush, dash; **-e** pl races

corsia f aisle; *di ospedale* ward; AUTO lane; **~ di emergenza** emergency lane; **~ di sorpasso** fast lane; **a tre -e** three-lane

Corsica f Corsica

corsivo m italics

corso¹ 1 agg Corsican **2** m, **-a** f Corsican

corso² **1** pp ☞ **correre 2** m course; *(strada)* main street; FIN *di moneta* circulation; *di titoli* rate; **~ d'acqua** watercourse; **~ di lingue** language course; FIN *fuori ~* out of circulation; *lavori* mpl *in* **~** work in progress

corte f court

corteccia f bark

corteggiare court

corteo m procession

cortese polite, courteous; **cortesia** f politeness, courtesy; **per ~!** please!

cortile m courtyard

corto short; **essere a ~ di** be short of; **cortocircuito** m short (circuit)

corvo m rook; **~ imperiale** raven

cosa f thing; *(che)* **~** what; **qualche ~** something; **dimmi una ~** tell me something; **una ~ da nulla** a trifle

coscia f thigh; GASTR leg

cosciente conscious; **coscienza** f conscience; *(consapevolezza)* consciousness; **coscienzioso** conscientious

così so; *(in questo modo)* like this; **~ ~** so-so; **e ~ via** and so on; **per ~ dire** so to speak; **proprio ~!** exactly!; **basta ~!** that's enough!; **cosicché** and so; **cosiddetto** so-called

cosmetico m/agg cosmetic

cosmo m cosmos

cosmopolita cosmopolitan

coso m F what-d'you-call-it F

cospargere sprinkle; *(coprire)* cover *(di* with); **cosparso** pp ☞ **cospargere**

cospiratore m, **-trice** f conspirator; **cospirazione** f conspiracy

costa f coast, coastline; *(pendio)* hillside; ANAT rib

costante constant, steady; **costanza** f perseverance

costare cost; **~ caro** be expensive, cost a lot; *fig* cost dear; **quanto costa?** how much is it?

costata f rib steak; **~ di agnello** lamb chop

costeggiare skirt, hug

costellazione f constellation

costiero coastal

costituire constitute; *società* form, create; **costituirsi** give o.s. up; **costituzionale** constitutional; **costituzione** f constitution

costo m cost; **~ della vita** cost of living; **ad ogni ~** at all costs

costola f rib; *di libro* spine; **costoletta** f GASTR cutlet

costoso expensive, costly

costretto pp ☞ **costringere**; **costringere** force, compel

costruire build, construct; **costruttivo** fig constructive; **costruttore** m, -trice f builder; (*fabbricante*) manufacturer; **costruzione** f building, construction; GRAM construction

costume m (*usanza*) custom; (*condotta*) morals; (*indumento*) costume; ~ **da bagno** swimming costume, swimsuit; *da uomo* (swimming) trunks

cotechino m kind of pork sausage

cotoletta f cutlet; ~ **alla milanese** breaded cutlet fried in butter

cotone m cotton; MED ~ **idrofilo** cotton wool, Am absorbent cotton

cotta f F crush

cottimo m: **lavorare a** ~ do piecework

cotto 1 pp ☞ **cuocere 2** agg done, cooked; F fig head over heels in love (*di* with); **cottura** f cooking

covare 1 v/t sit on, hatch; fig: *malattia* sicken for; *rancore* harbour, Am harbor 2 v/i sit on eggs; **covo** m den; (*nido*) nest; fig hideout

covone m sheaf

cozza f mussel

C.P. (= **Casella Postale**) PO Box (= Post Office Box)

crampo m cramp

cranio m skull

cratere m crater

cravatta f tie, Am anche necktie

creare create; fig (*causare*) cause; **creatività** f creativity; **creativo 1** agg creative **2** m copywriter; **creatore 1** agg creative **2** m Creator **3** m, -trice f creator; **creatura** f creature; **creazione** f creation

credente m/f believer

credenza[1] f belief

credenza[2] f mobile dresser

credenziali fpl credentials

credere 1 v/t believe; (*pensare*) believe, think; **lo credo bene!** I should think so too!; **credersi** believe o think o.s. to be **2** v/i believe; ~ **a qu** believe s.o.; ~ **in qu** believe in s.o; **non ci credo** I don't believe it; **credibile** credible; **credibilità** f credibility

credito m credit; fig trust; (*attendibilità*) reliability; **creditore** m, -trice f creditor

crema f cream; *di latte e uova* custard; ~ **da barba** shaving foam; ~ **idratante** moisturizer, moisturizing cream; ~ **solare** suntan lotion

cremare cremate; **cremazione** f cremation

79   **cruscotto**

cren m horseradish
crepa f crack; **crepaccio** m cleft; *di ghiacciaio* crevasse; **crepare** (*spaccarsi*) crack; F (*morire*) kick the bucket F
crêpe f inv pancake
crepitare crackle
crepuscolo m twilight
crescente growing; *luna* crescent; **crescere** 1 v/t bring up, raise 2 v/i grow
crescione m watercress
crescita f growth
cresima f confirmation
crespo *capelli* frizzy
cresta f crest; *di montagna* peak
creta f clay
cretino F 1 agg stupid, idiotic 2 m, -a f idiot, cretin
cric m inv AUTO jack
criminale agg, m/f criminal; **criminalità** f crime; **crimine** m crime
criniera f mane
cripta f crypt
crisantemo m chrysanthemum
crisi f inv crisis; MED fit
cristallizzare, cristallizzarsi crystallize; **cristallo** m crystal
cristianesimo m Christianity; **cristiano** 1 agg Christian 2 m, -a f Christian; **Cristo** m Christ
criterio m criterion; (*buon senso*) common sense
critica f criticism; **criticare** criticize; **critico** 1 agg criti-

cal 2 m, -a f critic
croato 1 agg Croatian 2 m, -a f Croat, Croatian; **Croazia** f Croatia
croccante 1 agg crisp, crunchy 2 m GASTR nut brittle
crocchetta f GASTR potato croquette
croce f cross; **Croce Rossa** Red Cross; **crociata** f crusade; **crociera** f cruise; **crocifiggere** crucify; **crocifisso** m crucifix
crollare collapse; **crollo** m collapse
cronaca f chronicle; *di partita* commentary; **fatto di** ~ news item; ~ **nera** crime news sg
cronico chronic
cronista m/f reporter; *di partita* commentator
cronologico chronological
cronometrare time; **cronometro** m chronometer; SP stopwatch
crosta f crust; MED scab; *di formaggio* rind
crostacei mpl shellfish pl
crostata f GASTR tart
crostino m GASTR crouton
cruciale crucial
cruciverba m inv crossword (puzzle)
crudele cruel; **crudeltà** f cruelty
crudo raw
crumiro m, -a f scab
crusca f bran
cruscotto m dashboard; *scomparto* glove compart-

ment

Cuba f Cuba; **cubano 1** agg Cuban **2** m, -a f Cuban

cubetto m (small) cube; **~ di ghiaccio** ice cube; **cubo 1** agg cubic **2** m cube

cuccagna f: (**paese** m **della**) **~** land of plenty

cuccetta f FERR couchette; MAR berth

cucchiaiata f spoonful; **cucchiaino** m teaspoon; **cucchiaio** m spoon; **~ da tavola** tablespoon

cuccia f dog's basket; esterna kennel

cucciolo m cub; di cane puppy

cucina f kitchen; (cibi) food; (il cucinare) cooking; **~ a gas** gas cooker; **cucinare** cook; **cucinino** m kitchenette

cucire sew; **cucito 1** agg sewn **2** m sewing; **cucitura** f seam

cuffia f **da piscina** swimming cap; RAD, TV headphones; **~ da bagno** shower cap

cugino m, -a f cousin

cui persona who, whom fml; cose which; **la casa in ~ abitano** the house they live in, the house in which they live; **il ~ nome** whose name; **per ~** so

culinario cookery attr, culinary; **arte** f **-a** culinary art, cookery

culla f cradle; **cullare** rock

culminante: punto m **~** cli-

max; **culmine** m peak

culo V m arse V, Am ass V

culto m cult; **religione** religion

cultura f culture; **culturale** cultural; **culturismo** m body-building

cumulativo cumulative; **biglietto** m **~** group ticket; **cumulo** m heap, pile

cuneo m wedge

cunetta f fondo stradale bump

cuocere cook; pane bake; **cuoco** m, -a f cook

cuoio m leather; **~ capelluto** scalp

cuore m heart; carte **-i** pl hearts; **di ~** wholeheartedly; **stare a ~ a qu** be very important to s.o.

cupo gloomy; suono deep

cupola f dome

cura f care; MED treatment; **~ dimagrante** diet; **avere ~ di qc** take care of sth; **curabile** curable; **curare** take care of; MED treat; **curarsi** look after o.s.; **non curarti di loro** don't bother about them

curiosare have a look around; spreg try (**in** into); **curiosità** f inv curiosity; **curioso** curious

cursore m INFOR cursor

curva f curve; **curvare** curve; **schiena** bend; **curvarsi** bend; **curvo** curved; persona bent

cuscinetto m TEC bearing; **~ a sfere** ball bearing; POL **stato** m **~** buffer state; **cuscino** m cushion; (guanciale)

81   **data**

pillow
custode m/f caretaker; di parco, museo attendant; **custodia** f care; DIR custody;
(astuccio) case; **custodire**

(conservare) keep
cute f skin
CV m (= **curriculum vitae**) CV
(= curriculum vitae), Am résumé

D

da stato in luogo at; moto da
luogo from; moto a luogo
to; tempo since; con verbo
passivo by; **viene ~ Roma**
he comes from Rome; **sono
~ mio fratello** I'm at my
brother's (place); **passo ~
Firenze** I'm going via Florence; **vado dal medico** I'm
going to the doctor's o Am
doctor; **~ ieri** since yesterday; **~ oggi in poi** from
now on; **~ bambino** as a
child; **l'ho fatto ~ me** I did
it myself; **qualcosa ~ mangiare** something to eat; **la
donna dai capelli grigi** the
woman with grey hair
dà ☞ **dare**
daccapo ☞ **capo**
dado m dice; GASTR stock
cube; TEC nut
dagli = **da** and art **gli**
dai¹ = **da** and art **i**
dai² ☞ **dare**
daino m deer; (pelle) buckskin
dal = **da** and art **il**
dall', **dalla**, **dalle**, **dallo** = **da**
and art **l'**, **la**, **le**, **lo**
daltonico colour-blind, Am
color-blind

(conservare) keep
cute f skin
dama f lady; gioco draughts
sg, Am checkers sg
damigiana f demijohn
danese 1 m/agg Danish **2** m/f
Dane; **Danimarca** f Denmark
danneggiare (rovinare) damage; (nuocere) harm; **danno**
m damage; (a persona) harm;
dannoso harmful
danza f dance; **~ classica** ballet; **danzare** dance
dappertutto everywhere
dappoco agg inv (inetto)
worthless; (irrilevante) minor, unimportant
dapprima at first
dare 1 v/t give; **~ qc a qu** give
s.o. sth, give sth to s.o.; **~ uno
sguardo a qc** have a look at
sth; **dammi del tu** call me
'tu' **2** v/i di finestra overlook
(su sth); di porta lead into
(su sth) **3** m FIN debit; **~ e
avere** debit and credit
darsena f dock
darsi give each other; (dedicarsi) devote o.s. (a to); **~
al commercio** go into business; **può ~** perhaps
data f date; **~ di nascita** date

of birth; ~ *di scadenza* expiry date, *Am* expiration date; **datare 1** v/t date **2** v/i: *a* ~ *da oggi* from today

dato 1 pp ☞ *dare* **2** *agg* (*certo*) given, particular; (*dedito*) addicted (*a* to); *in* -*i casi* in certain cases; ~ *che* given that **3** *m* piece of data; -*i pl* data *sg*

datore *m*, -**trice** *f*: ~ *di lavoro* employer

dattero *m* date; (*albero*) date palm

dattilografo *m*, -**a** *f* typist

davanti 1 *prp*: ~ *a* in front of **2** *avv* in front (*a* to); (*dirimpetto*) opposite **3** *m*/*agg inv* front

davanzale *m* window sill

davanzo more than enough

davvero really

d.C. (= *dopo Cristo*) AD (= *anno domini*)

dea *f* goddess

debito 1 *agg* due, proper **2** *m* debt; (*dovere*) duty; *avere un* ~ *con qu* be in debt to s.o.; **debitore** *m*, -**trice** *f* debtor

debole 1 *agg* weak; (*luce*) dim **2** *m* weakness; *avere un* ~ *per qu* have a soft spot for s.o.; **debolezza** *f* weakness

debutto *m* début

decadente decadent

decaffeinato decaffeinated, decaff F

decalcomania *f* transfer, *Am* decal

decennio *m* decade

decente decent

decentrare decentralize

decesso *m* death

decidere v/t (*questione*) settle; *data* decide on, settle on; ~ *di fare qc* decide to do sth **2** v/i decide; **decidersi** decide (*a* to), make up one's mind (*a* to)

decifrare decipher

decimale *m*/*agg* decimal

decimo tenth

decina *f* MAT ten; *una* ~ about ten

decisione *f* decision; (*risolutezza*) decisiveness; *prendere una* ~ make a decision; **decisivo** decisive; **deciso 1** pp ☞ *decidere* **2** *agg* (*definito*) definite; (*risoluto*) determined; (*netto*) clear; (*spiccato*) marked

declinare 1 v/t decline; *responsabilità* disclaim **2** v/i (*tramontare*) set; (*diminuire*) decline; **declinazione** *f* GRAM declension; **declino** *m* fig decline

decodificatore *m* decoder

decollare take off; **decollo** *m* take-off

decomposizione *f* decomposition; CHIM breaking down

decompressione *f* decompression

decorare decorate; **decoratore** *m*, -**trice** *f* decorator; **decorazione** *f* decoration

decorrenza f: *con immediata* ~ with immediate effect; **decorrere** pass; *a* ~ *da oggi* with effect from today; **decorso** 1 pp ☞ **decorrere** 2 m *di malattia* course

decrepito decrepit

decreto m decree; ~*-legge* m *decree passed in exceptional circumstances that has the force of law*

dedica f dedication; **dedicare** dedicate; **dedicarsi** dedicate o.s.; **dedito** dedicated (*a* to); *a un vizio* addicted (*a* to); **dedizione** f dedication

dedurre deduce; FIN deduct; (*derivare*) derive; **deduzione** f deduction

deficiente 1 agg (*mancante*) deficient, lacking (*di* in) 2 m/f idiot, moron

deficit m inv deficit; ~ *del bilancio pubblico* public spending deficit

definire define; (*risolvere*) settle; **definitivo** definitive; **definizione** f definition

deflettore m AUTO quarterlight

deformare deform; *legno* warp; *metallo* buckle; *fig* distort; **deformarsi** *di legno* warp; *di metallo* buckle; *di scarpe* lose their shape; **deformazione** f deformation; *di legno* warping; *di metallo* buckling; *fisica* deformity; *fig, visuale* distortion; **defor-**me deformed

defunto 1 agg dead; *fig* defunct 2 m, -a f DIR: *il* ~ the deceased

degenerare degenerate (*in* into)

degente m/f patient

degli = *di* and *art* **gli**

degnare 1 v/t: ~ *qu di una parola* deign to speak to s.o. 2 v/i e **degnarsi**: ~ *di* deign to, condescend to

degno worthy; ~ *di nota* noteworthy

degradare degrading; **degradarsi** demean o.s., lower o.s.; CHIM degrade; *di ambiente, edifici* deteriorate; **degradazione** f degradation; **degrado** m deterioration; ~ *ambientale* damage to the environment

degustazione f tasting

dei[1] = *di* and *art* **i**

dei[2] (pl di *dio*): **gli** ~ mpl the Gods

del = *di* and *art* **il**

delega f delegation; (*procura*) proxy; **delegare** delegate; **delegato** 1 agg: **amministratore** m ~ managing director 2 m, -a f delegate; ~ *sindacale* (trade) union delegate

delfino m dolphin

deliberare 1 v/t decide 2 v/i DIR deliberate (*su* on)

delicatezza f delicacy; **delicato** delicate

delimitare define

delineare

84

delineare outline

delinquente *m/f* criminal; *fig* scoundrel; **delinquenza** *f* crime; **~ minorile** juvenile delinquency; **~ organizzata** organized crime

delirare be in raptures; MED be delirious; **delirio** *m* delirium; *fig* frenzy

delitto *m* crime

delizioso delightful; *cibo* delicious

dell', della, delle, dello = di and *art* **l', la, le, lo**

delta *m* delta; **deltaplano** *m* hang-glider; *attività* hang-gliding

deludere disappoint; **delusione** *f* disappointment; **deluso** disappointed

demanio *m* State property

demente *m/f* MED person with dementia; F lunatic F

democratico 1 *agg* democratic **2** *m*, -*a f* democrat; **democrazia** *f* democracy

demografico demographic

demolire demolish (*anche fig*); *macchine* crush; **demolizione** *f* demolition; *di macchine* crushing

demonio *m* devil

demoralizzarsi become demoralized, lose heart

demotivato demotivated

denaro *m* money; **~ contante** cash

denaturato CHIM: **alcol** *m* **~** methlyated spirits *sg*

denominare name, call; **denominazione** *f* name; **~ di origine controllata** term signifying that a wine is of a certain origin and quality

denotare denote, be indicative of

densità *f* density; *della nebbia* thickness, density; **denso** dense; *fumo, nebbia* thick, dense

dentario dental; **dente** *m* tooth; **~ del giudizio** wisdom tooth; **mal** *m* **di -i** toothache; GASTR **al ~** al dente, still slightly firm

dentice *m* fish native to the Mediterranean

dentiera *f* dentures; **dentifricio** *m* toothpaste; **dentista** *m/f* dentist

dentro 1 *prp* in, inside; (*entro*) within **2** *avv* in, inside; (*nell' intimo*) inwardly; **qui / lì ~** in here / there

denuclearizzato nuclear-free, denuclearized

denuncia *f* denunciation; *alla polizia, alla società di assicurazione* complaint, report; *di nascita, morte* registration; **~ dei redditi** income tax return; **denunciare** denounce; *alla polizia, alla società di assicurazione* report; *nascita* register

denutrito undernourished

deodorante *m* deodorant

depilare *con pinzette* pluck; *con rasoio* shave; *con ceretta* wax

85 destro

depilatorio m/agg depilatory
dépliant m inv leaflet; (opuscolo) brochure
deplorevole deplorable
deporre 1 v/t put down; uova lay; re, presidente depose; ~ il falso commit perjury 2 v/i DIR testify, give evidence (a favore di for, a carico di against)
deportare deport
depositare deposit; (posare) put down, deposit; (registrare) register; depositato: marchio m ~ registered trademark; deposito m deposit; (magazzino) warehouse; rimessa m depot; FERR ~ bagagli left-luggage office, Am baggage checkroom
depravato m, -a f depraved person
depressione f depression; depresso 1 pp ☞ deprimere 2 agg depressed; deprimente depressing; deprimere depress; deprimersi get depressed
depurare purify; depuratore m purifier
deputato m, -a f Member of Parliament, Am Representative
deragliare FERR go off the rails; far ~ derail
deridere deride; derisione f derision; deriso pp ☞ deridere
deriva f MAR drift; andare al-

la ~ drift
derivare 1 v/t derive 2 v/i: ~ da come from, derive from
dermatologo m, -a f dermatologist
derubare rob
descritto pp ☞ descrivere; descrivere describe; descrizione f description
deserto 1 agg deserted 2 m desert
desiderare (volere) want, wish; intensamente long for; sessualmente desire; desidera? can I help you?; lascia a ~ it leaves a lot to be desired; desiderio m wish (di for); intenso longing (di for); sessuale desire (di for)
design m inv design
designare (nominare) appoint, name; (fissare) fix
desistere: ~ da desist from
desolato desolate; sono ~! I am so sorry
dessert m inv dessert
destinare destine; (assegnare) assign; con il pensiero mean, intend; dati fix; (indirizzare) address (a to); destinatario m, -a f di lettera addressee; destinazione f: (luogo m di) ~ destination
destino m destiny
destra f right; (mano) right hand; a ~ to the right
destreggiare manœuvre, Am maneuver
destrezza f skill, dexterity; destro right; (abile) skilful,

Am skillful, dexterous

detenere hold; **detenuto** *m*, **-a** *f* prisoner; **detenzione** *f* (*imprigionamento*) detention

detergente *m* detergent; *per cosmesi* cleanser

deteriorabile perishable; **deteriorarsi** deteriorate, get worse

determinare determine, establish; (*causare*) cause, lead to; **determinato** certain; (*specifico*) particular, specific; (*risoluto*) determined; **determinazione** *f* determination

detersivo *m* detergent; *per piatti* washing-up liquid, *Am* dishwashing liquid; *per biancheria* detergent, *Br anche* washing powder

detestare hate, detest

detonare detonate

detrarre deduct (*da* from); **detratto** *pp* ☞ **detrarre**; **detrazione** *f* deduction

detrito *m* debris; GEOL detritus

detta: *a ~ di* according to

dettaglio *m* detail; FIN **commercio** *m* **al ~** retail trade

dettare dictate; **dettato** *m* dictation

detto 1 *pp* ☞ **dire**; *~ fatto* no sooner said than done; **come non ~** let's forget it **2** *agg* said; (*soprannominato*) known as **3** *m* saying

devastare devastate

deve, devi ☞ **dovere**

deviare 1 *v/t* traffico, sospetti divert **2** *v/i* deviate; **deviazione** *f* deviation; *di traffico* diversion

devo ☞ **dovere**

devoto 1 *agg* devoted; REL devout **2** *m*, **-a** *f* devotee; REL *i -i* the devout *pl*

di 1 *prp* of; *con il comparativo* than; **~ ferro** (made of) iron; **io sono ~ Roma** I'm from Rome; **l'auto ~ mio padre** my father's car; **~ giorno** by day; **parlare ~ politica** talk about politics; **d'estate** in the summer; **di ~** on Sundays; **più bello ~** prettier than **2** *art* some; *interrogativo* any, some; *negativo* any; **del vino** some wine

di' ☞ **dire**

dia ☞ **dare**

diabete *m* diabetes *sg*; **diabetico 1** *agg* diabetic **2** *m*, **-a** *f* diabetic

diadema *m* diadem

diaframma *m* diaphragm

diagnosi *f inv* diagnosis; **diagnosticare** diagnose

diagonale *f/agg* diagonal

diagramma *m* diagram

dialetto *m* dialect

dialisi *f inv* dialysis

dialogo *m* dialogue, *Am* dialog

diamante *m* diamond

diametro *m* diameter

diapason *m inv* tuning fork

diapositiva *f* FOT slide

diario *m* diary

diarrea f diarrhoea, Am diarrhea

diavolo m devil; **mandare qu al ~** tell s.o. to get lost; F **ma che ~ fai?** what the heck are you doing? F

dibattersi struggle; **dibattito** m debate

dicembre m December

diceria f rumour, Am rumor

dichiarare state; ufficialmente declare; **dichiararsi** declare o.s.; **dichiarazione** f declaration; **~ dei redditi** income tax statement; **~ doganale** customs declaration

diciannove nineteen; **diciannovesimo** nineteenth; **diciassette** seventeen; **diciassettesimo** seventeenth; **diciottenne** m/f eighteen--year-old; **diciottesimo** eighteenth; **diciotto** eighteen; **dieci** ten; **alle / verso le ~** at / about ten (o'clock)

diesel m diesel

dieta f diet; **essere a ~** be on a diet; **dietetico** diet attr

dietro 1 prp behind; **~ l'angolo** around the corner; **~ di me** behind me **2** avv behind; **in auto** in the back; **di ~** stanza, porta back; zampe hind; AUTO rear **3** m inv back

difatti in fact

difendere defend; (proteggere) protect; **difensiva** f defensive; **stare sulla ~** be on the defensive; **difensivo** defensive; **difensore** m de-

fender; **~ d'ufficio** legal aid lawyer, Am public defender; **difesa** f defence, Am defense; **~ dei consumatori** consumer protection; **legittima ~** self-defence; **difeso** pp ☞ **difendere**

difetto m (imperfezione) defect; morale fault, flaw; (mancanza) lack; **difettoso** defective

diffamare slander; scrivendo libel; **diffamazione** f defamation of character

differente different (**da** from); **differenza** f difference; **~ di prezzo** difference in price, price difference; **a ~ di** unlike; **differenziarsi** differ (**da** from)

difficile difficult; (improbabile) unlikely; **difficoltà** f inv difficulty; **senza ~** easily, without any difficulty

diffidare 1 v/t DIR issue an injunction against; **~ qu dal fare qc** warn s.o. not to do sth **2** v/i: **~ di qu** distrust s.o.; **diffidente** distrustful; **diffidenza** f distrust

diffondere diffuse; fig spread; **diffondersi** fig spread; (dilungarsi) enlarge; **diffusione** f di luce, calore diffusion; di giornale circulation; **diffuso 1** pp ☞ **diffondere 2** agg widespread; luce diffuse

diga f fluviale dam; litoranea dyke; portuale breakwater

digerire digest; F (tollerare)

stomach F; **digestione** f digestion; **digestivo 1** agg digestive **2** m after-dinner drink, digestif

digitale digital; *impronta* f ~ fingerprint

digitare INFOR key

digiunare fast; **digiuno 1** agg fasting **2** m fast; *a* ~ on an empty stomach

dignità f dignity

digrignare gnash

dilagare flood; fig spread rapidly

dilaniare tear apart

dilatare expand; *occhi* open wide; **dilatarsi** di materiali expand; di pupilla dilate

dilazionare defer, delay

dileguarsi vanish, disappear

dilemma m dilemma

dilettante m/f amateur; spreg dilettante; **dilettarsi**: ~ *di qc* dabble in sth, do sth as a hobby; ~ *a fare qc* take delight in doing sth

diligente diligent; (accurato) accurate

diluire dilute

dilungarsi fig dwell (su on)

diluviare pour down; **diluvio** m downpour; fig deluge

dimagrante: *cura* f ~ diet; **dimagrire** lose weight

dimenare throw o.s. about

dimensione f dimension; (grandezza) size; (misure) dimensions

dimenticanza f forgetfulness, absent-mindedness; (svista)

oversight; **dimenticare** forget; **dimenticarsi** forget (*di* sth; *di fare qc* to do sth)

dimestichezza f familiarity

dimettere dismiss (*da* from); *da ospedali* discharge (*da* from); *da carceri* release (*da* from); **dimettersi** resign (*da* from)

dimezzare halve

diminuire 1 v/t reduce **2** v/i decrease, di prezzi, valore fall, go down; di vento, rumore die down; **diminuzione** f decrease; di prezzi, valore fall, drop (*di* in)

dimissioni fpl resignation; *dare le* ~ hand in one's resignation

dimora f residence

dimostrare demonstrate; (interesse) show; (provare) prove, show; **dimostrarsi** prove to be; **dimostrazione** f demonstration; (prova) proof

dinamica f dynamics; **dinamico** dynamic

dinamite f dynamite

dinanzi: ~ *a al cospetto di* before

dinastia f dynasty

dinosauro m dinosaur

dintorno 1 avv around **2** m: *-i* pl neighbourhood, Am neighborhood

dio m god; *grazie a Dio!* thank God!; *per l'amor di Dio* for God's sake

diocesi f inv diocese

89 dirittura

diossina f dioxin

dipartimento m department

dipendente 1 agg dependent **2** m/f employee; **dipendenza** f dependence; (edificio) annexe, Am annex; **essere alle ~ di** work for; **dipendere:** ~ **da** (essere subordinato a) depend on; (essere mantenuto da) be dependent on; (essere causato da) be due to; **dipende** it depends; **questo dipende da te** it's up to you; **dipeso** pp ☞ **dipendere**

dipingere paint; fig describe, depict; **dipinto 1** pp ☞ **dipingere 2** m painting, picture

diploma m diploma, certificate; ~ **di laurea** degree (certificate); **diplomarsi** obtain a diploma

diplomatico 1 agg diplomatic **2** m diplomat; **diplomato 1** agg qualified **2** m, -a f holder of a diploma; **diplomazia** f diplomacy

diporto: **imbarcazione** f **da ~** pleasure boat

diradare thin out; **diradarsi** thin out; di nebbia clear, lift

dire 1 v/t say; (raccontare) tell; ~ **qc a qu** tell s.o. sth; ~ **a qu di fare qc** tell s.o. to do sth; **vale a ~** that is, in other words; **a ~ il vero** to tell the truth; **come si dice ... in inglese?** what's the English for … ?, how do you say … in English?; **voler ~** mean

2 v/i ~ **bene di qu** speak highly of s.o.; **dico sul serio** I'm serious

direttiva f directive; **direttivo 1** agg managerial; comitato, consiglio, POL executive attr **2** m di società board (of directors); POL leadership

diretto 1 pp ☞ **dirigere 2** agg (immediato) direct; ~ **a** aimed at; lettera addressed to; **essere ~ a casa** be heading for home; RAD, TV **in** (ripresa) **-a** live **3** m direct train; SP straight

direttore m, **-trice** f manager; più in alto nella gerarchia director; EDU headmaster; donna headmistress; Am principal; di giornale, rivista editor (in chief); ~ **generale** CEO; ~ **d'orchestra** conductor

direzione f direction; di società management; di partito leadership; ufficio office; sede generale head office

dirigente 1 agg classe, partito ruling; personale managerial **2** m/f executive; POL leader

dirigere direct; azienda run, manage; orchestra conduct; **dirigersi** head (**a**, **verso** to, toward)

dirigibile m airship, dirigible

diritto 1 agg, avv straight **2** m right; DIR law; **aver ~ a** be entitled to; **di ~** by rights; **dirittura** f straight line; SP straight; fig rectitude; **in ~**

d'arrivo on the home straight

diroccato ramshackle

dirottare *traffico* divert; *aereo* reroute; *con intenzioni criminali* hijack; **dirottatore** *m*, **-trice** *f* hijacker

dirotto: *piove a ~* it's pouring

dirupo *m* precipice

disabile 1 *agg* disabled **2** *m/f* disabled person

disabitato uninhabited

disaccordo *m* disagreement

disadattato 1 *agg* maladjusted **2** *m/f* (social) misfit

disagio *m* (*difficoltà*) hardship; (*scomodità*) discomfort; (*imbarazzo*) embarrassment; *essere a ~* be ill at ease

disapprovare disapprove of; **disapprovazione** *f* disapproval

disappunto *m* disappointment

disarmato unarmed; *fig* defenceless, *Am* defenseless; **disarmo** *m* POL disarmament

disastro *m* disaster; **disastroso** disastrous

disattento inattentive; **disattenzione** *f* inattention; *errore* careless mistake

disavanzo *m* deficit

disavventura *f* misadventure

disboscamento *m* deforestation

discapito *m*: *a ~ di qu* to the detriment *o* disadvantage of s.o.

discarica *f* dumping; *luogo* dump

discendente 1 *agg inv* descending **2** *m/f* descendant; **discendere** descend; (*trarre origine*) be descended (*da* from); *da veicoli, da cavallo* get off (*da qc* sth)

discepolo *m* disciple

discesa *f* descent; (*pendio*) slope; *di bus* exit; *strada in ~* street that slopes downward

dischetto *m* INFOR diskette, floppy

disciplina *f* discipline; **disciplinato** disciplined

disco *m* disc, *Am* disk; SP discus; MUS record; INFOR disk; INFOR *~ rigido* hard disk; AUTO *~ orario* parking disc; *~ volante* flying saucer; **discobolo** *m* discus thrower

discolpare clear

discontinuo intermittent; (*disuguale*) erratic

discorde not in agreement, clashing; **discordia** *f* discord; (*differenza di opinioni*) disagreement; (*litigio*) argument

discorrere talk (*di* about); **discorso** *pp* ➤ **discorrere 2** *m* pubblico, ufficiale speech; (*conversazione*) conversation, talk

discoteca *f* locale disco; *raccolta* record library

discrepanza *f* discrepancy

discreto (*riservato*) discreet;
(*abbastanza buono*) fairly
good; (*moderato*) moderate,
fair; **discrezione** f discretion; **a ~ di** at the discretion
of
discriminare 1 *v/i* discriminate 2 *v/t* stranieri; discriminate against; **discriminazione** f discrimination
discussione f discussion; (*litigio*) argument; **discusso**
pp ☞ **discutere**; **discutere**
1 *v/t* discuss, talk about; *questione* debate; (*mettere in
dubbio*) question; (*contestare*) dispute 2 *v/i* talk; (*litigare*)
argue; (*negoziare*) negotiate;
discutibile debatable
disdegnare disdain
disdetto *pp* ☞ **disdire**; **disdire**
impegno cancel; *contratto*
terminate
disegnare draw; (*progettare*)
design; **disegno** m drawing;
(*progetto*) design; **~ di legge**
bill
diserbante m weed-killer
diseredare disinherit; **diseredato** underprivileged, disadvantaged
disertare desert; **disertore** m
deserter; **diserzione** f desertion
disfare undo; *letto* strip; (*distruggere*) destroy; **~ la valigia** unpack; **disfarsi di
ghiaccio** melt; **~ di** get rid
of; **disfatta** f defeat; **disfatto**
pp ☞ **disfare**

disgelo m thaw
disgrazia f misfortune; (*incidente*) accident; (*sfavore*) disgrace; **per ~** unfortunately;
disgraziato 1 *agg* (*sfortunato*) unlucky 2 m, **-a** f poor
soul; F (*farabutto*) bastard F
disgregare break up; **disgregarsi** break up, disintegrate
disguido m hiccup, hitch
disgustare disgust; **disgusto**
m disgust; **disgustoso** disgusting
disidratato dehydrated
disillusione f disillusionment; **disilluso** disillusioned
disinfettante m disinfectant;
disinfettare disinfect
disinibito uninhibited
disinnescare *bomba* defuse
disinserire disconnect
disinteressarsi take no interest (**di** in); **disinteressato**
disinterested; **disinteresse**
m lack of interest; (*generosità*) unselfishness
disintossicare detoxify; **disintossicazione** f treatment
for drug / alcohol addiction,
detox F
disinvolto confident; **disinvoltura** f confidence
dislessia f dyslexia; **dislessico** dyslexic
dislivello m difference in
height, height difference;
fig difference
disobbedire ☞ **disubbidire**
disoccupato 1 *agg* unem-

ployed, jobless **2** *m*, **-a** *f* unemployed person; **i** *-i* the unemployed *pl*, the jobless *pl*; **disoccupazione** *f* unemployment

disonestà *f* dishonesty; **disonesto** dishonest

disonore *m* dishonour, *Am* dishonor

disopra 1 *avv* above; **al ~ di** above **2** *agg* upper **3** *m* inv top

disordinato untidy, messy; **disordine** *m* untidiness, mess; **in ~** untidy, in a mess; **-i** *pl* riots, public disorder

disorganizzazione *f* disorganization

disorientamento *m* disorientation; **disorientare** disorientate, *Am* disorient; **disorientato** disorientated, *Am* disoriented

disotto 1 *avv* below; **al ~ di** beneath **2** *agg* lower **3** *m* underside

dispari *inv* odd; **disparità** *f* *inv* disparity

disparte: **in ~** aside

dispendio *m* waste; **dispendioso** expensive

dispensa *f stanza* larder; *mobile* cupboard; *pubblicazione* instalment, *Am* installment; DIR exemption; **dispensare** dispense; (*esonerare*) esonerate

disperare despair (*di* of); **far ~ qu** drive s.o. to despair; **disperarsi** despair; **disperato**

desperate; **disperazione** *f* despair, desperation

disperdere disperse; *energie, sostanze* squander; **dispersi** disperse; **disperso 1** *pp* → **disperdere 2** *agg* scattered; (*sperduto*) lost, missing

dispetto *m* spite; **per ~** out of spite; **a ~ di qc** in spite of sth; **fare i -i a qu** annoy *o* tease s.o.; **dispettoso** mischievous

dispiacere 1 *v/i* (*causare dolore*) upset (*a* s.o.); (*non piacere*) displease (*a* s.o.); **mi dispiace** I'm sorry; **le dispiace se apro la finestra?** do you mind if I open the window? **2** *m* (*rammarico*) regret, sorrow; (*dolore*) sadness; (*delusione*) disappointment; **-i** *pl* (*preoccupazioni*) worries, troubles

display *m* display

disponibile available; (*cortese*) helpful, obliging; **disponibilità** *f* availability; (*cortesia*) helpfulness

disporre 1 *v/t* arrange; (*stabilire*) order **2** *v/i* (*decidere*) make arrangements; **~ di qc** have sth (at one's disposal)

dispositivo *m* device

disposizione *f* arrangement; (*norma*) provision; (*attitudine*) aptitude (*a* for); **stare / mettere a ~ di qu** be / put at s.o.'s disposal

disposto 1 *pp* ☞ **disporre** 2
agg: ~ **a** ready to, willing
to; **essere ben** ~ **verso qu**
be well disposed to s.o.

dispotico despotic

disprezzare despise; **disprezzo** *m* contempt

disputa *f* dispute, argument;
disputare 1 *v/i* argue 2 *v/t*
SP take part in; **disputarsi**
qc compete for sth

disseminare scatter, dissem-
inate; *fig* spread

dissenso *m* dissent; *(dissapore)* argument, disagreement

dissenteria *f* dysentery

dissentire disagree (**da** with)

disservizio *m* poor service;
(inefficienza) inefficiency;
(cattiva gestione) mismanagement

dissestato *strada* uneven; *fi-
nanze* precarious

dissetante thirst-quenching;
dissetare: ~ **qu** quench
s.o.'s thirst; **dissetarsi**
quench one's thirst

dissimulare conceal, hide;
dissimulazione *f* concealment

dissociarsi dissociate o.s.
(**da** from)

dissolvere dissolve; *dubbi,
nebbia* dispel; **dissolversi**
dissolve; *(svanire)* vanish

dissuadere: ~ **qu da fare qc**
dissuade s.o. from doing
sth, persuade s.o. not to do
sth; **dissuaso** *pp* ☞ **dissuadere**

distaccare detach; SP leave
behind; **distaccarsi** *da persone* detach o.s. (**da** from);
distacco *m* detachment *(anche fig)*; *(separazione)* separation; SP lead

distante distant, far-off; ~ **da**
far from; **distanza** *f* distance
(anche fig); **distanziare** 1 *v/t*
space out; SP leave behind;
(superare) overtake; **distare**:
**l'albergo dista 100 metri
dalla stazione** the hotel is
100 metres from the station;
quanto dista da qui? how
far is it from here?

distendere *(adagiare)* lay;
gambe, braccia stretch out;
muscoli relax; *nervi* calm; **di-
stendersi** lie down; *(rilassarsi)* relax

distesa *f* expanse; **disteso** 1
pp ☞ **distendere** 2 *agg*
stretched out; *(rilassato)* relaxed

distinguere distinguish; **distintivo** 1 *agg* distinctive 2
m badge; **distinto** 1 *pp* ☞ **distinguere** 2 *agg* *(diverso)*
different, distinct; *(chiaro)*
distinct; *fig* distinguished; **-i
saluti** yours faithfully; **distinzione** *f* distinction

distorsione *f* distortion; MED
sprain

distrarre distract; *(divertire)*
entertain; **distrarsi** *(non essere attento)* get distracted;
(svagarsi) take one's mind
off things; **distratto** 1 *pp* ☞

distrarre 2 *agg* absent-minded; **distrazione** *f* absent-mindedness; (*errore*) inattention; (*svago*) amusement; *che distrae da un'attività* distraction

distribuire distribute; *premi* award, present; **distributore** *m* distributor; **~ (di benzina)** (petrol *o Am* gas) pump; **~ automatico** vending machine; **~ automatico di biglietti** ticket machine; **distribuzione** *f* distribution; *posta* delivery

distruggere destroy; **distruttivo** destructive; **distrutto** *pp* ☞ **distruggere**; **distruzione** *f* destruction

disturbare disturb; (*dare fastidio a*) bother; (*sconvolgere*) upset; **disturbarsi:** *non si disturbi* please don't bother; **disturbo** *m* trouble, bother; MED **-i** *pl* **di circolazione** circulation problems

disubbidiente disobedient; **disubbidire; ~ a** disobey

disumano inhuman

disuso: *in ~* in disuse, disused

ditale *m* thimble

dito *m* (*pl* **le dita**) finger; *del piede* toe; *un ~ di vino* a drop of wine

ditta *f* company, firm

dittatore *m* dictator; **dittatura** *f* dictatorship

diurno daytime *attr*; **albergo** *m ~* place where travellers can have a shower / shave

diva *f* diva

divagare digress

divampare *di rivolta, incendio* break out; *di passione* blaze

divano *m* couch; *Br anche* sofa; **~ letto** sofa bed

divaricare open (wide)

divario *m* difference

divenire become

diventare become; *rosso, bianco* turn, go

diverbio *m* argument

divergenza *f* divergence; *di opinioni* difference

diversamente differently; (*altrimenti*) otherwise

diversificare 1 *v/t* diversify **2** *v/i e* **diversificarsi** differ; **diversità** *f inv* difference; (*varietà*) diversity

diversivo *m* diversion, distraction

diverso (*differente*) different (*da* from, than); **-i** *pl* several; **da -i giorni** for the past few days

divertente amusing; **divertimento** *m* amusement; **buon ~!** have a good time!, have fun!; **divertire** amuse; **divertirsi** enjoy o.s., have a good time

dividere divide; (*condividere*) share; **dividersi** *di coppia* separate; (*scindersi*) be divided (*in* into)

divieto *m* ban; **~ di sosta** no parking

divincolarsi twist, wriggle

divinità *f inv* divinity; **divino**

divine
divisa f uniform; FIN currency
divisione f division; **divisorio 1** agg dividing **2** m partition
divo m star
divorare devour
divorziare get a divorce, get divorced; **divorziato** divorced; **divorzio** m divorce
divulgare divulge, reveal; (rendere accessibile) popularize
dizionario m dictionary
DNA m inv (= **acido deossiribonucleico**) DNA (= deoxyribonucleic acid)
do[1] → **dare**
do[2] m inv MUS C; nel solfeggio della scala doh
dobbiamo → **dovere**
D.O.C., doc (= **Denominazione d'Origine Controllata**) term signifying that a wine is of a certain origin and quality
doccia f shower; **fare la ~** (take a) shower
docente 1 agg teaching **2** m/f teacher
docile docile
documentario m documentary; **documentarsi** collect information; **documentazione** f documentation; **documento** m document
dodicesimo twelfth; **dodici** twelve
dogana f customs; (dazio) (customs) duty; **doganale** customs attr

doglie fpl: **avere le -e** be in labour o Am labor
dolce 1 agg sweet; carattere, voce, pendio gentle; acqua fresh; clima mild; ricordo pleasant; suono soft **2** m portata dessert; di sapore sweetness; torta cake; **-i** pl sweet things; **dolcezza** f sweetness; di carattere, voce gentleness; di clima mildness; di ricordo pleasantness; di suono softness; **dolciastro** sweetish; fig sugary; **dolcificante** m sweetener; **dolciumi** mpl sweets, Am candy
dolente painful, sore; **dolere** hurt, be painful; **mi duole la schiena** my back hurts
dollaro m dollar
dolo m malice
Dolomiti fpl Dolomites
dolore m pain; **doloroso** painful
doloso malicious
domanda f question; (richiesta) request; FIN demand; **fare una ~ a qu** ask s.o. a question; **domandare 1** v/t per sapere: nome, ora, opinione ecc ask; per ottenere: informazioni, aiuto ecc ask for; **~ un favore a qu** ask s.o. a favour; **~ scusa** apologize **2** v/i: **~ a qu** ask s.o.; **~ di qu** per sapere come sta ask after s.o.; per parlargli ask for s.o.; **domandarsi** wonder, ask o.s.
domani m/avv tomorrow; **~ mattina** tomorrow morning;

~ sera tomorrow evening; *a ~!* see you tomorrow

domare tame; *fig* control

domattina tomorrow morning

domenica *f* Sunday

domestico 1 *agg* domestic; *animale* ~ pet **2** *m*, -*a f* servant; *donna* maid

domiciliato: ~ *a* domiciled at; **domicilio** *m* domicile; *(casa)* home

dominante dominant; *idee* prevailing; *classe* ruling; **dominare 1** *v/t* dominate; *materia; passioni* master **2** *v/i* rule (*su* over); *fig: di confusione* reign; **dominio** *m (controllo)* control, power; *fig (campo)* domain, field; INFOR domain

domino *m* mask, domino

donare donate, give; *sangue* give; **donatore** *m*, -**trice** *f* donor; ~ *di sangue* blood donor

dondolare 1 *v/t culla* rock **2** *v/i* sway; *(oscillare)* swing; **dondolarsi** *su altalena* swing; *su sedia* rock; *fig* hang around; **dondolo** *m:* **cavallo** *m a* ~ rocking horse; **sedia** *f a* ~ rocking chair

donna *f* woman; *carte da gioco* queen; ~ *di servizio* home help

dono *m* gift

dopo 1 *prp* after; ~ *di te* after you; ~ *mangiato* after eating **2** *avv (in seguito)* afterwards,

after, *Am* afterward; *(poi)* then; *(più tardi)* later; *Il giorno* ~ the day after **3** *cong:* ~ *che* after; ~ *essere uscito* *ho visto* ... after I left, I saw ...; **dopobarba** *m inv* aftershave; **dopodomani** the day after tomorrow; **dopoguerra** *m inv* post-war period; **dopopranzo** *m* afternoon; **doposci** *m inv* après-ski; ~ *pl stivali* après-ski boots; **dopotutto** after all

doppiaggio *m di film* dubbing; **doppiare** *film* dub; SP lap; MAR round; **doppiatore** *m*, -**trice** *f* dubber

doppio 1 *agg* double **2** *m* double; SP doubles; **doppiopetto** *m* double-breasted jacket

dorato 1 *pp* ~ **dorare 2** *agg* gilded; *sabbia, riflessi* golden; GASTR browned

dormicchiare doze

dormiglione *m*, -**a** *f* late riser

dormire sleep; *dormita* (good) night's sleep; **dormitorio** *m* dormitory; **dormiveglia** *m:* **essere nel** ~ be only half awake

dorso *m* back; *(di libro)* spine; SP backstroke

dosare measure out; *fig* be sparing with; *parole* weigh; **dose** *f* quantity, amount; MED dose

dosso *m di strada* hump; *togliersi gli abiti di* ~ get undressed

dunque

dotare provide, supply (*di* with); *fig* provide, endow (*di* with); **dotato** gifted; ~ **di** equipped with; **dote** *f* dowry; *fig* gift

dott. (= *dottore*) Dr (= doctor)

dottore *m* doctor (*in* of); **dottoressa** *f* (woman) doctor

dottrina *f* doctrine

dott.ssa (= *dottoressa*) Dr (= doctor)

dove where; **di ~ sei?** where are you from?; **fin ~?** how far?; **per ~ si passa?** which way do you go?; **mettilo ~ vuoi** put it wherever you like

dovere 1 *v/i* have to, must; **non devo dimenticare** I mustn't forget; **deve arrivare oggi** she is supposed to arrive today; **come si deve** (*bene*) properly; *persona* very decent; **doveva succedere** it was bound to happen; **dovresti avvertirlo** you ought to *o* should let him know **2** *v/t denaro* owe **3** *m* duty

dovunque 1 *avv* (*dappertutto*) everywhere; (*in qualsiasi luogo*) anywhere **2** *cong* wherever

dovuto 1 *pp* → **dovere 2** *agg* due; ~ **a** because of, due to

dozzina *f* dozen; **una ~ di uova** a dozen eggs

dragare dredge

drago *m* dragon; **dragoncello** *m* tarragon

dramma *m* drama; **drammatico** dramatic

drastico drastic

dritto 1 *agg* straight **2** *avv* straight (ahead) **3** *m di abbigliamento, tessuto* right side **4** *m*, -**a** *f* F crafty devil F; **drizzare** (*raddrizzare*) straighten; (*erigere*) put up, erect; ~ **le orecchie** prick up one's ears; **drizzarsi:** ~ **in piedi** get to one's feet

droga *f* drug; **drogarsi** SP take drugs; **drogato** *m*, -**a** *f* drug addict

drogheria *f* grocer's, *Am* grocery store

dubbio 1 *agg* doubtful; (*equivoco*) dubious **2** *m* doubt; **essere in ~ fra** hesitate between; **mettere qc in ~** doubt sth; **senza ~** without a doubt; **dubbioso** doubtful; **dubitare** doubt (*di* sth); **dubito che venga** I doubt whether he'll come

duca *m* duke; **duchessa** *f* duchess

due two; **a ~ a ~** in twos, two by two; **tutt'e ~** both of them; **duecento 1** *agg* two hundred **2** *m*: **il Duecento** the thirteenth century

duello *m* duel

duemila two thousand; **due-pezzi** *m inv* bikini; *vestito* two-piece (suit)

duna *f* (sand) dune

dunque 1 *cong* so; (*allora*) well (then) **2** *m*: **venire al ~**

ing

duomo *m* cathedral

duplicato *m* duplicate; **duplice** double; **in ~ copia** in duplicate

durante during; **durare** last; (*conservarsi*) keep, last; **durata** *f* duration, length; *di prodotto* life; **duraturo** lasting

duro 1 *agg* hard; *carne, persona* tough; *inverno, voce* harsh; *congegno, meccanismo* stiff; *pane* stale; (*ostinato*) stubborn; **tieni ~!** hang in there! **2** *m* tough guy

durone *m* MED callus

DVD *m inv* DVD

E

e and; **sono le due ~ un quarto** it's (a) quarter past two, *Am* it's a quarter after two

è *☞* **essere**

ebano *m* ebony

ebbe, ebbi *☞* **avere**

ebbene well

ebbrezza *f* drunkenness; *fig* thrill

ebraico 1 *agg* Hebrew; *religione* Jewish **2** *m* Hebrew; **ebreo 1** *m*, **-a** *f* Jew; **2** *agg* Jewish

ecc. (= *eccetera*) etc (= et cetera)

eccedente excess; **eccedere 1** *v/t* exceed, go beyond **2** *v/i* go too far; **~ nel bere** drink too much

eccellente excellent

eccentrico eccentric

eccessivo excessive; **eccesso** *m* excess; **~ di velocità** speeding

eccetera et cetera

eccetto except; **eccezionale** exceptional; **eccezional-**

mente exceptionally; **eccezione** *f* exception

ecchimosi *f inv* bruise

eccitante 1 *agg* exciting **2** *m* stimulant; **eccitare** excite; **eccitarsi** get excited; **eccitazione** *f* excitement

ecclesiastico 1 *agg* ecclesiastical **2** *m* priest

ecco (*qui*) here; (*là*) there; **~ come** this is how; **~ fatto** that's that; **~ tutto** that's all; **~mi** here I am; **~li** here they are; **~ti il libro** here's your book

eclissarsi *fig* slip away; **eclisse** *f*, **eclissi** *f inv* eclipse

eco *m/f* echo

ecografia *f* scan

ecologia *f* ecology; **ecologico** ecological

economia *f* economy; *scienza* economics *sg*; **fare ~** economize (*di* on); **-e** *pl* savings; **economico** economic; (*poco costoso*) economical; **economizzare 1** *v/t* save **2** *v/i*

economize (**su** on)
ecosistema m ecosystem
eczema m eczema
ed and
edera f ivy
edicola f newspaper kiosk
edificare build; fig edify; **edificio** m building; fig structure
edile construction attr, building attr; **edilizia** f construction, building; (urbanistica) town planning
editore 1 agg publishing 2 m, **-trice** f publisher; (curatore) editor; **editoria** f publishing; **edizione** f edition
educare educate; (allevare) bring up; orecchio, mente train; **educativo** education attr; (istruttivo) educational; **educato** (ben) ~ well brought-up; **educazione** f education; dei figli upbringing; (buone maniere) (good) manners; ~ **fisica** physical education
effervescente effervescent; aspirina soluble
effettivamente in fact; per rafforzare un'affermazione really, actually; **effettivo** (reale) real, actual; (efficace) effective; **effetto** m effect; (impressione) impression; **fare** ~ (funzionare) work; (impressionare) make an impression; **-i** pl **personali** personal effects; **in -i** in fact; **effettuare** carry out; pagamento make;

effettuarsi take place; il servizio non si effettua la domenica there is no Sunday service
efficace effective
efficiente efficient; (funzionante) in working order; **efficienza** f efficiency
Egitto m Egypt; **egiziano** 1 agg Egyptian 2 m, -a f Egyptian; **egizio** ancient Egyptian
egli he
egocentrico egocentric
egoismo m selfishness, egoism
egoista 1 agg selfish 2 m/f selfish person
egr. (= **egregio**) form of address used in correspondence
egregio distinguished; nelle lettere ~ **signore** Dear Sir
eguale ☞ **uguale**
ehi! oi!
E.I. (= **Esercito Italiano**) Italian army
elaborare elaborate; dati process; piano work out; **elaborato** elaborate; **elaboratore** m: ~ **elettronico** computer; **elaborazione** f elaboration; ~ **elettronica dei dati** electronic data processing; ~ **dei testi** word processing
elastico 1 agg elastic; orari flexible 2 m rubber band
elefante m elephant
elegante elegant; **eleganza** f elegance

100

eleggere elect

elementare elementary; **scuola** ~ primary school, *Am* elementary school

elemento *m* element; (*componente*) component; **-i** *pl* (*rudimenti*) rudiments; (*fatti*) data *sg*

elemosina *f* charity; **chiedere l'~** beg

elencare list; **elenco** *m* list; ~ **telefonico** phone book, telephone directory

eletto 1 *pp* ☞ **eleggere 2** *agg* chosen; **elettore** *m*, **-trice** *f* voter

elettrauto *m* *inv* auto electrics garage; (*persona* automobile electrician; **elettricista** *m*/*f* electrician; **elettricità** *f* electricity; **elettrico** electric

elettrocardiogramma *m* electrocardiogram; **elettrodo** *m* electrode; **elettrodomestico** *m* household appliance; **elettromagnetico** electromagnetic

elettrone *m* electron; **elettronico** electronic; **libro** ~ e-book, electronic book; **commercio** ~ e-commerce

elettrotecnico 1 *agg* electrical **2** *m* electrical engineer

elevare raise; *costruzioni* erect; (*promuovere*) promote; *fig* (*migliorare*) better; **elevato** high; *fig* elevated, lofty

elezione *f* election

eliambulanza *f* air ambulance

elica *f* propeller

elicottero *m* helicopter

eliminare eliminate; **eliminatoria** *f* SP heat; **eliminazione** *f* elimination

eliporto *m* heliport

élite *f* élite

elmetto *m* helmet; **elmo** *m* helmet

elogio *m* praise

eloquente eloquent

eludere elude; *sorveglianza, domanda* evade

elvetico Swiss

e-mail *f* *inv* e-mail; **inviare un'~ a qc** e-mail s.o., send s.o. an e-mail

emanare 1 *v/t* give off; *legge* pass **2** *v/i* emanate, come (**da** from)

emanciparsi become emancipated; **emancipazione** *f* emancipation

emarginare marginalize; **emarginato** *m*, **-a** *f* person on the fringes of society

ematoma *m* haematoma, *Am* hematoma

embrione *m* embryo

emergenza *f* emergency; **emergere** emerge; (*distinguersi*) stand out; **emerso** *pp* ☞ **emergere**

emesso *pp* ☞ **emettere**; **emettere** *luce* give out, emit; *grido, verdetto* give; *calore* give off; FIN issue; TEC emit

emicrania *f* migraine

emigrante *m/f* emigrant; **emigrare** emigrate; **emigrato** *m*, **-a** *f* person who has emigrated, ex-pat; **emigrazione** *f* emigration

emisfero *m* hemisphere

emissione *f* emission; *di denaro, francobolli* issue; RAD broadcast; **emittente 1** *agg* issuing; (*trasmittente*) broadcasting **2** *f* RAD transmitter; TV channel

emoglobina *f* haemoglobin, *Am* hemoglobin

emorragia *f* haemorrhage, *Am* hemorrhage

emorroidi *fpl* haemorrhoids, *Am* hemorroids

emotivo emotional; (*sensibile*) sensitive

emozionante exciting, thrilling; **emozionarsi** get excited; (*commuoversi*) be moved; **emozionato** excited; (*agitato*) nervous; (*commosso*) moved; (*turbato*) upset; **emozione** *f* emotion; (*agitazione*) excitement

emporio *m negozio* department store

emulsione *f* emulsion

enciclopedia *f* encyclopedia

endovenoso intravenous

energetico *consumo ecc* energy *attr*, *alimento* energy-giving; **energia** *f* energy; **energico** strong, energetic

enfasi *f* emphasis

enigma *m* enigma

ennesimo MAT nth; F **per l'-a**

volta for the hundredth time F

enorme enormous

enoteca *f negozio* wine merchant (*specializing in fine wines*)

ente *m* organization; **gli enti locali** the local authorities

entrambi both

entrare (*andare dentro*) go in, enter; (*venire dentro*) come in, enter; *fig* **questo non c'entra** that has nothing to do with it; **~ in una stanza** enter a room, go into / come into a room; **entrata** *f* entrance; *in parcheggio* entrance, way in; *in un paese* entry; FIN **-e** *pl* (*reddito*) income; (*guadagno*) earnings; **~ libera** admission free

entro within

entroterra *m inv* hinterland

entusiasmare enthuse; **entusiasmo** *m* enthusiasm; **entusiasta** enthusiastic

enumerare enumerate

enzima *m* enzyme

epatite *f* hepatitis

epicentro *m* epicentre, *Am* epicenter; *fig* centre, *Am* center

epidemia *f* epidemic

epidermide *f* skin; MED epidermis

Epifania *f* Epiphany

epilessia *f* epilepsy; **epilettico 1** *agg* epileptic **2** *m*, **-a** *f* epileptic

episodio *m* episode

epoca *f* age; *(periodo)* period, time; **auto** *f* **d'~** vintage car; **mobili** *mpl* **d'~** period furniture

eppure (and) yet

equatore *m* equator; **equatoriale** equatorial

equazione *f* equation

equilibrare balance; **equilibrato** balanced; **equilibrio** *m* balance; *fig* common sense

equino horse *attr*

equinozio *m* equinox

equipaggiamento *m* equipment; **equipaggio** *m* crew

équipe *f inv* team

equitazione *f* horse riding

equivalente *m/agg* equivalent

equivoco 1 *agg* ambiguous; *(sospetto)* suspicious; F *(losco)* shady **F 2** *m* misunderstanding

era *f (epoca)* age, era; GEOL era; **~ atomica** atomic age; **~ glaciale** Ice Age

era, erano → **essere**

erba *f* grass; GASTR **-e** *pl* herbs; **-e aromatiche** herbs; **erbaccia** *f* weed; **erboristeria** *f* herbalist's, *Am* herbalist store

erede *m/f* heir; **donna** heiress; **eredità** *f* inheritance; BIO heredity; **ereditare** inherit; **ereditarietà** *f* heredity; **ereditario** hereditary; **ereditiera** *f* heiress

eremita *m* hermit

eretico 1 *agg* heretical **2** *m*, **-a** *f* heretic

eretto 1 *pp* → **erigere 2** *agg* erect; **erezione** *f* building; *di pene* erection

ergastolo *m* life sentence

ergonomico ergonomic

erica *f* heather

erigere erect; *fig (fondare)* establish, found

eritema *m cutaneo* rash; **~ solare** sunburn

ermafrodito *m* hermaphrodite

ermellino *m* ermine

ermetico *(a tenuta d'aria)* airtight; *fig* obscure

ernia *f* MED hernia; **~ del disco** slipped disc

ero → **essere**

eroe *m* hero

erogare *denaro* allocate; *gas, acqua* supply

eroina *f droga* heroin; *donna* eroica heroine

erosione *f* GEOL erosion

erotico erotic; **erotismo** *m* eroticism

errare wander, roam; *(sbagliare)* be mistaken; **errata corrige** *m inv* correction; **erroneamente** mistakenly; **errore** *m* mistake, error; **~ di ortografia** spelling mistake; **~ di stampa** misprint, typo; **per ~** by mistake

erta *f*: **stare all'~** be on the alert

erudito 1 *agg* erudite, learned **2** *m*, **-a** *f* erudite person, scholar

eruttare *di vulcano* erupt; **eruzione** *f* eruption; MED rash

es. (= *esempio*) eg (= for example)

esagerare 1 *v/t* exaggerate **2** *v/i* exaggerate; *(eccedere)* go too far; **esagerato** exaggerated; *zelo* excessive; *prezzo* exorbitant; **esagerazione** *f* exaggeration

esalare 1 *v/t odori* give off; **~ il respiro** exhale **2** *v/i* come, emanate *(da* from)

esaltare exalt; *(entusiasmare)* elate; **esaltarsi** become elated; **esaltato 1** *agg* elated; *(fanatico)* fanatical **2** *m* fanatic

esame *m* exam(ination); MED *(test)* test; *(visita)* examination; **esaminare** examine *(anche* MED)

esasperante exasperating; **esasperare** *(inasprire)* exacerbate; *(irritare)* exasperate; **esasperazione** *f* exasperation

esattezza *f* accuracy; **per l'~** to be precise; **esatto 1** *pp* ☞ **esigere 2** *agg* exact; *risposta* correct, right; *in punto* exactly; **~!** that's right!

esaudire grant; *speranze* fulfil, *Am* fullfil

esauriente exhaustive; **esaurimento** *m* exhaustion; COM **svendita** *f fino a* **~ della merce** clearance sale; **~ ner-**

voso nervous breakdown; **esaurire** exhaust; *merci* run out of; **esaurito** *(esausto)* exhausted; COM sold out; *pubblicazioni* out of print; **esausto** exhausted

esca *f* bait *(anche fig)*

esce ☞ **uscire**

eschimese *agg, m/f* Inuit, Eskimo

esclamare exclaim; **esclamazione** *f* exclamation

escludere exclude; **esclusione** *f* exclusion; **esclusiva** *f* exclusive right, sole right; **esclusivo** exclusive; **escluso 1** *pp* ☞ **escludere 2** *agg* excluded; *(impossibile)* out of the question **3** *m*, **-a** *f* person on the fringes of society

esco ☞ **uscire**

escogitare contrive

escoriazione *f* graze

escrementi *mpl* excrement

escursione *f* trip, excursion; *a piedi* hike; **escursionismo** *m* touring; *a piedi* hiking, walking; **escursionista** *m/f* tourist; *a piedi* hiker, walker

esecutivo *m/agg* executive; **esecutore** *m*, **-trice** *f* DIR executor; MUS performer; **esecuzione** *f (realizzazione)* carrying out; MUS performance; **~ (capitale)** execution; **eseguire** carry out; MUS perform

esempio *m* example; **per ~, ad ~** for example; **esemplare 1** *agg* exemplary **2** *m* specimen; (*copia*) copy

esentare exempt (*da* from); **esente** exempt; **~ da tasse** tax-free

esercente m/f shopkeeper, Am storekeeper

esercitare exercise; (*addestrare*) train; *professione* practise, Am practice; **esercitarsi** practise, Am practice; **esercitazione** f exercise

esercito m army

esercizio m exercise; (*pratica*) practice; (*anno finanziario*) financial year, Am fiscal year; FIN *azienda* business; *negozio* shop, Am anche store

esibire *documenti* produce; *mettere in mostra* display; **esibirsi** *in uno spettacolo* perform; *fig* show off; **esibizione** f exhibition; (*ostentazione*) showing off; (*spettacolo*) performance; **esibizionista** m/f show-off; PSI exhibitionist

esigente exacting, demanding; **esigenza** f demand; (*bisogno*) need; **esigere** demand; (*riscuotere*) exact

esile slender; *voce* faint

esiliare exile; **esilio** m exile

esistente existing; **esistenza** f existence; **esistere** exist

esitare hesitate; **esitazione** f hesitation

esito m result, outcome; FIN sales, turnover

esodo m exodus

esofago m œsophagus, Am esophagus

esonerare exempt (*da* from)

esordiente m/f beginner; **esordio** m introduction; (*inizio*) beginning; TEA début

esortare (*incitare*) urge; (*pregare*) beg; **esortazione** f urging

esotico exotic

espandere expand; **espandersi** expand; (*diffondersi*) spread; **espansivo** FIS, TEC expansive; *fig* warm, friendly

espatriare leave one's country; **espatrio** m expatriation

espediente m expedient

espellere expel

esperienza f experience

esperimento m experiment

esperto m/agg expert

espirare breathe out, exhale

esplicito explicit

esplodere 1 v/t *colpo* fire **2** v/i explode

esplorare explore; **esploratore** m, **-trice** f explorer; *giovane* m **~** boy scout

esplosione f explosion; **~ demografica** population explosion; **esplosivo** m/agg explosive; **esploso** pp **esplodere**

esponente m/f exponent; **esporre** expose (*anche* FOT); *avviso* put up; *in una mostra* exhibit, show; (*riferire*) present; *ragioni, caso* state; *teoria* explain; **esporsi**

expose o.s. (**a** to); (*compromettersi*) compromise o.s.

esportare export; **esportazione** *f* export

esposizione *f* (*mostra*) exhibition; (*narrazione*) presentation; FOT exposure; **esposto 1** *pp* ☞ **esporre 2** *agg* **in mostra** on show; **~ a** exposed to; **critiche** open to; **~ a sud** south facing **3** *m* statement; (*petizione*) petition

espressione *f* expression; **espressivo** expressive; **espresso 1** *pp* ☞ **esprimere 2** *agg* express **3** *m* posta express letter; FERR express; (**caffè** *m*) ~ espresso; **per** ~ express; **esprimere** express; **esprimersi** express o.s.

espropriare expropriate; **esproprio** *m* expropriation

espulsione *f* expulsion; **espulso** *pp* ☞ **espellere**

essa *pron f persona* she; *cosa, animale* it

essenza *f* essence; **essenziale 1** *agg* essential **2** *m*: **l'~ è** the main thing is

essere 1 *v/i* **~ di** (*provenire di*) be *o* come from; **~ di qu** (*appartenere a*) belong to s.o; **c'è** there is; **ci sono** there are; **sono io** it's me; **cosa c'è?** what's the matter?; **non c'è di che!** don't mention it!; **chi è?** who is it; **sono le tre** it's three o'clock; **siamo in quattro** there are four of us; **se fossi in te** if

I were you; **sarà!** if you say so! **2** *v/aus*: **siamo arrivati alle due** we arrived at two o'clock; **non siamo ancora arrivati** we haven't arrived yet; **è stato investito** he has been run over **3** *m* being

esso *pron m persona* he; *cosa, animale* it

est *m* east; **a** (*l*)**~ di** (to the) east of

estasi *f* ecstasy

estate *f* summer; **in ~, d'~** in (the) summer

estendere extend; **estendersi di territorio** extend; (*allungarsi*) stretch; *fig* (*diffondersi*) spread

estenuante exhausting

esteriore *m/agg* exterior, outside

esterno 1 *agg* external **2** *m* outside; **all'~** on the outside

estero 1 *agg* foreign **2** *m* foreign countries; **all'~** abroad

esteso 1 *pp* ☞ **estendere 2** *agg* extensive; (*diffuso*) widespread; **per ~** in full

estetista *f* beautician

estinguere extinguish, put out; *debito* pay off; **estinguersi** die out; **estinto 1** *pp* ☞ **estinguere 2** *agg* extinct; *debito* paid off **3** *m*, **-a** *f* deceased; **estintore** *m* fire extinguisher; **estinzione** *f* extinction; FIN paying off

estirpare uproot; *dente* extract; *fig* eradicate

estivo summer *attr*

estorcere *denaro* extort; estorsione *f* extortion; estorto *pp* ☞ **estorcere**
estradizione *f* extradition
estraneo 1 *agg* outside (*a qc* sth) 2 *m*, -a *f* stranger; *persona non autorizzata* unauthorized person
estrarre extract; *pistola* pull out; **~ a sorte** draw; estratto 1 *pp* ☞ **estrarre** 2 *m* extract; *documento* abstract; FIN **~ conto** statement (of account); estrazione *f* extraction
estremista *m/f* extremist; estremità *f inv* extremity; *di corda* end; *(punta)* tip; *(punto superiore)* top; estremo 1 *agg* extreme; *(più lontano)* farthest; *(ultimo nel tempo)* last, final 2 *m (estremità)* extreme; **gli -i** *pl di un documento* the main points
estro *m (ispirazione artistica)* inspiration
estroverso extrovert(ed)
estuario *m* estuary
esuberante *(vivace)* exuberant
esultare rejoice
età *f inv* age; **all'~ di** at the age of; **avere la stessa ~** be the same age; **di mezz'~** middle-aged
eternità *f* eternity; eterno eternal; *questione, problema* age-old; **in ~** for ever and ever

eterogeneo heterogen(e)ous
eterosessuale heterosexual
etica *f* ethics *sg*
etichetta *f* label; *cerimoniale* etiquette
etico ethical
etiope *agg, m/f* Ethiopian; Etiopia *f* Ethiopia
etnico ethnic
etrusco 1 *agg* Etruscan 2 *m*, -a *f* Etruscan
ettaro *m* hectare
etto *m* hundred grams; ettogrammo *m* hundred grams, hectogram
eucalipto *m* eucalyptus
eucaristia *f* REL Eucharist
euforia *f* euphoria
euro *m inv* euro; eurodeputato *m*, -a *f* Euro MP; Europa *f* Europe; europeo 1 *agg* European 2 *m*, -a *f* European; eurovisione *f* Eurovision
evacuare evacuate; evacuazione *f* evacuation
evadere 1 *v/t* evade; *(sbrigare)* deal with 2 *v/i* escape (*da* from)
evaporare evaporate
evasione *f* escape; *fig* escapism; **~ fiscale** *f* tax evasion; evasivo evasive; evaso 1 *pp* ☞ **evadere** 2 *m*, -a *f* fugitive; evasore *m*: **~ fiscale** tax evader
evenienza *f* eventuality
evento *m* event
eventuale possible; eventualità *f inv* eventuality; eventualmente if necessary

evidente evident; **evidenziatore** *m* highlighter
evitare avoid; *~ il fastidio a qu* spare s.o. the trouble
evoluto 1 *pp* ☞ **evolvere 2** *agg* developed; (*progredito*) progressive, advanced; *senza pregiudizi* open-minded; **evoluzione** *f* evolution; **evolvere 1** *v/t* develop **2** *v/i*

e **evolversi** evolve, develop
evviva hurray
ex ... ex-, former
extra *m/agg inv* extra
extracomunitario 1 *agg* non-EU **2** *m*, *-a f* non-EU citizen
extraconiugale extramarital
extraeuropeo non-European
extraterrestre *agg*, *m/f* extraterrestrial

F

fa 1 ☞ **fare 2** *avv*: **5 anni ~ 5** years ago **3** *m* MUS F; *nel solfeggio della scala* fa(h)
fabbisogno *m* needs
fabbrica *f* plant, factory; **fabbricante** *m/f* manufacturer; **fabbricare** manufacture; ARCHI build; *fig* fabricate; **fabbricato** *m* building
faccenda *f* matter; **faccende** *fpl* housework
faccia *f* face; (*risvolto, aspetto*) facet; (*lato*) side; *~ a faccia* cheek; *~ a ~* face to face; *gliel'ha detto in ~* he told him to his face; **facciata** *f* ARCHI front, façade; *di foglio* side; *fig* (*esteriorità*) appearance
faccio ☞ **fare**
facile easy; *di carattere* easygoing; (*incline*) prone (*a* to); *è ~ a dirsi* easier said than done!; *è ~ che venga* he is likely to come; **facilità** *f* ease; (*attitudine*) aptitude,

facility; **facilitare** facilitate; **facilmente** easily
facoltà *f inv* faculty; (*potere*) power; **facoltativo** optional
faggio *m* beech (tree)
fagiano *m* pheasant
fagiolini *mpl* green beans; **fagiolo** *m* bean
fagotto *m* bundle; MUS bassoon; *fig far ~* pack up and leave
fai da te *m inv* do-it-yourself, DIY, *Am* home improvement
fai ☞ **fare**
falciatrice *f* lawn-mower
falco *m* hawk
falegname *m* carpenter
falena *f* moth
falla *f* MAR leak
fallimento *m* failure; FIN bankruptcy; **fallire 1** *v/t* miss **2** *v/i* fail; FIN go bankrupt; **fallito 1** *agg* unsuccessful, failed; FIN bankrupt **2** *m* failure; FIN bankruptcy

fallo *m* fault; *(errore)* error, mistake; SP foul

falò *m inv* bonfire

falsario *m* forger; **falsificare** forge; **falso 1** *agg* false; *(sbagliato)* incorrect, wrong; *oro, gioielli* imitation, fake F; *(falsificato)* forged, fake F **2** *m (falsità)* falsehood; *oggetto falsificato* forgery, fake F

fama *f* fame; *(reputazione)* reputation

fame *f* hunger; *aver* ~ be hungry

famiglia *f* family; **familiare 1** *agg* family *attr*; *(conosciuto)* familiar; *(semplice)* informal **2** *m/f* relative, relation; **familiarità** *f* familiarity; **familiarizzarsi** familiarize o.s.

famoso famous

fanale *m* light; *(lampione)* street lamp

fanatico 1 *agg* fanatical **2** *m*, **-a** *f* fanatic

fanciullo *m*, **-a** *f* (young) boy; *ragazza* (young) girl

fango *m* mud; MED **-ghi** *pl* mud-baths; **fangoso** muddy

fannullone *m*, **-a** *f* lazy good-for-nothing

fantascienza *f* science fiction

fantasia *f* fantasy; *(immaginazione)* imagination; *(capriccio)* fancy; MUS fantasia

fantasma *m* ghost

fantasticare day-dream *(di* about); **fantastico** fantastic

fantoccio *m* puppet *(anche fig)*

farabutto *m* nasty piece of work

faraona *f*: *(gallina f)* ~ guinea fowl

farcire GASTR stuff; *torta* fill; **farcito** stuffed; *dolce* filled

fard *m inv* blusher

fardello *m* bundle; *fig* burden

fare 1 *v/t* do; *vestito, dolce, errore* make; *biglietto, benzina* buy, get; ~ *un bagno* have a bath; ~ *il medico* be a doctor; ~ *vedere qc a qu* show sth to s.o.; **farcela** manage; *non c'e la faccio più* I can't take any more; *2 più 2 fa 4* 2 and 2 make(s) 4; *quanto fa?* how much is it?; *far* ~ *qc a qu* get s.o. to do sth **2** *v/i*: *faccia pure!* go ahead!; *fa freddo / caldo* it's cold / warm

farfalla *f* butterfly

farina *f* flour; **farinaceo 1** *agg* starchy **2** *-cei mpl* starchy foodstuffs

faringe *f* pharynx; **faringite** *f* inflammation of the pharynx

farmaceutico pharmaceutical; **farmacia** *f* pharmacy, *Br* anche *negozio* chemist's; **farmacista** *m/f* pharmacist, *Br* anche chemist; **farmaco** *m* drug

faro *m* MAR lighthouse; AVIA beacon; AUTO headlight

farsi *(diventare)* grow; F *(drogarsi)* shoot up F; *si sta facendo tardi* it's getting late; ~ *male* hurt o.s.

fascia *f* band; MED bandage; ~

oraria (time) slot; **fasciare** MED bandage; **fasciatura** *f* (*fascia*) bandage; *azione* bandaging

fascicolo *m* (*opuscolo*) booklet, brochure; (*incartamento*) file

fascino *m* fascination, charm

fascio *m* bundle; *di fiori* bunch; *di luce* beam

fascismo *m* Fascism; **fascista** *agg*, *m/f* Fascist

fase *f* phase; AUTO stroke; *fig* **essere fuori ~** be out of sorts; **~ di lavorazione** production stage

fastidio *m* bother, trouble; **dare ~ a qu** bother s.o.; **le dà ~ se … ?** do you mind if …?; **fastidioso** (*irritante*) irritating, annoying; (*irritabile*) irritable

fata *f* fairy

fatale fatal; **fatalità** *f inv* fate; (*disavventura*) misfortune

fatica *f* (*sforzo*) effort; (*stanchezza*) fatigue; **a ~** with a great deal of effort; **faticare** toil; **~ a** find it difficult to; **faticoso** tiring; (*difficile*) laborious

fatto 1 *pp* ☞ **fare 2** *agg* done; AGR ripe; **~ a mano** handmade; **~ di legno** made of wood **3** *m* fact; (*avvenimento*) event; (*faccenda*) affair, business; **di ~** *agg* real; *avv* in fact, actually; **in ~ di** as regards

fattore *m* (*elemento*) factor;

AGR farm manager; **~ di protezione antisolare** (sun) protection factor

fattoria *f* farm; *casa* farmhouse

fattorino *m* messenger; *per consegne* delivery man

fattura *f* (*lavorazione*) workmanship; *di abiti* cut; FIN invoice; **fatturare** FIN invoice; **fatturato** *m* FIN (*giro d'affari*) turnover

fauna *f* fauna

fava *f* broad bean

favola *f* (*fiaba*) fairy tale; (*storia*) story; *morale* fable; (*meraviglia*) dream; **favoloso** fabulous

favore *m* favour; *Am* favor; **per ~ !** please!; **fare un ~ a qu** do s.o. a favour; **favorevole** favourable, *Am* favorable; **favorire 1** *v/t* favour, *Am* favor; (*promuovere*) promote **2** *v/i*: **vuol ~ ?** would you care to join me / us?; **favorito** *m/agg* favourite, *Am* favorite

fax *m inv* fax; **faxare** fax

fazione *f* faction

fazzolettino *m*: **~ di carta** tissue; **fazzoletto** *m* handkerchief; *per la testa* headscarf

febbraio *m* February

febbre *f* fever; **ha la ~** he has a temperature

fecondare fertilize; **fecondazione** *f* fertilization; **~ artificiale** artificial insemination

fede *f* faith; (*fedeltà*) loyalty; *anello* wedding ring; **fedele**

1 *agg* faithful; *(esatto, conforme all'originale)* true **2** *m* REL believer; **i -i** *pl* the faithful *pl*

federa *f* pillowcase

federazione *f* federation

fegato *m* liver; *fig* courage, guts F

felce *f* fern

felice happy; *(fortunato)* lucky; **felicità** *f* happiness; **felicitarsi: ~ con qu per qc** congratulate s.o. on sth

felino feline

felpa *f* sweatshirt

feltro *m* felt

femmina *(figlia)* girl, daughter; ZO, TEC female; **femminile 1** *agg* feminine; *(da donna)* women's **2** *m* GRAM feminine; **femminilità** *f* femininity; **femminismo** *m* feminism; **femminista** *m/f* feminist

femore *m* femur

fendinebbia *m inv* fog lamp *o* light

fenomeno *m* phenomenon

feriale: giorno *m* ~ weekday; **ferie** *fpl* holiday, *Am* vacation, **andare in** ~ go on holiday

ferire wound; *in incidente* injure; *fig* hurt; **ferirsi** injure o.s.; **ferita** *f* wound; *in incidente* injury; **ferito 1** *agg* wounded; *in incidente* injured; *fig: sentimenti* hurt; *orgoglio* injured **2** *m* casualty

fermacarte *m inv* paperweight

fermacravatta *m inv* tiepin

fermaglio *m* clasp; *per capelli* hair slide, *Am* barrette; *(gioiello)* brooch

fermare stop; DIR detain; **fermarsi** stop; *(restare)* stay, remain; **fermata** *f* stop; ~ **dell' autobus** bus stop

fermentare ferment; **fermento** *m* yeast; *fig* ferment

fermo 1 *agg* still; *veicolo* stationary; *(saldo)* firm; *mano* steady; **star ~** *(non muoversi)* keep still **2** *int* ~**!** *(alt!)* stop!; *(immobile!)* keep still!

feroce fierce, ferocious; *animale* wild; *(insopportabile)* dreadful

ferragosto *m* August 15 public holiday; *periodo* August holidays

ferramenta *f* hardware; *negozio* hardware store

ferro *m* iron; *(arnese)* tool; ~ **da calza** knitting needle; ~ **da stiro** iron; ~ **di cavallo** horseshoe; GASTR **ai -i** grilled, *Am* broiled; **ferrovia** *f* railway, *Am* railroad

fertile fertile; **fertilizzante** *m* fertilizer

fesso *m* F idiot F; **far ~ qu** con s.o F

fessura *f* *(spaccatura)* crack; *(fenditura)* slit, slot

festa *f* feast; REL *di santo* feast day; *(ricevimento)* party; *(compleanno)* birthday; ~ **della mamma / del papà** Mother's / Father's Day; ~

filare

nazionale national holiday;
festeggiamenti *mpl* celebrations; **festeggiare** celebrate; *persona* have a celebration for; **festival** *m inv* festival; **festività** *f inv* festival; **~** *pl* celebrations, festivities; **festivo** festive; ***giorno* ~** holiday

feto *m* fetus, *Br anche* foetus

fetta *f* slice; ***a -e*** sliced

fiaba *f* fairy tale

fiacca *f* weariness; *(svogliatezza)* laziness; ***battere la* ~** be a shirker

fiaccola *f* torch

fiamma *f* flame; MAR pennant; **fiammante**: ***rosso* ~** fiery red; ***nuovo* ~** brand new; **fiammifero** *m* match

fiancheggiare border; *fig* support

fianco *m* side; ANAT hip; **~ *a* ~** side by side; ***di ~ a qu*** beside s.o.

fiasco *m* flask; *fig* fiasco

fiato *m* breath; ***senza* ~** breathless; **riprendere ~** catch one's breath

fibbia *f* buckle

fibra *f* fibre, *Am* fiber; **~ *sintetica*** synthetic; **fibroso** fibrous

ficcanaso *m/f* F nosy parker F; **ficcare** thrust; F *(mettere)* shove F; **ficcarsi** get; ***dove s'è ficcato?*** where can it / he have got to?

fico *m* fig; *albero* fig (tree); **~ *d'India*** prickly pear

fidanzamento *m* engagement; **fidanzarsi** get engaged; **fidanzata** *f* fiancée; **fidanzato** *m* fiancé; **i -i** *pl* the engaged couple *pl*

fidarsi: **~ *di*** trust, rely on; **fidato** trustworthy; **fiducia** *f* confidence; ***avere ~ in qu*** have faith in s.o.; **fiduciaria** *f* **~** FIN trust company; **fiducioso** trusting

fienile *m* barn

fieno *m* hay

fiera *f* *mostra* fair

fiero proud

fifa F *f* jitters F; ***aver ~*** have the jitters

figlia *f* daughter; **figliastra** *f* stepdaughter; **figliastro** *m* stepson; **figlio** *m* son; ***avere -gli*** *fig* have children; ***essere ~ unico*** be an only child; **figlioccia** *f* goddaughter; **figlioccio** *m* godson

figura *f* figure; *(illustrazione)* illustration; *(apparenza)* appearance; ***far brutta ~*** make a bad impression; **figurare 1** *v/t fig* imagine; **figurati!** just imagine! **2** *v/i (apparire)* appear; *(far figura)* make a good impression; **figurato** illustrated; *linguaggio* figurative

fila *f* line, row; *(coda)* queue, *Am* line; ***tre giorni di ~*** three days running; ***fare la ~*** queue (up), *Am* wait in line; **filare 1** *v/t* spin **2** *v/i di ragionamento* make sense; *di for-*

maggio go stringy; *di veicolo* travel; F (*andarsene*) take off F; **~ diritto** (*comportarsi bene*) behave (o.s.)

filastrocca *f* nursery rhyme

filato 1 *agg* (*logico*) logical; **andare di ~ a casa** go straight home; **per 10 ore filate** for ten hours on the trot **2** *m* yarn; *per cucire* thread

file *m inv* INFOR file

filetto *m* GASTR fillet

filiale *f* branch; (*società affiliata*) affiliate

filigrana *f su carta* watermark; *in oreficeria* filigree

film *m inv* film, movie; **filmare** film; **filmato** *m* short (film)

filo *m* thread; *metallico* wire; *di lama* edge; *d'erba* blade; **~ interdentale** (*dental*) floss; **~ spinato** barbed wire; **filone** *m* MIN vein; *pane* French stick; *fig* tradition

filosofia *f* philosophy; **filosofico** philosophical; **filosofo** *m* philosopher

filtrare 1 *v/t* filter **2** *v/i fig* filter out; **filtro** *m* filter

fin → **fine, fino**

finale 1 *agg* final **2** *m* end **3** *f* SP final; **finalista** *m/f* finalist; **finalmente** (*alla fine*) at last; (*per ultimo*) finally

finanza *f* finance; **finanziamento** *m* funding; **finanziare** fund, finance; **finanziario** financial; **finanziere** *m* financier; (*guardia di finanza*) Customs officer; *lungo le co-*

ste coastguard

finché until; (*per tutto il tempo che*) as long as

fine 1 *agg* fine; (*sottile*) thin; *udito, vista* sharp, keen; (*raffinato*) refined **2** *m* aim; **al ~ di ...** in order to ... **3** *f* end; **alla ~** in the end; **fine settimana** *m inv* weekend

finestra *f* window; **finestrino** *m* window

fingere 1 *v/t*: **~ sorpresa** pretend to be surprised **2** *v/i*: **~ di** pretend to; **fingersi** pretend to be

finire finish, end; **finiscila!** stop it!; **finito** finished; (*venduto*) sold out

finlandese 1 *m/agg* Finnish **2** *m/f* Finn; **Finlandia** *f* Finland

fino¹ *agg* fine; (*acuto*) sharp; *oro* pure

fino² *prp tempo* till, until; *luogo* as far as; **~ a domani** until tomorrow; **~ a che** (*per tutto il tempo che*) as long as; (*fino al momento in cui*) until; **fin da ieri** since yesterday

fino³ *avv* even; **fin troppo** more than enough

finocchio *m* fennel

finora so far

finta *f* pretence, *Am* pretense, sham; SP feint; **far ~ di** pretend to; **finto 1** *pp* → **fingere 2** *agg* false; (*artificiale*) artificial; (*simulato*) feigned; **finzione** *f* pretence, *Am* pretense

flotta

fiocco m bow; **~ di neve** snowflake; **-cchi** pl **d'avena** oat flakes

fioco weak; *luce* dim

fionda f catapult

fioraio m, **-a** f florist; **fiore** m flower; *fig il* (*fior*) **~** the cream; *nelle carte* **-i** pl clubs; **fiorente** flourishing

fiorentino 1 agg Florentine **2** m, **-a** f Florentine; GASTR **alla -a** with spinach; *bistecca* charcoal grilled **3** f GASTR T-bone steak

fiorire flower; *fig* flourish

Firenze f Florence

firma f signature; **firmare** sign; **firmatario** m signatory; **firmato** *abito*, *borsa* designer *attr*

fisarmonica f accordion

fiscale tax attr, fiscal; *fig spreg* rigid, unbending

fischiare 1 v/t whistle; **~ qu** boo s.o. **2** v/i *di vento* whistle; **fischio** m whistle

fisco m tax authorities, Inland Revenue, *Am* IRS, *Am* Internal Revenue Service

fisica f physics; **fisico 1** agg physical **2** m physicist; ANAT physique

fisionomia f face; *fig: di popolo, città* appearance; (*carattere*) character

fisioterapia f physiotherapy; **fisioterapista** m/f physiotherapist

fissare (*fermare*) fix; (*guarda-*

re intensamente) stare at; (*stabilire*) arrange; (*prenotare*) book; **fissarsi** (*stabilirsi*) settle; (*ostinarsi*) set one's mind (**di** on); (*avere un'idea fissa*) become obsessed (**di** with); **fissazione** f (*mania*) fixation (**di** about); **fisso** 1 agg fixed; *stipendio*, *cliente* regular; *lavoro* permanent **2** avv fixedly

fitta f sharp pain

fitto (*denso*) thick

fiume m river; *fig* flood, torrent

fiutare smell; *cocaina* snort; **~ un imbroglio** smell a rat; **fiuto** m sense of smell; *fig* nose

flacone m bottle

flagrante flagrant; **cogliere qu in ~** catch s.o. red-handed

flash m inv FOT flash; *stampa* newsflash

flauto m flute

flemma f calm

flessibile flexible; **flessione** f bending; GRAM inflection; (*diminuzione*) dip, (*slight*) drop

flipper m inv pinball machine

flirtare flirt

F.lli (= **fratelli**) Bros (= brothers)

floppy disk m inv floppy (disk)

flora f flora

floscio limp; *muscoli* flabby

flotta f fleet

fluido

fluido *m/agg* fluid
fluorescente fluorescent
flusso *m* flow
fluttuazione *f* fluctuation
FMI *m* (= *Fondo Monetario Internazionale*) IMF (= International Monetary Fund)
foca *f* seal
focaccia *f* focaccia; *dolce: sweet type of bread*
foce *f* mouth
focoso fiery
fodera *f* interna lining; esterna cover; **foderare** *all'interno* line; *all'esterno* cover; **fodero** *m* sheath
foglia *f* leaf
foglio *m* sheet
fogna *f* sewer
folata *f* gust
folclore *m* folklore; **folcloristico** folk *attr*
folgorare *di fulmine, idea* strike; *di corrente elettrica* electrocute; **~ qu con lo sguardo** glare at s.o.
folla *f* crowd; *fig* host
folle[1] *agg* mad
folle[2] AUTO: *in ~* in neutral
follia *f* madness
folto thick
fondale *m* MAR sea bed; TEA backcloth
fondamentalista *m/f* fundamentalist; **fondamentale** fundamental; **fondamento** *m* foundation; **senza ~** unfounded; **fondare** found; **fondarsi** be based (*su* on); **fondato** founded; **fondato-**

re *m*, **-trice** *f* founder; **fondazione** *f* foundation
fondere 1 *v/t* (*liquefare*) melt; *metalli* smelt; *colori* blend **2** *v/i* melt; **fondersi** melt; FIN merge
fondo 1 *agg* deep **2** *m* bottom; (*sfondo*) background; *terreno* property; FIN fund; SP long-distance; SCI cross-country; **-i** *pl denaro* funds; **-i neri** illegal earnings; **a ~** (*profondamente*) in depth; *fig* **in ~** basically; **in ~ alla strada** at the end *o* bottom of the road; **andare a ~** (*affondare*) sink; (*approfondire*) get to the bottom (*di* of); **fondotinta** *m inv* foundation
fonduta *f* cheese fondue
fonetica *f* phonetics
fontana *f* fountain
fonte *m/f* spring; *fig* source
footing *m* jogging; **fare ~** go jogging
forare *di proiettile* pierce; *con il trapano* drill; *biglietto* punch; *pneumatico* puncture; **foratura** *f di pneumatico* puncture
forbici *fpl* scissors
forchetta *f* fork
forcina *f* hairpin
foresta *f* forest
foresteria *f* guest rooms; **forestiero 1** *agg* foreign **2** *m*, **-a** *f* foreigner
forfait *m inv* lump sum; **forfettario** flat-rate
forfora *f* dandruff

forma f form; (*sagoma*) shape; TEC (*stampo*) mould, Am mold; *essere in ~* be in good form

formaggino m processed cheese; **formaggio** m cheese

formale formal; **formalità** f inv formality

formare shape; **formarsi** form; (*svilupparsi*) develop; **formato** m size; *di libro* format; **formattare** INFOR format; **formazione** f formation; *fig:* addestramento training; SP line-up

formica¹ f ZO ant

formica²® Formica

formicaio m anthill

formicolare *di mano, gamba* tingle; *fig ~ di* teem with; **formicolio** m sensazione pins and needles

formidabile (*straordinario*) incredible; (*poderoso*) powerful

formula f formula; **formulare** *teoria* formulate; (*esprimere*) express

fornaio m baker; *negozio* bakery; **fornello** m oven

fornire supply (*qc a qu* s.o. with sth); **fornirsi** get (*di* sth); **fornitore** m supplier; **fornitura** f supply

forno m oven; (*panetteria*) bakery; *~ a microonde* microwave (oven); *al ~ carne, patate* roast; *mele, pasta* baked

foro¹ m (*buco*) hole

foro² m romano forum; DIR (*tribunale*) (law) court

forse perhaps, maybe

forte 1 agg strong; *suono* loud; *pioggia* heavy; *taglia, somma* large; *dolore* severe **2** avv (*con forza*) hard; (*ad alta voce*) loudly; (*velocemente*) fast **3** m (*fortezza*) fort; **fortezza** f MIL fortress

fortuito chance

fortuna f fortune; *avere ~* be successful; (*essere fortunato*) be lucky; *buona ~!* good luck!; *per ~* luckily; **fortunatamente** fortunately; **fortunato** lucky, fortunate

foruncolo m pimple

forza f strength; (*potenza*) power; *muscolare* force; *a ~ di ...* by dint of; *per ~* against my / our will; *per ~!* (*naturalmente*) of course!; *~!* come on!; *-e* pl (*armate*) MIL (armed) forces; **forzare** force

foschia f haze

fosforescente phosphorescent

fossa f pit, hole; (*tomba*) grave; **fossato** m ditch; *di fortezza* moat; **fossetta** f dimple

fossile m/agg fossil (*attr*)

fosso m ditch

foto f inv photo

fotocopia f photocopy; **fotocopiatrice** f photocopier

fotografare photograph; **fotografia** f arte photography;

(foto) photograph; **~ a colori** colour photograph; **fotografico** photographic; **macchina** f **-a** camera; **fotografo** m photographer

fotomontaggio m photomontage

fotoromanzo m graphic novel

fra between; *più persone o cose* among; *temporale* in; **~ questi ragazzi** out of all these boys; **~ l'altro** what's more; **~ breve** in a very short time, soon; **~ sé e sé** to himself / herself

frac m *inv* tails

fracassare smash; **fracasso** m din; *di oggetti che cadono* crash

fradicio rotten; *(bagnato)* soaking wet

fragile fragile; *persona* frail, delicate

fragola f strawberry

fragore m roar; *di tuono* rumble

fraintendere misunderstand

frammentario fragmentary; **frammento** m fragment

frana f landslide; **franare** collapse

francamente frankly

francese 1 m/agg French **2** m/f Frenchman; *donna* Frenchwoman; **i -i** pl the French pl; **Francia** f France

franco frank; FIN free; **farla -a** get away with it; **francobollo** m stamp

frangia f fringe, *Am* bangs

frantumare shatter; **frantumi** mpl splinters; **in ~** in smithereens; **mandare in ~** smash to smithereens

frappé m *inv* milkshake

frase f sentence; MUS phrase; **~ fatta** set phrase, idiom

frassino m ash (tree)

frastagliato *costa* jagged

frastuono m racket

frate m REL friar, monk

fratellastro m step-brother; *con un genitore in comune* half-brother; **fratello** m brother; **-i** pl fratello e sorella brother and sister; **fraterno** brotherly, fraternal

frattaglie fpl GASTR offal; *di pollo* giblets

frattanto meanwhile, in the meantime

frattempo: **nel ~** meanwhile, in the meantime

frattura f fracture; **fratturarsi:** **~ una gamba** break one's leg

frazione f fraction; POL small group; *(borgata)* hamlet

freccia f arrow; AUTO **~ (di direzione)** indicator, *Am* turn signal

freddo 1 agg cold **2** m cold; **ho ~** I'm cold; **fa ~** it's cold; **freddoloso: essere ~** feel the cold

freezer m *inv* freezer

fregare rub; F *(imbrogliare)* swindle; F *(rubare)* pinch F; P **me ne frego di quello**

che pensano I don't give a damn what they think F; **fregatura** *f* F (*imbroglio*) rip-off F; (*ostacolo, contrarietà*) pain F

fregio *m* ARCHI frieze

frenare AUTO brake; *folla, lacrime, risate* hold back; *impulso* restrain; **frenarsi** (*dominarsi*) restrain o.s.; **frenata** *f* braking; *fare una ~* brake; **freno** *m* AUTO brake; *del cavallo* bit; *~ a mano* handbrake, *Am* parking brake

frequentare *luoghi* frequent; *scuola, corso* attend; *persona* associate with; **frequentato** popular; *strada* busy; **frequente** frequent; *di ~* frequently; **frequenza** *f* frequency; *scolastica* attendance; *un'alta ~ di spettatori* a large audience; *con ~* frequently

fresco 1 *agg* fresh; *temperatura* cool **2** *m* coolness; *fa ~* it's cool; *mettere in ~* put in a cool place

fretta *f* hurry; *aver ~* be in a hurry; *non c'è ~* there's no hurry; **frettoloso** hurried; *lavoro* rushed; *persona* in a hurry

fricassea *f* GASTR fricassée

friggere 1 *v/t* fry **2** *v/i* sizzle; **friggitoria** *f* *shop that sells deep fried fish etc*

frigo *m* fridge, *Am* refrigerator; **frigorifero 1** *agg* cold

attr, *camion* refrigerated **2** *m* refrigerator

frittata *f* GASTR omelette, *Am* omelet; **frittella** *f* fritter; **fritto 1** *pp* ☞ **friggere 2** *agg* fried **3** *m* fried food; *~ misto* assortment of deep-fried food

frittura *f* metodo frying; *~ di pesce* fried fish

frivolo frivolous

frizionare rub; **frizione** *f* friction; AUTO clutch

frizzante *bevanda* fizzy, sparkling

frode *f* fraud

frontale frontal; *scontro ~* head-on collision; **fronte 1** *f* forehead; *di ~ a* (*dirimpetto*) opposite, facing; *in presenza di* before; *a confronto di* compared with **2** *m* front; *far ~ agli impegni* face up to one's responsibilities; **fronteggiare** face

frontiera *f* border, frontier

fronzolo *m* frill

frottola *f* F fib F

frugale frugal

frugare 1 *v/i* rummage **2** *v/t* (*cercare con cura*) search, rummage through

frullare GASTR blend, liquidize; *uova* whisk; **frullato** *m* milkshake; **frullatore** *m* liquidizer, blender; **frullino** *m* whisk

frumento *m* wheat

fruscio *m* rustle

frusta *f* whip; GASTR whisk;

frustare whip; **frustino** *m* riding crop

frustante frustrating; **frustrazione** *f* frustration

frutta *f* fruit; **~ secca** nuts

fruttare 1 *v/t* yield 2 *v/i* fruit; **frutteto** *m* orchard; **fruttivendolo** *m*, **-a** *f* greengrocer; **frutto** *m* fruit; **-i** *pl* **di mare** seafood

FS (= **Ferrovie dello Stato**) Italian State railways

f.to (= **firmato**) signed

fu ☞ **essere**

fucilare shoot; **fucile** *m* rifle

fuga[1] *f* escape; **~ di gas** gas leak

fuga[2] *f* MUS fugue

fuggifuggi *m inv* stampede; **fuggire** flee; **fuggitivo** *m* fugitive

fuliggine *f* soot

fulminare *di sguardo* glare at; **rimanere fulminato** *da fulmine* be struck by lightning; *da elettricità* be electrocuted; *fig* be thunderstruck; **fulminarsi** *di lampadina* blow; **fulmine** *m* lightning; **fulmineo** fast, rapid

fumare smoke; **fumatore** *m*, **-trice** *f* smoker; **scompartimento** *m* **per -i** / **non -i** smoking / non-smoking car

fumetto *m* comic strip; **-i** *pl* **per ragazzi** comics

fumo *m* smoke; *(vapore)* steam; **~ passivo** passive smoking; **fumoso** smoky; *fig (oscuro)* muddled

fune *f* rope; *(cavo)* cable

funebre funeral *attr*; *fig* gloomy, funeral

funerale *m* funeral

fungere act *(da* as*)*

fungo *m* mushroom; MED fungus

funicolare *f* funicular railway

funivia *f* cableway

funzionamento *m* operation, functioning; **funzionare** operate, function; **non ~** be out of order; *di orologio* have stopped; **funzionario** *m* official, civil servant; **funzione** *f* function; *(carica)* office; REL service; **mettere in ~** put into operation

fuoco *m* fire; FOT focus; **dar ~ a qc** set fire to sth; **~ fuoco** catch fire; **-chi** *pl* **d'artificio** fireworks; MIL **far ~** (open) fire; FOT **mettere a ~** focus

fuorché except

fuori 1 *prp stato* outside, out of; *moto* out of, away from; **~ città** out of town; **~ luogo** out of place; **~ di sé** beside o.s. 2 *avv* outside; **all'aperto** out of doors; SP out; **~!** out!; **fuoribordo** *m inv* motorboat; **motore** outboard motor; **fuorigioco** *m inv* offside; **essere nel ~** be offside; **fuoriserie** 1 *agg* made to order, custom 2 *f inv* AUTO custom-built model; **fuoristrada** *m inv* off-roader; **fuoriuscita** *f* **di gas** leakage; **fuor-**

garanzia

viare **1** v/i go astray **2** v/t lead astray

furbizia f cunning; **furbo** cunning, crafty

furgoncino m (small) van; **furgone** m van

furia f fury, rage; **a ~ di ...** by dint of ...; **furibondo** furious, livid; **furioso** furious; vento, lotta violent; **furore** m fury, rage; **far ~** be all the rage

furto m theft; **~ con scasso** burglary

fusa fpl: **fare le ~** purr

fuseaux mpl leggings

fusibile m EL fuse

fusione f fusion; FIN merger

fuso[1] pp **~ fondere**; metallo molten; burro melted

fuso[2] m spindle; **~ orario** time zone

fusto m (tronco) trunk; (stelo) stem, stalk; di metallo drum; di legno barrel

futile futile

futuristico futuristic; **futuro** m/agg future

G

gabbia f cage

gabbiano m (sea)gull

gabinetto m toilet, Am rest room

gaffe f blunder, gaffe

gala f (ricevimento) gala

galante gallant

galera f (prigione) jail, prison

galla f: **venire a ~** (come to the) surface; fig come to light; **galleggiante 1** agg floating **2** m (boa) buoy; **galleggiare** float

galleria f gallery; passaggio con negozi (shopping) arcade; FERR, MIN tunnel; TEA circle, Am balcony

Galles m Wales; **gallese 1** m/agg Welsh **2** m/f Welshman; donna Welshwoman

gallina f hen; **gallo** m cock

gallone m unità di misura gallon

galoppare gallop; **galoppo** m gallop; **al ~** at a gallop

gamba f leg; fig **in ~** (capace) smart, bright; persona anziana sprightly

gamberetto m shrimp; **gambero** m prawn

gambo m di fiore, bicchiere stem; di pianta, fungo stalk

gamma f range; MUS scale

gancio m hook

gara f competition; di velocità race; **fare a ~** compete

garage m inv garage

garantire 1 v/t guarantee; (assicurare) ensure **2** v/i (farsi garante) stand guarantor (**per** for); **garantito** guaranteed; **garanzia** f guarantee; **essere in ~** be under guarantee

gareggiare compete

gargarismo *m* gargle; *(collutorio)* mouthwash; **fare i -i** gargle

garofano *m* carnation; GASTR **chiodi di ~** cloves

garza *f* gauze

gas *m inv* gas; **a ~** gas *attr;* **~ lacrimogeno** tear gas; **gasato 1** *agg* bibita fizzy; F *(eccitato)* excited **2** *m,* **-a** *f* F bighead F

gasolio *m* per riscaldamento oil; AUTO diesel

gastrite *f* gastritis

gastronomia *f* gastronomy; **gastronomico** gastronomic

gatta *f*(female) cat; **gattino** *m* kitten; **gatto** *m* cat

gay *m/agg* gay

gazzella *f* gazelle

gazzetta *f* gazette

gazzosa *f* fizzy o *Am* carbonated drink, *Am* soda

G.d.F. (= *Guardia di Finanza*) Customs and Excise

gel *m inv* gel

gelare 1 *v/t* freeze **2** *v/i e* **gelarsi** freeze

gelateria *f* ice-cream parlour *o* parlor

gelatina *f* gelatine; **~ di frutta** fruit jelly

gelato 1 *agg* frozen **2** *m* ice cream

gelido freezing

gelo *m (brina)* frost; *fig* chill

gelosia *f* jealousy; **geloso** jealous (**di** of)

gelsomino *m* jasmine

gemellaggio *m* twinning; **gemello 1** *agg* twin **2** *m di camicia* cuff link **3** *m,* **-a** *f* twin; ASTR **Gemelli** *pl* Gemini

gemito *m* groan

gemma *f anche fig* gem; BOT bud

gene *m* BIO gene

genealogia *f* genealogy; **genealogico** genealogical

generale *m/agg* general; **in ~** in general; **generalità** *f inv* general nature; **in ~** personal details; **generalizzare** generalize; **generalmente** generally; **generare** *(dar vita a)* give birth to; *(causare)* generate, create; *sospetti* arouse; *elettricità, calore* generate; **generatore** *m* EL generator; **generazione** *f* generation

genere *m* kind; BIO genus; GRAM gender; **in ~** generally; **-i alimentari** foodstuffs; **~ umano** mankind, humanity; **generico** generic

genero *m* son-in-law

generoso generous (**con** to)

genetico genetic; **ingegneria** *f* **-a** genetic engineering

gengiva *f* gum

geniale ingenious; **genialità** *f* genius; *(ingegnosità)* ingeniousness

genio *m* genius; *(inclinazione)* talent

genitali *mpl* genitals

genitori *mpl* parents

gennaio *m* January

genocidio *m* genocide

Genova Genoa; **genovese**
m/agg Genoese
gentaglia *f* scum
gente *f* people *pl*
gentile kind; *nelle lettere* **~ Signora** Dear Madam; **genti-
lezza** *f* kindness
genuino genuine; *prodotto
alimentare* traditionally
made; *risata* spontaneous
genziana *f* gentian
geografia *f* geography; **geografico** geographic
geologico geological
geometra *m/f* surveyor, *Am*
structural engineer; **geometria** *f* geometry
geranio *m* geranium
gerarchia *f* hierarchy
gergo *m* slang; *di una professione anche* jargon
Germania *f* Germany
germe *m* germ; *fig (principio)*
seeds; **in ~** in embryo; **ger-
mogliare** sprout; **germoglio**
m shoot
geroglifico *m* hieroglyph
gesso *m* MIN gypsum; MED,
scultura plaster cast; *per scrivere* chalk
gesticolare gesticulate
gestione *f* management; **gestire** manage
gesto *m* gesture; *con la testa*
nod
gestore *m* manager
Gesù *m* Jesus; **~ bambino**
baby Jesus
gettare throw; *fondamenta*
lay; *grido* give, let out; **~**

via throw away; **gettarsi**
throw o.s.; *di fiume* flow (**in**
into)
getto *m* jet; **di ~** in one go
gettone *m* token; *per giochi*
counter; *per giochi d'azzardo*
chip
ghetto *m* ghetto
ghiacciaio *m* glacier; **ghiacciato** *lago, stagno* frozen; *bibita* ice-cold; **ghiaccio** *m* ice;
sulla strada black ice; **ghiacciolo** *m* icicle; *(gelato)* ice
lolly, *Am* Popsicle®
ghiaia *f* gravel
ghianda *f* acorn; **ghiandola** *f*
gland
ghigliottina *f* guillotine
ghiotto *persona* greedy; *fig: di
notizie ecc* avid (**di** for); *(appetitoso)* appetizing
ghirigoro *m* doodle
ghirlanda *f* garland
ghiro *m* dormouse; **dormire
come un ~** sleep like a log
già already; *(ex)* formerly; **~!**
of course!
giacca *f* jacket; **~ a vento**
windproof jacket
giacché since
giacenza *f per la vendita*
stock; *invenduta* unsold
goods; *periodo* stock time;
~ di cassa cash in hand; **-e**
pl **di magazzino** stock in
hand; **giacimento** *m* MIN deposit
giada *f* jade
giallo *m/agg* yellow; **libro ~,
film ~** thriller

Giappone m Japan; **giappo-nese** agg, m/f Japanese
giardinaggio m gardening; **giardiniera** f gardener; mobile plant stand; GASTR (mixed) pickles; **giardiniere** m gardener; **giardino** m garden; ~ **pubblico** park
gigante m/agg giant (attr); **gigantesco** gigantic
giglio m lily
gilè m inv waistcoat, Am vest
gin m inv gin
ginecologo m, -a f gynaecologist, Am gynecologist
ginepro m juniper
ginestra f broom
gingillarsi fiddle; (perder tempo) fool around
ginnastica f exercises; disciplina sportiva gymnastics; in palestra physical education
ginocchio m knee; **stare in ~** be on one's knees, be kneeling
giocare 1 v/i play; d'azzardo, in Borsa gamble; (scommettere) bet; ~ **a tennis, flipper** play 2 v/t play; (ingannare) trick; **giocarsi** (perdere al gioco) gamble away; (beffarsi) make fun; carriera throw away; **giocatore** m, **-trice** f player; d'azzardo gambler; **giocattolo** m toy; **gioco** m game; **il ~** gambling; ~ **d'azzardo** game of chance; **l'ho detto per ~** ! I was joking!; **giocoliere** m juggler
gioia f joy; (gioiello) jewel;

gioielleria f jeweller's (shop), Am jewelry store; **gioiello** m jewel
giornalaio m, **-a** f newsagent, Am news vendor; **giornale** m (news)paper; (rivista) magazine; (registro) journal; ~ **radio** news (bulletin); **giornaliero** daily; **abbonamento** ~ day pass; **giornalino** m per ragazzi comic; **giornalismo** m journalism; **giornalista** m/f journalist, reporter; **giornalistico** journalistic; agenzia, servizio news attr; **giornata** f day; **lo finiremo in ~** we'll finish it today; **giorno** m day; ~ **feriale** weekday, workday; ~ **festivo** (public) holiday; **l'altro** ~ the other day; **a -i** (fra pochi giorni) in a few days (time); **al** ~ a day; **al ~ d'oggi** nowadays; **di** ~ by day
giostra f carousel, merry-go-round
giovane 1 agg young; (giovanile) youthful 2 m/f young man, youth; ragazza young woman, girl; **i -i** young people pl, the young pl; **giovanotto** m young man, youth
giovare (essere utile) be useful (**a** to); (far bene) be good (**a** for)
Giove m Jupiter; **giovedì** m inv Thursday
gioventù f youth; (i giovani) young people pl; **giovinezza** f youth

gippone *m* AUTO SUV

giraffa *f* giraffe

girandola *f* fuoco d'artificio Catherine wheel, *Am* pinwheel; *(giocattolo)* windmill; *(banderuola)* weather vane; **girare 1** *v/t* turn; *città, negozi* go around; *paese* travel around; *film* shoot; *(mescolare)* mix; FIN endorse **2** *v/i* turn; *rapidamente* spin; *(andare in giro)* wander around; *con un veicolo* drive around; **mi gira la testa** I feel dizzy; **girarrosto** *m* GASTR spit; **girasole** *m* sunflower; **girata** *f* turn; *(passeggiata a piedi)* walk, stroll; *in macchina* drive; FIN endorsement; **girevole** revolving

girino *m* tadpole

giro *m* turn; *(circolo)* circle; *(percorso abituale)* round; *(deviazione)* detour; *(passeggiata a piedi)* walk, stroll; *in macchina* drive; *in bicicletta* ride; *di pista* lap; *di motore* rev; *(viaggio)* tour; **nel ~ di una settimana** within a week; **essere in ~** *(da qualche parte)* be around somewhere; *(fuori)* be out; **mettere in ~** spread; *fig* **prendere in ~ qu** pull s.o.'s leg

girocollo *m inv: maglione a ~* crewneck sweater; **gironzolare** hang around; **~ per negozi** wander around the stores; **girovagare** wander around

giù down; *(sotto)* below; *(da basso)* downstairs; *fig* **essere ~** be down *o* depressed; *di salute* be run down; **mandar ~** swallow *(anche fig)*; **su e ~** up and down

giubbotto *m* sports jacket; **~ di salvataggio** life jacket

giudicare judge; **~ male qu** misjudge s.o.; **lo hanno giudicato colpevole** he has been found guilty; **giudice** *m* judge; **giudizio** *m* judg(e)ment; *(senno)* wisdom; DIR *(causa)* trial; *(sentenza)* verdict; **a mio ~** in my opinion

giugno *m* June

giungere arrive *(a* in, at), reach *(a* sth)

giungla *f* jungle

giunta *f* addition; POL junta; **~ comunale** town council; **per ~** in addition, moreover; **giunto** *pp* ☞ **giungere**

giuramento *m* oath; **giurare** swear; **giurato 1** *agg* sworn **2** *m* member of the jury; **giuria** *f* jury

giuridico legal; **giurisprudenza** *f* jurisprudence

giustificare justify; **giustificazione** *f* justification

giustizia *f* justice; **giusto 1** *agg* just, fair; *(adatto)* right, appropriate; *(esatto)* correct, right **2** *avv* correctly; *mirare* accurately; *(proprio, per l'appunto)* just; **~!** that's right!

glassa f GASTR icing, Am frosting

gli 1 art mpl the; **avere gli occhi azzurri** have blue eyes **2** pron (a lui) (to) him; (a esso) (to) it; (a loro) (to) them; **dagli i libri** give him / them the books, give the books to him / them

glicemia f glycaemia, Am glycemia

glie: ~**la,** ~**lo,** ~**li,** ~**le,** ~**ne** = pron **gli** or **le** with pron **la, lo, li, le, ne**

globale global; **globalizzazione** f globalization; **globo** m globe; **globulo** m globule; MED corpuscle; ~ **rosso** red blood cell

gloria f glory

glossario m glossary

glucosio m glucose

gnocchi mpl (di patate) gnocchi (small potato dumplings)

gnorri m F: **fare lo** ~ act dumb F

goal m inv SP goal

gobba f hump; **gobbo 1** agg hunchbacked **2** m hunchback

goccia f drop; **a** ~ **a** ~ little by little; **gocciolare** drip

godere 1 v/t enjoy; **godersela** enjoy o.s. **2** v/i (rallegrarsi) be delighted (di at)

goffo awkward, clumsy

gol m inv SP goal

gola f throat; (ingordigia) greed(iness), gluttony; GEOG gorge; **mal** m **di** ~ sore throat

golf m inv golf; (cardigan) cardigan; (maglione) sweater

golfo m gulf

goloso greedy; **essere** ~ **di dolci** have a sweet tooth

golpe m inv coup

gomito m elbow

gomitolo m ball (of wool)

gomma f rubber; per cancellare eraser, Br anche rubber; (pneumatico) tyre, Am tire; ~ **da masticare** (chewing) gum; AUTO ~ **di scorta** spare tyre; **avere una** ~ **a terra** have a flat tyre; **gommapiuma®** f foam rubber; **gommista** m tyre o Am tire specialist; **gommone** m rubber dinghy

gondola f gondola; **gondoliere** m gondolier

gonfiare 1 v/t con aria inflate; le guance puff out; fig (esagerare) exaggerate, magnify **2** v/i e **gonfiarsi** swell up; gonfio swollen; pneumatico inflated; stomaco bloated; fig puffed up (di with); **gonfiore** m swelling

gonna f skirt

gorgogliare di stomaco rumble; dell'acqua gurgle

gorilla m inv gorilla; F (guardia del corpo) bodyguard, gorilla F

gotico m/agg Gothic

governante 1 f housekeeper **2** m ruler; **governare** POL govern, rule; **governativo** government attr; scuola state *attr*; **governo** *m* government

gozzovigliare make merry

gracchiare *di corvo* caw; *di rane* croak; *di persona* squawk

gracidare croak

gracile (*debole*) delicate

gradazione *f* gradation; (*sfumatura*) shade; ~ **alcolica** alcohol(ic) content

gradevole pleasant, agreeable; **gradimento** *m* liking

gradinata *f* flight of steps; (*stadio*) stand; *a teatro* gallery, balcony; **gradino** *m* step

gradire like; (*desiderare*) wish; *gradisce un po' di vino?* would you like some wine?; **gradito** pleasant; (*bene accetto*) welcome

grado[1] *m* degree; *in una gerarchia*, MIL rank; **in ~ di lavorare** capable of working, fit for work; **per -i** by degrees

grado[2] *m*: **di buon ~** willingly

graduale gradual

graduatoria *f* list

graffa *f* TIP brace

graffiare scratch; **graffio** *m* scratch; **graffiti** *mpl* graffiti *sg o pl*

grafica *f* graphics; **grafico 1** *agg* graphic **2** *m* (*diagramma*) graph; (*disegnatore*) graphic artist

grafologia *f* handwriting analysis, graphology

grammatica *f* grammar; **grammaticale** grammatical

grammo *m* gram(me)

Gran Bretagna *f* Great Britain

gran *☞* **grande**

grana 1 *f* grain; F (*seccatura*) trouble; F *soldi* dough F, cash **2** *m inv* cheese similar to Parmesan

granaio *m* barn

granchio *m* crab

grande big; (*largo*) wide; *fig* (*intenso, notevole*) great; (*adulto*) grown-up, big; (*vecchio*) old; **grandezza** *f* (*dimensione*) size; (*larghezza*) width; (*ampiezza*) breadth; (*altezza*) height; *fig* (*eccellenza*) greatness; (*grandiosità*) grandeur

grandinare hail; **grandine** *f* hail

grandioso grand

granducato *m* grand duchy

granello *m* grain; ~ **di pepe** peppercorn; ~ **di polvere** speck of dust

granita *f* type of ice made of frozen crystals of coffee or fruit syrup

granito *m* granite

grano *m* (*chicco*) grain; (*frumento*) wheat; *fig* grain, ounce

granturco *m* maize, corn

grappa *f* grappa, *brandy made from the remains of the grapes used in wine-making*

grappolo *m* bunch

grassetto *m* TIP bold

grasso 1 *agg* fat; (*unto*) greasy; *cibo* fatty **2** *m* fat;

grassoccio plump

grata f grating

gratella f, **graticola** f GASTR grill, Am broiler

gratifica f bonus

gratin m: **al** ~ au gratin; **gratinato** au gratin

gratis free (of charge)

gratitudine f gratitude; **grato** grateful

grattacapo m problem, headache F; **grattacielo** m skyscraper; **grattare** scratch; (raschiare) scrape; (grattugiare) grate; F pinch F; **grattugia** f grater; **grattugiare** grate

gratuito free (of charge); (infondato) gratuitous

gravare 1 v/t burden **2** v/i weigh (su on); **grave** (pesante) heavy; (serio) serious; (difficile) hard

gravidanza f pregnancy

gravità f seriousness, gravity; FIS (**forza** f **di**) ~ (force of) gravity

grazia f grace; (gentilezza) favour, Am favor; DIR pardon; **graziare** pardon; **grazie** thank you, thanks; ~ **tante**, ~ **mille** thank you so much; ~ **a** thanks to; **grazioso** charming; (carino) pretty

Grecia f Greece; **greco 1** agg Greek **2** m, -a f Greek

gregge m flock

greggio 1 agg (non lavorato) raw, crude **2** m crude (petroleum)

grembiule m apron; **grembo** m lap; materno womb; fig bosom

gretto (avaro) mean; (di mente ristretta) narrow-minded

gridare 1 v/i shout, yell; ~ **aiuto** shout for help **2** v/i shout, yell; (strillare) scream; **grido** m shout, cry

grigio grey, Am gray; fig (triste) sad; (scialbo) dreary

griglia f (grata) grating; GASTR grill; **alla** ~ grilled

grilletto m trigger

grillo m cricket; fig (capriccio) fancy, whim

grimaldello m lock pick

grinfie fpl fig clutches

grinta f grit; fig determination

grinza f di stoffa crease; **grinzoso** viso wrinkled; (spiegazzato) creased

grissino m bread stick

grondaia f gutter

grondare 1 v/i (colare) pour; (gocciolare) drip; ~ **di sudore** be dripping with sweat **2** v/t drip with

groppa f back

groppo m: **avere un** ~ **alla gola** have a lump in one's throat

grossezza f (dimensione) size; (spessore) thickness; (l'essere grosso) largeness

grossista m/f wholesaler

grosso 1 agg big, large; (spesso) thick; mare rough; sale, ghiaia coarse; **sbagliarsi di** ~ make a big mistake;

farla **-a** make a fine mess **2** *m* bulk; **grossolano** coarse; *errore* serious; **grossomodo** roughly

grotta *f* cave; *artificiale* grotto
grottesco grotesque
groviglio *m* tangle; *fig* muddle
gru *f inv* crane
gruccia *f* crutch; *per vestiti* hanger
grumo *m* clot; *di farina* lump
gruppo *m* group; **~ sanguigno** blood group
guadagnare earn; *(ottenere)* gain; **guadagno** *m* gain; *(profitto)* profit; *(entrate)* earnings
guaina *f* sheath; *(busto)* corset
guaio *m* trouble; *(danno)* damage; *essere nei* **-ai** be in trouble
guancia *f* cheek
guanciale *m* pillow
guanto *m* glove; **guantone** *m*: **~ da boxe** boxing glove
guardaboschi *m inv* forest ranger; **guardacoste** *m inv* MAR coastguard; **guardalinee** *m inv* SP assistant referee, linesman; **guardamacchine** *m* car park attendant, *Am* parking lot attendant
guardare 1 *v/t* look at; *(osservare, stare a vedere)* watch; *(custodire)* watch, look after; *(esaminare)* check **2** *v/i* look; *(controllare)* check; *di finestra* overlook (**su** sth); **~ a sud**

face south; **guardaroba** *m inv* cloakroom, *Am* checkroom; *armadio* wardrobe; **guardarsi** look at o.s.; **~ da** beware of; *(astenersi)* refrain from

guardia *f* guard; **~ forestale** forest ranger; **~ di finanza** Customs official; **~ del corpo** bodyguard; **~ medica, medico** *m* **di ~** duty doctor; *fare la* **~** keep guard; *stare in* **~** be on one's guard; **guardiano** *m*, **-a** *f (custode)* warden; *(portiere)* caretaker; *(guardia)* guard; *di parco* keeper; **~ notturno** night watchman; **guardone** *m* voyeur
guardrail *m inv* guardrail
guarigione *f* recovery; *in via di* **~** on the mend; **guarire 1** *v/t* cure **2** *v/i* recover; *di ferita* heal
guarnizione *f (abbellimento)* trimming; GASTR garnish; *di rubinetto* washer; AUTO **~ del freno** brake lining
guastafeste *m/f inv* spoilsport; **guastare** spoil, ruin; *meccanismo* break; **guastarsi** break down; *di tempo* change for the worse; *di cibi* go bad; **guasto 1** *agg* broken; *telefono, ascensore* out of order; AUTO broken down; *cibi* bad; *dente* rotten, decayed **2** *m* fault, failure; AUTO breakdown
guerra *f* war; **guerrafondaio**

m war-monger; **guerriglia** *f* guerrilla warfare; **guerrigliero** *m*, -a *f* guerrilla
gufo *m* owl
guida *f* guidance; (*persona, libro*) guide; AUTO driving; ~ **telefonica** phone book; ~ **turistica** tourist guide; AUTO ~ **a destra / a sinistra** right-hand / left-hand

drive; **guidare** guide; AUTO drive; **guidatore** *m*, -trice *f* driver
guinzaglio *m* lead, leash
guscio *m* shell
gustare taste; *fig* enjoy; **gusto** *m* taste; (*sapore*) flavour, *Am* flavor; *fig* (*piacere*) pleasure; **buon / cattivo** ~ good / bad taste

H

ha¹ (= *ettaro*) ha (= hectare)
ha² ☞ *avere*
habitat *m inv* BIO habitat
habitué *m/f inv* regular
hacker *m/f* INFOR *inv* hacker
hai ☞ *avere*
hall *f inv* foyer
hamburger *m inv* hamburger
handicap *m inv* handicap; **handicappato 1** *agg* disabled, handicapped **2** *m*, -a *f* disabled *o* handicapped person
hanno ☞ *avere*
hard disk *m inv* INFOR hard disk
hardware *m inv* INFOR hard-

ware
harem *m inv* harem
hashish *m* hashish
henné *m inv* henna
herpes *m inv* herpes
hinterland *m inv* hinterland
hit parade *f inv* hit parade, charts
ho ☞ *avere*
hobby *m inv* hobby
hockey *m inv* hockey; ~ **su ghiaccio** ice hockey
hostess *f inv* hostess; ~ **di terra** (*guida*) member of ground staff
hot dog *m inv* hot dog
hotel *m inv* hotel

I

i *art mpl* the
iceberg *m inv* iceberg
icona *f* icon
idea *f* idea; (*opinione*) opinion; **cambiare** ~ change

one's mind; **non avere la minima** ~ **di qc** not have the slightest idea about sth; **neanche per** ~**!** of course not!; **ideale** *m/agg* ideal; **idealiz-**

zare idealize; **ideare** *scherzo, scusa* think up; *metodo, oggetto nuovo* invent; *piano, progetto* devise; **ideatore** *m, -trice f* originator; *di metodo, oggetto nuovo* inventor

idem ditto

identico identical; **identificare** identify; **identikit** *m inv* Identikit®. *Am* composite drawing; **identità** *f inv* identity

ideologia *f* ideology

idiomatico idiomatic

idiota 1 *agg* idiotic, stupid **2** *m/f* idiot, fool; **idiozia** *f* stupidity; *(assurdità)* nonsense; *un'~* a stupid *o* idiotic thing to do / say

idolo *m* idol

idoneo suitable (*a* for)

idrante *m* hydrant

idratante *della pelle* moisturizing; **idratare** *la pelle* moisturize

idraulico 1 *agg* hydraulic; *impianto* *m* ~ plumbing **2** *m* plumber

idrico water *attr*

idroelettrico hydroelectric; **idrofilo:** *cotone* *m* ~ cotton wool, *Am* absorbent cotton; **idromassaggio** *m* Jacuzzi®, whirlpool; **idroplano** *m* hydroplane

iena *f* hyena

ieri yesterday; ~ *l'altro, l'altro* ~ the day before yesterday; ~ *mattina* yesterday morning

igiene *f* hygiene; **igienico** hy-

gienic; **carta** *f* ~*-a* toilet paper

ignaro unaware (*di* of); **ignorante** *(non informato)* ignorant; *(incolto)* uneducated; *(maleducato)* rude; **ignoranza** *f* ignorance; **ignorare** *(non considerare)* ignore; *(non sapere)* not know; **ignoto** unknown

il *art m sg* the; ~ *martedì* on Tuesdays; *2 euro* ~ *chilo 2* euros a kilo; *mi piace il caffè* I like coffee

illegale illegal

illeggibile illegible

illegittimo illegitimate

illeso unhurt

illimitato unlimited

illogico illogical

illudere deceive; **illudersi** delude o.s.

illuminare light up; *fig* enlighten; **illuminazione** *f* lighting; *fig* flash of inspiration

illusione *f* illusion; **illuso 1** *pp* ☞ **illudere 2** *m/f (sognatore)* dreamer

illustrare illustrate; **illustratore** *m, -trice f* illustrator; **illustrazione** *f* illustration

illustre illustrious

imballaggio *m operazione* packing; *(involucro)* package; **imballare** pack; *AUTO* ~ *il motore* race the engine

imbambolato *occhi, sguardo* blank; *dal sonno* bleary-eyed

imbarazzante embarrassing; **imbarazzare** embarrass; **im-**

barazzato embarrassed; **imbarazzo** *m* embarrassment; (*disturbo*) trouble; **mettere in ~ qu** embarrass s.o.

imbarcadero *m* landing stage; **imbarcarsi** go on board, embark; **imbarcazione** *f* boat; **~ da diporto** pleasure boat; **imbarco** *m di passeggeri* boarding, embarkation; *di carico* loading; (*banchina*) landing stage

imbattersi: ~ in qu bump into s.o.

imbattibile unbeatable

imbecille 1 *agg* idiotic, stupid **2** *m/f* imbecile, fool

imbiancare 1 *v/t* whiten; *con pitture* paint; *tessuti* bleach **2** *v/i e* **imbiancarsi** go white; **imbianchino** *m* (house) painter

imboccare *persona* feed; *fig* prompt; **~ una strada** turn into a road; **imboccatura** *f* (*apertura*) opening; (*ingresso*) entrance; MUS mouthpiece; **imbocco** *m* entrance

imboscata *f* ambush

imbottigliare *bottle*; *di veicoli* hold up

imbottito stuffed; *panino* filled; **imbottitura** *f* stuffing; *di giacca* padding

imbranato clumsy

imbrattare soil; (*macchiare*) stain

imbrogliare 1 *v/t* (*raggirare*) take in; (*truffare*) cheat; *fig* confuse **2** *v/i* cheat; **imbro-**

glio *m* (*truffa*) trick; *fig* (*pasticcio*) mess; **imbroglione** *m*, **-a** *f* cheat

imbronciato sulky

imbruttire 1 *v/t* make ugly **2** *v/i* get ugly

imbucare *posta* post, *Am* mail

imburrare butter

imbuto *m* funnel

imitare imitate; **imitazione** *f* imitation

immaginare imagine; (*supporre*) suppose; **immaginario** imaginary; **immaginazione** *f* imagination

immagine *f* image

immangiabile inedible

immaturo *persona* immature; (*precoce*) premature; *frutto* unripe

immedesimarsi identify (**in** with)

immediatamente immediately; **immediato** immediate; (*pronto*) prompt

immenso immense

immergere immerse; (*lasciare immerso*) soak; **immergersi** plunge; *di subacqueo, sottomarino* dive; *fig* immerse o.s. (**in** in); **immersione** *f* immersion; *di subacqueo, sottomarino* dive; **immerso 1** *pp* ➔ **immergere 2** *agg* immersed

immettere introduce (**in** into); INFOR *dati* enter; (*portare*) lead (**in** into); **immettersi: ~ in** get into

immigrante *m/f* immigrant; **immigrare** immigrate; **immigrato** *m*, **-a** *f* immigrant; **immigrazione** *f* immigration; (*immigrati*) immigrants; FIN inflow

imminente imminent; *pericolo* impending; *pubblicazione* forthcoming

immischiarsi meddle (*in* with), interfere (*in* in)

immissione *f* introduction; *di manodopera* intake; INFOR *di dati* entry

immobile 1 *agg* motionless **2** *mpl:* **-i** real estate; **immobiliare:** *agente m/f* ~ estate agent, *Am* realtor; *società f* ~ *di compravendita* property company; *di costruzione* construction company

immondizia *f* (*gen pl*) rubbish, *Am* trash

immorale immoral

immortale immortal; **immortalità** *f* immortality

immune MED immune (*a* to); (*esente*) free (*da* from); **immunità** *f* immunity; **immunitario:** *sistema m* ~ immune system; **immunodeficienza** *f* immunodeficiency

immutato unchanged

impacchettare (*confezionare*) wrap (up); (*mettere in pacchetti*) package

impacciare *movimenti* hamper; *persona* hinder; **impacciato** (*imbarazzato*) embarrassed; (*goffo*) awkward; im-

paccio *m* (*ostacolo*) hindrance; (*situazione difficile*) awkward situation; (*imbarazzo*) awkwardness

impacco *m* MED compress

impadronirsi: ~ *di qc* take possession of sth; *fig* master sth

impalcatura *f* temporanea scaffolding; *fig* framework

impallidire *di persona* turn pale

impanare GASTR coat with breadcrumbs; **impanato** in breadcrumbs, breaded

impaperarsi falter

imparare learn (*a* to)

imparentarsi: ~ *con qu* become related to s.o.

impari unequal; MAT odd

impartire give

imparziale impartial; **imparzialità** *f* impartiality

impassibile impassive

impastare mix; *pane* knead; **impasto** *m* GASTR dough; (*mescolanza*) mixture

impatto *m* impact

impaurire frighten; **impaurirsi** get frightened

impaziente impatient; **impazienza** *f* impatience

impazzata: *all'*~ correre at breakneck speed; *colpire* wildly

impazzire go mad *o* crazy; *far* ~ *qu* drive s.o. mad *o* crazy

impeccabile impeccable

impedire prevent; (*ostruire*) block, obstruct; (*impacciare*) hinder; ~ *a qu di fare qc* prevent s.o. from doing sth, keep s.o. from doing sth

impegnare (*dare come pegno*) pawn; (*riservare*) reserve; *spazio, corsia* take up; **impegnarsi** (*prendersi l'impegno*) commit o.s., undertake (*a* to); (*concentrarsi*) apply o.s. (*in* to); **impegnativo** (*che richiede impegno*) demanding; *pranzo, serata, abito* formal; (*vincolante*) binding; **impegnato** (*occupato*) busy; *fig* (politically) committed; *sono già* ~ I've made other arrangements; **impegno** *m* commitment; (*appuntamento*) engagement; *con* ~ in earnest

impensabile unthinkable; **impensato** unexpected

imperante (*dominante*) prevailing

imperativo *m/agg* imperative

imperatore *m*, **-trice** *f* emperor; *donna* empress

impercettibile imperceptible

imperdonabile unforgivable

imperfetto *m/agg* imperfect; **imperfezione** *f* imperfection

impermeabile 1 *agg* waterproof **2** *m* raincoat; **impermeabilizzare** waterproof

impero *m* empire; (*potere*) rule

impersonale impersonal; **impersonare** personify; (*interpretare*) play (the part of)

impertinente impertinent; **impertinenza** *f* impertinenze

imperturbabile imperturbabile

imperversare rage; *fig: di moda* be all the rage

impeto *m* impetus, force; (*accesso*) outburst; (*slancio*) passion; *parlare con* ~ speak forcefully; **impetuoso** impetuoso

impianto *m operazione* installation; (*apparecchiature*) plant; (*sistema*) system; MED implant; ~ *elettrico* wiring; ~ *di risalita* ski lift; ~ *di riscaldamento* heating system

impiccare hang; **impiccarsi** hang o.s.

impicciarsi: ~ *di o in qc* interfere *o* meddle in sth; **impiccio** *m* (*ostacolo*) hindrance; (*seccatura*) bother; *essere d'*~ be in the way; *essere in un* ~ be in trouble

impiegare (*usare*) use; *tempo, soldi* spend; (*metterci*) take; (*assumere*) employ; *ho impiegato un'ora* it took me an hour; **impiegato** *m*, **-a** *f* employee; ~ *di banca* bank employee; **impiego** *m* (*uso*) use; (*occupazione*) employment; (*posto*) job

impietosire move to pity; **impietosirsi** be moved to pity

impigliare entangle; **impigliarsi** get entangled

impigrire 1 v/t make lazy **2** v/i e impigrirsi get lazy

implacabile implacable

implicare (coinvolgere) implicate; (comportare) imply

implicito implicit

implorare implore

impolverato dusty, covered in dust

imponente imposing, impressive

imponibile 1 agg taxable **2** m taxable income

impopolare unpopular

imporre impose; prezzo fix; **imporsi** (farsi valere) assert o.s.; (avere successo) be successful, become established; (essere necessario) be necessary

importante important; **importanza** f importance; **senza ~** not important, unimportant; **importare 1** v/t FIN, INFOR import **2** v/i matter, be important; (essere necessario) be necessary; **non importa** it doesn't matter; **non gliene importa niente** he couldn't care less; **importatore** m, **-trice** f importer; **importazione** f import; **importo** m amount

importunare (assillare) pester; (disturbare) bother; **importuno** troublesome; domanda, osservazione ill-timed

impossessarsi: ~ di seize

impossibile impossible; im-

possibilità f impossibility

imposta[1] f tax; **~ sul reddito** income tax; **~ sul valore aggiunto** value added tax, Am sales tax

imposta[2] f di finestra shutter

impostare lavoro plan; problema set out; lettera post, Am mail

imposto pp ☞ imporre

impostore m impostor

impotente powerless; (inefficace) ineffectual; MED impotent

impraticabile strada impassable

impratichirsi get practice (in in)

imprecare curse, swear (contro at); **imprecazione** f curse

imprecisato quantità indeterminate; motivi, circostanze not clear; **imprecisione** f inaccuracy; **impreciso** inaccurate

impregnare impregnate; (imbevere) soak; **impregnarsi** become impregnated (di with)

imprenditore m, **-trice** f entrepreneur; **imprenditoriale** entrepreneurial

impreparato unprepared

impresa f (iniziativa) enterprise, undertaking; (azienda) business, firm

impresario m contractor; TEA impresario

impressionante impressive;

(*spaventoso*) frightening; (*sconvolgente*) upsetting, shocking; **impressionare** (*turbare*) upset, shock; (*spaventare*) frighten; (*colpire*) impress; **impressionato** FOT exposed; **~ favorevolmente** (favourably) impressed; **impressione** f impression; (*turbamento*) shock; (*paura*) fright; TIP printing; **impresso** pp ☞ **imprimere**

imprevedibile unforeseeable; *persona* unpredictable; **imprevisto 1** agg unexpected **2** m unforeseen event; **salvo imprevisti** all being well

imprigionare imprison

imprimere impress; fig: *nella mente* fix firmly, imprint; *movimento* impart; TIP print

improbabile unlikely, improbable

impronta f impression, mark; (*orma*) footprint; (*traccia*) track; fig mark; **-e pl digitali** fingerprints; **-e pl genetiche** genetic fingerprints

improprio improper

improvvisamente suddenly; **improvvisare** improvize; **improvvisata** f surprise; **improvvisato** improvized, impromptu; **improvviso** sudden; (*inaspettato*) unexpected; **all'~** suddenly; (*inaspettatamente*) unexpectedly

imprudente careless; (*non saggio*) imprudent, rash; **imprudenza** f carelessness; (*mancanza di saggezza*) imprudence, rashness

impugnare grasp; DIR contest; **impugnatura** f grip; (*manico*) handle

impulsivo impulsive; **impulso** m impulse

impunità f impunity

impuntarsi (*ostinarsi*) dig one's heels in

imputato m, **-a** f accused; **imputazione** f charge

imputridire rot

in in; *moto a luogo* to; **~ casa** at home; *va* **~ Inghilterra** he is going to England; **~ italiano** in Italian; **~ campagna** in the country; *viaggiare* **~ macchina** travel by car; **nel 1999** in 1999; **~ vacanza** on holiday

inabile unfit (*a* for); (*disabile*) disabled

inaccessibile inaccessible, out of reach; fig: *persona* unapproachable; *prezzi* exorbitant

inaccettabile unacceptable

inacidire, inacidirsi turn sour

inadatto unsuitable (*a* for)

inadeguato inadequate

inalare inhale; **inalatore** m inhaler; **inalazione** f inhalation

inalterabile *sentimento* unchangeable; *colore* fast; *metallo* non-tarnish

inalterato unchanged
inamidare starch
inammissibile inadmissible
inanimato inanimate; *(senza vita)* lifeless
inappetenza f lack of appetite
inarcare *schiena* arch; *sopracciglia* raise
inaridire 1 v/t parch **2** v/i dry up
inaspettato unexpected
inasprimento m *(intensificazione)* worsening; *di carattere* embitterment; **inasprire** exacerbate, make worse; *carattere* embitter
inattendibile unreliable
inatteso unexpected
inattività f inactivity; **inattivo** *persona, capitale* idle, inactive; *vulcano* dormant
inattuabile *(non fattibile)* impracticable; *(non realistico)* unrealistic
inaugurare *mostra* (officially) open, inaugurate; *lapide* unveil; F *oggetto nuovo* christen F; **inaugurazione** f *di mostra* (official) opening, inauguration; *di lapide* unveiling; F *di oggetto nuovo* christening F
inavvertenza f inadvertence
incagliarsi MAR run aground
incalcolabile incalculable
incalzare pursue; fig: *con richieste* ply
incamminarsi set out
incandescente incandescent; fig heated

incantare enchant; **incantarsi** *(restare affascinato)* be spellbound; *(sognare a occhi aperti)* be in a daze; TEC jam; **incantato** *per effetto di magia* enchanted; *(trasognato)* in a daze; *(affascinato)* spellbound; **incantesimo** m spell; **incantevole** delightful, charming
incanto[1] m *(incantesimo)* spell; **come per ~** as if by magic
incanto[2] m COM auction; **mettere all'~** put up for auction
incapace 1 agg incapable *(di* of); *(incompetente)* incompetent **2** m/f incompetent person; **incapacità** f *(inabilità)* inability; *(incompetenza)* incompetence
incappare: **~ in** nebbia, difficoltà run into
incapricciarsi: **~ di qu** take a liking to s.o.
incarcerare imprison
incaricare *(dare istruzioni a)* instruct; **~ qu di fare qc** tell o instruct s.o. to do sth; **incaricarsi**: **~ di qc** see to sth, deal with sth; **incaricato** m, **-a** f *(responsabile)* person in charge; *(funzionario)* official; **incarico** m *(compito)* task, assignment; *(nomina)* appointment
incarnare embody
incartare wrap (up) (in paper)

incassare COM (*riscuotere*) cash; *fig*: *colpi, insulti ecc* take; **incasso** *m* (*riscossione*) collection; (*somma incassata*) takings

incastonare set

incastrare fit in; F *fig* (*far apparire colpevole*) frame F; (*mettere in una posizione difficile*) corner F

incastro *m* joint

incatenare chain

incavato hollow; *occhi* deepset

incendiare set fire to; **incendiario** *m*, *-a f* arsonist; **incendio** *m* fire; ~ **doloso** arson

incenerire reduce to ashes; **inceneritore** *m* incinerator

incenso *m* incense

incensurato irreproachable; DIR **essere** ~ have a clean record

incentivare (*incrementare*) boost; **incentivo** *m* incentive

incerata *f* oilcloth

incertezza *f* uncertainty; **incerto 1** *agg* uncertain **2** *m* uncertainty

incessante incessant

incetta *f*: **fare** ~ **di qc** stockpile sth

inchiesta *f* investigation

inchinarsi bow; *di donna* curtsy; **inchino** *m* bow; *di donna* curtsy

inchiodare 1 *v/t* nail; *coperchio* nail down **2** *v/i* AUTO jam on the brakes

inchiostro *m* ink

inciampare trip (*in* over); ~ **in qu** run into s.o.

incidentale (*casuale*) accidental; (*secondario*) incidental; **incidente** *m* (*episodio*) incident; ~ **aereo** plane crash; ~ **stradale** road accident

incidere[1] *v/i* affect (**su** sth)

incidere[2] *v/t* engrave; (*tagliare*) cut; (*registrare*) record

incinta pregnant

incirca: **all'~** more or less

incisione *f* engraving; (*acquaforte*) etching; (*taglio*) cut; MED incision; (*registrazione*) recording; **incisivo 1** *agg* incisive **2** *m* (*dente*) incisor

incitare incite

incivile uncivilized; (*villano*) impolite

inclinare 1 *v/t* tilt **2** *v/i*: ~ **a** (*tendere a*) be inclined to; **inclinato** tilted; **inclinazione** *f* inclination; incline **inclined** (**a** to)

includere include; (*allegare*) enclose; **inclusivo** inclusive; **incluso 1** *pp* ☞ **includere 2** *agg* included; (*compreso*) inclusive; (*allegato*) enclosed

incoerente (*incongruente*) inconsistent; **incoerenza** *f* inconsistency

incognita *f* unknown quantity; **incognito**: **in** ~ incognito

incollare stick; *con colla liquida* glue; **incollarsi** stick (**a** to)

incolore colourless, *Am* colorless

incolpare blame

incolto uneducated; (*trascurato*) unkempt; AGR uncultivated

incolume unharmed; **incolumità** *f* safety

incombente *pericolo* impending; **incombenza** *f* task

incominciare start, begin (*a* to)

incomodare inconvenience; **incomodarsi** put o.s. out

incompatibile incompatible; **incompatibilità** *f* incompatibility

incompetente incompetent; **incompetenza** *f* incompetence

incompiuto unfinished

incompleto incomplete

incomprensibile incomprehensible; **incomprensione** *f* lack of understanding; (*malinteso*) misunderstanding; **incompreso** misunderstood

inconcepibile inconceivable

inconcludente inconclusive; *persona* ineffectual

inconfondibile unmistakable

inconfutabile indisputable

inconsapevole (*ignaro*) unaware

inconscio *m/agg* unconscious

inconsistente insubstantial; *fig* (*infondato*) unfounded; (*vago*) vague

inconsolabile inconsolable

inconsueto unusual

incontentabile hard to please; (*perfezionista*) perfectionist

incontestato undisputed

incontrare 1 *v/t* meet; *difficoltà* encounter **2** *v/i* e **incontrarsi** meet (**con** s.o.)

incontrario: *all'~* the other way round; (*nel modo sbagliato*) the wrong way round

incontrastato undisputed

incontro 1 *m* meeting; ~ *di calcio* football match *o* Am game **2** *prp:* ~ *a* towards; *andare* ~ *a qu* go and meet s.o.; *fig* meet s.o. halfway

inconveniente *m* (*svantaggio*) drawback; (*ostacolo*) hitch

incoraggiamento *m* encouragement; **incoraggiante** encouraging; **incoraggiare** encourage

incorniciare frame

incoronare crown

incorporare incorporate

incorreggibile incorrigible

incorrere: ~ *in sanzioni* incur; *errore* make

incorruttibile incorruptible

incosciente unconscious; (*irresponsabile*) reckless

incoscienza *f* unconsciousness; (*insensatezza*) recklessness

incostante changeable; *negli affetti* fickle

incostituzionale unconstitutional

incredibile incredible

incredulo incredulous, disbelieving

incrementare increase; incremento *m* increase, growth

increspare *acque* ripple; *capelli* frizz; *tessuto* gather

incriminare indict

incrociare 1 *v/t* cross **2** *v/i* MAR, AVIA cruise; **incrocio** *m* (*intersezione*) crossing; (*crocevia*) crossroads *sg*, *Am* intersection; *di razze animali* cross(-breed)

incubatrice *f* incubator; **incubazione** *f* incubation

incubo *m* nightmare

incudine *f* anvil

incurabile incurable

incurante heedless (*di* of)

incuriosire: ~ *qu* arouse s.o.'s curiosity

incursione *f* raid; ~ *aerea* air raid

incustodito unattended; *passaggio a livello* unmanned

indaco *m/agg* indigo

indaffarato busy

indagare investigate (*su*, *intorno a* sth); **indagine** *f* research; *della polizia* investigation; ~ *di mercato* market survey

indebitare, indebitarsi get into debt

indebolire weaken

indecente indecent

indecisione *f* indecision, in-

decisiveness; **indeciso** undecided; *abitualmente* indecisive

indefinito indefinite

indelebile indelible; *colore* fast

indenne *persona* uninjured; *cosa* undamaged; **indennità** *f inv* (*gratifica*) allowance, benefit; (*risarcimento*) compensation; ~ *di trasferta* travel allowance; **indennizzare** compensate (*per* for); **indennizzo** *m* (*compenso*) compensation

indescrivibile indescribable

indesiderato unwanted

indeterminato *tempo* unspecified, indefinite; *quantità* indeterminate

India *f* India; **indiano 1** *agg* Indian **2** *m*, -a *f* Indian

indicare show, indicate; *col dito* point at *o* to; (*consigliare*) suggest, recommend; (*significare*) mean; **indicativo** *m* GRAM indicative; **indicato** (*consigliabile*) advisable; (*adatto*) suitable

indicatore 1 *agg* indicative **2** *m* indicator; AUTO ~ *di direzione* indicator, *Am* turn signal; **indicazione** *f* indication; (*direttiva*) direction; (*informazione*) piece of information; MED *-i pl* directions (for use); *-i pl* **stradali** road signs

indice *m* index; ANAT index finger, forefinger

indicibile indescribable

indietreggiare draw back; *camminando all'indietro* step back; MIL retreat

indietro behind; *tornare, girarsi* back; *essere ~ con il lavoro* be behind; *mentalmente* be backward; *di orologio* be slow; *dare ~ (restituire)* give back; *tirarsi ~* draw back; *fig* back out; *all'~* backwards

indifeso undefended; *(inerme)* defenceless, *Am* defenseless

indifferente indifferent; *non ~* appreciable, considerable; *per me è ~* it's all the same to me; **indifferenza** *f* indifference

indigeno 1 *agg* native, indigenous **2** *m, -a f* native

indigestione *f* indigestion; **indigesto** indigestible

indignare: *~ qu* make s.o. indignant; **indignarsi** get indignant *(per* about)

indimenticabile unforgettable

indipendente independent *(da* of); **indipendentemente** independently; *~ dall'età* regardless of age; **indipendenza** *f* independence

indire *conferenza, elezioni, sciopero* call; *concorso* announce

indiretto indirect

indirizzare direct; *lettera* address; *(spedire)* send; **indirizzario** *m* address book; *per*

spedizione mailing list; **indirizzo** *m* address; *(direzione)* direction; *~ di posta elettronica* e-mail address

indisciplinato undisciplined

indiscreto indiscreet; **indiscrezione** *f* indiscretion

indiscriminato indiscriminate

indiscusso unquestioned

indiscutibile unquestionable

indispensabile 1 *agg* indispensable, essential **2** *m* essentials

indispettire irritate; **indispettirsi** get irritated; **indispettito** irritated

indisposto *(ammalato)* indisposed

indistinto indistinct

indistruttibile indestructible

indivia *f* endive

individuale individual; **individualista** *m/f* individualist; **individuo** *m* individual

indizio *m* clue; *(segno)* sign; *(sintomo)* symptom; DIR *-i pl* circumstantial evidence

indole *f* nature

indolente indolent

indolore painless

indomani: *l'~* the next day

indossare *(mettersi)* put on; *(portare)* wear; **indossatore** *m, -trice f* model

indotto *pp* ► **indurre**

indovinare guess; *futuro* predict; **indovinato** *(ben riuscito)* successful; *(ben scelto)* well chosen; **indovinello** *m* riddle; **indovino** m, -a f fortune-teller

indubbiamente undoubtedly
indugiare 1 v/t partenza delay **2** v/i (tardare) delay; (esitare) hesitate; (attardarsi) linger; **indugio** m delay; **senza ~** without delay
indulgente indulgent; giudice, sentenza lenient; **indulgenza** f indulgence; di giudice, sentenza leniency
indumento m item of clothing; **gli -i** pl clothes
indurire 1 v/t harden **2** v/i e **indurirsi** go hard, harden; **indurito** hardened
indurre induce
industria f industry; (operosità) industriousness; **industriale 1** agg industrial **2** m industrialist; **industrializzazione** f industrialization
ineccepibile irreproachable; ragionamento faultless
inedito unpublished; fig novel
inefficace ineffective
inefficiente inefficient; **inefficienza** f inefficiency
ineguagliabile (senza rivali) unrivalled; Am unrivaled; (senza confronto) incomparable; **ineguale** unequal; (discontinuo) uneven
inequivocabile unequivocal
inerte (inoperoso) idle; (immobile) inert, motionless; (senza vita) lifeless; FIS inert; **inerzia** f inertia; (inattività) inactivity

inesattezza f inaccuracy; **inesatto** inaccurate
inesauribile inexhaustible
inesperienza f inexperience; **inesperto** inexperienced
inesplorato unexplored
inesploso unexploded
inestimabile inestimable; bene invaluable
inetto inept
inevaso pending
inevitabile inevitable
inezia f trifle
infallibile infallible
infame 1 agg (turpe) infamous, foul; spir horrible **2** m/f P (delatore) grass P
infantile letteratura, giochi children's; malattie childhood attr; (immaturo) childish, infantile; **infanzia** f childhood; (primi mesi) infancy (anche fig); (bambini) children pl
infarinare (dust with) flour; **infarinatura** f fig smattering
infarto m cardiaco heart attack
infastidire annoy, irritate
infatti in fact
infatuarsi: ~ di qu become infatuated with s.o.
infedele 1 agg unfaithful; traduzione inaccurate **2** m/f REL infidel; **infedeltà** f inv unfaithfulness
infelice unhappy; (inopportuno) unfortunate; (malriuscito) bad; **infelicità** f unhappiness

inferiore 1 *agg* lower; *fig* inferior (*a* to); *essere* **~** *a qu* be inferior to s.o. **2** *m/f* inferior; (*subalterno*) subordinate; **inferiorità** *f* inferiority; **complesso** *m* **d'~** inferiority complex

infermeria *f* infirmary; **infermiere** *m*, **-a** *f* nurse; **infermo 1** *agg* (*ammalato*) ill; (*invalido*) invalid **2** *m*, **-a** *f* invalid

infernale infernal; **inferno** *m* hell

inferriata *f* grating; (*cancellata*) railings

infestare infest; **infettarsi** become infected; **infettivo** infectious; **infezione** *f* infection

infiammabile flammable; **infiammarsi** become inflamed; **infiammazione** *f* inflammation

inferire *di maltempo, malattie* rage; **~** *su o* **contro** savagely attack

infilare *fili, corde, ago* thread; (*inserire*) insert, put in; (*indossare*) put on; *strada* take; **infilarsi** *indumento* slip on; (*conficcarsi*) stick; (*introdursi*) slip (*in* into); (*stiparsi*) squeeze (*in* into)

infiltrarsi seep; *fig* infiltrate; **infiltrazione** *f* infiltration; *di liquidi* seepage

infilzare pierce; *perle* thread

infimo lowest

infine (*alla fine*) finally, eventually; (*insomma*) in short

infinità *f* infinity; **ho un'~ di cose da fare** I've got no end of things to do; **infinito 1** *agg* infinite **2** *m* infinity; GRAM infinitive

infischiarsi F: ~ di not give a hoot about F; **me ne infischio** I couldn't care less F

inflazione *f* inflation

inflessibile inflexible

infliggere inflict; **inflitto** *pp* **☞ infliggere**

influente influential; **influenza** *f* influence; MED flu, influenza; **influenzabile** easily influenced, impressionable; **influenzare** influence; **influire: ~ su** influence, have an effect on; **influsso** *m* influence

infondato unfounded

infondere *fig* instil, *Am* instill

inforcare *occhiali* put on; *bicicletta* get on, mount

informale informal

informare inform (*di* of); **informarsi** find out (*di, su* about); **informatica** *f* scienza information technology, IT; **informatico 1** *agg* computer *attr*, IT *attr* **2** *m*, **-a** *f* computer scientist, IT specialist

informato informed; **informatore** *m*, **-trice** *f* informant; *della polizia* informer; **informazione** *f* information; **un'~** a piece of information; **-i** information; **ufficio** *m* **-i** information office

informicolirsi have pins and needles

infortunio *m* accident; **~ sul lavoro** accident at work

infossato *occhi* deep-set, sunken

infrangere break; **infrangibile** unbreakable; *vetro m* ~ shatterproof glass

infranto *pp* ☞ **infrangere**

infrarosso infrared

infrasettimanale midweek

infrastruttura *f* infrastructure

infrazione *f* offence, *Am* offense

infreddatura *f* cold

infuocato *(caldissimo)* scorching; *discorso, tramonto* fiery

infuori: **all'~** outwards; **all'~ di** except

infuriarsi fly into a rage; **infuriato** furious

infusione *f*, infuso *m* infusion; *(tisana)* herbal tea

ingaggiare *(reclutare)* recruit; *attore, cantante lirico* engage; *SP* sign (up); *(iniziare)* start, begin; **ingaggio** *m* *(reclutamento)* recruitment; *SP* signing; *(somma)* fee

ingannare deceive; **~ il tempo** kill time; **inganno** *m* deception, deceit

ingarbugliare tangle; *fig* confuse, muddle; **ingarbugliarsi** get entangled; *fig* get confused

ingegnarsi do one's utmost

(a, per to)

ingegnere *m* engineer; **ingegneria** *f* engineering; **~ genetica** genetic engineering

ingegno *m* *(mente)* mind; *(intelligenza)* brains; *(genio)* genius; *(inventiva)* ingenuity

ingelosire 1 *v/t* make jealous **2** *v/i* be jealous

ingente enormous

ingenuo ingenuous

ingerire swallow

ingessare put in plaster; **ingessatura** *f* plaster

Inghilterra *f* England

inghiottire swallow

ingiallire turn yellow; **ingiallito** yellowed

inginocchiarsi kneel (down)

ingiù: **all'~** down(wards)

ingiunzione *f* injunction; **~ di pagamento** final demand

ingiuria *f* insult

ingiustificato unjustified

ingiustizia *f* injustice; **ingiusto** unjust, unfair

inglese 1 *m/agg* English **2** *m/f* Englishman; *donna* Englishwoman *f*

ingoiare swallow

ingolfare, ingolfarsi flood

ingombrante cumbersome, bulky; **ingombrare** *passaggio* block; *stanza, mente* clutter (up); **ingombro 1** *agg passaggio* blocked; *stanza, mente* cluttered (up) **2** *m* hindrance, obstacle; **essere d'~** be in the way

ingordo greedy

ingorgo *m* blockage; **~ stradale** traffic jam

ingozzare *cibo* devour, gobble up; *persona* stuff (*di* with); **ingozzarsi** stuff o.s (*di* with)

ingranaggio *m* gear; *fig* machine; **ingranare** engage; *fig* F **le cose cominciano a ~** things are beginning to work out

ingrandimento *m* enlargement; *di azienda, città* expansion, growth; **ingrandire** enlarge; *azienda, città* expand, develop; (*esagerare*) exaggerate; **ingrandirsi** grow

ingrassare 1 *v/t animali* fatten (up); (*lubrificare*) grease 2 *v/i* get fat, put on weight

ingratitudine *f* ingratitude; **ingrato** ungrateful; *lavoro, compito* thankless

ingrediente *m* ingredient

ingresso *m* entrance; (*atrio*) hall; (*accesso*) admittance; INFOR input; **~ libero** admission free; **vietato l'~** no entry, no admittance

ingrossare 1 *v/t* make bigger; (*gonfiare, accrescere*) swell 2 *v/i* **e ingrossarsi** get bigger; (*gonfiarsi*) swell; **ingrosso: all'~** (*all'incirca*) roughly, about; COM wholesale

inguaribile incurable

inguinale groin *attr*; **ernia** *f* **~** hernia; **inguine** *m* ANAT groin

ingurgitare gulp down

inibire prohibit, forbid; PSI inhibit; **inibito** inhibited; **inibizione** *f* PSI inhibition

iniettare inject; **~ qc a qu** inject s.o. with sth; **iniezione** *f* injection

inimicarsi fall out (*con* with); **inimicizia** *f* enmity

inimmaginabile unimaginable

ininterrotto continuous

iniziale *f/agg* initial; **iniziare** begin, start; *ostilità, dibattito* open; *fig* initiate; **~ a fare qc** begin *o* start doing sth, begin *o* start to do sth

iniziativa *f* initiative; **di mia ~** on my own initiative

inizio *m* start, beginning; **avere ~** start, begin; **dare ~ a qc** start sth

innaffiare water; **innaffiatoio** *m* watering can

innalzare raise; (*erigere*) erect

innamorarsi fall in love (*di* with); **innamorato** 1 *agg* in love (*di* with) 2 *m, -a f* boyfriend; *donna* girlfriend

innanzi 1 *prp* before; **~ a** in front of; **~ tutto** first of all; (*soprattutto*) above all 2 *avv stato in luogo in* front; (*avanti*) forward; (*prima*) before; **d'ora ~** from now on

innato innate, inborn

innervosire: ~ qu make s.o. nervous; (*irritare*) get on s.o.'s nerves; **innervosirsi** get nervous; (*irritarsi*) get irritated

innestare BOT, MED graft; EL *spina* insert; AUTO *marcia* engage

inno *m* hymn; ~ *nazionale* national anthem

innocente innocent; **innocenza** *f* innocence

innocuo innocuous, harmless

innovativo innovative; **innovazione** *f* innovation

inodore odourless, *Am* odorless

inoffensivo harmless, inoffensive

inoltrare forward; **inoltrarsi** advance, penetrate (*in* into); **inoltrato** late; **inoltre** besides

inondare flood; **inondazione** *f* flood

inopportuno (*inadatto*) inappropriate; (*intempestivo*) untimely; *persona* tactless

inorridire 1 *v/t* horrify **2** *v/i* be horrified; **inorridito** horrified

inosservato unobserved, unnoticed; (*non rispettato*) disregarded; *passare* ~ go unnoticed

inossidabile stainless

inquadrare *fotografia* frame; *fig* put into context; **inquadratura** *f* frame

inquietante (*che preoccupa*) worrying; (*che turba*) disturbing; **inquieto** restless; (*preoccupato*) worried; (*adirato*) angry

inquilino *m*, **-a** *f* tenant

inquinamento *m* pollution; **inquinante 1** *agg* polluting; *non* ~ environmentally friendly; *sostanza f* ~ pollutant **2** *m* pollutant; **inquinare** pollute; DIR *prove* tamper with

insabbiamento *m di porto* silting up; *fig* shelving

insaccati *mpl* sausages

insalata *f* salad; ~ *mista* mixed salad; ~ *verde* green salad; **insalatiera** *f* salad bowl

insanabile (*incurabile*) incurable; *fig* (*irrimediabile*) irreparable

insanguinato bloodstained

insaponare soap

insapore tasteless; **insaporire** flavour, *Am* flavor

insaputa: *all'* ~ *di qu* unknown to s.o.

insaziabile insatiable

inscenare stage

inscindibile inseparable

insegna *f* sign; (*bandiera*) flag; (*stemma*) symbol; (*decorazione*) decoration

insegnamento *m* teaching; **insegnante 1** *agg* teaching; *corpo m* ~ (~ teaching) staff **2** *m/f* teacher; **insegnare** teach; ~ *qc a qu* teach s.o. sth

inseguimento *m* chase, pursuit; **inseguire** chase, pursue

inseminazione *f* insemination; ~ *artificiale* artificial

145

insemination

insenatura f inlet

insensato 1 agg senseless, idiotic 2 m, -a f fool, idiot

insensibile insensitive (a to); parte del corpo numb; **insensibilità** f insensitivity; di parte del corpo numbness

inseparabile inseparable

inserire insert; (collegare: in elettrotecnica) connect; annuncio place; **inserirsi** fit in; in una conversazione join in; **inserto** m (pubblicazione) supplement; **inserviente** m/f attendant

inserzione f insertion; sul giornale ad, advertisement

insetticida m insecticide; **insettifugo** m insect repellent; **insetto** m insect

insicurezza f insecurity, lack of security; **insicuro** insecure

insieme 1 avv together; (contemporaneamente) at the same time 2 prp: ~ a, ~ con together with 3 m whole; di abiti outfit; nell'~ on the whole

insignificante insignificant

insinuare insert; fig: dubbio, sospetto sow the seeds of; ~ che insinuate that; **insinuarsi** penetrate; fig ~ in creep into; **insinuazione** f insinuation

insipido insipid

insistente insistent; **insistenza** f insistence; **insiste-**

re insist; (perseverare) perseverare; ~ a fare qc insist on doing sth

insoddisfacente unsatisfactory; **insoddisfatto** unsatisfied; (scontento) dissatisfied; **insoddisfazione** f dissatisfaction

insofferente intolerant

insolazione f sunstroke

insolente insolent

insolito unusual

insoluto unsolved; debito outstanding; **insolvenza** f insolvency

insomma briefly, in short; ~! well, really!

insonne sleepless; **insonnia** f insomnia; **insonnolito** sleepy

insopportabile unbearable, intolerable

insorgere rise (up) (contro against); di difficoltà come up, crop up

insormontabile insurmountable

insorto 1 pp ☞ **insorgere** 2 m rebel

insospettabile above suspicion; (impensato) unsuspected; **insospettire** 1 v/t: ~ qu make s.o. suspicious 2 v/i e **insospettirsi** become suspicious

insperato unhoped for; (inatteso) unexpected

inspiegabile inexplicable

inspirare breathe in, inhale

instabile unstable; tempo

installare

changeable
installare install; **installazio-ne** *f* installation
instancabile tireless
insù: **all'~** upwards
insuccesso *m* failure
insufficiente insufficient; (*inadeguato*) inadequate; **in-sufficienza** *f* insufficiency; (*inadeguatezza*) inadequacy
insulina *f* insulin
insulso *fig* (*privo di vivacità*) dull; (*vacuo*) inane; (*sciocco*) silly
insultare insult; **insulto** *m* insult
insurrezione *f* insurrection
intaccare (*corrodere*) corrode; *fig* (*danneggiare*) damage; *scorte, capitale* make inroads into
intanto (*nel frattempo*) meanwhile; (*per ora*) for the time being; (*invece*) yet; ~ **che** while
intasare block; **intasarsi** get blocked; **intasato** blocked
intascare pocket
intatto intact
integrale whole; MAT integral; *edizione* unabridged; **pane** *m* ~ wholemeal bread; Am wholewheat bread; **inte-grare** integrate; (*aumentare*) supplement; **integrarsi** integrate; **integrazione** *f* integration; **cassa** *f* ~ form of *income support*
intelaiatura *f* framework
intelletto *m* intellect; **intellet-**

tuale *agg, m/f* intellectual
intelligente intelligent; **intel-ligenza** *f* intelligence
intendere (*comprendere*) understand; (*udire*) hear; (*voler dire*) mean; (*avere intenzione*) intend; **s'intende!** of course!; **intendersi** (*capirsi*) understand each other; (*accordarsi*) agree; ~ **di qc** know a lot about sth; **intenditore** *m*, **-trice** *f* connoisseur, expert
intensificare intensify; **in-tensificarsi** intensify; **inten-sità** *f inv* intensity; EL strength; **intensivo** intensive; **intenso** intense
intento 1 *agg* engrossed (**a** in), intent (**a** on) **2** *m* aim, purpose; **intenzionale** intentional; **intenzione** *f* intention; **avere l'~ di fare qc** intend to do sth
interagire interact
interamente entirely
interattivo interactive
intercalare 1 *v/t* insert **2** *m* stock phrase
intercambiabile interchangeable
intercapedine *f* cavity
intercedere intercede (**presso** with; **per** on behalf of)
intercettare intercept; **inter-cettazione** *f* interception; **-i** *pl* **telefoniche** phone tapping
intercontinentale intercontinental

interdentale: *filo m ~* (dental) floss
interessante interesting; *in stato ~* pregnant; **interessare 1** *v/t* interest; (*riguardare*) concern **2** *v/i* matter; **interessarsi** be interested (*a, di* in); (*occuparsi*) take care (*di* of); **interessato 1** *agg* interested (*a* in); (*implicato*) involved (*a* in); *spreg parere, opinione* biased; *persona* self-interested **2** *m, -a f* person concerned; **interesse** *m* interest; (*tornaconto*) benefit; *per ~* out of self-interest; *senza ~* of no interest
interfaccia *f* INFOR interface
interferenza *f* interference; **interferire** *interfere*
interiezione *f interjection*
interiora *fpl* entrails
interiore *m/agg* interior
interlocutore *m*, **-trice** *f*: *la sua -trice* the woman he was talking to
intermediario *m*, **-a f** intermediary; **intermedio** intermediate; *bilancio, relazione* interim
interminabile interminable
intermittente intermittent
internazionale international
internet *m* Internet; *navigare su ~* surf the Net
interno 1 *agg* internal, inside *attr*; GEOG inland; POL, FIN domestic; *fig* inner **2** *m* (*parte interna*) inside, interior; GEOG interior; TELEC exten-

sion; *via Dante n. 6 ~ 9* 6 via Dante, Flat 9; *all'~* inside
intero whole, entire; (*completo*) complete; *latte m ~* whole milk; MAT *numero m ~* integer
interpellare consult
interpretare interpret; *personaggio* play; MUS play, perform; **interpretazione** *f* interpretation; TEA, MUS, *film* performance; **interprete** *m/f* interpreter; *attore, musicista* performer; *fare da ~* interpret, act as interpreter
interpunzione *f* punctuation
interrogare question; EDU test; **interrogativo 1** *agg* GRAM interrogative; *occhiata* questioning; *punto m ~* question mark **2** *m* (*domanda*) question; (*dubbio*) doubt; **interrogatorio** *m* questioning; **interrogazione** *f* questioning; *domanda* question; EDU oral (*test*)
interrompere interrupt; (*sospendere*) break off, stop; *comunicazioni, forniture* cut off; **interrotto** *pp* → **interrompere**; **interruttore** *m* EL switch; **interruzione** *f* interruption
interurbana *f* long-distance (phone) call; **interurbano** intercity; *chiamata f -a* long-distance (phone) call
intervallo *m* interval; *di scuola, lavoro* break
intervenire intervene; (*parte-*

cipare) take part, participate (**a** in); MED operate; **intervento** *m* intervention; (*partecipazione*) participation; MED operation; **pronto ~** emergency services

intervista *f* interview; **intervistare** interview; **intervistatore** *m*, **-trice** *f* interviewer

intesa *f* (*accordo*) understanding; (*patto*) agreement; SP team work; **inteso 1** *pp* **intendere 2** *agg* (*capito*) understood; (*destinato*) intended (**a** to); **siamo -i?** agreed

intestare *assegno* make out (**a** to); *proprietà* register (**a** in the name of); **intestatario** *m*, **-a** *f* *di assegno* payee; *di proprietà* registered owner

intestazione *f* heading; *su carta da lettere* letterhead

intestinale intestinal; **intestino** *m* intestine, gut

intimare order

intimidazione *f* intimidation; **intimidire** intimidate

intimità *f* privacy; *di un rapporto* intimacy; **intimo 1** *agg* intimate; (*segreto*) private; (*accogliente*) cosy, Am cozy; *amico* close, intimate **2** *m persona* close friend; (*abbigliamento*) underwear

intingere dip

intitolare call, entitle; (*dedicare*) dedicate (**a** to); **intitolarsi** be called

intollerabile intolerable; **intollerante** intolerant; **intol-**

leranza *f* intolerance

intonacare plaster; **intonaco** *m* plaster

intonarsi (*armonizzare*) go well (**a**, **con** with); **intonato** MUS in tune; **colori** *pl* **-i** colours that go well together

intontito dazed

intoppo *m* (*ostacolo*) hindrance; (*contrattempo*) snag

intorno 1 *prp:* **~ a** around; (*riguardo a*) about **2** *avv* around

intossicare poison; **intossicazione** *f* poisoning; **~ alimentare** food poisoning

intralciare hinder; **intralcio** *m* hindrance

intransigente intransigent

intransitivo intransitive

intraprendente enterprising; **intraprendenza** *f* enterprise; **intraprendere** undertake

intrattabile intractable; *prezzo* fixed, non-negotiable

intrattenere entertain; **~ buoni rapporti con qu** be on good terms with s.o.; **intrattenersi** dwell (**su** on)

intravedere glimpse; *fig* (*presagire*) anticipate, see; **intravisto** *pp* **intravedere**

intrecciare plait, braid; (*intessere*) weave; **intrecciarsi** intertwine

intreccio *m* *fig* (*trama*) plot

intricato tangled; *disegno* intricate; *fig* complicated

intrigante scheming; (*affasci-*

nante) intriguing; **intrigo** *m* plot

intrinseco intrinsic

introdurre introduce; (*inserire*) insert; **introdursi** get in; **introduzione** *f* introduction

introito *m* income; (*incasso*) takings

intromettersi interfere; (*interporsi*) intervene

introvabile impossible to find

introverso 1 *agg* introverted **2** *m*, *-a f* introvert

intrufolarsi sneak in

intruglio *m* concoction

intruso *m*, *-a f* intruder

intuire know instinctively; **intuito** *m* intuition; **intuizione** *f* intuition

inumano inhuman

inumidire dampen, moisten; **inumidirsi** get damp

inutile useless; (*superfluo*) unnecessary, pointless; **inutilizzabile** unusable; **inutilmente** pointlessly, needlessly

invadente 1 *agg* nosy **2** *m/f* busybody

invadere invade; (*occupare*) occupy; (*inondare*) flood

invaghirsi: ~ *di* take a liking to

invalido 1 *agg* disabled; DIR invalid **2** *m*, *-a f* disabled person

invano in vain

invariato unchanged

invasione *f* invasion (*di* of)

invecchiare 1 *v/t* age **2** *v/i*

age, get older; *di vini, cibi* mature; *fig* (*cadere in disuso*) date

invece instead; (*ma*) but; **~ *di* fare** instead of doing

inveire: ~ **contro** inveigh against

invenduto unsold

inventare invent

inventario *m* inventory

inventore *m*, *-trice f* inventor; **invenzione** *f* invention

invernale winter *attr*; **sport** *mpl* *-i* winter sports; **inverno** *m* winter; **d'~** in winter

inverosimile improbable, unlikely

inversione *f* (*scambio*) reversal; AUTO ~ *di marcia* U-turn

inverso 1 *agg* reverse **2** *m* opposite

invertire reverse; (*capovolgere*) turn upside down; **~ *la marcia*** turn around

investigare investigate; **investigatore** *m*, *-trice f* investigator

investimento *m* investment; *di pedone* running over; **investire** *pedone* run over; FIN, *fig* invest

inviare send; **inviato** *m*, *-a f* envoy; *di giornale* correspondent

invidia *f* envy; **invidiare** envy; **invidioso** envious

invincibile invincible

invio *m* dispatch

invisibile invisible

invitante *profumo* enticing; *offerta* tempting; **invitare** invite; invito *m*, **-a** *f* guest; **invito** *m* invitation

invocare invoke; (*implorare*) beg for

invogliare induce

involontario involuntary

involtini *mpl* GASTR rolled stuffed slices of meat

involucro *m* wrapping

inzaccherare spatter with mud

inzuppare soak; (*intingere*) dip

io 1 *pron* I; ~ **stesso** myself; **sono** ~! it's me! **2** *m inv* ego

iodio *m* iodine

ionico ARCHI Ionic

iosa: **a** ~ in abundance

iperattivo hyperactive

ipermercato *m* hypermarket, *Am* supermarket

ipersensibile hypersensitive

ipertensione *f* high blood pressure

ipnosi *f* hypnosis; **ipnotizzare** hypnotize

ipocalorico low-calorie

ipocrisia *f* hypocrisy; **ipocrita 1** *agg* hypocritical **2** *m/f* hypocrite

ipoteca *f* mortgage; **ipotecare** mortgage

ipotesi *f inv* hypothesis; **ipotetico** hypothetical; **ipotizzare** hypothesize

ippica *f* (horse) riding; **ippodromo** *m* race-course

ippopotamo *m* hippo(pota-

mus)

ira *f* anger

iracheno 1 *agg* Iraqi **2** *m*, **-a** *f* Iraqi

Iran *m* Iran; **iraniano 1** *agg* Iranian **2** *m*, **-a** *f* Iranian

Iraq *m* Iraq

irascibile irritable, irascible

iride *f* (*arcobaleno*) rainbow; ANAT, BOT iris

Irlanda *f* Ireland; **irlandese 1** *agg* Irish **2** *m* Irish Gaelic **3** *m/f* Irishman; **donna** Irishwoman

ironia *f* irony; **ironico** ironic(al); **ironizzare** be ironic

IRPEF *f* (= *Imposta sul Reddito delle Persone Fisiche*) income tax

irraggiungibile unattainable

irragionevole unreasonable

irrazionale irrational

irreale unreal

irrealizzabile unattainable

irregolare irregular; **irregolarità** *f inv* irregularity

irreparabile irreparable

irreperibile impossible to find

irreprensibile irreproachable

irrequieto restless

irresistibile irresistible

irresponsabile irresponsible

irrestringibile shrink-resistant

irrevocabile irrevocable

irriconoscibile unrecognizable

irrigare irrigate

irrigidire stiffen; *fig disciplina* tighten; **irrigidirsi** stiffen

irrilevante irrelevant

irrimediabile irremediable

irripetibile unrepeatable

irrisorio derisive; *quantità, somma di denaro* derisory; *prezzo* ridiculously low

irritabile irritable; **irritabilità** *f* irritability; **irritante** irritating; **irritare** irritate; **irritarsi** get irritated

irruzione *f: fare ~ in* burst into; *di polizia* raid

iscritto 1 *pp* ☞ **iscrivere 2** *m, -a f* member; *a gare, concorsi* entrant; EDU pupil, student 3 *m: per ~* in writing; **iscrivere** register; *a gare, concorsi* enter (*a* for, in); EDU enrol, *Am* enroll (*a* at); **iscriversi** *in un elenco* register; *~ a partito, associazione* join; *gara* enter; EDU enrol at, *Am* enroll at; **iscrizione** *f* inscription

islamico Islamic

Islanda *f* Iceland; **islandese 1** *m/agg* Icelandic **2** *m/f* Icelander

isola *f* island; *~ pedonale* pedestrian precinct

isolamento *m* isolation; TEC insulation; *~ acustico* soundproofing; **isolano** *m, -a f* islander

isolante 1 *agg* insulating **2** *m* insulator; **isolare** isolate; TEC insulate; **isolarsi** isolate o.s., cut o.s. off; **isolato 1**

agg isolated; TEC insulated **2** *m* outsider; *di case* block

ispettore *m, -trice f* inspector; **ispezionare** inspect; **ispezione** *f* inspection

ispirare inspire; **ispirarsi** *di artista* get inspiration (*a* from); **ispirazione** *f* inspiration; *(impulso)* impulse; *(idea)* idea

Israele *m* Israel; **israeliano** *m, -a f* Israeli

istallare ☞ **installare**

istantanea *f* snap; **istantaneo** instantaneous; **istante** *m* instant; *all'~* instantly

istanza *f (esigenza)* need; *(domanda)* application; DIR petition

isterico hysterical

istigare instigate

istintivo instinctive; **istinto** *m* instinct

istituire establish; **istituto** *m* institute; *assistenziale* institution, home; *~ di bellezza* beauty salon; **istituzione** *f* institution

istmo *m* isthmus

istruire educate, teach; *(dare istruzioni a, addestrare)* instruct; **istruito** educated; **istruttivo** instructive; **istruttore** *m, -trice f* instructor; **istruzione** *f* education; *(direttiva)* instruction; *-i pl per l'uso* instructions (for use)

Italia *f* Italy; **italiano 1** *m/agg* Italian; *parla ~?* do you

itinerario

speak Italian? **2** *m*, **-a** *f* Italian

itinerario *m* route, itinerary
ittico fish

iuta *f* jute
IVA *f* (= *Imposta sul Valore Aggiunto*) VAT (= value-added tax), *Am* sales tax

J

jazz *m* jazz; **jazzista** *m/f* jazz musician
jeans *mpl* jeans
jeep *f inv* jeep
jet-lag *m inv* jet lag
jogging *m* jogging; **fare** ~ jog, go for a jog
joint-venture *f inv* joint venture

jolly *m inv* joker
joy-stick *m inv* joystick
judo *m* judo
juke-box *m inv* jukebox
jumbo *m* jumbo
junior *m/agg* junior

K

kamikaze *m inv* suicide bomber
karatè *m* karate
killer *m inv* killer
kit *m inv* kit
kitsch *agg inv*, *m* kitsch
kiwi *m inv* BOT kiwi (fruit)

kmq (= *chilometri quadrati*) km² (= square kilometres)
k.o.: mettere qu ~ knock s.o. out; *fig* trounce s.o.
kolossal *m inv* epic
krapfen *m inv* GASTR doughnut, *Am* donut

L

l (= *litro*) l (= litre)
l' = **lo, la**
là there; **di** ~that way; (*in quel luogo*) in there; (**al**) **di** ~ **di** on the other side of; **più in** ~ further on; **nel tempo** later on
la¹ *art fsg* the; ~ **signora Rossi** Mrs Rossi; ~ **domenica** on

Sundays; **mi piace la birra** I like beer
la² *pron* **1** *sg* (*persona*) her; (*cosa, animale*) it; ~ **prenderò** I'll take it **2** *anche* **La** *sg* you
la³ *m* MUS A; **nel solfeggio della scala** la(h)
labbro *m* lip

labirinto *m* labyrinth

laboratorio *m* lab, laboratory; (*officina*) workshop

laborioso laborious; *persona* hard-working

laburista 1 *agg* Labour 2 *m/f* Labour Party member; *elettore* Labour supporter

lacca *f* lacquer; **laccare** lacquer

laccio *m* tie, (draw)string; **-cci** *pl* **delle scarpe** shoe laces

lacerante *dolore*, *grido* piercing; **lacero** tattered

lacrima *f* tear; **lacrimare** water; **lacrimevole** heart-rending; *film m* ~ tear-jerker; **lacrimogeno: gas** *m* ~ tear gas

lacuna *f* gap; **lacunoso** incomplete

ladino 1 *agg* South Tyrolean 2 *m*, *-a f* South Tyrolean

ladro *m*, *-a f* thief

laggiù down there; *distante* over there

laghetto *m* pond

lagna *f* (*lamentela*) whining; *persona* whiner; (*cosa noiosa*) bore; **lagnarsi** complain (*di* about)

lago *m* lake

laguna *f* lagoon

laico 1 *agg scuola*, *stato* secular 2 *m*, *-a f* layman; laywoman

lama *f* blade

lamentarsi complain (*di* about); **lamentela** *f* complaint; **lamento** *m* whimper

lametta *f*: ~ (*da barba*) razor blade

lamiera *f* metal sheet

lamina *f* foil; ~ **d'oro** gold leaf

lampada *f* lamp; **lampadario** *m* chandelier; **lampadina** *f* light bulb; ~ **tascabile** torch, *Am* flashlight

lampante blindingly obvious

lampeggiare flash; **lampeggiatore** *m* AUTO indicator, *Am* turn signal; FOT flashlight

lampione *m* streetlight

lampo *m* lightning

lampone *m* raspberry

lana *f* wool; **pura ~ vergine** pure new wool

lancetta *f* needle; *di orologio* hand

lancia *f* spear; MAR launch; **lanciare** throw; *prodotto* launch; ~ **un'occhiata** glance, take a quick look; ~ **un urlo** give a shout, shout; **lanciarsi** rush; ~ **contro** throw o.s at, attack; F ~ **in un'impresa** embark on a venture

lancinante *dolore* piercing

lancio *m* throwing; *di prodotto* launch; ~ **del disco** discus; ~ **del giavellotto** javelin; ~ **del peso** putting the shot

languore *m* languor; **ho un ~ allo stomaco** I'm feeling peckish

lapide *f* gravestone; *su monumento* plaque

lapis *m inv* pencil

lardo 154

lardo *m* lard

larghezza *f* width, breadth;
largo 1 *agg* wide, broad; *in
indumento* loose, big; *(abbondante)* large, generous **2** *m*
width; *(piazza)* square; *andare al ~* head for the open
sea; *farsi ~* elbow one's way
through; *stare alla -a da*
keep away from

laringe *f* larynx; **laringite** *f*
laryngitis

larva *f* ZO larva

lasagne *fpl* lasagne *sg*

lasciare leave; *(abbandonare)*
give up; *(concedere)* let;
(smettere di tenere) let go of;
*lascia andare!, lascia per-
dere!* forget it!; **lasciarsi**
separate, split; *~ andare* let
o.s. go

lascito *m* legacy

laser *m inv, agg inv* laser

lassativo *m/agg* laxative

lasso *m*: *~ di tempo* period of
time

lassù up there

lastra *f di pietra* slab; *di metallo, ghiaccio, vetro* sheet

latente latent

laterale lateral

laterizio *m* bricks and tiles

latino 1 *agg* Latin; *~-america-
no* Latin-American **2** *m* Latin; *~-americano, -a* Latin-
American

latitante *m/f* fugitive

latitudine *f* latitude

lato *m* side; *a ~ di, di ~ a* beside

latrato *m* barking

latrina *f* latrine

latta *f can, Br anche* tin

latte *m* milk; *~ intero* whole
milk; *~ scremato* skimmed
milk; *~ di soia* soy(a) milk;
latteo milk *attr*; *Via f Lattea*
Milky Way; **latteria** *f* dairy;
lattice *m* latex; **latticinio** *m*
dairy product

lattina *f can, Br anche* tin

lattosio *m* lactose

lattuga *f* lettuce

laurea *f* degree; *~ triennale/
magistrale* bachelor's/mas-
ter's degree; **laurearsi** graduate; **laureato** *m, -a f* graduate

lava *f* lava

lavabile washable; *~ in lavatrice* machine-washable

lavabo *m* basin

lavaggio *m* washing; *~ a secco* dry-cleaning

lavagna *f* blackboard, *Am*
chalkboard; GEOL slate

lavanda *f* BOT lavender

lavanderia *f* laundry; *~ a gettone* laundrette, *Am* laund-
romat®

lavandino *m* basin; *nella cucina* sink

lavapiatti *m/f inv* dishwasher;
lavare wash; *~ i panni* do the
washing; **lavarsi** wash; *~ le
mani* wash one's hands; *~ i
denti* brush o clean one's
teeth; **lavastoviglie** *f inv*
dishwasher; **lavatrice** *f*
washing machine

lavello *m* basin; *nella cucina* sink

lavorare 1 *v/i* work **2** *v/t materia prima* process; *legno* carve; *terra* work; **lavorativo: giorno** ~ *m* workday; *lavorato legno* carved; **lavoratore** *m*, **-trice** *f* worker; **lavorazione** *f di materia prima* processing; *di legno* carving; **lavoro** *m* work; *(impiego)* job; **per** ~ on business; **-i in corso** roadworks, work in progress; **senza** ~ unemployed, out of work

le¹ *art fpl* the

le² *pron fsg* to her; *fpl* them; *anche* **Le** you

leader *m/f inv* leader

leale loyal; **lealtà** *f* loyalty

lebbroso *m*, **-a** *f* leper

lecca-lecca *m inv* lollipop; **leccare** lick

leccio *m* holm oak

leccornia *f* delicacy

lecito legal, permissible

lega *f* league; *di metalli* alloy

legale 1 *agg* legal **2** *m/f* lawyer; **legalizzare** legalize

legame *m* tie, relationship; *(nesso)* link, connection; **legamento** *m* ANAT ligament; **legare** tie; *persona* tie up; *(collegare)* link; *fig di lavoro* tie down

legge *f* law; **fuori** ~ illegal

leggenda *f* legend; *di carta geografica ecc* key; **leggendario** legendary

leggere read

leggerezza *f* lightness; *fig* casualness; **con** ~ thoughtlessly; **leggero** light; *(lieve, di poca importanza)* slight; *(superficiale)* thoughtless; *caffè* weak; **alla -a** lightly

leggibile legible

leggio *m* lectern; MUS music stand

legislativo legislative; **legislatura** *f periodo* term of parliament

legittimare approve; **legittimo** legitimate

legna *f (fire)*wood; **legname** *m* timber; **legno** *m* wood; **di** ~ wooden

legumi *mpl* peas and beans; *secchi* pulses

lei *pron fsg soggetto* she; *oggetto, con preposizione* her; ~ **stessa** herself; *anche* **Lei** you; **dare del** ~ *a qu* address s.o. as 'lei'

lembo *m di gonna* hem, bottom; *di terra* stip

lente *f* lens; **-i** *pl* glasses, spectacles; **-i** *pl* (**a contatto**) contact lenses, contacts F; ~ **d'ingrandimento** magnifying glass

lenticchia *f* lentil

lentiggine *f* freckle

lento slow; *(allentato)* slack; *abito* loose

lenza *f* fishing rod

lenzuolo *m* sheet

leone *m* lion; ASTR **Leone** Leo; **leonessa** *f* lioness

leopardo *m* leopard

lepre f hare

lesbica f lesbian

lesionare damage; **lesione** f MED injury

lessare boil

lessico m vocabulary; (*dizionario*) glossary

lesso 1 agg boiled 2 m boiled beef

letale lethal

letame m manure, dung

letargo m lethargy

lettera f letter; **alla ~** to the letter; FIN **~ di cambio** bill of exchange; **letterale** literal; **letterario** literary; **letteratura** f literature

lettino m cot, Am crib; *dal medico* bed; *dallo psicologo* couch

letto[1] m bed; **~ a una piazza** single bed; **~ matrimoniale** double bed; **~i pl a castello** bunk beds; **andare a ~** go to bed

letto[2] pp **leggere**

lettore m, **-trice** f reader; *all'università* lecturer in a foreign language; INFOR disk drive; **~ compact disc, ~ CD** CD player

lettura f reading

leucemia f leukaemia, Am leukemia

leva f lever; MIL call-up, Am draft; AUTO **~ del cambio** gear lever, Am gear shift

levante m east

levare (*alzare*) raise, lift; (*togliere*) take, (re)move; (*ri-*

muovere) take out, remove; *macchia* remove, get out; *dente* take out, extract; **~ l'ancora** weigh anchor; **levarsi** get up, rise; *di sole* rise, come up; *indumento* take off; **levata** f di posta collection; **levatrice** f midwife

levigare smooth down; **levigato** smooth

lezione f lesson; *all'università* lecture

li pron mpl them

lì there; **~ per ~** there and then

libanese agg, m/f Lebanese; **Libano** m (the) Lebanon

libbra f pound

libellula f dragon-fly

liberale 1 agg generous; POL liberal 2 m/f liberal; **liberalizzare** liberalize; **liberalizzazione** f liberalization; **liberamente** freely; **liberare** release, free; (*sgomberare*) empty; *stanza* vacate; **liberarsi: ~ di** get rid of; **liberazione** f release; *di nazione* liberation; *libero* free; **libertà** f inv freedom, liberty

Libia f Libya; **libico** 1 agg Libyan 2 m, **-a** f Libyan

libreria f bookshop, Am bookstore; (*biblioteca*) library; *mobile* bookcase

libretto m booklet; MUS libretto; **~ degli assegni** cheque book, Am check book; AUTO **~ di circolazione** registration document; **~ di risparmio** bank book

libro *m* book

licenza *f* FIN licence, *Am* license; MIL leave; EDU school leaving certificate; **~ di costruzione** building permit; **~ di esercizio** trading licence; **licenziamento** *m* dismissal; **licenziare** dismiss; **licenziarsi** resign

liceo *m* high school

lido *m* beach

lieto happy; **~ di conoscerla** nice *o* pleased to meet you

lieve light; *(di poca gravità)* slight, minor; *sorriso, rumore* faint

lievitare rise; *fig* rise, be on the increase; **lievito** *m* yeast; **~ in polvere** baking powder

lilla *m/agg* lilac

lima *f* file; **limetta** *f* emery board; *di metallo* nail file

limitare limit (**a** to); limitato limited; **limitazione** *f* limitation; **~ delle nascite** birth control; **senza -i** without restriction; **limite** *m* limit; *(confine)* boundary; **~ di velocità** speed limit; **al ~** at most, at the outside

limitrofo bordering

limonata *f* lemonade; **limone** *m* lemon; *(albero)* lemon tree

limpido clear; *acqua* crystal-clear

lince *f* lynx

linciare lynch

linea *f* line; **~ dell'autobus** bus route; **mantenere la ~** keep one's figure; TELEC **restare in ~** stay on the line, not hang up; INFOR **in ~** on line

lineamenti *mpl (fisionomia)* features

lineare linear

lineetta *f* dash

linfonodo *m* lymph node

lingotto *m* ingot

lingua *f* tongue; *(linguaggio)* language; **~ madre** mother tongue; **~ straniera** foreign language; **linguaggio** *m* language

lino *m* BOT flax; *tessuto* linen

liofilizzato freeze-dried

lipidico: a basso contenuto ~ low-fat

liposuzione *f* liposuction

liquidare *(pagare)* pay; *merci* clear; *azienda* liquidate; *fig: questione* settle; *problema* dispose of; *persona* F dispose of F; **liquidazione** *f* liquidation; **~ totale** clearance sale; **liquidità** *f* liquid assets, liquidity; **liquido** *m/agg* liquid

liquirizia *f* liquorice

liquore *m* liqueur

lira *f* lira

lirica *f* lyric poem; MUS **la ~** opera; **lirico** lyric; *cantante* opera *attr*

lisca *f* fishbone

lisciare smooth; *(accarezzare)* stroke; *capelli* straighten; **liscio** smooth; *bevanda* straight, neat

liso worn

lista f (*elenco*) list; (*striscia*) strip; ~ *d'attesa* waiting list; ~ *dei vini* wine list

listino m: ~ *di borsa* share index; ~ *prezzi* price list

lite f quarrel, argument; **litigare** quarrel, argue; **litigio** m quarrel, argument

litografia f lithography

litorale 1 agg coastal **2** m coast; **litoranea** f coast road; **litoraneo** coast attr, coastal

litro m litre, Am liter

liuto m lute

livella f level; **livello** m level

livido 1 agg livid; *braccio, viso* black and blue; *occhio* black; *per il freddo* blue **2** m bruise

lo 1 art msg the **2** pron msg him; *cosa, animale* it; *non ~ so* I don't know

lobo m lobe

locale 1 agg local **2** m room; *luogo pubblico* place; FERR *local train*; **località** f inv town; ~ *balneare* seaside resort; **localizzare** localize; (*reperire*) locate

locandina f TEA bill

locatario m, -a f tenant; **locatore** m, -trice f landlord; *donna* landlady; **locazione** f rental

locomotiva f locomotive; **locomozione** f locomotion; *mezzo m di ~* means of transport

locuzione f fixed expression

lodare praise; **lode** f praise

loggia f loggia

loggione m TEA gallery

logica f logic; **logico** logical

logorare wear out; **logorio** m wear and tear; **logoro** *indumento* worn (out)

lombaggine f lumbago

Lombardia f Lombardy; **lombardo 1** agg of Lombardy **2** m, -a f native of Lombardy

lombata f loin

lombo m loin

lombrico m earthworm

Londra f London

longevo long-lived

longitudine f GEOG longitude

lontananza f distance; *tra persone* separation; **lontano 1** agg far; *nel tempo* far-off; *passato, futuro, parente* distant **2** avv far (away); *da ~* from a distance; *abita molto ~?* do you live very far away?

lontra f otter

loquace talkative

lordo dirty; *peso, reddito ecc* gross

loro 1 pron soggetto they; *oggetto* them; *forma di cortesia* you **2** possessivo their; *forma di cortesia* your; *il ~ amico* their / your friend; *i ~ genitori* their / your parents **3** pron: *il ~* theirs; *forma di cortesia* yours

lotta f struggle; SP wrestling; *fig* fight; **lottare** wrestle, struggle (**con** with); *fig* fight (**contro** against; **per** for);

lutto

lottatore *m* wrestler

lotteria *f* lottery

lotto *m* lottery; *di terreno* plot

lozione *f* lotion; **~ dopobarba** aftershave

L.st. (= *lira sterlina*) £ (= pound)

lubrificante *m* lubricant; AUTO lubricating oil; **lubrificare** lubricate

lucchetto *m* padlock

luccicare sparkle

luccio *m* pike

lucciola *f* glowworm

luce *f* light; *fig* **far ~ su qc** shed light on sth; AUTO **-i pl di posizione** side lights; **-i pl posteriori** rear lights

lucente shining

lucertola *f* lizard

lucidare polish; *disegno* trace; **lucido 1** *agg superficie* shiny; FOT glossy; *persona* lucid **2** *m* polish; *disegno* transparency; **~ da scarpe** shoe polish

lucro *m*: **a scopo di ~** profit-making

luglio *m* July

lugubre sombre, *Am* somber

lui *pron msg soggetto* he; *oggetto* him; **a ~** to him; **~ stesso** himself

lumaca *f* slug

luminosità *f* luminosity; FOT speed; **luminoso** luminous; *stanza* bright

luna *f* moon; **~ crescente / calante** crescent / waning moon; **~ piena** full moon; **~ di miele** honeymoon; **luna-park** *m inv* amusement park

lunario *m*: **sbarcare il ~** make ends meet

lunatico moody

lunedì *m inv* Monday

lunghezza *f* length; **lungo 1** *agg* long; *caffè* weak; **a ~** for a long time; *fig* **alla -a** in the long run; **andare per le -ghe** drag on; *di gran -a* by far **2** *prp* along; (*durante*) throughout; **lungolago** *m* lakeside; **lungomare** *m inv* sea front

lunotto *m* AUTO rear window

luogo *m* place; **~ di nascita** birthplace, place of birth; **avere ~** take place, be held; **fuori ~** out of place; **in primo ~** in the first place

lupo *m* wolf

lurido filthy

lusingare flatter

lussazione *f* dislocation

lusso *m* luxury; **albergo** *m* **di ~** luxury hotel; **lussuoso** luxurious

lustrare polish

lutto *m* mourning

M

ma but; (*eppure*) and yet; **~ va!** nonsense!

maccheroni *mpl* macaroni *sg*

macchia *f* spot; *di sporco* stain; (*bosco*) scrub; **macchiare** stain; **macchiato** stained; **caffè** *m* ~ espresso *with a splash of milk*

macchina *f* machine; (*auto*) car; *fig* machinery; **~ fotografica** camera; **~ da cucire** sewing machine; **~ da scrivere** typewriter; **macchinario** *m* machinery

macedonia *f*: **~ (di frutta)** fruit salad

macellaio *m*, **-a** *f* butcher; **macelleria** *f* butcher's

macerie *fpl* rubble

macigno *m* boulder

macinacaffè *m inv* coffee mill; **macinapepe** *m inv* pepper mill; **macinare** mill, grind

macrobiotica *f* health food; **negozio** *m di* ~ health food store; **macrobiotico** macrobiotic

Madonna *f* Madonna, Our Lady; **madonnaro** *m* pavement artist specializing in sacred images

madre *f* mother; **madrelingua 1** *f* mother tongue **2** *m/f* native speaker; **madreperla** *f* mother-of-pearl; **ma-**

drina *f* godmother

maestà *f* majesty

maestrale *m* north-west wind

maestro 1 *agg* (*principale*) main **2** *m* master; MUS, PITT maestro, master **3** *m*, **-a** *f* teacher; **~ di nuoto** swimming teacher *o* instructor; **~ di sci** ski instructor

mafia *f* Mafia

maga *f* witch

magari 1 *avv* maybe, perhaps **2** *int* ~! if only! **3** *cong* ~ **venisse** if only he would come

magazzino *m* warehouse; *di negozio* stock room; (*emporio*) factory shop; **grandi -i** *pl* department store

maggio *m* May

maggioranza *f* majority; **maggiore 1** *agg* bigger; (*più vecchio*) older; MUS major; **il ~** the biggest; *figlio* the oldest; *artista* the greatest; **la maggior parte di ...** most of the ..., the majority of the ...; **andare per la ~** be a crowd pleaser **2** *m* MIL major; **maggiorenne** adult *attr*; **maggioritario** majority; POL **sistema** *m* ~ first-past-the-post system

magia *f* magic; **magico** mag-ic(al)

magistrato DIR *m* magistrate

maglia *f* top; (*maglione*)

maligno

sweater; SP shirt, jersey; *ai ferri* stitch; *lavorare a ~* knit; **maglieria** *f* knitwear; **maglietta** *f* T-shirt; **maglione** *m* sweater

magnetico magnetic

magnifico magnificent

magnolia *f* magnolia

mago *m* wizard; *i re -gi* the Three Wise Men, the Magi

magro thin; *cibo* low-fat; *fig: consolazione* small; *guadagno* meagre, *Am* meager

mai never; *(qualche volta)* ever; *~ più* never again; *più che ~* more than ever; *se ~* if ever; *dove / perché ~?* where / why on earth?

maiale *m* pig, *Am* hog; *(carne f di) ~* pork

maiolica *f* majolica

maionese *f* mayonnaise

mais *m* maize

maiuscola *f* capital (letter); **maiuscolo** capital

mal ☞ **male**

malandato dilapidated; *persona* poorly

malanno *m* misfortune; *(malattia)* illness

malapena: *a ~* hardly

malato 1 *agg* ill; *essere ~ di cuore* have heart problems; *~ di mente* mentally ill **2** *m, -a f* sick person; **malattia** *f* illness; *essere / mettersi in ~* be / go on sick leave

malavita *f* underworld

malavoglia *f* unwillingness, reluctance; *di ~* unwillingly,

reluctantly

malconcio the worse for wear; *persona* not very well

maldestro awkward, clumsy

male 1 *m* evil; *che c'è di ~?* where's the harm in it?; *andare a ~* go bad; MED *mal di gola* sore throat; *mal di testa* headache; *mal di denti* toothache; *mal di mare* seasickness; *far ~ a qu* hurt s.o.; *mi fa ~ il braccio* my arm hurts; *il cioccolato mi fa ~* chocolate doesn't agree with me; *fare ~ alla salute* be bad for you; *farsi ~* hurt o.s. **2** *avv* badly; *capire ~* misunderstand; *meno ~!* thank goodness!; *stare ~* (*essere malato*) be ill; (*essere giù*) be depressed; *il giallo mi sta ~* yellow doesn't suit me

maledetto 1 *pp* ☞ **maledire 2** *agg* damn(ed); **maledire** curse; **maledizione** *f* curse; *~!* damn!

maleducato bad-mannered

malessere *m* indisposition; *fig* malaise

malfamato disreputable

malfatto *cosa* badly made; **malfattore** *m* criminal

malformazione *f* malformation

malgoverno *m* misgovernment

malgrado 1 *prp* in spite of; *mio ~* against my will **2** *cong* although

maligno malicious, spiteful;

MED malignant

malinconia f melancholy; **malinconico** melancholic

malincuore: *a* ~ reluctantly, unwilling

malintenzionato 1 *agg* shady, suspicious **2** *m*, **-a** *f* shady character

malinteso *m* misunderstanding

malizioso malicious; *sorriso* mischievous

malloppo *m* (*refurtiva*) loot

malmenare mistreat

malnutrito under-nourished; **malnutrizione** f malnutrition

malore *m*: **è stato colto da un ~** he was suddenly taken ill

malsano unhealthy

maltempo *m* bad weather

malto *m* malt

maltrattare ill-treat

malumore *m* bad mood; **essere di ~** be in a bad mood

malvagio evil, wicked

malvisto unpopular

malvivente *m* lout

malvolentieri unwillingly, reluctantly

mamma f mother, mum; **~ mia!** goodness!

mammella f breast

mammifero *m* mammal

mammografia f mammography

manager *m/f* manager; **manageriale** managerial, management *attr*

mancanza f lack (*di* of); (*er-*

rore) oversight

mancare 1 *v/i* be missing; *di coraggio* fail; (*euph: morire*) pass away; *a qu manca qc* s.o. lacks sth; **mi manchi molto** I miss you a lot; **mi mancano 10 euro** I'm 10 euros short; **mancano tre mesi a Natale** it's three months to Christmas; **mi mancano le parole** words fail me; **c'è mancato poco che cadesse** he almost fell; **ci mancherebbe altro!** no way!, you must be joking!; **~ di qc** (*non avere*) lack sth, be lacking in sth **2** *v/t* miss; **mancato** *occasione* missed, lost; *tentativo* unsuccessful

mancia f tip; **manciata** f handful

mancino 1 *agg* left-handed; *fig* **colpo** *m* ~ dirty trick **2** *m*, **-a** *f* left-hander

mandante *m/f* DIR client; **mandare** send; **~ qu a prendere qc** send s.o. for sth; *fig* **~ giù** digest, take in

mandarino *m* BOT mandarin (orange)

mandato *m* POL mandate; DIR warrant; **~ bancario** banker's order; **~ d'arresto** arrest warrant

mandibola f jaw

mandolino *m* mandolin

mandorla f almond; **mandorlo** *m* almond tree

mandria f herd

maneggevole manageable; **maneggiare** handle (*anche fig*); **maneggio** *m* handling; *per cavalli* riding school

manesco a bit too ready with one's fists

manette *fpl* handcuffs

manganello *m* truncheon, *Am* night stick

mangereccio edible

mangiabile edible; **mangia-cassette** *m inv*, **mangianastri** *m inv* cassette player; **mangiare 1** *v/t* eat; *fig* squander; **mangiarsi le parole** mumble **2** *m* food; **mangime** *m* fodder; **mangiucchiare** snack

mango *m* mango

mania *f* mania

manica *f* sleeve; **senza -che** sleeveless

Manica *f*: **la ~** the (English) Channel

manicaretto *m* delicacy

manichino *m* dummy

manico *m* handle

manicomio *m* mental home

manicure *f inv* manicure; (*persona*) manicurist

maniera *f* (*modo*) way, manner; (*stile*) manner; **-e** *pl* manners

manifestante *m/f* demonstrator; **manifestare 1** *v/t* (*esprimere*) express; (*mostrare*) show **2** *v/i* demonstrate; **manifestarsi** appear, show up; *di malattia* manifest itself; **manifestazione** *f* expres-

sion; *il mostrare* show; **~ di protesta** demonstration, demo F; **~ sportiva** sporting event; **manifesto 1** *agg* obvious **2** *m* poster

maniglia *f* handle; *di autobus, metro* strap

manipolare manipulate; *vino* adulterate; **manipolato geneticamente** genetically modified

mano *f* hand; **fuori ~** out of the way; *fig* **alla ~** approachable; **di seconda ~** secondhand; **dare una ~ a qu** give s.o. a hand; **tenersi per ~** hold hands; **man ~ che** as (and when); **manodopera** *f* labour, *Am* labor

manomettere tamper with

manopola *f* knob

manoscritto *m* manuscript

manovale *m* hod carrier

manovella *f* starting handle

manovra *f* manoeuvre, *Am* maneuver; **manovrare 1** *v/t* TEC operate; FERR shunt; *fig* manipulate **2** *v/i* manoeuvre, *Am* maneuver

mansarda *f* locale attic

mantello *m* (*cappa*) cloak; *di animale* coat; (*strato*) layer

mantenere keep; *in buono stato* maintain; **mantenersi in forma** keep in shape; **mantenimento** *m* maintenance; *di famiglia* keep

Mantova *f* Mantua; **mantovano 1** *agg* Mantuan **2** *m*, **-a** *f* Mantuan

manuale *m/agg* manual

manubrio *m* handlebars

manutenzione *f* maintenance

manzo *m* steer, bullock; *carne* beef

mappa *f* map; **mappamondo** *m* globe

maratona *f* marathon; **maratoneta** *m/f* marathon runner

marca *f* brand, make; (*etichetta*) label; **~ da bollo** revenue stamp; **marcare** *march*; *goal* score; **marcato** *accento*, *lineamenti* strong

marchio *m* COM brand; **~ depositato** registered trademark

marcia *f* march; SP walk; TEC AUTO *gear*; **~ indietro** reverse; **marciapiede** *m* pavement, *Am* sidewalk; FERR platform; **marciare** march

marcio bad, rotten; (*corrotto*) corrupt; **marcire** rot *anche fig*

mare *m* sea; **in alto ~** on the high seas; **marea** *f* tide; *fig* **una ~ di** loads of; **alta ~** high tide; **bassa ~** low tide; **mareggiata** *f* storm; **maremoto** *m* tidal wave

margarina *f* margarine

margherita *f* daisy

margine *m* margin; (*orlo*) edge, brink

marina *f* coast(line); MAR navy; PITT seascape; **marinaio** *m* sailor

marinare GASTR marinate; F

~ la scuola play truant, *Am* play hooky; **marinato** GASTR marinated

marino sea *attr*, marine

marionetta *f* puppet, marionette

marito *m* husband

marittimo maritime

marmellata *f* jam, *Am* jelly; **~ di arance** marmalade

marmitta *f* AUTO silencer, *Am* muffler

marmo *m* marble

marocchino 1 *agg* Moroccan **2** *m*, **-a** *f* Moroccan; **Marocco** *m* Morocco

marrone 1 *agg* (chestnut) brown **2** *m* colore (chestnut) brown; (*castagno*) chestnut

marsala *m* Marsala, *dessert wine*

Marte *m* Mars

martedì *m inv* Tuesday; **~ grasso** Shrove Tuesday, *Am* Mardi Gras

martello *m* hammer

martire *m/f* martyr; **martirio** *m* martyrdom

marzapane *m* marzipan

marziano *m* Martian

marzo *m* March

mascara *m inv* mascara

mascarpone *m* mascarpone

mascella *f* jaw

maschera *f* mask; *in teatro* usher; *donna* usherette; **~ antigas** gas mask; **mascherare** mask; *fig* camouflage, conceal; **mascherarsi** put on a mask; (*travestirsi*) dress up

(*da* as)

maschile spogliatoio, *abito* men's; *caratteristica* male; GRAM masculine; **maschilista** *m/agg* sexist; **maschio 1** *agg* male; **hanno tre figli -i** they have three sons *o* boys **2** *m* (*ragazzo*) boy; (*uomo*) man; ZO male; **mascolino** masculine

mascotte *f inv* mascot

mass media *mpl* mass media

massa *f* mass; EL earth, *Am* ground

massacrare massacre; **massacro** *m* massacre

massaggiare massage; **massaggiatore** *m*, **-trice** *f* masseur; *donna* masseuse; **massaggio** *m* massage

massaia *f* housewife

massiccio *1 agg* massive; *oro, noce ecc* solid **2** *m* massif

massima *f* saying, maxim; *temperatura* maximum; **in linea di ~** generally speaking;

massimo 1 *agg* greatest, maximum **2** *m* maximum; **al ~** at most

masso *m* rock

masticare chew

mastice *m* mastic; (*stucco*) putty

mastino *m* mastiff

mastodontico gigantic

masturbare, masturbarsi masturbate

matematica *f* mathematics, maths, *Am* math; **matematico 1** *agg* mathematical **2** *m*,

-a *f* mathematician

materassino *m* airbed; **materasso** *m* mattress

materia *f* matter; (*materiale*) material; (*disciplina*) subject; **~ prima** raw material; **materiale 1** *agg* material; (*rozzo*) coarse, rough **2** *m* material; TEC equipment

maternità *f inv* motherhood; *in ospedale* maternity; **materno** maternal; **scuola** *f* **-a** nursery school

matita *f* pencil

matrice *f* matrix

matricola *f* register; *all'università* first-year student

matrigna *f* stepmother

matrimoniale matrimonial; **matrimonio** *m* marriage; *rito* wedding *attr*

mattina *f* morning; **di ~** in the morning; **mattinata** *f* morning; TEA matinée; **mattiniero: essere ~** be an early bird; **mattino** *m* morning

matto 1 *agg* mad, crazy (**per** about) **2** *m*, **-a** *f* madman, lunatic; *donna* madwoman, lunatic; **mi piace da -i andare al cinema** I'm mad about the cinema

mattone *m* brick; **mattonella** *f* tile

maturare *interessi* accrue; **maturità** *f* maturity; *diploma: A* levels, *Am* final exams

maturo *frutto* ripe; *persona* mature

mazza *f* club; (*martello*)

mazzo 166

sledgehammer; *da baseball* bat; **~ da golf** golf club

mazzo *m* bunch; **~ di carte** pack *o* deck of cards

me (= *mi* before **lo, la, li, le, ne**) me; **dammelo** give me it, give it to me; **per ~** for me

meccanica *f* mechanics; *di orologio* mechanism; **meccanicamente** mechanically; **meccanico 1** *agg* mechanical **2** *m* mechanic; **meccanismo** *m* mechanism

mecenate *m/f* sponsor

mèche *f inv* streak, highlight

medaglia *f* medal

medesimo (very) same

media *f* average; *in ~* on average; **mediano 1** *agg* central, middle **2** *m* SP half-back; **mediante** by (means of); **mediatore** *m*, **-trice** *f* mediator; **mediazione** *f* mediation

medicare *persona* treat; *ferita* clean, disinfect; **medicazione** *f* treatment; (*bende*) dressing; **medicina** *f* medicine; **medicinale 1** *agg* medicinal **2** *m* medicine; **medico 1** *agg* medical **2** *m* doctor; **~ di guardia** duty doctor

medievale medieval

medio 1 *agg* middle *attr*; *statura, rendimento* average **2** *m* middle finger

mediocre mediocre

medioevo *m* Middle Ages

meditare 1 *v/t* think about; (*progettare*) plan **2** *v/i* medi-

tate; (*riflettere*) think; **~ su qc** think about sth; **meditazione** *f* meditation; (*riflessione*) reflection

mediterraneo *m/agg* Mediterranean

medium *m/f inv* medium

medusa *f* ZO jellyfish

meglio 1 *avv* better; **~!, tanto ~!** good!; **alla ~** to the best of one's ability **2** *agg* better; *superlativo* best **3** *m* best; **fare del proprio ~** do one's best **4** *f* **avere la ~ su** get the better of

mela *f* apple

melagrana *f* pomegranate

melanzana *f* aubergine, *Am* eggplant

melma *f* mud

melo *m* apple (tree)

melodia *f* melody

melodrammatico melodramatic

melone *m* melon

membrana *f* membrane; **~ del timpano** eardrum

membro *m* ANAT limb; *persona* member

memorabile memorable; **memoria** *f* memory; **a ~** by heart; **-e** *pl* memoirs; **memorizzare** memorize; INFOR save

menare lead; F (*picchiare*) hit

mendicante *m/f* beggar; **mendicare 1** *v/t* beg for **2** *v/i* beg

menefreghismo *m* couldn't--care-less attitude

meningite f meningitis
meno 1 avv less; superlativo least; MAT minus; il **~ possibile** as little as possible; **a ~ che** unless; **per lo ~** at least; **sono le sei ~ un quarto** it's a quarter to six, Am it's a quarter of six; **sempre ~** less and less; **fare a ~ di qc** do without sth **2** prp except; **menomato** damaged; (handicappato) disabled
mensa f di azienda canteen; MIL mess
mensile m/agg monthly; **mensilità** f inv salary
mensola f bracket
menta f mint
mentale mental; **mentalità** f inv mentality; **mentalmente** mentally; **mente** f mind; **avere in ~ di fare qc** be thinking about doing sth; **tenere a ~ qc** bear sth in mind; **non mi viene in ~ il nome di ...** I can't remember the name of ...
mentire lie
mento m chin
mentre while
menù m inv menu (anche IN-FOR)
menzionare mention
menzogna f lie
meraviglia f wonder; **a ~** wonderfully; **meravigliare** astonish; **meravigliarsi: ~ di** be astonished by; **meravigliato** astonished; **meraviglioso** marvellous, Am marvelous, wonderful
mercante m merchant; **mercantile 1** agg nave cargo attr; porto commercial **2** m cargo ship; **mercanzia** f merchandise
mercato m market; **~ coperto** indoor market; **~ delle pulci** flea market; **a buon ~** cheap, inexpensive
merce f goods
merceria f haberdashery, Am notions
mercoledì m inv Wednesday; **~ delle Ceneri** Ash Wednesday
mercurio m mercury; AST **Mercurio** Mercury
merda P shit P
merenda f snack
meridiana f sundial; **meridiano 1** agg midday attr **2** m meridian
meridionale 1 agg southern **2** m/f southerner; **meridione** m south; **il Meridione** southern Italy
meringa f meringue
meritare 1 v/t deserve **2** v/i: **un libro che merita** a worthwhile book; **merito** m merit; **in ~ a** as regards; **per ~ suo** thanks to him
merletto m lace
merlo m ZO blackbird
merluzzo m cod
meschino mean; (infelice) wretched
mescolanza f mixture; **mescolare** mix; insalata toss;

caffè stir; **mescolarsi** mix, blend

mese *m* month

messa¹: ~ *in piega* set; ~ *in scena* production

messa² *f* REL mass

messaggino *m* text, text message; **messaggio** *m* message

messicano 1 *agg* Mexican **2** *m*, **-a** *f* Mexican; **Messico** *m* Mexico

messinscena *f* production; *fig* act

messo *pp* ☞ **mettere**

mestiere *m* trade; (*professione*) profession

mestolo *m* ladle

mestruazione *f* menstruation

meta *f* destination; SP try; *fig* goal, aim

metà *f inv* half; *punto centrale* middle, centre, *Am* center; *a ~ prezzo* half price; *a ~ strada* halfway; *fare a ~* go halves (*di* on)

metabolismo *m* metabolism

metadone *m* methadone

metafora *f* metaphor; **metaforico** metaphorical

metallico metallic; **metallizzato** metallic; **metallo** *m* metal

metamorfosi *f inv* metamorphosis

metano *m* methane; **metanodotto** *m* gas pipeline

meteora *f* meteor; **meteorite** *m o f* meteorite; **meteorolo-**

-gico meteorological, weather *attr*

meticoloso meticulous

metodico methodical; **metodo** *m* method

metrico metric

metro *m* metre, *Am* meter; ~ *quadrato* square metre; ~ *cubo* cubic metre

metrò *m inv* (*metropolitana*) underground, *Am* subway

metronotte *m inv* night watchman

metropoli *f inv* metropolis; **metropolitana** *f* underground, *Am* subway

mettere put; *vestito* put on; ~ *in moto* start (up); ~ *in ordine* tidy up; *mettiamo che ...* let's assume that ...; **mettersi** *abito, cappello ecc* put on; *~ a sedere* sit down; AVIA, AUTO ~ *la cintura* fasten one's seat belt; *~ a fare qc* start to do sth

mezzaluna *f* half moon; GASTR two-handled chopper; **mezzanotte** *f* midnight; **mezzo 1** *agg* half; *mezz'ora* half-hour; *le ~* half past six, *Am* six thirty; ~ *chilo* a half kilo; *a ~ età* middle-aged **2** *avv* half **3** *m* (*parte centrale*) middle; (*metà*) half; (*strumento*) means *sg*; (*veicolo*) means *sg* of transport; *per ~ di* by means of; *in ~ a* between; *in ~ a quei documenti* in the middle of those papers, among those papers;

in ~ *alla stanza* in the middle of the room; *nel* ~ *di* in the middle of; *giusto* ~ happy medium; **mezzobusto** *m* half-length photograph / portrait; **mezzofondo** *m* middle distance; **mezzogiorno** *m* midday; GEOG **Mezzogiorno** south of (Italy)

mi[1] *m* MUS E; *nel solfeggio della scala* me, mi

mi[2] *pron* me; *riflessivo* myself; **eccomi** here I am

miagolare miaow; **miagolio** *m* miaowing

mica: *non ho* ~ *finito* I'm nowhere near finished; *non è* ~ *vero* there's not the slightest bit of truth in it; ~ *male* not bad at all

miccia *f* fuse

micidiale *veleno, clima* deadly; *fatica, sforza* exhausting

micio *m* (pussy) cat

micosi *f inv* mycosis

microbiologia *f* microbiology

microbo *m* microbe

microchip *m inv* microchip

microcamera *f* miniature camera

microchirurgia *f* microsurgery

microfilm *m inv* microfilm

microfono *m* microphone, mike F

microonda *f* microwave; *forno a* ~ *e* microwave (oven)

microprocessore *m* micro-

processor

microscopico microscopic; **microscopio** *m* microscope

midollo *m* marrow; ~ **spinale** spinal cord

miei *mpl di* **mio** my

miele *m* honey

mietere harvest

migliaio *m* thousand; *un* ~ *a o* one thousand; *a migliaia* in their thousands

miglio[1] *m misura* mile

miglio[2] *m grano* millet

miglioramento *m* improvement; **migliorare 1** *v/t* improve **2** *v/i e* **migliorarsi** improve, get better; **migliore** better; *il* ~ the best

mignolo *m* (*o* **dito** ~) little finger; *del piede* little toe

-**mila** thousand; *due* ~ two thousand

milanese 1 *agg* of Milan **2** *m/f* inhabitant of Milan; **Milano** *f* Milan

miliardario *m*, -*a f* billionaire, multimillionaire; **miliardo** *m* billion; **milionario** *m*, -*a f* millionaire; *donna* millionairess; **milione** *m* million

militare 1 *agg* military **2** *m* soldier; **milite** *m* soldier; **militesente** exempt from military service; **milizia** *f* militia

mille a thousand

millefoglie *m inv* vanilla slice; **millennio** *m* millennium; **millepiedi** *m inv* millipede; **millesimo** thousandth

milligrammo *m* milligram(me)

millimetro m millimetre, Am millimeter

milza f spleen

mimetizzare MIL camouflage; **mimetizzarsi** camouflage o.s.

mimo m mime

mina f mine; di matita lead

minaccia f threat; **minacciare** threaten; **minaccioso** threatening

minareto m minaret

minato: campo m ~ minefield; **minatore** m miner

minatorio threatening

minerale m/agg mineral

minestra f soup; ~ di verdura vegetable soup; **minestrina** f clear soup, broth; **minestrone** m minestrone

miniatura f miniature

miniera f mine (anche fig)

minigolf m inv minigolf

minigonna f mini(skirt)

minimizzare minimize; **minimo** 1 agg least, slightest; prezzo lowest; salario, temperatura minimum 2 m minimum

ministero m ministry; **ministro** m minister; ~ degli Esteri Foreign Secretary, Am Secretary of State; ~ degli Interni Home Secretary, Am Secretary of the Interior; primo ~ Prime Minister; **consiglio** m dei -i Cabinet

minoranza f minority

minorato 1 agg severely handicapped 2 m, -a f severely handicapped person

minore 1 agg minor; di età younger; distanza shorter; più piccolo smaller 2 m/f: vietato ai -i di 18 anni no admittance to those under 18 years of age; film X-rated; **minorenne** 1 agg underage 2 m/f minor

minuscola f small letter, lower case letter; **minuscolo** tiny, miniscule

minuto 1 agg tiny, minute; descrizione detailed 2 m minute; **minuzioso** descrizione detailed; ricerca meticulous

mio 1 agg my; un ~ amico a friend of mine, one of my friends 2 pron: il ~ mine; i miei my parents

miope short-sighted; **miopia** f short-sightedness, myopia

mira f aim; (obiettivo) target; prendere la ~ take aim; fig prendere di ~ qu have it in for s.o.

miracolo m miracle; per ~ by a miracle, miraculously

miraggio m mirage

mirare aim (a at)

mirino m MIL sight; FOT viewfinder

mirtillo m blueberry

mirto m myrtle

miscela f mixture; di caffè, tabacco blend; **miscelatore** m GASTR mixer; rubinetto mixer tap

mischia f (rissa) scuffle; SP,

molestia

(folla) scrum; **mischiare**
mix; *carte* shuffle; **mischiarsi** mix; **miscuglio** *m* mixture
miseria *f (povertà)* poverty;
costare una ~ cost next to
nothing; F **porca ~!** damn
and blast! F; **misero** wretched
missile *m* missile
missionario *m*, *-a f* mission-
ary; **missione** *f* mission
misterioso mysterious; **mistero** *m* mystery
mistico mystic(al)
misto 1 *agg* mixed 2 *m* mixture; **~ lana** wool mix
misura *f* measurement; *(taglia)* size; *(provvedimento)*,
fig measure; **su ~** made to
measure; **misurare** measure; *vestito* try on; **misurino**
m measuring spoon
mite mild; *condanna* light
mito *m* myth; **mitologia** *f* mythology; **mitologico** mytho-
logical
mitra *m inv*, **mitragliatrice** *f*
machine gun
mitt. (= **mittente**) from
mittente *m/f* sender
mixare mix
M.M. (= **Marina Militare**) Italian navy
mobile 1 *agg* mobile; *ripiano*,
pannello removeable 2 *m*
piece of furniture; **-i** *pl* furniture; **mobilia** *f* furnishings;
mobilificio *m* furniture factory; **mobilitare** mobilize
moca *m* mocha

mocassino *m* moccasin
moda *f* fashion; **alla ~** fashionable, in fashion; *vestirsi*
fashionably; **fuori ~** out of
fashion, unfashionable
modalità *f inv* method
modella *f* model; **modellare**
model; **modello** 1 *agg* model
2 *m* model; *di vestito* style;
(formulario) form
modem *m inv* INFOR modem
moderare moderate; **moderato** moderate; **moderazio-
ne** *f* moderation
modernizzare modernize;
moderno modern
modestia *f* modesty; **modesto** modest; *prezzo* very reasonable
modico reasonable
modifica *f* modification; **modificare** modify
modo *m (maniera)* way, manner; *(mezzo)* way; **~ di dire**
expression; **per ~ di dire** so
to speak; **a ~ mio** in my
own way; **ad ogni ~** anyway,
anyhow; **di ~ che** so that; **in
che ~?** how?
modulo *m* form; *(elemento)*
module
mogano *m* mahogany
moglie *f* wife
molare 1 *v/t* grind 2 *m* molar
mole *f (grandezza)* size
molecola *f* molecule
molestare bother; **sessualmente** sexually harass; **molestia** *f* bother, nuisance; **~
sessuale** sexual harassment

molla f spring; fig spur; **-e** pl
tongs; **mollare** corda release,
let go; F **schiaffo, ceffone**
give; F **fidanzato** dump; ~
la presa let go

molle soft; (bagnato) wet

molletta f hairgrip; da bucato
clothes peg, Am clothes pin

mollica f crumb

mollusco m mollusc, Am
mollusk

molo m pier

molteplice multifaceted

moltiplicare, moltiplicarsi
multiply

molto 1 agg a lot of; con nomi
plurali a lot of, many **2** avv a
lot; con aggettivi very; ~ **meglio** much better, a lot better; **da** ~ for a long time;
fra non ~ before long

momentaneo momentary,
temporary; **momento** m
moment; **dal** ~ **che** causale
since; **a -i** sometimes; **per il**
~ for the moment; **sul** ~ at
the time

monaca f nun; **monaco** m
monk

monarchia f monarchy

monastero m monastery; di
monache convent

mondano society attr, (terreno) worldly; **fare vita -a** go
out

mondare frutta peel

mondiale 1 agg world attr; fenomeno, scala worldwide; **di
fama** ~ world-famous **2** m: **i
-i** di calcio the World Cup;

mondo m world; **il più bello
del** ~ the most beautiful in
the world

monello m, **-a** f little devil

moneta f coin; (valuta) currency; (denaro) money; (spiccioli) change; **monetario**
monetary; **Fondo** ~ **internazionale** International
Monetary Fund

mongolfiera f hot-air balloon

monolocale m bedsit

monopattino m child's scooter

monopolio m monopoly;
monopolizzare monopolize

monoposto m single-seater

monotonia f monotony; mo-
notono monotonous

monouso disposable, throw-
away

montacarichi m inv hoist

montaggio m TEC assembly;
di film editing

montagna f mountain; fig **-e**
pl **russe** rollercoaster; mon-
tagnoso mountainous;
montanaro m, **-a** f mountain
dweller

montare 1 v/t go up, climb; cavallo get onto, mount; TEC
assemble; film edit; GASTR
whip **2** v/i go up; venire come
up; ~ **in macchina** get into; ~
su scala climb; pullman get
on

montarsi: ~ **la testa** get big-
headed

montatura f di occhiali frame;

di gioiello mount; *fig* frame-up F

monte *m* mountain (*anche fig*); *a ~* upstream; *fig* **mandare a ~** ruin

montone *m* ram; *pelle, giacca* sheepskin

montuoso mountainous

monumento *m* monument

moquette *f* fitted carpet

mora *f* BOT *del gelso* mulberry; *del rovo* blackberry

morale 1 *agg* moral **2** *f* morals; *di favola ecc* moral **3** *m* morale; **essere giù di ~** be feeling a bit down

morbido soft

morbillo *m* measles *sg*

morbo *m* disease; **morboso** *fig* unhealthy; *curiosità* morbid

mordere bite

morena *f* moraine

morfina *f* morphine

moribondo dying

morire die; *fig* **~ di paura** be scared to death

mormorare murmur; (*bisbigliare, lamentarsi*) mutter; **mormorio** *m* murmuring; (*brontolio*) muttering

morsetto *m* TEC clamp; EL terminal

morsicare bite; **morso 1** *pp* ☞ **mordere 2** *m* bite; *di cibo* bit, mouthful; *per cavallo* bit

mortale *malattia* fatal; *offesa, nemico* deadly; *uomo* mortal; **mortalità** *f* mortality

morte *f* death

mortificare mortify

morto 1 *pp* ☞ **morire 2** *agg* dead; **stanco ~** dead tired **3** *m*, **-a** *f* dead man; *donna* dead woman; **i -i** *pl* the dead *pl*

mortorio *m*: F **essere un ~** be deadly boring

mosaico *m* mosaic

mosca *f* fly

moscato 1 *agg* muscat **2** *m* muscatel

moscerino *m* gnat, midge

moschea *f* mosque

moscio thin, flimsy; *fig* washed out

moscone *m* ZO bluebottle; (*imbarcazione*) pedalo

mossa *f* movement; *fig e di judo, karate* move; **mosso 1** *pp* ☞ **muovere 2** *agg* *mare* rough

mostarda *f* mustard

mosto *m* must, *unfermented grape juice*

mostra *f* show; (*esposizione*) exhibition; *fig* **mettere in ~** show off; **mostrare** show; (*indicare*) point out; **mostrarsi** appear

mostro *m* monster; **mostruoso** monstrous

motel *m inv* motel

motivare cause; *personale* motivate; (*spiegare*) explain; **motivazione** *f* (*spiegazione*) explanation; (*stimolo*) motivation; **motivo** *m* reason; MUS theme, motif; *su tessuto* pattern; **per quale ~?** for what reason?

moto[1] *m* movement; **fare ~** get some exercise; **mettere in ~** *motore* start (up)

moto[2] *f* (motor)bike

motocicletta *f* motorcycle; **motociclista** *m/f* motorcyclist; **motociclo** *m* motorcycling

motore *m* engine; **accendere il ~** start the engine; **motorino** *m* moped; **motorizzato** motorized; F **sei ~** have you got wheels? F

motoscafo *m* motorboat

motto *m* motto

mouse *m inv* INFOR mouse

movente *m* motive

movimento *m* movement; (*vita*) life

mozione *f* motion; **~ di fiducia** vote of confidence

mozzarella *f* mozzarella

mozzicone *m* cigarette end, (cigarette) stub

mozzo *m* TEC hub

mq (= *metro quadrato*) sq m, m² (= square metre)

mucca *f* cow

mucchio *m* pile

muco *m* mucus

muffa *f* mould, *Am* mold; **fare la ~** go mouldy

mugolare whine

mulattiera *f* mule track

mulatto *m*, **-a** *f* mulatto

mulinello *m su canna da pesca* reel; *vortice d'acqua* eddy

mulino *m* mill; **~ a vento** windmill

mulo *m* mule

multa *f* fine; **multare** fine

multiculturale multicultural

multimediale multimedia

multinazionale *f/agg* multinational

multiplo multiple

multisala *m inv* multiplex

multiuso multipurpose

mungere milk

municipale municipal; **municipio** *m* town council, municipality; *edificio* town hall

munire: ~ di supply with; **munizioni** *fpl* ammunition

muovere 1 *v/t* move **2** *v/i partire* move off (**da** from); **~ incontro a qu** move towards s.o.; **muoversi** move; F (*sbrigarsi*) get a move on F

murare (*chiudere*) wall up; **muratore** *m* bricklayer; **muratura** *f* brickwork

murena *f* moray eel

muro *m* wall; **le -a** *fpl* the (city) walls

muschio *m* BOT moss

muscolare muscular; **strappo** *m* ~ strained muscle; **muscolo** *m* muscle; **muscoloso** muscular

museo *m* museum; **~ etnologico** folk museum; **~ d'arte** art gallery

museruola *f* muzzle

musica *f* music; **musicale** musical; **musicista** *m/f* musician

muso *m di animale* muzzle; **tenere il ~ a qu** be in a huff

with s.o.; **musone** *m* sulker
musulmano 1 *agg* Muslim **2**
m, **-a** *f* Muslim
muta *f di cani* pack; SP wetsuit
mutamento *m* change
mutande *fpl di donna* panties;
di uomo (under)pants, *Am*
briefs; **mutandine** *fpl* panties;~ **(da bagno)** (swimming) trunks, *Am* swimsuit
mutare change
mutilato *m* disabled ex-ser-

viceman
muto 1 *agg* dumb; *(silenzioso)*
silent, dumb; **film** *m* ~ silent
movie **2** *m*, **-a** *f* mute
mutua *f* fund *that pays out*
sickness benefit; **medico** *m*
della **~a** doctor recognized
by the 'mutua'; **mutuato** *m*,
-a *f* person entitled to sickness
benefit
mutuo 1 *agg* mutual **2** *m*
mortgage

N

n. (= **numero**) No. (= number)
nacchere *fpl* castanets
nafta *f* naphtha
nano 1 *agg* dwarf **2** *m*, **-a** *f*
dwarf
napoletano 1 *agg* Neapolitan
2 *m*, **-a** *f* Neapolitan; **Napoli**
f Naples
nappa *f* tassel; *pelle* nappa *(type of soft leather)*
narcotico *m* narcotic
narice *f* nostril
narrare tell, narrate; **narrato-**
re, -trice *f* narrator
nascere be born; BOT, *di sole*
come up; *fig* develop; **sono**
nato a Roma I was born in
Rome; **nascita** *f* birth
nascondere hide; **nascon-**
dersi hide; **nascondiglio**
m hiding place; **nascosto**
pp ☞ **nascondere 2** *avv*: *di*
~ in secret; *di* ~ *a qu* unbe-

knownst to s.o.
nasello *m pesce* hake
naso *m* nose
nastro *m* tape; *per capelli*, *di*
decorazione ribbon; ~
adesivo adhesive tape, Sel-
lotape®, *Am* Scotch tape®
Natale *m* Christmas; **buon ~!**
Merry Christmas!; **natalità** *f*
birth rate; **natalizio** Christmas
natante 1 *agg* floating **2** *m*
boat
nativo 1 *agg* native **2** *m*, **-a** *f*
native
NATO *f* (= **Organizzazione**
del Trattato nord-atlantico)
NATO (= North Atlantic
Treaty Organization)
nato ☞ **nascere**
natura *f* nature; PITT ~ **morta**
still life; **naturale** natural;
naturalezza *f* naturalness;
con ~ naturally; **naturaliz-**

zare: **è naturalizzato americano** he's a naturalized
American; **naturalmente**
naturally

naufragare *di nave* be
wrecked; *di persona* be shipwrecked; *fig* be ruined; **naufragio** *m* shipwreck; *fig* ruin;
fare ~ *di nave* be wrecked; *di
persona* be shipwrecked;
naufrago *m*, **-a** *f* survivor
of a shipwreck

nausea *f* nausea; **avere la ~**
feel sick, *Am* feel nauseous;
nauseare nauseate (*anche
fig*)

nautico nautical

navale naval; **cantiere** *m ~*
shipyard

navata *f* ARCHI: **~ centrale**
nave; **~ laterale** aisle

nave *f* ship; **~ da carico** cargo
ship; **~ passeggeri** passenger ship; **~ traghetto** ferry;
navetta *f agg inv*: **bus** *m ~*
shuttle bus **2** *f* shuttle; **~ spaziale** space shuttle

navigabile navigable; **navigare** sail; INFOR navigate; **~
in Internet** surf the Net; **navigatore** *m* navigator

nazionale 1 *agg* national **2** *f*
national team; **nazionali-
smo** *m* nationalism; **nazio-
nalista** *m/f* nationalist; **nazionalità** *f inv* nationality;
nazione *f* nation

ne 1 *pron* (*di lui*) about him;
(*di lei*) about her; (*di loro*)
about them; (*di ciò*) about

it; **~ sono contento** I'm happy about it; **~ ho abbastanza** I have enough **2** *avv* from
there; **~ vengo adesso** I've
just come back from there

né: **~ ... ~** neither ... nor; **non
l'ho trovato ~ a casa ~ in ufficio** I couldn't find him either at home or in the office

neanche neither; **neanch'io**
neither am I, me neither;
non l'ho ~ visto I didn't
even see him

nebbia *f* fog; **nebbioso** foggy

nebulosa *f* AST nebula

necessaire *m inv*: **~** (*da viaggio*) beauty case; **necessa-
rio 1** *agg* necessary **2** *m*: **il
~ per vivere** the basic neces-
sities; **necessità** *f inv* need;
in caso di ~ if need be;
per ~ out of necessity

nefrite *f* MED nephritis

negare deny; (*rifiutare*) refuse; **negativa** *f* negative;
negativo *m/agg* negative;
negato: **essere ~ per qc**
be hopeless at sth

negli = **in** and *art* **gli**

negligente careless, negligent; **negligenza** *f* carelessness, negligence

negoziante *m/f* shopkeeper,
Am storekeeper; **negoziare**
negotiate FIN **~ in** trade in;
negoziato *m* negotiation; **-i**
pl **di pace** peace negotiations; **negozio** *m* shop, *Am*
store

negro 1 *agg* black **2** *m*, **-a** *f*

nocciolina

black (man / woman)

nei, nel, nell', nella, nelle, nello = *in* and *art* **i, il, l', la, le, lo**

nemico 1 *agg* enemy *attr* **2** *m,* **-a** *f* enemy

nemmeno neither; **~ io** me neither; **~ per idea!** don't even think about it!

neo *m* mole; *fig* flaw

neonato *m,* **-a** *f* infant, new-born baby

neppure not even; **non ci vado-~ io** I'm not going – neither am I, me neither

nero 1 *m/agg* black *(anche fig)* **2** *m,* **-a** *f* black (man / woman)

nervo *m* nerve; **dare sui i a qu** get on s.o.'s nerves; **nervosismo** *m* nervousness; **nervoso 1** *agg* nervous; *(irritabile)* edgy **2** *m* F: **mi viene il ~** this is getting on my nerves

nespola *f* medlar; **nespolo** *m* medlar (tree)

nessuno 1 *agg* no; **non chiamare in nessun caso** don't call in any circumstances; **c'è -a notizia?** is there any news? **2** *pron* nobody, no one; **hai visto ~?** did you see anyone or anybody?

nettezza *f* cleanliness; **~ urbana** cleansing department; **netto** clean; *(chiaro)* clear; *reddito, peso* net

neurologico neurological; **neurologo** *m,* **-a** *f* neurologist

neutrale neutral; **neutralizzare** neutralize; **neutro** neutral; GRAM neuter

neve *f* snow; **nevicare** snow; **nevicata** *f* snowfall

nevralgia *f* neuralgia; **nevralgico** neuralgic; **punto** *m* ~ specially painful point; *fig* weak point

nevrotico 1 *agg* neurotic; F short-tempered **2** *m,* **-a** *f* neurotic

nicchia *f* niche

nicotina *f* nicotine

nido *m* nest

niente 1 *pron* nothing **2** *avv* nothing; **non ho ~ I** don't have anything, I have nothing; **non ho per ~ fame** I'm not at all hungry; **non fa niente** it doesn't matter; **niente(di)meno** no less; **~!** that's incredible!

ninfea *f* water-lily

nipote *m/f* di zio nephew; *donna, ragazza* niece; *di nonno* grandson; *donna, ragazza* granddaughter

nitido clear; FOT sharp

nitrire neigh

NO (= *nord-ovest*) NW (= northwest)

no no; **come ~!** of course!; **se ~** otherwise; **dire di ~** say no; **credo di ~** I don't think so

nobile 1 *agg* noble **2** *m/f* aristocrat; **nobiltà** *f* nobility

nocca *f* knuckle

nocciola *f* hazelnut; **(color** *m)* **~** hazel; **nocciolina** *f*: **~**

nocciolo 178

(*americana*) peanut
nocciolo¹ *m albero* hazel (tree)
nocciolo² *m di frutto* stone; *di questione* kernel
noce 1 *m* walnut (tree); *legno* walnut **2** *f* walnut; **~ di cocco** coconut; **~ moscata** nutmeg; **nocepesca** *f* nectarine
nocivo harmful
nodo *m* knot; *fig* crux; FERR junction
no-global *m/f inv* anti-globalist
noi *pron soggetto* we; *con prp* us; **a ~** to us; **con ~** with us
noia *f* boredom; **-e** *pl* trouble; **dar ~ a qu** annoy s.o.; **noioso** boring; (*molesto*) annoying
noleggiare rent, *Br anche* hire; (*dare a noleggio*) rent out, *Br* hire out; **noleggio** *m* rent, *Br anche* hire; **nolo** *m* rent, *Br anche* hire; **prendere a ~** rent; **dare a ~** rent out
nome *m* name; GRAM noun; **~ di battesimo** Christian name; **~ e cognome** full name; **in ~ di** in the name of
nomina *f* appointment; **nominare** (*menzionare*) mention; *a un incarico* appoint (**a** to)
non not; **~ ho fratelli** I don't have any brothers, I have no brothers
non stop *inv* nonstop

non vedente *m/f* blind person
nonché let alone; (*e anche*) as well as
noncurante nonchalant; **~ di** heedless of
nondimeno nevertheless
nonno *m*, **-a** *f* grandfather; *donna* grandmother; **-i** *pl* grandparents
nonnulla *m inv* trifle
nono ninth
nonostante despite; **ciò ~** however
nontiscordardimé *m inv* forget-me-not
nord *m* north; **a(l) ~ di** (to the) north of; **nordest** *m* northeast; **nordico** northern; *lingue* Nordic; **nordovest** *m* north-west
norma *f* (*precetto*) rule; TEC standard; **a ~ di legge** up to standard; **normale** normal; **normalità** *f* normality
norvegese *agg*, *m/f* Norwegian; **Norvegia** *f* Norway
nostalgia *f* nostalgia; **avere ~ di casa** feel homesick; **avere ~ di qu** miss s.o.
nostrano local, home *attr*
nostro 1 *agg* our; **i ~ -i genitori** our parents; **un ~ amico** a friend of ours **2** *pron*: **il ~** ours
nota *f* note; FIN bill; **~ spese** expense account; **prendere ~ di qc** make a note of sth; *situazione* take note of sth; **notaio** *m* notary (public)

notare (*osservare*) notice; (*annotare*) make a note of; *con segni* note; **notarile** notarial; **notevole** (*degno di nota*) notable, noteworthy; (*grande*) considerable; **notificare** serve (**a** on)

notizia f piece of news; *avere -e di qu* have news of s.o., hear from s.o.; **notiziario** m RAD, TV news sg

noto well-known; *rendere ~* announce; **notorietà** f fame; spreg notoriety

nottambulo m, -a f night owl; **nottata** f night; *fare la ~* stay up all night; **notte** f night; *di ~* at night; *buona ~!* good night!; **notturno** night(-time) attr; *animale* nocturnal

novanta ninety; **novantesimo** ninetieth; **nove** nine; **novecento 1** agg nine hundred **2** m: *il Novecento* the twentieth century

novella f short story

novembre m November

novità f inv novelty; (*notizia*) piece of news

nozione f notion, idea; *-i pl di base* rudiments

nozze fpl wedding; *~ d'argento* silver wedding (anniversary)

ns. (= *nostro*) our(s), *used in correspondence*

nube f cloud; **nubifragio** m cloudburst

nubile single, unmarried

nuca f nape of the neck

nucleare nuclear; **nucleo** m FIS nucleus (*anche fig*)

nudismo m naturism, nudism; **nudista** m/f naturist, nudist; **nudo 1** agg nude, naked; (*spoglio*) bare **2** m PITT nude

nulla nothing; *è una cosa da ~* it's nothing; *per ~* for nothing; **nullaosta** m: fig *ottenere il ~* get the green light; **nullo** invalid; gol disallowed; *voto* spoiled

numerale m numeral; **numerare** number; **numerato** numbered; **numero** m number; *arabo, romano* numeral; *di scarpa* size; *~ di targa* registration number, Am license number; *~ di telefono* phone number; *~ del volo* flight number; *~ verde* 0800 number, Am toll-free number; F *dare i -i* talk nonsense; **numeroso** numerous; *famiglia, classe* large

nuocere: *~ a* harm

nuora f daughter-in-law

nuotare swim; **nuotata** f swim; **nuoto** m swimming

nuovamente again; **nuovo 1** agg new; *di ~* again **2** m: *che c'è di ~?* what's new?

nutriente nourishing; **nutrimento** m food; **nutrire** feed; **nutrirsi** *di* live on; **nutritivo** nutritious

nuvola f cloud; fig *cadere dalle -e* be taken aback; **nuvoloso** cloudy

O

O (= *ovest*) W (= west)

o or; ~ ... ~ either ... or

oasi f inv oasis

obbedire ☞ **ubbidire**

obbligare: ~ qu a fare qc oblige s.o. to do sth; **obbligatorio** obligatory; **obbligazione** f obligation; FIN bond; **obbligo** m obligation; **d'~** obligatory

obesità f obesity; **obeso** obese

obiettare object (*a* to); **obiettivo 1** agg objective **2** m aim, objective; FOT lens; **obiettore** m: ~ **di coscienza** conscientious objector; **obiezione** f objection

obliquo oblique

obliterare *biglietto* punch

oblò m inv MAR porthole

oca f goose; *fig* silly woman

occasionale casual; **occasionalmente** occasionally; **occasione** f (*opportunità*) opportunity, chance; (*evento*) occasion; (*affare*) bargain; **automobile** f **d'~** second-hand car; **cogliere l'~** seize the opportunity; **all'~** if necessary; **in ~ di** on the occasion of

occhiaie fpl bags under the eyes

occhiali mpl glasses; ~ **da sole** sunglasses; **occhiata** f look; **dare un'~ a** have a look at it; (*sorvegliare*) keep an eye on; **occhiello** m buttonhole; **occhio** m eye; **a ~ nudo** to the naked eye; **a ~ e croce** roughly; **dare nell'~** attract attention; **a quattr'~-i** in private

occidentale western; occidente m west; **a ~ di** (to the) west of

occorrente 1 agg necessary **2** m necessary materials; **occorrenza** f: **all'~** if necessary, if need be; **occorrere** be necessary; (*accadere*) occur; **mi occorre** I need; **non occorre!** there's no need!

occupare *spazio* take up, occupy; *tempo* occupy, fill; *posto* have; *persona* keep busy; **occuparsi** take care (*di* of), deal (*di* with); **occupati degli affari tuoi!** mind your own business!; **occupato** TELEC busy, Br anche engaged; *posto, appartamento* taken; *gabinetto* engaged, Am occupied; *persona* busy; *città, nazione* occupied; **occupazione** f *di città, paese* occupation; (*attività*) pastime; (*impiego*) job

oceano m ocean; **Oceano Atlantico** Atlantic Ocean; **Oceano Pacifico** Pacific

Ocean

oculista m/f ophthalmologist

od = **o** (before a vowel)

odiare hate, detest

odierno modern-day attr, today's attr

odio m hatred; **odioso** hateful, odious

odontotecnico m, **-a** f dental technician

odorare smell (**di** of); **odorato** m sense of smell; **odore** m smell, odour, Am odor; **-i** pl GASTR herbs

offendere offend; **offendersi** take offence o Am offense

offensiva f offensive; **offensivo** offensive

offerente m bidder; **maggior** ~ highest bidder; **offerta** f offer; FIN supply; REL offering; (dono) donation; in asta bid; ~ **d'impiego** job offer; ~ **speciale** special offer

offesa f offence, Am offense; **offeso** pp ☞ **offendere**

officina f workshop; per macchine garage

offrire offer; **ti offro da bere** I'll buy you a drink; **posso offrirti qualcosa?** can I get you anything?

oggettivo objective; **oggetto** m object

oggi today; **d'~** of today; **da ~ in poi** from now on; ~ **stesso** today, this very day; ~ **come** ~ at the moment; ~ **pomeriggio** this afternoon;

oggigiorno nowadays

ogni every; ~ **tanto** every so often; ~ **sei giorni** every six days; **Ognissanti** m inv All Saints Day; **ognuno** everyone, everybody

Olanda f Holland; **olandese 1** agg m Dutch **2** m/f Dutchman; **donna** Dutchwoman

oleandro m oleander

oleoso oily

olfatto m sense of smell

oliera f type of cruet for oil and vinegar bottles

Olimpiadi fpl Olympic Games, Olympics; ~ **invernali** Winter Olympics

olio m oil; ~ **extra-vergine d'oliva** extra-virgin olive oil; ~ **solare** suntan oil

oliva f olive; **olivo** m olive (tree)

oltraggio m offence, Am offense, outrage

oltre 1 prp after, past; (più di) over; **vai ~ il semaforo** go past the traffic lights; ~ **a** apart from **2** avv nello spazio further; nel tempo longer

omaggio m homage; (dono) gift; **copia** (**in**) ~ free o complimentary copy; **essere in ~ con** come free with

ombelico m navel

ombra f shade; **zona non illuminata** shade; **all'~** in the shade; **ombrello** m umbrella; **ombrellone** m parasol; sulla spiaggia beach umbrella; **ombretto** m eye shadow

omeopatico 1 agg homeo-

pathic **2** *m,* **-a** *f* homeopath
omero *m* humerus
omesso *pp* ☞ **omettere;**
omettere omit, leave out
omicida 1 *agg* murderous **2**
m/f murderer; **omicidio** *m*
murder
omogeneizzato *m* baby
food; **omogeneo** homoge-
nous
omonimo 1 *agg* of the same
name **2** *m* homonym **3** *m,*
-a *f* namesake
omosessuale *agg, m/f* homosexual
on. (= *onorevole*) Hon (=
honourable)
onda *f* wave; **-e** *pl* **corte** short
wave; **-e** *pl* **lunghe** long
wave; **-e** *pl* **medie** medium
wave; RAD *andare in* ~ go
on the air; **ondata** *f* wave;
~ *di caldo* heat wave; ~ *di
freddo* cold spell; **ondeg-
giare** *di barca* rock; *di bandiera* flutter; **ondulato** *capelli* wavy; *superficie* uneven;
cartone, lamiera corrugated
onestà *f* honesty; **onesto**
honest; *prezzo, critica* fair
onice *m* onyx
onomastico *m* name day
onorare be a credit to; ~ *qu di
qc* honour *o Am* honor s.o.
with sth; **onorario 1** *agg*
honorary **2** *m* fee; **onore** *m*
honour, *Am* honor; *in* ~ *di*
in honour of; **onorevole 1**
agg honourable, *Am* hono-
rable **2** *Onorevole m/f*

Member of Parliament
ONU *f* (= *Organizzazione
delle Nazioni Unite*) UN
(= United Nations)
opaco opaque; *calze, rossetto*
dark
opera *f* work; MUS opera; ~
d'arte work of art; *mettersi
all'*~ set to work; **operaio 1**
agg working **2** *m,* **-a** *f* worker;
~ *specializzato* skilled
worker; **operare 1** *v/t* cam-
biamento make; *miracoli*
work; MED operate on **2** *v/i*
act; **operativo** operational;
ricerca applied; *ordine* operativo; *piano m* ~ plan of op-
erations; **operatore** *m,* **-trice**
f operator; *televisivo, cinematografico* cameraman; ~ *di
Borsa* market trader; ~ *sociale* social worker; ~ *turistico* tour operator; **operazione** *f* operation
opinione *f* opinion
oppio *m* opium
opporre offer; **opporsi** be
opposed
opportunista *m/f* opportunist; **opportunità** *f inv* opportunity; *di decisione* timeli-
ness; **opportuno** suitable
opposizione *f* opposition;
opposto 1 *pp* ☞ **opporre 2**
agg opposite **3** *m* POL opposition
oppressione *f* oppression;
oppresso 1 *pp* ☞ **opprimere 2** *agg* oppressed; **opprimere** oppress

oppure or (else)

optare: ~ *per* choose, opt for

opuscolo *m* brochure

opzione *f* option

ora[1] *f* time; *unità di misura* hour; *che ~ è?, che -e sono?* what's the time?; ~ *legale* daylight saving time; ~ *locale* local time; ~ *di punta* rush hour; TELEC peak time; *di buon'~* early

ora[2] **1** *avv* now; *per ~* for the moment, for the time being; ~ *come ~* at the moment; *d'~ in poi* from now on **2** *cong* now

orale *m/agg* oral

orario 1 *agg tariffa* hourly; *velocità* per hour **2** *m di treno, bus* timetable, *Am* schedule; *di negozio* business hours; *al lavoro* hours of work; ~ *di apertura / chiusura* opening / closing time; *in* ~ on time

orata *f* bream

orbita *f* AST orbit; ANAT eyesocket; *in* ~ in orbit

orchestra *f* orchestra; *luogo* (orchestra) pit

orchidea *f* orchid

ordigno *m* device

ordinale *m/agg* ordinal

ordinamento *m* rules and regulations; ~ *sociale* rules governing society; **ordinare** order; *stanza* tidy up

ordinario ordinary; *mediocre* pretty average

ordinato tidy; **ordinazione** *f*

order; **ordine** *m* order; *mettere in* ~ tidy up; *di prim'~* first-rate; ~ *del giorno* agenda; *l'~ dei medici* the medical association

orecchino *m* earring; **orecchio** *m* ear; MUS *a* ~ by ear; **orecchioni** *mpl* mumps *sg*

oreficeria *f* goldsmith work; *(gioielleria)* jeweller's, *Am* jewelry store

orfano 1 *agg* orphan **2** *m, -a f* orphan; **orfanotrofio** *m* orphanage

organismo *m* organism; *fig* body

organizzare organize; **organizzazione** *f* organization

organo *m* organ

orgasmo *m* orgasm

orgoglio *m* pride; **orgoglioso** proud

orientale 1 *agg* eastern; *(dell'Oriente)* Oriental **2** *m/f* Oriental

orientamento *m*: *senso d'~* sense of direction; ~ *professionale* professional advice; **orientarsi** get one's bearings

oriente *m* east; *l'Oriente* the Orient; *Medio Oriente* Middle East; *Estremo Oriente* Far East; *ad ~ di* (to the) east of

origano *m* oregano

originale *m/agg* original; **originalmente** originally; **originario** original; *essere* ~

di come from; *popolo* originate in; **origine** *f* origin; **in**
~ originally

origliare eavesdrop

orizzontale horizontal; **orizzonte** *m* horizon

orlo *m* edge; *di vestito* hem

orma *f* footprint; *fig* **seguire
le -e di qu** follow in s.o.'s
footsteps

ormai by now

ormonale hormonal; **ormone** *m* hormone

ornamentale ornamental;
ornamento *m* ornament; **ornare** decorate

oro *m* gold; **d'~** (made of)
gold

orologiaio *m* (clock- and)
watch-maker; **orologio** *m*
clock; *da polso* watch

oroscopo *m* horoscope

orrendo horrendous

orribile horrible

orrore *m* horror (**di** of)

orsacchiotto *m* bear cub;
giocattolo teddy (bear)

orso *m* bear; *fig* hermit; ~
bianco polar bear

ortaggio *m* vegetable

ortica *f* nettle; **orticaria** *f* nettle rash

orto *m* vegetable garden,
kitchen garden; ~ **botanico**
botanical gardens

ortodosso orthodox

ortografia *f* spelling

ortopedico 1 *agg* orthopae-
dic, *Am* orthopedic 2 *m*, -a
f orthopaedist, *Am* orthope-

dist

orzaiolo *m* stye

orzo *m* barley

osare dare

osceno obscene

oscillare *di corda* sway,
swing; *di barca* rock; FIS os-
cillate; *fig: di persona* waver;
di prezzi fluctuate

oscurare *di: luce* block
out; **oscurità** *f* darkness; *fig*
obscurity; **nell'~** in the dark;
oscuro 1 *agg* dark; *(sconosciuto)* obscure 2 *m*: **essere
all'~ di qc** be in the dark
about sth

ospedale *m* hospital

ospitale hospitable; **ospitalità** *f* hospitality; **ospitare** put
up; **ospite** *m/f* guest; *chi
ospita* host; *donna* hostess;
ospizio *m* old folk's home

osservare *(guardare)* look at,
observe; *(notare)* see, observe; *(far notare)* point
out; *(seguire)* obey; ~ **una
dieta** keep to a diet; **osservatore** *m*, **-trice** *f* observer;
osservatorio *m* AST observatory; **osservazione** *f* observation

ossessione *f* obsession (**di**
with); **avere l'~ di** be obsessed with; **ossessivo** obsessive

ossia or rather

ossidare tarnish

ossigeno *m* oxygen

osso *m* bone; ~ **sacro** sac-
rum; **in carne e -a** in the

flesh; **ossobuco** m marrow-
bone; GASTR ossobuco, *stew
made with knuckle of
veal*

ostacolare hinder; **ostacolo**
m obstacle; *nell'atletica* hurdle; *nell'equitazione* fence,
jump; *fig* stumbling block,
obstacle

ostaggio m hostage; *prendere qu in ~* take s.o. hostage

ostello m: ~ *della gioventù*
youth hostel

osteoporosi f osteoporosis

osteria f inn

ostetrica f obstetrician; (*levatrice*) midwife; **ostetrico** 1
agg obstetric(al) 2 m obstetrician

ostia f Host

ostile hostile; **ostilità** f inv
hostility

ostinarsi dig one's heels in; ~
a fare qc persist in doing sth;
ostinato obstinate

ostrica f oyster

ostruire block, obstruct;
ostruito blocked

otite f ear infection

otorinolaringoiatra m/f ear,
nose and throat specialist

ottagono octagon; **ottanta**
eighty; **ottantesimo** eighti-

eth; **ottavo** eighth

ottenere get, obtain; **ottengo**
☞ **ottenere**

ottica f optics; *fig* viewpoint;
ottico 1 *agg* optical 2 m optician

ottimismo m optimism; **ottimista** m/f optimist

ottimizzare optimize; **ottimo**
excellent

otto eight

ottobre m October

ottocento 1 *agg* eight hundred 2 m: *l'Ottocento* the
nineteenth century

ottone m brass; MUS *-i pl* brass

otturare block; *dente* fill; **otturatore** m FOT shutter; **otturazione** f blocking; *di dente* filling

ottuso obtuse

ovaia f ANAT ovary

ovale m/agg oval

overdose f inv overdose

ovest m west; *a(l) ~ di* (to the)
west of

ovini mpl sheep

ovunque everywhere

ovvero or rather; (*cioè*) that is

ovvio obvious

ozio m laziness, idleness

ozono m ozone; *la fascia d'~*
the ozone layer

P

pacato calm, unhurried

pacchetto *m* package; *di sigaretta, biscotti* packet

pacchiano vulgar, in bad taste

pacco *m* parcel, package; ~ **postale** parcel

pace *f* peace; *lasciare in* ~ *qu* leave s.o. alone *o* in peace

pacifista *m/f* pacifist

padano of the Po; *pianura f -a* Po Valley

padella *f di cucina* frying pan

padiglione *m* pavilion; ~ **auricolare** auricle

Padova *f* Padua; **padovano 1** *agg* Paduan **2** *m*, **-a** Paduan

padre *m* father; **padrino** *m* godfather; **padronanza** *f* control; *(conoscenza)* mastery; ~ *di sé* self-control; **padrone** *m*, **-a** *f* boss; *(proprietario)* owner; *di cane* master; **donna** mistress; ~ *di casa* man / lady of the house; *per inquilino* landlord; **donna** landlady

paesaggio *m* scenery; PITT, GEOG landscape; **paesaggista** *m/f* PITT landscape painter; **paese** *m* country; *(villaggio)* village; *(territorio)* region; *i Paesi Bassi* pl the Netherlands; *-i pl in via di sviluppo* developing countries

paga *f* pay; **pagabile** payable; **pagamento** *m* payment; **pagare 1** *v/t* pay for; *conto, fattura* pay; *gliela faccio* ~ he'll pay for this **2** *v/i* pay

pagella *f* report, *Am* report card

paghetta *f* pocket money

pagina *f* page; **-e gialle** Yellow Pages; ~ *web* webpage

paglia *f* straw

paio *m*: *un* ~ *di* a pair of; *un* ~ *di volte* a couple of times

pala *f* shovel; *di elica, turbina* blade

palasport *m inv* indoor sports arena

palato *m* palate

palazzina *f* luxury home; **palazzo** *m* palace; *(edificio)* building; *con appartamenti* block of flats, *Am* apartment block; ~ *di giustizia* courthouse; ~ *dello sport* indoor sports arena

palco *m* dais; TEA stage; **palcoscenico** *m* stage

palese obvious

Palestina *f* Palestine; **palestinese** *agg*, *m/f* Palestinian

paletta *f* shovel; *per la spiaggia* spade; **paletto** *m* tent peg

palla *f* ball; ~ *di neve* snowball; **pallacanestro** *f* basketball; **pallanuoto** *f* water po-

lo; **pallavolo** f volley ball
palliativo m palliative
pallido pale
pallina f di vetro marble; **~ da golf** golf ball; **~ da tennis** tennis ball; **pallino** m nel biliardo cue ball; nelle bocce jack; munizione pellet; fig avere il **~** della pesca be mad about fishing; **a -i** pl spotted; **palloncino** m balloon; **pallone** m ball; (calcio) football, soccer; AVIA balloon; **pallottola** f pellet; di pistola bullet
palma f palm
palmare m PDA
palmo m hand's breadth; ANAT palm
palo m polc; nel calcio (goal) post
palombaro m diver
palpare feel; MED palpate
palpebra f eyelid
paltò m inv overcoat
palude f swamp; **paludoso** swampy; **palustre** swampy; pianta swamp attr
panca f bench; in chiesa pew
pancarré m sliced loaf
pancetta f pancetta, cured belly of pork
panchetto m footstool; **panchina** f bench
pancia f m stomach; **mal** m **di ~** stomach-ache; **panciotto** m waistcoat, Am vest
pancreas m inv pancreas
pane m bread; **~ integrale** wholemeal o Am whole-

wheat bread; **panetteria** f bakery; **panettiere** m/f baker; **panettone** m panettone, cake made with candied fruit
panfilo m yacht; **~ a motore** motor yacht
pangrattato m breadcrumbs
panico m panic
paniere m basket
panificio m bakery
panino m roll; **~ imbottito** filled roll; **paninoteca** f sandwich shop
panna f cream; **~ montata** whipped cream
panne f: **essere in ~** have broken down
pannello m panel; **~ solare** solar panel
panno m (pezzo di stoffa) cloth; **-i** pl clothes; **se fossi nei tuoi -i** if I were in your shoes
pannocchia f cob
pannolino m nappy, Am diaper; per donne sanitary towel, Am sanitary napkin
panorama m panorama; fig overview
pantaloncini mpl shorts; **pantaloni** mpl trousers, Am pants
pantera f ZO panther
pantofola f slipper
papà m inv daddy, dad
papa m Pope
papavero m poppy
papera f fig (errore) slip of the tongue
papero m, **-a** f gosling

papillon *m inv* bow tie
pappa *f* food
pappagallo *m* parrot
paprica *f* paprika
parabola *f* TV satellite dish
parabrezza *m inv* windscreen, *Am* windshield
paracadute *m inv* parachute; **paracadutista** *m/f* parachutist
paracarro *m* post
paradiso *m* heaven, paradise
paradossale paradoxical; **paradosso** *m* paradox
parafango *m* AUTO wing; *di bici* mudguard
parafulmine *m* lightning rod
paraggi *mpl* neighbourhood, *Am* neighborhood; **nei ~ di** (somewhere) near
paragonare compare; **paragone** *m* comparison
paragrafo *m* paragraph
paralisi *f* paralysis; **paralizzare** paralyze
parallela *f* parallel line; **-e** *pl* parallel bars; **parallelo** *m/agg* parallel
paralume *m* lampshade
parametro *m* parameter
paranoia *f* paranoia; **paranoico** paranoid
paranormale *m/agg* paranormal
paraocchi *mpl* blinkers (*anche fig*)
parapetto *m* parapet; MAR rail
paraplegico 1 *agg* paraplegic **2** *m*, **-a** *f* paraplegic

parare 1 *v/t* ornare decorate; *proteggere* shelter; *occhi* shield; *scansare* parry **2** *v/i* save
parassita *m/f* parasite (*anche fig*)
parata *f* parade
paraurti *m inv* bumper
parcheggiare park; **parcheggio** *m* parking; *luogo* car park, *Am* parking lot
parchimetro *m* parking meter
parco *m* park; **~ naturale** nature reserve
parecchio 1 *agg* a lot of **2** *pron* **parecchi** *mpl*, **parecchie** *fpl* quite a few **3** *avv* quite a lot
pareggiare 1 *v/t* even up; (*uguagliare*) match; *conto* balance **2** *v/i* SP draw, *Am* tie; **pareggio** *m* SP draw, *Am* tie
parente *m/f* relative
parentesi *f* bracket, *Am* parenthesis
parere *v/i* seem, appear; *che te ne pare?* what do you think?; *non ti pare?* don't you think?; *a quanto pare* by all accounts **2** *m* opinion; *a mio ~* in my opinion
parete *f* wall
pari 1 *agg* equal; *numero* even; *alla ~* the same; SP *finire alla ~* end in a draw *o Am* tie **2** *m* (social) equal, peer
Parigi Paris; **parigino** Parisian

parità f equality, parity; **~ di diritti** equal rights; **a ~ di condizioni** all things being equal

parlamentare 1 agg Parliamentary **2** v/i negotiate **3** m/f Member of Parliament, MP; **parlamento** m Parliament

parlare talk, speak (**a qu** to s.o.; **di qc** about sth); **parla inglese?** do you speak English?

parmigiano m formaggio Parmesan

parodia f parody

parola f word; facoltà speech; **~ d'ordine** password; **-e pl crociate** crossword; **~ chiave** keyword; **essere di ~** keep one's word; **parolaccia** f swear word

parquet m parquet floor

parrocchia f parish; **parroco** m parish priest

parrucca f wig; **parrucchiere** m, **-a** f hairdresser; **~ per signora** ladies' hairdresser

part time 1 agg part-time **2** avv part time

parte f part; (porzione) portion; (lato) side; DIR party; **prendere ~ a** take part in; **a ~** separate; **mettere da qc** put sth aside; **da nessuna ~** nowhere; **da tutte le -i** everywhere; **da~ mia** regalo ecc from me; **in ~** in part, partly

partecipante m/f participant;

partecipare 1 v/t announce **2** v/i: **~ a gara** take part in; dolore, gioia share; **partecipazione** f (intervento) participation; (annunzio) announcement; FIN holding; **~ agli utili** profit-sharing

partenza f departure; SP start

participio m participle

particolare 1 agg particular; segretario private; **in ~** in particular **2** m particular, detail; **particolareggiato** detailed; **particolarità** f inv special nature

partigiano m, **-a** f partisan

partire leave; AUTO, SP start

partita f SP match; di carte game; di merce shipment; **~ IVA** VAT registration number

partito m POL party

partner m/f inv partner

parto m birth; **partorire** give birth to

parziale partial; fig biased

Pasqua f Easter; **pasquale** Easter attr; **Pasquetta** f Easter Monday

passaggio m passage; in macchina lift, Am ride; atto passing; SP pass; **essere di ~** be passing through; **~ a livello** level crossing, Am grade crossing; **dare un ~ a qu** give s.o. a lift; **passante** m/f passer-by; **passaporto** m passport; **passare 1** v/i (trasferirsi) go (**in** into); SP pass; di legge be passed; di *tempo* go by, pass; **~ da / per Milano** go through Milan; **~ dal panettiere** drop by the baker's; **mi è passato di mente** it slipped my mind; **~ per imbecille** be taken for a fool **2** *v/t confine* cross; (*sorpassare*) overstep; (*porgere*) pass; (*trascorrere*) spend; TELEC **ti passo Claudio** here's Claudio; **passata** *f* quick wipe; GASTR **~ (di pomodoro)** passata, *sieved tomato pulp*; **passatempo** *m* pastime, hobby; **passato 1** *agg past*; *alimento* puréed; **l'anno ~** last year **3** *m past*; GASTR purée

passeggero 1 *agg passing*, short-lived **2** *m*, **-a** *f passenger*; **passeggiare** stroll, walk; **passeggiata** *f* stroll, walk, (*percorso*) walk; **passeggino** *m* pushchair, *Am* baby buggy; **passeggio** *m*: **andare a ~** go for a walk

passe-partout *m inv chiave* master key

passerella *f* (*foot*)bridge; MAR gangway; AVIA ramp; *per sfilate* catwalk, *Am* runway

passero *m* sparrow

passionale passionate; *delitto* of passion; **passione** *f* passion; REL Passion

passivo 1 *agg passive* **2** *m* GRAM passive; FIN liabilities

passo *m* step; (*impronta*) footprint; *di libro* passage;

GEOG pass; **~ carrabile** driveway; **fare due -i** go for a walk or a stroll; *fig* **fare il primo ~** take the first step

pasta *f* paste; (*pastasciutta*) pasta; (*impasto*) dough; (*dolce*) pastry; **~ frolla** shortcrust pastry; **~ sfoglia** puff pastry; **pastasciutta** *f* pasta; **pastella** *f* batter

pastello *m* pastel

pasticca *f* pastille

pasticceria *f* pastries, cakes; *negozio* cake shop; **pasticcino** *m* pastry; **pasticcio** *m* GASTR pie; *fig* mess; **essere nei -i** be in a mess

pastiglia *f* MED tablet, pill

pasto *m* meal

pastore *1 m*, **-a** *f* shepherd **2** *m* REL: **~ (evangelico)** pastor; **pastorizzato** pasteurized

patata *f* potato; **-e** *pl* **fritte** (French) fries; **patatine** *fpl* crisps, *Am* chips; (*fritte*) French fries

patente *f*: **~ (di guida)** driving licence, *Am* driver's license

paternità *f* paternity; **paterno** paternal, fatherly

patetico pathetic

patire 1 *v/i suffer* (*di* from) **2** *v/t suffer* (from); **patito 1** *agg* of suffering **2** *m*, **-a** *f* fan

patria *f* homeland

patrigno *m* stepfather

patrimonio *m* estate; **~ artistico** artistic heritage

patriottismo *m* patriotism

patrocinio *m* support, patronage

patrono *m*, **-a** *f* REL patron saint

patteggiare negotiate

pattinaggio *m* skating; **~ su ghiaccio** ice skating; **pattinare** skate; AUTO skid; **pattinatore** *m*, **-trice** *f* skater; **pattino** *m* SP skate; **~ a rotelle** roller skate; **~ in linea** roller blade

patto *m* pact; **a ~ che** on condition that

pattuglia *f* patrol

pattumiera *f* dustbin, *Am* trashcan

paura *f* fear; **avere ~ di** be frightened of; **mettere ~ a qu** frighten s.o.; **pauroso** fearful; (*che fa paura*) frightening

pausa *f* pause; *durante il lavoro* break

pavimento *m* floor

pavone *m* peacock

pazientare be patient; **paziente** *agg*, *m/f* patient; **pazienza** *f* patience

pazzesco crazy; **pazzia** *f* madness; **pazzo 1** *agg* mad, crazy; **andare ~ per** be mad *o* crazy about **2** *m*, **-a** *f* madman; *donna* madwoman

p.c. (= **per conoscenza**) cc (= carbon copy)

peccare sin; **~ di** be guilty of; **peccato** *m* sin; (**che**) **~!** what a pity!

pecora *f* sheep

pecorino *m*/*agg*: (**formaggio** *m*) **~** pecorino (*ewe's milk cheese*)

peculiarità *f inv* special feature, peculiarity

pedaggio *m* toll

pedalare pedal; **pedale** *m* pedal; **pedalò** *m inv* pedalo

pedana *f* footrest; SP springboard

pedata *f* kick; *impronta* footprint

pediatra *m/f* paediatrician, *Am* pediatrician

pedicure 1 *m/f* chiropodist, *Am* podiatrist **2** *m inv* pedicure

pedina *f* draughtsman, *Am* draftsman; *fig* cog in the wheel; **pedinare** shadow, follow

pedofilo *m*, **-a** *f* paedophile, *Am* pedophile

pedonale pedestrian; **pedone** *m* pedestrian

peggio 1 *avv* worse **2** *m*: **il ~ è che** the worst of it is that; **avere la ~** get the worst of it; **peggioramento** *m* deterioration, worsening; **peggiorare** *v/t* make worse, worsen **2** *v/i* get worse, worsen; **peggiore** worse; *superlativo* worst; **il ~** the worst

pelare peel; *pollo* pluck; *fig F* fleece F

pelle *f* skin; **avere la ~ d'oca** have gooseflesh

pellegrinaggio *m* pilgrimage; **pellegrino** *m*, **-a** *f* pilgrim

pelletteria *f* leatherwork

pellicano *m* pelican

pelliccia *f* fur; *cappotto* fur coat

pellicola *f* film

pelo *m* hair, coat; (*pelliccia*) coat; *fig per un* ~ by the skin of one's teeth

pena *f* (*sofferenza*) pain, suffering; (*punizione*) punishment; ~ *di morte* death penalty; *stare in* ~ *per qu* worry about s.o.; *non ne vale la* ~ it's not worth it; *mi fa* ~ I feel sorry for him / her; **penale 1** *agg* criminal; *codice penal* **2** *f* penalty; **penalità** *f inv* penalty; **penalizzare** penalize

pendenza *f* slope; **pendere** hang; (*essere inclinato*) slope; *pendio m* slope

pendolare *m/f* commuter

pendolo *m* pendulum

pene *m* penis

penetrante *dolore*, *freddo* piercing; *fig*: *sguardo* piercing, penetrating; *analisi* penetrating; **penetrare 1** *v/t* penetrate **2** *v/i*: ~ *in* enter

penisola *f* peninsula

penitenza *f* REL penance; *in gioco* forfeit; **penitenziario** *m* prison

penna *f* pen; *di uccello* feather; ~ *stilografica* fountain pen; **pennarello** *m* felt-tip (pen); **pennello** *m* brush

penombra *f* half-light

penoso painful

pensare think; ~ *a* think about o of; ~ *a fare qc* (*ricordarsi di*) remember to do sth; ~ *di fare qc* think of doing sth; *ci penso io* I'll take care of it; **pensiero** *m* thought; (*preoccupazione*) worry; *stare in* ~ be worried (*per* about); **pensieroso** pensive

pensile hanging

pensilina *f* shelter

pensionamento *m* retirement; **pensionato** *m*, **-a** *f* pensioner, retired person; *alloggio* boarding house; **pensione** *f* pension; *albergo* boarding house; ~ *completa* full board; *mezza* ~ half board; *andare in* ~ retire

Pentecoste *f* Pentecost, *Br anche* Whitsun

pentirsi *di peccato* repent, ~ *di aver fatto qc* be sorry for doing sth

pentola *f* pot, pan

penultimo last but one, penultimate

penzolare dangle; **penzoloni** dangling

pepare pepper; **pepato** peppered; **pepe** *m* pepper; **peperone** *m* pepper

per for; *mezzo* by; ~ *qualche giorno* for a few days; ~ *tutta la notte* throughout the night; *dieci* ~ *cento* ten per cent; *uno* ~ *uno* one by one; ~ *fare qc* (in order) to do sth; *stare* ~ be about to

pera *f* pear

peraltro however

perbene 1 *agg* respectable **2** *avv* properly

percento 1 *m* percentage **2** *avv* per cent; **percentuale** *f*/*agg* percentage

percepire perceive; *(riscuotere)* cash

perché because; *(affinché)* so that; **~?** why?

perciò so, therefore

percorrere *distanza* cover; *strada*, *fiume* travel along; **percorso 1** *pp* ☞ **percorrere 2** *m* (*tragitto*) route

percossa *f* blow; **percosso** *pp* ☞ **percuotere**; **percuotere** strike

percussione *f* percussion; MUS **-i** *pl* percussion

perdere 1 *v*/*t* lose; *treno*, *occasione* miss; **~ tempo** waste time **2** *v*/*i* lose; *di rubinetto*, *tubo* leak; **perdersi** get lost; **~ d'animo** lose heart; **mi sono perduto** I'm lost; **perdita** *f* loss; *di gas*, *di acqua* leak; **~ di tempo** waste of time; **perditempo 1** *m*/*f inv* idler **2** *m inv* waste of time

perdonare forgive; **perdono** *m* forgiveness

perenne eternal; BOT perennial

perfettamente perfectly; **perfetto** perfect; **perfezionamento** *m* perfection, further improvement; **corso** *m di* **~** further training; **per-**

-fezionare perfect; **perfezione** *f* perfection; **perfezionista** *m*/*f* perfectionist

perfido treacherous

perfino even

perforare drill through

pergolato *m* pergola

pericolante on the verge of collapse; **pericolo** *m* danger; *(rischio)* risk; **fuori ~** out of danger; **pericoloso** dangerous

periferia *f* periphery; *di città* outskirts; **periferico** peripheral; *quartiere* outlying; INFOR **unità** *f inv* **-a** peripheral

perifrasi *f inv* circumlocution

periodico 1 *agg* periodic **2** *m* periodical; **~ mensile** monthly; **periodo** *m* period

peripezia *f* misadventure

perito 1 *agg* expert **2** *m*, **-a** *f* expert

peritonite *f* peritonitis

perizia *f* skill, expertise; *esame* examination (by an expert)

perla *f* pearl; **perlina** *f* bead

perlomeno at least

perlopiù usually

perlustrare patrol

permaloso easily offended, touchy

permanente 1 *agg* permanent **2** *f* perm; **permanenza** *f* permanence; *in un luogo* stay

permesso 1 *pp* ☞ **permettere 2** *m* permission; *(breve licenza)* permit; MIL leave; **~**

di soggiorno residence permit; *(è) ~?* may I?; **permettere** allow, permit; **permettersi** afford

pernacchia f F raspberry F, Am bronx cheer F

perno m pivot

pernottamento m night, overnight stay

però but

pero m pear (tree)

perpendicolare f/agg perpendicular

perplesso perplexed

perquisire search; **perquisizione** f search; *~ personale* body search; *mandato m di ~* search warrant

persecuzione f persecution; *mania f di ~* persecution complex; **perseguitare** persecute; **perseguitato** m: *~ politico* person persecuted for their political views

perseverante persevering; **perseverare** persevere

persiana f shutter

persino ☞ **perfino**

persistente persistent; **persistere** persist

perso pp ☞ **perdere**

persona f person; *a (o per) ~* a head, each; *in ~, di ~* in person; **personaggio** m character; *(celebrità)* personality; **personale 1** agg personal **2** m staff, personnel; **personalità** f inv personality; **personalmente** personally

perspicace shrewd

persuadere persuade, convince; *~ qu a fare qc* persuade s.o. to do sth; **persuasivo** persuasive; **persuaso** pp ☞ **persuadere**

pertanto and so, therefore

pertinente relevant, pertinent

perturbazione f disturbance

Perù m Peru; **peruviano 1** agg Peruvian **2** m, *-a* f Peruvian

pervenire arrive; *far ~* send

p.es. (= *per esempio*) eg (= for example)

pesante heavy; fig: *libro, film* boring; **pesantezza** f heaviness; *~ di stomaco* indigestion; **pesapersone** f inv scales; *in negozio ecc* weighing machine; **pesare** weigh

pesca[1] f *frutto* peach

pesca[2] f fishing

pescare fish for; *(prendere)* catch; fig dig up; *ladro, svaligiatore ecc* catch (red-handed); **pescatore** m fisherman; **pesce** m fish; *~ d'aprile* April Fool; ASTR *Pesci* pl Pisces; **pescecane** m shark; **peschereccio** m fishing boat; **pescheria** f fishmonger's, Am fish store; **pescivendolo** m, *-a* f fishmonger, Am fish seller

pesco m peach (tree)

peso m weight; *a ~* by weight

pessimismo m pessimism; **pessimista 1** agg pessimistic **2** m/f pessimist

pessimo very bad, terrible

piazzare

pestaggio *m* F going-over F; **pestare** *carne, prezzemolo* pound; *con piede* step on; *(picchiare)* beat up

peste *f* plague; *persona* pest F

pesticida *m* pesticide

pesto *m* pesto, paste of basil, olive oil and pine nuts

petalo *m* petal

petardo *m* fire-cracker

peto *m* fart F

petroliera *f* (oil) tanker; **petrolifero** *oil attr*; **petrolio** *m* oil, petroleum

pettegolezzo *m* piece of gossip; **pettegolo 1** *agg* gossipy **2** *m*, **-a** *f* gossip

pettinare comb; **pettinarsi** comb one's hair; **pettinatura** *f* hairstyle, hairdo; **pettine** *m* comb

petto *m* chest; *(seno)* breast; **~ di pollo** chicken breast; *a doppio* ~ double-breasted

pezza *f* cloth; *(toppa)* patch

pezzo *m* piece; *di motore* part; *da / per un* ~ for a long time; **~ di ricambio** spare (part); *andare in -i* break into pieces

piacere 1 *v/i*: **le piace il vino?** do you like wine?; **non mi piace il cioccolato** I don't like chocolate; **mi piacerebbe saperlo** I'd really like to know **2** *m* pleasure; *(favore)* favour, Am favor; **~!** pleased to meet you!; **mi fa ~** I'm happy to; **con ~** with pleasure; **per ~** please; **piacevole**

pleasant; **piacimento**: *a* ~ as much as you like

piaga *f (ferita)* wound

piallare plane

pianerottolo *m* landing

pianeta *m* planet

piangere 1 *v/i* cry, weep **2** *v/t* mourn

pianificare plan

pianista *m/f* pianist; **piano 1** *agg* flat **2** *avv (adagio)* slowly; *(a voce bassa)* quietly **3** *m* plan; *(pianura)* plane; *di edificio* floor; MUS piano; **~ rialzato** mezzanine; **primo** ~ foreground; FOT close-up; **pianoforte** *m* piano

pianta *f* plant; *di città* map; *del piede* sole; **piantare** plant; *chiodo* hammer in; F **piantala!** cut it out! F; F **~ qu** dump s.o. F

pianterreno *m* ground floor, Am first floor

pianto 1 *pp* → **piangere 2** *m* crying, weeping; *(lacrime)* tears

pianura *f* plain

piastra *f* plate; **piastrella** *f* tile

piattaforma *f* platform; **~ di lancio** launch pad; **piattino** *m* saucer; **piatto 1** *agg* flat **2** *m* plate; GASTR dish; MUS **-i** *pl* cymbals; **primo** ~ first course; **~ del giorno** day's special

piazza *f* square; COM market (place); **piazzale** *m* large square; *in autostrada* toll-booth area; **piazzare** place,

put; (*vendere*) sell; **piazzola** *f*
small square; **~ di sosta** lay-
by

piccante spicy, hot

picchiare beat

piccione *m* pigeon

picco *m* peak; MAR **colare a ~**
sink

piccolo 1 *agg* small, little; *di
statura* short **2** *m*, -a *f* child;
la gatta con i suoi -i the
cat and her young; **da ~** as
a child

piccozza *f* ice axe, *Am* ice ax

picnic *m inv* picnic

pidocchio *m* louse

piede *m* foot; **a -i** on foot; **stare in -i** stand; **a -i nudi** barefoot, with bare feet

piedistallo *m* pedestal

piega *f* wrinkle; *di pantaloni*
crease; *di gonna* pleat; **piegare 1** *v/t* bend; (*ripiegare*)
fold **2** *v/i* bend; **piegarsi**
bend; *fig* **~ a** comply with;
pieghevole sedia folding

Piemonte *m* Piedmont; **pie-
montese** *agg*, *m/f* Piedmon-
tese

piena *f* flood; *a teatro* full
house; **pieno 1** *agg* full (**di**
of); (*non cavo*) solid **2** *m*:
AUTO **fare il ~** fill up

pietà *f* pity (**di** for); PITT pietà;
avere ~ di qu take pity on
s.o.

pietanza *f* dish

pietra *f* stone; **pietrina** *f* flint;
pietroso stony

pigiama *m* pyjamas, *Am* pa-

jamas

pigiare crush

pigliare catch

pigna *f* pinecone

pignolo pedantic

pigrizia *f* laziness; **pigro** lazy

pilastro *m* pillar

pila *f* EL battery; (*catasta*) pile

pillola *f* pill; **prendere la ~** be
on the pill

pilone *m* pier; EL pylon

pilota *m/f* AVIA, MAR pilot;
AUTO driver; **pilotare** pilot;
AUTO drive

pinacoteca *f* art gallery

pineta *f* pine forest

ping-pong *m* ping-pong

pinna *f di pesce* fin; SP flipper

pino *m* pine; **pinolo** *m* pine
nut

pinza *f* pliers; **pinzare** staple;
pinzatrice *f* stapler; **pinzette**
fpl tweezers

pioggia *f* rain

piombare fall; *precipitarsi*
rush (**su** at); **mi è piombato
in casa** he dropped in unexpectedly; **piombino** *m* sink-
er; **piombo** *m* lead

pioppo *m* poplar

piovere rain; **piovigginare**
drizzle; **piovoso** rainy

piovra *f* octopus

pipa *f* pipe

pipì *f* F pee F; F **fare la ~** go
for a pee F

pipistrello *m* bat

piramide *f* pyramid

pirata *m* pirate

pirofila *f* oven-proof dish

piroscafo *m* steamer

pisciare P piss P

piscina *f* (swimming) pool; ~ **coperta** indoor pool

pisello *m* pea

pisolino *m* nap

pista *f di atletica* track; (*traccia*) trail; ~ **d'atterraggio** runway; ~ **da ballo** dance floor; ~ **da sci** slope; ~ **ciclabile** bike path

pistacchio *m* pistachio

pistola *f* pistol

pittore *m*,-**trice** *f* painter; **pittura** *f* painting; **pitturare** paint

più 1 *avv* more (**di, che** than); *superlativo* most; *MAT* plus; ~ **grande** bigger; *il* ~ **grande** the biggest; **di** ~ more; **non** ~ no more; *tempo* no longer; ~ **o meno** more or less; **per di** ~ what's more; **mai** ~ never again; **al** ~ **presto** as soon as possible; **al** ~ **tardi** at the latest **2** *agg* more; *superlativo* most; ~ **volte** several times **3** *m* most; **per lo** ~ mainly; *i* ~, *le* ~ the majority

piuma *f* feather

piumino *m* down; *giacca* quilted jacket

piumone® *m* Continental quilt, duvet

piuttosto rather

pizza *f* pizza; **pizzaiolo** *m* pizza maker; **pizzeria** *f* pizzeria

pizzicare 1 *v/t braccio, persona* pinch; F *ladro* catch (redhanded) **2** *v/i* pinch; **pizzico**

m pinch; **pizzicotto** *m* pinch

pizzo *m* (*merletto*) lace

placare placate; *dolore* ease

placca *f* plate; (*targhetta*) plaque; ~ **dentaria** plaque; **placcare** plate; *nel rugby* tackle; **placcato d'oro** gold-plated

planetario 1 *agg* planetary **2** *m* planetarium

plasma *m* plasma; ~ **sanguigno** blood plasma; **plasmare** mould; *Am* mold

plastica *f* plastic; *MED* plastic surgery; **plastico 1** *agg* plastic **2** *m* *ARCHI* scale model; **esplosivo** *m* *al* ~ plastic bomb

plastilina® *f* Plasticine®

platano *m* plane (tree)

platea *f* *TEA* stalls

platino *m* platinum

plausibile plausible

plenilunio *m* full moon

plettro *m* plectrum

pleurite *f* pleurisy

plico *m* envelope

plurale *m*/*agg* plural

plutonio *m* plutonium

pneumatico 1 *agg* pneumatic **2** *m* tyre, *Am* tire

po': *un* ~ a little (**di** sth), a little bit (**di** of); *un bel* ~ quite a lot

poco 1 *agg* little; *con nomi plurali* few **2** *avv* not much; *con aggettivi* not very; **senti un po'!** just listen!; *a* ~ *a* ~ little by little, gradually; ~ **fa** a little while ago; **fra**

in a little while; soon; ~ *dopo* a little while later, soon after; *per* ~ cheap; (*quasi*) almost, nearly

podere *m* farm

podio *m* podium

podismo *m* walking

poesia *f* poetry; *componimento* poem; **poeta** *m*, **-essa** *f* poet; **poetico** poetic

poggiare lean; (*posare*) put, place; **poggiatesta** *m inv* head rest

poi then; *d'ora in* ~ from now on

poiché since

polacco 1 *m/agg* Polish 2 *m*, **-a** *f* Pole

polare Polar; *circolo* *m* ~ *artico* / *antartico* Arctic / Antarctic circle

polemica *f* argument; **polemico** argumentative; **polemizzare** argue

polenta *f* polenta, *kind of porridge made from cornmeal*

policlinico *m* general hospital

poliglotta 1 *agg* multilingual 2 *m/f* polyglot

poligono *m* MAT polygon; MIL ~ *di tiro* firing range

poliomielite *f* poliomyelitis

polipo *m* polyp

politica *f* politics; (*strategia*) policy; **politico** 1 *agg* political 2 *m*, **-a** *f* politician

polizia *f* police; **poliziesco** police *attr*; *romanzo* *m* ~ detective story; **poliziotto** 1 *m*

policeman 2 *agg*: *donna* *f* **-a** policewoman; *cane* *m* ~ police dog

polizza *f* policy

pollame *m* poultry

pollice *m* thumb; *unità di misura* inch

polline *m* pollen

pollo *m* chicken

polmone *m* lung; **polmonite** *f* pneumonia

polo¹ *m* GEOG pole; ~ *nord* North Pole; ~ *sud* South Pole

polo² 1 *m* SP polo 2 *f inv* polo shirt

Polonia *f* Poland

polpa *f* flesh; *di manzo, vitello* meat

polpaccio *m* calf

polpastrello *m* fingertip

polpetta *f di carne* meatball; **polpettone** *m* meat loaf

polpo *m* octopus

polsino *m* cuff; **polso** *m* ANAT wrist; *di camicia* cuff; *pulsazione* pulse

poltiglia *f* mush

poltrire laze around

poltrona *f* armchair; TEA stall (seat)

poltrone *m*, **-a** *f* lazybones *sg*

polvere *f* dust; (*sostanza polverizzata*) powder; *latte* *m in* ~ powdered milk; **polverina** *f* powder; **polveroso** dusty

pomata *f* cream

pomello *m* cheek; *di porta* knob

pomeridiano afternoon *attr*;
pomeriggio *m* afternoon;
di ~, nel ~ in the afternoon
pomice *f* agg: *(pietra f) ~*
pumice (stone)
pomo *m* knob; *~ d'Adamo*
Adam's apple
pomodoro *m* tomato
pompa[1] *f* pomp; *impresa f di
-e funebri* undertaker's, *Am*
mortician
pompa[2] *f* TEC pump
pompelmo *m* grapefruit
pompiere *m* fireman; *-i pl* fire
brigade, *Am* fire depart-
ment
pone ☞ *porre*
ponente *m* west
pongo ☞ *porre*
ponte *m* bridge; ARCHI scaffolding; MAR deck; *fare il ~*
make a long weekend of it
pontefice *m* pontiff
ponteggio *m* scaffolding
pontificio papal; *Stato m ~*
Papal States
pontile *m* jetty
pop: *musica f ~* pop (music)
popolare 1 *agg* popular; *quartiere* working-class; *ballo m ~*
folk dance **2** *v/t* populate;
popolarità *f* popularity; **popolato** populated; *(abitato)*
inhabited; *(pieno)* crowded;
popolazione *f* population;
popolo *m* people
poppa *f* MAR stern
porcellana *f* porcelain, china
porcellino *m* piglet; *~ d'India*
guinea-pig

porcheria *f* disgusting thing;
è una ~ it's disgusting; *-e
pl* junk food; **porchetta** *f*
suckling pig, *roasted whole
in the oven*
porcile *m* pigsty, *Am* pigpen
porcino *m* cep
porco *m* pig; **porcospino** *m*
porcupine
porgere *mano, oggetto* hold
out; *aiuto, saluto ecc* offer
porno *m* agg F porn F; **pornografico** pornographic
poro *m* pore
porre place, put; *domanda*
ask; *poniamo che …* let's
suppose that …
porro *m* leek; MED wart
porta *f* door
portabagagli *m inv* luggage
rack; AUTO roof rack; **portacenere** *m inv* ashtray; **portachiavi** *m inv* keyring; **porta-
finestra** *f* French window;
portafoglio *m* wallet; **porta-
fortuna** *m inv* good luck
charm
portale *m* door; INFOR portal
portamonete *m inv* purse;
portaombrelli *m inv* umbrella stand; **portapacchi**
m inv di macchina roof rack;
di bicicletta carrier; **porta-
penne** *m inv* pencil case
portare *(trasportare)* carry;
(accompagnare) take; *(avere
addosso)* wear; *(condurre)*
lead; *~ via* take away; *mi
ha portato un regalo* he
brought me a present; *por-*

tale un regalo take her a present; **essere portato per qc / per fare qc** have a gift for sth / for doing sth

portasci *m inv* AUTO ski rack

portata *f* GASTR course; *di cannocchiale* range; **alla ~ di** *film, libro ecc* suitable for; **a ~ di mano** within reach

portatile portable; **(computer** *m***) ~** portable (computer); **(telefono** *m***) ~** mobile (phone), *Am* cell(ular) phone

portatore *m*, **-trice** *f* bearer; *di malattia* carrier

portauovo *m inv* eggcup

portavoce *m/f inv* spokesperson

portico *m* porch; **-i** *pl* arcades

portiera *f* door; **portiere** *m* doorman; **(portinaio)** caretaker; SP goalkeeper

portinaio *m*, **-a** *f* caretaker; **portineria** *f* caretaker's flat, *Am* superintendent's apartment

porto¹ *pp* ☞ **porgere**

porto² *m posta* postage; **~ d'armi** gun licence *o Am* license

porto³ *m* MAR port

Portogallo *m* Portugal; **portoghese** *agg*, *m/f* Portuguese

portone *m* main entrance

porzione *f* share; GASTR portion

posa *f di cavi, tubi* laying; FOT exposure; FOT **mettersi in ~**

pose; **posacenere** *m inv* ashtray; **posare** 1 *v/t* put, place 2 *v/i* rest on; *fig* **~ su** rest on; *fig* **~ da intellettuale** pose as an intellectual; **posarsi** alight; **posate** *fpl* cutlery, *Am* flatware

positivo positive

posizione *f* position

possedere own, possess; **possessivo** possessive; **possesso** *m* possession

possiamo ☞ **potere**

possibile 1 *agg* possible; **il più presto ~** as soon as possible 2 *m*: **fare il ~** do everything one can; **possibilità** *f inv* possibility; *(occasione)* opportunity, chance; **possibilmente** if possible

posso ☞ **potere**

posta *f* mail, *Br anche* post; *(ufficio postale)* post office; **~ aerea** airmail; **per ~** by post; INFOR **~ elettronica** e-mail; **~ lumaca** snail mail; **postale** postal

postdatare postdate

posteggiare park; **posteggio** *m* carpark, *Am* parking lot; **~ dei taxi** taxi rank, *Am* cab stand

posteriore back *attr*, rear *attr*; *(successivo)* later

posticipare postpone; **posticipato: pagamento** *m* **~** payment in arrears

postino *m*, **-a** *f* postman, *Am* mailman; *donna* postwoman, *Am* mailwoman

posto[1] pp ☞ **porre**; ~ **che** supposing that

posto[2] m place; (*lavoro*) job, position; **mettere a ~ stanza** tidy up; ~ **macchina** parking space; ~ **finestrino / corridoio** window / aisle seat; ~ **a sedere** seat; ~ **di polizia** police station; **vado io al ~ tuo** I'll go in your place, I'll go instead of you; **fuori ~** out of place

postoperatorio postoperative

postumo posthumous

potabile fit to drink; **acqua** f ~ drinking water

potare prune

potente powerful; (*efficace*) potent; **potenza** f world power; ~ **mondiale** world power; ~ **del motore** engine power; **potenziare** strengthen

potere 1 v/i can, be able to; **non posso andare** I can't go; **non ho potuto farlo** I couldn't do it, I wasn't able to do it; **può darsi** perhaps, maybe **2** m power

poveraccio m, -a f poor thing; **poveretto** m, **poverino** m poor man; **povero 1** agg poor **2** m, -a f poor man; **donna** f poor woman; **i -i** pl the poor pl; **povertà** f poverty

pozzanghera f puddle

pozzo m well; ~ **petrolifero** oil well

PP.TT. (= **Poste e Telecomu-**

nicazioni) Italian Post Office

pranzare have lunch; **la sera** have dinner; **pranzo** m lunch; **la sera** dinner

prassi f inv standard procedure

pratica f practice; (*esperienza*) experience; (*atto*) file; **mettere in ~** put into practice; **-che** pl papers; **in ~** in practice; **avere ~ di qc** have experience of sth; **praticabile** sport which can be done; **strada** passable; **praticantato** m apprenticeship; **praticare** professione practise; **locale** frequent; ~ **molto sport** do a lot of sport; **pratico** practical; **essere ~ di conoscere bene** know a lot about

prato m meadow

preavviso m notice

precauzione f caution; **-i** pl precautions

precedente 1 agg preceding **2** m precedent; **avere dei -i penali** have a record; **precedenza** f precedence; **avere la ~** AUTO have right of way; **dare la ~** AUTO give way; Am yield; **precedere** precede

precipitare 1 v/t throw; fig rush **2** v/i fall, plunge; **precipitarsi** (*affrettarsi*) rush; **precipitazione** f (*fretta*) haste; **-i** pl **atmosferiche** atmospheric precipitation; **precipitoso** hasty

precipizio *m* precipice
precisamente precisely; **precisare** specify; **precisione** *f* precision; **con** ~ precisely; **preciso** accurate; *persona* precise
precoce precocious; *pianta* early
precotto *m* ready-made, pre-cooked
preda *f* prey
predica *f* sermon
prediletto 1 *pp* ☞ **prediligere 2** *agg* favourite, *Am* favorite; **prediligere** prefer
predire predict
predisporre draw up in advance; ~ **a** encourage; **predisposto** *pp* ☞ **predisporre**
predominare predominate; **predominio** *m* predominance
prefabbricato 1 *agg* prefabricated **2** *m* prefabricated building
prefazione *f* preface
preferenza *f* preference; **preferenziale** preferential; **preferire** prefer
preferito favourite, *Am* favorite
prefettura *f* prefecture
prefiggersi set o.s.; **prefisso 1** *pp* ☞ **prefiggersi 2** *m* TELEC code
pregare beg (**di fare** to do); *divinità* pray to; **ti prego di ascoltarmi** please listen to me
preghiera *f* request; REL

prayer
pregiato *pietra* precious
pregio *m* (*qualità*) good point
pregiudicato *m*, -a *f* previous offender; **pregiudizio** *m* prejudice
prego please; ~? I'm sorry (what did you say)?; **grazie! -** ~! thank you! - you're welcome!, not at all!
preistoria *f* prehistory; **preistorico** prehistoric
prelavaggio *m* pre-wash
prelevamento *m* *di sangue, campione* taking; FIN withdrawal; ~ **in contanti** cash withdrawal; **prelevare** *sangue, campione* take; *denaro* withdraw
prelibato exquisite
prelievo *m* (*prelevamento*) taking; FIN withdrawal; ~ **del sangue** blood sample
pre-maman 1 *agg* maternity *attr* **2** *m inv* maternity dress
prematuro premature
premeditato premeditated
premere press
premessa *f* introduction
premesso *pp* ☞ **premettere**; **premettere** say first
premiare give an award *o* prize to; *onestà, coraggio* reward; **premiazione** *f* awards ceremony; **premio** *m* prize, award; FIN premium
premura *f* (*fretta*) hurry, rush; **mettere** ~ **a qu** hurry s.o. along; **premuroso** attentive
prenatale prenatal

prendere 1 v/t take; *malattia,
treno* catch; **cosa prendi?**
what will you have; **andare / venire a ~ qu** fetch
s.o.; **~ il sole** sunbathe; **prendersela** get upset (**per**
about; **con** with); **che ti
prende?** what's got into
you? **2** v/i: **~ a destra** turn
right; **prendisole** m inv sun-
dress

prenotare book, reserve;
prenotazione f booking,
reservation

preoccupare worry; **preoc-
cuparsi** worry; **preoccupato** worried; **preoccupazione** f worry

preparare prepare; **prepararsi** get ready (**a** to), prepare
(**a** to); **preparativi** mpl pre-
parations; **preparazione** f
preparation

preposizione f preposition

prepotente domineering; *bisogno* pressing

presa f grip, hold; EL **~ di corrente** socket, Am outlet; **essere alle -e con qc** be grap-
pling with sth

presagio m omen

presbite far-sighted

prescindere: **~ da** have nothing to do with

prescritto pp ☞ **prescrivere**;
prescrivere prescribe

presentare *documenti, biglie-
to* show, present; *domanda*
submit; *scuse* make; TEA present; (*contenere*) contain; (*far

conoscere*) introduce (**a** to);
presentarsi look; (*esporre*)
show itself; *occasione* occur;
presentatore m, **-trice** f presenter; **presentazione** f
presentation; *di richiesta*
submission; **fare le -i** make
the introductions; **presente
1** agg present; **hai ~ il negozio …?** do you know the
shop …? **2** m present; **i -i**
pl those present

presentimento m premoni-
tion

presenza f presence; **alla** (o
in) **~ di** in the presence of

presepe m, **presepio** m na-
tivity (scene)

preservare protect, keep (**da**
from); **preservativo** m condom

presidente m/f chairman;
POL President; **~ del Consi-
glio (dei ministri)** Prime
Minister

preso pp ☞ **prendere**

pressappoco more or less

pressione f pressure; **far ~ su**
put pressure on, pressure

presso 1 prp (*vicino a*) near;
nella sede di on the premises
of; *posta* care of; **vive ~ i genitori** he lives with his parents; **lavoro ~ la FIAT** I work
for Fiat **2** m: **nei -i di** in the
vicinity of; **pressoché** almost

prestare lend; **~ ascolto / aiuto a qu** listen to /
help s.o.; **prestarsi** offer

one's services; (*essere adatto*) lend itself (*a* to); **prestazione** *f* service; **prestito** *m* loan; **in ~** on loan; **dare in ~** lend; **prendere in ~** borrow

presto (*fra poco*) soon; (*in fretta*) quickly; (*di buon'ora*) early; **a ~!** see you soon!; **far ~** be quick

presumere presume; **presuntuoso** presumptuous

prete *m* priest

pretendere claim; **pretesa** *f* pretension

pretesto *m* pretext

pretura *f* magistrates' court, *Am* circuit court

prevalenza *f* prevalence; **in ~** prevalently; **prevalere** prevail

prevedere foresee, predict; *tempo* forecast; *di legge* provide for; **prevedibile** predictable

prevendita *f* advance sale

prevenire *domanda, desiderio* anticipate; (*evitare*) prevent; **preventivo 1** *agg* preventive **2** *m* estimate; **prevenzione** *f* prevention

previdenza *f* foresight; **~ sociale** social security, *Am* welfare

previsione *f* forecast; **-i** *pl* **del tempo** weather forecast; **previsto** *pp* ☞ **prevedere**

prezioso precious

prezzemolo *m* parsley

prezzo *m* price; **a buon ~** cheap

prigione *f* prison; **prigioniero** *m*, **-a** *f* prisoner

prima[1] *avv* before; (*in primo luogo*) first; **~ di** before; **~ di fare qc** before doing sth; **~ o poi** sooner or later; **~ che** before; **quanto ~** as soon as possible

prima[2] *f* FERR first class; AUTO first; TEA first night

primavera *f* spring

primitivo primitive; (*iniziale*) original

primizia *f* early crop

primo 1 *agg* first **2** *m*, **-a** *f* first; **ai -i del mese** at the beginning of the month; **sulle -e** in the beginning, at first **3** *m* GASTR first course, starter; **primogenito 1** *agg* firstborn **2** *m*, **-a** *f* first-born

principale 1 *agg* main **2** *m* boss

principato *m* principality; **principe** *m* prince; **principessa** *f* princess

principiante *m/f* beginner; **principio** *m* start, beginning; (*norma*) principle; **al ~** at the start, in the beginning; **per ~** as a matter of principle

privare deprive (*di* of); **privarsi** deprive o.s. (*di* of)

privatizzare privatize; **privato 1** *agg* private; **in ~** in private **2** *m* private citizen

privilegiare favour, *Am* favor, prefer; **privilegiato** privileged; **privilegio** *m* privilege

privo: ~ **di** lacking in; ~ **di grassi** fat-free

pro 1 m inv: **i ~ e i contro** the pros and cons; **a che ~?** what's the point? **2** prp for; ~ **capite** per capita, each

probabile probable; **probabilità** f inv probability

problema m problem

proboscide f trunk

procedere carry on; fig (agire) proceed; **procedimento** m process

procedura f procedure; DIR proceedings

processare try

processione f procession

processo m process; DIR trial

procinto m: **essere in ~ di** be about to

proclamare proclaim

procura f power of attorney; **Procura di Stato** public prosecutor's office; **per ~** by proxy; **procurare** (causare) cause; ~ **qc a qu** cause s.o. sth; **procurarsi** get hold of; **procuratore** m, **-trice** f person with power of attorney; DIR lawyer for the prosecution; ~ **generale** Attorney General

prodotto 1 pp ☞ **produrre 2** m product; **produco** ☞ **produrre**; **produrre** produce; danni cause; **produttivo** productive; **produttore** m, **-trice** f producer; **produzione** f production

prof. ssa (= **professoressa**)

Prof. (= Professor)

profanare desecrate

professionale professional; scuola, corso vocational; **professione** f profession; **professionista** m/f professional; **libero** ~ self-employed person

professore m, **-essa** f teacher; d'università professor

proficuo profitable

profilattico prophylactic

profilo m profile

profitto m (vantaggio) advantage

profondità f inv depth; FOT ~ **di campo** depth of field; **profondo** deep

profugo m, **-a** f refugee

profumare perfume; **profumeria** f perfume shop; **profumo** m perfume

progettare plan; **progetto** m design; di costruzione project; ~ **di legge** bill

prognosi f inv prognosis

programma m programme, Am program; INFOR program; ~ **televisivo** TV programme; **avere in ~** have planned; **programmare** plan; INFOR program; **programmatore** m, **-trice** f programmer; **programmazione** f programming; FIN ~ **economica** economic planning; INFOR **linguaggio** m **di** ~ programming language

progredire progress; **progressivo** progressive; progresso *m* progress; **fare -i** make progress

proibire ban, prohibit; **~ a qu di fare qc** forbid s.o. to do sth

proiettare throw; *film* screen, show; *fig* project; **proiettile** *m* projectile

proiettore *m* projector; **~ per diapositive** slide projector

proletario 1 *agg* proletariat **2** *m* proletarian

pro loco *f inv* local tourist board

prologo *m* prologue

prolunga *f* EL extension cord; **prolungare** extend; *nel tempo* prolong, extend; **prolungarsi** *di strada* extend; *di riunione* go on

promemoria *m inv* memo

promessa *f* promise; **promesso** *pp* ☞ **promettere**; **promettere** promise; **~ bene** look promising

promontorio *m* promontory, headland

promosso *pp* ☞ **promuovere**; **promozione** *f* promotion; EDU year; **~ delle vendite** sales promotion; **promuovere** promote; EDU move up

pronome *m* pronoun

prontezza *f* readiness, promptness; *(rapidità)* speediness, promptness; **~ di spirito** quick thinking; **pronto** *(preparato)* ready (*a fare qc* to do sth; *per qc*

for sth); TELEC **~!** hello!; **~ soccorso** first aid; *in ospedale* accident and emergency, A&E

pronuncia *f* pronunciation; **pronunciare** pronounce; **pronunciarsi** give an opinion (*su* on)

propaganda *f* propaganda; **propagare** propagate; *fig* spread; **propagarsi** spread *(anche fig)*

propenso inclined (*a fare qc* to do sth)

propongo ☞ **proporre**; **proporre** propose; **proporsi** stand (*come* as); **~ di fare qc** intend to do sth

proporzionato in proportion (*a* to); **proporzione** *f* proportion; **in ~** in proportion (*a, con* to)

proposito *m* intention; **a ~** by the way; **a ~ di** about, with reference to; **di ~** on purpose

proposizione *f* GRAM sentence

proposta *f* proposal; **proposto** *pp* ☞ **proporre**

proprietà *f inv* property; *diritto* ownership; **proprietario** *m*, **-a** *f* owner

proprio 1 *agg* own; *(caratteristico)* typical; *(adatto)* proper; **nome ~** proper noun; **amor ~** pride **2** *avv* *(davvero)* really **3** *m* *(beni)* personal property; **lavorare in ~** be self-employed

propulsore *m* propeller

prora *f* prow

proroga *f* postponement; (*prolungamento*) extension; **prorogare** (*rinviare*) postpone; (*prolungare*) extend

prosa *f* prose

prosciogliere release; DIR acquit

prosciugare drain; *di sole* dry up

prosciutto *m* ham; ~ **cotto** cooked ham; ~ **crudo** salted air-dried ham

proseguimento *m* continuation; **proseguire 1** *v/t* continue **2** *v/i* continue, carry on

prospettiva *f* perspective; (*panorama*) view; (*possibilità*) prospect; *fig* point of view

prospetto *m disegno* elevation; (*facciata*) facade; (*tabella*) table

prossimamente shortly, soon; **prossimità** *f* inv proximity; **in ~ di** near; **prossimo 1** *agg* close; **la -a volta** the next time **2** *m* fellow human being

prostituta *f* prostitute

protagonista *m/f* protagonist

proteggere protect (*da* from)

proteina *f* protein

protesi *f inv* prosthesis; ~ **dentaria** false teeth

protesta *f* protest; **protestante**, *m/f* Protestant; **protestare** protest

protetto *pp* ☞ **proteggere**; **protezione** *f* protection

prova *f* (*esame*) test; (*tentativo*) attempt; (*testimonianza*) proof; *di abito* fitting; SP heat; TEA **-e** *pl* rehearsal; TEA **-e** *pl* **generali** dress rehearsal; **mettere alla ~** put to the test; **provare** test, try out; *vestito* try (on); (*dimostrare*) prove; TEA rehearse; **~ a fare qc** try to do sth

provengo ☞ **provenire**; **provenienza** *f* origin; **provenire** come (*da* from); **proventi** *mpl* income

proverbio *m* proverb

provetta *f* test-tube

provincia *f* province; **provinciale 1** *agg* provincial **2** *m/f* provincial **3** *f* A road, *Am* highway

provino *m* screen-test; (*campione*) sample

provocante provocative; **provocare** (*causare*) cause; (*sfidare*) provoke; *invidia* arouse

provvedere 1 *v/t* provide (*di* with) **2** *v/i:* ~ **a** take care of; **provvedimento** *m* measure

provvigione *f* commission

provvisorio provisional

provvista *f:* **far ~ di qc** stock up on sth; **provvisto 1** *pp* ☞ **provvedere 2** *agg:* **essere ~ di** be provided with

prozio *m*, **-a** *f* great-uncle; *donna* great-aunt

prua *f* prow

prudente careful, cautious;

prudenza *f* care, caution
prudere: **mi prude la mano** my hand itches
prugna *f* plum; **~ secca** prune
prurito *m* itch
P.S. (= **Pubblica Sicurezza**) police; (= **post scriptum**) PS (= post scriptum)
pseudo ... pseudo ...
pseudonimo *m* pseudonym
psicanalisi *f* psychoanalysis; psicanalista *m/f* psychoanalyst
psiche *f* psyche
psichiatra *m/f* psychiatrist
psicologia *f* psychology; psicologico psychological; psicologo *m*, -a *f* psychologist
psicosi *f inv* psychosis
psicoterapia *f* psychotherapy
P.T.P. (= **Posto Telefonico Pubblico**) public telephone
pubblicare publish; pubblicazione *f* publication; **-i** *pl* (**matrimoniali**) banns; pubblicità *f inv* publicity; annuncio advert; **fare ~ a** evento publicize; prodotto advertise; pubblicitario **1** *agg* advertising **2** *m*, -a *f* publicist; pubblico **1** *agg* public **2** *m* public; (spettatori) audience; **in ~** in public
pube *m* pubis
pubertà *f* puberty
pudore *m* modesty
pugilato *m* boxing; pugile *m* boxer
pugnalare stab; pugnale *m* dagger

pugno *m* fist; (colpo) punch; quantità handful; **fare a -i** come to blows
pulce *f* flea
pulcino *m* chick
puledro *m*, -a *f* colt; femmina filly
pulire clean; pulito clean; fig cleaned-out; pulitura *f* cleaning; **~ a secco** dry cleaning; pulizia *f* cleanliness; **fare le -e** do the cleaning
pullman *m inv* bus, Br anche coach
pullover *m inv* pullover
pullulare: **~ di** be swarming with
pulpito *m* pulpit
pulsante *m* button; pulsazione *f* pulsation
pungere prick; di ape sting; pungiglione *m* sting
punibile punishable (**con** by); punire punish; punizione *f* punishment; SP (**calcio** *m* di) **~** free kick
punta *f* di spillo, coltello point; di dita, lingua tip; GEOG peak; fig touch, trace; puntare **1** *v/t* pin (**su** to); (dirigere) point (**verso** at); (scommettere) bet (**su** on); fig **~ i piedi** dig one's heels in **2** *v/i:* **~ a** successo aspire to; puntata *f* instalment, Am instalment; (scommessa) bet
punteggiatura *f* punctuation; punteggio *m* score
puntiglioso punctilious

puntina f di giradischi stylus; ~ (**da disegno**) drawing pin, Am thumbtack; **puntino** m dot; **a** ~ perfectly; **punto 1** pp ☞ **pungere 2** m point; MED, (**maglia**) stitch; ~ **di vista** point of view; ~ **cardinale** point of the compass; **fino a che** ~ **sei arrivato?** how far have you got?; **alle dieci in** ~ at ten o'clock exactly o on the dot; ~ (**fermo**) full stop, Am period; **due -i** colon; ~ **e virgola** semi-colon; ~ **esclamativo** exclamation mark, Am exclamation point; ~ **interrogativo** question mark; **essere sul** ~ **di fare qc** be on the point of doing sth

puntuale punctual; **puntualità** f punctuality; **puntualizzare** make clear

puntura f di ape sting; di ago prick

può, puoi ☞ **potere**

pupazzo m puppet; ~ **di neve** snowman

pupilla f pupil

purché provided

pure 1 cong even if; (**tuttavia**) (and) yet **2** avv too, as well; **pur di** in order to; **venga** ~ **avanti!** do come in!

purè m inv purée

purga f purge; **purgante** m laxative

puro pure

purtroppo unfortunately

pus m pus

pustola f pimple

puttana f P whore

puzza f stink; **puzzare** stink (**di** of); **puzzo** m stink; **puzzola** f ZO polecat; **puzzolente** stinking

p.v. (= **prossimo venturo**) next

Q

q (= **quintale**) 100 kilos

qua here; **passa di** ~ come this way; **al di** ~ **di** on this side of

quaderno m exercise book

quadrante m quadrant; di orologio dial

quadrare di conti balance; fig **i conti non quadrano** there's something fishy going on; **quadrato** m/agg square

quadrifoglio m four-leaf clover

quadro 1 agg square **2** m painting, picture; MAT square; **a -i** check attr, Am checkered

quadruplo m/agg quadruple

quaggiù down here

quaglia f quail

qualche a few; (**un certo**)

some; *interrogativo* any; ~ **cosa** something; ~ **volta** sometime; *alcune volte* a few times; *a volte* sometimes; *in ~ luogo* somewhere; *in ~ modo* somehow

qualcosa something; *interrogativo* anything, something; **qualcos'altro** something else; ~ **da mangiare** something to eat; ~ **di bello** something beautiful

qualcuno someone, somebody; *in interrogazioni anche* anyone, anybody; *c'è ~?* is anybody there?

quale 1 *agg* what; ~ *libro vuoi?* which book do you want? **2** *pron: prendi un libro –~?* take a book – which one?; *il / la ~ persona* who, that; *cosa* which, that; *la persona della ~ stai parlando* the person you're talking about **3** *avv* as

qualifica f qualification; **qualificare** qualify; (*definire*) describe; **qualificarsi** give one's name (**come** as); *a esame, gara* qualify; **qualificato** qualified

qualità f *inv* quality; *di prima ~* top quality

qualora in the event that

qualsiasi any; *non importa quale* whatever; ~ **persona** anyone; ~ **cosa faccia** whatever I do

qualunque any; *uno ~* any one; ~ **cosa** anything; ~ **co-sa faccia** whatever I do; *in ~ stagione* whatever the season

qualvolta: *ogni ~* every time that

quando when; *da ~?* how long?; ~ **vengo** when I come; *ogni volta che* whenever I come

quantità f *inv* quantity, amount; **quantitativo** m quantity, amount

quanto 1 *agg* how much; *con nomi plurali* how many; *tutti -i pl* every single one *sg*; *-i pl* how many are we? *quanto ne abbiamo oggi?* what is the date today? **2** *avv*: ~ **dura ancora?** how long will it go on for?; ~ **a me** as for me; ~ **costa?** how much is it; *in ~* since, because; *per ~ ne sappia* as far as I know

quaranta forty

quarantena f quarantine

quarantenne 1 *agg* forty or so **2** m/f person in his / her forties; **quarantesimo** fortieth

quaresima f Lent

quarta f AUTO fourth (gear)

quartiere m district; MIL quarters; ~ **generale** headquarters

quarto 1 *agg* fourth **2** m fourth; (*quarta parte*) quarter; ~ **d'ora** quarter of an hour

quarzo m quartz

quasi almost; ~ **mai** hardly ever

quassù up here

quattordicesimo fourteenth; **quattordici** fourteen

quattrini *mpl* money

quattro four; **farsi in ~ per fare** qc go to a lot of trouble to do sth; **quattrocchi: a ~ in** private; **quattrocento 1** *agg* four hundred **2** *m*: **il Quattrocento** the fifteenth century; **quattromila** four thousand

quegli, quei ↪ **quello**

quello 1 *agg* that, *pl* those **2** *pron* that (one), *pl* those (ones); **~ che** the one that; **tutto ~ che** all (that), everything (that)

quercia *f* oak

querela *f* legal action; **sporgere ~ contro** s.o take legal action against s.o

quesito *m* question

questi ↪ **questo**

questionario *m* questionnaire; **questione** *f* question; **è fuori ~** it is out of the question

questo 1 *agg* this, *pl* these **2** *pron* this (one), *pl* these (ones); **~ qui** this one here; **per ~** for that reason; **-a**

poi! well I'm blowed

questore *m* chief of police; **questura** *f* police headquarters

qui here; **~ vicino** near here; **passa di ~!** come this way!; **di ~ a un mese** a month from now

quiete *f* peace and quiet

quindi 1 *avv* then **2** *cong* therefore

quindicesimo fifteenth; **quindici** fifteen; **quindicina** *f*: **una ~** about fifteen; **quinta** *f* AUTO fifth (gear); TEA **le -e** the wings; **quintale** *m* hundred kilos; **quinto** fifth

quota *f* share, quota; (*altitudine*) altitude; **quotare** (*valutare*) value; FIN **quotate in borsa** listed o quoted on the Stock Exchange; **quotato** respected; **quotazione** *f* di *azioni* value, price; **~ d'acquisto** bid price; **~ di vendita** offer price

quotidianamente daily; **quotidiano 1** *agg* daily **2** *m* daily (newspaper)

quoziente *m*: **~ d'intelligenza** IQ

R

rabarbaro *m* rhubarb

rabbia *f* rage; (*stizza*) anger; MED rabies *sg*; **fare ~ a** qu make s.o. angry

rabbino *m* rabbi

rabbioso *gesto*, *sguardo* of rage; *cane* rabid

rabbrividire shudder; *per paura* shiver

raccapricciante appalling

raccattare (*tirar su*) pick up

racchetta *f* racquet; **~ da sci** ski pole

raccogliere (*tirar su*) pick up; (*radunare*) gather; AGR harvest; **raccoglitore** *m* ring binder; **~ del vetro** bottle bank; **raccolgo** ☞ **raccogliere**; **raccolta** *f* collection; AGR harvest; **fare la ~ di francobolli** collect stamps; **raccolto 1** *pp* ☞ **raccogliere 2** *m* harvest

raccomandabile: un tipo poco ~ a shady character; **raccomandare 1** *v/t* recommend **2** *v/i*: **~ a qu di fare qc** tell s.o. to do sth; **raccomandata** *f* recorded delivery (letter), *Am* certified mail; **raccomandazione** *f* recommendation

raccontare tell; **racconto** *m* story

raccordo *m* TEC connection; *strada* slip road, *Am* ramp; **~ anulare** ring road, *Am* beltway

radar *m inv* radar

raddoppiare double; *sforzi* redouble

raddrizzare straighten

radere shave; *sfiorare* skim; **~ al suolo** raze to the ground; **radersi** shave

radiare strike off

radiatore *m* radiator

radicale radical; **radice** *f* root; **~ quadrata** square root

radio *f inv* radio; (*stazione*) radio station; **radioascoltatore** *m*, **-trice** *f* (radio) listener; **radioattività** *f* radioactivity; **radioattivo** radioactive; **radiocronaca** *f* (radio) commentary; **radiofonico** radio *attr*; **radiografia** *f* X-ray; **radiosveglia** *f* clock radio; **radiotaxi** *m inv* taxi, cab; **radiotelefono** *m* radio; **radioterapia** *f* radiation treatment; **radiotrasmittente** *f apparecchio* radio transmitter; *stazione* radio station

rado *pettine* wide-toothed; *alberi, capelli* sparse; **di ~** seldom

radunare, radunarsi collect, gather; **raduno** *m* rally

rafano *m* horseradish

raffermo *pane* stale

raffica *f* gust; *di mitragliatrice* burst

raffigurare represent

raffinatezza *f* refinement; **raffinato** *fig* refined; **raffineria** *f* refinery

rafforzare strengthen

raffreddare cool; **raffreddarsi** cool down; MED catch cold; **raffreddato: essere ~** have a cold; **raffreddore** *m* cold; **~ da fieno** hay fever

rag. (= **ragioniere**) accountant

ragazza *f* girl; **la mia ~** my girlfriend

ragazzo *m* boy; **il mio ~** my boyfriend

raggio *m* ray; MAT radius; **~**

d'azione range; *fig* duties; *-i pl* **X** X-rays

raggirare fool, take in; **raggiro** *m* trick

raggiungere *luogo* reach, get to; *persona* join; *scopo* achieve

raggomitolarsi curl up

raggrinzito wrinkled

ragionamento *m* reasoning; **ragionare** reason; **ragione** *f* reason; (*diritto*) right; **aver** ~ be right; **dare** ~ *a qu* admit that s.o. is right; **ragioneria** *f* book-keeping; EDU *high school specializing in business studies*; **ragionevole** reasonable; **ragioniere** *m*, *-a f* accountant

ragnatela *f* spider's web; **ragno** *m* spider

ragù *m inv* meat sauce for pasta

rallegramenti *mpl* congratulations; **rallegrare** cheer up; **rallegrarsi** cheer up; ~ *con qu di qc* congratulate s.o. on sth

rallentare slow down; **rallentatore**: *al* ~ in slow motion

ramanzina *f* lecture

rame *m* copper

rammaricarsi be disappointed (*di* at)

rammendare darn

ramo *m* branch; **ramoscello** *m* twig

rampa *f* flight; ~ *d'accesso* slip road, *Am* ramp; **rampicante 1** *agg* climbing; **pianta**

f ~ climber **2** *m* climber

rampone *m* crampon

rana *f* frog

rancore *m* rancour, *Am* rancor

randagio stray

rango *m* rank

rannicchiarsi huddle up

rannuvolarsi cloud over

ranocchio *m* frog

rapa *f* turnip

rapace 1 *m* bird of prey **2** *agg fig* predatory

rapida *f* rapids; **rapidità** *f* speed, rapidity; **rapido 1** *agg* quick, fast; *crescita, aumento* rapid **2** *m* (*treno m*) ~ intercity train

rapimento *m* abduction, kidnapping

rapina *f* robbery; **rapinare** rob; **rapinatore** *m*, *-trice f* robber

rapire abduct, kidnap; **rapitore** *m*, *-trice f* abductor, kidnapper

rappacificazione *f* reconciliation

rapporto *m* (*resoconto*) report; (*relazione*) relationship; (*nesso*) connection; *in* ~ *a* in connection with

rappresentante *m/f* representative; **rappresentanza** *f* agency; ~ *esclusiva* sole agency; **rappresentare** represent; TEA perform; **rappresentazione** *f* representation; TEA performance

rarità *f inv* rarity; **raro** rare

rasare shave; **rasatura** f shaving

raschiare scrape; *ruggine*, *sporco* scrape off; **raschiarsi**: ~ *la gola* clear one's throat

rasentare (*sfiorare*) scrape; fig (*avvicinarsi*) verge on; ~ *il muro* hug the wall; **rasente**: ~ *a* very close to

rasoio m razor

rassegna f festival; *di pittura ecc* exhibition; *passare in ~* review; **rassegnarsi** resign o.s (*a* to)

rasserenarsi *di tempo* clear up

rassicurare reassure

rassomigliare: ~ *a* look like, resemble; **rassomigliarsi** look like o resemble each other

rastrellare rake; fig comb; **rastrelliera** f rack; ~ *per biciclette* bike rack; **rastrello** m rake

rata f instalment, *Am* installment; *a-e* in instalments; **rateale**: *pagamento* m ~ payment in instalments o *Am* installments; *vendita* f ~ hire purchase, *Am* installment plan

ratto m ZO rat

rattoppare patch; **rattoppo** m patch

rattrappito stiff

rattristare sadden; **rattristarsi** become sad

raucedine f hoarseness; **rau-co** hoarse

ravanello m radish

ravioli mpl ravioli sg

ravvicinare move closer; (*riappacificare*) reconcile

ravvivare revive

razionale rational; **razionare** ration; **razione** f ration

razza f race; fig sort, kind; ZO breed

razzia f raid

razziale racial; **razzismo** m racism; **razzista** agg, m/f racist

razzo m rocket

re m inv king; MUS D

reagire react (*a* to)

reale (*vero*) real; (*regale*) royal; **realista** m/f realist

realizzabile feasible; **realizzare** realize; *progetto* carry out; **realizzarsi** *di sogno* come true; *di persona* find, find fulfilment o *Am* fulfillment

realmente really; **realtà** f inv reality; *in* ~ in fact, actually

reato m (criminal) offence o *Am* offense

reattore m AVIA jet engine; *aereo* jet; ~ *nucleare* nuclear reactor; **reazione** f reaction

recapitare deliver; **recapito** m delivery; (*indirizzo*) address; ~ *telefonico* phone number

recarsi go

recensione f review; **recensire** review

recente recent; **recentemen-**

215

remoto

te recently

recintare enclose; **recinto** *m* enclosure; **steccato** fence

recipiente *m* container, recipient

reciproco mutual, reciprocal

recita *f* performance; **recitare 1** *v/t* recite; TEA play (the part of); *preghiera* say **2** *v/i* act

reclamare 1 *v/i* complain **2** *v/t* claim

réclame *f inv* advert; **reclamizzare** advertise

reclamo *m* complaint

reclusione *f* seclusion

record *m inv* record

recuperare ☞ *ricuperare*

redatto *pp* ☞ *redigere*; **redattore** *m*, **-trice** *f* editor; *di articolo* writer; **~ capo** editor-in-chief

reddito *m* income

redigere *testo, articolo* write; *lista* draw up

redini *fpl* reins

referendum *m inv* referendum

referenza *f* reference

referto *m* (official) report

refettorio *m* refectory

refurtiva *f* stolen property

regalare give; **regalino** *m* little gift *o* present; **regalo** *m* gift, present

regata *f* (boat) race

reggere 1 *v/t* (*sostenere*) support; (*tenere in mano*) hold; (*sopportare*) bear **2** *v/i* *di ragionamento* stand up; **reg-**

gersi stand

reggia *f* palace

reggipetto *m*, **reggiseno** *m* bra, *Am* brassiere

regia *f* production; *di film* direction

régime *m* régime; MED diet

regina *f* queen

regionale regional; **regione** *f* region

regista *m/f* director; TEA producer

registrare record; (*rilevare*) show, register; **registratore** *m*: **~ (a cassetta)** cassette recorder; **registrazione** *f* recording; **registro** *m* register

regno *m* kingdom; *periodo* reign

regola *f* rule; **in ~** in order; **regolabile** adjustable, **regolamento** *m* regulation; **regolare 1** *v/t* regulate; *spese* cut down on; TEC adjust; *questione* sort out; *conto, debito* settle **2** *agg* regular

regredire regress

relativo relative (**a** to); (*corrispondente*) relevant; **relatore** *m*, **-trice** *f* speaker; **relazione** *f* relationship; (*esposizione*) report; **avere una ~ con qu** have a relationship with s.o.

religione *f* religion; **religiosa** *f* nun; **religioso 1** *agg* religious **2** *m* monk

relitto *m* wreck

remare row; **remo** *m* oar

remoto remote

remunerare pay; **remunera-zione** *f* payment, remuneration

rendere (*restituire*) give back, return; (*fruttare*) yield; *senso, idea* render; ~ **felice** make happy; **rendimento** *m di macchina, impiegato* performance; **rendita** *f* income

rene *m* kidney

reparto *m* department

repentaglio: mettere a ~ risk, endanger

reperibile available; **difficilmente ~** difficult to find; **reperire** find; **reperto** *m* find; DIR exhibit

replica *f* replica; TV, TEA repeat; (*risposta*) answer, reply; **replicare** repeat; (*ribattere*) reply, answer

reportage *m inv* report

represso *pp* ☞ **reprimere**; **reprimere** repress

repubblica *f* republic

reputare consider; **reputarsi** consider o.s.; **reputazione** *f* reputation

requisire requisition; **requisito** *m* requirement

resa *f* surrender; (*restituzione*) return; **~ dei conti** settling of accounts

residence *m inv* block of service flats *o Am* apartments; **residente** resident; **residenza** *f* (official) address; (*sede*) seat; (*soggiorno*) stay; **residenziale** residential; **zona** *f* **~** residential area

residuo *m* remainder

resina *f* resin

resistente sturdy, strong; **resistere** *al freddo ecc* stand up to; (*opporsi*) resist

reso *pp* ☞ **rendere**

resoconto *m* report

respingere *richiesta* reject, turn down; *nemico, attacco* repel; **respinto** *pp* ☞ **respingere**

respirare 1 *v/t* breathe (in) **2** *v/i* breathe; *fig* draw breath; **respiratore** *m* respirator; *per apnea* snorkel; **respirazione** *f* breathing; **~ artificiale** artificial respiration; **respiro** *m* breathing; **trattenere il ~** hold one's breath

responsabile responsible (**di** for); DIR liable (**di** for); **responsabilità** *f inv* responsibility; DIR liability

ressa *f* crowd

restare stay, remain; (*avanzare*) be left; **~ indietro** stay behind; **~ perplesso / vedovo** be puzzled / widowed

restaurare restore; **restauro** *m* restoration

restituire return; *salute* restore

resto *m* rest, remainder; (*soldi*) change; **-i** *pl* remains; **del ~** anyway, besides

restringere narrow; *vestito* take in; **restringersi** *di strada* narrow; *di stoffa* shrink

rete *f per pescare ecc* net; SP goal; INFOR, TELEC, FERR network

retina f ANAT retina

retribuire pay; **retribuzione** f payment

retroattivo retroactive

retrobottega m inv back shop

retrocedere retreat; fig lose ground

retrodatare backdate

retromarcia f AUTO reverse (gear)

retroscena mpl fig background

retrospettivo mostra retrospective

retroterra m inv hinterland

retrovisivo: specchietto m ~ rearview mirror

retta[1] f somma fee

retta[2] f MAT straight line

retta[3] f: **dare ~ a qu** listen to s.o.

rettangolare rectangular; **rettangolo** m rectangle

rettificare correct

rettile m reptile

rettilineo straight

rettore m rector

reumatismo m rheumatism

revisionare conti audit; automobile MOT; testo revise; **revisione** f di conti audit; di automobile MOT; di testo revision

revoca f repeal; **revocare** repeal

ri- re-

riabilitazione f rehabilitation

riacquistare get back, regain; casa buy back

riagganciare TELEC hang up

riallacciare refasten; TELEC reconnect

rialzare (alzare di nuovo) pick up; (aumentare) raise, increase; **rialzo** m rise, increase

rianimare speranze, entusiasmo revive; (rallegrare) cheer up; MED resuscitate; **rianimazione** f resuscitation; **centro** m **di ~** intensive care unit

riapertura f reopening; **riaprire** reopen

riassumere re-employ; (riepilogare) summarize; **riassunto** 1 pp ☞ **riassumere** 2 m summary

riavere get back, regain

ribaltabile folding; **ribaltare** overturn

ribassare 1 v/t lower 2 v/i fall, drop; **ribasso** m fall, drop; (sconto) discount

ribattere (replicare) answer back; (insistere) insist

ribellarsi rebel (a against); **ribelle** 1 agg rebellious 2 m/f rebel; **ribellione** f rebellion

ribes m inv currant; **~ nero** blackcurrant; **~ rosso** redcurrant

ribrezzo m horror; **fare ~ a** disgust

ricadere fall; (cadere di nuovo) fall back; fig relapse; **ricaduta** f relapse

ricamare embroider

ricambiare change; (contrac-

cambiare) return, reciprocate; **ricambio** *m* change;
(*sostituzione*) replacement;
pezzo (spare) part

ricamo *m* embroidery

ricapitolare sum up, recapit-
ulate

ricaricare *batteria* recharge

ricattare blackmail; **ricatto** *m*
blackmail

ricavare derive; *denaro* get;
ricavato *m di vendita* proceeds

ricchezza *f* wealth

riccio[1] *m* ZO hedgehog; ~ *di*
mare sea urchin

riccio[2] **1** *agg* curly **2** *m* curl

ricciolo *m* curl

ricco 1 *agg* rich; ~ *di* rich in **2**
m, -*a f* rich man / woman

ricerca *f* research; *di persona*
scomparsa, informazione ecc
search (*di* for); EDU project;
alla ~ *di* in search of; **ricer-
care** (*cercare di nuovo*) look
again for; (*cercare con cura*)
search for; **ricercato 1** *agg*
oggetto, *artista* sought-after
2 *m* man wanted by the police

ricetta *f* prescription; GASTR
recipe

ricevere receive; *di medico*
see patients; **ricevimento**
m receipt; *festa* reception; **ricevitore** *m* receiver; **ricevuta** *f* receipt

richiamare (*chiamare di nuovo*) call again; (*chiamare indietro*) call back; (*attirare*)

draw; *fig* (*rimproverare*) reprimand

richiedere ask for again; (*ne-
cessitare di*) take, require; *documento* apply for; **richiesta**
f request (*di* for); **a** (*a
su*) ~ *di* at the request of; **richiesto** *pp* ← **richiedere**

riciclare recycle; **riciclabile**
recyclable

ricompensa *f* reward; **ricompensare** reward (**qu di qc**
s.o. for sth)

riconciliarsi be reconciled

riconoscente grateful; **riconoscenza** *f* gratitude; **riconoscere** recognise; **riconoscimento** *m* recognition

riconquistare reconquer

ricordare remember; (*menzionare*) mention; ~ **qc a qu**
remind s.o. of sth; **ricordarsi**
remember (**di qc** sth; **di fare
qc** to do sth); **ricordo** *m*
memory; *oggetto* memento;
~ (**di viaggio**) souvenir

ricorrenza *f* recurrence; *di
evento* anniversary; **ricorrere** *di date*, *di festa* take place;
~ **a qu** turn to s.o.; ~ **a qc**
have recourse to sth; **ricorso
1** *pp* ← **ricorrere 2** *m* DIR appeal; **avere** ~ **a** avvocato, *medico* see

ricostruire rebuild; *fig* reconstruct; **ricostruzione** *f* re-
building; *fig* reconstruction

ricotta *f* ricotta, *soft cheese
made from ewe's milk*

ricoverare admit; **ricovero** *m*

in ospedale admission; (*rifugio*) shelter
ricreazione *f* recreation; *nelle scuole* break, *Am* recess
ricredersi change one's mind
ricuperare 1 *v/t* get back, recover; *libertà, fiducia* regain; *spazio* gain; *tempo* make up **2** *v/i* catch up; **ricupero** *m* recovery; **~ del centro storico** development of the old town; **~ di debiti** debt collection; EDU **corso m di ~** remedial course; **materiale m di ~** scrap; SP **partita f di ~** rescheduled match
ridare (*restituire*) give back, return; *fiducia, forze* restore
ridere laugh (*di* at)
ridicolo 1 *agg* ridiculous **2** *m* ridicule
ridimensionare downsize; *fig* get into perspective
ridotto 1 *pp* ↗ **ridurre 2** *agg:* **a prezzi -i** at reduced prices; **riduco** ↗ **ridurre**; **ridurre** reduce (**a** to); *prezzi* reduce, cut; *personale* reduce, cut back; **ridursi** decrease; **~ a fare qc** be reduced to doing sth; **~ male** be in a bad way; **~ in miseria** ruin o.s.; **riduzione** *f* reduction, cut
riempire fill (up); *formulario* fill in
rientrare come back; *a casa* come home; **questo non rientrava nei miei piani** that didn't come in to the plan; **rientro** *m* return; **al tuo ~**

when you get back
rifare do again; (*rinnovare*) do up; *stanza* tidy up; *letto* make; **rifarsi** rebuild; *casa* renovate; *guardaroba* replace; **~ di qc** make up for sth
riferimento *m* reference; **riferire** report; **riferirsi:** **~ a** refer to
rifiutare, rifiutarsi refuse; **rifiuto** *m* refusal; **-i** *pl* waste, refuse; (*spazzatura*) rubbish
riflessione *f anche* FIS reflection; **riflessivo** thoughtful; GRAM reflexive; **riflesso 1** *pp* ↗ **riflettere 2** *m* reflection; (*gesto istintivo*) reflex (movement); **riflettere 1** *v/t* reflect **2** *v/i* think; **~ su qc** think about sth, reflect on sth; **riflettersi** be reflected; **riflettore** *m* floodlight
riforma *f* reform; **riformare** (*rifare*) re-shape, re-form; (*cambiare*) reform; MIL declare unfit
rifornimento *m* AVIA refuelling, *Am* refueling; **-i** *pl* supplies; **fare ~ di cibo** stock up on food; **fare ~ di benzina** fill up; **rifornire** *macchina* fill up; *frigo* restock, fill (*di* with); **~ il magazzino** restock; **rifornirsi** stock up (*di* on)
rifugiarsi take refuge; **rifugiato** *m*, **-a** *f* refugee; **rifugio** *m* shelter; **~ alpino** mountain hut

riga f line; (fila) row; (regolo) rule; in stoffa stripe; nei capelli parting, Am part; **stoffa f a -ghe** striped fabric

rigatoni mpl rigatoni sg

rigenerare regenerate; **rigenerazione** f regeneration

rigetto m MED rejection; fig mental block

rigido (duro) rigid; muscolo, articolazione stiff; clima harsh; fig (severo) strict

rigirare 1 v/i walk around **2** v/t turn over and over; denaro launder; **~ il discorso** change the subject; **rigirarsi** turn around; nel letto toss and turn

rigoglioso lush, luxuriant

rigore m di clima harshness; (severità) strictness; SP **(calcio m di) ~** penalty (kick); **rigoroso** rigorous

riguardare look at again; (rivedere) review, look at; (riferirsi) be about; **non ti riguarda** it doesn't concern you; **riguardarsi** take care of o.s.; **riguardo** m (attenzione) care; (rispetto) respect; **~ a** as regards

rilasciare release; documento issue; **rilascio** m release; di passaporto issue

rilassare, rilassarsi relax; **rilassato** relaxed

rilegare libro bind

rilevare (ricavare) find; (osservare) notice; ditta buy up

rilievo m relief; fig **dare ~ a**

qc, **mettere qc in ~** emphasize o highlight sth

rima f rhyme; fig ~ rhyme

rimandare send again; (restituire) send back; palla return; (rinviare) postpone

rimanente 1 agg remaining **2** m rest, balance; rimanere stay, remain; (avanzare) be left (over); **rimanerci male** be hurt; **rimango** ☞ **rimanere**

rimarginare, rimarginarsi heal

rimasto pp ☞ rimanere

rimbalzare bounce

rimboccare coperte tuck in; **rimboccarsi le maniche** roll up one's sleeves

rimborsare reimburse, pay back; **rimborso** m reimbursement, repayment; **~ spese** reimbursement of expenses

rimboschire reforest

rimediare 1 v/i: **~ a** make up for, remedy **2** v/t find, scrape together; **rimedio** m remedy; MED medicine

rimescolare mix again; più volte mix thoroughly; caffè stir again

rimessa f di auto garage; degli autobus depot; SP **~ laterale** throw-in

rimettere put back, return; (affidare) refer; (vomitare) bring up; **~ a posto** put back; **ci ho rimesso molti soldi** I lost a lot of money; **rimetter-**

rinvenire

si *di tempo* improve; **~ da qc** get over sth

rimodernare modernize

rimorchiare AUTO tow (away); **rimorchiatore** *m* MAR tug; **rimorchio** *m* AUTO tow; *veicolo* trailer

rimorso *m* remorse

rimozione *f* removal

rimpatriare 1 *v/t* repatriate **2** *v/i* go home

rimpiangere regret (**di avere fatto qc** doing sth); *tempi passati, giovinezza* miss; **rimpianto 1** *pp* ☞ **rimpiangere 2** *m* regret

rimpiazzare replace

rimpicciolire 1 *v/t* make smaller **2** *v/i* become smaller, shrink

rimproverare scold; *impiegato* reprimand; **~ qc a qu** reproach s.o. for sth; **rimprovero** *m* scolding

rimuovere remove; (*muovere di nuovo*) move again

rinascere be born again; *di passione, speranza* be revived; *fig* **sentirsi ~** feel rejuvenated; **Rinascimento** *m* Renaissance

rincarare 1 *v/t* increase, put up; **~ la dose** make matters worse **2** *v/i* increase in price; **rincaro** *m* price increase

rincasare *venire* come home; *andare* go home

rinchiudere shut up; **rinchiudersi** shut o.s. up

rincorrere run after; **rincorsa**

f run-up; **rincorso** *pp* ☞ **rincorrere**

rincrescere: mi rincresce I'm sorry

rinfacciare: ~ qc a qu cast sth up to s.o.

rinforzare strengthen; **rinforzo** *m* reinforcement; MIL **-i** *pl* reinforcements

rinfrescare cool down; **rinfrescarsi** freshen up; **rinfresco** *m* buffet (party)

rinfusa: alla ~ any which way, all higgledy-piggledy

ringhiare growl

ringhiera *f* railing

ringiovanire 1 *v/t* make feel younger; *di aspetto* make look younger **2** *v/i* feel younger; *di aspetto* look younger

ringraziamento: un ~ a word of thanks; **i miei -i** *pl* my thanks; **ringraziare** thank (**di** for)

rinnovare renovate; *guardaroba* replace; *abbonamento* renew; (*ripetere*) renew, repeat; **rinnovarsi** renew itself; (*ripetersi*) be repeated; **rinnovo** *m* renovation; *di guardaroba* replacement; *di abbonamento* renewal; *di richiesta* repetition

rintracciare track down

rinuncia *f* renunciation (**a** of); **rinunciare** give up (**a** sth)

rinvenire 1 *v/t* recover; *resti* discover **2** *v/i* regain con-

rinviare   222

sciousness, come round

rinviare (*mandare indietro*)
return; (*posticipare*) postpone; *a letteratura* refer; **rinvio** *m* return; *di riunione*
postponement; *in un testo*
cross-reference

rione *m* district

riordinare tidy up

riorganizzare reorganize

riparare 1 *v/t* (*proteggere*) protect (*da* from); (*aggiustare*)
repair; *un torto* make up
for 2 *v/i* escape; ripararsi
dalla pioggia take shelter
(*da* from); riparato sheltered; riparazione *f* repair;
fig di torto putting right; **riparo** *m* shelter; **mettersi al
~** take shelter

ripartire¹ *v/i* leave again

ripartire² *v/t* divide up

ripassare 1 *v/i* ☞ passare 2
v/t col ferro iron; *lezione* revise, *Am* review

ripensamento *m*: avere un ~
have second thoughts; **ripensare**: *~ a qc* think about
sth again; **ci ho ripensato**
I've changed my mind

ripetere repeat; ripetizione *f*
repetition; *dare -i a qu* tutor
s.o.

ripido steep

ripiegare 1 *v/t* fold up again 2
v/i fall back; **ripiego** *m*
makeshift (solution)

ripieno 1 *agg* full; GASTR
stuffed 2 *m* stuffing

riporre put away; *speranze*

place

riportare take back; (*riferire*)
report; *vittoria, successo*
achieve; MAT carry over;
danni sustain

riposarsi rest; **riposo** *m* rest

ripostiglio *m* boxroom, store-
room

riprendere take again; (*prendere indietro*) take back; *lavoro* go back to; FOT record;
~ a fare qc start doing sth
again; **riprendersi**: *~ da qc*
get over sth; **ripresa** *f* resumption; *di vestito* altera-
tion; *film* shot; AUTO acceleration; *a più -e* several
times

riproduco ☞ riprodurre; riprodurre reproduce; riprodursi *di animali* breed, reproduce; *di situazione* happen again; **riproduzione** *f*
reproduction; *~ vietata* copy-
right

riprovare 1 *v/t* feel again; *vestito* try on again 2 *v/i* try
again

ripugnante disgusting, re-
pugnant; **ripugnare**: *~ a qu*
disgust s.o.

ripulire clean again; (*rimettere
in ordine*) tidy (up)

risa *fpl* laughter

risalire *v/t scale* go back up 2
v/i (*rincarare*) go up again; *~
a* go back to; **risalita** *f* ascent; **impianti** *mpl di ~* ski
lifts

risaltare stand out; **risalto** *m*

rissa

mettere in ~, dare ~ a highlight

risanamento *m* redevelopment; FIN improvement

risarcimento *m* compensation; **risarcire** *persona* compensate (*di* for); *danno* compensate for

risata *f* laugh

riscaldamento *m* heating; ~ *della temperatura terrestre* global warming

riscaldare heat *o* warm up; **riscaldarsi** warm o.s.

rischiararsi clear (up); *di cielo* clear (up); ~ *in volto* cheer up

rischiare 1 *v/t* risk 2 *v/i*: ~ *di sbagliare* risk making a mistake; **rischio** *m* risk; **rischioso** risky

riscontrare (*confrontare*) compare; (*controllare*) check; (*incontrare*) come up against; *errori* come across

riscuotere FIN *soldi* draw; *assegno* cash; *fig* earn

risentimento *m* resentment; **risentire** 1 *v/t* hear again 2 *v/i* feel the effects; **risentirsi** TELEC talk again; (*offendersi*) take offence *o* Am offense

riserva *f* reserve; *fig* reservation; AUTO *essere in* ~ be running out of fuel; *fare* ~ *di* qc stock up on; **riservare** keep; (*prenotare*) book, reserve; **riservarsi** reserve; *mi riservo di non accettare*

I reserve the right to not to accept; **riservato** reserved; (*confidenziale*) confidential

risiedere be resident, reside

riso[1] *pp* ☞ *ridere* 2 *m* laughing

riso[2] *m* rice

risolto *pp* ☞ *risolvere*; **risoluto** determined; **risoluzione** *f* resolution; (*soluzione*) solution; *di contratto* cancellation; *prendere una* ~ make a decision; **risolvere** solve; (*decidere*) resolve; **risolversi** be solved; (*decidersi*) decide, resolve; ~ *in nulla* come to nothing

risorgere rise; *fig*: *di industria ecc* experience a rebirth; **Risorgimento** *m* Risorgimento, *the reunification of Italy*

risorsa *f* resource

risotto *m* risotto

risparmiare save; *fig* spare; **risparmio** *m* saving; *-i pl* savings

rispettare respect; *legge, contratto* abide by; **rispettivo** respective; **rispetto** 1 *m* respect 2 *prp*: ~ *a* (*confronto a*) compared with; (*in relazione a*) as regards

risplendere shine, glitter

rispondere answer (*a* sth), reply (*a* to); (*reagire*) respond; *saluto* acknowledge; ~ *di qc* be accountable for sth (*a* to); **risposta** *f* answer, reply; (*reazione*) response

rissa *f* brawl

ristabilire 224

ristabilire *ordine* restore; *regolamento* re-introduce; **ristabilirsi** recover

ristampa *f* reprint

ristorante *m* restaurant

ristretto: *caffè* **m** *inv* ~ very strong coffee

ristrutturare restructure; **ristrutturazione** *f* restructuring

risultare result; *(rivelarsi)* turn out; **risultato** *m* result

risurrezione *f* REL Resurrection

risvegliare, risvegliarsi *fig* reawaken

ritardare 1 *v/t* delay **2** *v/i* be late; *di orologio* be slow; **ritardatario** *m*, *-a f* latecomer; **ritardo** *m* delay; *essere in* ~ be late

ritenere *(credere)* believe; **ritenersi:** *si ritiene molto intelligente* he thinks he is very intelligent; **ritenuta** *f* deduction *(su* from)

ritirare withdraw, pull back; *(tirare di nuovo)* throw again; *proposta* withdraw; *(prelevare)* collect; **ritirarsi** *(restringersi)* shrink; ~ *da gara, esame ecc* withdraw from; **ritiro** *m* withdrawal

ritmo *m* rhythm

rito *m* ceremony

ritoccare touch up

ritornare *venire* get back, come back, return; *andare* go back, return; *su argomento* go back (*su* over); ~ *verde*

turn green again

ritornello *m* refrain

ritorno *m* return; *essere di* ~ be back

ritrarre pull away; PITT paint

ritrattare retract

ritratto *m* portrait

ritrovare find; *(riacquistare)* regain; **ritrovarsi** meet again; *(capitare)* find o.s.; *(orientarsi)* get one's bearings; **ritrovo** *m* meeting; *luogo* meeting place

riunione *f* meeting; *di amici, famiglia* reunion; **riunire** gather; **riunirsi** meet

riuscire succeed; *(essere capace)* manage; *non riesco a capire* I can't understand; ~ *in qc* be successful in sth; **riuscita** *f* success; **riuscito** successful

riutilizzare re-use

riva *f* shore

rivale *m/f, agg* rival *attr,* rivalità *f inv* rivalry

rivalutare revalue; *persona* change one's mind about

rivedere see again; *(ripassare)* review, look at again; *(verificare)* check

rivelare reveal

rivendere resell

rivendicare demand

rivendita *f* negozio retail outlet; **rivenditore** *m*, *-trice f* retailer; ~ *specializzato* dealer

rivestimento *m* covering; **rivestire** *(foderare)* cover; *ruo-*

lo play; *carica* fill

rivincita *f* return game; **prendersi la** ~ get one's revenge

rivista *f* magazine; TEA revue; MIL review

rivolgere turn; *domanda* address (*a qu* to s.o.); ~ *la parola a qu* speak to s.o., address s.o; **rivolgersi**: ~ *a qu* apply to s.o. (*per* for)

rivolta *f* revolt; **rivoltare** turn; (*mettere sottosopra*) turn upside down; (*disgustare*) revolt; **rivoltella** *f* revolver; **rivoluzione** *f* revolution

rizzare put up; *bandiera* raise; *orecchie* prick up; **rizzarsi** straighten up; *mi si sono rizzati i capelli in testa* my hair stood on end

roba *f* things, stuff; ~ *da matti!* would you believe it!

robot *m inv* robot; *da cucina* food processor

robusto sturdy

rocca *f* fortress

roccia *f* rock; **roccioso** rocky

rock *m inv* MUS rock

roco hoarse

rodaggio *m* running in; *fig sono ancora in* ~ I'm still finding my feet

rodere gnaw at; **rodersi**: ~ *dalla gelosia* be eaten up with jealousy; **roditore** *m* rodent

rogna *f* F *di cane* mange; *problema* hassle

rognone *m di animale* kidney

Roma *f* Rome

Romania *f* Romania

romanico Romanesque; **romano** 1 *agg* Roman 2 *m, -a f* Roman

romantico 1 *agg* romantic 2 *m, -a f* romantic

romanzo 1 *agg* Romance 2 *m* novel; ~ *giallo* thriller

rombo¹ *m* rumble

rombo² *m* MAT rhombus

romeno 1 *agg* Romanian 2 *m, -a f* Romanian

rompere 1 *v/t* break; F ~ *le scatole a qu* get on s.o.'s nerves F 2 *v/i* F be a pain F; **rompersi** break; ~ *un braccio* break one's arm

rompicapo *m inv* puzzle; (*problema*) headache

rondine *f* swallow

ronzare buzz; **ronzio** *m* buzzing

rosa 1 *f* rose 2 *m/agg inv* pink; **rosario** *m* REL rosary; **rosato** *m* rosé; **rosmarino** *m* rosemary

rosolare brown

rosolia *f* German measles *sg*

rosone *m* ARCHI rose window

rospo *m* toad

rossetto *m* lipstick

rosso 1 *agg* red 2 *m* red; ~ *d'uovo* egg yolk; *passare col* ~ go through a red light

rosticceria *f* rotisserie (*shop selling roast meat*)

rotaia *f* rail

rotatoria *f* roundabout, *Am* traffic circle

rotella *f* castor

rotolare roll; **rotolarsi** roll (around); **rotolino** m FOT film; **rotolo** m roll; FOT film; **andare a -i** go to rack and ruin
rotondo round
rotta f MAR, AVIA course
rottame m wreck
rotto 1 pp ☞ **rompere 2** agg broken; **rottura** f breaking; F **tra innamorati** break-up; F **che ~!** what a pain! F
rotula f kneecap
roulotte f inv caravan, Am trailer
routine f routine
rovesciare liquidi spill; oggetto knock over; (capovolgere) overturn; fig turn upside down; **rovesciarsi** overturn, capsize; **rovescio** reverse; in tennis backhand; **mettersi una maglia al ~** put a sweater on inside out
rovina f ruin; **andare in ~** go to rack and ruin; **rovinare** ruin; **rovinarsi** ruin o.s.
rovo m bramble
rozzo rough and ready
ruba: **andare a ~** sell like hot cakes; **rubare** steal
rubinetto m tap, Am faucet

rubino m ruby
rubrica f di libro table of contents; quaderno address book; di giornale column; TV report
rudere m ruin
rudimentale rudimentary
ruga f wrinkle, line
ruggine f rust
ruggire roar
rugiada f dew
rullino m FOT film; **rullo** m roll
rum m rum
rumore m noise; **rumoroso** noisy
ruolo m role
ruota f wheel; **~ di scorta** spare wheel
rupe f cliff
rupestre rock attr; **arte** f **~** wall painting
ruscello m stream
russare snore
Russia f Russia; **russo 1** agg Russian **2** m, **-a** f Russian
rustico rural, rustic; fig unsophisticated
ruttare belch; **rutto** m belch
ruvido rough
ruzzolare fall; **ruzzolone** m fall; **fare un ~** fall

S

S. (= *santo*) St (= Saint)

sa ☞ *sapere*

sabato *m* Saturday

sabbia *f* sand; **sabbioso** sandy

sabotaggio *m* sabotage; **sabotare** sabotage

sacca *f* bag; ANAT, BIO sac

saccheggiare sack; *spir* raid

sacchetto *m* bag; **sacco** *m* sack; *fig* F **un ~ di** piles of F; **costa un ~** it costs a fortune; **~ a pelo** sleeping bag; **saccopelista** *m/f* backpacker

sacerdote *m* priest

sacramento *m* sacrament

sacrificare sacrifice; **sacrificarsi** sacrifice o.s.; **sacrificio** *m* sacrifice

sacro sacred

sadico 1 *agg* sadistic **2** *m*, -a *f* sadist

safari *m inv* safari

saggio[1] **1** *agg* wise **2** *m* wise man, sage

saggio[2] *m* test; (*campione*) sample; *scritto* essay; *di danza, musica* end of term show

Sagittario *m* ASTR Sagittarius

sahariana *f* safari jacket

sala *f* room; (*soggiorno*) living room; **~ da pranzo** dining room; **~ giochi** amusement arcade; **~ operatoria** (operating) theatre, *Am* operat-

ing room

salame *m* salami

salamoia *f*: **in ~** in brine

salariale pay *attr*; **salario** *m* salary, wages

salatino *m* savoury, *Am* savory; **salato** savoury, *Am* savory; **acqua** salt; **cibo** salted; F (*caro*) steep F; **troppo ~** salty

saldare weld; *ossa* set; *fattura* pay; **saldo 1** *agg* steady, secure **2** *m* payment; *in svendita* sale item; (*resto*) balance; **-i** *pl* **di fine stagione** end-of-season sales

sale *m* salt

salgo ☞ *salire*

salice *m* willow; **~ piangente** weeping willow

saliera *f* salt cellar; **salina** *f* salt works

salire 1 *v/i* climb; *di livello, prezzi, temperatura* rise; **~ in macchina** get in; **~ su scala** climb; *treno, autobus* get on **2** *v/t scale* climb; **salita** *f* climb; *strada* slope; **strada** *f* **in ~** steep street

saliva *f* saliva

salma *f* corpse, body

salmastro 1 *agg* briny **2** *m* salt

salmone *m* salmon; **~ affumicato** smoked salmon

salone *m* living room; (*esposi*-

zione) show
salotto *m* lounge
salpare sail
salsa *f* sauce; **~ di pomodoro** tomato sauce
salsiccia *f* sausage
saltare 1 *v/t* jump; (*omettere*) skip; **~ (in padella)** sauté **2** *v/i* jump; *di bottone* come off; *di fusibile* blow; F *di impegno* be cancelled *o Am* canceled; **~ fuori** turn up
saltellare hop
salto *m* jump; (*dislivello*) change in level; **~ in alto** high jump; **~ in lungo** long jump, *Am* broad jump; **faccio un ~ da te** I'll drop in
saltuariamente occasionally; **saltuario** occasional
salumeria *f* shop that sells '*salumi*'; **salumi** *mpl* cold meat
salutare 1 *agg* healthy **2** *v/t* say hello to, greet; **salute** *f* health; **~!** cheers!; **saluto** *m* wave; **tanti -i** greetings
salvagente *m inv* lifebelt; (*giubbotto*) life jacket; *per bambini* ring; (*isola spartitraffico*) traffic island; **salvaguardare** protect, safeguard; **salvaguardia** *f* protection; **salvare** save, rescue; **salvataggio** *m* salvage; **barca f di ~** lifeboat; **salve!** hello!; **salvezza** *f* salvation
salvia *f* sage
salvietta *f* napkin
salvo 1 *agg* safe **2** *prp* except;

~ che unless; **~ imprevisti** all being well **3** *m*: **mettersi in ~** take shelter
San = **Santo**
sandalo *m* sandal; BOT sandalwood
sangue *m* blood; **a ~ freddo** in cold blood; GASTR *al ~* rare; **sanguigno: gruppo** *m* **~** blood group; **sanguinare** bleed; **sanguinoso** bloody; **sanguisuga** *f* leech
sanità *f* health; **amministrazione** health care; **sanitario** health *attr*; **assistenza** *f* **-a** health care
sanno ☞ **sapere**
sano healthy; **~ e salvo** safe and sound
santo 1 *agg* holy **2** *m*, **-a** *f* saint; *davanti al nome* St
santuario *m* sanctuary
sanzione *f* sanction
sapere 1 *v/t* know; (*essere capace di*) be able to; (*venire a*) **~** hear; **sai nuotare?** can you swim?; **lo so** I know **2** *v/i*: **far ~ qc a qu** let s.o. know sth; **~ di** (*avere sapore di*) taste of **3** *m* knowledge
sapone *m* soap; **saponetta** *f* toilet soap
sapore *m* taste; **-i** *pl* aromatic herbs; **saporito** tasty
saracinesca *f* roller shutter
sarcastico sarcastic
sarcofago *m* sarcophagus
Sardegna *f* Sardinia
sardina *f* sardine
sardo 1 *agg* Sardinian **2** *m*, **-a**

f Sardinian

sarò ☞ *essere*

sarto *m*, **-a** *f* tailor; *per donne* dressmaker; **sartoria** *f* tailor's; *per donne* dressmaker's

sasso *m* stone

sassofono *m* saxophone

satellite *m* satellite

satira *f* satire; **satirico** satirical

saturo saturated

sauna *f* sauna

sazietà *f*: **mangiare a** ~ eat one's fill; **sazio** full (up)

sbadato absent-minded

sbadigliare yawn; **sbadiglio** *m* yawn

sbagliare 1 *v/i e* **sbagliarsi** make a mistake **2** *v/t* make a mistake in; TELEC **sbagliare** ~ dial the wrong number; ~ **strada** go the wrong way; **sbagliato** wrong; **sbaglio** *m* mistake; **per** ~ by mistake

sbalordire amaze; **sbalorditivo** amazing

sbalzare throw; **sbalzo** *m* jump; ~ *di temperatura* sudden change in temperature

sbandare AUTO skid; FERR, *fig* go off the rails; **sbandata** *f* AUTO skid; F *prendersi* **una** ~ *per* get a crush on s.o.

sbarazzare clear; **sbarazzarsi**: ~ *di* get rid of

sbarcare 1 *v/t merci* unload; *persone* disembark **2** *v/i* disembark; **sbarco** *m di merci* unloading; *di persone* disem-

barkation

sbarra *f* bar

sbarramento *m* fence; (*ostacolo*) barrier; **sbarrare** bar; *assegno* cross; *occhi* open wide; **sbarrato** *assegno* crossed; *occhi* wide open

sbattere 1 *v/t porta* slam, bang; (*urtare*) bang; GASTR beat **2** *v/i* bang

sberla *f* F slap

sbiadire fade; **sbiadito** faded

sbilanciarsi lose one's balance; *fig* commit o.s.

sbizzarrirsi indulge o.s.

sbloccare clear; *macchina* unblock; *prezzi* deregulate

sboccare: ~ *in di fiume* flow into; *di strada* lead to

sbocciare come (out)

sbocco *m di situazione* way out

sbornia *f* F: *prendersi* **una** ~ get drunk

sborsare F cough up F

sbottonare unbutton; **sbottonarsi**: ~ *la giacca* unbutton one's jacket

sbraitare shout, yell

sbranare tear apart

sbriciolarsi crumble

sbrigare attend to; **sbrigarsi** hurry up; **sbrigativo** (*rapido*) hurried, rushed; (*brusco*) brusque

sbrinare *frigorifero* defrost; **sbrinatore** *m* defrost control

sbrogliare untangle; **sbrogliarsela** sort things out

sbronza *f* F hangover; **sbronzarsi** F get drunk; **sbronzo** F tight F

sbucare emerge; *da dove sei sbucato?* where did you spring from?

sbucciare *frutta, patate* peel; *sbucciarsi le ginocchia* skin one's knees; **sbucciatura** *f* graze

scabroso rough, uneven; *fig* offensive

scacchiera *f* chessboard

scacciare chase away

scacco *m* (chess) piece; **-cchi** *pl* chess; *a -cchi* checked, *Am* checkered

scadente 1 ☞ **scadere** 2 *agg* second-rate; **scadenza** *f* deadline; *su alimento* best before date; **scadere** *di passaporto* expire; *di cambiale* fall due; *(perdere valore)* decline (in quality); **scaduto** expired; *alimento* past its sell-by date

scaffale *m* shelves

scaglia *f* flake; *di legno* chip; *di pesce* scale

scagliare hurl; **scagliarsi**: ~ *contro* attack

scala *f* staircase; GEOG, MUS scale; ~ *(a pioli)* ladder; ~ *mobile* escalator; *disegno in* *m* in ~ scale drawing; *fare le -e* climb the stairs; **scalare** climb; **scalata** *f* climb; *fare ~ al successo* rise to fame; **scalatore** *m*, **-trice** *f* climber

scaldabagno *m* water heat-

er; **scaldare** heat (up); **scaldarsi** warm up; *fig* get worked up

scalinata *f* steps; **scalino** *m* step

scalo *m* AVIA stop; MAR port of call; *fare ~ a* call at

scalogna *f* bad luck; **portare** ~ be unlucky; **scalognato** unlucky

scaloppina *f* escalope

scalpello *m* chisel

scalzo barefoot

scambiare *(confondere)* mistake *(per* for); *(barattare)* exchange, swap *(con* for); **scambio** *m* exchange; *di persona* mistake; FERR points; *-i pl commerciali* trade

scampagnata *f* day out in the country

scampanellata *f* ring

scampi *mpl* scampi

scampo *m* escape, way out

scampolo *m* remnant

scandagliare sound; *fig* sound out

scandalistico scandal-mongering; **scandalizzare** scandalize; **scandalizzarsi** be scandalized *(di* by); **scandalizzato** scandalized; **scandalo** *m* scandal; **scandaloso** scandalous

scandinavo 1 *agg* Scandinavian 2 *m*, **-a** *f* Scandinavian

scanner *m inv* INFOR scanner; **scannerizzare** INFOR scan

scansare *(allontanare)* move;

scegliere

(*evitare*) avoid; **scansarsi** move out of the way

scansionare scan

scantinato *m* cellar

scapito: **a ~ di** to the detriment of

scapola *f* shoulder blade, ANAT scapula

scapolo 1 *agg* single, unmarried **2** *m* bachelor

scappamento *m* TEC exhaust

scappare (*fuggire*) run away; (*affrettarsi*) rush, run

scappatella *f di bambino* escapade; **fare delle -lle** get into mischief

scappatoia *f* way out

scarabocchiare scribble; **scarabocchio** *m* scribble

scarafaggio *m* cockroach

scaraventare throw, hurl; **scaraventarsi** throw *o* hurl o.s. (**contro** at)

scarcerare release; **scarcerazione** *f* release

scarica *f* discharge; **scaricamento** *m* INFOR download; **scaricare** unload; *batteria* run down; *rifiuti, sostanze nocive* dump; *responsabilità* offload; INFOR download; **scaricarsi** *di batteria* run down; **scarico 1** *agg camion* empty; *batteria* run-down **2** *m di merci* unloading; *luogo* dump; **divieto di ~** no dumping

scarlattina *f* scarlet fever

scarpa *f* shoe

scarpata *f* (*burrone*) escarp-

ment

scarpinata *f* trek

scarpone *m* (heavy) boot; **~ da sci** ski boot

scarseggiare become scarce; **~ di qc** be short of sth; **scarso** scarce, in short supply; **quattro chilometri -si** barely four kilometres

scartare (*svolgere*) unwrap; (*eliminare*) reject; **scarto** *m* rejection; (*cosa scartata*) reject

scassare F ruin, wreck; **scassarsi** F give up the ghost F; **scassato** F done for F

scassinare force open; **scasso** *m* forced entry; **furto** *m* **con ~** breaking and entering

scatenare *fig* unleash; **scatenarsi** *di tempesta* break; *di collera* break out; *di persona* let one's hair down

scatola *f* box; *di tonno, piselli* can, Br *anche* tin; **in ~** *cibo* canned, Br *anche* tinned

scattare 1 *v/t* FOT take **2** *v/i* go off; *di serratura* catch; (*arrabbiarsi*) lose one's temper; *di atleta* put on a spurt; **scatto** *m* click; SP spurt; FOT exposure; *di foto* taking; TELEC unit; **uno ~ di rabbia** an angry gesture

scavalcare *muro* climb (over)

scavare *con pala* dig; *con trivella* excavate; **scavi** *mpl* archeologici dig

scegliere choose, select;

scelgo ☞ *scegliere*; scelta *f* choice, selection; *di prima ~* first-rate; scelto 1 *pp* ☞ *scegliere* 2 *agg* handpicked; *merce, pubblico* selected

scemo 1 *agg* stupid, idiotic 2 *m*, -a *f* idiot

scena theatre, *Am* theater; *(scenata)* scene; scenata *f* scene

scendere 1 *v/i andare* go down, descend; *venire* come down, descend; *da cavallo* get down, dismount; *dal treno, dall' autobus* get off; *dalla macchina* get out; *di temperatura, prezzi* go down, drop 2 *v/t*: ~ *le scale andare* go down the stairs; *venire* come down the stairs

sceneggiatura *f* screenplay

scenografo *m*, -a *f* set designer

scettico 1 *agg* sceptical, *Am* skeptical 2 *m*, -a *f* sceptic, *Am* skeptic

scheda *f* card; *(formulario)* form; ~ *telefonica* phonecard; schedario *m* file; schedina *f* pools coupon

scheggia *f* sliver

scheletro *m* skeleton

schema *m* diagram; *(abbozzo)* outline; schematico general; *disegno* schematic

scherma *f* fencing

schermo *m* screen; *(riparo)* shield; ~ *piatto* flat screen; ~ *a contatto* touchscreen

scherzare play; *(burlare)*

joke; scherzo *m* joke; *-i a parte* joking aside; *per ~ fare, dire qc* as a joke

schiaccianoci *m inv* nutcrackers; schiacciare 1 *v/t* crush; *noce* crack 2 *v/i* SP smash the ball; schiacciato crushed, squashed

schiaffeggiare slap; schiaffo *m* slap

schiamazzo *m* yell, scream

schiantare, schiantarsi crash

schiarire lighten; schiarirsi brighten up; schiarita *f* bright spell

schiavitù *f* slavery; schiavo 1 *agg*: *essere ~ di* be a slave to 2 *m*, -a *f* slave

schiena *f* back; *mal m di ~* back ache; schienale *m di sedile* back

schiera *f* group; *a ~* in ranks; schierarsi: ~ *in favore di qu* come out in favour *o Am* favor of s.o.

schietto pure; *fig* frank

schifezza: *che ~!* how disgusting!; schifo *m* disgust; *fare ~ a* qu disgust s.o.; schifoso disgusting; *(pessimo)* dreadful

schiuma *f* foam; ~ *da bagno* bubble bath; ~ *da barba* shaving foam

schivare avoid, dodge F; schivo shy

schizzare 1 *v/t (spruzzare)* squirt; *(abbozzare)* sketch 2 *v/i* squirt; *(saltare)* jump schizzinoso fussy

schizzo *m* squirt; *(abbozzo)* (lightning) sketch

sci *m inv* ski; *attività* skiing; ~ **acquatico** water ski / skiing; ~ **di fondo** cross-country ski / skiing

sciacquare rinse

sciagura *f* disaster; sciagurato unfortunate

scialle *m* shawl

scialuppa *f* dinghy; ~ *di salvataggio* lifeboat

sciame *m* swarm

sciare ski

sciarpa *f* scarf

sciatica *f* sciatica

sciatore *m*, -trice *f* skier

sciatto untidy, sloppy

scientifico scientific; scienza *f* science; scienziato *m*, -a *f* scientist

scimmia *f* monkey; scimmiottare ape

scimpanzé *m inv* chimpanzee, chimp F

scintilla *f* spark; scintillante sparkling; scintillare sparkle

sciocchezza *f* (*idiozia*) stupidity; sciocco 1 *agg* silly 2 *m*, -a *f* silly thing

sciogliere untie; *capelli* let down; *neve* melt; *dubbio*, *problema* clear up; sciogliersi *di corda, nodo* come undone; *di burro, neve* melt; scioglilingua *m inv* tonguetwister

scioltezza *f* nimbleness; *fisica*

agility

sciolto 1 *pp ☞* sciogliere 2 *agg ghiaccio* melted

scioperare strike; sciopero *m* strike; *fare* ~ go on strike

sciovia *f* ski-lift

scippatore *m*, -trice *f* bagsnatcher; scippo *m* bagsnatching

scirocco *m* sirocco

sciroppo *m* syrup

scissione *f* splitting

sciupare (*logorare*) wear out; *salute* ruin; *tempo, denaro* waste; sciupato *persona* drawn; *cosa* worn out

scivolare slide; (*cadere*) slip; scivolo *m* slide; *gioco* chute; scivoloso slippery

sclerosi *f* MED sclerosis; ~ *multipla* multiple sclerosis, MS

scocciare F bother, hassle F; scocciatore F *m*, -trice *f* pest F, nuisance; scocciatura F *f* nuisance

scodella *f* bowl

scogliera *f* cliff; scoglio *m* rock

scoiattolo *m* squirrel

scolapasta *m inv* colander; scolare drain

scolaro *m*, -a *f* schoolboy; *ragazza* schoolgirl; scolastico *attr*

scoliosi *f inv* curvature of the spine

scollato low-necked; *donna* wearing a low neckline; scollatura *f* neck(line);

scollo *m* neck
scolo *m* drainage
scolorire, scolorirsi fade;
scolorito faded
scolpire *statua* sculpt; *legno*
carve; *fig* engrave
scommessa *f* bet; scom-
messo *pp* ☞ **scommettere**;
scommettere bet
scomodare disturb; scomo-
darsi put o.s. out; **non si
scomodi** please don't go
to any bother; scomodo uncomfortable; (*non pratico*)
inconvenient
scomparire   disappear;
scomparsa *f* disappear-
ance; scomparso *pp* ☞
scomparire
scompartimento *m* com-
partment
scompigliare *persona* ruffle
the hair of; *capelli* ruffle;
scompiglio *m* confusion
scomporre   break   down;
scomporsi: *senza ~* without
showing any emotion
sconcertante disconcerting
sconcio indecent;   *parola*
filthy
sconclusionato incoherent
sconfiggere defeat
sconfinato vast, boundless
sconfitta *f* defeat; sconfitto
pp ☞ *sconfiggere*
sconforto *m* discouragement
scongelare thaw
scongiurare beg;   *pericolo*
avert
sconosciuto 1 *agg* unknown

2 *m*, -a *f* stranger
sconsigliare advise against;
~ qc a qu advise s.o. against
sth
scontare FIN deduct, dis-
count; *pena* serve; scontato
discounted; (*previsto*) expected; *~ del 30%* with a
30% discount
scontento 1 *agg* unhappy,
not satisfied (*di* with) 2 *m*
unhappiness, dissatisfaction
sconto *m* discount
scontrarsi collide (*con* with);
fig clash (*con* with)
scontrino *m* receipt
scontro *m* AUTO collision; *fig*
clash; scontroso unpleas-
ant, disagreeable
sconvolgente upsetting, distressing; *di un'intelligenza ~*
incredibly intelligent; sconvolgere upset; sconvolto 1
pp ☞ *sconvolgere* 2 *agg paese* in upheaval
scopa *f* broom; scopare
sweep; P shag P
scoperchiare *pentola* take
the lid off
scoperta *f* discovery; scoperto 1 *pp* ☞ *scoprire* 2 *agg*: *assegno* ~ dud cheque 3 *m*:
allo ~ in the open
scopo *m* aim, purpose; *allo ~
di fare qc* in order to do sth
scoppiare *di bomba* explode;
di palloncino, pneumatico
burst; *~ in lacrime* burst into
tears; *~ a ridere* burst out
laughing; scoppio *m* explo-

fig outbreak

scoprire *contenitore* take the
lid off; (*denudare*) uncover;
piani, verità discover

scoraggiare discourage;
scoraggiarsi become discouraged, lose heart; **scoraggiato** discouraged

scorciatoia f short cut

scordare, scordarsi di forget; **scordato** MUS out of
tune

scoreggia f F fart F; **scoreggiare** F fart F

scorgere see, make out

scoria f waste

scorpione m scorpion; ASTR
Scorpione Scorpio

scorrere v/i flow, run; *di
tempo* go past, pass **2** v/t *giornale* skim

scorretto (*errato*) incorrect;
(*non onesto*) unfair

scorrevole *porta* sliding; *stile*
flowing

scorso 1 pp ☞ **scorrere 2**
agg: **l'anno** ~ last year

scorta f escort; (*provvista*)
supply; **scortare** escort

scortese rude, discourteous;
scortesia f rudeness

scorto pp ☞ **scorgere**

scorza f peel; *fig* exterior

scossa f shake; ~ **di terremoto** (earth) tremor; ~ **elettrica**
electric shock; **scosso** pp ☞
scuotere

scostare move away (**da**
from); **scostarsi** move

(aside)

scottare 1 v/t burn; GASTR
verdure blanch **2** v/i burn;
scotta! it's hot!; **scottato**
verdure blanched; **scottatu-
ra** f burn

Scozia f Scotland; **scozzese
1** *agg* Scottish **2** m/f Scot

screditare discredit

scremato skimmed

screpolare, **screpolarsi**
crack; **screpolatura** f crack

scricchiolare creak; **scric-
chiolio** m creak

scritta f inscription; **scritto 1**
pp ☞ **scrivere 2** m writing;
scrittore m, **-trice** f writer;
scrittura f writing; REL
scripture

scrivania f desk; **scrivere**
write; (*annotare*) write down;
come si scrive … ? how do
you spell … ?

scroccare F scrounge F

scrollare shake; ~ **le spalle**
shrug (one's shoulders)

scrosciare *di pioggia* fall in
torrents

scrupolo m scruple; **scrupo-
losità** f scrupulousness;
scrupoloso scrupulous

scrutare look at intently; *orri-
zonte* scan

scrutinio m POL counting;
EDU *teachers' meeting to discuss pupils' performance*

scucire unpick; F **scuci i soldi!** cough up! F; **scucirsi**
come apart at the seams

scuderia f stable

scudetto *m* SP championship;
scudo *m* shield

sculacciare spank

scultore *m*, **-trice** *f* sculptor;
scultura *f* sculpture

scuola *f* school; **~ media** secondary school; **~ superiore**
high school; **~ guida** driving
school; **andare a ~** go to
school

scuotere shake

scure *f* axe, *Am* ax

scurire darken; **scuro** dark

scusa *f* excuse; **chiedere ~**
apologize; **scusare** forgive;
(*giustificare*) excuse; **mi scusi** I'm sorry; **scusi, scusa**
excuse me; **scusarsi** apologize

sdebitarsi pay one's debts

sdegno *m* moral indignation

sdentato toothless

sdoganare clear through
customs

sdolcinato sloppy

sdraiarsi lie down; **sdraiato**
lying down; **sdraio** *m*: (**sedia f a) ~** deck chair

sé oneself; *lui* himself; *lei* herself; *loro* themselves; *esso,
essa* itself; **da ~** (by) himself / herself / themselves

se¹ *cong* if; **~ mai** if need be;
~ mai arrivasse ... should he
arrive ...; **come ~** as if; **~
no** if not

se² *pron* = **si** in front of **lo, la,
li, le, ne**

sebbene even though

secca *f* shallows

seccante *fig* annoying; **seccare 1** *v/t* dry; *fig* annoy **2**
v/i dry; **seccarsi** dry; *fig*
get annoyed; **seccatore** *m*,
-trice *f* nuisance, pest F;
seccatura *f* nuisance

secchio *m* bucket

secco dry; *fiori, pomodori*
dried; *tono* curt

secolo *m* century

seconda *f* AUTO second
(gear); FERR second class;
EDU second year; **secondario** secondary; **secondo 1**
agg second; **di -a mano** second-hand; **~ fine** ulterior
motive **2** *prp* according to;
~ me in my opinion **3** *m* second; GASTR main course

sedano *m* celery

sedare calm (down); **sedativo** *m* sedative

sede *f* headquarters

sedentario sedentary; **sedere 1** *m* F rear end F **2** *v/i* **e
sedersi** sit down; **sedia** *f*
chair; **~ a dondolo** rocking
chair; **~ a rotelle** wheelchair

sedicesimo sixteenth; **sedici**
sixteen

sedile *m* seat

seducente attractive; **sedurre** seduce; (*attrarre*) attract

seduta *f* session; **seduto** seat-
ed

seduzione *f* seduction

sega *f* saw

segale *f* rye

segare saw; **segatura** *f* sawdust

seggio *m* seat; ~ **(elettorale)** polling station; **seggiola** *f* chair; **seggiolino** *m di bicicletta* child's seat; **seggiolone** *m* high chair; **seggiovia** *f* chair lift

segnalare signal; *(annunciare)* report; **segnale** *m* signal; *(segno)* sign; ~ **d'allarme** alarm; **segnaletica** *f* signs; **segnalibro** *m* bookmark; **segnare** *(marcare)* mark; *(annotare)* note down; SP score; **segno** *m* sign; *(traccia)* mark, trace; *(cenno)* gesture, sign

segretaria *f* secretary; **segretario** *m* secretary; **segreteria** *f carica* secretaryship; *ufficio* administrative office; *attività* secretarial duties; ~ **telefonica** answering machine, voicemail

segreto *m/agg* secret

seguace *m/f* disciple, follower; **seguente** next, following; **seguire 1** *v/t* follow; *corso* take **2** *v/i* follow **(a qc** sth); **seguito** *m persone* retinue; *(sostenitori)* followers; *di film* sequel; **di** ~ one after the other, in succession; **in** ~ after that

sei[1] ➞ **essere**

sei[2] six

seicento 1 *agg* six hundred **2** *m*: **il Seicento** the seventeenth century

selciato *m* paving

selezione *f* selection

self-service *m inv* self-service (café)

sella *f* saddle; **sellino** *m* saddle

seltz *m*: **acqua** *f* **di** ~ soda (water)

selvaggina *f* game; **selvaggio 1** *agg animale, fiori* wild; *tribù, omicidio* savage **2** *m*, **-a** *f* savage; **selvatico** wild

semaforo *m* traffic lights

sembrare seem; *(assomigliare a)* look like

seme *m* seed

semestre *m* six months; EDU term, *Am* semester

semicerchio *m* semi-circle; **semicircolare** semi-circular

semifinale *f* semi-final

semifreddo *m* soft ice cream

seminare SOW

seminario *m* seminar

seminudo half-naked

seminuovo practically new

semolino *m* semolina

semplice simple; *(non doppio)* single; *(spontaneo)* natural; **semplicità** *f* simplicity; **semplificare** simplify

sempre always; **per** ~ for ever; ~ **più** more and more; ~ **più vecchio** older and older; **piove** ~ **di più** the rain's getting heavier and heavier; ~ **che** as long as

senape *f* mustard

senato *m* senate; **senatore** *m*, **-trice** *f* senator

senno *m* common sense; **uscire di** ~ lose one's mind;

(*arrabbiarsi*) lose control

seno *m* breast

sensato sensible

sensazionale sensational; **sensazione** *f* sensation, feeling; (*impressione*) feeling; **fare ~** cause a sensation

sensibile sensitive; (*evidente*) significant; **sensibilità** *f* sensitivity; **sensibilizzare** make more aware (**a** of)

senso *m* sense; (*significato*) meaning; (*direzione*) direction; **buon ~** common sense; **~ unico** one way; **~ vietato** no entry; **in ~ orario** clockwise; **perdere i -i** faint; **sensore** *m* TEC sensor

sensuale sensual

sentenza *f* DIR verdict

sentiero *m* path

sentimentale sentimental; **sentimento** *m* feeling, sentiment

sentire feel; (*udire*) hear; (*ascoltare*) listen to; *odore* smell; *cibo* taste; **sentirsi** feel; **sentirsela di fare qc** feel up to doing sth

senza without; **senz'altro** definitely; **~ di me** without me; **~ ridere** without laughing; **senzatetto** *m/f inv* homeless person; **i -i** *pl* the homeless *pl*

separare separate; **separarsi** separate, split up F; **separazione** *f* separation

sepolto *pp* ☞ **seppellire**; **sepoltura** *f* burial; **seppellire**

bury

seppia *f* cuttlefish

seppure even if

sequestrare confiscate; DIR impound, seize; (*rapire*) kidnap; **sequestro** *m* kidnap(ping); DIR impounding, seizure

sera *f* evening; **di ~** in the evenings; **serale** evening *attr*; **serata** *f* evening; *festa* party

serbatoio *m* tank

Serbia *f* Serbia

serbo[1] **1** *agg* Serbian **2** *m*, **-a** *f* Serb

serbo[2] *m*: **avere qc in ~** have sth in store

serenata *f* serenade

sereno serene; *fig* relaxed, calm

sericoltura *f* silk-worm farming

serie *f inv* series *sg*

serietà *f* seriousness; **serio 1** *agg* serious; (*affidabile*) reliable **2** *m*: **sul ~** seriously

serpe *f* grass snake; **serpente** *m* snake

serra *f* greenhouse

serramanico: **coltello a ~** *m* a ~ flick knife, *Am* switchblade

serranda *f* shutter; **serrare** close; *denti, pugni* clench; **serratura** *f* lock

servire 1 *v/i* be useful; **non mi serve** I don't need it; **a che serve questo?** what's this for? **2** *v/t* serve; **~ da bere a qu** pour s.o. a drink; **ser**-

239

virsi (*usare*) use (*di* sth); **prego, si serva!** a tavola please
help yourself!
servizio *m* service; (*favore*)
favour, *Am* favor; (*dipartimento*) department; *in giornale* feature (story); ~ *militare* military service; ~ *da tavola* dinner service; *fuori* ~
out of order; *in* ~ on duty;
-zi pl (*igienici*) toilets, *Am*
rest room
servofreno *m* servo brake;
servosterzo *m* power steering
sesamo *m* sesame
sessanta sixty; **sessantenne**
sixty-year-old; **sessantesimo** sixtieth; **sessantina** *f*:
una ~ about sixty (*di* sth)
sesso *m* sex; **sessuale** sexual
sesto sixth
seta *f* silk
sete *f* thirst; *aver* ~ be thirsty
setta *f* sect
settanta seventy; **settanten-
ne** seventy-year-old; **settantesimo** seventieth; **settanti-
na** *f*: *una* ~ about seventy
(*di* sth)
settare *macchina, computer*
set up
sette seven; **settecento 1** *agg*
seven hundred **2** *m: il Settecento* the eighteenth century
settembre *m* September
settentrionale 1 *agg* northern **2** *m/f* northerner; **set-
tentrione** *m* north

setticemia *f* septicaemia, *Am*
septicemia
settimana *f* week; ~ *santa*
Easter week, Holy week;
settimanale *m/agg* weekly
settimo seventh
settore *m* sector
severo severe
sezione *f* section
sfacchinata *f* backbreaking
job
sfacciato cheeky, *Am* fresh
sfamare feed
sfarzo *m* splendour, *Am*
splendor
sfarzoso magnificent
sfasciare smash; **sfasciarsi**
smash
sfavore *m* disadvantage; **sfavorevole** unfavourable, *Am*
unfavorable
sfera *f* sphere
sfida *f* challenge; **sfidare**
challenge
sfiducia *f* distrust
sfigurare 1 *v/t* disfigure **2** *v/i*
look out of place; **sfigurato**
disfigured
sfilare 1 *v/t* unthread; (*togliere*) take off **2** *v/i* parade; **sfilata** *f*: ~ *di moda* fashion
show
sfinimento *m* exhaustion; **sfinito** exhausted
sfiorare brush; *argomento*
touch on
sfitto empty, not rented
sfocato *foto* blurred, out of
focus
sfociare flow

sfogare *rabbia, frustrazione* vent, get rid of (**con**, **su** on); **sfogarsi** vent one's feelings; **~ con qu** confide in s.o.

sfoglia *pasta f ~* puff pastry; **sfogliare** *libro* leaf through

sfogo *m* outlet; MED rash

sfoltire thin

sfondare break; *porta* break down; *pavimento* break through

sfondo *m* background

sformare stretch out of shape; **sformato** *m* GASTR soufflé

sfortuna *f* bad luck, misfortune; **sfortunatamente** unfortunately; **sfortunato** unlucky, unfortunate

sforzare strain; **sforzarsi** try very hard; **sforzo** *m* effort; *fisico* strain; *fare uno ~* make an effort

sfrattare evict; **sfratto** *m* eviction

sfregare rub

sfruttamento *m* exploitation; **sfruttare** exploit

sfuggire (*scampare*) escape (**a** from); *mi è sfuggito di mente* it slipped my mind; **sfuggita: di ~** in passing

sfumatura *f* nuance; *di colore* shade

sfuriata *f* (angry) tirade

sfuso loose; *vino* in bulk

sgabello *m* stool

sgabuzzino *m* cupboard

sgambetto *m: fare lo ~ a qu

trip s.o. up

sganciare unhook; F *soldi* fork out F; **sganciarsi** come unhooked

sgarbato rude

sgobbare slave; **sgobbone** *m*, -a *f* F swot F

sgocciolare drip

sgombere → **sgombrare**; **sgombrare** *strada, stanza* clear; *ostacolo* remove

sgombro[1] *agg strada, stanza* empty

sgombro[2] *m* mackerel

sgomentarsi be frightened

sgonfiare 1 *v/t* let the air out of 2 *v/i e* sgonfiarsi become deflated; *il braccio si è sgonfiato* the swelling in the arm has gone down; **sgonfio** flat; MED not swollen

sgradevole unpleasant

sgradito unwelcome

sgranchire, sgranchirsi: *~ le gambe* stretch one's legs

sgraziato awkward

sgridare scold, tell off F

sguaiato raucous

sguardo *m* look; (*occhiata*) glance

sguazzare splash about; *fig* F *~ nei soldi* be rolling in it F

sgusciare 1 *v/t* shell 2 *v/i* slip away; *mi è sgusciato di mano* it slipped out of my hand

shampoo *m inv* shampoo

shock *m inv* shock

sì yes; *dire di ~* say yes; *penso di ~* I think so

si[1] *pron* oneself; *lui* himself; *lei* herself; *esso, essa* itself; *loro* themselves; *reciproco* each other; **spazzolarsi i capelli** brush one's hair; **~ dice** they say; **cosa ~ può dire?** what can one say?, what can I say?

si[2] *m* MUS B

sia: ~ ... ~ ... both ... and ...; *(o l'uno o l'altro)* either ... or ...; **~ che ... ~ che ...** whether ... or whether ...

siamo → **essere**

sibilare hiss; *di vento* whistle

sicario *m* hired killer, hit man F

sicché (and) so

siccità *f inv* drought

siccome since

Sicilia *f* Sicily; **siciliano 1** *agg* Sicilian **2** *m*, **-a** *f* Sicilian

sicura *f* safety catch

sicurezza *f* security; *(protezione)* safety; *(certezza)* certainty; **sicuro 1** *agg* safe; *(certo)* sure; **~ di sé** sure of o.s.; **di ~** definitely **2** *m*: **mettere al ~** put in a safe place

sidro *m* cider

siedo → **sedere**

siepe *f* hedge

siero *m* MED serum; **sieropositivo** HIV positive

siesta *f* siesta

siete → **essere**

sig. (= **signore**) Mr (= mister)

sigaretta *f* cigarette; **sigaro** *m* cigar

sigg. (= **signori**) Messrs

sigillare seal; **sigillo** *m* seal

sigla *f* initials *pl*; *musicale* theme (tune)

sig.na (= **signorina**) Miss, Ms

significare mean; **significato** *m* meaning

signora *f* lady; **mi scusi, ~!** excuse me!; **la ~ Rossi** Mrs Rossi; **-e e signori** ladies and gentlemen

signore *m* gentleman; **mi scusi, ~!** excuse me!; **il signor Rossi** Mr Rossi; **i -i Rossi** Mr and Mrs Rossi

signorina *f* young lady; **la ~ Rossi** Miss Rossi

sig.ra (= **signora**) Mrs

silenziatore *m* silencer, *Am* muffler

silenzio *m* silence; **silenzioso** silent

sillaba *f* syllable

siluro *m* MAR torpedo

simboleggiare symbolize; **simbolico** symbolic; **simbolismo** *m* symbolism; **simbolo** *m* symbol

simile similar

simmetria *f* symmetry; **simmetrico** symmetrical

simpatia *f* liking; *(affinità)* sympathy; **simpatico** likeable; **simpatizzare** become friends

simulare feign; TEC simulate; **simulazione** *f* pretence, *Am* pretense; TEC simulation

sinagoga *f* synagogue

sinceramente sincerely; *(in verità)* honestly; **sincerità** *f* sincerity; **sincero** sincere

sindacalista m/f trade unionist, Am labor unionist; **sindacato** m trade union, Am labor union

sindaco m mayor

sinfonia f symphony; **sinfonico** symphonic

singhiozzare sob; **singhiozzo** m: **avere il ~** have hiccups; **-zi** pl sobs

single m/f inv single

singolare 1 agg singular; (insolito) unusual; (strano) strange 2 m singular; SP singles; **singolo** 1 agg individual; camera, letto single 2 m individual; SP singles

sinistra f left; **a ~** on the left; andare to the left; **sinistro** 1 agg left, left-hand; fig sinister 2 m accident

sino ☞ **fino**

sinonimo 1 agg synonymous 2 m synonym

sintesi f inv synthesis; (riassunto) summary; **sintetico** synthetic; (riassunto) brief; **sintetizzare** synthesize; (riassumere) summarize

sintomo m symptom

sintonia f RAD tuning; fig **essere in ~** be on the same wavelength (con as); **sintonizzare** RAD tune; **sintonizzarsi** tune in (su to)

sinusite f sinusitis

sipario m curtain

sirena f siren; mitologica mermaid; **~ d'allarme** alarm

siringa f MED syringe

sismico seismic

sistema m system; **sistemare** put; (mettere in ordine) arrange; casa do up; **sistemarsi** tidy o.s. up; (trovare casa, sposarsi) settle down; **sistemazione** f place; (lavoro) job; in albergo accommodation, Am accommodations

sito site; **in ~** on the premises

situato: **essere ~** be situated; **situazione** f situation

sito web m website

slacciare undo

slalom m slalom

slanciato slender

slancio m impulse

slavo 1 agg Slav, Slavonic 2 m, **-a** f Slav

sleale disloyal

slegare untie

slip m inv underpants, Am briefs; da donna panties

slitta f sledge

slittino m sled; SP bobsleigh

slogan m inv slogan

slogare dislocate; **slogarsi**: **~ una caviglia** sprain one's ankle; **slogatura** f sprain

sloggiare move out

Slovacchia f Slovakia; **slovacco** 1 agg Slovak(ian) 2 m, **-a** f Slovak(ian)

Slovenia f Slovenia; **sloveno** 1 agg Slovene 2 m, **-a** f Slovene

smacchiare take the stains out of; **smacchiatore** m stain remover

smagliatura *f* ladder, *Am* run; MED stretch mark

smaltire dispose of

smalto *m* enamel; *per ceramiche* glaze; **~ per unghie** nail varnish

smantellare dismantle

smarrimento *m* loss; *smarrire* lose; **smarrirsi** get lost; **smarrito 1** *pp* ☞ **smarrire 2** *agg* lost

smascherare unmask

smemorato forgetful

smentire prove to be wrong; **smentita** *f* denial

smeraldo *m/agg* emerald

smesso *pp* ☞ **smettere**; **smettere 1** *v/t* stop; *abiti* stop wearing **2** *v/i* stop (*di fare qc* doing sth)

smilitarizzare demilitarize

sminuire *problema* a downplay; *persona* belittle

smisurato boundless

smontabile which can be taken apart, *Am* knockdown; **smontare 1** *v/i da cavallo* dismount **2** *v/t* dismantle

smorfia *f* grimace; **smorfioso** affected

smorzare *colore* tone down; *luce* dim; *entusiasmo* dampen

SMS *m inv* text, text message; **mandare un ~ a qc** text s.o., send s.o. a text

smuovere shift, move

snello slim, slender

snervante irritating

snob 1 *agg* snobbish **2** *m/f inv* snob

SO (= *sud-ovest*) SW (= southwest)

so ☞ *sapere*

sobborgo *m* suburb

sobrio sober

Soc. (= *società*) Co (= company); soc. (= society)

socchiudere half-close; **socchiuso 1** *pp* ☞ **socchiudere 2** *agg* half-closed; *porta* ajar

soccorrere help; **soccorritore** *m* rescue worker; **soccorso 1** *pp* ☞ **soccorrere 2** *m* rescue; **pronto ~** first aid; **~ stradale** breakdown service, *Am* wrecking service

sociale social; **socialismo** *m* socialism; **socialista** *agg*, *m/f* socialist; **socializzare** socialize

società *f inv* company; (*associazione*) society; **~ per azioni** joint stock company

socievole sociable

socio *m*, **-a** *f* member; FIN partner

soddisfacente satisfying; **soddisfare** satisfy; **soddisfatto 1** *pp* ☞ **soddisfare 2** *agg* satisfied; **essere ~ di qu** be satisfied with s.o.; **soddisfazione** *f* satisfaction

sodo *uovo* hard-boiled

sofà *m inv* sofa

sofferenza *f* suffering

soffermarsi dwell (*su* on)

sofferto *pp* ☞ **soffrire**

soffiare blow; F swipe F; **soffiarsi**: **~ il naso** blow one's nose

soffice soft

soffio *m* puff

soffitta *f* attic

soffitto *m* ceiling

soffocante suffocating; **soffocare** suffocate

soffriggere fry gently

soffrire 1 *v/t* suffer; *persone* bear, stand **2** *v/i* suffer (*di* from)

soffritto *pp* ☞ **soffriggere**

sofisticato sophisticated

software *m inv* software

soggettivo subjective; **soggetto 1** *agg* subject; *essere ~ a qc* suffer from sth **2** *m* GRAM subject; **soggezione** *f* subjection

soggiornare stay; **soggiorno** *m* stay

soglia *f* threshold

sogliola *f* sole

sognare, sognarsi dream (*di* about, of); **sognatore** *m*, **-trice** *f* dreamer; **sogno** *m* dream

soia *f* soya

sol *m inv* MUS G

solaio *m* attic, loft

solamente only

solare solar

solco *m* furrow

soldato *m* soldier

soldi *mpl* money

sole *m* sun; *c'è il ~* it's sunny; *prendere il ~* sunbathe; **soleggiato** sun-dried

solenne solemn

solere: *~ fare* be in the habit of doing

soletta *f* insole

solidale *fig* in agreement; **solidarietà** *f* solidarity

solido solid; (*robusto*) sturdy

solista *m/f* soloist

solitario 1 *agg* solitary; *luogo* lonely **2** *m* solitaire; *gioco* patience, *Am* solitaire

solito 1 *agg* usual, same **2** *m di ~* usually; *come al ~* as usual

solitudine *f* solitude

sollecitare (*stimolare*) urge; *risposta* ask for

solletico *m* tickling; *fare il ~ a qu* tickle s.o.; *soffrire il ~* be ticklish

sollevamento *m* lifting; (*insurrezione*) rising; *~ pesi* weightlifting; **sollevare** lift; *obiezione* bring up; **sollevarsi** *di popolo* rise up; AVIA climb

sollievo *m* relief

solo 1 *agg* lonely; (*non accompagnato*) alone; (*unico*) only; MUS solo; *da ~* by myself / yourself etc, on my / your etc own **2** *avv* only **3** *m* MUS solo

solstizio *m* solstice

soltanto only

solubile soluble; **soluzione** *f* solution; **solvente 1** *agg* FIN solvent **2** *m* CHIM solvent

somigliante similar; **somiglianza** *f* resemblance; **somigliare:** *~ a qu* resemble s.o.

soprintendente

somma f (*addizione*) addition; (*risultato*) sum; (*importo*) amount, sum; **sommare** add; **sommario 1** *agg* summary **2** *m* summary; *di libro* table of contents; **sommato: tutto ~** all things considered

sommergere submerge; *fig* overwhelm (**di** with); **sommergibile** *m* submarine; **sommerso** pp ☞ **sommergere**

somministrare MED administer

sommossa f uprising

sondaggio m: **~ (d'opinione)** (opinion) poll

sondare sound; *fig* test

sonnambulo m, **-a** f sleepwalker; **sonnecchiare** doze; **sonnifero** m sleeping pill; **sonno** m sleep; **aver ~** be sleepy; **sonnolenza** f drowsiness

sono ☞ **essere**

sonoro sound *attr*; *risa, applausi* loud; **colonna** f **-a** sound-track

sontuoso sumptuous

soppesare weigh; *fig* weigh up

sopportabile bearable, tolerable; **sopportare** *peso* bear; *fig* bear, stand F

soppressione f deletion; *di regola* abolition; **soppresso** pp ☞ **sopprimere**; **sopprimere** delete; *regola* abolish

sopra 1 *prp* on; (*più in alto di*) above; **l'uno ~ l'altro** one on top of the other; **i bambini ~ cinque anni** children over five; **al di ~ di qc** over sth **2** *avv* on top; (*al piano superiore*) upstairs; **vedi ~** see above

soprabito m (over)coat

sopracciglio m eyebrow

sopraccoperta f *di letto* bedspread; *di libro* dustjacket

sopraffare overwhelm

sopraggiungere *di persona* turn up; *di difficoltà* come up

sopralluogo m inspection (of the site)

soprammobile m ornament

soprannaturale supernatural

soprannome m nickname

soprannumero: in ~ overcrowded

soprano m soprano; **mezzo ~** mezzo(-soprano)

soprappensiero ☞ **sovrapensiero**

soprattassa f surcharge

soprattutto particularly, above all

sopravvalutare overvalue; *fig* overestimate

sopravvento m: **avere** o **prendere il ~** have the upper hand

sopravvissuto 1 *agg* surviving **2** m, **-a** f survivor; **sopravvivenza** f survival; **sopravvivere** survive, outlive (**a qu** s.o.)

soprintendente m/f supervisor

sopruso *m* abuse of power

soqquadro *m*: *mettere a ~* turn upside down

sorbetto *m* sorbet

sorbirsi put up with

sordina *f* mute; *in ~* in secret, on the quiet

sordità *f* deafness; **sordo** deaf; **sordomuto** deaf and dumb

sorella *f* sister; **sorellastra** *f* stepsister

sorgente *f* spring; *fig* source; **sorgere** *di sole* rise, come up; *fig* arise, come up

sorpassare go past; AUTO pass, *Br anche* overtake; *fig* exceed; **sorpassato** out of date; **sorpasso** *m*: *fare un ~* pass, *Br anche* overtake

sorprendente surprising; **sorprendere** surprise; (*cogliere sul fatto*) catch; **sorpresa** *f* surprise; **sorpreso** *pp* ☞ *sorprendere*

sorridere smile; **sorriso 1** *pp* ☞ *sorridere* **2** *m* smile

sorseggiare sip

sorso *m* mouthful

sorta *f* sort, kind

sorte *f* fate; *tirare a ~* draw lots; **sorteggiare** draw

sorto *pp* ☞ *sorgere*

sorveglianza *f* supervision; *di edificio* security; **sorvegliare** supervise; *bagagli ecc* look after

sorvolare 1 *v/t* AVIA fly over **2** *v/i fig*: *~ su* skim over; (*omettere*) skip

sosia *m inv* double

sospendere suspend; (*appendere*) hang; **sospensione** *f* suspension; **sospeso 1** *pp* ☞ *sospendere* **2** *agg* hanging; *fig*: *questione* pending; *tenere in ~ persona* keep in suspense

sospettare suspect; *~ qu o di qu* suspect s.o.; **sospetto 1** *agg* suspicious **2** *m*, *-a f* suspect; **sospettoso** suspicious

sospirare 1 *v/i* sigh **2** *v/t* long for; **sospiro** *m* sigh

sosta *f* stop; (*pausa*) break, pause; *divieto di ~* no parking

sostantivo *m* noun

sostanza *f* substance

sostare stop

sostegno *m* support

sostenere support; (*affermare*) maintain; **sostengo** ☞ *sostenere*; **sostenitore** *m*, *-trice f* supporter

sostituibile replaceable; **sostituire**: *~ X con Y* replace X with Y, substitute Y for X; **sostituto** *m*, *-a f* substitute, replacement; **sostituzione** *f* substitution, replacement

sottaceti *mpl* pickles

sottana *f* slip, underskirt; (*gonna*) skirt; REL cassock

sotterraneo 1 *agg* underground *attr* **2** *m* cellar

sotterrare bury

sottile fine; *fig* subtle; *udito* keen

sottintendere imply; **sottinteso 1** *pp* ☞ **sottintendere 2** *m* allusion

sotto 1 *prp* under; **5 gradi ~ zero** 5 degrees below (zero); **al di ~ di qc** under sth **2** *avv* below; (*più in basso*) lower down; (*al di sotto*) underneath; (*al piano di ~*) downstairs

sottobanco under the counter

sottobraccio: **camminare ~** walk arm-in-arm; **prendere qu ~** take s.o.'s arm

sottocchio: **tenere ~ qc** keep an eye on sth

sottoesposto FOT underexposed

sottofondo *m* background

sottolineare *anche fig* underline

sottomarino 1 *agg* underwater *attr* **2** *m* submarine

sottomesso 1 *pp* ☞ **sottomettere 2** *agg* submissive; *popolo* subject *attr*; **sottomettere** submit; *popolo* subdue

sottopassaggio *m* underpass

sottoporre submit; **sottoporsi**: **~ a** undergo

sottoscritto 1 *pp* ☞ **sottoscrivere 2** *m* undersigned; **sottoscrivere** *documento* sign; *teoria* subscribe to; *abbonamento* take out; **sottoscrizione** *f* signing; (*abbonamento*) subscription

sottosopra *fig* upside-down

sottosuolo *m* subsoil

sottosviluppato underdeveloped

sottovalutare undervalue; *persona* underestimate

sottoveste *f* slip, underskirt

sottovoce quietly, sotto voce

sottrarre MAT subtract; *denaro* embezzle; **sottrarsi**: **~ a qc** avoid sth; **sottratto** ☞ **sottrarre**; **sottrazione** *f* MAT subtraction; *di denaro* embezzlement

souvenir *m inv* souvenir

sovrabbondante overabundant

sovraccarico 1 *agg* overloaded (**di** with) **2** *m* overload

sovrano 1 *agg* sovereign **2** *m*, **-a** *f* sovereign

sovrappensiero: **essere ~** be lost in thought

sovrappeso 1 *agg* overweight **2** *m* excess weight

sovrappopolato overpopulated

sovrapporre overlap

sovrastare overlook, dominate

sovrintendente *m/f* ☞ **soprintendente**

sovrumano superhuman

sovvenzionare give a grant to; **sovvenzione** *f* grant

sovversivo subversive

S.P. (= **Strada Provinciale**) A road, *Am* highway

S.p.A. *f* (= **Società per Azio-**

ni) joint stock company

spaccare break in two; *legna* split, chop; **spaccarsi** break in two

spacciare *droga* deal in, push F; **spacciarsi**: ~ *per* pass o.s. off as; **spacciatore** *m*, **-trice** *f di droga* dealer; **spaccio** *m di droga* dealing; *negozio* general store

spacco *m in gonna* slit; *in giacca* vent; **spaccone** *m*, **-a** *f* braggart

spada *f* sword

spaesato disoriented, confused

spaghetti *mpl* spaghetti *sg*

Spagna *f* Spain; **spagnolo 1** *m/agg* Spanish **2** *m*, **-a** *f* Spaniard

spago *m* string

spalancare open wide

spalla *f* shoulder; *era di* **-e** he had his back to me

spalliera *f* wallbars

spallina *f* shoulder pad

spalmare spread

spalti *mpl* terraces

spandere spread; **spandersi** spread; **spanto** *pp* ☞ **spandere**

sparare 1 *v/i* shoot (*a* at) **2** *v/t*: ~ *un colpo* fire a shot; **sparatoria** *f* gunfire

sparecchiare clear

spareggio *m* SP play-off

spargere spread; *lacrime, sangue* shed

sparire disappear; **sparizione** *f* disappearance

sparo *m* (gun)shot

sparpagliare scatter

sparso *pp* ☞ **spargere 2** *agg* scattered

spartire divide (up), split; **spartito** *m* score; **spartitraffico** *m* traffic island

spasimante *m/f* admirer

spasmo *m* MED spasm

spasso *m* fun; *andare a* ~ go for a walk; *è uno* ~ he / it's a good laugh; **spassoso** very funny

spavaldo cocky, over-confident

spaventapasseri *m inv* scarecrow; **spaventare** frighten, scare; **spaventarsi** be frightened, be scared; **spavento** *m* fright, scare; **spaventoso** frightening

spaziale space *attr*

spazientirsi get impatient

spazio *m* space; **spazioso** spacious

spazzaneve *m inv* snow-plough, *Am* snowplow; **spazzare** sweep; **spazzatura** *f* rubbish, *Am* garbage; **spazzino** *m*, **-a** *f* street sweeper; **spazzola** *f* brush; **spazzolare** brush; **spazzolino** *m* brush; ~ *da denti* toothbrush

specchiarsi look at o.s.; (*riflettersi*) be mirrored; **specchietto** *m* mirror; (*prospetto*) table; AUTO ~ *retrovisore* rear-view mirror; **specchio** *m* mirror

speciale special; **specialista**
m/f specialist; **specialità** *f*
inv speciality, *Am* specialty;
specializzarsi specialize;
specialmente especially

specie 1 *f inv* species *sg*; **una**
~ di a sort *o* kind of **2** *avv* especially

specificare specify; **specifico** specific

speculatore *m*, **-trice** *f* speculator; **speculazione** *f* speculation

spedire send; **spedizione** *f*
dispatch; *di merce* shipping;
(viaggio) expedition; **spedizioniere** *m* courier

spegnere put out; *luce, motore, radio* turn off, switch off;
spegnersi *di fuoco* go out;
di motore stop

spellare skin; **spellarsi** peel

spendere spend; *fig* invest

spennare *pollo* pluck

spensierato carefree

spento *pp* ☞ **spegnere**

speranza *f* hope; **sperare 1**
v/t hope for **2** *v/i* trust (**in** in)

sperduto lost; *luogo* isolated

sperimentare try; *in laboratorio* test; *fig: fatica, dolore*
feel; *droga* experiment with

sperma *m* sperm

sperperare fritter away,
squander

spesa *f* expense; **fare la ~** do
the shopping; **fare -e** go
shopping; **a proprie -e** at
one's own expense

spesso 1 *agg* thick **2** *avv* often, frequently; **spessore**
m thickness

spett. (= **spettabile**) Messrs;
in lettera **Spett. Ditta** Dear
Sirs

spettacolare spectacular;
spettacolo *m* show; *(panorama)* spectacle, sight; **~ teatrale** show

spettare: **questo spetta a te**
this is yours; **non spetta a**
te giudicare it's not up to
you to judge

spettatore *m*, **-trice** *f* spectator; *TEA* member of the audience

spettinare: **~ qu** ruffle s.o.'s
hair

spettro *m* ghost; *FIS* spectrum

spezie *fpl* spices

spezzare break in two; **spezzarsi** break; **spezzatino** *m*
stew; **spezzato 1** *agg* broken
(in two) **2** *m* co-ordinated
two-piece suit; **spezzettare**
break up

spia *f* spy; *TEC* pilot light; **fare**
la ~ tell, sneak

spiacente: **essere ~** be sorry;
spiacere: **mi spiace** I am
sorry

spiacevole unpleasant

spiaggia *f* beach

spiare spy on

spiazzo *m* empty space

spiccato strong

spicchio *m di frutto* section; **~**
d'aglio clove of garlic

spicciarsi hurry up

spiccioli *mpl* (small) change

spiedo

spiedo *m* spit; **allo ~** spit-roasted

spiegare (*stendere*) spread; (*chiarire*) explain; **spiegarsi** explain what one means; **spiegazione** *f* explanation

spiegazzare crease

spietato pitiless

spiga *f* di grano ear; **spigato** herring-bone *attr*

spigliato confident

spigola *f* sea bass

spigolo *m* corner

spilla *f* gioiello brooch; **~ da balia** safety pin

spillo *m* pin

spina *f* BOT thorn; ZO spine; *di pesce* bone; EL plug; ANAT **~ dorsale** spine

spinaci *mpl* spinach

spinale spinal

spinello F *m* joint F

spingere push; *fig* drive

spinoso thorny

spinta *f* push

spinterogeno *m* AUTO distributor

spinto *pp* ☞ **spingere**

spionaggio *m* espionage

spiraglio *m* crack; *di luce, speranza* glimmer

spirale *f* spiral; *contraccettivo* coil

spirare blow; *fig* die

spirito *m* spirit; (*disposizione*) mind; (*umorismo*) wit; **spiritoso** witty; **spirituale** spiritual

splendente bright; **splendere** shine; **splendido** wonderful, splendid

spogliare undress; (*rubare*) rob; **spogliarello** *m* striptease; **spogliarsi** undress, strip; **spogliatoio** *m* dressing room, locker room; **spoglio** bare

spola *f*: **fare la ~ da un posto all'altro** shuttle backwards and forwards between two places

spolverare dust

sponda *f* di letto edge, side; *di fiume* bank; *nel biliardo* cushion

sponsor *m inv* sponsor; **sponsorizzare** sponsor

spontaneo spontaneous

sporadico sporadic

sporcare dirty; **sporcarsi** get dirty; **sporcizia** *f* dirt; **sporco 1** *agg* dirty **2** *m* dirt

sporgere 1 *v/t* hold out; *denuncia* make **2** *v/i* jut out; **sporgersi** lean out

sport *m inv* sport

sportello *m* door; **~ automatico** ATM, cash dispenser

sportivo 1 *agg* sports *attr*, *persona* sporty **2** *m*, **~a** *f* sportsman; *donna* sportswoman

sporto *pp* ☞ **sporgere**

sposa *f* bride; **sposare** marry; **sposarsi** get married; **sposato** married; **sposo** *m* bridegroom; **~i** *pl* newlyweds

spostare (*trasferire*) move, shift; (*rimandare*) postpone; **spostarsi** move

spranga *f* bar; **sprangare** bar

sprecare waste, squander; **spreco** *m* waste

spregevole despicable

spremere squeeze; **spremilimoni** *m inv* lemon squeezer; **spremuta** *f* juice; **~ d'arancia** orange juice

sprofondare sink

sproporzionato out of proportion (**a** to)

sproposito *m* blunder; **costare uno ~** cost a fortune; **a ~** out of turn

sprovveduto inexperienced

sprovvisto: ~ di lacking; **alla -a** unexpectedly

spruzzare spray; **spruzzatore** *m* spray; **spruzzo** *m* spray; **di fango** splatter

spudorato shameless

spugna *f* sponge

spuma *f* foam; **spumante:** (**vino** *m*) ~ sparkling wine

spuntare stick out; BOT come up; **di sole** appear; **di giorno** break

spuntino *m* snack

spunto *m* suggestion; **prendere ~ da** be inspired by

sputare 1 *v/i* spit 2 *v/t* spit out; **sputo** *m* spittle

squadra *f strumento* set square; (**gruppo**) squad; SP team

squalifica *f* disqualification; **squalificare** disqualify

squallido squalid; **squallore** *m* squalor

squalo *m* shark

squama *f* flake; **di pesce** scale

squarcio *m in stoffa* rip, tear; **in nuvole** break

squilibrato 1 *agg* insane 2 *m*, **-a** *f* lunatic; **squilibrio** *m* imbalance

squillare ring; **squillo** *m* ring

squisito *cibo* delicious

sradicare uproot; *fig (eliminare)* eradicate; *persona, pianta* uproot

S.r.l. *f* (= **Società a responsabilità limitata**) Ltd (= limited)

SS. (= **santi**) Saints

stabile 1 *agg* steady; (*duraturo*) stable; *tempo* settled 2 *m* building

stabilimento *m* (*fabbrica*) plant, Br factory

stabilire *data, obiettivi, record* set; (*decidere*) decide, settle; **stabilirsi** settle; **stabilità** *f* steadiness; *di relazione, moneta* stability

staccare remove, detach; EL unplug

stadio *m* stage; SP stadium

staffa *f* stirrup; **perdere le -e** blow one's top

staffetta *f* SP relay; **corsa** *f* **a ~** relay race

stage *m inv* training period

stagionale seasonal; **stagionare** age, mature; *legno* season; **stagionato** aged, mature; *legno* seasoned; **stagione** *f* season; **alta ~** high season; **bassa ~** low season

stagnante stagnant

stagno 1 *m* pond; TEC tin 2

agg watertight

stalla *f per bovini* cowshed; *per cavalli* stable

stamani, stamattina this morning

stambecco *m* ibex

stampa *f* press; *tecnica* printing; FOT print; *posta* **-e** *pl* printed matter; **stampante** *f* INFOR printer; **~ a getto di inchiostro** ink-jet printer; **stampare** print; **stampatello** *m* block letters; **stampato** *m* INFOR printout, hard copy

stampella *f* crutch

stampo *m* mould, *Am* mold

stancare tire (out); **stancarsi** get tired, tire; **stanchezza** *f* tiredness; **stanco** tired; **~ morto** dead beat

stanghetta *f* leg

stanotte tonight; *(la notte scorsa)* last night

stanza *f* room

stanziare *somma di denaro* allocate, earmark

stanzino *m* boxroom

stappare take the top off

stare be; *(restare)* stay; *(abitare)* live; **~ in piedi** stand; **~ bene** be well; *di vestiti* suit; **~ per fare qc** be about to do sth; **lascialo ~** let him be; **~ telefonando** be making a phonecall; **come sta?** how are you?, how are things?; **ben ti sta!** serves you right!

starnutire sneeze; **starnuto** *m* sneeze

stasera this evening, tonight

statale 1 *agg* state *attr* **2** *m/f* civil servant **3** *f* main road;

statistica *f* statistics

stato 1 *pp* **~ essere** *e* **stare 2** *m anche* POL state; **~ civile** marital status

statua *f* statue

statunitense 1 *agg* US *attr*, American **2** *m/f* US citizen

statura *f* height; *fig* stature

stavolta this time

stazionario stationary; **stazione** *f* station; **~ di servizio** service station; **~ balneare** seaside resort; **~ termale** spa

stecca *f di biliardo* cue; *di sigarette* carton; MED splint; MUS wrong note; **stecchino** *m* toothpick

stella *f* star; **~ di mare** starfish

stelo *m* stem, stalk

stemma *m* coat of arms

stendere spread; *braccio* stretch out; *biancheria* hang up; *verbale* draw up; **stendersi** stretch out; **stendibiancheria** *m inv* clothes dryer

stenodattilografa *f* shorthand typist

stentare: ~ a fare qc find it hard to do sth; **stento: a ~** with difficulty

stereo *m inv* stereo

stereotipo 1 *agg* stereotypical **2** *m* stereotype

sterile sterile; **sterilità** f sterility; **sterilizzare** sterilize; **sterilizzazione** f sterilization

sterlina f sterling

sterminare exterminate

sterminato vast

sterminio m extermination

sterno m breastbone, ANAT sternum

sterzare steer; **sterzata** f swerve; **sterzo** m AUTO steering

steso pp ☞ **stendere**

stesso same; **lo ~, la stessa** the same one; **è lo ~** it's all the same; **oggi ~** this very day; **io ~** myself; **se ~** himself

stile m style

stilografica f fountain pen

stima f (ammirazione) esteem; (valutazione) estimate; **stimare** persona esteem; oggetto value; (ritenere) consider; **stimato** respected

stimolante 1 agg stimulating **2** m stimulant; **stimolare** stimulate

stinco m shin

stingere, stingersi fade; **stinto** pp ☞ **stingere**

stipare cram; **stipato** crammed (di with)

stipendiato m, -a f salaryearner; **stipendio** m salary

stipulare stipulate

stiramento m MED pulled muscle

stirare iron; **stirarsi** pull; **stiro**: ferro m da ~ iron; non ~

non-iron

stirpe f (origine) birth

stitichezza f constipation

stivale m boot; **-i** pl **di gomma** wellingtons, Am rubber boots

sto ☞ **stare**

stoccafisso m stockfish (airdried cod)

stoffa f material

stomaco m stomach

stonare di cantante sing out of tune; fig be out of place; di colori clash; **stonato** persona tone deaf; nota false; strumento out of tune

stop m inv AUTO brake light; cartello stop sign; **stoppare** stop

storcere twist; ~ **il naso** make a face; **storcersi** bend; ~ **un piede** twist one's ankle

stordimento m dizziness; **stordire** stun; **stordito** stunned

storia f history; (narrazione) story; non far-e! don't make a scene!; **storico 1** agg historical; (memorabile) historic **2** m, -a f historian

stormo m di uccelli flock

storpio 1 agg crippled **2** m -a f cripple

storta f: prendere una ~ twist one's ankle; **storto** crooked

stoviglie fpl dishes

strabico cross-eyed; **strabismo** m strabismus

stracarico overloaded

stracciare tear up

stracciatella *f* type of soup;
gelato chocolate chip

stracciato in shreds

straccio *m* *per pulire* cloth;
per spolverare duster

strada *f* road; *per ~* down the
road; *sono* (*già*) *per ~* I'm
on my way; *a metà ~* half-
way; **stradale** road *attr*; **stra-
dario** *m* street-finder, street
map

strafare exaggerate

strage *f* slaughter

stragrande: *la ~ maggioranza* the vast majority

strangolare strangle

straniero 1 *agg* foreign **2** *m*, **-a**
f foreigner

strano strange

straordinario 1 *agg* special;
(*eccezionale*) extraordinary
2 *m* overtime

strapazzare treat badly; **stra-
pazzarsi** overdo it; **strapaz-
zo** *m* strain; *essere uno ~* be
exhausting; *da ~* third-rate

strapieno crowded

strapiombo: *a ~* overhanging

strappare tear, rip; (*staccare*)
tear down; (*togliere*) snatch
(*a qu* from s.o.); **strappo** *m*
tear, rip; *MED* torn ligament

straripare overflow its banks

strascico *m* train; *fig* after-ef-
fects

stratagemma *m* stratagem

strategia *f* strategy; **strategico** strategic

strato *m* layer

stravagante extravagant

stravecchio ancient

stravedere: *~ per qu* worship
s.o.

stravolgere change radically;
(*travisare*) twist; (*stancare*) exhaust; **stravolto 1** *pp* ☞ *stravolgere* **2** *agg* (*stanco*) exhausted

strazio *m*: *era uno ~* it was
painful

strega *f* witch; **stregone** *m*
wizard

stremare exhaust; **stremato**
exhausted

stress *m inv* stress; **stressante** stressful; **stressare** stress

stretta *f* hold; *~ di mano*
handshake; *mettere qu alle
-e* put s.o. in a tight corner;
strettamente closely; *tenere qc ~* (*in mano*) clutch
sth (in one's hand); **stretto
1** *pp* ☞ *stringere* **2** *agg* narrow; *vestito* too tight; *lo ~ necessario* the bare minimum
3 *m* *GEOG* strait; **strettoia** *f*
bottleneck

stridere *di porta* squeak; *di
colori* clash

stridulo shrill

strillare scream; **strillo** *m*
scream

striminzito skimpy

strimpellare strum

stringa *f* lace

stringere 1 *v/t* make narrower; *abito* take in; *vite*
tighten; *~ amicizia* become
friends **2** *v/i* *di tempo* press;
stringersi *intorno a tavolo*

squeeze up

striscia f strip; *dipinta* stripe; **-sce** pl **pedonali** zebra crossing, *Am* crosswalk; **a -sce** striped

strisciare 1 v/t *piedi* scrape; (*sfiorare*) brush, smear (*contro* against) **2** v/i crawl; **striscio** m MED smear

striscione m banner

strizzare wring; **~ l'occhio a qu** wink at s.o.

strofa f verse

strofinaccio m dish towel; **strofinare** rub

stroncare *vita* snuff out; F *idea* shoot down

stropicciare crush, wrinkle

strozzare strangle

strozzino m **-a** f loan shark F

strumentalizzare make use of; **strumento** m instrument

strutto m lard

struttura f structure

struzzo m ZO ostrich

stuccare plaster; **stucco** m plaster

studente m, **-essa** f student; **studiare** study; **studio** m study; *di artista*, RAD, TV studio; *di professionista* office; *di medico* surgery, *Am* office

stufa f stove; **~ elettrica / a gas** electric / gas heater

stufare GASTR stew; *fig* bore; **stufarsi** get bored (*di* with); **stufato** m stew; **stufo**: **essere ~ di qc** be bored with sth

stuolo m host

stupefacente 1 agg amazing,

stupefying **2** m narcotic; **stupefatto** amazed, stupefied; **stupendo** stupendous

stupidaggine f stupidity; **stupidità** f stupidity; **stupido 1** agg stupid **2** m, **-a** f idiot

stupire 1 v/t amaze **2** v/i e **stupirsi** be amazed; **stupore** m amazement

stuprare rape; **stupro** m rape

sturare clear, unblock

stuzzicadenti m inv toothpick

stuzzicare tease; *appetito* whet

su 1 prp on; *argomento* about; (*circa*) about; **sul tavolo** on the table; **sul mare** by the sea; **sui trecento euro** about three hundred euros; **nove volte ~ dieci** nine times out of ten **2** avv up; (*al piano di sopra*) upstairs; **~!** come on!; **guardare in ~** look up

sub m/f inv skin diver

subacqueo 1 agg underwater **2** m, **-a** f skin diver

subaffittare sublet; **subaffitto** m sublet

subentrare: **~ a qu** take s.o.'s place

subire *danni*, *perdita* suffer

subito immediately

suburbano suburban

succedere (*accadere*) happen; **~ in carica** succeed; **successione** f succession; **successivo** successive

successo 1 pp ☞ **succedere** **2** m success; **di ~** successful;

successore *m* successor

succhiare suck; **succo** *m* juice; **~ d'arancia** orange juice

succursale *f* branch

sud *m* south; **a(l) ~ di** (to the) south of; **~ ovest** south-west; **~ est** south-east; **a ~ di** (to the) south of

sudare perspire, sweat; **sudato** sweaty

suddividere subdivide

sudicio 1 *agg* dirty **2** *m* dirt; **sudiciume** *m* dirt

sudore *m* perspiration, sweat

sufficiente sufficient; **sufficienza** *f* sufficiency; **a ~** enough

suffragio *m* suffrage

suggerimento *m* suggestion; **suggerire** suggest; TEA prompt; **suggeritore** *m* TEA prompter; **suggestionare** influence; **suggestivo** picturesque

sughero *m* cork

sugli = su and *art* **gli**

sugo *m* sauce; *di arrosto* juice

sui = su and *art* **i**

suicida *m/f* suicide (victim); **suicidarsi** commit suicide, kill o.s.; **suicidio** *m* suicide

suino pork *attr*

sul = su and *art* **il**

sull', sulla, sulle, sullo = su and *art* **l', la, le, lo**

suo 1 *agg* ◇ *di lui* his; *di lei* her; *di cosa* its; **il ~ maestro** his / her teacher; **questo libro è ~** this is his / her book

◇ *forma di cortesia* your; **il ~, la sua, i suoi, le sue** your **2** *pron*: **il ~, la sua, i suoi, le sue** *di lui* his; *di lei* hers; *di cosa* its; *forma di cortesia* yours

suocera *f* mother-in-law; **suocero** *m* father-in-law; **-i** *pl* mother- and father-in--law, in-laws F

suola *f* sole

suolo *m* ground; *(terreno)* soil

suonare 1 *v/t* play; *campanello* ring **2** *v/i* play; *alla porta* ring; **suono** *m* sound

suora *f* REL nun

super 1 *inv* F 4-star; *Am* premium

superare go past; *fig* overcome; *esame* pass

superbo haughty

superficiale superficial; **superficie** *f* surface

superfluo superfluous

superiore 1 *agg* top; *qualità* superior **2** *m* superior; **superiorità** *f* superiority

superlativo *m/agg* superlative

supermarket *m inv*, **supermercato** *m* supermarket

superstite 1 *agg* surviving **2** *m/f* survivor

superstizione *f* superstition; **superstizioso** superstitious

superstrada *f* motorway, *Am* highway

suppergiù about

supplementare supplementary; **supplemento** *m* supplement; **supplente** *m/f* replacement; EDU supply teacher

supplicare beg

suppongo ☞ **supporre**; **supporre** suppose

supporto *m* TEC support

supposizione *f* supposition

supposta *f* MED suppository

supposto *pp* ☞ **supporre**

suppurare MED suppurate

surf *m inv* surfboard; **fare ~** surf, go surfing; **surfista** *m/f* surfer

surgelato 1 *agg* frozen **2** *m: -i pl* frozen food

suscettibile touchy

suscitare arouse

susina *f* plum

sussidio *m* grant, allowance

sussultare start, jump; **sussulto** *m* start, jump

sussurrare whisper

svagarsi take one's mind off things; **svago** *m* distraction

svaligiare burgle, *Am* burglarize

svalutare devalue; **svalutazione** *f* devaluation

svanire vanish

svantaggio *m* disadvantage; **svantaggioso** disadvantageous

svariato varied

svedese 1 *m/agg* Swedish **2** *m/f* Swede

sveglia *f* alarm clock; **sve-**

gliare wake (up); **svegliarsi** waken up; **sveglio** awake; *fig* alert

svelare *segreto* reveal

svelto quick; *alla -a* quickly

svendere sell at a reduced price; **svendita** *f* clearance

svenire faint

sventolare wave

svenuto *pp* ☞ **svenire**

svestire undress; **svestirsi** get undressed, undress

Svezia *f* Sweden

sviare deflect; *fig* divert

svignarsela slip away

sviluppare develop; **svilupparsi** develop; **sviluppato** developed; **sviluppo** *m* development

svincolo *m di strada* junction

svista *f* oversight

svitare unscrew; **svitato** unscrewed; *fig* F *essere ~* have a screw loose F

Svizzera *f* Switzerland; **svizzero 1** *agg* Swiss **2** *m, -a f* Swiss

svogliato lazy

svolgere *rotolo* unwrap; *tema* develop; *attività* carry out; **svolgersi** happen; *di film* be set

svolta *f* turning; *fig* turning point; **svoltare**: *~ a destra* turn right; **svolto** *pp* ☞ **svolgere**

svuotare empty

T

tabaccheria *f* tobacconist's, *Am* tobacco store; **tabacco** *m* tobacco

tabella *f* table; **tabellina** *f* multiplication table

tabellone *m* board; *per avvisi* notice board, *Am* bulletin board

tabù *m/agg inv* taboo

tabulato *m* printout

taccagno mean, stingy F

tacchino *m* turkey

tacco *m* heel

taccuino *m* notebook

tacere 1 *v/t* keep quiet about, say nothing about **2** *v/i* not say anything, be silent

tachicardia *f* tachycardia

tachimetro *m* speedometer

taciturno taciturn

tafano *m* ZO horsefly

tafferuglio *m* scuffle

taglia *f (misura)* size; **~ unica** one size; **tagliacarte** *m inv* paper-knife; **tagliando** *m* coupon; AUTO service; **tagliare** cut; *albero* cut down; *legna* chop; **tagliarsi i capelli** have one's hair cut; *fig* **la strada a qu** cut in front of s.o.; **mi sono tagliata un dito** I've cut my finger; **tagliatelle** *fpl* tagliatelle *sg*; **tagliente** sharp; **tagliere** *m* chopping board; **taglierini** *mpl* type of noo-

dles; **taglio** *m* cut

tailleur *m inv* suit

talco *m* talcum powder

tale such a; **~ e quale** just like; **un ~** someone

talento *m* talent

talloncino *m* coupon

tallone *m* heel

talmente so

talora sometimes

talpa *f* mole

talvolta sometimes

tamburo *m* drum

tamponamento *m* AUTO collision; **~ a catena** multi-vehicle pile-up; **tamponare** *falla* plug; AUTO collide with; **tampone** *m* MED swab; *per donne* tampon; *per timbri* (ink) pad

tana *f* den

tandem *m inv* tandem

tangente *f* MAT tangent; F *(bustarella)* bribe; **tangenziale** *f* ring road

tanica *f* container

tanto 1 *agg* so much; **-i** *pl* so many; **-i saluti** best wishes; **-e grazie** thank you so much **2** *pron* much; **-i** *pl* many **3** *avv* *(così)* so; *con verbi* so much; **di ~ in ~** from time to time; **~ quanto** as much as; **è da ~ (tempo) che non lo vedo** I haven't seen him for a long time

tappa 1 v/t delay; *di viaggio* stage; **tappare** plug; *bottiglia* put the cork in; **tapparella** f rolling shutter

tappeto m carpet

tappezzare (wall)paper; **tappezzeria** f wallpaper; *di sedili* upholstery

tappo m cap, top; *di sughero* cork; *di lavandini, vasche* plug

tarchiato stocky

tardare 1 v/t delay **2** v/i be late; **tardi** late; **più ~** later (on); **al più ~** at the latest; **a più ~!** see you!; **far ~** (*arrivare in ritardo*) be late; (*stare alzato*) stay up late; *in ufficio* work late; **tardo** late

targa f nameplate; AUTO numberplate, *Am* license plate; **targhetta** f tag; *su porta* nameplate

tariffa f rate; *nei trasporti* fare

tarlato worm-eaten

tarlo m woodworm

tarma f (clothes) moth

tartaro m tartar

tartaruga f tortoise; *aquatica* turtle

tartina f canapé

tartufo m truffle

tasca f pocket; **tascabile 1** agg pocket attr **2** m paperback

tassa f tax; **tassametro** m meter; **tassare** tax

tassello m nel muro plug

tassista m/f taxi driver, cab driver

tasso m FIN rate; **~ d'interesse** interest rate

tastare feel; fig **~ il terreno** see how the land lies

tastiera f keyboard; **tasto** m key

tattica f tactics

tatto m (senso) touch; fig tact

tatuaggio m tattoo

tavola f table; (asse) plank, board; *in libro* plate; **~ calda** snackbar; **mettersi a ~** sit down to eat; **tavoletta** f: **~ di cioccolata** bar of chocolate; **tavolo** m table

taxi m inv taxi, esp Am cab

tazza f cup; **tazzina** f espresso cup

tè m inv tea; **~ freddo** iced tea

te you

teatrale theatre attr, Am theater attr, fig theatrical; **rappresentazione** f ~ play; **teatro** m theatre, Am theater; **~ lirico** opera (house)

tecnica f technique; (tecnologia) technology; **tecnico 1** agg technical **2** m technician; **tecnologia** f technology; **alta ~** high tech; **tecnologico** technological

tedesco 1 m/agg German **2** m, -a f German

tegame m (sauce)pan

teglia f baking tin

tegola f tile

teiera f teapot

tela f cloth; PITT canvas; **~ cerata** oilcloth

telaio m loom; di automobile

chassis; *di bicicletta, finestra* frame

telecamera *f* television camera

telecomando *m* remote control

telecomunicazioni *fpl* telecommunications, telecomms

teleferica *f* cableway

telefilm *m inv* television film

telefonare (tele)phone, call (*a qu* s.o.); **telefonata** *f* (tele)phone call; *fare una ~ a qu* phone *o* call s.o.; **telefonico** (tele)phone *attr*; **telefonino** *m* mobile (phone), *Am* cell(ular) phone; **telefono** *m* (tele)phone; *~ a scheda (magnetica)* cardphone; *~ cellulare* mobile phone, *Am* cellular phone

telegiornale *m* news *sg*

telelavoro *m* teleworking

teleobiettivo *m* telephoto lens

telepatia *f* telepathy

teleschermo *m* TV screen

telescopio *m* telescope

telespettatore *m*, **-trice** *f* TV viewer

televisione *f* television, TV; **televisivo** television *attr*, TV *attr*; **televisore** *m* television (set), TV (set)

tema *m* theme, subject

temere be afraid *o* frightened of

temperamatite *m inv* pencil sharpener

temperamento *m* temperament

temperare *acciaio* temper; *matita* sharpen; **temperato** *acciaio* tempered; *clima* temperate

temperatura *f* temperature; *~ ambiente* room temperature

tempesta *f* storm

tempia *f* temple

tempio *m* temple

tempo *m* time; *meteorologico* weather; *~ libero* free time; *a ~ pieno* full-time; *in ~* in time; *un ~* once, long ago; *lavora da molto ~* he has been working for a long time; *fa bel / brutto ~* the weather is lovely / nasty

temporale *m* thunderstorm; **temporaneo** temporary

tenace tenacious

tenaglie *fpl* pincers

tenda *f* curtain; *da campeggio* tent

tendenza *f* tendency; **tendere 1** *v/t elastico, muscoli* stretch; *corde del violino* tighten; *mano* hold out; *fig: trappola* lay; **2** *v/i: ~ a (aspirare a)* aim at; *(essere portati a)* tend to; *(avvicinarsi a)* verge on

tendina *f* net curtain

tendine *m* tendon

tenente *m* lieutenant

tenere 1 *v/t* hold; *(conservare, mantenere)* keep; *(gestire)* run; *conferenza* give; *~ d'oc-*

tesoro

chio keep an eye on **2** *v/i* hold (on); **~ a** (*dare importanza a*) care about; SP support

tenero *m* tender; *pietra, legno* soft

tenersi (*reggersi*) hold on (**a** to); (*mantenersi*) keep o.s.; **~ in piedi** stand (up)

tengo ↝ **tenere**

tennis *m* tennis; **~ da tavolo** table tennis; **tennista** *m/f* tennis player

tenore *m* MUS tenor

tensione *f* voltage; *fig* tension

tentare try, attempt; (*allettare*) tempt; **tentativo** *m* attempt; **tentazione** *f* temptation

tenuta *f* (*capacità*) capacity; (*resistenza*) stamina; (*divisa*) uniform; (*abbigliamento*) outfit; AGR estate

teologo *m*, **-a** *f* theologian

teorema *m* theorem; **teoria** *f* theory; **teorico** theoretical

tepore *m* warmth

teppista *m/f* hooligan

terapia *f* therapy

tergicristallo *m* AUTO windscreen *o* *Am* windshield wiper

termale thermal; **terme** *fpl* baths

terminal *m inv* AVIA terminal; **terminale** *m/agg* terminal; **terminare** end, terminate; **termine** *m* end; (*confine*) limit; FIN (*scadenza*) deadline; (*parola*) term; **a breve / lungo ~** in the short / long term

termocoperta *f* electric blanket

termometro *m* thermometer

termos *m inv* thermos®

termosifone *m* radiator

termostato *m* thermostat

terra *f* earth; (*regione, proprietà, terreno agricolo*) land; (*superficie del suolo*) ground; (*pavimento*) floor; **a ~** on the ground; AVIA, MAR **scendere a ~** get off; **terracotta** *f* terracotta; **terraferma** *f* dry land, terra firma

terrazza *f*, **terrazzo** *m* balcony, terrace

terremoto *m* earthquake

terreno *agg* earthly; *piano* ground, *Am* first **2** *m* (*superficie*) ground; (*suolo, materiale*) soil; (*appezzamento*) plot of land; *fig* (*settore, tema*) field, area; **terrestre** terrestrial

terribile terrible

terrina *f* bowl

territorio *m* territory

terrore *m* terror; **terrorismo** *m* terrorism; **terrorista** *m/f* terrorist; **terrorizzare** terrorize

terza *f* AUTO third (gear); **terziario** *m* tertiary sector, services; **terzino** *m* SP back; **terzo** third

teschio *m* skull

tesi *f inv*: **~ (di laurea)** thesis

teso 1 *pp* ↝ **tendere 2** *agg* taut; *fig* tense

tesoro *m* treasure; (*tesoreria*)

treasury
tessera f card
tessile 1 agg textile **2** -i mpl textiles
tessuto m fabric, material
test m inv test
testa f head; **a** ~ a head; **essere in** ~ lead, be ahead
testamento m will
testardo stubborn
testata f (giornale) newspaper; di letto headboard
teste m/f witness
testicolo m testicle
testimone m/f witness; **testimoniare 1** v/i testify, give evidence **2** v/t testify to; DIR ~ **il falso** commit perjury
testo m text
tetano m tetanus
tetro gloomy
tetto m roof; **tettoia** f roof
Tevere m Tiber
TG m (= **Telegiornale**) TV news sg
thermos ☞ **termos**
ti you; riflessivo yourself
tibia f shinbone, tibia
tic m inv di orologio tick; MED tic
ticket m inv MED prescription charge
tiene ☞ **tenere**
tiepido lukewarm, tepid
tifo m MED typhus; fig **fare il ~ per** be a fan o supporter of; **tifoso** m, -a f fan, supporter
tigre f tiger
timbrare stamp; **timbro** m stamp; MUS timbre; ~ **posta-**

le postage stamp
timidezza f shyness, timidity; **timido** shy, timid
timo m BOT thyme
timone m MAR, AVIA rudder
timore m fear
timpano m MUS kettledrum; ANAT eardrum
tingere dye
tinta f (colorante) dye; (colore) colour, Am color; **tintarella** f (sun)tan
tinto pp ☞ **tingere**
tintoria f dry-cleaner's
tintura f dyeing; (colorante) dye; ~ **di iodio** iodine
tipico typical
tipo m sort, type; F fig guy
tipografia f printing; stabilimento printer's
tir m heavy goods vehicle, Am truck
tiranno m tyrant
tirare 1 v/t pull; (tendere) stretch; (lanciare) throw; (sparare) fire; (tracciare) draw; ~ **fuori** take out; ~ **su** da terra pick up; bambino bring up; ~ **giù** take down **2** v/i pull; di abito be too tight; di vento blow; (sparare) shoot; **tirarsi:** ~ **indietro** back off; fig back out; **tiratura** f di libro print run; di giornale circulation
tirchio 1 agg mean **2** m, -a f miser, skinflint F
tiro m (lancio) throw; (sparo) shot; ~ **con l'arco** archery
tirocinante m/f trainee; **tiro-**

cinio m training

tiroide f thyroid

tirolese agg, m/f Tyrolean, Tyrolese; **Tirolo** m Tyrol

tisana f herbal tea, tisane

titolare m/f owner; **titolo** m title; dei giornali headline; FIN security; ~ **di studio** qualification

titubare hesitate

tizio m, -a f: **un ~** somebody, some man; **una -a** somebody, some woman

toccare 1 v/t touch; (riguardare) be about **2** v/i happen (**a** to); **tocca a me** it's my turn; **mi tocca partire** I have to go; **tocco** m touch

togliere take (away), remove; (eliminare) take off; (revocare) lift; dente take out, extract; ~ **di mezzo** get rid of; **togliersi** giacca take off, remove; (spostarsi) take o.s. off; ~ **dai piedi** get out of the way; **tolgo** ☞ **togliere**

tollerante tolerant; **tollerare** tolerate

tolto pp ☞ **togliere**

tomba f grave

tombola f bingo

tonaca f habit

tonalità f inv tonality

tondo round

tonfo m in acqua splash

tonificare tone up

tonnellata f tonne

tonno m tuna

tono m tone

tonsille fpl ANAT tonsils; **ton-**

sillite f tonsillitis

topazio m topaz

topo m mouse; **Topolino** m Mickey Mouse

toppa f (serratura) keyhole; (rattoppo) patch

torace m chest

torbido liquido cloudy

torcere twist; biancheria wring; **torchio** m press

torcia f torch

torcicollo m stiff neck

tordo m thrush

torinese of Turin; **Torino** f Turin

tormenta f snowstorm; **tormentare** torment; **tormentarsi** torment o.s.

tornaconto m benefit

tornante m hairpin bend

tornare venire come back, return; andare go back, return; (quadrare) balance; ~ **utile** prove useful

torneo m tournament

tornio m lathe

toro m bull; ASTR **Toro** Taurus

torre f tower

torrefazione f roasting

torrente m stream

torrido torrid

torrone m nougat

torso m torso

torsolo m core

torta f cake; **tortellini** mpl tortellini sg

torto m wrong; **aver ~** be wrong; **a ~** wrongly

tortora f turtledove

tortuoso (sinuoso) winding;

(*ambiguo*) devious

tortura f torture; **torturare** torture

tosaerba f o m lawnmower; **tosare** *pecore* shear

Toscana f Tuscany; **toscano** Tuscan

tosse f cough; **aver la ~** have a cough

tossico 1 *agg* toxic **2** m, -a f F druggie F; **tossicodipendente** m/f drug addict; **tossicodipendenza** f drug addiction; **tossicomane** m/f drug addict

tossire cough

tostapane m toaster; **tostare** *pane* toast; *caffè* roast

totale m/agg total; **totalità** f (*interezza*) totality; **nella ~ dei casi** in all cases

totip m *competition similar to football pools, based on horse racing*

totocalcio m *competition similar to football pools*

tovaglia f tablecloth; **tovagliolo** m napkin, serviette

tozzo 1 *agg* stocky **2** m *di pane* crust

tra ☞ **fra**

traballare stagger; *di mobile* wobble

traboccare overflow (*anche fig*)

traccia f (*orma*) footprint; *di veicolo* track; (*indizio*) clue; (*segno*) trace; (*abbozzo*) sketch; **tracciare** *linea* draw; (*delineare*) outline; (*abbozza-*re) sketch

trachea f windpipe

tracolla f (shoulder) strap; **a ~** slung over one's shoulder; **borsa f a ~** shoulder bag

tradimento m betrayal; **tradire** betray; *coniuge* be unfaithful to; **tradirsi** give o.s. away; **traditore 1** *agg* (*infedele*) unfaithful **2** m, **-trice** f traitor

tradizionale traditional; **tradizione** f tradition

tradotto pp ☞ **tradurre**; **tradurre** translate (*in* into); **traduttore** m, **-trice** f translator; **traduzione** f translation

trafficante m/f *spreg* dealer; **~ di droga** drug dealer; **trafficare** deal, trade (*in* in); *spreg* traffic (*in* in); (*armeggiare*) tinker; (*affaccendarsi*) bustle about; **traffico** m traffic

traforo m tunnel

tragedia f tragedy

traghetto m ferry

tragico tragic

tragitto m journey

traguardo m finishing line

traiettoria f trajectory

trainare (*rimorchiare*) tow; *di animali* pull, draw; **traino** m towing; *veicolo* vehicle on tow; **a ~** on tow

tralasciare (*omettere*) omit, leave out; (*interrompere*) interrupt

traliccio m EL pylon; TEC trellis

tram m *inv* tram

trama f fig plot
tramandare hand down
tramare fig plot
trambusto m (confusione) bustle; (tumulto) commotion
tramezzino m sandwich
tramite 1 m (collegamento) link; (intermediario) go-between **2** prp through
tramontana f north wind
tramontare set; **tramonto** m sunset; fig decline
trampolino m diving board; SCI ski jump
tranello m trap
tranne except
tranquillante m tranquillizer, Am tranquilizer; **tranquillità** f peacefulness, tranquillity; **tranquillizzare: ~ qu** set s.o.'s mind at rest; **tranquillo** calm, peaceful
transatlantico 1 agg transatlantic **2** m liner
transazione f DIR settlement; FIN transaction
transenna f barrier
transgenico genetically modified
transitabile strada passable
transitivo GRAM transitive
transito m transit; **divieto di ~** no thoroughfare
trantran m F routine
tranviere m (manovratore) tram driver; (controllore) tram conductor
trapanare drill; **trapano** m drill
trapezio m trapeze; **trapezi-**

sta m/f trapeze artist
trapiantare transplant; **trapianto** m transplant
trappola f trap
trapunta f quilt
trarre conclusioni draw; vantaggio derive
trasalire jump
trasandato scruffy; lavoro slipshod
trasbordo m transfer
trascinare drag; (travolgere) sweep away; fig (entusiasmare) carry away
trascorrere 1 v/t spend **2** v/i pass, go by; **trascorso** pp ☞ **trascorrere**
trascrivere transcribe
trascurabile unimportant; **trascurare** neglect; (tralasciare) ignore; **trascurato** careless, negligent; (trasandato) slovenly; (ignorato) neglected
trasferibile transferable; **trasferimento** m transfer; **trasferire** transfer; **trasferirsi** move; **trasferta** f transfer; SP away game
trasformare transform; TEC process; **trasformarsi** change, turn (in into); **trasformatore** m transformer; **trasformazione** f transformation
trasfusione f transfusion
trasgredire disobey; **trasgressore** m transgressor
traslocare move; **trasloco** m move

trasmettere 266

trasmettere pass on; RAD, TV broadcast, transmit; **trasmissione** f transmission; RAD, TV broadcast, transmission; (*programma*) programme, *Am* program
trasparente 1 *agg* transparent **2** f transparency
trasportare transport; **trasporto** m transport; **-i** pl **pubblici** public transport, *Am* mass transit
trasversale 1 *agg* transverse **2** f MAT transversal
tratta f trade; FIN draft
trattamento m treatment; **trattare 1** v/t treat; TEC treat, process; FIN deal in; (*negoziare*) negotiate **2** v/i deal; **~ di** be about; **trattarsi**: *di che si tratta?* what's it about?; **trattative** fpl negotiations, talks; **trattato** m treatise; DIR, POL treaty
trattenere (*far restare*) keep, hold; (*far perder tempo*) hold up; (*frenare*) restrain; *fiato, respiro* hold; *lacrime* hold back; *somma* withhold; **trattenersi** (*rimanere*) stay; (*frenarsi*) restrain o.s.; **~ dal fare qc** refrain from doing sth; **trattenuta** f deduction
trattino m dash; *in parole composte* hyphen; **tratto 1** pp ☞ **trarre 2** m *di spazio, tempo* stretch; *di penna* stroke; (*linea*) line; **a un ~** all of a sudden; **-i** pl (*lineamenti*) features

trattore m tractor
trattoria f restaurant
trauma m trauma; **traumatico** traumatic
travaglio m MED labour, *Am* labor
travasare decant
trave f beam
traversa f crossbeam; **traversare** cross; **traversata** f crossing; **traverso**: *andare di ~ di cibi* go down the wrong way
travestire disguise; **travestirsi** disguise o.s., dress up (*da* as); **travestito** m transvestite
travolgere carry away (*anche fig*); *con un veicolo* run over; **travolto** pp ☞ **travolgere**
trazione f TEC traction; AUTO **~ anteriore / posteriore** front- / rear-wheel drive
tre three
treccia f plait
trecento 1 *agg* three hundred **2** m: *il Trecento* the fourteenth century; **tredicesimo** thirteenth; **tredici** thirteen
tregua f truce; *fig* break, let-up
trekking m hiking
tremare tremble, shake (*di, per* with)
tremendo terrible, tremendous
tremila three thousand
treno m train; *in ~* by train
trenta thirty; **trentenne** *agg, m/f* thirty-year-old; **trentesimo** thirtieth; **trentina**: *una ~*

tuffo

about thirty

treppiedi *m inv* tripod

triangolare triangular; **triangolo** *m* triangle; AUTO warning triangle

tribù *f inv* tribe

tribuna *f* platform; **tribunale** *m* court

tributo *m* tax; *fig* tribute

tricheco *m* walrus

triciclo *m* tricycle

tricolore *m* Italian flag

triennale *contratto* three-year; *mostra* three-yearly; **triennio** *m* three-year period

trifoglio *m* clover

triglia *f* red mullet

trillo *m* trill

trimestrale quarterly

trincea *f* trench

trio *m* trio

trionfare triumph (**su** over); **trionfo** *m* triumph

triplicare triple; **triplo 1** *agg* triple **2** *m: il* ~ **three** times as much (**di** as)

trippa *f* tripe

triste sad; **tristezza** *f* sadness

tritare mince, *Am* ground meat; **tritatutto** *m inv* mincer, *Am* meat grinder

trittico *m* triptych

triturare grind

trivella *f* drill

triviale trivial

trofeo *m* trophy

tromba *f* MUS trumpet; ~ *d'aria* whirlwind; ~ *delle scale* stairwell

trombone *m* trombone

trombosi *f* thrombosis

troncare cut off; *fig* break off

tronco *m* ANAT, BOT trunk; FERR section

trono *m* throne

tropicale tropical; **tropici** *mpl* tropics

troppo 1 *agg* too much; **-i** *pl* too many **2** *avv* too much; *con agg* too; **è ~ tardi** it's too late

trota *f* trout

trottare trot; **trotto** *m* trot

trovare find; (*inventare*) find, come up with; **andare a ~ qu** (go and) see s.o.; **trovarsi** be; ~ *bene* be happy; **trovata** *f* good idea

truccare make up; *motore* soup up F; *partita, elezioni* fix; **truccarsi** put on one's make-up; **trucco** *m* make-up; (*inganno, astuzia*) trick

truffa *f* fraud; **truffare** defraud (**di** of); **truffatore** *m*, **-trice** *f* trickster, con artist F

truppa *f* troops

tu you; **dammi del ~** call me 'tu'

tubatura *f*, **tubazione** *f* pipes, piping

tubercolosi *f* tuberculosis

tubetto *m* tube

tubo *m* pipe; *flessibile* hose; AUTO ~ *di scappamento* exhaust (pipe)

tuffarsi (*immergersi*) dive; (*buttarsi dentro*) throw o.s. (*anche fig*); **tuffo** *m* dip; SP dive

tugurio *m* hovel

tulipano *m* tulip

tumore *m* tumour, *Am* tumor

tumulto *m* riot

tunica *f* tunic

Tunisia *f* Tunisia; **tunisino 1** *agg* Tunisian **2** *m*, -**a** *f* Tunisian

tunnel *m inv* tunnel

tuo 1 *agg* your; *il ~ amico* your friend; *un ~ amico* a friend of yours **2** *pron*: *il ~* yours

tuonare thunder; **tuono** *m* thunder

tuorlo *m* yolk

turbante *m* turban

turbare upset, disturb; **turbolenza** *f* turbulence

turchese *m/agg* turquoise

Turchia *f* Turkey; **turco 1** *m/agg* Turkish **2** *m*, -**a** *f* Turk

turismo *m* tourism; **turista** *m/f* tourist; **turistico** tourist *attr*

turno *m* turn; *di lavoro* shift; *a ~* in turn; *~ di riposo* rest day; *darsi il ~* take turns

tuta *f* da lavoro overalls; *~ da ginnastica* track suit, *Am* sweats; *~ da sci* ski suit

tutela *f* protection; DIR guardianship; **tutelare** protect; **tutore** *m*, -**trice** *f* guardian

tuttavia still

tutto 1 *agg* whole; -**i**, -**e** *pl* all; *~ il libro* the whole book; -**i i giorni** every day; -**i e tre** all three; *noi* -**i** all of us **2** *avv* all; *era ~ solo* he was all alone; *del ~* quite; *in ~* altogether, in all **3** *pron* all; *gente* everybody, everyone; *cose* everything

tuttora still

TV *f inv* TV

U

ubbidiente obedient; **ubbidire** obey

ubriacare: *~ qu* get s.o. drunk; **ubriacarsi** get drunk; **ubriaco 1** *agg* drunk **2** *m*, -**a** *f* drunk

uccello *m* bird

uccidere kill; **uccidersi** kill o.s.; **ucciso** *pp ☞* **uccidere**

udienza *f* audience; DIR hearing; **udire** hear; **udito** *m* hearing

Ue *f* (= *Unione europea*) EU

(= European Union)

ufficiale 1 *agg* official **2** *m* official; MIL officer; **ufficio** *m* office; *~ cambi* bureau de change; *~ postale* post office; *~ turistico* tourist information office; **ufficioso** unofficial

ufo *m* UFO

uguaglianza *f* equality; **uguagliare** make equal; (*livellare*) level; (*essere pari a*) equal; **uguale** equal; (*lo stes-*

so) the same; *terreno* level

ulcera *f* ulcer

ulteriore further

ultimamente recently; **ultimare** complete; **ultimatum** *m inv* ultimatum; **ultimo 1** *agg* last; (*più recente*) latest; ~ **piano** top floor **2** *m*, -**a** *f* last; *fino all'~* till the end

ultrasuono *m* ultrasound

ultravioletto ultraviolet

ululare howl

umanità *f* humanity; **umanitario** humanitarian; **umano** human; *trattamento ecc* humane

umidificatore *m* humidifier; **umidità** *f* dampness; *di clima* humidity; **umido 1** *agg* damp **2** *m* dampness; GASTR *in* ~ stewed

umile (*modesto*) humble; *mestiere* menial; **umiliante** humiliating; **umiliare** humiliate; **umiliazione** *f* humiliation; **umiltà** *f* humility

umore *m* mood; *di buon* ~ in a good mood; *di cattivo* ~ in a bad mood

umorismo *m* humour, *Am* humor

un, una → **uno**

unanime unanimous; **unanimità** *f* unanimity; *all'~* unanimously

uncinetto *m* crochet hook; **uncino** *m* hook

undicesimo eleventh; **undici** eleven

ungere grease

ungherese *agg*, *m/f* Hungarian; **Ungheria** *f* Hungary

unghia *f* nail

unico only; (*senza uguali*) unique

unifamiliare: *casa f* ~ detached house

unificazione *f* unification

uniformare standardize; **uniformarsi**: ~ *a* conform to; *regole* comply with; **uniforme** *f* /*agg* uniform

unione *f* union; *fig* unity; **Unione europea** European Union; **unire** unite; (*congiungere*) join; **unirsi** unite; **unità** *f inv* unit; INFOR ~ *disco* disk drive; ~ *di misura* unit of measurement; **unito** united

universale universal; **università** *f inv* university; **universitario** *agg* university *attr* **2** *m*, -**a** *f* university student; (*professore*) university lecturer; **universo** *m* universe

uno 1 *art* a; *before a vowel or silent* h *an*; *un uovo* an egg **2** *agg* a, one **3** *m* one; ~ *e mezzo* one and a half **4** *pron* one; *a* ~ *a* ~ one by one; *l'un l'altro* each other, one another

unto 1 *pp* → **ungere 2** *agg* greasy **3** *m* grease

uomo *m* man; *d'affari* businessman; *da* ~ *abbigliamento ecc* for men, men's

uovo *m* egg; ~ *alla coque* soft-boiled egg; ~ *di Pasqua* Easter egg; ~ *al tegame* fried egg; *-a pl* **strapazzate** scrambled eggs

uragano *m* hurricane

uranio *m* uranium

urbano urban; *fig* urbane

urgente urgent; **urgenza** *f* urgency; *in caso d'~* in an emergency

urina *f* urine

urlare scream; **urlo** *m* scream

urna *f* urn; *elettorale* ballot box

urrà! hooray!

urtare bump into; *fig* offend **urto** *m* bump; *(scontro)* collision

usa: *~ e getta* disposable, throw-away

usanza *f* custom, tradition; **usare 1** *v/t* use **2** *v/i* use; *(essere di moda)* be in fashion; **usato** used; *(di seconda mano)* second-hand

uscire come out; *(andare fuo-* *ri)* go out; **uscita** *f* exit, way out; *~ di sicurezza* emergency exit

usignolo *m* nightingale

uso *m* use; *(abitudine)* custom; *fuori ~* out of use; *per esterno* not to be taken internally

ustionarsi burn o.s.; **ustione** *f* burn

usuale usual

usufruire: *~ di qc* have the use of sth

usuraio *m* loan shark

utensile *m* utensil

utente *m/f* user

utero *m* womb

utile 1 *agg* useful **2** *m* FIN profit; **utilità** *f* usefulness; **utilitaria** *f* economy car; **utilizzare** use; **utilizzazione** *f* use

utopia *f* utopia

uva *f* grapes; *~ passa* raisins *pl*; *~ spina* gooseberry

V

V. (= *via*) St (= street)

va *→* **andare**

vacanza *f* holiday, *Am* vacation; *andare in ~* go on holiday

vacca *f* cow

vaccinare vaccinate; **vaccinazione** *f* vaccination; **vaccino** *m* vaccine

vado *→* **andare**

vagabondo 1 *agg* *(girovago)* wandering; *(fannullone)* idle **2** *m*, *-a f* *(giramondo)* wanderer; *(fannullone)* idler, layabout F; *(barbone)* tramp, *Am* hobo; **vagare** wander (aimlessly)

vagina *f* ANAT vagina

vaglia *m inv: ~ (postale)* postal order

vago vague

vagone *m* carriage, car; *per merci* wagon; *~ letto* sleeper; *~ ristorante* dining car

vai ☞ *andare*
valanga *f* avalanche
valere be worth; (*essere valido*) be valid; **far** ~ *diritti, autorità* assert; **valersi:** ~ *di qc* avail o.s. of sth; **valevole** valid
valgo ☞ *valere*
valico *m* pass
validità *f* validity; **valido** valid; *persona* fit
valigia *f* suitcase; **fare le -e** pack
valle *f* valley
valore *m* value; (*coraggio*) bravery, valour, *Am* valor; **-i** *pl* securities; **di** ~ valuable; **valorizzare** increase the value of; (*far risaltare*) show off
valuta *f* currency; **valutare** value
valvola *f* valve; *EL* fuse
valzer *m inv* waltz
vandalo *m* vandal
vanga *f* spade
vangelo *m* gospel
vaniglia *f* vanilla
vanità *f* vanity; **vanitoso** vain
vanno ☞ *andare*
vano 1 *agg* minacce, promesse empty; (*inutile*) vain 2 *m* (*spazio vuoto*) hollow; (*stanza*) room
vantaggio *m* advantage; *in gara* lead; **vantaggioso** advantageous
vantarsi boast (**di** about)
vapore *m* vapour, *Am* vapor; *MAR* steamer; ~ (*acqueo*) steam; **vaporetto** *m* water

bus; **vaporoso** floaty; (*vago*) woolly, *Am* wooly
variabile 1 *agg* changeable 2 *f* *MAT* variable; **variare** vary; **variazione** *f* variation
varice *f* varicose vein
varicella *f* chickenpox
varietà 1 *f inv* variety 2 *m inv* variety, *Am* vaudeville; (**spettacolo** *m* **di**) ~ (variety o *Am* vaudeville) show; **vario** varied; **-ri** *pl* various
variopinto multicoloured, *Am* multicolored
vasca *f* (*serbatoio, cisterna*) tank; (*lunghezza di piscina*) length; *di fontana* basin; ~ (**da bagno**) bath, (bath)tub
vaselina *f* vaseline
vasellame *m* dishes
vaso *m* pot; *ANAT* vessel
vassoio *m* tray
vasto vast
V.d.F. (= *vigili del fuoco*) fire brigade, *Am* fire department
ve = *vi* (*before lo, la, li, le, ne*)
vecchiaia *f* old age; **vecchio** 1 *agg* old 2 *m*, **-a** *f* old man; *donna* old woman
vece *f*: **fare le -i di qu** take s.o.'s place
vedere see; **far** ~ show
vedovo 1 *agg* widowed 2 *m*, **-a** *f* widower; *donna* widow
veduta *f* view (**su** of)
vegetale 1 *agg* vegetable *attr*, *vita* plant *attr* 2 *m* vegetable; **vegetariano** 1 *agg* vegetarian *attr* 2 *m*, **-a** *f* vegetarian;

vegetazione f vegetation

vegeto vecchio spry; **vivo e ~** hale and hearty

veglia f (l'essere svegli) wakefulness; (il vegliare) vigil

veicolo m vehicle

vela f sail; attività sailing

veleno m poison; di animali venom (anche fig); **velenoso** poisonous; fig venomous

veliero m sailing ship

velina: **carta f ~** per imballaggio tissue paper

velista m/f sailor

velluto m velvet; **~ a coste** corduroy

velo m veil

veloce fast, quick; **velocemente** quickly; **velocità** f inv speed

vena f vein

vendemmia f (grape) harvest; **vendemmiare** harvest

vendere sell

vendetta f revenge; **vendicare** avenge; **vendicarsi** get one's revenge (**di qu** on s.o.; **di qc** for sth)

vendita f sale; **venditore** m, **-trice** f salesman; donna saleswoman

venerare revere

venerdì m inv Friday; **Venerdì Santo** Good Friday

Venere f Venus

Venezia f Venice; **veneziano 1** agg Venetian **2** m, -a f Venetian

vengo → **venire**; **venire** come; (riuscire) turn out; come ausiliare be; **mi sta venendo fame** I'm getting hungry

ventaglio m fan

ventenne agg, m/f twenty-year-old; **ventesimo** twentieth; **venti** twenty

ventilatore m fan

ventina f: **una ~** about twenty; **ventiquattrore** f inv valigetta overnight bag

vento m wind; **c'è ~** it's windy; **ventoso** windy

ventre m stomach

venuta f arrival; **venuto** pp → **venire**

veramente really

veranda f veranda

verbale 1 agg verbal **2** m record; di riunione minutes

verbo m GRAM verb

verde 1 agg green **2** m green; POL **i -i** pl the Greens

verdura f vegetables

vergine 1 agg virgin attr **2** f virgin; ASTR **Vergine** Virgo

vergogna f shame; (timidezza) shyness; **vergognarsi** be ashamed; (essere timido) be shy; **vergognoso** ashamed; (timido) shy; azione shameful

verifica f check; **verificare** check; **verificarsi** (accadere) occur, take place; (avverarsi) come true

verità f inv truth

verme m worm

vermut m vermouth

vernice f paint; trasparente

varnish; **pelle** patent leather; **~ fresca** wet paint; **verniciare** paint; **con vernice trasparente** varnish

vero 1 *agg* true; *(autentico)* real; **sei contento, ~?** you're happy, aren't you?; **ti piace il gelato, ~?** you like ice cream, don't you? **2** *m* truth

veronese *f agg* of Verona **2** *m/f* inhabitant of Verona

verosimile likely

verruca *f* wart

versamento *m* payment

versante *m* slope

versare *vino* pour; *denaro* pay; *(rovesciare)* spill

versione *f* version; *(traduzione)* translation

verso 1 *prp* towards; **andare ~ casa** head for home; **~ le otto** about eight o'clock **2** *m di poesie* verse

vertebra *f* vertebra; **vertebrale: colonna** *f* **~** spinal column

verticale 1 *agg* vertical **2** *f* vertical (line); *in ginnastica* handstand

vertice *m* summit

vertigine *f* vertigo, dizziness; **ho le -i** I feel dizzy; **vertiginoso** *altezza* dizzy; *prezzi* sky-high; *velocità* breakneck

verza *f* savoy (cabbage)

vescica *f* ANAT bladder

vescovo *m* bishop

vespa *f* ZO wasp; *(scooter)* Vespa® scooter; **vespista** *m/f* Vespa® rider

vestaglia *f* dressing gown, *Am* robe

veste *f* fig *(capacità, funzione)* capacity; **in ~ ufficiale** in an offical capacity; **vestiario** *m* wardrobe; **vestire** dress; *(portare)* wear; **vestirsi** get dressed; *in un certo modo* dress; **~ da** *(travestirsi)* dress up as; **vestito** *m* da uomo suit, *da donna* dress, *(capo di vestiario)* item of clothing, garment; **-i pl** clothes; **-i pl da uomo** menswear

veterinario *m*, **-a** *f* veterinary surgeon, vet F

veto *m* veto; **porre il ~ a** veto

vetrata *f finestra* large window; *porta* glass door; *di chiesa* stained-glass window; **vetrina** *f* (shop) window; *mobile* display cabinet; *di museo, fig* showcase; **vetrinista** *m/f* window dresser; **vetro** *m* glass; *di finestra, porta* pane; **di ~** glass *attr*

vetta *f* top; *di montagna* peak

vettura *f* AUTO car; FERR carriage, car

vi 1 *pron* you; *riflessivo* yourselves; *reciproco* each other **2** *avv* → **ci**

via 1 *f* street, road; *fig* way; **per ~ di** by; *(a causa di)* because of **2** *m* off, starting signal; SP **dare il ~** give the off **3** *avv* away; *andar* **~** go away, leave; **e così ~** and so on; **~!** go away!; *(suvvia)* come on! **4** *prp* via, by way of

viabilità f road conditions; *(rete stradale)* road network; *(traffico stradale)* road traffic

viadotto m viaduct

viaggiare travel; **viaggiatore** m,-**trice** f traveller; *Am* traveler; **viaggio** m journey; ~ *di nozze* honeymoon; ~ *d'affari* business trip; ~ *di studio* study trip; *essere in* ~ be away, be travelling

viale m avenue

viavai m inv coming and going

vibrare vibrate; **vibrazione** f vibration

vice m/f inv deputy

vice- prefisso vice-

vicedirettore m assistant manager

vicenda f *(episodio)* event; *(storia)* story; *a* ~ *(a turno)* in turn; *(scambievolmente)* each other, one another

viceversa vice versa

vicinanza f nearness, proximity; -**e** pl neighbourhood, *Am* neighborhood, vicinity; **vicinato** m neighbourhood, *Am* neighborhood, *(persone)* neighbours, *Am* neighbors; **vicino 1** agg near, close; ~ *a* near, close to; *(accanto a)* next to; *da* ~ *esaminare* closely; *visto* close up **2** avv nearby, close by **3** m, -**a** f neighbour, *Am* neighbor

vicolo m lane; ~ *cieco* dead end

videata f INFOR display

video m video; F *(schermo)* screen; **videocamera** f videocamera, camcorder; **videocassetta** f video (cassette); **videogioco** m video game; **videoregistratore** m video (recorder); **videoteca** f video library; *negozio* video shop o *Am* store; **videotel** m inv Italian Videotex®; **videotelefono** m videophone

vietare forbid; ~ *a qu di fare qc* forbid s.o. to do sth; **vietato** forbidden; ~ *fumare* no smoking

vigilanza f vigilance; **sotto** ~ under surveillance; **vigile 1** agg watchful **2** m/f: ~ *(urbano)* local police officer; ~ *del fuoco* firefighter; **vigilia** f night before, eve; ~ *di Natale* Christmas Eve

vigliacco 1 agg cowardly **2** m, -**a** f coward

vigna f *(small)* vineyard; **vigneto** m vineyard

vignetta f cartoon

vigore m vigour, *Am* vigor

vile 1 agg vile; *(codardo)* cowardly **2** m coward

villa f villa

villaggio m village; ~ *turistico* holiday village

villeggiatura f holiday, *Am* vacation

villino m house

vincere 1 v/t win; *avversario* defeat, beat; *difficoltà* overcome **2** v/i win; **vincita** f win; **vincitore** *m*, **-trice** *f* winner

vincolare bind; *capitale* tie up; **vincolo** *m* bond

vino *m* wine; **~ bianco** white wine; **~ rosso** red wine

vinto *pp* ☞ **vincere**

viola 1 *m/agg inv* purple **2** *f* MUS viola; BOT violet

violare violate; *legge* break; **violazione** *f* violation; *di leggi, accordi* breach; **~ di domicilio** unlawful entry

violentare rape; **violento** violent; **violenza** *f* violence

violino *m* violin; **violoncello** *m* cello

vipera *f* viper

virgola *f* comma; MAT decimal point

virile manly, virile

virtù *f inv* virtue

virus *m inv* virus

vischio *m* mistletoe

viscido slimy

viscosa *f* viscose

visibile visible; **visibilità** *f* visibility

visiera *f* di *berretto* peak; *di casco* visor

visione *f* sight, vision

visita *f* visit; **~ medica** medical (examination); **far ~ a qu** visit s.o.; **visitare** visit; MED examine; **visitatore** *m*, **-trice** *f* visitor

visivo visual

viso *m* face

visone *m* mink

vissuto *pp* ☞ **vivere**

vista *f* sight; (*veduta*) view; **a prima ~** at first sight; **conoscere qu di ~** know s.o. by sight; *fig* **perdere qu di ~** lose touch with s.o.; **visto 1** *pp* ☞ **vedere**; **~ che** seeing that **2** *m* visa; **vistoso** eye-catching

visuale 1 *agg* visual **2** *f* (*veduta*) view

vita *f* life; (*durata della vita*) lifetime; ANAT waist; **vitale** vital; *persona* lively

vitamina *f* vitamin

vite[1] *f* TEC screw

vite[2] *f* AGR vine

vitello *m* calf; GASTR veal

viticoltura *f* vinegrowing

vitreo *fig*: *sguardo* glazed

vittima *f* victim

vitto *m* diet food; **~ e alloggio** bed and board

vittoria *f* victory

viva voce *m inv* speakerphone, hands-free phone

vivace lively; *colore* bright

vivaio *m* di *pesci* tank; *di piante* nursery; *fig* breeding ground

vivanda *f* food

vivente living; **vivere 1** *v/i* live (*di* on) **2** *v/t* (*passare, provare*) experience; *vita* live, lead; **viveri** *mpl* food (supplies)

vivisezione *f* vivisection

vivo 1 *agg* (*in vita*) alive; (*vivente*) living; *colore* bright; **farsi ~** get in touch; (*arrivare*) turn up **2** *m*: **dal ~** *trasmissione* live; **i -i** *pl* the living *pl*

viziare *persona* spoil; **viziato** *persona* spoiled; *aria* f *-a* stale air; *vizio* m vice; (*cattiva abitudine*) (bad) habit; (*dipendenza*) addiction; *vizioso persona* dissolute; *circolo* m ~ vicious circle

v.le (= *viale*) St (= street)

vocabolario m vocabulary; (*dizionario*) dictionary; **vocabolo** m word

vocale 1 *agg* vocal **2** f vowel

vocazione f vocation

voce f voice; *fig* rumour, *Am* rumor; *in dizionario, elenco* entry

voglia f (*desiderio*) wish, desire; (*volontà*) will; *sulla pelle* birthmark; **avere ~ di fare qc** feel like doing sth; **contro ~, di mala ~** unwillingly; **voglio** ☞ *volere*

voi you; *riflessivo* yourselves; *reciproco* each other

volano m shuttlecock

volante 1 *agg* flying **2** m AUTO (steering) wheel; **volantino** m leaflet; **volare** fly

volentieri willingly; **~!** with pleasure!

volere 1 *v/t & v/i* want; **vorrei ...** I would *o* I'd like ...; **vorrei partire** I'd like to leave; **~ dire** mean; **~ bene a qu** (*amare*) love s.o.; **ci vogliono dieci mesi** it takes ten months; **senza ~** without meaning to **2** m will

volgare vulgar

volgere 1 *v/t:* **~ le spalle** turn

one's back **2** *v/i:* **~ al termine** draw to a close

volo m flight; (*caduta*) fall; **~ di linea** scheduled flight; *fig* **afferrare qc al ~** be quick to grasp sth

volontà f will; **a ~** as much as you like; **buona ~** goodwill; **volontariato** m voluntary work; **volontario 1** *agg* voluntary **2** m, -a f volunteer

volpe f fox; *femmina* vixen

volt m *inv* volt

volta f time; (*turno*) turn; ARCHI vault; **una ~** once; **due ~e** twice; **qualche ~** sometimes; **poco per ~** little by little; **un'altra ~** (*ancora una volta*) one more time; **lo faremo un'altra** we'll do it some other time

voltaggio m voltage

voltare turn; **~ a destra** turn right; **voltarsi** turn (round)

volto[1] m face

volto[2] *pp* ☞ *volgere*

volume m volume; **voluminoso** bulky

vomitare vomit; **vomito** m vomit

vongola f ZO, GASTR clam

vortice m whirl; *in acqua* whirlpool; *di vento* whirlwind

vostro 1 *agg* your; *i -i amici* your friends **2** *pron:* *il ~* yours; *questi libri sono -i* these books are yours

votare vote; **votazione** f vote; **voto** m POL vote; EDU mark,

Am grade; REL vow
v.r. (= *vedi retro*) see over
v.s. (= *vedi sopra*) see above
Vs. (= *vostro*) your
V.U. (= *Vigili Urbani*) police
vulcanico volcanic; **vulcano**
   m volcano
vulnerabile vulnerable

vuole ☞ *volere*
vuotare empty; **vuotarsi**
   empty; **vuoto 1** *agg* empty;
   (*non occupato*) vacant **2** *m*
   (*spazio*) empty space; (*recipiente*) empty; FIS vacuum;
   fig void; *andare a* ~ fall
   through

W

W (= *watt*) W (= watt); (= *viva*) long live
walkman *m inv* Walkman®
watt *m inv* watt
WC *m inv* WC
week-end *m inv* weekend

western *m inv* Western
whisky *m inv* whisky
windsurf *m inv* (*tavola*) sailboard; *attività* windsurfing;
   fare ~ go windsurfing

X

X, x *f* x; **raggi** *mpl* ~ X-rays
xenofobia *f* xenophobia

xilofono *m* xylophone

Y

yacht *m inv* yacht
yoga *m* yoga

yogurt *m inv* yoghurt

Z

zafferano *m* saffron
zaffiro *m* sapphire
zaino *m* rucksack, backpack
zampa *f* ZO (*piede*) paw; *di uccello* claw; (*arto*) leg; GASTR
   di maiale trotter

zampillare gush; **zampillo** *m*
   spurt
zampone *m* GASTR stuffed
   pig's trotter
zanzara *f* mosquito; **zanzariera** *f* mosquito net; *su fine-*

stre insect screen
zappa f hoe; **zappare** hoe
zapping m inv: **fare lo ~** zap, channel-punch
zattera f raft
zebra f zebra
zecca[1] f ZO tick
zecca[2] f Mint
zelo m zeal
zenzero m ginger
zeppo: **pieno ~** crammed (**di** with)
zerbino m doormat
zero m zero; **nel tennis** love; **nel calcio** nil; **2 gradi sotto ~** 2 degrees below zero
zigomo m cheekbone
zigzag m inv zigzag
zimbello m decoy; *fig* laughing stock
zinco m zinc
zingaro m, **-a** f gipsy
zio m, **-a** f uncle; **donna** aunt

zitto quiet; **sta ~!** be quiet!
zoccolo m clog; ZO hoof
zodiacale: **segni** mpl **-i** signs of the Zodiac
zolfo m sulphur, Am sulfur
zona f zone, area; **~ disco** short-stay parking area; **~ industriale** industrial area; **~ pedonale** pedestrian precinct
zoo m inv zoo
zoppicare limp; *di mobile* wobble
zoppo lame; (*zoppicante*) limping; *mobile* wobbly
zucca f marrow; *fig* F (*testa*) nut F
zuccherare sugar; **zucchero** m sugar
zucchini mpl courgettes, Am zucchini(s)
zuffa f scuffle
zuppa f soup; **~ inglese** trifle
zuppo soaked

English-Italian
Inglese-Italiano

A

a [ə] un *m*, una *f*; *masculine before s + consonant, gn, ps, x, y, z* uno; *feminine before vowel* un'; *five flights ~ day* cinque voli al giorno

aback [ə'bæk]: *taken ~* preso alla sprovvista

abandon [ə'bændən] abbandonare; *scheme* rinunciare a

abate [ə'beɪt] *of storm* calmarsi

abbey ['æbɪ] abbazia *f*

abbreviate [ə'briːvɪeɪt] abbreviare; **abbreviation** abbreviazione *f*

abdicate ['æbdɪkeɪt] abdicare

abdomen ['æbdəmən] addome *m*

abduct [əb'dʌkt] sequestrare

◆ **abide by** [ə'baɪd] attenersi a

ability [ə'bɪlətɪ] abilità *f inv*

ablaze [ə'bleɪz] in fiamme

able ['eɪbl] (*skilful*) capace; *be ~ to do sth* poter fare qc

abnormal [æb'nɔːml] anormale

aboard [ə'bɔːd] **1** *prep* a bordo di **2** *adv* a bordo

abolish [ə'bɒlɪʃ] abolire; **abolition** abolizione *f*

abort [ə'bɔːt] annullare; *program* interrompere; **abortion** aborto *m*; *have an ~* abortire; **abortive** fallito

about [ə'baʊt] **1** *prep* (*concerning*) su; *talk ~ sth* parlare di qc; *be angry ~ sth* essere arrabbiato per qc; *what's it ~? of book, film* di cosa parla?; *of complaint, problem* di cosa si tratta? **2** *adv* (*roughly*) intorno a; (*nearly*) quasi; *it's ~ ready* è quasi pronto; *be ~ to ... (be going to)* essere sul punto di ...; *be ~ (somewhere near)* essere nei paraggi; *there are a lot of people ~* c'è un sacco di gente qui

above [ə'bʌv] sopra; *on the floor ~* al piano di sopra; **above-mentioned** suddetto

abrasive [ə'breɪsɪv] *personality* ruvido

abreast [ə'brest] fianco a fianco; *keep ~ of* tenere al corrente di

abridge [ə'brɪdʒ] ridurre

abroad [ə'brɔːd] all'estero

abrupt [ə'brʌpt] brusco

abscess ['æbsɪs] ascesso *m*

absence ['æbsəns] assenza f; **absent** assente; **absentee** assente m/f; **absenteeism** assenteismo m; **absent-minded** distratto

absolute ['æbsəluːt] assoluto; *idiot* totale; **absolutely** assolutamente; **absolution** REL assoluzione f; **absolve** assolvere

absorb [əb'sɔːb] assorbire; **absorbent** assorbente; **absorbing** avvincente

abstain [əb'steɪn] *from voting* astenersi; **abstention** *in voting* astensione f

abstract ['æbstrækt] astratto

absurd [əb'sɜːd] assurdo; **absurdity** assurdità f inv

abundance [ə'bʌndəns] abbondanza f; **abundant** abbondante

abuse¹ [ə'bjuːs] n abuso m; *(ill treatment)* maltrattamento m; *(insults)* insulti mpl

abuse² [ə'bjuːz] v/t abusare di; *(treat badly)* maltrattare; *(insult)* insultare

abusive [ə'bjuːsɪv] *language* offensivo; **become ~** diventare aggressivo

abysmal [ə'bɪzml] F *(very bad)* pessimo

academic [ækə'demɪk] **1** n docente m/f universitario, -a **2** adj accademico; *person* portato per lo studio; **academy** accademia f

accelerate [ək'seləreɪt] accelerare; **acceleration** accele-

razione f; **accelerator** acceleratore m

accent ['æksənt] accento m; **accentuate** accentuare

accept [ək'sept] accettare; **acceptable** accettabile; **acceptance** accettazione f

access ['ækses] **1** n accesso m **2** v/t accedere a; **accessible** accessibile

accessory [ək'sesərɪ] accessorio m; LAW complice m/f

accident ['æksɪdənt] incidente m; **by~** per caso; **accidental** accidentale; **accidentally** accidentalmente

acclimatize [ə'klaɪmətaɪz] acclimatarsi

accommodate [ə'kɒmədeɪt] ospitare; *needs* tenere conto di; **accommodation**, Am **accommodations** sistemazione f

accompaniment [ə'kʌmpənɪmənt] MUS accompagnamento m; **accompany** accompagnare

accomplice [ə'kʌmplɪs] complice m/f

accomplished [ə'kʌmplɪʃt] dotato; **accomplishment** *of task* realizzazione f; *(talent)* talento m; *(achievement)* risultato m

accord [ə'kɔːd] accordo m; **of his own ~** di sua spontanea volontà

accordance [ə'kɔːdəns]: **in ~ with** conformemente a

according [ə'kɔːdɪŋ]: **~ to** secondo; **accordingly** di conseguenza

accordion [ə'kɔːdıən] fisarmonica *f*

account [ə'kaʊnt] *financial* conto *m*; (*report, description*) resoconto *m*; **give an ~ of** fare un resoconto di; **on no ~** per nessuna ragione; **on ~** a causa di; **take into ~** tenere conto di

◆ **account for** (*explain*) giustificare; (*make up*) ammontare a

accountable [ə'kaʊntəbl] responsabile; **accountant** contabile *m/f*; *running own business* commercialista *m/f*; **account number** numero *m* di conto; **accounts** contabilità *f*

accumulate [ə'kjuːmjʊleɪt] **1** *v/t* accumulare **2** *v/i* accumularsi; **accumulation** accumulazione *f*

accuracy ['ækjʊrəsɪ] precisione *f*; **accurate** preciso; **accurately** con precisione

accusation [ækjuː'zeɪʃn] accusa *f*; **accuse:** **~ s.o. of sth** accusare qn di qc; **accused** LAW accusato *m*, -a *f*; **accusing** accusatorio

accustom [ə'kʌstəm]: **get ~ed to** abituarsi a

ace [eɪs] *in cards* asso *m*; (*in tennis: shot*) ace *m inv*

ache [eɪk] **1** *n* dolore *m* **2** *v/i* fare male

achieve [ə'tʃiːv] realizzare;

success ottenere; **achievement** *of ambition* realizzazione *f*; (*thing achieved*) successo *m*

acid ['æsɪd] acido *m*

acknowledge [ək'nɒlɪdʒ] riconoscere; **~ receipt of** accusare ricezione di; **acknowledg(e)ment** riconoscimento *m*; (*letter*) lettera *f* di accusata ricezione

acorn ['eɪkɔːn] ghianda *f*

acoustics [ə'kuːstɪks] acustica *f*

acquaint [ə'kweɪnt]: **be ~ed with** *fml* conoscere; **acquaintance** *person* conoscenza *f*

acquire [ə'kwaɪə(r)] acquisire; **acquisition** acquisizione *f*

acquit [ə'kwɪt] LAW assolvere; **acquittal** LAW assoluzione *f*

acre ['eɪkə(r)] acro *m* (4.047m²)

acrobat ['ækrəbæt] acrobata *m/f*

across [ə'krɒs] **1** *prep on other side of* dall'altro lato di; **walk ~ the street** attraversare la strada; **a bridge ~ the river** un ponte sul fiume; **~ Europe** *all over* in tutta Europa **2** *adv to other side* dall'altro lato **10 m ~** largo 10 m; **swim ~** attraversare a nuoto

act [ækt] **1** *v/i* agire; THEA recitare **2** *n* (*deed*) atto *m*; *of play* atto *m*; *in variety show* numero *m*; (*pretence*) finta

action 284

f; (*law*) atto m
action ['ækʃn] azione f; *take ~*
agire; **action replay** TV replay m inv
active ['æktɪv] attivo; **activist**
POL attivista m/f; **activity** attività f inv
actor ['æktə(r)] attore m; **actress** attrice f
actual ['æktʃʊəl] reale; *cost effettivo*; **actually** in realtà; *expressing surprise* veramente; *stressing the converse* a dire il vero
acute [ə'kjuːt] acuto
ad [æd] ☞ **advertisement**
AD [eɪ'diː] (= **anno domini**) d.C. (= dopo Cristo)
adamant ['ædəmənt] categorico
adapt [ə'dæpt] 1 v/t adattare 2 v/i *of person* adattarsi; **adaptability** adattabilità f; **adaptable** adattabile; **adaptation** *of play etc* adattamento m; **adapter** *electrical* adattatore m
add [æd] 1 v/t aggiungere; MATH addizionare 2 v/i *of person* fare le somme
◆ **add on** aggiungere
◆ **add up** 1 v/t sommare 2 v/i fig quadrare
addict ['ædɪkt] *to football, chess* maniaco m, -a f; *drug ~* tossicomane m/f, TV ~ teledipendente m/f; **addicted** dipendente; *be ~ to drugs, alcohol* essere dedito a; **addiction** dipendenza f; **addic-**

tive: *be ~* provocare dipendenza
addition [ə'dɪʃn] MATH addizione f; *to list, company etc* aggiunta f; *in ~ to* in aggiunta a; **additional** aggiuntivo; **additive** additivo m; **add-on** complemento m
address [ə'dres] 1 n indirizzo m 2 v/t *letter* indirizzare; *audience* tenere un discorso a; **address book** indirizzario m; **addressee** destinatario m, -a f
adequate ['ædɪkwət] adeguato; **adequately** adeguatamente
◆ **adhere to** [æd'hɪə(r)] *surface* aderire a; *rules* attenersi a
adhesive [əd'hiːsɪv] adesivo m
adjacent [ə'dʒeɪsnt] adiacente
adjective ['ædʒɪktɪv] aggettivo m
adjoining [ə'dʒɔɪnɪŋ] adiacente
adjourn [ə'dʒɜːn] aggiornare; **adjournment** aggiornamento m
adjust [ə'dʒʌst] 1 v/t regolare 2 v/i: *~ to* adattarsi a; **adjustable** regolabile; **adjustment** regolazione f; *psychological* adattamento m
ad lib [æd'lɪb] 1 *adj* a braccio F 2 v/i improvvisare
administer [əd'mɪnɪstə(r)] *country* governare; **adminis-**

tration amministrazione *f*; (*government*) governo *m*; administrative amministrativo; administrator amministratore *m*, -trice *f*

admirable ['ædmərəbl] ammirevole

admiral ['ædmərəl] ammiraglio *m*

admiration [ædmə'reɪʃn] ammirazione *f*; admire ammirare; admirer ammiratore *m*, -trice *f*; admiring ammirativo; admiringly con ammirazione

admissible [əd'mɪsəbl] ammissibile; admission (confession) ammissione *f*; ~ free entrata *f* libera; admit ammettere; *to a place* lasciare entrare; *to school, club etc* ammettere; *to hospital* ricoverare; admittance: no ~ vietato l'accesso

adolescence [ædə'lesns] adolescenza *f*; adolescent 1 *n* adolescente *m/f* 2 *adj* adolescenziale

adopt [ə'dɒpt] adottare; adoption adozione *f*

adorable [ə'dɔːrəbl] adorabile; adoration adorazione *f*; adore adorare

adrenalin [ə'drenəlɪn] adrenalina *f*

adrift [ə'drɪft] alla deriva; *fig* sbandato

adult ['ædʌlt] 1 *n* adulto *m*, -a *f* 2 *adj* adulto; adultery adulterio *m*

advance [əd'vɑːns] 1 *n* (money) anticipo *m*; *in science etc* progresso *m*; MIL avanzata *f*; in ~ in anticipo; make ~s (progress) fare progressi; *sexually* fare delle avances 2 *v/i* MIL avanzare; (make progress) fare progressi 3 *v/t theory* avanzare; *money* anticipare; *knowledge, cause* fare progredire; advanced avanzato; *learner* di livello avanzato

advantage [əd'vɑːntɪdʒ] vantaggio *m*; take ~ of *opportunity* approfittare di; advantageous vantaggioso

adventure [əd'ventʃə(r)] avventura *f*; adventurous avventuroso

adverb ['ædvɜːb] avverbio *m*

adversary ['ædvəsərɪ] avversario *m*, -a *f*

adverse ['ædvɜːs] avverso

advertise ['ædvətaɪz] *v/t job* mettere un annuncio per; *product* reclamizzare 2 *v/i* *for job* mettere un annuncio; *for product* fare pubblicità; advertisement annuncio *m*; *for product* pubblicità *f* *inv*; advertiser *in newspaper etc* inserzionista *m/f*; advertising pubblicità *f*; advertising agency agenzia *f* pubblicitaria; advertising campaign campagna *f* pubblicitaria

advice [əd'vaɪs] consigli *mpl*; a bit of ~ un consiglio;

advisable consigliabile; **advise** *person* consigliare a

advocate ['ædvəkeɪt] propugnare

aerial ['eərɪəl] antenna *f*; **aerial photograph** fotografia *f* aerea

aerobics [eə'rəʊbɪks] aerobica *f*

aerodynamic [eərəʊdaɪ'næmɪk] aerodinamico

aeronautical [eərəʊ'nɔːtɪkl] aeronautico

aeroplane ['eərəpleɪn] aeroplano *m*

aerosol ['eərəsɒl] spray *m inv*

aesthetic [iːs'θetɪk] estetico

affair [ə'feə(r)] (*matter*) affare *m*; (*love*) relazione *f*

affect [ə'fekt] *v/t* colpire; (*influence*) influire su; (*concern*) riguardare

affection [ə'fekʃn] affetto *m*; **affectionate** affettuoso; **affectionately** affettuosamente

affirmative [ə'fɜːmətɪv] affermativo

affluence ['æfluəns] benessere *m*; **affluent** benestante

afford [ə'fɔːd]: **be able to ~ sth** potersi permettere qc; **affordable** abbordabile

afloat [ə'fləʊt] *boat* a galla

afraid [ə'freɪd]: **be ~** avere paura (**of** di); **I'm ~** *expressing regret* sono spiacente

afresh [ə'freʃ] da capo

Africa ['æfrɪkə] Africa *f*; **African 1** *n* africano *m*, -a *f* **2** *adj*

africano; **African-American 1** *n* afroamericano *m*, -a *f* **2** *adj* afroamericano

after ['ɑːftə(r)] **1** *prep* dopo; ~ **her** / **me** dopo di lei / me; ~ **all** dopo tutto; ~ **that** dopo; **the day ~ tomorrow** dopodomani **2** *adv* dopo; **the day ~** il giorno dopo **3** *conj*: **after I left, I saw ...** dopo essere uscito ho visto ...; **after I left, she saw ...** dopo che io sono uscito, lei ha visto ...; **aftermath**: **the ~ of war** il dopoguerra; **in the ~ of** nel periodo immediatamente successivo a; **afternoon** pomeriggio *m*; **this ~** oggi pomeriggio; **good ~** buon giorno; **after sales service** servizio *m* dopovendita; **aftershave** dopobarba *m inv*; **afterwards** dopo

again [ə'geɪn] di nuovo; **I never saw him ~** non l'ho mai più visto

against [ə'geɪnst] contro

age [eɪdʒ] **1** *n* (*also* era) età *f inv*; **she's five years of ~** ha cinque anni; **I've been waiting for ~s F** ho aspettato un secolo **F 2** *v/i* invecchiare; **aged**: **a boy ~ 16** un ragazzo di 16 anni; **he was ~ 16** aveva 16 anni; **age group** fascia *f* d'età; **age limit** limite *m* d'età

agency ['eɪdʒənsɪ] agenzia *f*

agenda [ə'dʒendə] ordine *m* del giorno

ajar

agent ['eɪdʒənt] agente *m/f*

aggravate ['ægrəveɪt] aggravare; (*annoy*) seccare

aggression [ə'greʃn] aggressione *f*; **aggressive** aggressivo; **aggressively** con aggressività

aghast [ə'ɡɑːst] inorridito

agile ['ædʒaɪl] agile; **agility** agilità *f*

agitated ['ædʒɪteɪtɪd] agitato; **agitation** agitazione *f*; **agitator** agitatore *m*, -trice *f*

agnostic [æg'nɒstɪk] agnostico *m*, -a *f*

ago [ə'ɡəʊ]: **2** *days* ~ due giorni fa; *long* ~ molto tempo fa

agonize ['ægənaɪz] angosciarsi (*over* per); **agonizing** angosciante; **agony** agonia *f*, *mental* angoscia *f*

agree [ə'ɡriː] **1** *v/i* essere d'accordo; (*of figures*) quadrare; (*reach agreement*) mettersi d'accordo; *I* ~ sono d'accordo **2** *v/t price* concordare; **agreeable** (*pleasant*) piacevole; **agreement** accordo *m*

agricultural [æɡrɪ'kʌltʃərəl] agricolo; **agriculture** agricoltura *f*

ahead [ə'hed] davanti; (*in advance*) avanti; *be* ~ *of* essere davanti a; *plan* ~ programmare per tempo

aid [eɪd] **1** *n* aiuto *m* **2** *v/t* aiutare

aide [eɪd] assistente *m/f*

Aids [eɪdz] Aids *m*

ailing ['eɪlɪŋ] *economy* malato

ailment ['eɪlmənt] disturbo *m*

aim [eɪm] **1** *n* (*objective*) obiettivo *m* **2** *v/i in shooting* mirare; ~ *to do sth* aspirare a fare qc **3** *v/t*: *be* ~*ed at of remark etc* essere rivolto a; *of guns* essere puntato contro; **aimless** senza obiettivi; *wandering* senza meta

air [eə(r)] **1** *n* aria *f*; *by* ~ *travel* in aereo; *send mail* per via aerea; *in the open* ~ all'aperto; *on the* ~ RAD, TV in onda **2** *v/t room* arieggiare; *views* rendere noto; **airbag** airbag *m inv*; **air-conditioned** con aria condizionata; **air-conditioning** aria *f* condizionata; **aircraft** aereo *m*; **aircraft carrier** portaerei *f inv*; **air fare** tariffa *f* aerea; **air force** aeronautica *f* militare; **air hostess** hostess *f inv*; **airline** compagnia *f* aerea; **airliner** aereo *m* di linea; **airmail**: *by* ~ per via aerea; **airplane** *Am* aeroplano *m*; **airport** aeroporto *m*; **air rage** comportamento di estrema irascibilità dei passeggeri di un aereo; **air terminal** terminal *m*; **air-traffic control** controllo *m* del traffico aereo; **air-traffic controller** controllore *m* di volo

aisle [aɪl] corridoio *m*; *in supermarket* corsia *f*; *in church* navata *f* laterale

ajar [ə'dʒɑː(r)]: *be* ~ essere socchiuso

alarm [ə'lɑːm] **1** n allarme m **2** v/t allarmare; **alarm clock** sveglia f; **alarming** allarmante; **alarmingly** in modo allarmante

Albania [æl'beɪnɪə] Albania f; **Albanian 1** adj albanese **2** n albanese m/f; *language* albanese m

album ['ælbəm] album m inv

alcohol ['ælkəhɒl] alcol m; **alcoholic 1** n alcolizzato m, -a f **2** adj alcolico

alert [ə'lɜːt] **1** n (signal) allarme m **2** v/t mettere in guardia **3** adj all'erta inv

A-level ['eɪlevl] diploma di scuola media superiore in Gran Bretagna che permette di accedere all'università

alibi ['ælɪbaɪ] alibi m inv

alien ['eɪlɪən] **1** n straniero m, -a f; from space alieno m, -a f **2** adj estraneo; **alienate** alienarsi

align [ə'laɪn] allineare

alike [ə'laɪk] **1** adj simile; be ~ assomigliarsi **2** adv: old and young ~ vecchi e giovani allo stesso tempo

alimony ['ælɪmənɪ] alimenti mpl

alive [ə'laɪv]: be ~ essere vivo

all [ɔːl] **1** adj tutto; (any whatever) qualsiasi; ~ day tutto il giorno; beyond ~ doubt al di là di qualsiasi dubbio **2** pron tutto; ~ of us / them tutti noi / loro; he ate ~ of it lo ha mangiato tutto; for

~ I know per quel che ne so; ~ at once tutto in una volta; (suddenly) tutt'a un tratto; ~ but (nearly) quasi; ~ but John agreed (except) erano tutti d'accordo tranne John; ~ the better molto meglio; they're not at ~ alike non si assomigliano affatto; not at ~! niente affatto!; ~ two due pari; ~ right ☞ alright

allegation [ælɪ'geɪʃn] accusa f; allege dichiarare; alleged presunto; allegedly a quanto si suppone

allegiance [ə'liːdʒəns] fedeltà f inv

allergic [ə'lɜːdʒɪk] allergico (to a); allergy allergia f

alleviate [ə'liːvɪeɪt] alleviare

alley ['ælɪ] vicolo m

alliance [ə'laɪəns] alleanza f

allocate ['æləkeɪt] assegnare; allocation assegnazione f; (amount) parte f

allot [ə'lɒt] assegnare

allow [ə'laʊ] permettere; (calculate for) calcolare; it's not ~ed è vietato

◆ allow for tenere conto di

allowance [ə'laʊəns] (money) sussidio m; (pocket money) paghetta f

alloy ['ælɔɪ] lega m

'all-purpose multiuso inv; all-round generale; person eclettico; all-time: be at an ~ low aver raggiunto il minimo storico

◆ **allude to** [ə'luːd] alludere a

alluring [ə'lʊːrɪŋ] attraente

'all-wheel drive quattro per quattro *m inv*

ally ['ælaɪ] alleato *m*, -a *f*

almond ['ɑːmənd] mandorla *f*

almost ['ɔːlməʊst] quasi

alone [ə'ləʊn] solo

along [ə'lɒŋ] **1** *prep* lungo; **walk ~ the street** camminare lungo la strada *2 adv:* ~ **with** insieme con; **all ~** *(all the time)* per tutto il tempo; ~, **you can have one!** va bene, puoi averne uno!

alongside [ə'lɒŋ'saɪd] di fianco a; **person** al fianco di

aloof [ə'luːf] in disparte

aloud [ə'laʊd] ad alta voce

alphabet ['ælfəbet] alfabeto *m*; **alphabetical** alfabetico

alpine ['ælpaɪn] alpino; **Alps** Alpi *fpl*

already [ɔːl'redɪ] già

alright [ɔːl'raɪt] *I'm* ~ *(not hurt)* sto bene; *(have got enough)* va bene così; **is the monitor ~?** *(in working order)* funziona il monitor?; **is it ~ with you if I ...?** ti va bene se ...?; ~, **you can have one!** va bene, puoi averne uno!; **that's** ~ *(don't mention it)* non c'è di che; *(I don't mind)* non fa niente; ~, **that's enough!** basta così!

Alsatian [æl'seɪʃn] pastore *m* tedesco

also ['ɔːlsəʊ] anche

altar ['ɒltə(r)] altare *m*

alter ['ɒltə(r)] modificare; *clothes* aggiustare; **altera-**

tion modifica *f*

alternate 1 ['ɒltəneɪt] *v/i* alternare **2** ['ɒltənət] *adj* alternato; **on ~ Mondays** un lunedì su due; **alternative 1** *n* alternativa *f* **2** *adj* alternativo; **alternatively** alternativamente

although [ɔːl'ðəʊ] benché (+ *subj*), sebbene (+ *subj*)

altitude ['æltɪtjuːd] altitudine *f*

altogether [ɔːltə'geðə(r)] *(completely)* completamente; *(in all)* complessivamente

altruism ['æltruːɪzm] altruismo *m*; **altruistic** altruistico

aluminium [ælju'mɪnɪəm], *Am* **aluminum** [ə'luːmɪnəm] alluminio *m*

always ['ɔːlweɪz] sempre

a.m. [eɪ'em] (= *ante meridiem*) di mattina

amass [ə'mæs] accumulare

amateur ['æmətə(r)] *n* *(unskilled)* dilettante *m/f*; SP non professionista *m/f*; **amateurish** *pej* dilettantesco

amaze [ə'meɪz] stupire; **amazed** stupito; **amazement** stupore *m*; **amazing** sorprendente; F *(good)* incredibile; **amazingly** incredibilmente

ambassador [æm'bæsədə(r)] ambasciatore *m*, -trice *f*

amber ['æmbə(r)] *n* ambra *f*; **at ~** giallo

ambience ['æmbɪəns] atmosfera *f*

ambiguity [æmbɪ'gjuːətɪ]
ambiguità f inv; **ambiguous**
ambiguo

ambition [æm'bɪʃn] ambizione f; **ambitious** ambizioso

ambivalent [æm'bɪvələnt]
ambiguo

amble ['æmbl] camminare
con calma

ambulance ['æmbjuləns] ambulanza f

ambush ['æmbʊʃ] **1** n agguato m **2** v/t tendere un agguato a

amend [ə'mend] emendare;
amendment emendamento
m; **amends**: **make ~** fare ammenda

amenities [ə'miːnɪtɪz] comodità fpl

America [ə'merɪkə] America
f; **American 1** n americano
m, -a f **2** adj americano

amicable ['æmɪkəbl] amichevole; **amicably** amichevol-
mente

ammunition [æmjʊ'nɪʃn]
munizioni fpl

amnesia [æm'niːzɪə] amnesia
f

amnesty ['æmnəstɪ] amnistia
f

among(st) [ə'mʌŋ(st)] tra

amoral [eɪ'mɒrəl] amorale

amount [ə'maʊnt] quantità f
inv; (sum of money) importo
m

◆ **amount to** ammontare a;
(be equal to) equivalere a

amphibian [æm'fɪbɪən] anfi-

bio m

ample ['æmpl] abbondante

amplifier ['æmplɪfaɪə(r)] amplificatore m; **amplify** sound
amplificare

amputate ['æmpjuːteɪt] amputare; **amputation** amputa-
zione f

amuse [ə'mjuːz] (make laugh
etc) divertire; (entertain) intrattenere; **amusement**
(merriment) divertimento
m; (entertainment) intratteni-
mento m; **amusement park**
parco m giochi; **amusing** divertente

an [æn] ☞ **a**

anaemia [ə'niːmɪə] anemia f;
anaemic anemico

anaesthetic [ænəs'θetɪk]
anestetico m

analog ['ænəlɒg] COMPUT
analogico; **analogy** analogia
f

analyse, Am **analyze**
['ænəlaɪz] analizzare; (psy-
choanalyse) psicanalizzare;
analysis analisi f inv; **analyst** PSYCH analista m/f; **ana-
lytical** analitico

anarchy ['ænəkɪ] anarchia f

ancestor ['ænsestə(r)] antenato m, -a f

anchor ['æŋkə(r)] **1** n NAUT
ancora f **2** v/i NAUT gettare
l'ancora; **anchorman** conduttore m; **anchorwoman**
conduttrice f

ancient ['eɪnʃənt] antico

and [ænd] e

antipathy

anemia *Am* ☞ **anaemia**

anesthetic *Am* ☞ **anaesthetic**

angel ['eɪndʒl] angelo *m*

anger ['æŋgə(r)] **1** *n* rabbia *f* **2** *v/t* fare arrabbiare

angle ['æŋgl] angolo *m*; (*position, fig*) angolazione *f*

angry ['æŋgrɪ] arrabbiato

animal ['ænɪml] animale *m*

animated ['ænɪmeɪtɪd] animato; **animated cartoon** cartone *m* animato; **animation** animazione *f*

animosity [ænɪ'mɒsətɪ] animosità *f inv*

ankle ['æŋkl] caviglia *f*

annexe, *Am* **annex** [ə'neks] *state* annettere

annihilate [ə'naɪəleɪt] annientare; **annihilation** annientamento *m*

anniversary [ænɪ'vɜːsərɪ] anniversario *m*

announce [ə'naʊns] annunciare; **announcement** annuncio *m*; **announcer** TV, RAD annunciatore *m*, -trice *f*

annoy [ə'nɔɪ] infastidire; **annoyance** (*anger*) irritazione *f*; (*nuisance*) fastidio *m*; **annoying** irritante

annual ['ænjʊəl] annuale

annul [ə'nʌl] annullare; **annulment** annullamento *m*

anonymous [ə'nɒnɪməs] anonimo

anorak ['ænəræk] giacca *f* a vento

anorexia [ænə'reksɪə] anoressia *f*

another [ə'nʌðə(r)] **1** *adj* un altro *m*, un'altra *f* **2** *pron* un altro *m*, un'altra *f*; **one ~** l'un l'altro; **do they know one ~?** si conoscono?

answer ['ɑːnsə(r)] **1** *n* risposta *f* **2** *v/t* rispondere a; **~ the door** aprire la porta; **answering machine**, **answerphone** segreteria *f* telefonica

ant [ænt] formica *f*

antagonism [æn'tægənɪzm] antagonismo *m*; **antagonistic** ostile; **antagonize** contrariare

Antarctic [ænt'ɑːktɪk] Antartico *m*

antenatal [æntɪ'neɪtl]: **~ classes** corso *m* di preparazione al parto; **~ clinic** clinica *f* per gestanti

antenna [æn'tenə] antenna *f*

antibiotic [æntɪbaɪ'ɒtɪk] antibiotico *m*

anticipate [æn'tɪsɪpeɪt] prevedere; **anticipation** previsione *f*

anticlockwise ['æntɪklɒkwaɪz] **1** *adj* antiorario **2** *adv* in senso antiorario

antics ['æntɪks] buffonate *fpl*

antidote ['æntɪdəʊt] antidoto *m*

antifreeze ['æntɪfriːz] antigelo *m inv*

anti-globalist [æntɪ'gləʊbəlɪst] no-global *m/f inv*

antipathy [æn'tɪpəθɪ] antipatia *f*

antiquated ['æntɪkweɪtɪd] antiquato

antique [æn'tiːk] *n* pezzo *m* d'antiquariato

antiseptic [æntɪ'septɪk] **1** *adj* antisettico **2** *n* antisettico *m*

antisocial [æntɪ'səʊʃl] asociale

antivirus program [æntɪ'vaɪrəs] COMPUT programma *m* antivirus

anxiety [æŋ'zaɪətɪ] ansia *f*; **anxious** ansioso

any ['enɪ] **1** *adj* qualche; *are there ~ glasses?* ci sono dei bicchieri?; *is there ~ bread?* c'è del pane?; *is there ~ improvement?* c'è qualche miglioramento?; *there isn't ~ bread* non c'è pane; *take ~ one you like* prendi quello che vuoi **2** *pron: do you have ~?* ne hai?; *there aren't ~ left* non ce ne sono più; *there isn't ~ left* non ce n'è più; *~ of them could be guilty* chiunque di loro potrebbe essere colpevole **3** *adv is that ~ easier?* è un po più facile?

anybody ['enɪbɒdɪ] qualcuno; *with negative* nessuno; *(whoever)* chiunque; *there wasn't ~ there* non c'era nessuno; *~ could do it* lo potrebbe fare chiunque

anyhow ['enɪhaʊ] comunque

anyone ['enɪwʌn] ☞ *anybody*

anything ['enɪθɪŋ] qualcosa; *with negatives* niente, nulla; *I didn't hear ~* non ho sentito niente *or* nulla; *~ but* per niente

anyway ['enɪweɪ] ☞ *anyhow*

anywhere ['enɪweə(r)] da qualche parte; *with negative* da nessuna parte; *(wherever)* dovunque; *I can't find it ~* non riesco a trovarlo da nessuna parte

apart [ə'pɑːt] *in distance* distante; *~ from (excepting)* a parte; *(in addition to)* oltre a

apartment [ə'pɑːtmənt] appartamento *m*; **apartment block** *Am* palazzo *m* (d'appartamenti)

ape [eɪp] scimmia *f*

Apennines ['æpənaɪnz] Appennini *mpl*

aperitif [ə'perɪtiːf] aperitivo *m*

apologize [ə'pɒlədʒaɪz] scusarsi *(to s.o.* con qu); **apology** scusa *f*

apostrophe [ə'pɒstrəfɪ] GRAM apostrofo *m*

app [æp] COMPUT app *f*

appalling [ə'pɔːlɪŋ] sconvolgente

apparatus [æpə'reɪtəs] apparecchio *m*

apparent [ə'pærənt] evidente; *(seeming)* apparente; **apparently** apparentemente

appeal [ə'piːl] *(charm)* attrativa *f*; *for funds etc*, LAW appello *m*

◆ **appeal for** fare un appello per

◆ **appeal to** (*be attractive to*) attirare

appealing [ə'pi:lɪŋ] *idea, offer* allettante

appear [ə'pɪə(r)] apparire; *in court* comparire; *it ~s that ...* sembra che ...; **appearance** apparizione *f*, *in court* comparizione *f*; (*look*) aspetto *m*

appendicitis [əpendɪ'saɪtɪs] appendicite *f*; **appendix** MED, *of book etc* appendice *f*

appetite ['æpɪtaɪt] appetito *m*; **appetizer** *food* stuzzichino *m*; *drink* aperitivo *m*; **appetizing** appetitoso

applaud [ə'plɔ:d] applaudire; **applause** applauso *m*; (*praise*) approvazione *f*

apple ['æpl] mela *f*; **apple pie** torta *f* di mele

appliance [ə'plaɪəns] apparecchio *m*; *household* elettrodomestico *m*

applicable [ə'plɪkəbl] applicabile; **applicant** candidato *m*, -a *f*; **application** *for job etc* candidatura *f*; *for passport* domanda *f*; *for university* domanda *f* di iscrizione; **apply 1** *v/t* applicare **2** *v/i of rule* applicarsi

◆ **apply for** *job, passport* fare domanda per; *university* fare domanda di iscrizione a

◆ **apply to** (*contact*) rivolgersi a; (*affect*) applicarsi a

appoint [ə'pɔɪnt] *to position* nominare; **appointment** *to position* nomina *f*; (*meeting*) appuntamento *m*

appraisal [ə'preɪz(ə)l] valutazione *f*

appreciable [ə'pri:ʃəbl] notevole; **appreciate 1** *v/t* apprezzare; (*acknowledge*) rendersi conto di **2** *v/i* FIN rivalutarsi; **appreciative** (*showing gratitude*) riconoscente; (*showing pleasure*) soddisfatto

apprehensive [æprɪ'hensɪv] apprensivo

approach [ə'prəʊtʃ] **1** *n* avvicinamento *m*; (*proposal*) contatto *m*; *to problem* approccio *m* **2** *v/t* (*get near to*) avvicinarsi a; (*contact*) contattare; *problem* abbordare; **approachable** abbordabile

appropriate [ə'prəʊprɪət] appropriato

approval [ə'pru:vl] approvazione *f*, **approve** approvare

◆ **approve of** approvare

approximate [ə'prɒksɪmət] approssimativo; **approximately** approssimativamente

apricot ['eɪprɪkɒt] albicocca *f*

April ['eɪprəl] aprile *m*

apt [æpt] *remark* appropriato; **aptitude** attitudine *f*

aqualung ['ækwəlʌŋ] autorespiratore *m*

aquarium [ə'kweərɪəm] acquario *m*

Aquarius [ə'kweərɪəs] ASTR
Acquario *m*

Arab ['ærəb] **1** *n* arabo *m*, -a *f*
2 *adj* arabo; **Arabic 1** *n* arabo
m **2** *adj* arabo

arbitrary ['ɑːbɪtrərɪ] arbitrario

arbitrate ['ɑːbɪtreɪt] arbitrare;
arbitration arbitrato *m*

arch [ɑːtʃ] arco *m*

archaeological [ɑːkɪə'lɒd-
ʒɪkl] archeologico; **archaeologist** archeologo *m*, -a *f*;
archaeology archeologia *f*

archaic [ɑː'keɪk] arcaico

archbishop [ɑːtʃ'bɪʃəp] arcivescovo *m*

archeology *Am* ☞ **archaeology**

architect ['ɑːkɪtekt] architetto *m*; **architectural** architettonico; **architecture** architettura *f*

archives ['ɑːkaɪvz] archivi
mpl

Arctic ['ɑːktɪk] Artico *m*

ardent ['ɑːdənt] ardente

arduous ['ɑːdjʊəs] arduo

area ['eərɪə] area *f*; (*region*)
zona *f*; **area code** TELEC
prefisso *m* telefonico

arena [ə'riːnə] SP arena *f*

Argentina [ɑːdʒən'tiːnə] Argentina *f*; **Argentinian 1**
adj argentino **2** *n* argentino
m, -a *f*

arguably ['ɑːgjʊəblɪ] probabilmente; **it was ~ ...** si
può dire che ...; **argue**
(*quarrel*) litigare; (*reason*) so-

stenere; **argument** (*quarrel*)
litigio *m*; (*reasoning*) argomento *m*; **argumentative**
polemico

arid ['ærɪd] land arido

Aries ['eəriːz] ASTR Ariete *m*

arise [ə'raɪz] *of situation*
emergere

aristocracy [ærɪ'stɒkrəsɪ] ari-
stocrazia *f*; **aristocrat** aristocratico *m*, -a *f*; **aristocratic**
aristocratico

arithmetic [ə'rɪθmətɪk] aritmetica *f*

arm¹ [ɑːm] *n* braccio *m*; *of*
chair bracciolo *m*

arm² [ɑːm] *v/t* armare

armaments ['ɑːməmənts] ar-
mamenti *mpl*

armchair ['ɑːmtʃeə(r)] poltrona *f*

armed [ɑːmd] armato; **armed
forces** *fpl* armate; **armed
robbery** rapina *f* a
mano armata

armour, *Am* **armor** ['ɑːmə(r)]
armatura *f*; *metal plates* blin-
datura *f*

armpit ['ɑːmpɪt] ascella *f*

arms [ɑːmz] (*weapons*) armi
fpl

army ['ɑːmɪ] esercito *m*

around [ə'raʊnd] **1** *prep* (*in
circle*, *roughly*) intorno a;
room, *world* attraverso; **it's
~ the corner** è dietro l'angolo **2** *adv* (*in the area*) qui intorno; (*encircling*) intorno;
he lives ~ here abita da queste parti; *walk ~* andare in gi-

ro; **she has been ~** (*has travelled, is experienced*) ha girato; **he's still ~** F (*alive*) è ancora in circolazione

arouse [əˈrauz] suscitare; (*sexually*) eccitare

arrange [əˈreɪndʒ] (*put in order*) sistemare; *music* arrangiare; *meeting, party etc* organizzare; *time and place combinare*; **I've ~d to meet her** ho combinato di incontrarla; **arrangement** (*agreement*) accordo *m*; *of party, meeting* organizzazione *f*; *of furniture etc* disposizione *f*; *of music* arrangiamento *m*; **~s** *for party, meeting* preparativi *mpl*

arrears [əˈrɪəz] arretrati *mpl*

arrest [əˈrest] **1** *n* arresto *m*; **be under ~** essere in arresto **2** *v/t* arrestare

arrival [əˈraɪvl] arrivo *m*; **arrive** arrivare

♦ **arrive at** arrivare a

arrogance [ˈærəgəns] arroganza *f*; **arrogant** arrogante

arrow [ˈærəu] freccia *f*

arse [ɑːs] P culo *m* P

arson [ˈɑːsn] incendio *m* doloso

art [ɑːt] arte *f*

artery [ˈɑːtəri] arteria *f*

'art gallery galleria *f* d'arte

arthritis [ɑːˈθraɪtɪs] artrite *f*

artichoke [ˈɑːtɪtʃəuk] carciofo *m*

article [ˈɑːtɪkl] articolo *m*

articulate [ɑːˈtɪkjulət] chiaro; **be ~** *of person* esprimersi bene

artificial [ɑːtɪˈfɪʃl] artificiale; (*not sincere*) finto

artillery [ɑːˈtɪləri] artiglieria *f*

artist [ˈɑːtɪst] artista *m/f*; **artistic** artistico

'arts degree laurea *f* in discipline umanistiche

as [æz] **1** *conj* (*while, when*) mentre; (*because*) dato che; (*like*) come; **~ if** come se; **~ usual** come al solito **2** *adv*: **~ high …** alto come …; **~ much ~ that?** così tanto?; **run ~ fast ~ you can** corri più veloce che puoi **3** *prep* come; **~ a child** da bambino; **dressed ~ a policeman** vestito da poliziotto; **work ~ a translator** essere traduttore; **~ for** quanto a; **~ Hamlet** nel ruolo di Amleto

Ascension [əˈsenʃn] REL Ascensione *f*; **ascent** *path* salita *f*; *of mountain* ascensione *f*; *fig* ascesa *f*

ash [æʃ] cenere *f*

ashamed [əˈʃeɪmd]: **be ~ of** vergognarsi di

ashore [əˈʃɔː(r)] a terra; **go ~** sbarcare

ashtray [ˈæʃtreɪ] portacenere *m*; **Ash Wednesday** mercoledì *m inv* delle Ceneri

Asia [ˈeɪʒə] Asia *f*; **Asian 1** *n* asiatico *m*, -a *f*; (*Indian, Pakistani*) indiano *m*, -a *f* **2** *adj* asiatico; (*Indian, Pakistani*) indiano; **Asian-American** americano *m*, -a *f* di origine asiatica

aside [ə'saɪd] da parte; **~ from** a parte

ask [ɑːsk] **1** v/t person chiedere a; (invite) invitare; question fare; favour chiedere; **~ s.o. for ...** chiedere a qu ...; **~ s.o. to ...** chiedere a qu di ... **2** v/i chiedere

◆ **ask after** person chiedere di

◆ **ask for** chiedere; person chiedere di

◆ **ask out** chiedere di uscire a

asleep [ə'sliːp]: **he's ~** sta dormendo; **fall ~** addormentarsi

asparagus [ə'spærəgəs] asparagi mpl

aspect ['æspekt] aspetto m

aspirations [æspə'reɪʃnz] aspirazioni fpl

aspirin ['æsprɪn] aspirina f

ass¹ [æs] F (idiot) cretino m, -a

ass² [æs] Am P (bum) culo m P

assassin [ə'sæsɪn] assassino m, -a f; **assassinate** assassinare; **assassination** assassinio m

assault [ə'sɒlt] **1** n assalto m **2** v/t aggredire

assemble [ə'sembl] **1** v/t parts assemblare **2** v/i of people radunarsi; **assembly** assemblea f; of parts assemblaggio m; **assembly line** catena f di montaggio

assent [ə'sent] acconsentire

assertive [ə'sɜːtɪv] person si-

curo di sé

assess [ə'ses] valutare; **assessment** valutazione f

asset ['æset] FIN attivo m; fig: thing vantaggio m; person elemento m prezioso

assign [ə'saɪn] person destinare; thing assegnare; **assignment** (task) compito m

assimilate [ə'sɪmɪleɪt] assimilare; person into group integrare

assist [ə'sɪst] assistere; **assistance** assistenza f; **assistant** assistente m/f; in shop commesso m, -a f; **assistant manager** vice-responsabile m/f; of hotel, restaurant vice-direttore m

associate 1 [ə'səʊʃɪeɪt] v/t associare **2** [ə'səʊʃɪət] n socio m, -a f; **association** associazione f

assortment [ə'sɔːtmənt] assortimento m

assume [ə'sjuːm] (suppose) supporre; **assumption** supposizione f

assurance [ə'ʃʊərəns] assicurazione f; (confidence) sicurezza f; **assure** (reassure): **~ s.o. of sth** assicurare qc a qu

asterisk ['æstərɪsk] asterisco m

asthma ['æsmə] asma f

astonish [ə'stɒnɪʃ] sbalordire; **astonishing** sbalorditivo; **astonishment** stupore m

astound [ə'staʊnd] stupefare

astride [ə'straɪd] a cavalcioni

di

astrology [ə'strɒlədʒi] astrologia f

astronaut ['æstrənɔːt] astronauta m/f

astronomer [ə'strɒnəmə(r)]
astronomo m, -a f; **astronomical** price etc astronomico; **astronomy** astronomia f

astute [ə'stjuːt] astuto

asylum [ə'sailəm] mental manicomio m; political asilo m

at [æt] (with places) a; **he
works ~ the hospital** lavora
in ospedale; **~ the baker's**
dal panettiere, in panetteria;
~ Joe's da Joe; **~ the door**
alla porta; **~ 10 pounds** a
10 sterline; **~ the age of 18**
all'età di 18 anni; **~ 5 o'clock**
alle cinque; **~ night** di notte;
~ 150 km / h a 150 km/h; **be
good / bad ~ sth** essere / -
non essere bravo in qc

atheist ['eiθiist] ateo m, -a f

athlete ['æθliːt] atleta m/f;
athletic atletico; **athletics**
atletica f

Atlantic [ət'læntik] Atlantico
m

atlas ['ætləs] atlante m

ATM [etti:'em] (= **automatic
teller machine**) (sportello
m) Bancomat® m

atmosphere ['ætməsfiə(r)]
atmosfera f

atom ['ætəm] atomo m; **atom
bomb** bomba f atomica;
atomic atomico

◆ **atone for** [ə'təun] scontare

atrocious [ə'trəuʃəs] atroce;
atrocity atrocità f inv

attach [ə'tætʃ] attaccare; importance attribuire; document, file allegare; **attachment** to email allegato m

attack [ə'tæk] **1** n aggressione
f; MIL attacco m **2** v/t aggredire; MIL attaccare

attempt [ə'tempt] **1** n tentativo m **2** v/t tentare

attend [ə'tend] partecipare a;
school frequentare

◆ **attend to** (deal with) sbrigare; customer, patient assistere

attendance [ə'tendəns] partecipazione f; at school frequenza f; **attendant** in museum etc sorvegliante m/f

attention [ə'tenʃn] attenzione
f; **pay ~** fare attenzione; **attentive** attento

attic ['ætik] soffitta f

attitude ['ætitjuːd] atteggiamento m

attorney [ə'tɜːni] avvocato m

attract [ə'trækt] attirare; **attraction** attrazione f; **attractive** attrattivo; person attraente

aubergine ['əubəʒiːn] melanzana f

auction ['ɔːkʃn] asta f

audacity [ɔː'dæsəti] audacia f

audible ['ɔːdəbl] udibile

audience ['ɔːdiəns] pubblico
m; TV telespettatori mpl;
with the Pope etc udienza f

audio ['ɔːdiəu] audio inv;

audiovisual audiovisivo

audit ['ɔːdɪt] 1 n revisione f contabile 2 v/t verificare

audition [ɔː'dɪʃn] 1 n audizione f 2 v/i fare un'audizione

auditor ['ɔːdɪtə(r)] revisore m contabile

auditorium [ɔːdɪ'tɔːrɪəm] of theatre sala f

August ['ɔːɡəst] agosto m

aunt [ɑːnt] zia f

au pair [əʊ'peə(r)] ragazza f alla pari

aura ['ɔːrə]; **she has an ∼ of confidence** emana sicurezza

auspicious [ɔː'spɪʃəs] propizio

austere [ɔː'stɪə(r)] austero; austerity austerità f inv

Australia [ɒ'streɪlɪə] Australia f; Australian 1 adj australiano 2 n australiano m, -a f

Austria ['ɒstrɪə] Austria f; Austrian 1 adj austriaco 2 n austriaco m, -a f

authentic [ɔː'θentɪk] autentico; authenticity autenticità f

author ['ɔːθə(r)] autore m, autrice f

authoritarian [ɔːθɒrɪ'teərɪən] autoritario; authoritative autoritario; information autorevole; authority autorità f inv; (permission) autorizzazione f; authorization autorizzazione f; authorize autorizzare

autistic [ɔː'tɪstɪk] autistico

autobiography [ɔːtəbaɪ'ɒgrə-fɪ] autobiografia f

autocratic [ɔːtə'krætɪk] autocratico

autograph ['ɔːtəgrɑːf] autografo m

automate ['ɔːtəmeɪt] automatizzare; automatic 1 adj automatico 2 n car macchina f con il cambio automatico; automatically automaticamente; automation automazione f

automobile ['ɔːtəməbiːl] automobile f

autonomous [ɔː'tɒnəməs] autonomo

autopilot ['ɔːtəʊpaɪlət] pilota m automatico

autopsy ['ɔːtɒpsɪ] autopsia f

autumn ['ɔːtəm] autunno m

auxiliary [ɔːg'zɪlɪərɪ] ausiliario

available [ə'veɪləbl] disponibile

avalanche ['ævəlɑːnʃ] valanga f

avenue ['ævənjuː] corso m; fig strada f

average ['ævərɪdʒ] 1 adj medio; (mediocre) mediocre 2 n media f; **on ∼** in media ◆ **average out at** risultare in media a

averse [ə'vɜːs]: **not be ∼ to** non avere niente contro; aversion avversione f (**to** per)

avid ['ævɪd] avido

avocado [ævə'kɑːdəʊ] avocado m inv

avoid [əˈvɔɪd] evitare
await [əˈweɪt] attendere
awake [əˈweɪk] sveglio; **it's keeping me ~** mi impedisce di dormire
award [əˈwɔːd] **1** n (prize) premio m **2** v/t assegnare; damages riconoscere; **awards ceremony** cerimonia f di premiazione
aware [əˈweə(r)] conscio; **become ~ of** rendersi conto di; **awareness** consapevolezza f
away [əˈweɪ] fuori casa; **be ~** travelling, sick etc essere via; **run ~** correre via; **look ~**

guardare da un'altra parte; **it's 2 miles ~** dista 2 miglia; **away game** SP partita f fuori casa
awesome [ˈɔːsm] F (terrific) fantastico
awful [ˈɔːfʊl] tremendo, terribile; **awfully** F (very) da matti F
awkward [ˈɔːkwəd] (clumsy) goffo; (difficult) difficile; (embarrassing) scomodo; **feel ~** sentirsi a disagio
axe, Am **ax** [æks] **1** n scure f, accetta f **2** v/t project, job sopprimere
axle [ˈæksl] asse f

B

BA [biːˈeɪ] (= **Bachelor of Arts**) (degree) laurea f in lettere; (person) laureato m, -a f in lettere
baby [ˈbeɪbɪ] n bambino m, -a f; **baby-sit** fare il / la baby--sitter
bachelor [ˈbætʃələ(r)] scapolo m; UNIV **~'s degree** laurea f triennale (di primo livello)
back [bæk] **1** n of person schiena f; of animal, hand dorso m; of car, bus parte f posteriore; of book, house retro m; of clothes rovescio m; of drawer fondo m; of chair schienale m; SP terzino m; **in the ~** (of the car) (nei sedili) di dietro; **at the ~ of**

the bus in fondo all'autobus; **~ to front** al contrario **2** adj door, steps di dietro; wheels, legs posteriore; garden sul retro **3** adv: **please move ~** indietro, per favore; **give sth ~ to s.o.** restituire qc a qu; **she'll be ~ tomorrow** sarà di ritorno domani **4** v/t (support) appoggiare; car guidare in retromarcia; horse puntare su
◆ **back down** fare marcia indietro
◆ **back off** spostarsi indietro; from danger tirarsi indietro
◆ **back out** of commitment tirarsi indietro
◆ **back up 1** v/t (support) con-

fermare; *claim, argument* supportare; *file* fare un back-up di **2** *v/i in car* fare retromarcia

'backache mal *m inv* di schiena; **backbone** spina *f* dorsale; **backdate** retrodatare; **backdoor** porta *f* di dietro; **backer** FIN finanziatore *m*, -trice *f*; **background** sfondo *m*; *of person* background *m inv*; *of story* retroscena *mpl*; **backhand** *in tennis* rovescio *m*; **backing** *moral* appoggio *m*; MUS accompagnamento *m*; **backing group** gruppo *m* d'accompagnamento; **backlash** reazione *f* violenta; **backlog**: ~ **of work** lavoro *m* arretrato; **backpack** zaino *m*; **backpacker** sacco-pelista *m/f*; **back seat** sedile *m* posteriore; **backside** F sedere *m*; **backspace (key)** (tasto di) ritorno *m*; **back streets** vicoli *mpl*; **backstroke** SP dorso *m*; **backtrack** tornare indietro; **backup** (*support*) rinforzi *mpl*; COMPUT backup *m inv*; **backup disk** COMPUT disco *m* di backup; **backward** *child* tardivo; *society* arretrato; *glance* all'indietro; **backwards** indietro; **backyard** cortile *m*

bacon ['beɪkn] pancetta *f*

bacteria [bæk'tɪərɪə] batteri *mpl*

bad [bæd] *news, manners* cat-

tivo; *weather, headache* brutto; *mistake* grave; *food* guasto; **it's not** ~ non è male; **that's too** ~ *shame* peccato!

badge [bædʒ] distintivo *m*

bad 'language parolacce *fpl*; **badly** male; *injured* gravemente; *he* ~ *needs* ... ha urgente bisogno di ...

badminton ['bædmɪntən] badminton *m*

bad-tempered [bæd'tempəd] irascibile

baffle ['bæfl]: *be* ~*d* essere perplesso

bag [bæg] borsa *f*; *plastic, paper* busta *f*

baggage ['bægɪdʒ] bagagli *mpl*; **baggage check** *Am* deposito *m* bagagli; **baggage trolley** carrello *m*

baggy ['bægɪ] senza forma

bail [beɪl] LAW cauzione *f*; **on** ~ su cauzione

bait [beɪt] esca *f*

bake [beɪk] cuocere al forno; **baked potatoes** patate cotte *al forno con la buccia*; **baker** fornaio *m*, -a *f*; **bakery** panetteria *f*

balance ['bæləns] **1** *n* equilibrio *m*; (*remainder*) resto *m*; *of bank account* saldo *m* **2** *v/t* tenere in equilibrio **3** *v/i* stare in equilibrio; **balanced** (*fair*) obiettivo; *diet, personality* equilibrato; **balance sheet** bilancio *m* (di esercizio)

balcony ['bælkənɪ] balcone

m; *in theatre* prima galleria *f*

bald [bɔːld] *man* calvo; **bald-ing** stempiato

Balkans ['bɔːlkənz]: **the ~** i Balcani *mpl*

ball [bɔːl] palla *f*; *football* pallone *m*; **be on the ~** essere sveglio; **play ~** *fig* collaborare; **the ~'s in his court** la prossima mossa è sua

ballad ['bæləd] ballata *f*

ballerina [bælə'riːnə] ballerina *f*

ballet ['bæleɪ] *art* danza *f* classica; *dance* balletto *m*; **ballet dancer** ballerino *m* classico, ballerina *f* classica

'ball game F: **that's a different ~** è un altro paio di maniche

ballistic missile [bə'lɪstɪk] missile *m* balistico

balloon [bə'luːn] *child's* palloncino *m*; *for flight* mongolfiera *f*

ballot ['bælət] **1** *n* votazione *f* **2** *v/t members* consultare tramite votazione; **ballot box** urna *f* elettorale

'ballpark F: **be in the right ~** essere nell'ordine corretto di cifre; **ballpark figure** F cifra *f* approssimativa; **ballpoint (pen)** penna *f* a sfera

balls [bɔːlz] V palle *fpl* V

bamboo [bæm'buː] bambù *m inv*

ban [bæn] **1** *n* divieto *m* (**on** di) **2** *v/t* proibire

banal [bə'nɑːl] banale

banana [bə'nɑːnə] banana *f*

band [bænd] banda *f*; *pop* gruppo *m*; *of material* nastro *m*

bandage ['bændɪdʒ] **1** *n* benda *f* **2** *v/t* bendare

'Band-Aid® *Am* cerotto *m*

B&B [biː'n'biː] (= **bed and breakfast**) pensione *f* familiare, bed and breakfast *m inv*

bandit ['bændɪt] brigante *m*

bandy ['bændɪ] *legs* storto

bang [bæŋ] **1** *n* colpo *m* **2** *v/t door* chiudere violentemente; (*hit*) sbattere

bangle ['bæŋgl] braccialetto *m*

bangs [bæŋz] *Am* frangia *f*

banisters ['bænɪstəz] ringhiera *fsg*

banjo ['bændʒəʊ] banjo *m inv*

bank¹ [bæŋk] *of river* riva *f*

bank² [bæŋk] FIN banca *f*

◆ **bank on** contare su

'bank account conto *m* bancario; **banker** banchiere *m*; **banker's card** carta *f* assegni; **bank holiday** giorno *m* festivo; **banking** professione *f* bancaria; **bank loan** prestito *m* bancario; **bank manager** direttore *m* di banca; **bank rate** tasso *m* ufficiale di sconto; **bankroll** finanziare; **bankrupt** fallito; **go ~** fallire; **bankruptcy** bancarotta *f*

banner ['bænə(r)] striscione *m*

banquet ['bæŋkwɪt] banchetto *m*

baptism ['bæptɪzm] battesimo *m*; **baptize** battezzare

bar¹ [bɑː(r)] *n* of iron spranga *f*; of chocolate tavoletta *f*; for drinks bar *m inv*; (counter) bancone *m*

bar² [bɑː(r)] *v/t* vietare l'ingresso a

barbaric [bɑːˈbærɪk] barbaro

barbecue ['bɑːbɪkjuː] **1** *n* barbecue *m inv* **2** *v/t* cuocere al barbecue

barbed 'wire [bɑːbd] filo *m* spinato

barber ['bɑːbə(r)] barbiere *m*

'bar code codice *m* a barre

bare [beə(r)] (naked) nudo; room) spoglio; **barefoot**: *be* ~ essere scalzo; **bare-headed** senza cappello; **barely** appena

bargain ['bɑːgɪn] **1** *n* (deal) patto *m*; (good buy) affare *m* **2** *v/i* tirare sul prezzo

barge [bɑːdʒ] NAUT chiatta *f*
◆ **barge into** piombare su

baritone ['bærɪtəʊn] *n* baritono *m*

bark¹ [bɑːk] **1** *n* of dog abbaiare *m* **2** *v/i* abbaiare

bark² [bɑːk] *n* of tree corteccia *f*

'barmaid barista *f*; **barman** barista *m*

barn [bɑːn] granaio *m*

barometer [bəˈrɒmɪtə(r)] also fig barometro *m*

barracks ['bærəks] MIL caserma *fsg*

barrel ['bærəl] (container) barile *m*

barren ['bærən] land arido

barrette [bəˈret] *Am* molletta *f*

barricade [bærɪˈkeɪd] barricata *f*

barrier ['bærɪə(r)] barriera *f*

barrister ['bærɪstə(r)] avvocato *m*

'bar tender barista *m/f*

barter ['bɑːtə(r)] **1** *n* baratto *m* **2** *v/i* barattare

base [beɪs] **1** *n* base *f* **2** *v/t* basare (**on** su); **baseball** baseball *m*; **ball** palla *f* da baseball; **baseball cap** berretto *m* da baseball; **baseboard** *Am* battiscopa *m inv*; **basement** seminterrato *m*

basic ['beɪsɪk] (rudimentary) rudimentale; salary di base; beliefs fondamentale; **basically** essenzialmente

basin ['beɪsn] for washing lavandino *m*

basis ['beɪsɪs] base *f*

bask [bɑːsk] crogiolarsi

basket ['bɑːskɪt] cestino *m*; in basketball cesto *m*; **basketball** basket *m*, pallacanestro *f*; **ball** pallone *m* da pallacanestro

bass [beɪs] (part) voce *f* di basso; (singer, guitar) basso *m*; (double bass) contrabbasso *m*

bastard ['bɑːstəd] F bastardo *m*, -a *f* F

303 **bear**

bat¹ [bæt] **1** *n* mazza *f*; *for table tennis* racchetta *f* **2** *v/i* SP battere

bat² [bæt] *animal* pipistrello *m*

batch [bætʃ] *n of students* gruppo *m*; *of goods* lotto *m*; *of bread* infornata *f*

bath [bɑːθ] bagno *m*

bathe [beɪð] (*swim, have bath*) fare il bagno; **bathing costume** costume *m* da bagno

'**bathrobe** accappatoio *m*; **bathroom** (stanza *f* da) bagno *m*; **bath towel** asciugamano *m* da bagno; **bathtub** vasca *f* da bagno

batter ['bætə(r)] pastella *f*; **battered** maltrattato; *suitcase etc* malridotto

battery ['bætrɪ] pila *f*, MOT batteria *f*

battle ['bætl] **1** *n also fig* battaglia *f* **2** *v/i against illness etc* lottare; **battleship** corazzata *f*

bawl [bɔːl] (*shout*) urlare; (*weep*) strillare

bay [beɪ] (*inlet*) baia *f*; **bay window** bovindo *m*

BC [biːˈsiː] (= *before Christ*) a. C. (= avanti Cristo)

be [biː] essere; *it's me* sono io; *how much is / are ...?* quant'è / quanto sono ...?; *there is, there are* c'è, ci sono; *don't ~ sad* non essere triste; *how are you?* come stai?; *he's very well* sta bene; *I'm hot / cold* ho freddo / caldo; *it's hot / cold* fa freddo / caldo; *he's seven* ha sette anni ◇ *has the postman been?* è passato il postino?; *I've never been to Japan* non sono mai stato in Giappone; *I've been here for hours* sono qui da tanto ◇ *tags: that's right, isn't it?* giusto, no?; *she's American, isn't she?* è americana, vero? ◇ *v/aux: I am thinking* sto pensando; *he's working in London* lavora a Londra ◇ *obligation: you are to do what I tell you* devi fare quello che ti dico ◇ *passive* essere; *he was killed* è stato ucciso

beach [biːtʃ] spiaggia *f*; **beachwear** abbigliamento *m* da spiaggia

beads [biːdz] perline *fpl*

beak [biːk] becco *m*

'**be-all**: *the ~ and end-all* la cosa più importante

beam [biːm] **1** *n in ceiling etc* trave *f* **2** *v/i* (*smile*) fare un sorriso radioso **3** *v/t* (*transmit*) trasmettere

bean [biːn] (*vegetable*) fagiolo *m*; *of coffee* chicco *m*; *be full of ~s* F essere particolarmente vivace

bear¹ [beə(r)] *n animal* orso *m*

bear² [beə(r)] **1** *v/t weight* portare; *costs* sostenere; (*tolerate*) sopportare; *child* dare alla luce **2** *v/i: bring pressure to ~ on* fare pressione su

bearable ['beərəbl] sopportabile

beard [biəd] barba *f*

beat [bi:t] **1** *n of heart* battito
m; *of music* ritmo *m* **2** *v/i of
heart* battere; *of rain* pic-
chiettare; **~ about the bush**
menar il can per l'aia **3** *v/t in
competition* battere; *(hit)* picchiare; *drum* suonare; **~ it!** F
fila!; **it ~s me** non capisco

♦ **beat up** picchiare

beaten ['bi:tən] **off the ~
track** fuori mano; **beating**
physical botte *fpl*; **beat-up**
F malconcio

beautiful ['bju:tɪfʊl] bello;
thanks, that's just ~! grazie,
così va bene; **beautifully**
stupendamente; **beauty** bellezza *f*; **beauty salon** istituto
m di bellezza

beaver ['bi:və(r)] castoro *m*

because [bɪ'kɒz] perché; **~ of**
a causa di

become [bɪ'kʌm] diventare;
what's ~ of her? che ne è
stato di lei?; **becoming** grazioso

bed [bed] letto *m*; **~ of flowers**
aiuola *f*; **go to ~** andare a letto; **bedding** materasso *m* e
lenzuola *fpl*; **bedridden** costretto a letto; **bedroom** camera *f* da letto; **bed-sit, bed-
-sitter** monolocale *m*; **bed-
time** ora *f* di andare a letto

bee [bi:] ape *f*

beech [bi:tʃ] faggio *m*

beef [bi:f] manzo *m*; **beefbur-**

ger hamburger *m inv*

beep [bi:p] **1** *n* bip *m inv* **2** *v/i*
suonare

beer [bɪə(r)] birra *f*

beet [bi:t] barbabietola *f*

beetle ['bi:tl] coleottero *m*

before [bɪ'fɔ:(r)] **1** *prep* prima
di **2** *adv* prima; **I've seen
this film ~** questo film l'ho
già visto **3** *conj* prima che
(+ *subj*); **I saw him ~ he left**
l'ho visto prima che partisse;
I saw him ~ I left l'ho visto
prima di partire; **beforehand** prima

befriend [bɪ'frend] fare amicizia con

beg [beg] **1** *v/i* mendicare **2**
v/t: **~ s.o. to ...** pregare qu
di ...; **beggar** mendicante
m/f

begin [bɪ'gɪn] cominciare; **beginner** principiante *m/f*; **beginning** inizio *m*; *(origin)*
origine *f*

behalf [bɪ'hɑ:f]: **on ~ of** a nome di

behave [bɪ'heɪv] comportarsi;
~ (yourself)! comportati bene!; **behaviour**, *Am* behavio-
r comportamento *m*

behind [bɪ'haɪnd] **1** *prep* dietro; *in order* dietro a; **be ~** *(responsible for)* essere dietro a;
(support) appoggiare **2** *adv*
(at the back) dietro; **she
had to stay ~** è dovuta rimanere; **be ~ in match** essere in
svantaggio;

beige [beɪʒ] beige *inv*

305

best

being ['bi:ɪŋ] (*existence*) esistenza *f*; (*creature*) essere *m*

belated [bɪ'leɪtɪd] in ritardo

belch [beltʃ] **1** *n* rutto *m* **2** *v/i* ruttare

Belgian ['beldʒən] **1** *adj* belga **2** *n* belga *m/f*; **Belgium** Belgio *m*

belief [bɪ'li:f] convinzione *f*; *in God* fede *f*; **believe** credere

◆ **believe in** *God, person* credere in; *ghost, person* credere a

believer [bɪ'li:və(r)] REL credente *m/f*; *I'm a great ~ in ...* credo fermamente in ...

bell [bel] *in church, school* campana *f*; *on door, bicycle* campanello *m*; **bellhop** *Am* fattorino *m* d'albergo

belligerent [bɪ'lɪdʒərənt] bellicoso

bellow ['beləʊ] urlare; *of bull* muggire

belly ['belɪ] pancia *f*

belong [bɪ'lɒŋ] *v/i*: *where does this ~?* dove va questo?; *I don't ~ here* mi sento un estraneo

◆ **belong to** appartenere a

be'longings cose *fpl*

beloved [bɪ'lʌvɪd] adorato

below [bɪ'ləʊ] **1** *prep* sotto **2** *adv* di sotto; *in text* **10 degrees ~** 10 gradi sotto zero

belt [belt] cintura *f*

bench [bentʃ] *seat* panchina *f*; **benchmark** punto *m* di rife-

rimento

bend [bend] **1** *n* curva *f* **2** *v/t* piegare **3** *v/i* curvarsi; *of person* inchinarsi

◆ **bend down** chinarsi

beneath [bɪ'ni:θ] **1** *prep* sotto **2** *adv* di sotto

benefactor ['benɪfæktə(r)] benefattore *m*, -trice *f*

beneficial [benɪ'fɪʃl] vantaggioso

benefit ['benɪfɪt] **1** *n* vantaggio *m* **2** *v/t* andare a vantaggio di **3** *v/i* trarre vantaggio (*from* da)

benevolent [bɪ'nevələnt] benevolo

benign [bɪ'naɪn] benevolo; MED benigno

bequeath [bɪ'kwi:ð] *also fig* lasciare in eredità

bequest [bɪ'kwest] lascito *m*

bereaved [bɪ'ri:vd] **1** *adj* addolorato **2** *n*: *the~* i familiari *mpl* del defunto

beret ['bereɪ] berretto *m*

berry ['berɪ] bacca *f*

berth [bɜːθ] *on ship, train* cuccetta *f*; *for ship* ormeggio *m*

beside [bɪ'saɪd] accanto a; *be ~ o.s.* essere fuori di sé; *that's ~ the point* questo non c'entra

besides [bɪ'saɪdz] **1** *adv* inoltre **2** *prep* (*apart from*) oltre a

best [best] **1** *adj* migliore **2** *adv* meglio; *it would be ~ if ...* sarebbe meglio se ...; *I like her ~* lei è quella che mi piace di più **3** *n*: *do one's*

~ fare del proprio meglio; **the** ~ il meglio; (*outstanding thing or person*) il / la migliore; **they've done the ~ they can** hanno fatto tutto il possibile; **make the ~ of** cogliere il lato buono di; **all the ~!** tanti auguri!; **best before date** scadenza *f*; **best man** *at wedding* testimone *m* dello sposo

bet [bet] **1** *n* scommessa *f* **2** *v/i* scommettere; **you ~!** ci puoi scommettere!

betray [bɪ'treɪ] tradire; **betrayal** tradimento *m*

better ['betə(r)] **1** *adj* migliore; **get** ~ migliorare **2** *adv* meglio; **you'd ~ ask permission** faresti meglio a chiedere il permesso; **I'd really not** sarebbe meglio di no; **all the ~ for us** tanto meglio per noi; **I like her** ~ lei mi piace di più; **better off be** ~ stare meglio finanziariamente

between [bɪ'twiːn] tra

beware [bɪ'weə(r)]: ~ **of ...!** (stai) attento a ...!

bewilder [bɪ'wɪldə(r)] sconcertare; **bewilderment** perplessità *f*

beyond [bɪ'jɒnd] oltre, al di là di

bias ['baɪəs] *against* pregiudizio *m*; *in favour of* preferenza *f*; **bias(s)** parziale

Bible ['baɪbl] bibbia *f*; **biblical** biblico

bicentenary [baɪsen'tiːnərɪ] bicentenario *m*

bicker ['bɪkə(r)] bisticciare

bicycle ['baɪsɪkl] bicicletta *f*

bid [bɪd] **1** *n at auction* offerta *f*; (*attempt*) tentativo *m* **2** *v/t & v/i at auction* offrire; **bidder** offerente *m/f*

biennial [baɪ'enɪəl] biennale

big [bɪg] **1** *adj* grande; **my ~ brother** / **sister** mio fratello / mia sorella maggiore **2** *adv*: **talk** ~ spararle grosse

bigamist ['bɪɡəmɪst] bigamo *m*, -a *f*

'**bighead** F pallone *m* gonfiato F

bigot ['bɪɡət] fanatico *m*, -a *f*

bike [baɪk] F bici *f inv* F **2** *v/i* andare in bici; **biker** motociclista *m/f*; (*courier*) corriere *m*

bikini [bɪ'kiːnɪ] bikini *m inv*

bilingual [baɪ'lɪŋɡwəl] bilingue

bill [bɪl] **1** *n in hotel, restaurant* conto *m*; (*gas* / *electricity* ~) bolletta *f*; (*invoice*) fattura *f*; *Am: money* banconota *f*; POL disegno *m* di legge; (*poster*) avviso *m*

'**billboard** *Am* tabellone *m* per affissioni pubblicitarie; **billfold** *Am* portafoglio *m*

billiards ['bɪljədz] biliardo *m*

billion ['bɪljən] (*1,000,000,000*) miliardo *m*

bin [bɪn] bidone *m*; **bin lorry** camion *m* della nettezza urbana

bind [baɪnd] *also fig* legare; LAW obbligare; **binding** *agreement* vincolante

binoculars [bɪ'nɒkjʊləz] binocolo *msg*

biodegradable [baɪəʊdɪ'greɪdəbl] biodegradabile

biographer [baɪ'ɒgrəfə(r)] biografo *m*, -a *f*; **biography** biografia *f*

biological [baɪə'lɒdʒɪkl] biologico; **biology** biologia *f*; **biotechnology** biotecnologia *f*

bird [bɜːd] uccello *m*

biro® ['baɪrəʊ] biro *f*

birth [bɜːθ] *also fig* nascita *f*; (*labour*) parto *m*; **give ~ to** *child* partorire; **date of ~** data di nascita; **birth certificate** certificato *m* di nascita; **birth control** controllo *m* delle nascite; **birthday** compleanno *m*; **happy ~!** buon compleanno!; **birthplace** luogo *m* di nascita

biscuit ['bɪskɪt] biscotto *m*

bisexual ['baɪseksjʊəl] bisessuale

bishop ['bɪʃəp] vescovo *m*

bit [bɪt] *n* (*piece*) pezzo *m*; (*part*) parte *f*; **a ~** (*a little*) un po'; **a ~ of advice** un consiglio; **~ by ~** poco a poco; **I'll be there in a ~** (*in a little while*) sarò lì tra poco

bitch [bɪtʃ] 1 *n dog* cagna *f*; *F woman* bastarda *f* F 2 *v/i* F (*complain*) lamentarsi

bite [baɪt] 1 *n* morso *m* 2 *v/t*

mordere; *one's nails* mangiarsi 3 *v/i* mordere

bitter ['bɪtə(r)] *taste* amaro; *person* amareggiato

black [blæk] 1 *adj* nero; *tea* senza latte 2 *n colour* nero *m*; *person* nero *m*, -a *f*
♦ **black out** (*faint*) svenire

blackberry mora *f* di rovo; **blackbird** merlo *m*; **blackboard** lavagna *f*; **black box** scatola *f* nera; **black coffee** caffè *m* nero; **black economy** economia *f* sommersa; **black eye** occhio *m* nero; **blacklist** lista *f* nera; **blackmail** 1 *n* ricatto *m* 2 *v/t* ricattare; **black market** mercato *m* nero; **blackness** oscurità *f*; **blackout** ELEC black-out *m inv*; MED svenimento *m*

bladder ['blædə(r)] vescica *f*

blade [bleɪd] *of knife* lama *f*; *of helicopter* pala *f*; *of grass* filo *m*

blame [bleɪm] 1 *n* colpa *f*; (*responsibility*) responsabilità *f* 2 *v/t*; **~ s.o. for sth** ritenere qu responsabile di qc

bland [blænd] *smile* insulso; *food* insipido

blank [blæŋk] 1 *adj* (*not written on*) bianco; *tape* vergine; *look* vuoto 2 *n* (*empty space*) spazio *m*; **blank cheque**, *Am* **blank check** assegno *m* in bianco

blanket ['blæŋkɪt] coperta *f*

blasphemy ['blæsfəmɪ] bestemmia *f*

blast [blɑːst] **1** n (explosion) esplosione f; (gust) raffica f **2** v/t far esplodere; ~! accidenti!; **blast-off** lancio m

blatant ['bleɪtənt] palese

blaze [bleɪz] **1** n (fire) incendio m **2** v/i of fire ardere

blazer ['bleɪzə(r)] blazer m inv

bleach [bliːtʃ] **1** n for clothes varechina f; for hair acqua f ossigenata **2** v/t hair ossigenarsi

bleak [bliːk] countryside desolato; weather cupo; future deprimente

bleary-eyed ['blɪəraɪd]: be ~ avere lo sguardo appannato

bleat [bliːt] of sheep belare

bleed [bliːd] sanguinare; **bleeding** emorragia f

bleep [bliːp] **1** n blip m inv **2** v/i suonare

blemish ['blemɪʃ] on skin imperfezione f; on fruit ammaccatura f

blend [blend] **1** n miscela f **2** v/t miscelare; **blender** machine frullatore m

bless [bles] benedire; ~ you! (in response to sneeze) salute!; **blessing** benedizione f

blind [blaɪnd] **1** adj cieco **2** n: the ~ i ciechi **3** v/t accecare; **blind alley** vicolo m cieco; **blind date** appuntamento m al buio; **blindfold** n benda f **2** v/t bendare (gli occhi a); **blinding** atroce; light accecante; **blindly** a tastoni; fig ciecamente; **blind spot** in

road punto m cieco

blink [blɪŋk] of person sbattere le palpebre; of light tremolare

blister ['blɪstə(r)] vescichetta f

blizzard ['blɪzəd] bufera f di neve

bloc [blɒk] POL blocco m

block [blɒk] **1** n blocco m; in town isolato m; ~ of flats palazzo m (d'appartamenti) **2** v/t bloccare

◆ **block out** light impedire

blockage ['blɒkɪdʒ] ingorgo m; **blockbuster** successone m; **block letters** maiuscole fpl

bloke [bləʊk] F tipo m F

blond [blɒnd] biondo; **blonde** woman bionda f

blood [blʌd] sangue m; **blood donor** donatore m, -trice f di sangue; **blood group** gruppo m sanguigno; **blood poisoning** setticemia f; **blood pressure** pressione f del sangue; **blood sample** prelievo m di sangue; **bloodshed** spargimento m di sangue; **bloodshot** iniettato di sangue; **bloodstained** macchiato di sangue; **blood test** analisi f inv del sangue; **bloodthirsty** assetato di sangue; **bloody 1** adj hands etc insanguinato; F maledetto; ~ **hell!** porca miseria! F; **you're a ~ genius!** sei un geniaccio! F **2** adv: **I'm ~ tired**

sono stanco morto

bloom [blu:m] *also fig* fiorire

blossom ['blɒsəm] **1** *n* fiori *mpl* **2** *v/i also fig* fiorire

blot [blɒt] macchia *f*

◆ **blot out** *memory* cancellare; *view* nascondere

blouse [blauz] camicetta *f*

blow¹ [bləu] *n* colpo *m*

blow² [bləu] **1** *v/t of wind* spingere; *smoke* soffiare; ~ **a whistle** fischiare; ~ **one's nose** soffiarsi il naso **2** *v/i of wind, person* soffiare; *of fuse* saltare; *of tyre* scoppiare

◆ **blow out 1** *v/t candle* spegnere **2** *v/i of candle* spegnersi

◆ **blow over 1** *v/t* abbattere **2** *v/i* rovesciarsi; *of storm, argument* calmarsi

◆ **blow up 1** *v/t with explosives* far saltare; *balloon* gonfiare; *photograph* ingrandire **2** *v/i also fig* esplodere

'**blow-dry** asciugare col phon; **blow-out** *of tyre* scoppio *m*

blue [blu:] blu; *film* porno; **blue chip** sicuro; *company* di alto livello; **blues** MUS blues *m inv*; **have the** ~ essere giù

bluff [blʌf] **1** *n* (*deception*) bluff *m inv* **2** *v/i* bluffare

blunder ['blʌndə(r)] **1** *n* errore *m* **2** *v/i* fare un errore

blunt [blʌnt] spuntato; *person* diretto; **bluntly** senza mezzi termini

blur [blɜ:(r)] **1** *n* massa *f* indi-

stinta **2** *v/t* offuscare

◆ **blurt out** [blɜ:t] spiattellare

blush [blʌʃ] **1** *n* rossore *m* **2** *v/i* arrossire; **blusher** *cosmetic* fard *m inv*

blustery ['blʌstəri] ventoso

BO [bi:'əu] (= *body odour*) odori *mpl* corporei

board [bɔ:d] **1** *n* asse *f*; *for chess* scacchiera *f*; *for notices* tabellone *m*; ~ (*of directors*) consiglio *m* (d'amministrazione); **on** ~ a bordo **2** *v/t aeroplane etc* salire a bordo di **3** *v/i of passengers* salire a bordo

◆ **board up** chiudere con assi

boarder ['bɔ:də(r)] pensionante *m*, *f*; EDU convittore *m*, *-trice f*; **board game** gioco *m* da tavolo; **boarding card** carta *f* d'imbarco; **boarding pass** carta *f* d'imbarco; **boarding school** collegio *m*; **board meeting** riunione *f* di consiglio; **board room** sala *f* del consiglio

boast [bəust] vantarsi

boat [bəut] *(small, for leisure)* barca *f*; *(ship)* nave *f*

bodily ['bɒdili] **1** *adj* corporale **2** *adv eject* di peso; **body** corpo *m*; *dead* cadavere *m*; **body double** controfigura *f*; **bodyguard** guardia *f* del corpo; **body language** linguaggio *m* del corpo; **bodywork** MOT carrozzeria *f*

bogus ['bəugəs] fasullo

boil 310

boil[1] [bɔɪl] (*swelling*) foruncolo *m*

boil[2] [bɔɪl] **1** *v/t* far bollire **2** *v/i* bollire

◆ **boil down to** ridursi a

boiler ['bɔɪlə(r)] caldaia *f*

boisterous ['bɔɪstərəs] turbolento

bold [bəʊld] **1** *adj* (*brave*) audace **2** *n print* neretto *m*; **in ~** in neretto

bolster ['bəʊlstə(r)] *confidence* rafforzare

bolt [bəʊlt] **1** *n on door* catenaccio *m*; (*metal pin*) bullone *m* **2** *adv*: **~ upright** diritto come un fuso **3** *v/t* (*fix with bolts*) fissare con bulloni; (*close*) chiudere col catenaccio **4** *v/i* (*run off*) scappare via

bomb [bɒm] **1** *n* bomba *f* **2** *v/t* bombardare; (*blow up*) far saltare; **bombard** *also fig* bombardare; **bomb attack** attacco *m* dinamitardo; **bomber** *airplane* bombardiere *m*; *terrorist* dinamitardo *m*, -a *f*; **bomb scare** allarme-bomba *m*; **bombshell** *fig*: *news* bomba *f*

bond [bɒnd] **1** *n* (*tie*) legame *m*; FIN obbligazione *f* **2** *v/i* aderire

bone [bəʊn] osso *m*; *in fish* lisca *f*

bonfire ['bɒnfaɪə(r)] falò *m* *inv*

bonnet ['bɒnɪt] *of car* cofano *m*

bonus ['bəʊnəs] *money* gratifica *f*; (*something extra*) vantaggio *m* in più

boo [buː] **1** *n* fischio *m* **2** *v/t & v/i* fischiare

boob[1] [buːb] F (*mistake*) errore *m*

boob[2] [buːb] P (*breast*) tetta *f* P

booboo ['buːbuː] F gaffe *m* *inv*

book [bʊk] **1** *n* libro *m* **2** *v/t* (*reserve*) prenotare; *of policeman* multare; SP ammonire; **bookcase** scaffale *m*; **booked up** tutto esaurito; *person* occupatissimo; **bookie** F allibratore *m*; **booking** (*reservation*) prenotazione *f*; **booking office** biglietteria *f*; **bookkeeper** contabile *m/f*; **bookkeeping** contabilità *f*; **booklet** libretto *m*; **bookmaker** allibratore *m*; **books** (*accounts*) libri *mpl* contabili; **bookseller** libraio *m*, -a *f*; **bookshop**, *Am* **bookstore** libreria *f*

boom[1] [buːm] **1** *n* boom *m* *inv* **2** *v/i of business* andare a gonfie vele

boom[2] [buːm] *n* (*bang*) rimbombo *m*

boost [buːst] **1** *n* spinta *f* **2** *v/t sales* incrementare; *confidence* aumentare

boot[1] [buːt] stivale *m*; (*climbing ~*) scarpone *m*; *for football* scarpetta *m*

◆ **boot up** COMPUT inizializzare

booth [bu:ð] *at market, fair* bancarella *f; (telephone ~)* cabina *f*

booze [bu:z] F alcolici *mpl;* **booze-up** F bevuta *f*

border ['bɔ:də(r)] **1** *n* confine *m; (edge)* bordo *m* **2** *v/t country* confinare con

◆ **border on** *country* confinare con; *(be almost)* rasentare

bore[1] [bɔ:(r)] *v/t hole* praticare

bore[2] [bɔ:(r)] **1** *n person* persona *f* noiosa **2** *v/t* annoiare

bored [bɔ:d] annoiato; *I'm ~* mi sto annoiando; **boredom** noia *f;* **boring** noioso

born [bɔ:n]: *be ~* essere nato

borrow ['bɒrəʊ] prendere in prestito

bosom ['bʊzm] *of woman* seno *m*

boss [bɒs] boss *m inv*

◆ **boss around** dare ordini a

bossy ['bɒsɪ] prepotente

botanical [bə'tænɪkl] botanico; **botany** botanica *f*

botch [bɒtʃ] fare un pasticcio con

both [bəʊθ] **1** *adj pron* entrambi, tutti *mpl* e due, tutte *fpl* e due, tutt'e due; *~ (of the)* **brothers were there** tutt'e due i fratelli erano lì; *~ of them* entrambi **2** *adv:* *~ my mother and I* sia mia madre che io; *is it business or pleasure? – ~* per piacere o per affari? – tutt'e due

bother ['bɒðə(r)] **1** *n* disturbo *m; it's no ~* non c'è problema **2** *v/t (disturb)* disturbare; *(worry)* preoccupare **3** *v/i: don't ~ (you needn't do it)* non preoccuparti

bottle ['bɒtl] bottiglia *f; for baby* biberon *m*

◆ **bottle up** *feelings* reprimere

'**bottle bank** contenitore *m* per la raccolta del vetro; **bottled water** acqua *f* in bottiglia; **bottleneck** ingorgo *m;* **bottle-opener** apribottiglie *m inv*

bottom ['bɒtəm] **1** *adj* più basso **2** *n* fondo *m; (buttocks)* sedere *m; at the ~ of the screen* in basso sullo schermo; *at the ~ of the page* in fondo alla pagina

◆ **bottom out** toccare il fondo

bottom 'line *financial* risultato *m* finanziario; *the ~ (the real issue)* l'essenziale *m*

boulder ['bəʊldə(r)] macigno *m*

bounce [baʊns] **1** *v/t ball* far rimbalzare **2** *v/i of ball* rimbalzare; *on sofa etc* saltare; *of cheque* essere protestato; **bouncer** buttafuori *m inv*

bound[1] [baʊnd] *adj: be ~ to do sth (sure to)* dover fare per forza qc; *(obliged to)* essere obbligato a fare qc; *the train is ~ to be late* il treno sarà senz'altro in ritardo

bound² [baʊnd] *adj:* **be ~ for**
of ship essere diretto a
bound³ [baʊnd] *n (jump)* balzo *m*
boundary ['baʊndərɪ] confine *m*
bouquet [bu'keɪ] bouquet *m inv*
bourbon ['bɜːbən] bourbon *m inv*
bout [baʊt] MED attacco *m; in boxing* incontro *m*
bow¹ [baʊ] **1** *n as greeting* inchino *m* **2** *v/i* inchinarsi **3** *v/t head* chinare
bow² [bəʊ] *n (knot)* fiocco *m;* MUS archetto *m*
bow³ [baʊ] *n of ship* prua *f*
bowels ['baʊəlz] intestino *msg*
bowl¹ [bəʊl] *n container* bacinella *f; for soup, cereal* ciotola *f; for cooking, salad* terrina *f*
bowl² [bəʊl] **1** *n ball* boccia *f* **2** *v/i in bowling* lanciare
bowling ['bəʊlɪŋ] bowling *m;* **bowling alley** pista *f* da bowling; **bowls** *nsg (game)* bocce *fpl*
bow 'tie (cravatta *f* a) farfalla *f*
box¹ [bɒks] *n container* scatola *f; on form* casella *f*
box² [bɒks] *v/i* fare pugilato
boxer ['bɒksə(r)] pugile *m;* **boxing** pugilato *m,* boxe *f;* **Boxing Day** Santo Stefano; **boxing glove** guantone *m* da pugile; **boxing match** in-

contro *m* di pugilato
'box number *at post office* casella *f;* **box office** botteghino *m*
boy [bɔɪ] *child* bambino *m; youth* ragazzo *m; son* figlio *m*
boycott ['bɔɪkɒt] **1** *n* boicottaggio *m* **2** *v/t* boicottare
'boyfriend ragazzo *m;* boy-scout boy-scout *m inv*
bra [brɑː] reggiseno *m*
bracelet ['breɪslɪt] braccialetto *m*
bracket ['brækɪt] *for shelf* staffa *f; in text* parentesi *f inv*
brag [bræg] vantarsi
braid [breɪd] *trimming* passamaneria *f; Am in hair* treccia *f*
braille [breɪl] braille *m*
brain [breɪn] cervello *m;* **brainless** F deficiente; **brains** (*intelligence*) cervello *msg;* **brain surgeon** neurochirurgo *m;* **brain tumour,** *Am* **brain tumor** tumore *m* al cervello; **brainwash** fare il lavaggio del cervello a; **brainy** F geniale
brake [breɪk] **1** *n* freno *m* **2** *v/i* frenare; **brake light** MOT fanalino *m* d'arresto; **brake pedal** MOT pedale *m* del freno
branch [brɑːntʃ] *of tree* ramo *m; of company* filiale *f*
◆ **branch out** diversificarsi
brand [brænd] **1** *n* marca *f* **2** *v/t:* **be ~ed a traitor** essere tacciato di tradimento;

breakup

brand image brand image *f inv*

brandish ['brændɪʃ] brandire

brand 'leader marca *f* leader di mercato; **brand name** marca *f*; **brand-new** nuovo di zecca

brandy ['brændɪ] brandy *m inv*

brass [brɑːs] *(alloy)* ottone *m*; **the ~** MUS gli ottoni; **brass band** fanfara *f*

brassière [brə'zɪə(r)] reggiseno *m*

brat [bræt] *pej* marmocchio *m*

brave [breɪv] coraggioso; **bravery** coraggio *m*

brawl [brɔːl] **1** *n* rissa *f* **2** *v/i* azzuffarsi

Brazil [brə'zɪl] Brasile *m*; **Brazilian 1** *adj* brasiliano **2** *n* brasiliano *m*, -a *f*

breach [briːtʃ] *(violation)* violazione *f*; *in party* rottura *f*; **breach of contract** inadempienza *f* di contratto

bread [bred] pane *m*

breadth [bredθ] larghezza *f*

'breadwinner *be the ~* mantenere la famiglia

break [breɪk] **1** *n also fig* rottura *f*; *(rest)* pausa *f* EDU intervallo *m* **2** *v/t china, egg, bone* rompere; *rules, law* violare; *promise* non mantenere; *news* comunicare; *record* battere **3** *v/i of china, egg, toy* rompersi; *of news* diffondersi; *of storm* scoppiare

◆ **break down 1** *v/i of vehicle, machine* avere un guasto; *of talks* arenarsi; *in tears* scoppiare in lacrime; *mentally* avere un esaurimento **2** *v/t door* buttare giù; *figures* analizzare

◆ **break even** coprire le spese

◆ **break in** *(interrupt)* interrompere; *of burglar* entrare con la forza

◆ **break off 1** *v/t* staccare; *engagement* rompere; **they've broken it off** si sono lasciati **2** *v/i (stop talking)* interrompersi

◆ **break up 1** *v/t into parts* scomporre; *fight* far cessare **2** *v/i of ice* spaccarsi; *of couple* separarsi; *of band, meeting* sciogliersi

breakable ['breɪkəbl] fragile; **breakage** danni *mpl*; **breakdown** *of vehicle, machine* guasto *m*; *of talks* rottura *f*; *(nervous ~)* esaurimento *m* (nervoso); *of figures* analisi *f inv*; **breakdown lorry** carro *m* attrezzi; **breakdown service** servizio *m* di soccorso stradale; **breakdown truck** carro *m* attrezzi

breakfast ['brekfəst] colazione *f*; *have ~* fare colazione

'break-in furto *m* (con scasso); **breakthrough** *in negotiations* passo *m* avanti; *of technology* scoperta *f*; **breakup** *of partnership* rottura *f*

breast

h fiatospan

breast [brest] seno m; **breast-feed** allattare; **breaststroke** nuoto m a rana

breath [breθ] respiro m; **be out of ~** essere senza fiato

breathe [briːð] respirare
◆ **breathe in** inspirare
◆ **breathe out** espirare

breathing [ˈbriːðɪŋ] respiro m

breathless [ˈbreθlɪs] senza fiato; **breathtaking** mozzafiato

breed [briːd] **1** n razza f **2** v/t allevare; fig generare **3** v/i of animals riprodursi; **breeding** allevamento m; of person educazione f

breeze [briːz] brezza f; **breezy** ventoso; fig brioso

brew [bruː] **1** v/t beer produrre **2** v/i of storm prepararsi; **there's trouble ~ing** ci sono guai in vista; **brewery** fabbrica f di birra

Brexit [ˈbreksɪt] POL, EU Brexit f

bribe [braɪb] **1** n bustarella f **2** v/t corrompere; **bribery** corruzione f

brick [brɪk] mattone m

bride [braɪd] sposa f; **bridegroom** sposo m; **bridesmaid** damigella f d'onore

bridge [brɪdʒ] **1** n ponte m; of ship ponte m di comando **2** v/t gap colmare

◆ **brighten up** [ˈbraɪtn] **1** v/t ravvivare **2** v/i of weather schiarirsi; of face, person rallegrarsi

bridle [ˈbraɪdl] briglia f

brief [briːf] adj breve

brief² [briːf] **1** n (mission) missione f **2** v/t: **~ s.o. on sth** instruct dare istruzioni a qu su qc; inform mettere qu al corrente di qc

'briefcase valigetta f; **briefing** briefing m; **briefly** brevemente; (to sum up) in breve; **briefs** slip m inv

bright [braɪt] colour vivace; smile, future radioso; (sunny) luminoso; (intelligent) intelligente; **~ red** rosso vivo; **brightly** smile in modo radioso; shine, lit intensamente; coloured in modo sgargiante

brilliance [ˈbrɪljəns] of person genialità f; of colour vivacità f; of sunshine etc sfolgorante; (very good) eccezionale; (very intelligent) brillante

brim [brɪm] of container orlo m; of hat falda f

bring [brɪŋ] portare
◆ **bring back** (return) restituire; (re-introduce) reintrodurre; memories risvegliare
◆ **bring down** also fig abbattere; price far scendere
◆ **bring on** illness provocare
◆ **bring out** book pubblicare; new product lanciare
◆ **bring up** child allevare; subject sollevare

brink [brɪŋk] orlo m

brisk [brɪsk] person, tone spic-

315 **bucket**

cio; *walk* svelto; *trade* vivace
bristles ['brɪslz] peli *mpl*
Brit [brɪt] F britannico *m*, -a *f*;
Britain Gran Bretagna *f*;
British 1 *adj* britannico **2**
n: **the ~** i britannici
brittle ['brɪtl] fragile
broad [brɔːd] largo; *(general)*
generale; **in ~ daylight** in
pieno giorno; **broadband**
banda *f* larga; **broadcast 1**
n trasmissione *f* **2** *v/t* trasmettere; **broadcaster** giornalista *m/f* radiotelevisivo,
-a; **broad jump** *Am* salto
m in lungo; **broadly:**
~ speaking parlando in senso
lato; **broadminded** di larghe
vedute
broccoli ['brɒkəlɪ] broccoli
mpl
brochure ['brəʊʃə(r)] dépliant *m inv*, opuscolo *m*
broil [brɔɪl] *Am* fare alla griglia; **broiler** *Am* on stove
grill *m inv*
broke [brəʊk] al verde; **bro-**
ken 1 *adj* rotto; *marriage* fallito; **she's**
from a ~ home i suoi sono
separati; **broken-hearted**
col cuore spezzato; **broker**
mediatore *m*, -trice *f*
bronchitis [brɒŋ'kaɪtɪs] bronchite *f*
bronze [brɒnz] bronzo *m*
brooch [brəʊtʃ] spilla *f*
brothel ['brɒθl] bordello *m*
brother ['brʌðə(r)] fratello *m*;
brother-in-law cognato *m*;

brotherly fraterno
brow [braʊ] *(forehead)* fronte
f; *of hill* cima *f*
brown [braʊn] **1** *n* marrone *m*
2 *adj* marrone; *eyes, hair* castano; *(tanned)* abbronzato;
Brownie giovane esploratrice *f*; **brownie** *Am* dolcetto *m*
al cioccolato con noci;
brown sugar zucchero *m*
non raffinato
browse [braʊz] *in shop* curiosare; COMPUT navigare; **~**
through a book sfogliare
un libro; **browser** COMPUT
browser *m inv*
bruise [bruːz] livido *m*; *on*
fruit ammaccatura *f*
brunette [bruː'net] brunetta *f*
brunt [brʌnt]: **bear the ~ of ...**
subire il peggio di ...
brush [brʌʃ] **1** *n* spazzola *f*;
(paint~) pennello *m*; *(tooth~)*
spazzolino *m* da denti; *(con-*
flict) scontro *m* **2** *v/t* spazzolare; *(touch lightly)* sfiorare
◆ **brush aside** ignorare
◆ **brush up** ripassare
brusque [brʌsk] brusco
Brussels 'sprout ['brʌslz] ca-
volino *m* di Bruxelles
brutal ['bruːtl] brutale; **bru-**
tality brutalità *f inv*; **brutally**
brutalmente; **brute** bruto *m*
bubble ['bʌbl] bolla *f*
buck¹ [bʌk] *n Am* F *(dollar)*
dollaro *m*
buck² [bʌk] *v/i of horse* sgrop-
pare
bucket ['bʌkɪt] secchio *m*

buckle 316

buckle¹ ['bʌkl] **1** n fibbia f **2** v/t belt allacciare

buckle² ['bʌkl] v/i of wood, metal cedere

bud [bʌd] BOT bocciolo m

buddy ['bʌdɪ] F amico m, -a f

budge [bʌdʒ] **1** v/t smuovere **2** v/i muoversi

budgerigar ['bʌdʒərɪgɑː(r)] pappagallino m

budget ['bʌdʒɪt] budget m inv; of company bilancio m preventivo; of state bilancio m dello Stato

buff [bʌf] appassionato m, -a f

buffalo ['bʌfələʊ] bufalo m

buffer ['bʌfə(r)] RAIL respingente m; COMPUT buffer m inv; fig cuscinetto m

buffet ['bʊfeɪ] meal buffet m inv

bug [bʌg] **1** n (insect) insetto m; (virus) virus m inv; (spying device) microspia f; COMPUT bug m inv **2** v/t room installare microspie in; telephone mettere sotto controllo; F (annoy) seccare

buggy ['bʌgɪ] for baby passeggino m

build [bɪld] **1** n of person corporatura f **2** v/t costruire

◆ build up **1** v/t relationship consolidare; **build up one's strength** rimettersi in forze **2** v/i of tension, traffic aumentare

builder ['bɪldə(r)] muratore m; company impresario m edile; **building** edificio m,

palazzo m; (activity) costruzione f; **building site** cantiere m edile; **building society** istituto m di credito immobiliare; **building trade** edilizia f; **build-up** of traffic, pressure aumento m; of arms, forces ammassamento m; (publicity) pubblicità f inv; **built-in** wardrobe a muro; flash incorporato; **built-up area** abitato m

bulb [bʌlb] BOT bulbo m; (light ~) lampadina f

bulge [bʌldʒ] **1** n rigonfiamento m **2** v/i sporgere

bulky ['bʌlkɪ] voluminoso

bull [bʊl] toro m; **bulldozer** bulldozer m inv

bullet ['bʊlɪt] proiettile m, pallottola f

bulletin ['bʊlɪtɪn] bollettino m; **bulletin board** COMPUT bulletin board m inv; Am: on wall bacheca f

'bullet-proof a prova di proiettile

'bull's-eye centro m del bersaglio; **hit the ~** fare centro; bullshit V stronzate fpl V

bully ['bʊlɪ] **1** n prepotente m/f **2** v/t tiranneggiare; bullying mobbing m

bum [bʌm] n F worthless person mezza calzetta f F; (bottom) sedere m; (Am: tramp) barbone m **2** v/t F cigarette etc scroccare

bump [bʌmp] **1** n (swelling) gonfiore m; (lump) bernoccolo *m*; *on road* cunetta *f* **2** *v/t* battere

◆ **bump into** *table* battere contro; *(meet)* incontrare

bumper ['bʌmpə(r)] MOT paraurti *m inv*; **bumpy** *road* accidentato; *flight* movimentato

bunch [bʌntʃ] *of people* gruppo *m*; *of keys, flowers* mazzo *m*; **a ~ of grapes** un grappolo d'uva; **thanks a ~** *ironic* grazie tante!

bundle ['bʌŋələʊ] bungalow *m inv*

bungle ['bʌŋɡl] pasticciare

bunk [bʌŋk] cuccetta *f*; **bunk beds** letti *mpl* a castello

buoy [bɔɪ] NAUT boa *f*; **buoyant** allegro; *economy* sostenuto

burden ['bɜːdn] **1** *n also fig* peso *m* **2** *v/t*: **~ s.o. with sth** *fig* opprimere qu con qc

bureau ['bjʊərəʊ] *(office)* ufficio *m*

bureaucracy [bjʊə'rɒkrəsɪ] burocrazia *f*; **bureaucrat** burocrate *m/f*; **bureaucratic** burocratico

burger ['bɜːɡə(r)] hamburger *m inv*

burglar ['bɜːɡlə(r)] ladro *m*; **burglar alarm** antifurto *m*; **burglarize** *Am* svaligiare; **burglary** furto *m* (con scasso); **burgle** svaligiare

burial ['berɪəl] sepoltura *f*

burn [bɜːn] **1** *n* bruciatura *f* **2** *v/t* bruciare; *of sun* scottare **3**

v/i ardere; *of house* bruciare; *of toast, get sunburnt* scottarsi, bruciarsi

◆ **burn down 1** *v/t* dare alle fiamme **2** *v/i* essere distrutto dal fuoco

burp [bɜːp] **1** *n* rutto *m* **2** *v/i* ruttare

burst [bɜːst] **1** *n in pipe* rottura *f* **2** *adj* *tyre* bucato **3** *v/t* *balloon* far scoppiare **4** *v/i* *of balloon, tyre* scoppiare; **~ into tears** scoppiare in lacrime; **~ out laughing** scoppiare a ridere

bury ['berɪ] seppellire; *hide* nascondere

bus [bʌs] autobus *m inv*; *(long distance)* pullman *m inv*; **bus driver** autista *m/f* di autobus

bush [bʊʃ] *plant* cespuglio *m*; *land* boscaglia *f*; **bushy** *eyebrows* irsuto

business ['bɪznɪs] *(trade)* affari *mpl*; *(company)* impresa *f*; *(work)* lavoro *m*; *(affair, matter)* faccenda *f*; *(as subject of study)* economia *f* aziendale; **on ~** per affari; **mind your own ~!** fatti gli affari tuoi!; **business card** biglietto *m* da visita (della ditta); **business class** business class *f*; **business hours** orario *msg* di apertura; **businesslike** efficiente; **businessman** uomo *m* d'affari; **business meeting** riunione *f* d'affari; **business school** istituto *m* commerciale;

business studies (*course*) economia *f* aziendale; **business trip** viaggio *m* d'affari; **businesswoman** donna *f* d'affari

'**bus station** autostazione *f*; **bus stop** fermata *f* dell'autobus

bust[1] [bʌst] *n of woman* petto *m*

bust[2] [bʌst] *adj* F (*broken*) scassato

'**bust-up** F rottura *f*; **busty** prosperoso

busy ['bɪzɪ] **1** *adj also* TELEC occupato; *day* intenso; *street* animato; *shop, restaurant* affollato; **busybody** impiccione *m*, -a *f*

but [bʌt] **1** *conj* ma **2** *prep*: *all him* tutti tranne lui; *the last ~ one* il penultimo; *~ for you* se non fosse per te; *nothing ~ the best* solo il meglio

butcher ['butʃə(r)] macellaio *m*, -a *f*; **butcher's** macelleria *f*

butt [bʌt] **1** *n of cigarette* mozzicone *m*; *Am* P (*backside*)

culo *m* P **2** *v/t* dare una testata a

butter ['bʌtə(r)] burro *m*; **buttercup** ranuncolo *m*; **butterfly** *also swimming* farfalla *f*

buttocks ['bʌtəks] natiche *fpl*

button ['bʌtn] bottone *m*; *on machine* pulsante *m*

buy [baɪ] comprare
◆ **buy out** COM rilevare

buyer ['baɪə(r)] acquirente *m/f*

buzz [bʌz] **1** *n* ronzio *m* **2** *v/i of insect* ronzare; **buzzer** cicalino *m*

by [baɪ] *agency* da; (*near, next to*) vicino a; (*no later than*) entro, per; (*past*) davanti a; (*mode of transport*) in; *~ day* di giorno; *~ bus* in autobus; *~ my watch* secondo il mio orologio; *a book ~ ...* un libro di ...; *~ myself / herself* da solo

bye(-bye) [baɪ] ciao

'**bypass** circonvallazione *f*; MED by-pass *m inv*; **by-product** sottoprodotto *m*; **bystander** astante *m/f*

C

cab [kæb] taxi *m inv*; *of truck* cabina *f*

cabbage ['kæbɪdʒ] cavolo *m*

'**cab driver** *esp Am* tassista *m/f*

cabin ['kæbɪn] *of plane, ship* cabina *f*; **cabin attendant**

assistente *m/f* di volo; **cabin crew** equipaggio *m*

cabinet ['kæbɪnɪt] armadietto *m*; POL Consiglio *m* dei ministri; **cabinet minister** membro *m* del Consiglio dei ministri

319

camp

cable ['keɪbl] ELEC, *for securing* cavo *m*; ~ (*TV*) TV *f* via cavo; cable car funivia *f*; cable television televisione *f* via cavo

'cab stand *Am* stazione *f* dei taxi

cactus ['kæktəs] cactus *m inv*

cadaver [kə'dævə(r)] *Am* cadavere *m*

caddie ['kædɪ] *in golf* portamazze *m inv*

Caesarean [sɪ'zeərɪən] parto *m* cesareo

café ['kæfeɪ] caffè *m inv*, bar *m*; cafeteria tavola *f* calda

caffeine ['kæfi:n] caffeina *f*

cage [keɪdʒ] gabbia *f*; cagey evasivo

cake [keɪk] 1 *n* dolce *m*, torta *f*

calamity [kə'læmətɪ] calamità *f inv*

calcium ['kælsɪəm] calcio *m*

calculate ['kælkjʊleɪt] calcolare; calculating calcolatore; calculation calcolo *m*; calculator calcolatrice *f*

calendar ['kælɪndə(r)] calendario *m*

calf[1] [kɑːf] *young cow* vitello *m*

calf[2] [kɑːf] *of leg* polpaccio *m*

call [kɔːl] 1 *n* (*phone* ~) telefonata *f*; (*shout*) grido *m*; (*demand*) richiesta *f*; (*visit*) visita *f* 2 *v/t on phone*, (*summon*) chiamare; (*shout*) gridare; *meeting* convocare; be ~ed chiamarsi 3 *v/i on phone* chiamare; (*shout*) gridare;

(*visit*) passare

◆ call back 1 *v/t also* TELEC richiamare 2 *v/i on phone* richiamare; (*make another visit*) ripassare

◆ call for (*collect*) passare a prendere; (*demand*) reclamare; (*require*) richiedere

◆ call off *strike* revocare; *wedding* disdire

◆ call out (*shout*) chiamare ad alta voce; (*summon*) chiamare

calm [kɑːm] 1 *adj* calmo 2 *n* calma *f*

◆ calm down 1 *v/t* calmare 2 *v/i* calmarsi

calmly ['kɑːmlɪ] con calma

calorie ['kælərɪ] caloria *f*

camcorder ['kæmkɔːdə(r)] videocamera *f*

camera ['kæmərə] macchina *f* fotografica; (*video* ~) videocamera *f*; (*television* ~) telecamera *f*; cameraman cameraman *m inv*; camera phone cellulare *m* con fotocamera

camouflage ['kæməflɑːʒ] 1 *n* mimetizzazione *f*; *of soldiers* tuta *f* mimetica 2 *v/t* mimetizzare

camp [kæmp] 1 *n* campo *m* 2

v/i accamparsi

campaign [kæm'peɪn] **1** *n* campagna *f* **2** *v/i* militare

'camp-bed letto *m* da campo; **camper** *person* campeggiatore *m*, -trice *f*; *vehicle* camper *m inv*; **camping** campeggio *m*; **campsite** camping *m inv*, campeggio *m*

campus ['kæmpəs] campus *m*

can[1] [kæn] ◇ (*ability*) potere; **~ you hear me?** mi senti?; **I can't see** non vedo; **~ you speak French?** sai parlare il francese?; **as well as you ~** meglio che puoi ◇ (*permission*) potere; **~ I help you?** posso aiutarla?; **~ you help me?** mi può aiutare?

can[2] [kæn] *for drinks* lattina *f*; *for food* scatola *f*

Canada ['kænədə] Canada *m*; **Canadian 1** *adj* canadese **2** *n* canadese *m/f*

canal [kə'næl] (*waterway*) canale *m*

canary [kə'neərɪ] canarino *m*

cancel ['kænsl] annullare; **cancellation** annullamento *m*

cancer ['kænsə(r)] cancro *m*

Cancer ['kænsə(r)] ASTR Cancro *m*

candid ['kændɪd] franco

candidacy ['kændɪdəsɪ] candidatura *f*; **candidate** candidato *m*, -a *f*

candle ['kændl] candela *f*

candour, *Am* candor

['kændə(r)] franchezza *f*

candy ['kændɪ] *Am* (*sweet*) caramella *f*; (*sweets*) dolciumi *mpl*; **candy floss** zucchero *m* filato

cane [keɪn] canna *f*; *for walking* bastone *m*

canister ['kænɪstə(r)] barattolo *m*; *spray* bombola *f*

cannabis ['kænəbɪs] hashish *m*

canned [kænd] in scatola; (*recorded*) registrato

cannot ['kænɒt] ☞ **can not**

canny ['kænɪ] (*astute*) arguto

canoe [kə'nuː] canoa *f*

'can opener apriscatole *m inv*

can't [kɑːnt] = **can not**

canteen [kæn'tiːn] *in factory* mensa *f*

canvas ['kænvəs] tela *f*

canyon ['kænjən] canyon *m inv*

cap [kæp] *hat* berretto *m*; *for lens* coperchio *m*

capability [keɪpə'bɪlətɪ] *of person* capacità *f inv*; **capable** capace

capacity [kə'pæsətɪ] capacità *f inv*; *of engine* potenza *f*

capital ['kæpɪtl] *of country* capitale *f*; **capital letter** maiuscola *f*; *money* capitale *m*; **capitalism** capitalismo *m*; **capitalist 1** *adj* capitalista **2** *n* capitalista *m/f*; **capital letter** lettera *f* maiuscola; **capital punishment** pena *f* capitale

Capricorn ['kæprɪkɔːn] ASTR Capricorno *m*

capsize [kæp'saɪz] ribaltarsi

capsule ['kæpsjʊl] *of medicine* cachet *m inv*; *(space ~)* capsula *f*

captain ['kæptɪn] capitano *m*

caption ['kæpʃn] didascalia *f*

captivate ['kæptɪveɪt] affascinare; **captive** prigioniero; **captivity** cattività *f*; **capture 1** *n of building, city* occupazione *f*; *of city* presa *f*; *of criminal, animal* cattura *f* **2** *v/t person, animal* catturare; *city, building* occupare; *city* prendere; *market share* conquistare

car [kɑː(r)] macchina *f*, auto *f inv*; *of train* vagone *m*; **by ~** in macchina

caravan ['kærəvæn] roulotte *f inv*

'**car bomb** autobomba *f*

carbon monoxide [kɑːbən-mɒn'ɒksaɪd] monossido *m* di carbonio

carburetor [kɑːbju'retə(r)] carburatore *m*

carcass ['kɑːkəs] carcassa *f*

card [kɑːd] *to mark special occasion* biglietto *m*; *(post~)* cartolina *f*; *(business ~)* biglietto *m* (da visita); *(playing ~)* carta *f*; COMPUT scheda *f*; **cardboard** cartone *m*

cardiac ['kɑːdɪæk] cardiaco; **cardiac arrest** arresto *m* cardiaco

cardinal ['kɑːdɪnl] REL cardinale *m*

care [keə(r)] **1** *n of baby, pet* cure *fpl*; *of the elderly* assistenza *f*; *of the sick* cura *f*; *(worry)* preoccupazione *f*; **take ~** *(be cautious)* fare attenzione; **take ~ (of yourself)!** *(goodbye)* stammi bene; **take ~ of** *baby, dog* prendersi cura di; *tool, house, garden* tenere bene; *(deal with)* occuparsi di **2** *v/i* interessarsi; **I don't ~!** non mi importa
◆ **care about** interessarsi a
◆ **care for** *(look after)* prendersi cura di

career [kə'rɪə(r)] carriera *f*; *(path through life)* vita *f*

careful ['keəfʊl] **(be) ~** (stai) attento!; **carefully** con cautela; **careless** incurante; *driver, worker* sbadato; *work* fatto senza attenzione; **carelessly** senza cura; **carer** accompagnatore *m*, -trice *f*

caress [kə'res] accarezzare

'**car ferry** traghetto *m* (per le macchine)

cargo ['kɑːgəʊ] carico *m*

'**car hire** autonoleggio *m*

caricature ['kærɪkətjʊə(r)] caricatura *f*

carnation [kɑː'neɪʃn] garofano *m*

carnival ['kɑːnɪvl] carnevale *m*

'**car park** parcheggio *m*

carpenter ['kɑːpɪntə(r)] falegname *m*

carpet ['kɑːpɪt] tappeto *m*;

(fitted ~) moquette *f inv*

'car phone telefono *m* da automobile; **car rental** autonoleggio *m*

carrier ['kærɪə(r)] *(company)* compagnia *f* di trasporto; *of disease* portatore *m* sano, portatrice *f* sana

carrot ['kærət] carota *f*

carry ['kærɪ] **1** *v/t* portare; *of ship, bus etc* trasportare **2** *v/i of sound* sentirsi

◆ **carry on 1** *v/i (continue)* andare avanti, continuare **2** *v/t (conduct)* portare avanti

◆ **carry out** *survey etc* effettuare; *orders etc* eseguire

cart [kɑːt] carretto *m*; *Am:* in *supermarket, at airport* carrello *m*

carton ['kɑːtn] cartone *m*; *of cigarettes* stecca *f*

cartoon [kɑːˈtuːn] fumetto *m*; *on TV, film* cartone *m* animato

cartridge ['kɑːtrɪdʒ] *for gun, printer* cartuccia *f*

carve [kɑːv] *meat* tagliare; *wood* intagliare

case¹ [keɪs] *for glasses, pen* astuccio *m*; *of wine* cassa *f*; *(suitcase)* valigia *f*

case² [keɪs] *(instance, for police),* MED caso *m*; LAW causa *f*; **in** ~ ... in caso; **in any** ~ in ogni caso

cash [kæʃ] **1** *n* contanti *mpl*; *(money)* soldi *mpl* **2** *v/t cheque* incassare; **cash desk** cassa *f*; **cash flow** flusso *m* di cassa; **cashier** *in shop etc* cassiere *m*, -a *f*; **cash machine**, **cashpoint** (sportello *m*) Bancomat® *m*; **cash register** cassa *f*

casino [kəˈsiːnəʊ] casinò *m inv*

casket ['kæskɪt] *Am (coffin)* bara *f*

casserole ['kæsərəʊl] *meal* stufato *m*; *container* casseruola *f*

cassette [kəˈset] cassetta *f*; **cassette recorder** registratore *m* (a cassette)

cast [kɑːst] **1** *n of play* cast *m inv*; *(mould)* stampo *m* **2** *v/t doubt, suspicion* far sorgere **(on** su); *metal* colare (in uno stampo)

cast 'iron ghisa *f*

castle ['kɑːsl] castello *m*

casual ['kæʒʊəl] *(chance)* casuale; *(offhand)* disinvolto; *remark* poco importante; *clothes* casual *inv*; **casually** *dressed* (in modo) casual; *say* con disinvoltura; **casualty** *dead person* vittima *f*; *injured* ferito *m*

cat [kæt] gatto *m*

catalogue, *Am* **catalog** ['kætəlɒg] catalogo *m*

catalyst ['kætəlɪst] catalizzatore *m*

catastrophe [kəˈtæstrəfɪ] catastrofe *f*; **catastrophic** catastrofico

catch [kætʃ] **1** *n* presa *f*; *of fish* pesca *f*; *on bag, box* chiusura *f* *f*; *on door, window* fermo *m*; (*problem*) inghippo *m* **2** *v/t* ball, escapee, bus, fish, illness prendere; (*hear*) afferrare

◆ **catch on** (*become popular*) fare presa; (*understand*) afferrare

◆ **catch up** recuperare; *catch up with s.o.* raggiungere qu; *catch up with sth* work, studies mettersi in pari con qc

catching ['kætʃɪŋ] *also fig* contagioso; **catchy** *tune* orecchiabile

categoric [kætə'gɒrɪk] categorico; **category** categoria *f*

caterer ['keɪtərə(r)] ristoratore *m*, -trice *f*

caterpillar ['kætəpɪlə(r)] bruco *m*

cathedral [kə'θiːdrəl] cattedrale *f*, duomo *m*

Catholic ['kæθəlɪk] **1** *adj* cattolico **2** *n* cattolico *m*, -a *f*; **Catholicism** cattolicesimo *m*

cattle ['kætl] bestiame *m*

cauliflower ['kɒlɪflaʊə(r)] cavolfiore *m*

cause [kɔːz] **1** *n* causa *f*; (*grounds*) motivo *m* **2** *v/t* causare

caution ['kɔːʃn] **1** *n* (*carefulness*) cautela *f*, prudenza *f* **2** *v/t* (*warn*) mettere in guardia; **cautious** cauto, prudente; **cautiously** con cautela

cave [keɪv] caverna *f*, grotta *f*

caviar ['kævɪɑː(r)] caviale *m*

cavity ['kævɪtɪ] cavità *f inv*; *in tooth* carie *f inv*

CD [siː'diː] (= *compact disc*) CD *m inv*; **CD player** lettore *m* CD; **CD-ROM** CD-ROM *m inv*

cease [siːs] cessare; **cease-fire** cessate il fuoco *m inv*

ceiling ['siːlɪŋ] soffitto *m*; (*limit*) tetto *m*, plafond *m inv*

celeb [seleb] vip *m/f inv*

celebrate ['selɪbreɪt] festeggiare; **celebrated** acclamato; **celebration** celebrazione *f*, festeggiamento *m*; **celebrity** celebrità *f inv*

celibate ['selɪbət] *man* celibe; *woman* nubile

cell [sel] *for prisoner* cella *f*; BIO cellula *f*; *in spreadsheet* casella *f*, cella *f*

cellar ['selə(r)] cantina *f*; *of wine* collezione *f* di vini

cellist ['tʃelɪst] violoncellista *m/f*; **cello** violoncello *m*

'cell phone, cellular phone ['seljʊlə(r)] *Am* telefono *m* cellulare, cellulare *m*

cement [sɪ'ment] cemento *m*

cemetery ['semətrɪ] cimitero *m*

censor ['sensə(r)] censurare; **censorship** censura *f*

census ['sensəs] censimento *m*

cent [sent] centesimo *m*

centenary [sen'tiːnərɪ] centenario *m*

center *Am* ☞ *centre*

centigrade ['sentɪgreɪd] centigrado

centimetre, *Am* **centimeter** ['sentɪmiːtə(r)] centimetro *m*

central ['sentrəl] centrale; **central heating** riscaldamento *m* autonomo; **centralize** accentrare; **central locking** MOT chiusura *f* centralizzata; **central reservation** MOT banchina *f* spartitraffico

centre ['sentə(r)] **1** *n* centro *m* **2** *v/t* centrare

century ['sentʃərɪ] secolo *m*

CEO [siːiːˈəʊ] (= *Chief Executive Officer*) direttore *m* generale

ceramic [sɪˈræmɪk] ceramico

cereal ['sɪərɪəl] cereale *m*; (*breakfast* ~) cereali *mpl*

ceremonial [serɪˈməʊnɪəl] **1** *adj* da cerimonia **2** *n* cerimoniale *m*; **ceremony** cerimonia *f*

certain ['sɜːtn] (*sure, particular*) certo; **certainly** certamente; ~ **not!** certo che no!; **certainty** certezza *f*; **it's a** ~ è una cosa certa

certificate [səˈtɪfɪkət] *qualification* certificazione *f*; *official paper* certificato *m*

certify ['sɜːtɪfaɪ] dichiarare ufficialmente

Cesarean *Am* ☞ **Caesarean**

chain [tʃeɪn] **1** *n* catena *f* **2** *v/t*: ~ **sth to sth** incatenare qc a qc; **chain reaction** reazione *f* a catena

chair [tʃeə(r)] **1** *n* sedia *f*; (*arm* ~) poltrona *f*; *at university* cattedra *f* **2** *v/t meeting* presiedere; **chair lift** seggiovia *f*; **chairman** presidente *m*; **chairmanship** presidenza *f*; **chairperson** presidente *m/f*

chalet ['ʃæleɪ] chalet *m inv*

chalk [tʃɔːk] gesso *m*

challenge ['tʃælɪndʒ] **1** *n* sfida *f* **2** *v/t* sfidare; (*call into question*) mettere alla prova; **challenger** sfidante *m/f*; **challenging** *job, undertaking* stimolante

chambermaid ['tʃeɪmbəmeɪd] cameriera *f*; **Chamber of Commerce** Camera *f* di Commercio

champagne [ʃæmˈpeɪn] champagne *m inv*

champion ['tʃæmpɪən] **1** *n* SP campione *m*, -essa *f* **2** *v/t cause* difendere; **championship** *event* campionato *m*; *title* titolo *m* di campione

chance [tʃɑːns] (*possibility*) probabilità *f inv*; (*opportunity*) opportunità *f inv*; (*luck*) caso *m*; **by** ~ per caso; **take a** ~ correre un rischio

change [tʃeɪndʒ] **1** *n* cambiamento *m*; *small coins* moneta *f*; *from purchase* resto *m*; **for a** ~ per cambiare **2** *v/t* cambiare **3** *v/i* cambiare; (*put on different clothes*) cambiarsi; **changeable** incostante; *weather* variabile; **change-**

over passaggio *m*; *period* fase *f* di transizione; **changing room** *m* spogliatoio *m*; *in shop* camerino *m*

channel *on TV, in water* canale *m*; **Channel Tunnel** tunnel *m* della Manica

chant [tʃɑːnt] **1** *n* slogan *m inv*; REL canto *m* **2** *v/i* gridare; *of demonstrators* gridare slogan; REL cantare

chaos ['keɪɒs] caos *m*; **chaotic** caotico

chap [tʃæp] *n* F tipo *m* F

chapel ['tʃæpl] cappella *f*

chapter ['tʃæptə(r)] capitolo *m*

character ['kærɪktə(r)] carattere *m*; *(person)* tipo *m*; *in book* personaggio *m*; **characteristic 1** *n* caratteristica *f* **2** *adj* caratteristico; **characterize** caratterizzare

charge [tʃɑːdʒ] **1** *n (fee)* costo *m*; LAW accusa *f*; *free of ~* gratis; *be in ~* essere responsabile **2** *v/t sum of money* far pagare; *Am (put on account)* addebitare; LAW accusare; *battery* caricare **3** *v/i (attack)* attaccare; **charge account** conto *m* (spese); **charge card** carta *f* di addebito

charger ['tʃɑːdʒə(r)] *battery*, TEL caricabatteria *m*

charitable ['tʃærɪtəbl] *institution* di beneficenza; *person* caritatevole; **charity** carità *f*; *organization* associazione *f* di beneficenza

charm [tʃɑːm] **1** *n* fascino *m*; *on bracelet etc* ciondolo *m* **2** *v/t (delight)* conquistare; **charming** affascinante; *house, village* incantevole

charred [tʃɑːd] carbonizzato

chart [tʃɑːt] diagramma *m*; *(map)* carta *f*

'**charter flight** volo *m* charter *inv*

chase [tʃeɪs] **1** *n* inseguimento *m* **2** *v/t* inseguire

◆ **chase away** cacciare (via)

chassis ['tʃæsɪ] *of car* telaio *m*

chat [tʃæt] **1** *n* chiacchierata *f* **2** *v/i* chiacchierare

◆ **chat up** F abbordare F

'**chatline** chat line *f inv*; **chat room** chat room *f inv*; **chat show** talk show *m inv*

chatter ['tʃætə(r)] **1** *n* parlantina *f* **2** *v/i talk* fare chiacchiere; *of teeth* battere; **chatterbox** chiacchierone *m*, -a *f*

chauffeur ['ʃəʊfə(r)] autista *m/f*

chauvinist ['ʃəʊvɪnɪst] *(male ~)* maschilista *m*

cheap [tʃiːp] economico; *(nasty)* cattivo; *(mean)* tirchio

cheat [tʃiːt] **1** *n person* imbroglione *m*, -a *f* **2** *v/t* imbrogliare **3** *v/i* imbrogliare; *in cards* barare

check¹ [tʃek] **1** *adj shirt* a quadri **2** *n* quadro *m*

check² [tʃek] *n Am* FIN assegno *m*

check³ [tʃek] **1** *n to verify sth* verifica *f* **2** *v/t* & *v/i* verificare

◆ **check in** registrarsi
◆ **check out 1** *v/i of hotel* saldare il conto **2** *v/t* (*look into*) verificare; *club, restaurant etc* provare
◆ **check up on** fare dei controlli su

checked ['tʃekt] *material* a quadri

checkered ['tʃekərd] *Am material* a quadri; **checkers** *Am* dama *f*

'**check-in** (**counter**) banco *m* dell'accettazione; **checking account** conto *m* corrente; **check-in time** check in *m inv*; **checklist** lista *f* di verifica; **checkmark** *Am* segno *m*; **check-mate** *n* scacco *m* matto; **check-out** cassa *f*; **check-point** posto *m* di blocco; **checkroom** *Am for coats* guardaroba *m inv*; **checkup** *medical* check up *m inv*; *dental* visita *f* di controllo

cheek [tʃiːk] guancia *f*; (*impudence*) sfacciataggine *f*; **cheeky** sfacciato

cheer [tʃɪə(r)] **1** *n* acclamazione *f*; ~**s!** (*toast*) salute!; ~**s!** *F* (*thanks*) grazie! **2** *v/t* acclamare **3** *v/i* fare acclamazioni
◆ **cheer up 1** *v/i* consolarsi; **cheer up!** su con la vita! **2** *v/t* tirare su

cheerful ['tʃɪəful] allegro; **cheering** acclamazioni *fpl*

cheerio [tʃɪərɪ'əʊ] *F* ciao *m*

'**cheerleader** ragazza *f* pon

pon

cheese [tʃiːz] formaggio *m*; **cheesecake** dolce *m* al formaggio

chef [ʃef] chef *m/f inv*

chemical ['kemɪkl] **1** *adj* chimico **2** *n* sostanza *f* chimica

chemist farmacista *m/f*; *in laboratory* chimico *m*, -a *f*; **chemistry** chimica *f*

chemotherapy [kiːməʊ'θerəpɪ] chemioterapia *f*

cheque [tʃek] assegno *m*; **chequebook** libretto *m* degli assegni

cherry ['tʃerɪ] *fruit* ciliegia *f*; *tree* ciliegio *m*

chess [tʃes] scacchi *mpl*

chest [tʃest] *of person* petto *m*; (*box*) cassa *f*

chew [tʃuː] masticare; *of dog, rats* rosicchiare; **chewing gum** gomma *f* da masticare

chic [ʃiːk] chic *inv*

chick [tʃɪk] pulcino *m*; F (*girl*) ragazza *f*

chicken ['tʃɪkɪn] **1** *n* pollo *m*; **chickenpox** varicella *f*

chief [tʃiːf] **1** *n* principale *m/f*; *of tribe* capo *m* **2** *adj* principale; **chiefly** principalmente

child [tʃaɪld] (*pl* **children** ['tʃɪldrən]) *also pej* bambino *m*, -a *f*; **they have two children** hanno due figli; **childhood** infanzia *f*; **childish** *pej* infantile, puerile; **childlike** innocente; **childminder** baby-sitter *m/f inv*

children ['tʃɪldrən] *pl* ☞ **child**

Chile ['tʃɪlɪ] Cile m; **Chilean 1** adj cileno **2** n cileno m, -a f

chill [tʃɪl] **1** n in air freddo m; illness colpo m di freddo; **there's a ~ in the air** l'aria è fredda **2** v/t wine mettere in fresco

◆ **chill out** rilassarsi

chilli (pepper) ['tʃɪlɪ] peperoncino m

chilly ['tʃɪlɪ] weather, welcome freddo

chimney ['tʃɪmnɪ] camino m

chimpanzee [tʃɪmpæn'ziː] scimpanzé m inv

chin [tʃɪn] mento m

china ['tʃaɪnə] porcellana f

China ['tʃaɪnə] Cina f; **Chinese 1** adj cinese **2** n language cinese m; person cinese m/f

chip [tʃɪp] **1** n fragment scheggia f; damage scheggiatura f; in gambling fiche f inv; COMPUT chip m inv; **~s** patate fpl fritte; Am patatine fpl **2** v/t damage scheggiare

chisel ['tʃɪzl] scalpello m

chlorine ['klɔːriːn] cloro m

chock-full ['tʃɒkfʊl] F strapieno

chocolate ['tʃɒkələt] cioccolato m; in box cioccolatino m; **chocolate cake** dolce m al cioccolato

choice [tʃɔɪs] **1** n scelta f; **I had no ~** non avevo scelta **2** adj (top quality) di prima scelta

choir ['kwaɪə(r)] coro m

choke [tʃəʊk] **1** n MOT starter m inv **2** v/t & v/i soffocare

cholesterol [kə'lestərɒl] colesterolo m

choose [tʃuːz] scegliere; **choosey** F selettivo

chop [tʃɒp] **1** n meat braciola f **2** v/t wood spaccare; meat, vegetables tagliare a pezzi

◆ **chop down** tree abbattere

chord [kɔːd] MUS accordo m

chore [tʃɔː(r)] household faccenda f domestica

choreographer [kɒrɪ'ɒgrəfə(r)] coreografo m, -a f; **choreography** coreografia f

chorus ['kɔːrəs] singers, of song coro m

Christ [kraɪst] Cristo m; **~!** Cristo!

christen ['krɪsn] battezzare

Christian ['krɪstʃən] **1** n cristiano m, -a f **2** adj cristiano; **Christianity** cristianesimo m; **Christian name** nome m di battesimo

Christmas ['krɪsməs] Natale m; **Merry ~!** Buon Natale!; **Christmas card** biglietto m di auguri natalizi; **Christmas Day** giorno m di Natale; **Christmas Eve** vigilia f di Natale; **Christmas present** regalo m di Natale; **Christmas tree** albero m di Natale

chrome, chromium [krəʊm, 'krəʊmɪəm] cromo m

chronic ['krɒnɪk] cronico

chrysanthemum [krɪ'sænθəməm] crisantemo m

chubby ['tʃʌbɪ] paffuto

chuck [tʃʌk] F buttare

chuckle ['tʃʌkl] **1** *n* risatina *f* **2** *v/i* ridacchiare

chunk [tʃʌŋk] pezzo *m*

church [tʃɜːtʃ] chiesa *f*; **church service** funzione *f* religiosa; **churchyard** cimitero *m* (di una chiesa)

chute [ʃuːt] scivolo *m*; *for waste disposal* canale *m* di scarico

cider ['saɪdə(r)] sidro *f*

cigar [sɪˈgɑː(r)] sigaro *m*

cigarette [sɪgəˈret] sigaretta *f*; **cigarette lighter** accendino *m*

cinema ['sɪnɪmə] cinema *m inv*; **cinema goer** frequentatore *m*, -trice *f* di cinema

cinnamon ['sɪnəmən] canella *f*

circle ['sɜːkl] **1** *n* cerchio *m*; (*group*) cerchia *f* **2** *v/i* of *plane* girare in tondo; *of bird* volteggiare

circuit ['sɜːkɪt] ELEC circuito *m*; (*lap*) giro *m*; **circuit board** COMPUT circuito *m* stampato

circular ['sɜːkjʊlə(r)] **1** *n giving information* circolare *f* **2** *adj* circolare; **circulate 1** *v/i* circolare **2** *v/t memo* far circolare; **circulation** BIO circolazione *f*; *of newspaper* tiratura *f*

circumstances ['sɜːkəmstənsɪz] circostanze *fpl*; (*financial*) situazione *fsg* (economica)

circus ['sɜːkəs] circo *m*

cistern ['sɪstən] cisterna *f*; *of WC* serbatoio *m*

citizen ['sɪtɪzn] cittadino *m*, -a *f*; **citizenship** cittadinanza *f*

city ['sɪtɪ] città *f inv*; **city centre**, *Am* **city center** centro *m* (della città); **city hall** sala *f* municipale

civic ['sɪvɪk] civico

civil ['sɪvl] civile; **civil ceremony** cerimonia *f* civile; **civil engineer** ingegnere *m* civile; **civilian 1** *n* civile *m/f* **2** *adj clothes* civile; **civilization** civilizzazione *f*; **civilize** civilizzare; **civil rights** diritti *mpl* civili; **civil servant** impiegato *m*, -a *f* statale; **civil service** pubblica amministrazione *f*; **civil war** guerra *f* civile

claim [kleɪm] **1** *n* (*request*) richiesta *f*; (*right*) diritto *m*; (*assertion*) affermazione *f* **2** *v/t* (*ask for as a right*) rivendicare; *damages* richiedere; (*assert*) affermare; *lost property* reclamare; **claimant** richiedente *m/f*

clairvoyant [kleəˈvɔɪənt] chiaroveggente *m/f*

clam [klæm] vongola *f*

clammy ['klæmɪ] *hands* appiccicaticcio; *weather* afoso

clamp [klæmp] *fastener* morsa *f*; *for wheel* ceppo *m* (bloccaruote)

♦ **clamp down** usare il pu-

cleavage

gno di ferro
♦ **clamp down on** mettere un freno a

clandestine [klænˈdestɪn] clandestino

clap [klæp] (*applaud*) applaudire

clarification [klærɪfɪˈkeɪʃn] chiarimento *m*; **clarify** chiarire

clarinet [klærɪˈnet] clarinetto *m*

clarity [ˈklærɪtɪ] chiarezza *f*

clash [klæʃ] **1** *n* scontro *m* **2** *v/i* scontrarsi; *of opinions* essere in contrasto; *of colours* stonare; *of events* coincidere

clasp [klɑːsp] **1** *n fastener* chiusura *f* **2** *v/t in hand* stringere

class [klɑːs] **1** *n* (*lesson*) lezione *f*; (*group of people, category*) classe *f* **2** *v/t* classificare

classic [ˈklæsɪk] **1** *adj* classico **2** *n* classico *m*; **classical** classico; **classification** classificazione *f*; **classified** *information* riservato; **classified ad(vertisement)** inserzione *f*, annuncio *m*; **classify** (*categorize*) classificare

'**classroom** aula *f*; **classy** F d'alta classe

clause [klɔːz] *in agreement* articolo *m*; GRAM proposizione *f*

claustrophobia [klɔːstrəˈfəʊbɪə] claustrofobia *f*

claw [klɔː] **1** *n* artiglio *m*; *of lobster* chela *m* **2** *v/t* (*scratch*)

graffiare

clay [kleɪ] argilla *f*

clean [kliːn] **1** *adj* pulito **2** *adv* F (*completely*) completamente **3** *v/t* pulire; *teeth* lavarsi; *car, hands, face* lavare; *clothes* lavare *or* pulire a secco

cleaner [ˈkliːnə(r)] *male* uomo *m* delle pulizie; *female* donna *f* delle pulizie; (*dry ~*) lavanderia *f*, tintoria *f*

cleanse [klenz] *skin* detergere; **cleanser** *for skin* detergente *m*; **cleansing cream** latte *f* detergente

clear [klɪə(r)] **1** *adj* chiaro; *sky* sereno; *water, eyes* limpido; *skin* uniforme; *conscience* pulito **2** *v/t roads etc* sgombe(e)rare; (*acquit*) scagionare; (*authorize*) autorizzare **3** *v/i of sky* schiarirsi; *of mist* diradarsi

♦ **clear off** F filarsela F
♦ **clear out 1** *v/t cupboard* sgomb(e)rare **2** *v/i* sparire
♦ **clear up 1** *v/i* (*tidy up*) mettere in ordine; *of weather* schiarirsi; *of illness* sparire **2** *v/t* (*tidy*) mettere in ordine; *mystery* risolvere

clearance [ˈklɪərəns] *space* spazio *m* libero; (*authorization*) autorizzazione *f*; **clearance sale** liquidazione *f*; **clearing** *in woods* radura *f*; **clearly** chiaramente

cleavage [ˈkliːvɪdʒ] décolleté *m inv*

clench [klentʃ] serrare

clergy ['klɜːdʒɪ] clero *m*; **clergyman** ecclesiastico *m*

clerk [klɑːk, *Am* klɜːk] impiegato *m*, -a *f*; *Am in store* commesso *m*, -a *f*

clever ['klevə(r)] intelligente; *gadget* ingegnoso

click [klɪk] **1** *n* COMPUT click *m inv* **2** *v/i of camera etc* scattare

◆ **click on** COMPUT cliccare su

client ['klaɪənt] cliente *m/f*; **clientele** clientela *f*

cliff [klɪf] scogliera *f*

climate ['klaɪmət] clima *m*; **climate change** mutazione *f* climatica

climax ['klaɪmæks] punto *m* culminante

climb [klaɪm] **1** *n up mountain* scalata *f*, arrampicata *f* **2** *v/t* salire su **3** *v/i* salire; **climber** alpinista *m/f*

clinch [klɪntʃ] *deal* concludere

cling [klɪŋ] *of clothes* essere attillato

◆ **cling to** *of child* avvinghiarsi a; *tradition* aggrapparsi a

clingy ['klɪŋɪ] *person* appiccicoso

clinic ['klɪnɪk] clinica *f*; **clinical** clinico

clip¹ [klɪp] **1** *n fastener* fermaglio *m*; *for hair* molletta *f* **2** *v/t*: ~ **sth to sth** attaccare qc a qc

clip² [klɪp] **1** *n from film* spez-

zone *f* **2** *v/t hair, grass* tagliare

clipping ['klɪpɪŋ] *from newspaper* ritaglio *m*

cloakroom ['kləʊkruːm] *for coats* guardaroba *m inv*

clock [klɒk] orologio *m*; **clock radio** radiosveglia *f*; **clockwise** in senso orario

clone [kləʊn] **1** *n* clone *m* **2** *v/t* clonare; **cloning** clonazione *f*

close¹ [kləʊs] **1** *adj family, friend* intimo **2** *adv* vicino; ~ **at hand** a portata di mano; ~ **by** nelle vicinanze

close² [kləʊz] *v/t* chiudere **2** *v/i of door, eyes* chiudersi; *of shop* chiudere

closed-circuit 'television televisione *f* a circuito chiuso; **close-knit** affiatato; **closely** *listen, watch* attentamente; *cooperate* fianco a fianco

closet ['klɒzɪt] *Am* armadio *m*

close-up ['kləʊsʌp] primo piano *m*

closing date ['kləʊzɪŋ] termine *m*

closure ['kləʊʒə(r)] chiusura *f*

clot [klɒt] **1** *n of blood* grumo *m* **2** *v/i of blood* coagularsi

cloth [klɒθ] tessuto *m*; *for cleaning* straccio *m*

clothes [kləʊðz] vestiti *mpl*; **clothes hanger** attaccapanni *m inv*; **clothes peg** molletta *f* per i panni; **clothing** abbigliamento *m*

cloud [klaʊd] *n* nuvola *f*
♦ **cloud over** rannuvolarsi
cloudless ['klaʊdlɪs] sereno;
cloudy nuvoloso
clout [klaʊt] *fig (influence)* impatto *m*
clove of 'garlic [kləʊv] spicchio *m* d'aglio
clown [klaʊn] *also pej* pagliaccio *m*
club [klʌb] *weapon* clava *f*; *in golf* mazza *f*; *organization* club *m inv*
clue [kluː] indizio *m*
clumsiness ['klʌmzɪnɪs] goffaggine *f*; **clumsy** goffo, maldestro
cluster ['klʌstə(r)] gruppo *m*
clutch [klʌtʃ] **1** *n* MOT frizione *f* **2** *v/t* stringere
♦ **clutch at** cercare di afferrare
Co. (= *Company*) Cia (= compagnia)
c/o (= *care of*) presso
coach [kəʊtʃ] **1** *n (trainer)* allenatore *m*, -trice *f*; *on train* vagone *m*; *(bus)* pullman *m inv* **2** *v/t* allenare; **coaching** allenamento *m*; **coach station** stazione *f* dei pullman
coagulate [kəʊ'æɡjʊleɪt] coagularsi
coal [kəʊl] carbone *m*
coalition [kəʊə'lɪʃn] coalizione *f*
'coalmine miniera *f* di carbone
coarse [kɔːs] *skin, fabric* ruvido; *hair* spesso; *(vulgar)*

grossolano; **coarsely** *(vulgarly)* grossolanamente; **ground** a grani grossi
coast [kəʊst] costa *f*; **coastal** costiero
'coastguard *organization*, *person* guardia *f* costiera; **coastline** costa *f*, litorale *m*
coat [kəʊt] **1** *n (over-~)* cappotto *m*; *of animal* pelliccia *f*; *of paint etc* mano *f* **2** *v/t (cover)* ricoprire; **coathanger** attaccapanni *m inv*, gruccia *f*; **coating** strato *m*
coax [kəʊks] convincere con le moine
cobweb ['kɒbweb] ragnatela *f*
cocaine [kə'keɪn] cocaina *f*
cock [kɒk] *chicken* gallo *m*; *any male bird* maschio *m* (di uccelli); **cockpit** *of plane* cabina *f* (di pilotaggio); **cockroach** scarafaggio *m*; **cocktail** cocktail *m inv*
cocoa ['kəʊkəʊ] *drink* cioccolata *f* calda
coconut ['kəʊkənʌt] cocco *m*; **coconut palm** palma *f* di cocco
code [kəʊd] codice *m*
coeducational [kəʊedjuː'keɪʃnl] misto
coerce [kəʊ'ɜːs] costringere
coexist [kəʊɪɡ'zɪst] coesistere; **coexistence** coesistenza *f*
coffee ['kɒfɪ] caffè *m inv*; **coffee maker** caffettiera *f*; **coffee pot** caffettiera *f*; **coffee**

shop caffetteria *f*

coffin ['kɒfɪn] bara *f*

cog [kɒg] dente *m*

cohabit [kəʊ'hæbɪt] convivere

coherent [kəʊ'hɪərənt] coerente

coil [kɔɪl] **1** *n* of rope rotolo *m* **2** *v/t:* ~ (*up*) avvolgere

coin [kɔɪn] moneta *f*

coincide [kəʊɪn'saɪd] coincidere; **coincidence** coincidenza *f*

Coke® [kəʊk] Coca® *f*

cold [kəʊld] **1** *adj* freddo; *I'm* ~ ho freddo; *it's* ~ *of weather* fa freddo **2** *n* freddo *m*; MED raffreddore *m*; **cold-blooded** *also murder* a sangue freddo; *person* spietato; **cold calling** porta-a-porta *m*; *by phone* televendite *fpl*; **coldly** freddamente; **coldness** freddezza *f*; **cold sore** febbre *f* del labbro

collaborate [kə'læbəreɪt] collaborare; **collaboration** collaborazione *f*; *with enemy* collaborazionismo *m*; **collaborator** collaboratore *m*, -trice *f*; *with enemy* collaborazionista *m/f*

collapse [kə'læps] crollare; *of person* accasciarsi; **collapsible** pieghevole

collar ['kɒlə(r)] collo *m*, colletto *m*; *of dog* collare *m*; **collar-bone** clavicola *f*

collateral [kə'lætərəl] *for loan* garanzia *f* collaterale; **collat-**

eral **damage** danni *mpl* collaterali

colleague ['kɒliːg] collega *m/f*

collect [kə'lekt] **1** *v/t person* andare / venire a prendere; *tickets, cleaning etc* ritirare; *as hobby* collezionare; (*gather*) raccogliere **2** *v/i* (*gather together*) radunarsi **3** *adv Am:* **call** ~ telefonare a carico del destinatario; **collection** collezione *f*; *in church* colletta *f*; *of poems, stories* raccolta *f*; **collective** collettivo; **collector** collezionista *m/f*

college ['kɒlɪdʒ] istituto *m* di studi superiori; *for professional training* scuola *f* professionale; *of British university* college *m inv*; **technical college** istituto *m* tecnico

collide [kə'laɪd] scontrarsi; **collision** collisione *f*, scontro *m*

colon ['kəʊlən] *punctuation* due punti *mpl*

colonel ['kɜːnl] colonnello *m*

colonial [kə'ləʊnɪəl] coloniale; **colonize** colonizzare; **colony** colonia *f*

color *Am* ☞ **colour**

colossal [kə'lɒsl] colossale

colour ['kʌlə(r)] colore *m*; **colour-blind** daltonico; **coloured** *person* di colore; **colourful** pieno di colori; *account* pittoresco

colt [kəʊlt] puledro *m*

column ['kɒləm] colonna f; in newspaper rubrica f; **columnist** giornalista m/f che cura una rubrica

coma ['kəʊmə] coma m inv

comb [kəʊm] **1** n pettine m **2** v/t pettinare; area rastrellare

combat ['kɒmbæt] **1** n combattimento m **2** v/t combattere

combination [kɒmbɪ'neɪʃn] combinazione f

combine [kəm'baɪn] **1** v/t unire; ingredients mescolare **2** v/i combinarsi

come [kʌm] venire; of train, bus arrivare

◆ **come about** (happen) succedere

◆ **come across** (find) trovare

◆ **come along** (come too) venire; (turn up) presentarsi; (progress) fare progressi

◆ **come back** ritornare

◆ **come down** venire giù; in price, amount etc, (descend) scendere; of rain, snow cadere

◆ **come for** (attack) assalire; (collect) venire a prendere

◆ **come forward** farsi avanti

◆ **come from** venire da; *where do you come from?* di dove sei?

◆ **come in** entrare; of train, in race arrivare; of tide salire

◆ **come in for** attirare; *come in for criticism* attirare delle critiche

◆ **come off** of handle etc staccarsi

◆ **come on** (progress) fare progressi; *how's the work coming on?* come sta venendo il lavoro?; *come on!* dai!; in disbelief ma dai!

◆ **come out** of person, book, sun uscire; of results, product venir fuori; of stain venire via

◆ **come to 1** v/t place arrivare a; *that comes to £70* fanno 70 sterline **2** v/i (regain consciousness) rinvenire

◆ **come up** salire; of sun sorgere

◆ **come up with** new idea etc venir fuori con

comeback ritorno m; *make a ~* tornare alla ribalta

comedian [kə'miːdɪən] comico m, -a f; pej buffone m; **comedy** commedia f

comfort ['kʌmfət] **1** n comodità f inv; (consolation) conforto m **2** v/t confortare; **comfortable** chair, room comodo

comic ['kɒmɪk] **1** n to read fumetto m; (comedian) comico m, -a f **2** adj comico; **comical** comico; **comic book** fumetto m; **comic strip** striscia f (di fumetti)

comma ['kɒmə] virgola f

command [kə'mɑːnd] **1** n comando m **2** v/t person comandare a

commandeer [kɒmən'dɪə(r)]

appropriarsi di

commander [kə'mɑːndə(r)] comandante *m*; **commander-in-chief** comandante *m* in capo

commemorate [kə'meməreıt] commemorare

commence [kə'mens] cominciare

commendable [kə'mendəbl] lodevole; **commendation** *for bravery* riconoscimento *m*

comment ['kɒment] **1** *n* commento *m* **2** *v/i* fare commenti; **commentary** cronaca *f*; **commentator** *on TV* telecronista *m/f*; *on radio* radiocronista *m/f*

commerce ['kɒmɜːs] commercio *m*; **commercial 1** *adj* commerciale **2** *n* (*advert*) pubblicità *f inv*; **commercial break** interruzione *f* pubblicitaria; **commercialize** *Christmas etc* commercializzare

commission [kə'mıʃn] (*payment*, *committee*) commissione *f*; (*job*) incarico *m*

commit [kə'mıt] *crime* commettere; *money* assegnare; ~ **o.s.** impegnarsi; **commitment** impegno *m*; **committee** comitato *m*

commodity [kə'mɒdətı] prodotto *m*

common ['kɒmən] comune; **have sth in** ~ **with s.o.** avere qc in comune con qu; **com-**

monly comunemente; **common sense** buon senso *m*

commotion [kə'məʊʃn] confusione *f*

communal ['kɒmjunl] comune

communicate [kə'mjuːnıkeıt] comunicare; **communication** comunicazione *f*; **communications** comunicazioni *fpl*; **communicative** comunicativo

Communion [kə'mjuːnıən] REL comunione *f*

Communism ['kɒmjunızm] comunismo *m*; **Communist 1** *adj* comunista **2** *n* comunista *m/f*

community [kə'mjuːnətı] comunità *f inv*

commute [kə'mjuːt] **1** *v/i* fare il / la pendolare **2** *v/t* LAW commutare; **commuter** pendolare *m/f*; **commuter traffic** traffico *m* dei pendolari; **commuter train** treno *m* dei pendolari

compact 1 [kəm'pækt] *adj* compatto **2** ['kɒmpækt] *n* MOT compact *m inv*

companion [kəm'pænjən] compagno *m*, -a *f*

company ['kʌmpənı] compagnia *f*; COM società *f inv*; **company car** auto *f inv* della ditta

comparable ['kɒmpərəbl] paragonabile; (*similar*) simile; **comparative 1** *adj* (*relative*) relativo; *study*, *method* comparato; **comparatively** relativamente; **compare 1** v/t paragonare (**with** a); **~d with ...** rispetto a ... **2** v/i: **how did he ~?** com'era rispetto agli altri?; **comparison** paragone *m*, confronto *m*

compartment [kəmˈpɑːtmənt] scomparto *m*

compass [ˈkʌmpəs] bussola *f*; *for geometry* compasso *m*

compassion [kəmˈpæʃn] compassione *f*; **compassionate** compassionevole

compatibility [kəmpætəˈbɪlɪtɪ] compatibilità *f*; **compatible** compatibile

compel [kəmˈpel] costringere

compensate [ˈkɒmpənseɪt] **1** v/t *with money* risarcire **2** v/i: **~ for** compensare; **compensation** *money* risarcimento *m*; *reward* vantaggio *m*; *comfort* consolazione *f*

compete [kəmˈpiːt] competere; (*take part*) gareggiare; **~ for** contendersi

competence [ˈkɒmpɪtəns] competenza *f*; **competent** competente

competition [kɒmpəˈtɪʃn] (*contest*) concorso *m*; SP gara *f*; (*competing, competitors*) concorrenza *f*; **competitive** competitivo; *sport* agonistico; *price, offer* concorrenziale; **competitiveness** competitività *f*; **competitor** *in contest* concorrente *m/f*; **our ~s** COM la concorrenza

complain [kəmˈpleɪn] lamentarsi; *to shop* reclamare; **complaint** lamentela *f*; *to shop* reclamo *m*; MED disturbo *m*

complementary [kɒmplɪˈmentərɪ] complementare

complete [kəmˈpliːt] **1** adj (*total*) completo; (*finished*) terminato **2** v/t *task, building etc* completare; *form* compilare; **completely** completamente; **completion** completamento *m*

complex [ˈkɒmpleks] **1** adj complesso **2** n also PSYCH complesso *m*; **complexion** *facial* carnagione *f*; **complexity** complessità *f unv*

compliance [kəmˈplaɪəns] conformità *f*

complicate [ˈkɒmplɪkeɪt] complicare; **complicated** complicato; **complication** complicazione *f*

compliment [ˈkɒmplɪmənt] **1** n complimento *m* **2** v/t fare i complimenti a; **complimentary** lusinghiero; (*free*) in omaggio

comply [kəmˈplaɪ] ubbidire; **~ with** osservare; *of products, equipment* essere conforme a

component [kəmˈpəʊnənt] componente *m*

compose [kəmˈpəʊz] *also* MUS comporre; **composed**

(calm) calmo; **composer**
MUS compositore *m*, -trice
f; **composition** *also* MUS
composizione *f*; *(essay)* tema
m; **composure** calma *f*

compound ['kɒmpaʊnd] *n*
CHEM composto *m*

comprehend [kɒmprɪ'hend]
(understand) capire; **com-**
prehension comprensione
f; **comprehensive** esauriente; **comprehensive insur-**
ance polizza *f* casco

compress ['kɒmpres] comprimere; *information* condensare

comprise [kəm'praɪz] comprendere; *(make up)* costituire; **be ~d of** essere composto da

compromise ['kɒmprəmaɪz]
1 *n* compromesso *m* **2** *v/i* arrivare a un compromesso **3**
v/t (jeopardize) compromettere; **~ o.s.** compromettersi

compulsion [kəm'pʌlʃn]
PSYCH coazione *f*; **compul-**
sive *behaviour* patologico;
reading avvincente; **compul-**
sory obbligatorio

computer [kəm'pjuːtə(r)]
computer *m inv*; **computer**
game computer game *m*
inv; **computerize** computerizzare; **computer literate**
che ha dimestichezza con il
computer; **computer sci-**
ence informatica *f*; **comput-**
er scientist informatico *m*,
-a *f*; **computing** informatica

f

comrade ['kɒmreɪd] *also* POL
compagno *m*, -a *f*; **comrade-**
ship cameratismo *m*

conceal [kən'siːl] nascondere; **concealment** occultazione *f*

conceit [kən'siːt] presunzione *f*; **conceited** presuntuoso

conceivable [kən'siːvəbl]
concepibile; **conceive of**
woman concepire

concentrate ['kɒnsəntreɪt] **1**
v/i concentrarsi **2** *v/t energies*
concentrare; **concentration**
concentrazione *f*

concept ['kɒnsept] concetto
m; **conception** *of child* concepimento *m*

concern [kən'sɜːn] **1** *n (anxiety)* preoccupazione *f*; *(care)*
interesse *m*; *(business)* affare
m; *(company)* impresa *f* **2** *v/t*
(involve) riguardare; *(worry)*
preoccupare; **concerned**
(anxious) preoccupato; *(caring)* interessato; *(involved)*
in questione; **as far as I'm**
~ per quanto mi riguarda;
concerning riguardo a

concert ['kɒnsət] concerto *m*;
concerted congiunto

concession [kən'seʃn] *(compromise)* concessione *f*

concise [kən'saɪs] conciso

conclude [kən'kluːd] concludere; *(from* da); **conclusion**
conclusione *f*; **conclusive**
conclusivo

concrete ['kɒŋkriːt] concreto

concussion [kənˈkʌʃn] commozione f cerebrale

condemn [kənˈdem] condannare; **condemnation** condanna f

condensation [kɒndenˈseɪʃn] *on walls, windows* condensa f

condescend [kɒndɪˈsend] *he ~ed to speak to me* si è degnato di rivolgermi la parola; **condescending** borioso

condition [kənˈdɪʃn] **1** *n* (*state, requirement*) condizione f; MED malattia f; *in / out of ~* in / fuori forma **2** *v/t* PSYCH condizionare; **conditioner** *for hair* balsamo m; *for fabric* ammorbidente m; **conditioning** PSYCH condizionamento m

condo [ˈkɒndəʊ] *Am* condominio m

condolences [kənˈdəʊlənsɪz] condoglianze *fpl*

condom [ˈkɒndɒm] preservativo m

condominium [kɒndəˈmɪnɪəm] *Am* condominio m

condone [kənˈdəʊn] *actions* scusare

conduct 1 [ˈkɒndʌkt] *n* (*behaviour*) condotta f **2** [kənˈdʌkt] *v/t* (*carry out*) ELEC condurre; MUS dirigere; **conducted tour** visita f guidata; **conductor** MUS direttore *m d'orchestra; *on bus* bigliettaio m; PHYS conduttore m

cone [kəʊn] cono m; *of pine*

tree pigna f

conference [ˈkɒnfərəns] congresso m; **conference room** sala f riunioni

confess [kənˈfes] **1** *v/t* confessare **2** *v/i* confessare; REL confessarsi; **confession** confessione f

confide [kənˈfaɪd] **1** *v/t* confidare **2** *v/i: ~ in s.o.* confidarsi con qu; **confidence** (*assurance*) sicurezza f (di sé); (*trust*) fiducia f; *in ~* in confidenza; **confident** sicuro; *person* sicuro di sé; **confidential** riservato, confidenziale; *adviser* di fiducia; **confidently** con sicurezza

confine [kənˈfaɪn] (*imprison*) richiudere; (*restrict*) limitare; **confined** *space* ristretto

confirm [kənˈfɜːm] confermare; **confirmation** conferma f

confiscate [ˈkɒnfɪskeɪt] sequestrare

conflict 1 [ˈkɒnflɪkt] *n* conflitto m **2** [kənˈflɪkt] *v/i* *of statements* essere in conflitto; *of dates* coincidere

conform [kənˈfɔːm] conformarsi; *~ to* *of products, acts etc* essere conforme a

confront [kənˈfrʌnt] (*face*) affrontare; *~ s.o. with sth* mettere qu di fronte a qc; **confrontation** scontro m

confuse [kənˈfjuːz] confondere; *~ s.o. with s.o.* confondere qu con qu; **confused** confuso; **confusing** che confonde; **confusion** confusione *f*

congested [kən'dʒestɪd] congestionato; **congestion** congestione *f*

congratulate [kən'grætjuleɪt] congratularsi con; **congratulations** congratulazioni *fpl*

congregate ['kɒngrɪgeɪt] (*gather*) riunirsi; **congregation** REL fedeli *mpl*

congress ['kɒngres] (*conference*) congresso *m*; **Congress** *in USA* il Congresso; **Congressional** del Congresso; **Congressman** membro *m* del Congresso

conjecture [kən'dʒektʃə(r)] (*speculation*) congettura *f*

conjurer, conjuror ['kʌndʒərə(r)] (*magician*) prestigiatore *m*, -trice *f*

con man ['kɒnmæn] F truffatore *m*

connect [kə'nekt] (*join, link*) collegare; *to power supply* allacciare; **connected: be well-~** avere conoscenze influenti; **be ~ with ...** essere collegato con; **connecting flight** coincidenza *f* (volo); **connection** (*link*) collegamento *m*; *when travelling* coincidenza *f*; (*personal contact*) conoscenza *f*; **in ~ with** a proposito di

connoisseur [kɒnə'sɜː(r)] intenditore *m*, -trice *f*

conquer ['kɒŋkə(r)] conquistare; *fear etc* vincere; **conqueror** conquistatore *m*, -trice *f*; **conquest** conquista *f*

conscience ['kɒnʃəns] coscienza *f*; **conscientious** coscienzioso; **conscientiousness** coscienziosità *f*

conscious ['kɒnʃəs] (*aware*) consapevole; (*deliberate*) conscio; MED cosciente; **consciously** consapevolmente; **consciousness** consapevolezza *f*; **lose / regain ~** perdere / riprendere conoscenza

consecutive [kən'sekjutɪv] consecutivo

consensus [kən'sensəs] consenso *m*

consent [kən'sent] **1** *n* consenso *m* **2** *v/i* acconsentire

consequence ['kɒnsɪkwəns] conseguenza *f*; **consequently** di conseguenza

conservation [kɒnsə'veɪʃn] tutela *f*; **conservationist** ambientalista *m/f*; **conservative 1** *adj* (*conventional*) conservatore; *clothes* tradizionale; *estimate* cauto; **Conservative** Br POL conservatore **2** *n* Br POL **Conservative** conservatore *m*, -trice *f*; **conserve 1** *n* (*jam*) marmellata *f* **2** *v/t energy* risparmiare

consider [kən'sɪdə(r)] considerare; (*show regard for*) tener conto di; (*think about*) pensare a; **considerable** considerevole; **considerably** considerevolmente; **considerate** premuroso; *be ~ of* avere riguardo per; **considerately** premurosamente; **consideration** (*thought*) considerazione *f*; (*thoughtfulness, concern*) riguardo *m*; (*factor*) fattore *m*; *take sth into ~* prendere in considerazione qc

consignment [kən'saɪnmənt] COM consegna *f*

◆ **consist of** [kən'sɪst] consistere in

consistency [kən'sɪstənsɪ] (*texture*) consistenza *f*; (*unchangingness*) coerenza *f*; **consistent** coerente

consolidate [kən'sɒlɪdeɪt] consolidare

consonant ['kɒnsənənt] GRAM consonante *f*

conspicuous [kən'spɪkjʊəs]: *be* / *look ~* spiccare

conspiracy [kən'spɪrəsɪ] cospirazione *f*; **conspirator** cospiratore *m*, -trice *f*; **conspire** cospirare

constant ['kɒnstənt] costante; **constantly** costantemente

constipated ['kɒnstɪpeɪtɪd] stitico; **constipation** stitichezza *f*

constituency [kən'stɪtjʊənsɪ] POL circoscrizione *f* elettorale

constitute ['kɒnstɪtjuːt] costi-

tuire; **constitution** costituzione *f*; **constitutional** POL costituzionale

constraint [kən'streɪnt] restrizione *f*

construct [kən'strʌkt] costruire; **construction** costruzione *f*; **construction industry** edilizia *f*; **construction worker** operaio *m* edile; **constructive** costruttivo

consul ['kɒnsl] console *m*; **consulate** consolato *m*

consult [kən'sʌlt] (*seek advice of*) consultare; **consultancy** (*company*) società *f inv* di consulenza; (*advice*) consulenza *f*; **consultant** consulente *m*/*f*; **consultation** consultazione *f*

consume [kən'sjuːm] consumare; **consumer** consumatore *m*, -trice *f*; **consumer confidence** fiducia *f* dei consumatori; **consumption** consumo *m*

contact ['kɒntækt] **1** *n* contatto *m*; (*person*) conoscenza *f* **2** *v/t* mettersi in contatto con; **contact lens** lente *f* a contatto

contagious [kən'teɪdʒəs] contagioso

contain [kən'teɪn] contenere; **container** contenitore *m*; COM container *m inv*; **container ship** nave *f* portacontainer

contaminate [kən'tæmɪneɪt]

contamination   340

contaminare; **contamination** contaminazione f
contemporary [kən'tempərə-rɪ] **1** adj contemporaneo **2** n coetaneo m, -a f
contempt [kən'tempt] disprezzo m; **contemptible** spregevole; **contemptuous** sprezzante
contender [kən'tendə(r)] concorrente m/f; against champion sfidante m/f; POL candidato m, -a f
content¹ ['kɑːntent] n contenuto m
content² [kən'tent] **1** adj contento **2** v/t: **~ o.s. with** accontentarsi di
contented [kən'tentɪd] contento; **contentment** soddisfazione f
contents ['kɒntents] of container contenuto m
contest¹ ['kɒntest] n (competition) concorso m; (struggle, for power) lotta f
contest² [kən'test] v/t leadership etc essere in lizza per; will impugnare
contestant [kən'testənt] concorrente m/f
context ['kɒntekst] contesto m
continent ['kɒntɪnənt] continente m; **the~** l'Europa f continentale; **continental** continentale
continual [kən'tɪnjʊəl] continuo; **continually** continuamente; **continuation** segui-

to m; **continue** continuare (**doing** a fare); **continuous** ininterrotto; **continuously** ininterrottamente
contort [kən'tɔːt] contorcere
contraception [kɒntrə'sepʃn] contraccezione f; **contraceptive** anticoncezionale m, contraccettivo m
contract¹ ['kɒntrækt] n contratto m
contract² [kən'trækt] **1** v/i (shrink) contrarsi **2** v/t illness contrarre
contractor [kən'træktə(r)] appaltatore m, -trice f; **building ~** ditta f di appalti (edili)
contractual [kən'træktjʊəl] contrattuale
contradict [kɒntrə'dɪkt] contraddire; **contradiction** contraddizione f; **contradictory** contraddittorio
contrary¹ ['kɒntrərɪ] **1** adj contrario; **~ to** contrariamente a **2** n: **on the ~** al contrario
contrary² [kən'treərɪ]: **be ~** (perverse) essere un bastian contrario
contrast ['kɒntrɑːst] **1** n contrasto m **2** v/t confrontare **3** v/i contrastare; **contrasting** contrastante
contravene [kɒntrə'viːn] contravvenire a
contribute [kən'trɪbjuːt] **1** v/i contribuire; to magazine collaborare (**to** con); to discus-

cool

sion intervenire (*to* in) 2 *v/t money* contribuire con; **contribution:** *money* offerta *f*; *to political party, church* donazione *f*; *of time, effort* contributo *m*; *to debate* intervento *m*; *to magazine* collaborazione *f*; **contributor** *of money* finanziatore *m*, -trice *f*; *to magazine* collaboratore *m*, -trice *f*

control [kən'trəʊl] 1 *n* controllo *m*; **be in ~ of sth** tenere qc sotto controllo; **~s** *of aircraft, vehicle* comandi *m*; *(restrictions)* restrizioni 2 *v/t (govern)* controllare; *(regulate)* regolare; **~ o.s.** controllarsi

controversial [kɒntrə'vɜːʃl] controverso; **controversy** polemica *f*

convalescence [kɒnvə'lesns] convalescenza *f*

convenience [kən'viːnɪəns] comodità *f inv*; **at your ~** a tuo comodo; **convenience store** negozio *m* alimentari; **convenient** comodo; **whenever it's ~** quando ti va bene

convent ['kɒnvənt] convento *m*

convention [kən'venʃn] *(tradition)* convenzione *f*; *(conference)* congresso *m*; **conventional** convenzionale; **method** tradizionale

conversation [kɒnvə'seɪʃn] conversazione *f*; **conversational** colloquiale

conversely [kən'vɜːslɪ] per contro

conversion [kən'vɜːʃn] conversione *f*; *of house* trasformazione *f*; **convert** 1 *n* convertito *m*, -a *f* 2 *v/t* convertire; **convertible** *car* cabriolet *f inv*, decappottabile *f*

convey [kən'veɪ] *(transmit)* comunicare; *(carry)* trasportare; **conveyor belt** nastro *m* trasportatore

convict 1 ['kɒnvɪkt] *n* carcerato *m*, -a *f* 2 [kən'vɪkt] *v/t* LAW condannare; **conviction** LAW condanna *f*; *(belief)* convinzione *f*

convince [kən'vɪns] convincere

convoy ['kɒnvɔɪ] convoglio *m*

cook [kʊk] 1 *n* cuoco *m*, -a *f* 2 *v/t food* cucinare; *meal* preparare 3 *v/i of person* cucinare; *of food* cuocere; **cookbook** ricettario *m*; **cooker** cucina *f*; **cookery** cucina *f*; **cookie** *Am* biscotto *m*; **cooking** cucina *f*

cool [kuːl] 1 *n* F: **keep one's ~** conservare la calma 2 *adj* fresco; *(calm)* calmo; *(unfriendly)* freddo; F *(great)* grande 3 *v/i of food* raffreddarsi; *of tempers* calmarsi; *of interest* raffreddarsi 4 *v/t* F: **~ it!** calma!

◆ **cool down** 1 *v/i* raffreddarsi; *of weather* rinfrescare; *fig: of tempers* calmarsi 2 *v/t food* raffreddare; *fig* calmare

cooperate [kəʊˈɒpəreɪt] cooperare; **cooperation** cooperazione f; **cooperative** f; **cooperative** (*helpful*) disponibile (a collaborare)

coordinate [kəʊˈɔːdɪneɪt] coordinare; **coordination** of activities coordinamento m; of body coordinamento f

cop [kɒp] F poliziotto m

cope [kəʊp] farcela; **~ with** farcela con

copier [ˈkɒpɪə(r)] machine fotocopiatrice f

copper [ˈkɒpə(r)] metal rame m

copy [ˈkɒpɪ] **1** n copia f **2** v/t copiare

cord [kɔːd] (string) corda f; (cable) filo m; **cordless (phone)** cordless m inv

cordon [ˈkɔːdn] cordone m

cords [kɔːdz] trousers pantaloni mpl di velluto a coste

corduroy [ˈkɔːdərɔɪ] velluto m a coste

core [kɔː(r)] **1** n of fruit torsolo m; of problem nocciolo m; of organization, party cuore m **2** adj issue essenziale

cork [kɔːk] in bottle tappo m di sughero; (material) sughero m; **corkscrew** cavatappi m inv

corn [kɔːn] grain frumento m; Am (maize) granturco m

corner [ˈkɔːnə(r)] **1** n of page, room, street angolo m; of table spigolo m; in football calcio m d'angolo, corner m

inv; **in the ~** nell'angolo; **on the ~** of street all'angolo **2** v/t person bloccare; **~ a market** prendersi il monopolio di un mercato **3** v/i of driver, car affrontare una curva

coronary [ˈkɒrənərɪ] **1** adj coronario **2** n infarto m

coroner [ˈkɒrənə(r)] ufficiale pubblico che indaga sui casi di morte sospetta

corporal [ˈkɔːpərəl] caporale m maggiore; **corporal punishment** punizione f corporale

corporate [ˈkɔːpərət] COM aziendale; **sense of ~ loyalty** corporativismo m; **corporation** (business) corporation f inv

corpse [kɔːps] cadavere m

correct [kəˈrekt] **1** adj giusto; **she's ~** ha ragione **2** v/t correggere; **correction** correzione f; **correctly** giustamente

correspond [kɒrɪˈspɒnd] (match, write) corrispondere; **correspondence** corrispondenza f; **correspondent** corrispondente m/f

corridor [ˈkɒrɪdɔː(r)] corridoio m

corroborate [kəˈrɒbəreɪt] corroborare

corrosion [kəˈrəʊʒn] corrosione f

corrupt [kəˈrʌpt] **1** adj also COMPUT corrotto **2** v/t mor-

als, *youth* traviare; (*bribe*) corrompere; **corruption** corruzione *f*

Corsica ['kɔːsɪkə] Corsica *f*; **Corsican 1** *adj* corso **2** *n* corso *m*, -a *f*

cosmetic [kɒz'metɪk] cosmetico; *surgery* estetico; *fig* di facciata; **cosmetics** cosmetici *mpl*; **cosmetic surgery** chirurgia *f* estetica

cosmopolitan [kɒzmə'pɒlɪtən] cosmopolitano

cost [kɒst] **1** *n also fig* costo *m* **2** *v/t* costare; FIN *proposal* fare il preventivo di; **how much does it ~?** quanto costa?; **cost-effective** conveniente; **cost of living** costo *m* della vita; **cost price** prezzo *m* di costo

costume ['kɒstjuːm] *for actor* costume *m*

cosy ['kəʊzɪ] (*comfortable*) gradevole; (*intimate and friendly*) intimo

cot [kɒt] *for child* lettino *m*; *Am* (*camp-bed*) letto *m* da campo

cottage ['kɒtɪdʒ] cottage *m inv*

cotton ['kɒtn] **1** *n* cotone *m* **2** *adj* di cotone; **cotton candy** *Am* zucchero *m* filato; **cotton wool** ovatta *f*

couch [kaʊtʃ] divano *m*

couchette [kuː'ʃet] cuccetta *f*

couch po'tato F teledipendente *m/f*

cough [kɒf] **1** *n* tosse *f* **2** *v/i*

tossire; *to get attention* tossicchiare; **cough medicine**, **cough syrup** sciroppo *m* per la tosse

could [kʊd]: **~ I have my key?** mi dà la chiave?; **~ you help me?** mi puoi dare una mano?; **you ~ be right** magari hai ragione; **you ~ have warned me!** avresti potuto avvisarmi!; **I ~n't say for sure** non potrei giurarci

council ['kaʊnsl] (*assembly*) consiglio *m*; (*city ~*) comune *m*; **councillor**, *Am* **councilor** consigliere *m*, -a *f* (comunale)

counsel ['kaʊnsl] **1** *n* (*advice*) consiglio *m*; (*lawyer*) avvocato *m* **2** *v/t action* consigliare; *person* offrire consulenza a; **counselling**, *Am* **counseling** terapia *f*; **counsellor**, *Am* **counselor** (*adviser*) consulente *m/f*

count [kaʊnt] **1** *n* conteggio *m* **2** *v/t & v/i* contare; **~ yourself lucky** considerati fortunato

◆ **count on** contare su

'countdown conto *m* alla rovescia

counter ['kaʊntə(r)] *in shop, café* banco *m*; *in game* segalino *m*

'counteract neutralizzare; **counter-attack 1** *n* contrattacco *m* **2** *v/i* contrattaccare; **counterclockwise** *Am* **1** *adj* antiorario **2** *adv* in senso antiorario; **counteresponage** controspionaggio *m*; **counterfeit 1** *v/t* falsificare **2** *adj* falso; **counterpart** *person* omologo *m*, -a *f*; **counter-productive** controproducente

countess ['kauntes] contessa *f*

countless ['kauntlis] innumerevole

country ['kʌntrɪ] paese *m*; *as opposed to town* campagna *f*; **countryside** campagna *f*

county ['kauntɪ] contea *f*

coup [kuː] POL colpo *m* di stato, golpe *m inv*; *fig* colpo *m*

couple ['kʌpl] coppia *f*; *just a ~* solo un paio; *a ~ of* un paio di

coupon ['kuːpɒn] buono *m*

courage ['kʌrɪdʒ] coraggio *m*; **courageous** coraggioso

courgette [kʊəˈʒet] zucchino *m*

courier ['kʊrɪə(r)] (*messenger*) corriere *m*; *with tourist party* accompagnatore *m* turistico accompagnatrice *f* turistica

course *f* stages of lessons corso *m*; *of meal* portata *f*; *of ship, plane* rotta *f*; *for golf* campo *m*; *for race, skiing* pista *f*; *of ~* (*certainly*) certo; (*naturally*) ovviamente; *of ~* not certo che no; *first ~* primo *m*

court [kɔːt] LAW corte *f*; (*courthouse*) tribunale *m*; SP campo *m*; *take s.o. to ~* fare causa a qu; *out of ~* in via

amichevole; **court case** caso *m* (giudiziario)

courtesy ['kɜːtəsɪ] cortesia *f*

'**courthouse** tribunale *m*, palazzo *m* di giustizia; **courtroom** aula *f* del tribunale; **courtyard** cortile *m*

cousin ['kʌzn] cugino *m*, -a *f*

cover ['kʌvə(r)] **1** *n protective* fodera *f*; *of book, magazine* copertina *f*; (*shelter*) riparo *m*; *insurance* copertura *f* **2** *v/t* coprire; *distance* percorrere

♦ **cover up 1** *v/t* coprire; *fig* insabbiare **2** *v/i*: *cover up for s.o.* coprire qu

coverage ['kʌvərɪdʒ] *by media* copertura *f*

covert ['kəʊvɜːt] segreto

'**cover-up** insabbiamento *m*

cow [kaʊ] mucca *f*

coward ['kaʊəd] vigliacco *m*, -a *f*; **cowardice** vigliaccheria *f*

'**cowboy** cow-boy *m inv*

co-worker ['kəʊwɜːkə(r)] collega *m/f*

cozy *Am* → **cosy**

crab [kræb] granchio *m*

crack [kræk] **1** *n* crepa *f*; (*joke*) battuta *f* **2** *v/t cup, glass* incrinare; *nut* schiacciare; *code* decifrare; F (*solve*) risolvere **3** *v/i* incrinarsi

♦ **crack down on** prendere serie misure contro

cracked [krækt] *cup* incrinato; **cracker** *to eat* cracker *m inv*

cradle ['kreɪdl] *for baby* culla *f*
craft¹ [krɑːft] NAUT imbarcazione *f*
craft² [krɑːft] *(skill)* attività *f inv* artigiana; *(trade)* mestiere *m*
'craftsman artigiano *m*
crafty ['krɑːftɪ] astuto
crag [kræg] *rock* rupe *f*
cram [kræm] *papers, food* infilare; *people* stipare
cramps [kræmps] crampo *m*
crane [kreɪn] **1** *n machine* gru *f inv* **2** *v/t:* ~ **one's neck** allungare il collo
crank [kræŋk] *person* tipo *m* strambo; COMPUT crank *m*
crank [kræŋk] *person* tipo *m* strambo; *(eccentric)* strampalato; *Am (bad-tempered)* irascibile
crap [kræp] P merda *f*; *don't talk* ~ non dire cazzate
crash [kræʃ] **1** *n noise* fragore *m*; *accident* incidente *m*; COM crollo *m*; COMPUT crash *m inv* **2** *v/i fall noisily* fracassarsi; *of car* schiantarsi; *of two cars* scontrarsi, schiantarsi; *of plane* precipitare; *of market* crollare; COMPUT fare un crash **3** *v/t car* avere un incidente con; **crash course** corso *m* intensivo; **crash diet** dieta *f* lampo; **crash helmet** casco *m* (di protezione); **crash-land** fare un atterraggio di fortuna
crate [kreɪt] cassetta *f*
crater ['kreɪtə(r)] cratere *m*
crave [kreɪv] smaniare dalla voglia di; **craving** voglia *f*;

pej smania *f*
crawl [krɔːl] **1** *n in swimming* crawl *m* **2** *v/i on floor* andare (a) carponi; *(move slowly)* avanzare lentamente
crayon ['kreɪən] matita *f* colorata; *wax* pastello *m* a cera
craze [kreɪz] moda *f*; **crazy** pazzo
creak [kriːk] scricchiolare; **creaky** che scricchiola
cream [kriːm] **1** *n for skin* crema *f*; *for coffee, cake* panna *f*; *colour* color *m* panna **2** *adj* color panna
crease [kriːs] **1** *n* grinza *f*; *deliberate* piega *f* **2** *v/t accidentally* sgualcire
create [kriːˈeɪt] creare; **creation** creazione *f*; **creative** creativo; **creator** creatore *m*, -trice *f*
creature ['kriːtʃə(r)] creatura *f*
credibility [kredəˈbɪlətɪ] credibilità *f*; **credible** credibile
credit ['kredɪt] **1** *n* FIN credito *m*; *(honour)* merito *m* **2** *v/t amount* accreditare; **creditable** lodevole; **credit card** carta *f* di credito; **credit limit** limite *m* di credito; **creditor** creditore *m*, -trice *f*; **creditworthy** solvibile
creep [kriːp] **1** *n pej* tipo *m* odioso **2** *v/i quietly* avanzare quatto quatto; *slowly* avanzare lentamente; **creepy** F che dà i brividi
cremate [krɪˈmeɪt] cremare; **cremation** cremazione *f*

crest [krest] *of hill, bird* cresta *f*

crevasse [krəˈvæs] voragine *f*

crevice [ˈkrevɪs] crepa *f*

crew [kruː] *of ship, plane* equipaggio *m*; **crew cut** taglio *m* a spazzola

crib [krɪb] *Am for baby* lettino *m*

crime [kraɪm] reato *m*; *(criminality)* criminalità *f*; *(shameful act)* crimine *m*; **criminal 1** *n* delinquente *m/f* **2** *adj* LAW penale; *(shameful)* vergognoso

crimson [ˈkrɪmzn] cremisi *inv*

cripple [ˈkrɪpl] **1** *n* invalido *m*, -a *f* **2** *v/t person* rendere invalido; *fig* paralizzare

crisis [ˈkraɪsɪs] crisi *f inv*

crisp [krɪsp] *weather, lettuce, new shirt* fresco; *bacon, toast* croccante; **crisps** patatine *fpl*

criterion [kraɪˈtɪərɪən] criterio *m*

critic [ˈkrɪtɪk] critico *m*, -a *f*; **critical** critico; **criticism** critica *f*; **criticize** criticare

Croatia [kəʊˈeɪʃə] Croazia *f*; **Croatian 1** *adj* croato **2** *n* croato *m/f*; *language* croato *m*

crockery [ˈkrɒkərɪ] stoviglie *fpl*

crocodile [ˈkrɒkədaɪl] coccodrillo *m*

crony [ˈkrəʊnɪ] F amico *m*, -a *f*

crook [krʊk] truffatore *m*, -trice *f*; **crooked** *streets* tortuoso; *picture* storto; *(dishonest)* disonesto

crop [krɒp] **1** *n* raccolto *m*; *type of grain etc* coltura *f* **2** *v/t hair, photo* tagliare
◆ **crop up** saltar fuori

cross [krɒs] **1** *adj (angry)* arrabbiato **2** *n* croce *f* **3** *v/t (go across)* attraversare; **~ o.s.** REL farsi il segno della croce **4** *v/i (go across)* attraversare; *of lines* intersecarsi
◆ **cross off, cross out** depennare

crosscheck 1 *n* controllo *m* incrociato **2** *v/t* fare un controllo incrociato su; **cross-country** *(skiing)* sci *m* di fondo; **cross-examine** LAW interrogare in contraddittorio; **cross-eyed** strabico; **crossing** NAUT traversata *f*; **crossroads** incrocio *m*; *fig* bivio *m*; **crosswalk** *Am* passaggio *m* pedonale; **crossword (puzzle)** cruciverba *m inv*

crotch [krɒtʃ] *of person* inguine *m*; *of trousers* cavallo *m*

crouch [kraʊtʃ] accovacciarsi

crow [krəʊ] *bird* corvo *m*; **as the ~ flies** in linea d'aria

crowd [kraʊd] folla *f*; **crowded** affollato

crown [kraʊn] corona *f*; *on tooth* capsula *f*

crucial [ˈkruːʃl] essenziale

crucifix [ˈkruːsɪfɪks] crocifis-

curl

so *m*; **crucifixion** crocifissio-
ne *f*; **crucify** REL crocifiggere; *fig* fare a pezzi
crude [kru:d] **1** *adj* (*vulgar*)
volgare; (*unsophisticated*) rudimentale **2** *n*: ~ (**oil**) (petrolio *m*) greggio *m*
cruel ['kru:əl] crudele; **cruelty** crudeltà *f inv*
cruise [kru:z] **1** *n* crociera *f*
2 *v/i of people* fare una crociera; *of car, plane* viaggiare a
velocità di crociera
crumb [krʌm] briciola *f*
crumble ['krʌmbl] *of bread*
sbriciolarsi; *of stonework*
sgretolarsi; *fig: of opposition*
etc crollare
crumple ['krʌmpl] **1** *v/t*
(*crease*) sgualcire **2** *v/i* (*collapse*) accasciarsi
crush [krʌʃ] **1** *n* (*crowd*) ressa
f **2** *v/t* schiacciare; (*crease*)
sgualcire
crust [krʌst] *on bread* crosta *f*
crutch [krʌtʃ] *for injured person* stampella *f*
cry [kraɪ] **1** *n* (*call*) grido *m* **2**
v/t (*call*) gridare **3** *v/i* (*weep*)
piangere
◆ **cry out** gridare
cryptic ['krɪptɪk] sibillino
crystal ['krɪstl] cristallo *m*
cube [kju:b] cubo *m*; **cubic**
cubico
cubicle ['kju:bɪkl] cabina *f*
cucumber ['kju:kʌmbə(r)]
cetriolo *m*
cuddle ['kʌdl] coccolare
cue [kju:] *for actor etc* imbec-

cata *f*; *for pool* stecca *f*
cuff [kʌf] *of shirt* polsino *m*;
(*blow*) schiaffo *m*; Am (*of
trousers*) risvolto *m*
culminate ['kʌlmɪneɪt]: ~ *in*
culminare in; **culmination**
culmine *m*
culprit ['kʌlprɪt] colpevole
m/f
cult [kʌlt] culto *m*
cultivate ['kʌltɪveɪt] *land* coltivare; *person* coltivarsi; **cul-
tivated** *person* colto; **cultivation** *of land* coltivazione *f*
cultural ['kʌltʃərəl] culturale;
culture cultura *f*; **cultured**
colto
cumulative ['kju:mjʊlətɪv]
cumulativo
cunning ['kʌnɪŋ] **1** *n* astuzia *f*
2 *adj* astuto
cup [kʌp] tazza *f*; (*trophy*)
coppa *f*
cupboard ['kʌbəd] armadio
m
'**cup final** finale *f* di coppa
curb [kɜ:b] **1** *n on powers etc*
freno *m* **2** *v/t* tenere a freno
cure [kjʊə(r)] **1** *n* MED cura *f* **2**
v/t MED guarire; *by drying* es-
siccare; *by salting* salare; *by
smoking* affumicare
curiosity [kjʊərɪ'ɒsɪtɪ] curiosità *f inv*; **curious** (*inquisitive*) curioso; (*strange*) strano
curl [kɜ:l] **1** *n* in hair ricciolo
m; *of smoke* spirale *f* **2** *v/t* arricciare **3** *v/i of hair* arriccia-
si; *of leaf etc* accartocciarsi
◆ **curl up** acciambellarsi

curly ['kɜːlɪ] *hair* riccio; *tail* a ricciolo

currant ['kʌrənt] uva *f* passa

currency ['kʌrənsɪ] *money* valuta *f*; **foreign** ~ valuta estera; **current** **1** *n in sea*, ELEC corrente *f* **2** *v/t* (*present*) attuale; **current account** conto *m* corrente; **current affairs** attualità *f*

curry ['kʌrɪ] *dish* piatto *m* al curry; *spice* curry *m*

curse [kɜːs] **1** *n spell* maledizione *f*; (*swearword*) imprecazione *f* **2** *v/t* maledire; (*swear at*) imprecare contro **3** *v/i* (*swear*) imprecare

cursor ['kɜːsə(r)] COMPUT cursore *m*

cursory ['kɜːsərɪ] di sfuggita

curt [kɜːt] brusco

curtain ['kɜːtn] tenda *f*; THEA sipario *m*

curve [kɜːv] **1** *n* curva *f* **2** *v/i* (*bend*) fare una curva

cushion ['kʊʃn] **1** *n* cuscino *m* **2** *v/t blow, fall* attutire

custody ['kʌstədɪ] *of children* custodia *f*; **in** ~ LAW in detenzione preventiva

custom ['kʌstəm] usanza *f*; COM clientela *f*; **customer** cliente *m/f*; **customer service** servizio *m* assistenza al cliente

customs ['kʌstəmz] dogana *f*; **Customs and Excise** Ufficio *m* Dazi e Dogana; **customs officer** doganiere *m*, -a *f*

cut [kʌt] **1** *n with knife, of hair, clothes* taglio *m*; (*reduction*) riduzione *f* **2** *v/t* tagliare; (*reduce*) ridurre; **get one's hair** ~ tagliarsi i capelli
♦ **cut down 1** *v/t tree* abbattere **2** *v/i in smoking etc* limitarsi
♦ **cut off** tagliare; (*isolate*) isolare
♦ **cut up** *meat etc* sminuzzare

'cutback *in production* riduzione *f*; *in spending* taglio *m*

cute [kjuːt] (*pretty*) carino; (*smart, clever*) furbo

cutlery ['kʌtlərɪ] posate *fpl*

'cut-off date scadenza *f*; **~-price** *goods* a prezzo ridotto; *store of* articoli scontati; **cut-throat** *competition* spietato; **cutting 1** *n from newspaper etc* ritaglio *m* **2** *adj remark* tagliente

CV [siː'viː] (= *curriculum vitae*) curriculum vitae *m inv*

cycle ['saɪkl] **1** *n* (*bicycle*) bicicletta *f*; *of events* ciclo *m* **2** *v/i to work* andare in bicicletta; **cycling** ciclismo *m*; **cyclist** ciclista *m/f*

cylinder ['sɪlɪndə(r)] cilindro *m*; **cylindrical** cilindrico

cynic ['sɪnɪk] cinico *m*, -a *f*; **cynical** cinico; **cynicism** cinismo *m*

cypress ['saɪprəs] cipresso *m*

Czech [tʃek] **1** *adj* ceco; **the** ~ **Republic** la Repubblica Ceca **2** *n person* ceco *m*, -a *f*; *language* ceco *m*

D

DA *Am* (= **district attorney**) procuratore *m* distrettuale
◆ **dabble in** dilettarsi di
dad [dæd] papà *m inv*
daddy ['dædɪ] papà *m inv*; **daddy longlegs** zanzarone *m*
daffodil ['dæfədɪl] trombone *m*
daft [dɑːft] stupido
dagger ['dægə(r)] pugnale *m*
daily ['deɪlɪ] **1** *n* (*paper*) quotidiano *m* **2** *adj* quotidiano
dairy: ~ *products* latticini *mpl; food* ~ *free* senza latticini *mpl*
daisy ['deɪzɪ] margherita *f*
dam [dæm] *for water* diga *f*
damage ['dæmɪdʒ] **1** *n also fig* danno *m* **2** *v/t* danneggiare; *fig: reputation etc* compromettere; **damages** LAW risarcimento *msg;* **damaging** *evidence* schiacciante; *report* incriminante
damp [dæmp] umido
dance [dɑːns] **1** *n* ballo *m* **2** *v/i* ballare; *of ballerina* danzare; **dancer** (*performer*) ballerino *m*, -a *f; be a good* ~ ballare bene; **dancing** ballo *m*, danza *f*

damn [dæm] **1** *int* F accidenti **2** *adj* F maledetto **3** *adv* F incredibilmente; **damning** *evidence* schiacciante; *report* incriminante

dandelion ['dændɪlaɪən] dente *m* di leone
dandruff ['dændrʌf] forfora *f*
Dane [deɪn] danese *m/f*
danger ['deɪndʒə(r)] pericolo *m;* **dangerous** pericoloso
dangle ['dæŋgl] **1** *v/t* dondolare **2** *v/i* pendere
Danish ['deɪnɪʃ] **1** *adj* danese **2** *n* (*language*) danese *m*
dare [deə(r)] **1** *v/i* osare; ~ *to do sth* osare fare qc; *how* ~ *you!* come osi! **2** *v/t*: ~ *s.o. to do sth* sfidare qu a fare qc; **daring** audace
dark [dɑːk] **1** *n* buio *m*, oscurità *f* **2** *adj room, night* buio; *hair, eyes, colour* scuro; **dark glasses** occhiali *mpl* scuri; **darkness** oscurità *f*
darling ['dɑːlɪŋ] tesoro *m*
dart [dɑːt] **1** *n for throwing* freccetta *f* **2** *v/i* scagliarsi; **darts** *game* freccette *fpl*
dash [dæʃ] **1** *n in punctuation* trattino *m; of whisky, milk* goccio *m; of salt* pizzico *m* **2** *v/i* precipitarsi **3** *v/t hopes* stroncare; **dashboard** cruscotto *m*
data ['deɪtə] dati *mpl;* **database** base *f* dati; **data protection** protezione *f* dati
date¹ [deɪt] (*fruit*) dattero *m*
date² [deɪt] data *f; (meeting)* appuntamento *m;* **what's**

dated   350

the ~ today? quanti ne abbiamo oggi?; **out of ~** *clothes* fuori moda; *passport* scaduto; **up to ~** aggiornato; *(fashionable)* attuale; **dated** superato

daughter ['dɔːtə(r)] figlia *f*; **daughter-in-law** nuora *f*

dawdle ['dɔːdl] ciondolare

dawn [dɔːn] alba *f; fig: of new age* albori *mpl*

day [deɪ] giorno *m; emphasizing duration* giornata *f*; **the ~ after** il giorno dopo; **the ~ after tomorrow** dopodomani; **the ~ before** il giorno prima; **the ~ before yesterday** l'altro ieri; **in those ~s** a quei tempi; **the other ~** *(recently)* l'altro giorno; **daybreak: at ~** allo spuntare del giorno; **daydream 1** *n* sogno *m* ad occhi aperti **2** *v/i* essere sovrappensiero; **daylight** luce *f* del giorno; **daytime: in the ~** durante il giorno; **day return** biglietto *m* di andata e ritorno in giornata; **daytrip** gita *f* di un giorno

dazed [deɪzd] *by news* sbalordito; *by blow* stordito

dazzle ['dæzl] *of light, fig* abbagliare

dead [ded] **1** *adj* morto; *battery* scarica; *phone* muto **2** *adv* F *(very)* da matti F; **~ beat, ~ tired** stanco morto **3** *n*: **the ~** *(dead people)* i morti; **dead end** *street* vicolo *m* cieco; **dead heat** pareggio

m; **deadline** scadenza *f; for newspaper* termine *m* per l'invio in stampa; **deadlock** *in talks* punto *m* morto; **deadly** mortale

deaf [def] sordo; **deafening** assordante; **deafness** sordità *f*

deal [diːl] **1** *n* accordo *m*; **a great ~ of** un bel po' di **2** *v/t cards* distribuire

◆ **deal in** trattare; *drugs* trafficare

◆ **deal with** *(handle)* occuparsi di; *situation* gestire; *(do business with)* trattare con

dealer ['diːlə(r)] *(merchant)* commerciante *m/f*; *(drug ~)* spacciatore *m*, -trice *f*; **dealing** *(drug ~)* spaccio *m*; **dealings** *(business)* rapporti *mpl*

dear [dɪə(r)] caro; **Dear Sir** Egregio Signore

death [deθ] morte *f*; **death penalty** pena *f* di morte; **death toll** numero *m* delle vittime

debatable [dɪ'beɪtəbl] discutibile; **debate 1** *n* dibattimento *m*; POL dibattito *m* **2** *v/i* dibattere **3** *v/t* dibattere su

debit ['debɪt] **1** *n* addebito *m* **2** *v/t* addebitare; **debit card** bancomat *m inv*

debris ['debriː] *of plane* rottami *mpl; of building* macerie *fpl*

debt [det] debito *m*; **be in ~**

avere dei debiti; **debtor** debitore *m*, -trice *f*

debug [diː'bʌg] COMPUT togliere gli errori da

decade ['dekeɪd] decennio *m*, decade *f*

decadent ['dekədənt] decadente

decaffeinated [diː'kæfɪneɪtɪd] decaffeinato

decay [dɪ'keɪ] **1** *n of matter* decomposizione *f*; *of civilization* declino *m*; *(decayed matter)* marciume *m*; *in teeth* carie *f* **2** *v/i of organic matter* decomporsi; *of civilization* declinare; *of teeth* cariarsi

deceased [dɪ'siːst]: **the ~** il defunto *m*, la defunta *f*

deceit [dɪ'siːt] falsità *f*, disonestà *f*, **deceitful** falso, disonesto; **deceive** ingannare

December [dɪ'sembə(r)] dicembre *m*

decency ['diːsənsɪ] decenza *f*; **decent** *price, proposition* corretto; *meal, sleep* decente; **a ~ guy** un uomo per bene

decentralize [diː'sentrəlaɪz] decentralizzare

deception [dɪ'sepʃn] inganno *m*; **deceptive** ingannevole; **deceptively**: **it looks ~ simple** sembra semplice solo all'apparenza

decide [dɪ'saɪd] decidere (**to do** di fare); **decided** (*definite*) deciso

decimal ['desɪml] decimale

decipher [dɪ'saɪfə(r)] decifrare

decision [dɪ'sɪʒn] decisione *f*; **decisive** risoluto; *(crucial)* decisivo

deck [dek] *of ship* ponte *m*; *of bus* piano *m*; *of cards* mazzo *m*; **deckchair** sedia *f* a sdraio, sdraio *f inv*

declaration [deklə'reɪʃn] dichiarazione *f*; **declare** dichiarare

decline [dɪ'klaɪn] **1** *n in number, standards* calo *m*; *in health* peggioramento *m* **2** *v/t invitation* declinare; **~ to comment** esimersi dal commentare **3** *v/i (refuse)* declinare; *(decrease)* diminuire; *of health* peggiorare

decode [diː'kəʊd] decodificare

decompose [diːkəm'pəʊz] decomporsi

décor ['deɪkɔː(r)] arredamento *m*

decorate ['dekəreɪt] *with paint* imbiancare; *with paper* tappezzare; *(adorn)*, MIL decorare; **decoration** *paint* vernice *f*; *paper* tappezzeria *f*; *(ornament)* addobbi *mpl*; MIL decorazione *f*; **decorator** *(interior ~)* imbianchino *m*

decoy ['diːkɔɪ] *n* esca *f*

decrease ['diːkriːs] **1** *n* diminuzione *f* **2** *v/t* ridurre **3** *v/i* ridursi

dedicate ['dedɪkeɪt] *book etc* dedicare; **dedicated** dedito;

dedication *in book* dedica *f*; *to cause, work* dedizione *f*

deduce [dɪˈdjuːs] dedurre

deduct [dɪˈdʌkt] detrarre (*from* da); **deduction** *from salary* trattenuta *f*; (*conclusion*) deduzione *f*

deed [diːd] (*act*) azione *f*; LAW atto *m*

deep [diːp] profondo; *colour* intenso; **deepen 1** *v/t* rendere più profondo **2** *v/i* diventare più profondo; *of crisis* aggravarsi; *of mystery* infittirsi; **deep freeze** congelatore *m*

deer [dɪə(r)] cervo *m*

deface [dɪˈfeɪs] vandalizzare

defamation [defəˈmeɪʃn] diffamazione *f*; **defamatory** diffamatorio

default [ˈdiːfɒlt] COMPUT di default

defeat [dɪˈfiːt] **1** *n* sconfitta *f* **2** *v/t* sconfiggere

defect [ˈdiːfekt] difetto *m*; **defective** difettoso

defence [dɪˈfens] difesa *f*; **defenceless** indifeso

defend [dɪˈfend] difendere; **defendant** accusato *m*, -a *f*; *in criminal case* imputato *m*, -a *f*; **defense** *Am* ☞ **defence**; **Defense Secretary** *Am* POL ministro *m* della difesa; **defensive 1** *n*: **go on the ∼** mettersi sulla difensiva **2** *adj weaponry* difensivo; *person* sulla difensiva

deference [ˈdefərəns] deferenza *f*

defiance [dɪˈfaɪəns] sfida *f*; **defiant** provocatorio

deficiency [dɪˈfɪʃənsɪ] carenza *f*

deficit [ˈdefɪsɪt] deficit *m inv*

define [dɪˈfaɪn] definire

definite [ˈdefɪnɪt] *date, time, answer* preciso; *improvement* netto; (*certain*) certo; **definite article** GRAM articolo *m* determinativo; **definitely** senza dubbio; *smell, hear* distintamente

definition [defɪˈnɪʃn] definizione *f*

definitive [dɪˈfɪnətɪv] *biography* più completo; *performance* migliore

deformity [dɪˈfɔːmɪtɪ] deformità *f inv*

defrost [diːˈfrɒst] *food* scongelare; *fridge* sbrinare

defuse [diːˈfjuːz] *bomb* disinnescare; *situation* placare

defy [dɪˈfaɪ] (*disobey*) disobbedire a

degrading [dɪˈgreɪdɪŋ] degradante

degree [dɪˈgriː] grado *m*; *from university* laurea *f*

dehydrated [diːhaɪˈdreɪtɪd] disidratato

deign [deɪn]: **∼ to ...** degnarsi di ...

dejected [dɪˈdʒektɪd] sconfortato

delay [dɪˈleɪ] **1** *n* ritardo **2** *v/t* ritardare; **be ∼ed** (*be late*) essere in ritardo **3** *v/i* tardare

delegate ['delɪgeɪt] **1** *n* delegato *m*, -a *f* **2** *v/t* delegare; **delegation** *of task* delega *f*; *(people)* delegazione *f*

delete [dɪ'liːt] cancellare; **delete key** COMPUT tasto *m* cancella; **deletion** *act* cancellazione *f*; *that deleted* cancellatura *f*

deliberate [dɪ'lɪbərət] *adj* deliberato **2** [dɪ'lɪbəreɪt] *v/i* riflettere; **deliberately** deliberatamente

delicate ['delɪkət] delicato

delicatessen [delɪkə'tesn] gastronomia *f*

delicious [dɪ'lɪʃəs] delizioso, ottimo

delight [dɪ'laɪt] gioia *f*; **delighted** lieto, **delightful** molto piacevole

deliver [dɪ'lɪvə(r)] consegnare; *message* trasmettere; *baby* far nascere; *speech* tenere; **delivery** *of goods, mail* consegna *f*; *of baby* parto *m*; **delivery date** termine *m* di consegna; **delivery van** furgone *m* delle consegne

de luxe [də'lʌks] di lusso

demand [dɪ'mɑːnd] **1** *n* rivendicazione *f*; COM domanda *f*; **in ~** richiesto **2** *v/t* esigere; *(require)* richiedere; **demanding** *job* impegnativo; *person* esigente

demented [dɪ'mentɪd] demente

demo ['deməʊ] *(protest)* manifestazione *f*; *of video etc* di-

mostrazione *f*

democracy [dɪ'mɒkrəsɪ] democrazia *f*; **democrat** democratico *m*, -a *f*; **democratic** democratico

demolish [dɪ'mɒlɪʃ] demolire; **demolition** demolizione *f*

demonstrate ['demənstreɪt] **1** *v/t (prove)* dimostrare; *machine* fare una dimostrazione di **2** *v/i politically* manifestare; **demonstration** dimostrazione *f*; *(protest)* manifestazione *f*; **demonstrator** *(protester)* manifestante *m/f*

demoralized [dɪ'mɒrəlaɪzd] demoralizzato; **demoralizing** demoralizzante

demote [diː'məʊt] retrocedere; MIL degradare

den [den] *(study)* studio *m*

denial [dɪ'naɪəl] negazione *f*

denim ['denɪm] denim *m*; **denims** *(jeans)* jeans *m inv*

Denmark ['denmɑːk] Danimarca *f*

denomination [dɪnɒmɪ-'neɪʃn] *of money* banconota *f*; REL confessione *f*

dense [dens] fitto; **density** *of population* densità *f inv*

dent [dent] **1** *n* ammaccatura *f* **2** *v/t* ammaccare

dental ['dentl] *treatment* dentario, dentale; *hospital* dentistico

dented ['dentɪd] ammaccato

dentist ['dentɪst] dentista *m/f*; **dentures** dentiera *f*

Denver boot ['denvə(r)] *Am* ceppo *m* bloccaruote

deny [dɪ'naɪ] negare; *rumour* smentire

deodorant [di:'əʊdərənt] deodorante *m*

depart [dɪ'pɑːt] partire; ~ **from** (*deviate from*) allontanarsi da

department [dɪ'pɑːtmənt] *of university* dipartimento *m*; *of government* ministero *m*; *of store, company* reparto *m*; **Department of State** *Am* Ministero *m* degli esteri; **department store** grande magazzino *m*

departure [dɪ'pɑːtʃə(r)] partenza *f*; (*deviation*) allontanamento *m*; **departure lounge** sala *f* partenze; **departure time** ora *f* di partenza

depend [dɪ'pend] *that* ~**s** dipende; *it* ~**s on the weather** dipende dal tempo; **dependable** affidabile; **dependence, dependency** dipendenza *f*; **dependent 1** *n* persona *f* a carico; *a married man with* ~**s** un uomo sposato con famiglia a carico **2** *adj* dipendente; ~ **children** figli *mpl* a carico

depict [dɪ'pɪkt] raffigurare

deplorable [dɪ'plɔːrəbl] deplorevole; **deplore** deplorare, lamentarsi di

deploy [dɪ'plɔɪ] (*use*) spiegare; (*position*) schierare

deport [dɪ'pɔːt] deportare; **deportation** deportazione *f*

deposit [dɪ'pɒzɪt] **1** *n in bank* versamento *m*, deposito *m*; *of mineral* deposito *m*; *on purchase* acconto *m*; (*against loss, damage*) cauzione *f* **2** *v/t money* versare, depositare; (*put down*) lasciare; *silt, mud* depositare; **deposit account** libretto *m* di risparmio

depot ['depəʊ] (*bus station*) rimessa *f* degli autobus; *for storage* magazzino *m*; *Am* (*train station*) stazione *f* ferroviaria

depreciate [dɪ'priːʃɪeɪt] FIN svalutarsi; **depreciation** FIN svalutazione *f*

depress [dɪ'pres] *person* deprimere; **depressed** depresso; **depressing** deprimente; **depression** depressione *f*

deprivation [deprɪ'veɪʃn] privazione *f*; (*lack: of sleep, food*) carenza *f*; **deprive** *s.o. of sth* privare qu di qc; **deprived** socialmente svantaggiato

depth [depθ] profondità *f inv*; *in* ~ (*thoroughly*) a fondo

deputy ['depjʊtɪ] vice *m/f inv*; **deputy leader** *of party* vice segretario *m*

derail [dɪ'reɪl]: *be* ~**ed** *of train* essere deragliato

derelict ['derəlɪkt] desolato

deride [dɪ'raɪd] deridere; **derision** derisione *f*; **derisory**

355

detail

amount irrisorio
derivative [dɪ'rɪvətɪv] deriva-to; **derive** trarre; **be ~d from** *of word* derivare da
dermatologist [dɜːmə'tɒlə-dʒɪst] dermatologo *m*, -a *f*
derogatory [dɪ'rɒgətrɪ] peggiorativo
descend [dɪ'send] **1** *v/t* scendere; **be ~ed from** discendere da **2** *v/i* scendere; *of mood, darkness* calare; **descendant** discendente *m/f*; **descent** discesa *f*; *(ancestry)* discendenza *f*
describe [dɪ'skraɪb] descrivere; **description** descrizione *f*
desegregate [diː'segrəgeɪt] eliminare la segregazione in
desert[1] ['dezət] *n* deserto *m*
desert[2] [dɪ'zɜːt] **1** *v/t (abandon)* abbandonare **2** *v/i of soldier* disertare
deserted [dɪ'zɜːtɪd] deserto; **deserter** MIL disertore *m*; **desertion** abbandono *m*; MIL diserzione *f*
deserve [dɪ'zɜːv] meritare
design [dɪ'zaɪn] **1** *n* design *m*; *technical* progettazione *f*; *(pattern)* motivo *m* **2** *v/t house, car* progettare; *clothes* disegnare
designate ['dezɪgneɪt] *person* designare
designer [dɪ'zaɪnə(r)] designer *m/f inv*; *of building, car, ship* progettista *m/f*; **fashion ~** stilista *m/f*; **designer**

clothes abiti *mpl* firmati
desirable [dɪ'zaɪrəbl] desiderabile; *(advisable)* preferibile; **desire** desiderio *m*
desk [desk] scrivania *f*; *in hotel* reception *f inv*; **desk clerk** receptionist *m/f inv*; **desktop publishing** editoria *f* elettronica
desolate ['desələt] *place* desolato
despair [dɪ'speə(r)] **1** *n* disperazione *f*; **in ~** disperato **2** *v/i* disperare; **desperate** disperato; **be ~ for sth** morire dalla voglia di qc; **desperation** disperazione *f*
despicable [dɪs'pɪkəbl] deplorevole; **despise** disprezzare
despite [dɪ'spaɪt] malgrado, nonostante
dessert [dɪ'zɜːt] dolce *m*, dessert *m inv*
destination [destɪ'neɪʃn] destinazione *f*
destiny ['destɪnɪ] destino *m*
destitute ['destɪtjuːt] indigente
destroy [dɪ'strɔɪ] distruggere; **destroyer** NAUT cacciatorpediniere *m*; **destruction** distruzione *f*; **destructive** distruttivo; *child* scalmanato
detach [dɪ'tætʃ] staccare; **detached** *(objective)* distaccato; **detached house** villetta *f*; **detachment** *(objectivity)* distacco *m*
detail ['diːteɪl] dettaglio *m*; **in**

~ dettagliatamente; **detailed** dettagliato

detain [dɪˈteɪn] trattenere; **detainee** detenuto *m*, -a *f*

detect [dɪˈtekt] rilevare; *anxiety, irony* cogliere; **detection** *of crime* investigazione *f*; *of smoke etc* rilevamento *m*; **detective** agente *m/f*/investigativo; **detector** rilevatore *m*

détente [ˈdeɪtɒnt] POL distensione *f*

deter [dɪˈtɜː(r)] dissuadere

detergent [dɪˈtɜːdʒənt] detergente *m*

deteriorate [dɪˈtɪərɪəreɪt] deteriorarsi

determination [dɪtɜːmɪˈneɪʃn] (*resolution*) determinazione *f*; **determine** (*establish*) determinare; **determined** determinato, deciso

deterrent [dɪˈterənt] deterrente *m*

detest [dɪˈtest] detestare; **detestable** detestabile

detour [ˈdiːtʊə(r)] deviazione *f*

◆ **detract from** [dɪˈtrækt] *merit, value* sminuire; *enjoyment* rovinare

devaluation [diːvæljʊˈeɪʃn] svalutazione *f*; **devalue** svalutare

devastate [ˈdevəsteɪt] *also fig* devastare

develop [dɪˈveləp] **1** *v/t film, business* sviluppare; *land, site* valorizzare; (*originate*) sco-

prire; *illness* contrarre **2** *v/i* (*grow*) svilupparsi; ~ **into** diventare; **developing country** paese *m* in via di sviluppo; **development** sviluppo *m*; *of land, site* valorizzazione *f*; (*origination*) scoperta *f*

device [dɪˈvaɪs] dispositivo *m*; (*tool*) apparecchio *m*

devil [ˈdevl] diavolo *m*

devious [ˈdiːvɪəs] (*sly*) subdolo

devise [dɪˈvaɪz] escogitare

devoid [dɪˈvɔɪd]: *be ~ of* essere privo di

devolution [diːvəˈluːʃn] POL decentramento *m*

devote [dɪˈvəʊt] dedicare; **devoted** *son etc* devoto; **devotion** *to a person* attaccamento *m*; *to one's job* dedizione *f*

devour [dɪˈvaʊə(r)] *food, book* divorare

devout [dɪˈvaʊt] devoto; *a ~ Catholic* un cattolico fervente

dew [djuː] rugiada *f*

diabetes [daɪəˈbiːtiːz] diabete *m*; **diabetic** diabetico *m*, -a *f*

diagnose [ˈdaɪəgnəʊz] diagnosticare; **diagnosis** diagnosi *f inv*

diagonal [daɪˈægənl] diagonale; **diagonally** diagonalmente

diagram [ˈdaɪəgræm] diagramma *m*

dial [ˈdaɪəl] **1** *n of clock, meter* quadrante *m* **2** *v/i* TELEC comporre il numero **3** *v/t* TELEC comporre

dialect ['daɪəlekt] dialetto *m*

'dialling tone, *Am* **'dial tone** segnale *m* di linea libera

dialogue, *Am* **dialog** ['daɪəlɒg] dialogo *m*

diameter [daɪ'æmɪtə(r)] diametro *m*

diamond ['daɪəmənd] diamante *m*; (*shape*) losanga *f*; **~s** in cards quadri *mpl*

diaper ['daɪəpə(r)] *Am* pannolino *m*

diaphragm ['daɪəfræm] diaframma *m*

diarrhoea, *Am* **diarrhea** [daɪə'riːə] diarrea *f*

diary ['daɪərɪ] *for thoughts* diario *m*; *for appointments* agenda *f*

dice [daɪs] dado *m*

dictate [dɪk'teɪt] dettare; **dictator** POL dittatore *m*; **dictatorship** dittatura *f*

dictionary ['dɪkʃənrɪ] dizionario *m*

die [daɪ] morire

◆ **die down** *of noise, fire* estinguersi; *of storm, excitement* placarsi

◆ **die out** *of custom* scomparire; *of species* estinguersi

diesel ['diːzl] (*fuel*) diesel *m*

diet ['daɪət] **1** *n* dieta *f* **2** *v/i to lose weight* essere a dieta

differ ['dɪfə(r)] differire; (*disagree*) non essere d'accordo; **difference** differenza *f*; (*disagreement*) divergenza *f*; **dif-**

ferent diverso, different; **differentiate** distinguere; **~ between** *things* distinguere tra; *people* fare distinzioni tra; **differently** diversamente, differentemente

difficult ['dɪfɪkəlt] difficile; **difficulty** difficoltà *f inv*; **with ~** a fatica

dig [dɪg] scavare

digest [daɪ'dʒest] *also fig* digerire; **digestion** digestione *f*

digit ['dɪdʒɪt] cifra *f*; **digital** digitale

dignified ['dɪgnɪfaɪd] dignitoso; **dignity** dignità *f*

dilapidated [dɪ'læpɪdeɪtɪd] rovinato; *house* cadente

dilemma [dɪ'lemə] dilemma *m*

dilute [daɪ'luːt] diluire

dim [dɪm] **1** *adj room* buio; *light* fioco; *outline* indistinto; (*stupid*) idiota; *prospects* vago **2** *v/i of lights* abbassarsi

dime [daɪm] *Am* moneta da dieci centesimi

dimension [daɪ'menʃn] dimensione *f*

diminish [dɪ'mɪnɪʃ] diminuire

din [dɪn] baccano *m*

dine [daɪn] cenare

dinghy ['dɪŋgɪ] *small yacht* dinghy *m*; *rubber boat* gommone *m*

dining car ['daɪnɪŋ] RAIL vagone *m* ristorante; **dining room** *in house* sala *f* da pranzo; *in hotel* sala *f* ristorante

dinner ['dɪnə(r)] *in the evening* cena *f*; *at midday* pranzo *m*; *formal gathering* ricevimento *m*; **dinner jacket** smoking *m inv*; **dinner party** cena *f*

dinosaur ['daɪnəsɔː(r)] dinosauro *m*

dip [dɪp] **1** *n for food* salsa *f*; *in road* pendenza *f* **2** *v/i of road* scendere

diploma [dɪ'pləʊmə] diploma *m*

diplomacy [dɪ'pləʊməsɪ] diplomazia *f*; **diplomat** diplomatico *m*, -a *f*; **diplomatic** diplomatico

direct [daɪ'rekt] **1** *adj* diretto **2** *v/t play* mettere in scena; *film* curare la regia di; **could you please ~ me to ...?** mi può per favore indicare la strada per ...?; **direction** direzione *f*; *of film, play* regia *f*; **~s** (*instructions*), *to a place* indicazioni *fpl*; *for use* istruzioni *fpl*; **directly** (*straight*) direttamente; (*soon, immediately*) immediatamente; **director** *of company* direttore *m*, -trice *f*; *of play, film* regista *m/f*; **directory** elenco *m*; TELEC guida *f* telefonica

dirt [dɜːt] sporco *m*, sporcizia *f*; **dirty 1** *adj* sporco; (*pornographic*) sconcio **2** *v/t* sporcare

disability [dɪsə'bɪlətɪ] handicap *m inv*, invalidità *f inv*; **disabled** handicappato *m*, -a *f*; **the ~** i disabili

disadvantage [dɪsəd'vɑːntɪdʒ] svantaggio *m*; **disadvantaged** penalizzato

disagree [dɪsə'griː] *of person* non essere d'accordo

◆ **disagree with** *of person* non essere d'accordo con; *of food* fare male a

disagreeable [dɪsə'griːəbl] sgradevole; **disagreement** disaccordo *m*; (*argument*) discussione *f*

disallow [dɪsə'laʊ] *goal* annullare

disappear [dɪsə'pɪə(r)] sparire, scomparire; **disappearance** sparizione *f*, scomparsa *f*

disappoint [dɪsə'pɔɪnt] deludere; **disappointed** deluso; **disappointing** deludente; **disappointment** delusione *f*

disapproval [dɪsə'pruːvl] disapprovazione *f*; **disapprove** disapprovare; **~ of** disapprovare; **disapproving** di disapprovazione

disarm [dɪs'ɑːm] **1** *v/t* disarmare **2** *v/i* disarmarsi; **disarmament** disarmo *m*

disaster [dɪ'zɑːstə(r)] disastro *m*; **disastrous** disastroso

disband [dɪs'bænd] **1** *v/t* sciogliere **2** *v/i* sciogliersi

disbelief [dɪsbə'liːf] incredulità *f*

disc [dɪsk] disco *m*

discard [dɪ'skɑːd] sbarazzarsi di

disciplinary [dɪsɪ'plɪnərɪ] disciplinare; **discipline** disciplina f

'**disc jockey** disc jockey m/f inv

disclaim [dɪs'kleɪm] negare; responsibility declinare

disclose [dɪs'kləʊs] svelare, rivelare

disco ['dɪskəʊ] discoteca f

discomfort [dɪs'kʌmfət] disagio m; (pain) fastidio m

disconcert [dɪskən'sɜːt] sconcertare

disconnect [dɪskə'nekt] (detach) sconnettere; supply, telephones staccare

disconsolate [dɪs'kɒnsələt] sconsolato

discontent [dɪskən'tent] malcontento m, **discontented** scontento

discontinue [dɪskən'tɪnjuː] interrompere; be a ~d line essere fuori produzione

discotheque ['dɪskətek] discoteca f

discount ['dɪskaʊnt] sconto m

discourage [dɪs'kʌrɪdʒ] (dissuade) scoraggiare

discover [dɪs'kʌvə(r)] scoprire; **discovery** scoperta f

discredit [dɪs'kredɪt] screditare

discreet [dɪs'kriːt] discreto

discrepancy [dɪs'krepənsɪ] incongruenza f

discretion [dɪs'kreʃn] discrezione f

discriminate [dɪs'krɪmɪneɪt]: ~ **against** discriminare; **discriminating** esigente; **discrimination** sexual, racial etc discriminazione f

discus ['dɪskəs] SP object disco m; event lancio m del disco

discuss [dɪs'kʌs] discutere; of article trattare di; **discussion** discussione f

disease [dɪ'ziːz] malattia f

disembark [dɪsɪm'bɑːk] sbarcare

disentangle [dɪsən'tæŋgl] districare

disfigure [dɪs'fɪgə(r)] sfigurare; fig deturpare

disgrace [dɪs'greɪs] **1** n vergogna f **2** v/t disonorare; **disgraceful** vergognoso

disgruntled [dɪs'grʌntld] scontento

disguise [dɪs'gaɪz] **1** n travestimento m **2** v/t voice etc camuffare; fear, anxiety dissimulare; ~ **o.s. as** travestirsi da

disgust [dɪs'gʌst] **1** n disgusto m **2** v/t disgustare; **disgusting** disgustoso

dish [dɪʃ] piatto m; for cooking recipiente m

disheartening [dɪs'hɑːtnɪŋ] demoralizzante

disheveled [dɪ'ʃevld] person, appearance arruffato; after effort scompigliato

dishonest [dɪs'ɒnɪst] disonesto; **dishonesty** disonestà f

dishonor etc Am ➡ **dishonour** etc

dishonour [dɪsˈɒnə(r)] disonore m; **dishonourable** disdicevole

'dishwasher machine lavastoviglie f inv; person lavapiatti m/f inv; **dishwashing liquid** Am detersivo m per i piatti

disillusion [dɪsɪˈluːʒn] disilludere; **disillusionment** disillusione f

disinfect [dɪsɪnˈfekt] disinfettare; **disinfectant** disinfettante m

disinherit [dɪsɪnˈherɪt] diseredare

disintegrate [dɪsˈɪntəgreɪt] disintegrarsi; of marriage, building andare in pezzi

disinterested [dɪsˈɪntərestɪd] (unbiased) disinteressato

disjointed [dɪsˈdʒɔɪntɪd] sconnesso

disk [dɪsk] disco m; (diskette) dischetto m; **disk drive** COMPUT lettore m or drive m inv di dischetti; **diskette** dischetto m

dislike [dɪsˈlaɪk] **1** n antipatia f **2** v/t: **I ~ cats** non mi piacciono i gatti

dislocate ['dɪsləkeɪt] lussare

disloyal [dɪsˈlɔɪəl] sleale; **disloyalty** slealtà f

dismal ['dɪzməl] weather, news deprimente; person (sad), failure triste; person (negative) ombroso

dismantle [dɪsˈmæntl] smontare; organization demolire

dismay [dɪsˈmeɪ] costernazione f

dismiss [dɪsˈmɪs] employee licenziare; suggestion scartare; idea accantonare; **dismissal** of employee licenziamento m

disobedience [dɪsəˈbiːdɪəns] disobbidienza f; **disobedient** disobbidiente; **disobey** disobbedire a

disorder [dɪsˈɔːdə(r)] (untidiness) disordine m; (unrest) disordini mpl; MED disturbo m

disorganized [dɪsˈɔːgənaɪzd] disorganizzato

disoriented [dɪsˈɔːrɪəntɪd], **disorientated** [dɪsˈɔːrɪənteɪtɪd] disorientato

disown [dɪsˈəʊn] disconoscere

disparaging [dɪˈspærɪdʒɪŋ] dispregiativo

disparity [dɪˈspærətɪ] disparità f inv

dispassionate [dɪˈspæʃənət] spassionato

dispatch [dɪˈspætʃ] (send) spedire

disperse [dɪˈspɜːs] of crowd disperdersi; of mist dissiparsi

display [dɪˈspleɪ] **1** n esposizione f, mostra f; in shop window articoli mpl in esposizione; COMPUT visualizzazione f **2** v/t emotion manifestare; at exhibition esporre;

(for sale) esporre in vendita; COMPUT visualizzare

displease [dɪs'pliːz] contrariare; **displeasure** disappunto *m*

disposable [dɪ'spəʊzəbl] usa e getta *inv*; **disposable income** reddito *m* disponibile; **disposal** eliminazione *f*; *of waste* smaltimento *m*; **put sth at s.o.'s ~** mettere qc a disposizione di qu

◆ **dispose of** [dɪ'spəʊz] *(get rid of)* sbarazzarsi di

disposed [dɪ'spəʊzd]: **be ~ to do sth** *(willing)* essere disposto a fare qc; **be well ~ towards** essere ben disposto verso

disprove [dɪs'pruːv] smentire

dispute [dɪ'spjuːt] **1** *n* controversia *f*; *industrial* contestazione *f* **2** *v/t* contestare; *(fight over)* contendersi

disqualification [dɪskwɒlɪfɪ'keɪʃn] squalifica *f*; **disqualify** squalificare

disregard [dɪsrə'gɑːd] **1** *n* mancanza *f* di considerazione **2** *v/t* ignorare

disreputable [dɪs'repjʊtəbl] depravato; *area* malfamato

disrespect [dɪsrə'spekt] mancanza *f* di rispetto; **disrespectful** irriverente

disrupt [dɪs'rʌpt] *train service* creare disagi a; *meeting, class* disturbare; **disruption** *of train service* disagio *m*; *of meeting, class* disturbo *m*

dissatisfaction [dɪssætɪs'fækʃn] insoddisfazione *f*; **dissatisfied** insoddisfatto

dissident ['dɪsɪdənt] dissidente *m/f*

dissimilar [dɪs'sɪmɪlə(r)] dissimile

dissolute ['dɪsəluːt] *adj* dissoluto

dissolve [dɪ'zɒlv] **1** *v/t substance* sciogliere **2** *v/i of substance* sciogliersi

distance ['dɪstəns] distanza *f*; **in the ~** in lontananza; **distant** lontano

distaste [dɪs'teɪst] avversione *f*; **distasteful** spiacevole

distinct [dɪ'stɪŋkt] *(clear)* netto; *(different)* distinto; **distinction** *(differentiation)* distinzione *f*; **hotel of ~** hotel d'eccezione; **distinctive** caratteristico; **distinctly** distintamente; *(decidedly)* decisamente

distinguish [dɪ'stɪŋgwɪʃ] *(see)* distinguere; **~ between X and Y** distinguere tra X e Y; **distinguished** *(famous)* insigne; *(dignified)* distinto

distort [dɪ'stɔːt] distorcere

distract [dɪ'strækt] *person* distrarre; *attention* distogliere

distraught [dɪ'strɔːt] affranto

distress [dɪ'stres] **1** *n* sofferenza *f* **2** *v/t (upset)* angosciare; **distressing** sconvolgente

distribute [dɪ'strɪbjuːt] distribuire; **distribution** distribuzione f; **distributor** COM distributore m

district ['dɪstrɪkt] quartiere m; **district attorney** Am procuratore m distrettuale

distrust [dɪs'trʌst] diffidenza f

disturb [dɪ'stɜːb] disturbare; **disturbance** (interruption) fastidio m; ~s (civil unrest) disordini mpl; **disturbed** turbato; psychologically malato di mente; **disturbing** inquietante

disused [dɪs'juːzd] inutilizzato

ditch [dɪtʃ] **1** n fosso m **2** v/t F boyfriend scaricare F; F car sbarazzarsi di

dive [daɪv] **1** n tuffo m; underwater immersione f; of plane picchiata f; F bar etc bettola f F **2** v/i tuffarsi; underwater fare immersione; of submarine immergersi; of plane scendere in picchiata; **diver** off board tuffatore m, -trice f; underwater sub m/f inv, sommozzatore m, -trice f

diverge [daɪ'vɜːdʒ] divergere

diversification [daɪvɜːsɪfɪ-'keɪʃn] COM diversificazione f; **diversify** COM diversificare; **diversion** for traffic deviazione f; to distract attention diversione m; **diversity** varietà f inv

divert [daɪ'vɜːt] traffic deviare; attention sviare

divide [dɪ'vaɪd] dividere

dividend ['dɪvɪdend] FIN dividendo m

divine [dɪ'vaɪn] REL, F divino

diving ['daɪvɪŋ] from board tuffi mpl; underwater immersione f; **diving board** trampolino m

division [dɪ'vɪʒn] divisione f; of company sezione f

divorce [dɪ'vɔːs] **1** n divorzio m **2** v/t divorziare da **3** v/i divorziare; **divorced** divorziato; **divorcee** divorziato m, -a f

divulge [daɪ'vʌldʒ] divulgare

DIY [diːaɪ'waɪ] (= do it yourself) fai da te m inv, bricolage m

dizziness ['dɪzɪnɪs] giramento m di testa, vertigini fpl; **dizzy** stordito; I feel ~ mi gira la testa

DJ [diː'dʒeɪ] (= disc jockey) dj m/f inv; (= dinner jacket) smoking m inv

DNA [diːen'eɪ] (= deoxyribonucleic acid) DNA m inv (= acido m deossiribonucleico)

do [duː] **1** v/t fare; one's hair farsi; 100mph etc andare a; ~ the ironing / cooking stirare / cucinare; have one's hair done farsi fare i capelli **2** v/i (be suitable, enough) andare bene; that will ~! basta così!; ~ well (do a good job) essere bravo; (be in good health) stare bene; of busi-

ness andare bene; **well done!** bravo!; **how ~ you ~?** molto piacere

♦ **do away with** abolire

♦ **do up** (*renovate*) restaurare; (*fasten*) allacciare

♦ **do with: I could do with ...** mi ci vorrebbe ...

♦ **do without 1** *v/i* farne a meno **2** *v/t* fare a meno di

docile ['dəʊsaɪl] docile

dock¹ [dɒk] **1** *n* NAUT bacino *m* **2** *v/i* of ship entrare in porto; *of spaceship* agganciarsi

dock² [dɒk] LAW banco *m* degli imputati

doctor ['dɒktə(r)] MED dottore *m*, -essa *f*; **doctorate** ['dɒktərət] dottorato *m*

doctrine ['dɒktrɪn] dottrina *f*

document ['dɒkjʊmənt] documento *m*; **documentary** documentario *m*; **documentation** documentazione *f*

dodge [dɒdʒ] *blow* schivare; *person, issue* evitare; *question* aggirare

dog [dɒg] **1** *n* cane *m* **2** *v/t* of bad luck perseguitare

dogged ['dɒgɪd] accanito

dogma ['dɒgmə] dogma *m*; **dogmatic** dogmatico

'dog-tired F stravolto

do-it-yourself [du:ɪtjə'self] fai da te *m*

doldrums ['dɒldrəmz]: **be in the ~** of economy essere in stallo; of person essere giù di corda

doll [dɒl] *toy*, F *woman* bam-

bola *f*

dollar ['dɒlə(r)] dollaro *m*

Dolomites ['dɒləmaɪts] Dolomiti *mpl*

dolphin ['dɒlfɪn] delfino *m*

dome [dəʊm] of building cupola *f*

domestic [də'mestɪk] domestico; *news, policy* interno; **domestic flight** volo *m* nazionale

dominant ['dɒmɪnənt] dominante; *member* principale; **dominate** dominare; **domination** dominio *m*; **domineering** autoritario

donate [dəʊ'neɪt] donare; **donation** donazione *f*

donkey ['dɒŋkɪ] asino *m*

donor ['dəʊnə(r)] donatore *m*, -trice *f*

donut ['dəʊnʌt] Am bombolone *m*, krapfen *m inv*

doodle ['du:dl] scarabocchiare

doom [du:m] (*fate*) destino *f*; (*ruin*) rovina *f*; **doomed** project condannato al fallimento

door [dɔ:(r)] porta *f*; of car portiera *f*; **doorbell** campanello *m*; **doorman** usciere *m*; **doorway** vano *m* della porta

dope [dəʊp] (*drugs*) droga *f* leggera; F (*idiot*) cretino *m*, -a *f*

dormant ['dɔ:mənt]: **~ volcano** vulcano *m* inattivo

dormitory ['dɔ:mɪtrɪ] dormi-a *f*

dose 364

torio *m*; *Am* casa *f* dello studente

dose [dəʊs] dose *f*

dot [dɒt] puntino *m*; *in email address* punto *m*

double ['dʌbl] **1** *n amount* doppio; (*person*) sosia *m inv*; *of film star* controfigura *f* **2** *adj* doppio **3** *adv*: **~ the amount** il doppio della quantità **4** *v/t & v/i* raddoppiare; **double-bass** contrabbasso *m*; **double bed** letto *m* matrimoniale; **doublecheck** ricontrollare; **double-click** cliccare due volte (**on** su); **doublecross** fare il doppio gioco con; **double glazing** doppi vetri *mpl*; **double park** parcheggiare in doppia fila; **double room** camera *f* doppia; *with double bed* camera *f* matrimoniale; **doubles** *in tennis* doppio *msg*

doubt [daʊt] **1** *n* dubbio *m*; **be in ~** essere in dubbio; **no ~** (*probably*) senz'altro **2** *v/t* dubitare di; **doubtful** *look* dubbio; **be ~** *of person* essere dubbioso; **doubtless** senza dubbio

dough [dəʊ] impasto *m*; **doughnut** bombolone *m*, krapfen *m inv*

dove [dʌv] colomba *f*; *fig* pacifista *m/f*

down [daʊn] **1** *adv* (*downwards*) giù; **~ there** laggiù; **£200 ~** *as deposit* un acconto

di £200; **~ south** a sud; **be ~** *of price, rate* essere diminuito; (*not working*) non funzionare; F (*depressed*) essere giù **2** *prep* giù da; (*along*) lungo; **walk ~ a street** percorrere una strada; **down-and-out** senza tetto *m/f inv*; **downhill** in discesa; **go ~** *fig* peggiorare; **downhill skiing** discesa *f* libera; **download** COMPUT **1** *v/t* scaricare **2** *n* scaricamento *m*; **downmarket** di fascia medio-bassa; **down payment** deposito *m*, acconto *m*; **downplay** minimizzare; **downpour** acquazzone *m*; **downright 1** *adj*: **it's a ~ lie** è una bugia bella e buona; **he's a ~ idiot** è un perfetto idiota **2** *adv dangerous etc* assolutamente; **downscale** *Am* di fascia medio-bassa; **downside** (*disadvantage*) contropartita *f*; **downsize** *company* ridimensionare; **the ~d version** *of car* la versione ridotta; **downstairs** al piano di sotto; **downtown** in centro; **downwards** verso il basso

doze [dəʊz] fare un sonnellino

◆ **doze off** assopirsi

dozen ['dʌzn] dozzina *f*

drab [dræb] *adj* scialbo

draft [drɑːft] *of document* bozza *f*; *Am* MIL leva *f*; *Am = **draught** 2 *v/t document* fare una bozza di; *Am* MIL arruo-

dress

lare; **draft dodger** *Am* MIL renitente *m* alla leva

drag [dræg] **1** *v/t* (*pull*) trascinare; (*search*) dragare **2** *v/i of time* non passare mai; *of show, film* trascinarsi

drain [dreɪn] **1** *n* (*pipe*) tubo *m* di scarico; *under street* tombino *m* **2** *v/t water* fare colare; *oil* fare uscire; *vegetables* scolare; *land* drenare; *glass, tank* svuotare; (*exhaust: person*) svuotare; **drainage** (*drains*) fognatura *f*; *of water from soil* drenaggio *m*; **drainpipe** tubo *m* di scarico

drama ['drɑːmə] *of air* arte *f* drammatica; (*excitement*) dramma *m*; (*play: on TV*) sceneggiato *m*; **dramatic** drammatico; (*exciting*) sorprendente; *gesture* teatrale; **dramatist** drammaturgo *m*, -a *f*; **dramatize** *story* adattare; *fig* drammatizzare

drapes [dreɪps] *Am* tende *fpl*

drastic ['dræstɪk] drastico

draught [drɑːft] *of air* corrente *f* (d'aria); ~ (*beer*) birra *f* alla spina; **draught beer** birra *f* alla spina; **draughts** *game* dama *f*; **draughtsman** disegnatore *m* industriale; *of plan* disegnatore *m*, -trice *f*; **draughty** pieno di correnti d'aria

draw [drɔː] **1** *n in game* pareggio *m*; *in lottery* estrazione *f*; (*attraction*) attrazione *f* **2** *v/t picture* disegnare; *curtain, ti-*

rare; *in lottery, gun, knife* estrarre; (*attract*) attirare; (*lead*) tirare; *from bank account* ritirare **3** *v/i* disegnare; *in game* pareggiare

◆ **draw back 1** *v/i* (*recoil*) tirarsi indietro **2** *v/t hand* ritirare; *curtains* aprire

◆ **draw out** *wallet etc* estrarre; *money from bank* ritirare

◆ **draw up 1** *v/t document* redigere; *chair* accostare **2** *v/i of vehicle* fermarsi

'drawback inconveniente *m*

drawer ['drɔː(r)] *of desk etc* cassetto *m*

drawing ['drɔːɪŋ] disegno *m*; **drawing pin** puntina *f*

drawl [drɔːl] pronuncia *f* strascicata

dread [dred] aver il terrore di; **dreadful** terribile; **dreadfully** F (*extremely*) terribilmente; *behave* malissimo

dream [driːm] **1** *n* sogno *m* **2** *v/i* sognare; *I ~t about you* ti ho sognato

◆ **dream up** sognare

dreary ['drɪərɪ] deprimente; (*boring*) noioso

dredge [dredʒ] *canal* dragare

◆ **dredge up** *fig* scovare

dregs [dregz] *of coffee* fondi *mpl*; *the ~ of society* la feccia della società

dress [dres] **1** *n for woman* vestito *m*; (*clothing*) abbigliamento *m* **2** *v/t person* vestire; *wound* medicare; *salad* condire; *get~ed* vestirsi **3** *v/i* vestirsi

◆ **dress up** vestirsi elegante;
(*wear a disguise*) travestirsi

'dress circle prima galleria *f*;
dresser *in kitchen* credenza
f; **dressing** *for salad* condimento *m*; *for wound* medicazione *f*; **dressing gown** vestaglia *f*; **dress rehearsal**
prova *f* generale

dribble ['drɪbl] *of person* sbavare; *of water* gocciolare; SP
dribblare

dried [draɪd] *fruit etc* essicato

drier ['draɪr] = **dryer**

drift [drɪft] *of snow* accumularsi; *of ship* andare alla deriva; (*go off course*) uscire
dalla rotta; *of person* vagabondare

◆ **drift apart** *of couple* allontanarsi (l'uno dall'altro)

drifter ['drɪftər] vagabondo
m, -a *f*

drill [drɪl] **1** *n* (*tool*) trapano *m*;
(*exercise*), MIL esercitazione *f*
2 *v/t tunnel* scavare; **~ a hole**
fare un foro col trapano **3** *v/i*
for oil trivellare; MIL adde-
strarsi

drily ['draɪlɪ] *remark* ironica-
mente

drink [drɪŋk] **1** *n* bevanda *f*;
non-alcoholic ~ bibita *f*
(analcolica); **a ~ of ...** un bicchiere di ... **2** *v/t* & *v/i* bere

◆ **drink up 1** *v/i* (*finish drink*)
finire il bicchiere **2** *v/t* (*drink
completely*) finire di bere

drinkable ['drɪŋkəbl] potabi-

le; **drinker** bevitore *m*, -trice
f; **drinking water** acqua *f* potabile

drip [drɪp] **1** *n* goccia *f*; MED
flebo *f inv* **2** *v/i* gocciolare

drive [draɪv] **1** *n outing* giro *m*
in macchina; (*driveway*) via-
le *m*; (*energy*) grinta *f*; COM-
PUT lettore *m*; (*campaign*)
campagna *f* **2** *v/t vehicle* guidare; (*take in car*) portare (in
macchina); TECH azionare **3**
v/i guidare; **I ~ to work** vado
al lavoro in macchina

◆ **drive in** *nail* piantare

drivel ['drɪvl] sciocchezze *fpl*

driver ['draɪvər] guidatore
m, -trice *f*, conducente *m/f*;
of train macchinista *m/f*;
COMPUT driver *m inv*; **driver's license** *Am* patente *f*
(di guida); **driveway** viale
m; **driving 1** *n* guida *f* **2**
adj rain violento; **driving
lesson** lezione *f* di guida;
driving licence patente *f*
(di guida); **driving school**
scuola *f* guida; **driving test**
esame *m* di guida

drizzle ['drɪzl] **1** *n* pioggerella
f **2** *v/i* piovviginare

drop [drɒp] **1** *n of rain* goccia
f; *in price, temperature* calo *m*
2 *v/t* far cadere; *from plane*
sganciare; *person from car*
lasciare; *person from team*
scartare; (*stop seeing*) smettere di frequentare; *charges,
demand etc* abbandonare;
(*give up*) lasciare perdere **3**

v/i cadere; (*decline*) calare

◆ **drop in** passare

◆ **drop off 1** *v/t person, goods* lasciare **2** *v/i* (*fall asleep*) addormentarsi; (*decline*) calare

◆ **drop out** *from competition, school* ritirarsi

drought [draʊt] siccità *f inv*

drown [draʊn] annegare

drowsy ['draʊzɪ] sonnolento

drug [drʌg] **1** *n* droga *f*; **be on ~s** drogarsi **2** *v/t* drogare; **drug addict** tossicodipendente *m/f*; **drug dealer** spacciatore *m*, -trice *f* (di droga); **druggist** *Am* farmacista *m/f*; **drugstore** *Am* negozio-bar che vende articoli vari, inclusi medicinali; **drug trafficking** traffico *m* di droga

drum [drʌm] MUS tamburo *m*; (*container*) bidone *m*; **~s** in *pop music* batteria *f*; **drummer** batterista *m/f*; *in brass band* percussionista *m/f*; **drumstick** bacchetta *f*

drunk [drʌŋk] **1** *n* ubriacone *m*, -a *f* **2** *adj* ubriaco; **get ~** ubriacarsi; **drunk driving** guida *f* in stato di ebbrezza

dry [draɪ] **1** *adj* secco **2** *v/t & v/i* asciugare; **dry-clean** pulire *or* lavare a secco; **dry cleaner** tintoria *f*; **dryer** *machine* asciugatrice *f*

dual ['dju:əl] doppio; **dual carriageway** carreggiata *f* a due corsie

dub [dʌb] *movie* doppiare

dubious ['dju:brəs] equivoco; (*having doubts*) dubbioso

duchess ['dʌtʃɪs] duchessa *f*

duck [dʌk] **1** *n* anatra *f* **2** *v/i* piegarsi

dud [dʌd] F (*false bill*) falso *m*

due [dju:] dovuto; *the rent is ~ tomorrow* domani scade la rata dell'affitto

duke [dju:k] duca *m*

dull [dʌl] *weather* grigio; *sound, pain* sordo; (*boring*) noioso

duly ['dju:lɪ] (*as expected*) come previsto; (*properly*) debitamente

dumb [dʌm] (*mute*) muto; *Am* F (*stupid*) stupido

dummy ['dʌmɪ] *for clothes* manichino *m*; *for baby* succhiotto *m*

dump [dʌmp] **1** *n for rubbish* discarica *f*; (*unpleasant place*) postaccio *m* **2** *v/t* (*deposit*) lasciare; (*dispose of*) scaricare; *waste* sbarazzarsi di

dune [dju:n] duna *f*

duplex (apartment) ['du:pleks] appartamento *m* su due piani

duplicate ['dju:plɪkət] duplicato *m*

durable ['djʊərəbl] *material* resistente

during ['djʊərɪŋ] durante

dusk [dʌsk] crepuscolo *m*

dust [dʌst] **1** *n* polvere *f* **2** *v/t* spolverare; **dustbin** bidone *m* della spazzatura; **duster**

straccio *m* (per spolverare);
dustpan paletta *f*; **dusty** *table* impolverato; *road* polveroso

Dutch [dʌtʃ] **1** *adj* olandese **2** *n language* olandese *m*; **the** ~ gli Olandesi

duty ['dju:tɪ] dovere *m*; *on goods* tassa *f* doganale, dazio *m*; **be on** ~ essere di servizio; **duty free** duty free *inv*

DVD [di:vi:'di:] (= *digital versatile disk*) DVD *m inv*

dwarf [dwɔ:f] **1** *n* nano *m*, -a *f*

2 *v/t* fare scomparire

dwindle ['dwɪndl] diminuire

dye [daɪ] **1** *n* tintura *f*; *for food* colorante *m* **2** *v/t* colorare, tingere

dying ['daɪɪŋ] morente; *tradition* in via di disparizione

dynamic [daɪ'næmɪk] dinamico; **dynamism** dinamismo *m*

dynasty ['dɪnəstɪ] dinastia *f*

dyslexic [dɪs'leksɪk] **1** *adj* dislessico **2** *n* dislessico *m*, -a *f*

E

each [i:tʃ] **1** *adj* ogni **2** *adv* ciascuno; **they're £1.50** ~ costano £1,50 ciascuno **3** *pron* ciascuno *m*, -a *f*, ognuno *m*, -a *f*; ~ **other** l'un l'altro *m*, l'una l'altra *f*; **we know** ~ **other** ci conosciamo

eager ['i:gə(r)] entusiasta; **be** ~ **to do sth** essere ansioso di fare qc; **eagerly** ansiosamente; **eagerness** smania *f*

eagle ['i:gl] aquila *f*; **eagle-eyed: be** ~ **eyed** avere l'occhio di falco

ear¹ [ɪə(r)] orecchio *m*

ear² [ɪə(r)] *of corn* spiga *f*

earache ['ɪəreɪk] mal d'orecchi

early ['ɜ:lɪ] **1** *adj* (*not late*) primo; *arrival* anticipato; (*farther back in time*) antico; ~ *October* inizio ottobre; **at an** ~ **age** in giovane età; **let's**

have an ~ **supper** ceniamo presto **2** *adv* (*not late*) presto; (*ahead of time*) in anticipo; **early bird** (*early riser*) persona *f* mattiniera

earmark ['ɪəmɑ:k] riservare

earn [ɜ:n] guadagnare; *interest* fruttare; *holiday, respect etc* guadagnarsi

earnest ['ɜ:nɪst] serio

earnings ['ɜ:nɪŋz] guadagno *m*

'earphones cuffie *fpl* (d'ascolto); **earring** orecchino *m*; **earshot**: **within** ~ a portata d'orecchio; **out of** ~ fuori dalla portata d'orecchio

earth [ɜ:θ] **1** *n also* ELEC terra *f* **2** *v/t* ELEC mettere a terra; **earthenware** terracotta *f*; **earthly** terreno; **it's no** ~

use ... F è perfettamente inutile ...; **earthquake** terremoto *m*

ease [iːz] **1** *n* facilità *f*; *feel at ~* sentirsi a proprio agio **2** *v/t* (*relieve*) alleviare; *it will ~ my mind* mi darà sollievo **3** *v/i of pain* alleviarsi

◆ **ease off 1** *v/t* (*remove*) togliere con cautela **2** *v/i of pain, rain* diminuire

easel [ˈiːzl] cavalletto *m*

easily [ˈiːzəlɪ] facilmente; (*by far*) di gran lunga

east [iːst] **1** *n* est **2** *adj* orientale **3** *adv travel* a est; *~ of* a est di

Easter [ˈiːstə(r)] Pasqua *f*; **Easter Day** il giorno *or* la domenica di Pasqua; **Easter egg** uovo *m* di Pasqua

easterly [ˈiːstəlɪ]: *~ wind* vento *m* dell'est; *in an ~ direction* verso est

Easter 'Monday lunedì *m inv* di Pasqua, Pasquetta *f*

eastern [ˈiːstən] orientale

Easter 'Sunday il giorno *or* la domenica di Pasqua

eastward [ˈiːstwəd] verso est

easy [ˈiːzɪ] facile; (*relaxed*) tranquillo; **easy chair** poltrona *f*; **easy-going**: *he's very ~* gli va bene quasi tutto

eat [iːt] mangiare

◆ **eat out** mangiare fuori

eatable [ˈiːtəbl] commestibile; *lunch, dish* mangiabile

eavesdrop [ˈiːvzdrɒp]: *~ on s.o.* origliare qu

ebb [eb] *of tide* rifluire

e-bike [ˈiːbaɪk] bici *f* elettrica

e-book [ˈiːbʊk] e-book *m inv*, libro *m* elettronico; **e-business** e-commerce *m*, commercio *m* elettronico

eccentric [ɪkˈsentrɪk] **1** *adj* eccentrico **2** *n* eccentrico *m*, -a *f*; **eccentricity** eccentricità *f inv*

echo [ˈekəʊ] **1** *n* eco *f* **2** *v/i* risuonare **3** *v/t words* ripetere; *views* condividere

eclipse [ɪˈklɪps] **1** *n* eclissi *f inv* **2** *v/t fig* eclissare

ecofriendly [ˈiːkəʊfrendlɪ] ecologico

ecological [iːkəˈlɒdʒɪkl] ecologico; **ecologically** ecologicamente; **ecologically friendly** ecologico; **ecologist** ecologista *m/f*; **ecology** ecologia *f*

economic [iːkəˈnɒmɪk] economico; **economical** (*cheap*) economico; (*thrifty*) parsimonioso; **economics** *science* economia *f*; *financial aspects* aspetti *mpl* economici; **economist** economista *m/f*; **economize** risparmiare, fare economia

◆ **economize on** risparmiare su

economy [ɪˈkɒnəmɪ] economia *f*; **economy class** classe *f* economica

ecosystem [ˈiːkəʊsɪstm] ecosistema *m*; **ecotourism** agriturismo *m*

ecstasy ['ekstəsɪ] estasi f inv; **ecstatic** in estasi

eczema ['eksmə] eczema m

edge [edʒ] **1** n of knife filo m; of table, seat, lawn bordo m; of road ciglio m; of cliff orlo m; **on ~** teso **2** v/i (move slowly) muoversi con cautela; **edgeways: I couldn't get a word in ~** non sono riuscito a piazzare una parola; **edgy** teso

edible ['edɪbl] commestibile

edit ['edɪt] text rivedere; prepare for publication curare; newspaper dirigere; TV program, film montare; COMPUT editare; **edition** edizione f; **editor** of text revisore m; of publication curatore m, -trice f; of newspaper direttore m, -trice; of TV program responsabile m/f del montaggio; of film tecnico m del montaggio; **editorial 1** adj editoriale; **the ~ staff** la redazione **2** n editoriale m

educate ['edjʊkeɪt] child istruire; consumers educare; **he was ~d at ...** ha studiato a ...; **educated** istruito; **education** istruzione f; **the ~ system** la pubblica istruzione; **educational** didattico; (informative) istruttivo

eerie ['ɪərɪ] inquietante

effect [ɪ'fekt] effetto m; **effective** efficace; (striking) d'effetto

effeminate [ɪ'femɪnət] effe-

minato

efficiency [ɪ'fɪʃənsɪ] efficienza f; of machine rendimento m; **efficient** efficiente; machine ad alto rendimento; **efficiently** con efficienza

effort ['efət] sforzo m; **effortless** facile

e.g. [iː'dʒiː] ad or per esempio

egg [eg] uovo m; **eggcup** portauovo m inv; **egghead** F intellettualoide m/f; **eggplant** Am melanzana f

ego ['iːgəʊ] ego m; **egocentric** egocentrico; **egoism** egoismo m; **egoist** egoista m/f

eiderdown ['aɪdədaʊn] (quilt) piumino m

eight [eɪt] otto m; **eighteen** diciotto; **eighteenth** diciottesimo; **eighth** ottavo; **eighth note** Am MUS croma f; **eightieth** ottantesimo; **eighty** ottanta

either ['aɪðə(r)] **1** adj l'uno o l'altro; (both) entrambi pl **2** pron l'uno o l'altro m, l'una o l'altra f **3** adv nemmeno, neppure; **I won't go ~** non vado nemmeno or neppure io **4** conj: **~ my mother or my sister** mia madre o mia sorella; **he doesn't like ~ wine or beer** non gli piacciono né il vino, né la birra

eject [ɪ'dʒekt] **1** v/t espellere **2** v/i from plane eiettarsi

◆ **eke out** [iːk] usare con par-

simonia; *grant etc* arrotondare; *eke out a living* tirare
avanti

el [el] *Am* ferrovia *f* sopraelevata

elaborate 1 [ɪˈlæbərət] *adj*
elaborato **2** [ɪˈlæbəreɪt] *v/i*
fornire particolari

elapse [ɪˈlæps] trascorrere

elastic [ɪˈlæstɪk] **1** *adj* elastico
2 *n* elastico *m*; **elasticated**
elasticizzato; **elastic band**
elastico *m*

Elastoplast® [ɪˈlæstəplɑːst]
cerotto *m*

elated [ɪˈleɪtɪd] esultante; **el-
ation** esultanza *f*

elbow [ˈelbəʊ] gomito *m*

elder [ˈeldə(r)] **1** *adj* maggiore
2 *n* maggiore *m/f*; **elderly 1**
adj anziano; **2** *npl* **the ~** gli
anziani; **eldest 1** *adj* maggiore **2** *n* maggiore *m/f*

elect [ɪˈlekt] eleggere; **elected**
eletto; **election** elezione *f*;
election campaign campagna *f* elettorale; **election
day** giorno *m* delle elezioni;
electorate elettorato *m*

electric [ɪˈlektrɪk] *also fig*
elettrico; **electrical** elettrico; **electric chair** sedia *f*
elettrica; **electrician** elettricista *m/f*; **electricity** elettricità *f*; **electrify** elettrificare;
fig elettrizzare

electrocute [ɪˈlektrəkjuːt]
fulminare

electron [ɪˈlektron] elettrone
m; **electronic** elettronico;

electronics elettronica *f*

elegance [ˈelɪɡəns] eleganza
f; **elegant** elegante

element [ˈelɪmənt] elemento
m; **elementary** elementare;
elementary school *Am*
scuola *f* elementare

elephant [ˈelɪfənt] elefante *m*

elevate [ˈelɪveɪt] elevare; **elevated railroad** *Am* ferrovia *f*
sopraelevata; **elevation** (*altitude*) altitudine *f*; **elevator**
Am ascensore *m*

eleven [ɪˈlevn] undici; **eleventh** undicesimo

eligible [ˈelɪdʒəbl]: *be ~ to do
sth* avere il diritto di fare qc

eliminate [ɪˈlɪmɪneɪt] eliminare; **elimination** eliminazione
f

elite [eɪˈliːt] **1** *n* elite *f inv* **2** *adj*
elitario

eloquence [ˈeləkwəns] elo-
quenza *f*; **eloquent** eloquente

else [els]: *anything ~* qualco-
s'altro; *nothing ~* nient'altro; *nobody ~* nessun altro;
everyone ~ is going tutti
gli altri vanno; *someone ~*
qualcun altro; *something ~*
qualcos'altro; *let's go
somewhere ~* andiamo da
qualche altra parte; *or ~* altrimenti; *elsewhere* altrove

elude [ɪˈluːd] sfuggire a; **elu-
sive** *person* difficile da trovare; *quality* raro

emaciated [ɪˈmeɪsɪeɪtɪd]
emaciato

e-mail ['iːmeɪl] **1** *n* e-mail *m inv* **2** *v/t person* mandare un e-mail a; *text* mandare per e-mail; **e-mail address** indirizzo *m* e-mail

emancipation [ɪmænsɪ'peɪʃn] emancipazione *f*

embalm [ɪm'bɑːm] imbalsamare

embankment [ɪm'bæŋkmənt] *of river* argine *m*; RAIL massicciata *f*

embargo [em'bɑːgəu] embargo *m inv*

embark [ɪm'bɑːk] imbarcarsi

embarrass [ɪm'bærəs] imbarazzare; **embarrassed** imbarazzato; **embarrassing** imbarazzante; **embarrassment** imbarazzo *m*

embassy ['embəsɪ] ambasciata *f*

embezzle [ɪm'bezl] appropriarsi indebitamente di; **embezzlement** appropriazione *f* indebita

emblem ['embləm] emblema *f*

embodiment [ɪm'bɒdɪmənt] incarnazione *f*; **embody** incarnare

embrace [ɪm'breɪs] **1** *n* abbraccio *m* **2** *v/t (hug, include)* abbracciare **3** *v/i of two people* abbracciarsi

embroider [ɪm'brɔɪdə(r)] ricamare; *fig* ricamare su

embryo ['embrɪəu] embrione *m*; **embryonic** *fig* embrionale

emerald ['emərəld] smeraldo *m*; *colour* verde *m* smeraldo

emerge [ɪ'mɜːdʒ] *(appear)* emergere; *it has ~d that ...* è emerso che ...

emergency [ɪ'mɜːdʒənsɪ] emergenza *f*; **emergency exit** uscita *f* di sicurezza; **emergency landing** atterraggio *m* di fortuna; **emergency services** servizi *mpl* di soccorso

emigrant ['emɪgrənt] emigrante *m/f*; **emigrate** emigrare; **emigration** emigrazione *f*

Eminence ['emɪnəns]: REL **His ~** Sua Eminenza; **eminent** eminente

emission [ɪ'mɪʃn] *of gases* emanazione *f*; **emit** *heat, gases* emanare; *light, smoke* emettere; *smell* esalare

emotion [ɪ'məuʃn] emozione *f*; **emotional** *problems, development* emozionale; *(causing emotion)* commovente; *(showing emotion)* commosso

emperor ['empərə(r)] imperatore *m*

emphasis ['emfəsɪs] enfasi *f*; *on word* rilievo *m*; **emphasize** enfatizzare; *word* dare rilievo a; **emphatic** enfatico

empire ['empaɪə(r)] impero *m*

employ [ɪm'plɔɪ] dare lavoro a; *(take on)* assumere; *(use)* impiegare; **employee** dipendente *m/f*; **employer** datore

m, **-trice** *f* di lavoro; **employment** occupazione *f*; *(work)*
impiego *m*

emptiness ['emptɪnɪs] vuoto
m; **empty 1** *adj* vuoto **2** *v/t*
vuotare **3** *v/i* of room, street
svuotarsi

emulate ['emjʊleɪt] emulare

enable [ɪ'neɪbl] *person* permettere a; *thing* permettere

enchanting [ɪn'tʃɑːntɪŋ] incantevole

encircle [ɪn'sɜːkl] circondare

enclose [ɪn'kləʊz] *in letter* allegare; *area* recintare; **enclosure** *with letter* allegato *m*

encore ['ɒŋkɔː(r)] bis *m inv*

encounter [ɪn'kaʊntə(r)] **1** *n*
incontro *m* **2** *v/t* incontrare

encourage [ɪn'kʌrɪdʒ] incoraggiare; **encouragement**
incoraggiamento *m*; **encouraging** incoraggiante

encyclopedia [ɪnsaɪklə'piː-
dɪə] enciclopedia *f*

end [end] **1** *n* *(conclusion, purpose)* fine *m*; *(extremity)*
estremità *f inv*; **in the ~** alla
fine **2** *v/t* terminare **3** *v/i* finire

◆ **end up** finire

endanger [ɪn'deɪndʒə(r)]
mettere in pericolo; **endan-
gered species** specie *f* in
via d'estinzione

endeavor, *Am* **endeavor**
[ɪn'devə(r)] **1** *n* tentativo *m*
2 *v/t* tentare

endemic [ɪn'demɪk] endemi-
co

ending ['endɪŋ] finale *m*;
GRAM desinenza *f*; **endless**
interminabile

endorse [ɪn'dɔːs] *candidacy*
appoggiare; *product* fare
pubblicità a; **endorsement**
of candidacy appoggio *m*;
of product pubblicità *f*

end 'product prodotto *m* finale

endurance [ɪn'djʊərəns] resistenza *f*; **endure 1** *v/t* sopportare **2** *v/i* *(last)* resistere;
enduring durevole

end-'user utente *m* finale

enemy ['enəmɪ] nemico *m*, -a
f

energetic [enə'dʒetɪk] energico; **energy** energia *f*; **energy supply** rifornimento di
energia elettrica

enforce [ɪn'fɔːs] far rispettare

engage [ɪn'geɪdʒ] **1** *v/t* *(hire)*
ingaggiare **2** *v/i* TECH ingranare; **engaged** *to be married*
fidanzato; **get ~** fidanzarsi;
TELEC occupato; **engage-
ment** *(appointment)* impegno *m*; *to be married* fidanzamento *m*; MIL scontro *m*; **engagement ring** anello *m* di
fidanzamento

engine ['endʒɪn] motore *m*;
engineering ingegneria *f*;
engineer ingegnere *m*; *for
sound, software* tecnico *m*;
NAUT macchinista *m*

England ['ɪŋglənd] Inghilterra *f*; **English 1** *adj* inglese
2 *n* *(language)* inglese *m*;

the ~ gli inglesi; **English Channel** Manica *f*; **Englishman** inglese *m*; **Englishwoman** inglese *f*

engrave [ɪn'greɪv] incidere; **engraving** *(drawing)* stampa *f*; *(design)* incisione *f*

engrossed [ɪn'grəʊst]: ~ *in* assorto in

engulf [ɪn'gʌlf] avvolgere

enhance [ɪn'hɑːns] accrescere; *performance, reputation* migliorare

enigma [ɪ'nɪgmə] enigma *m*

enjoy [ɪn'dʒɔɪ]: *did you ~ the film?* ti è piaciuto il film?; *I ~ reading* mi piace leggere; ~ *(your meal)* buon appetito!; ~ *o.s.* divertirsi; **enjoyable** piacevole; **enjoyment** piacere *m*, divertimento *m*

enlarge [ɪn'lɑːdʒ] ingrandire; **enlargement** ingrandimento *m*

enlighten [ɪn'laɪtn] illuminare

enlist [ɪn'lɪst] MIL arruolarsi

enmity ['enmətɪ] inimicizia *f*

enormous [ɪ'nɔːməs] enorme; **enormously** enormemente

enough [ɪ'nʌf] **1** *adj* sufficiente, abbastanza *inv* **2** *pron* abbastanza; *will £50 be ~?* saranno sufficienti £50?; *that's ~!* basta! **3** *adv* abbastanza; *strangely* ~ per quanto strano

enquire [ɪn'kwaɪə(r)] chiedere informazioni, informarsi

enrol, *Am* **enroll** [ɪn'rəʊl] iscriversi

en suite (bathroom) ['ɒnswiːt] bagno *m* in camera

ensure [ɪn'ʃʊə(r)] assicurare

entail [ɪn'teɪl] comportare

entangle [ɪn'tæŋgl] *in rope* impigliare

enter ['entə(r)] **1** *v/t room, house* entrare in; *competition* iscriversi a; COMPUT inserire **2** *v/i* entrare; *in competition* iscriversi **3** *n* COMPUT invio *m*

enterprise ['entəpraɪz] *(initiative)* intraprendenza *f*; *(venture)* impresa *f*; **enterprising** intraprendente

entertain [entə'teɪn] *(amuse)* intrattenere; *(consider: idea)* considerare; **entertainer** artista *m/f*; **entertaining** divertente; **entertainment** divertimento *m*

enthusiasm [ɪn'θjuːzɪæzm] entusiasmo *m*; **enthusiast** appassionato *m*, -a *f*; **enthusiastic** entusiasta; **enthusiastically** con entusiasmo

entire [ɪn'taɪə(r)] intero; **entirely** interamente

entitle [ɪn'taɪtl] dare il diritto a; *be ~d to do sth* avere il diritto di fare qc

entrance ['entrəns] entrata *f*, ingresso *m*; THEA entrata *f* in scena

entranced [ɪn'trɑːnst] incantato

'entrance   exam(ination)

esame *m* di ammissione

entrant ['entrənt] concorrente *m/f*

entrepreneur [ɒntrəprə'nɜː] imprenditore *m*, -trice *f*; **entrepreneurial** imprenditoriale

entrust [ɪn'trʌst] affidare

entry ['entrɪ] (*way in*) entrata *f*; *in diary* annotazione *f*; *in accounts, dictionary* voce *f*; **entryphone** citofono *m*

envelop [ɪn'veləp] avviluppare

envelope ['envələʊp] busta *f*

enviable ['envɪəbl] invidiabile; **envious** invidioso; **be ~ of s.o.** essere invidioso di qu

environment [ɪn'vaɪərənmənt] ambiente *m*; **environmental** ambientale; **environmentalist** ambientalista *m/f*; **environmentally friendly** ecologico; **environmental protection** tutela *f* dell'ambiente; **environs** dintorni *mpl*

envoy ['envɔɪ] inviato *m*, -a *f*

envy ['envɪ] **1** *n* invidia *f* **2** *v/t*: **~ s.o. sth** invidiare qc a qu

epic ['epɪk] **1** *n* epopea *f* **2** *adj journey* mitico

epicentre *Am* **epicenter** ['episentr] epicentro *m*

epidemic [epɪ'demɪk] epidemia *f*

episode ['episəʊd] episodio *m*

epitaph ['epɪtɑːf] epitaffio *m*

epoch ['iːpɒk] epoca *f*

equal ['iːkwl] **1** *adj* uguale **2** *n*: **be the ~ of** essere equivalente a; **treat s.o. as his ~** trattare qualcuno alla pari **3** *v/t* (*be as good as*) uguagliare; **equality** uguaglianza *f*, parità *f*; **equalize 1** *v/t* uniformare **2** *v/i* SP pareggiare; **equalizer** SP gol *m* *inv* del pareggio; **equally** ugualmente; **equal rights** parità *f* di diritti

equation [ɪ'kweɪʒn] MATH equazione *f*

equator [ɪ'kweɪtə(r)] equatore *m*

equip [ɪ'kwɪp] equipaggiare; **equipment** equipaggiamento *m*; *electrical, electronic* apparecchiature *fpl*

equity ['ekwətɪ] FIN capitale *m* azionario

equivalent [ɪ'kwɪvələnt] **1** *adj* equivalente **2** *n* equivalente *m*

era ['ɪərə] era *f*

eradicate [ɪ'rædɪkeɪt] sradicare

erase [ɪ'reɪz] cancellare; **eraser** gomma *f* (da cancellare)

e-reader ['iːriːdər] lettore *m* di e-book

erect [ɪ'rekt] **1** *adj* eretto **2** *v/t* erigere; **erection** erezione *f*

ergonomic [ɜːgəʊ'nɒmɪk] ergonomico

erode [ɪ'rəʊd] erodere; *fig* intaccare; **erosion** erosione *f*; *fig* diminuzione *f* erotic [ɪˈrɒtɪk] erotico

errand [ˈerənd] commissione f

erratic [ɪˈrætɪk] irregolare

error [ˈerə(r)] errore m; error message COMPUT messaggio m di errore

erupt [ɪˈrʌpt] of volcano eruttare; of violence esplodere; of person dare in escandescenze; eruption of volcano eruzione f; of violence esplosione f

escalate [ˈeskəleɪt] of costs aumentare; of war intensificarsi; escalation escalation f inv; escalator scala f mobile

escape [ɪˈskeɪp] 1 n of prisoner, animal, gas fuga f 2 v/i of prisoner, animal scappare, fuggire; of gas fuoriuscire

escort 1 [ˈeskɔːt] n accompagnatore m, -trice f; (guard) scorta f 2 [ɪˈskɔːt] v/t socially accompagnare; act as guard to scortare

especially [ɪˈspeʃlɪ] specialmente

espionage [ˈespɪənɑːʒ] spionaggio m

espresso (coffee) [esˈpresəʊ] espresso m

essay [ˈeseɪ] saggio m; in school tema m

essential [ɪˈsenʃl] essenziale

establish [ɪˈstæblɪʃ] company fondare; (create, determine) stabilire; establishment firm azienda f; restaurant lo-

cale m

estate [ɪˈsteɪt] land tenuta f; of dead person patrimonio m; estate agent agente m/f immobiliare; estate car giardiniera f

esthetic Am ☞ aesthetic

estimate [ˈestɪmət] 1 n stima f, valutazione f; COM preventivo m 2 v/t stimare

estuary [ˈestjʊərɪ] estuario m

etc [etˈsetrə] (= et cetera) ecc. (= eccetera)

eternal [ɪˈtɜːnl] eterno; eternity eternità f inv

ethical [ˈeθɪkl] etico; ethics etica f

ethnic [ˈeθnɪk] etnico; ethnic minority minoranza f etnica

e-ticket [ˈiːtɪkɪt] biglietto m acquistato su Internet

EU [iːˈjuː] (= European Union) UE f (= Unione europea)

euphemism [ˈjuːfəmɪzm] eufemismo m

euro [ˈjʊərəʊ] euro m inv; Euro MP eurodeputato m, -a f

Europe [ˈjʊərəp] Europa f; European 1 adj europeo 2 n europeo m, -a f; European Parliament Parlamento m europeo; European Union Unione f europea

euthanasia [juːθəˈneɪzɪə] eutanasia f

evacuate [ɪˈvækjʊeɪt] evacuare

evade [ɪˈveɪd] eludere; taxes evadere

evaluate [ɪ'væljʊət] valutare; **evaluation** valutazione f

evaporate [ɪ'væpəreɪt] evaporare; *of confidence* svanire; **evaporation** evaporazione f

evasion [ɪ'veɪʒn] elusione f; *of taxes* evasione f; **evasive** evasivo

eve [iːv] vigilia f

even ['iːvn] **1** *adj* (*regular*) omogeneo; *breathing* regolare; *surface* piano; (*number*) pari *inv*; *players, game* alla pari; **get ~ with ...** farla pagare a ... **2** *adv* persino; **~ bigger** ancora più grande; **not ~** nemmeno, neppure; **~ so** nonostante questo; **~ if** anche se **3** *v/t:* **~ the score** pareggiare

evening ['iːvnɪŋ] sera f; *in the* ~ di sera; *this* ~ stasera; *good* ~ buona sera; **evening class** corso *m* serale; **evening dress** *for woman* vestito *m* da sera; *for man* abito *m* scuro

evenly ['iːvnlɪ] (*regularly*) in modo omogeneo; *breathe* regolarmente

event [ɪ'vent] evento *m*, avvenimento *m*; SP prova f; **eventful** movimentato

eventually [ɪ'ventjʊəlɪ] finalmente, alla fine

ever ['evə(r)] mai; **have you ~ been to ...?** sei mai stato in ...?; *for* ~ per sempre; *as* ~ come sempre; **~ since he**

left da quando è partito; **everlasting** eterno

every ['evrɪ] ogni; **~ other day** un giorno sì, uno no; **~ now and then** ogni tanto; **everybody** tutti; **everyday** di tutti i giorni; **everyone** tutti *pl*; **everything** tutto; **everywhere** dovunque, dappertutto; (*wherever*) dovunque

evict [ɪ'vɪkt] sfrattare

evidence ['evɪdəns] prova f; **give ~** testimoniare; **evident** evidente; **evidently** evidentemente

evil ['iːvl] **1** *adj* cattivo **2** *n* male *m*

evolution [iːvə'luːʃn] evoluzione f; **evolve** evolvere

ex [eks] F *wife / husband* ex *m/f inv* F

exact [ɪg'zækt] esatto; **exacting** *task* impegnativo; *employer* esigente; *standards* rigido; **exactly** esattamente

exaggerate [ɪg'zædʒəreɪt] esagerare; **exaggeration** esagerazione f

exam [ɪg'zæm] esame *m*; **examination** esame *m*; *of patient* visita f; **examine** esaminare; *patient* visitare

example [ɪg'zɑːmpl] esempio *m*; *for* ~ ad o per esempio

excavate ['ekskəveɪt] (*dig*) scavare; *of archaeologist* riportare alla luce; **excavation** scavo *m*

exceed [ɪk'siːd] (*be more than*) eccedere, superare;

(*go beyond*) oltrepassare, superare; **exceedingly** estremamente

excel [ɪkˈsel] **1** *v/i* eccellere; ~ **at** eccellere in **2** *v/t:* ~ **o.s.** superare se stesso; **excellence** eccellenza *f*; **excellent** eccellente

except [ɪkˈsept] eccetto; ~ **for** fatta eccezione per; **exceptional** eccezionale; **exceptionally** (*extremely*) eccezionalmente; **exception** eccezione *f*

excerpt [ˈeksɜːpt] estratto *m*

excess [ɪkˈses] **1** *n* eccesso *m* **2** *adj* in eccesso; **excess baggage** eccedenza *f* di bagaglio; **excessive** eccessivo

exchange [ɪksˈtʃeɪndʒ] **1** *n* scambio *m* **2** *v/t* cambiare (**for** con); **exchange rate** FIN tasso *m* di cambio

Exchequer [ɪksˈtʃekə(r)] tesoro *m*

excite [ɪkˈsaɪt] (*make enthusiastic*) eccitare; **excited** eccitato; **get** ~ eccitarsi; **excitement** eccitazione *f*; **exciting** eccitante, emozionante

exclaim [ɪkˈskleɪm] esclamare; **exclamation** esclamazione *f*; **exclamation mark**, *Am* **exclamation point** punto *m* esclamativo

exclude [ɪkˈskluːd] escludere; **excluding** ad esclusione di; **exclusive** esclusivo

excuse 1 [ɪkˈskjuːs] *n* scusa *f* **2** [ɪkˈskjuːz] *v/t* scusare; ~ **me**

to get attention, interrupting scusami; *to get past* permesso

ex-di'rectory: **be** ~ non comparire sull'elenco telefonico

execute [ˈeksɪkjuːt] *criminal* giustiziare; *plan* attuare; **execution** *of criminal* esecuzione *f*; *of plan* attuazione *f*; **executive** dirigente *m/f*

exempt [ɪgˈzempt]: **be** ~ **from** essere esente da

exercise [ˈeksəsaɪz] **1** *n* esercizio *m*; MIL esercitazione *f* **2** *v/t muscle* fare esercizio con; *dog* far fare esercizio a; *caution* adoperare **3** *v/i* fare esercizio; **exercise bike** cyclette *f inv*; **exercise book** EDU quaderno *m* di esercizi

exhale [eksˈheɪl] esalare

exhaust [ɪgˈzɔːst] **1** *n fumes* gas *mpl* di scarico; *pipe* tubo *m* di scappamento **2** *v/t* (*tire*) estenuare; (*use up*) esaurire; **exhausted** (*tired*) esausto; **exhausting** estenuante; **exhaustion** spossatezza *f*; **exhaustive** esauriente; **exhaust pipe** tubo *m* di scappamento

exhibit [ɪgˈzɪbɪt] **1** *n in exhibition* oggetto *m* esposto; LAW prova *f* **2** *v/t of artist* esporre; (*give evidence of*) manifestare; **exhibition** esposizione *f*; *of bad behaviour* manifestazione *f*; *of skill* dimostrazione *f*

exhilarating [ɪgˈzɪləreɪtɪŋ] emozionante

exile ['eksaɪl] **1** *n* esilio *m*; *person* esiliato *m*, -a *f* **2** *v/t* esiliare

exist [ɪg'zɪst] esistere; **~ on** vivere di; **existence** esistenza *f*; **in ~** esistente; **existing** attuale

exit ['eksɪt] **1** *n* uscita *f* **2** *v/i* COMPUT uscire

exonerate [ɪg'zɒnəreɪt] scagionare

exorbitant [ɪg'zɔːbɪtənt] esorbitante

exotic [ɪg'zɒtɪk] esotico

expand [ɪk'spænd] **1** *v/t* espandere **2** *v/i* espandersi; *of metal* dilatarsi; **expanse** distesa *f*; **expansion** espansione *f*; *of metal* dilatazione *f*

expect [ɪk'spekt] **1** *v/t* aspettare; (*suppose, demand*) aspettarsi **2** *v/i*: **be ~ing** aspettare un bambino; **I ~ so** immagino di sì; **expectant mother** donna *f* in stato interessante; **expectation** aspettativa *f*

expedition [ekspɪ'dɪʃn] spedizione *f*

expel [ɪk'spel] espellere

expendable [ɪk'spendəbl] *person* sacrificabile

expenditure [ɪk'spendɪtʃə(r)] spesa *f*

expense [ɪk'spens] spesa *f*; **expenses** spese *fpl*; **expensive** caro

experience [ɪk'spɪərɪəns] **1** *n* esperienza *f* **2** *v/t pain, pleasure* provare; *difficulty* incontrare; **experienced** con esperienza

experiment [ɪk'sperɪmənt] **1** *n* sperimento *m* **2** *v/i* fare esperimenti; **experimental** sperimentale

expert ['ekspɜːt] **1** *adj* esperto **2** *n* esperto *m*, -a *f*; **expertise** competenza *f*

expiration date [ɪkspɪ'reɪʃn] *Am* data *f* di scadenza; **expire** scadere; **expiry** scadenza *f*; **expiry date** data *f* di scadenza

explain [ɪk'spleɪn] spiegare; **explanation** spiegazione *f*; **explanatory** esplicativo

explicit [ɪk'splɪsɪt] *instructions* esplicito; **explicitly** *state, forbid* esplicitamente

explode [ɪk'spləʊd] **1** *v/i of bomb* esplodere **2** *v/t bomb* fare esplodere

exploit[1] ['eksplɔɪt] *n* exploit *m inv*

exploit[2] [ɪk'splɔɪt] *v/t person, resources* sfruttare

exploitation [eksplɔɪ'teɪʃn] sfruttamento *m*

exploration [eksplə'reɪʃn] esplorazione *f*; **exploratory** *surgery* esplorativo; **explore** *country, possibility etc* esplorare; **explorer** esploratore *m*, -trice *f*

explosion [ɪk'spləʊʒn] *also in population* esplosione *f*; **explosive** esplosivo *m*

export ['ekspɔːt] **1** *n* esportazione *f*; *item* prodotto *m* di esportazione **2** *v/t goods*, COMPUT esportare; **exporter** esportatore *m*, -trice *f*

expose [ɪk'spəʊz] (*uncover*) scoprire; *scandal, person* denunciare; **exposure** esposizione *f*; *to cold weather* esposizione *f* prolungata al freddo; *of dishonest behaviour* denuncia *f*; PHOT posa *f*

express [ɪk'spres] **1** *adj* (*fast, explicit*) espresso **2** *n* (*train*) espresso *m* **3** *v/t* esprimere; **expression** espressione *f*; **expressive** espressivo; **expressly** espressamente; **expressway** autostrada *f*

expulsion [ɪk'spʌlʃn] espulsione *f*

extend [ɪk'stend] **1** *v/t* estendere; *house, repertoire* ampliare; *runway* prolungare; *contract, visa* prorogare **2** *v/i of garden etc* estendersi; **extension** *to house* annesso *m*; *of contract, visa* proroga *f*; TELEC interno *m*; **extension cable** prolunga *f*; **extensive** ampio; **extent** ampiezza *f*; **to a certain ~** fino a un certo punto

exterior [ɪk'stɪərɪə(r)] **1** *adj* esterno **2** *n of building* esterno *m*; *of person* aspetto *m* esteriore

exterminate [ɪk'stɜːmɪneɪt] sterminare

external [ɪk'stɜːnl] (*outside*) esterno

extinct [ɪk'stɪŋkt] *species*

estinto; **extinction** *of species* estinzione *f*; **extinguish** spegnere; **extinguisher** estintore *m*

extortion [ɪk'stɔːʃn] estorsione *f*

extra ['ekstrə] **1** *n* extra *m inv* 2 *adj* in più; **be ~** (*cost more*) essere a parte **3** *adv* particolarmente

extract[1] ['ekstrækt] *n* estratto *m*

extract[2] [ɪk'strækt] *v/t* estrarre; *information* estorcere

extraction [ɪk'strækʃn] estrazione *f*

extradite ['ekstrədaɪt] estradare; **extradition** estradizione *f*

extramarital [ekstrə'mærɪtl] extraconiugale

extraordinary [ɪk'strɔːdɪnərɪ] straordinario

extra 'time SP tempi *mpl* supplementari

extravagance [ɪk'strævəgəns] stravaganza *f*; **extravagant** *with money* stravagante

extreme [ɪk'striːm] **1** *n* estremo *m* **2** *adj* estremo; **extremely** estremamente; **extremist** estremista *m/f*

extrovert ['ekstrəvɜːt] estroverso *m*, -a *f*

exuberant [ɪg'zjuːbərənt] esuberante

eye [aɪ] **1** *n* occhio *m* **2** *v/t* scrutare; **eyeball** bulbo *m* oculare; **eyebrow** sopracciglio *m*; **eyecatching** appari-

fall

scente; **eyeglasses** *Am* occhiali *mpl*; **eyelid** palpebra *f*; **eyeliner** eyeliner *m inv*; **eyeshadow** ombretto *m*;

eyesight vista *f*; **eyesore** pugno *m* in un occhio; **eyewitness** testimone *m/f* oculare

F

fabric ['fæbrɪk] tessuto *m*
fabulous ['fæbjʊləs] fantastico
façade [fə'sɑːd] facciata *f*
face [feɪs] **1** *n* viso *m*, faccia *f*; **~ to ~** faccia a faccia; **lose ~** perdere la faccia **2** *v/t person, sea etc* essere di fronte a; *facts* affrontare
♦ **face up to** affrontare
'facecloth guanto *m* di spugna; **facelift** lifting *m inv* del viso; **facial** pulizia *f* del viso
facilitate [fə'sɪlɪteɪt] facilitare; **facilities** strutture *fpl*
fact [fækt] fatto *m*; **in ~, as a matter of ~** in realtà
faction ['fækʃn] fazione *f*
factor ['fæktə(r)] fattore *m*
factory ['fæktərɪ] fabbrica *f*
faculty ['fækəltɪ] facoltà *f inv*
fad [fæd] mania *f* passeggera
fade [feɪd] *v/i of colours* svanire; *of light* smorzarsi; *of memories* svanire; **faded** *colour, jeans* sbiadito
fag [fæg] F *Br cigarette* sigaretta *f*; *Am pej homosexual* finocchio *m*
fail [feɪl] **1** *v/i* fallire **2** *v/t test* essere bocciato a; *he never*

~s to write non manca mai di scrivere **2** *n*: **without ~** con certezza; **failing** difetto *m*; **failure** fallimento *m*
faint [feɪnt] **1** *adj* vago **2** *v/i* svenire; **faintly** vagamente
fair[1] [feə(r)] *(fun ~)* luna park *m inv*; COM fiera *f*
fair[2] [feə(r)] **1** *adj hair* biondo; *complexion* chiaro; *(just)* giusto **2** *adv*: **~ enough** e va bene
fairly ['feəlɪ] *treat* giustamente; *(quite)* piuttosto; **fairness** *of treatment* giustizia *f*
fairy ['feərɪ] fata; **fairy tale** fiaba *f*, favola *f*
faith [feɪθ] fede *f*; **faithful** fedele
fake [feɪk] **1** *n* falso *m* **2** *adj* falso **3** *v/t (forge)* falsificare; *(feign)* simulare
fall[1] [fɔːl] *n Am* autunno *m*
fall[2] [fɔːl] *v/i of person, night* cadere; *of prices, temperature* calare; **~ ill** ammalarsi **2** *n of person, government* caduta *f*; *in price, temperature* calo *m*
♦ **fall back on** ricorrere a
♦ **fall behind** *with work* rimanere indietro
♦ **fall for** *(fall in love with)* in-

namorarsi di; (*be deceived by*) abboccare a

◆ **fall through** *of plans* andare a monte

fallible ['fæləbl] fallibile

falling star ['fɔːlɪŋ] stella *f* cadente

false [fɔːls] falso; **false start** *in race* falsa partenza *f*; **false teeth** dentiera *f*; **falsify** falsificare

fame [feɪm] fama *f*

familiar [fə'mɪljə(r)] familiare; (*intimate*) intimo; **be ~ with sth** conoscere bene qc; **familiarity** *with subject etc* buona conoscenza *f* (**with** di); **familiarize**: **~ o.s. with ...** familiarizzarsi con ...

family ['fæmǝlɪ] famiglia *f*; **family doctor** medico *m* di famiglia; **family name** cognome *m*; **family planning** pianificazione *f* familiare; **family planning clinic** consultorio *m* per la pianificazione familiare; **family tree** albero *m* genealogico

famine ['fæmɪn] fame *f*

famous ['feɪməs] famoso; **be ~ for ...** essere noto per ...

fan¹ [fæn] *n* (*supporter*) fan *m/f*

fan² [fæn] **1** *n for cooling: electric* ventilatore *m*; *handheld* ventaglio *m* **2** *v/t*: **~ o.s.** farsi aria

fanatical [fə'nætɪkl] fanatico; **fanaticism** fanatismo *m*

'fan belt MOT cinghia *f* della ventola

fancy ['fænsɪ] **1** *adj design* stravagante **2** *n*: **as the ~ takes you** quanto ti va; **take a ~ to s.o.** prendere a benvolere qu **3** *v/t* F avere voglia di; **he fancies you** gli piaci; **fancy dress** costume *m*

fantasize ['fæntəsaɪz] fantasticare; **fantastic** (*very good*) fantastico; (*very big*) enorme; **fantasy** fantasia *f*

far [fɑː(r)] lontano; (*much*) molto; **~ away** lontano; **how ~ is it to ...?** quanto dista ...?; **as ~ as the corner** fino all'angolo; **as ~ as I know** per quanto ne so; **you've gone too ~** *in behaviour* sei andato troppo oltre; **so ~ so good** fin qui tutto bene

farce [fɑːs] farsa *f*

fare [feə(r)] *n for travel* tariffa *f*

Far East Estremo Oriente *m*

farewell [feə'wel] addio *m*

farfetched [fɑː'fetʃt] inverosimile

farm [fɑːm] fattoria *f*

◆ **farm out** dare in appalto

farmer ['fɑːmə(r)] agricoltore *m*, -trice *f*; **farmhouse** cascina *f*; **farming** agricoltura *f*; **farmworker** bracciante *m/f*; **farmyard** cortile *m* di una cascina

far-'off lontano; **farsighted** previdente; *optically* presbi-

fear

te

fart [fɑːt] **1** *n* F scoreggia *f* F, peto *m* **2** *v/i* F scoreggiare F, petare

farther ['fɑːðə(r)] più lontano; **farthest** più lontano

fascinate ['fæsɪneɪt] affascinare; **fascinating** affascinante; **fascination** *with subject* fascino *m*

fascism ['fæʃɪzm] fascismo *m*; **fascist 1** *n* fascista *m/f* **2** *adj* fascista

fashion ['fæʃn] moda *f*; (*manner*) maniera *f*, modo *m*; **in** ~ alla moda; **out of** ~ fuori moda; **fashionable** alla moda; **fashionably** alla moda; **fashion-conscious** fanatico della moda; **fashion designer** stilista *m/f*; **fashion show** sfilata *f* di moda

fast[1] [fɑːst] **1** *adj* veloce, rapido; **be** ~ *of clock* essere avanti **2** *adv* velocemente, in fretta; ~ **asleep** profondamente addormentato

fast[2] [fɑːst] *n not eating* digiuno *m*

fasten ['fɑːsn] **1** *v/t* chiudere; *dress, seat-belt* allacciare; ~ **sth onto sth** attaccare qc a qc **2** *v/i of dress etc* allacciarsi; **fastener** chiusura *f*

'fast food fast food *m*; **fast forward 1** *n on video etc* avvolgimento *m* rapido **2** *v/i* riavvolgere rapidamente; **fast lane** *on road* corsia *f* di sorpasso; **in the** ~ *fig: of life* a

cento all'ora; **fast train** rapido *m*

fat [fæt] **1** *adj* grasso **2** *n* grasso *m*

fatal ['feɪtl] fatale

fatality [fə'tælətɪ] vittima *f*; **fatally**: ~ **injured** ferito a morte

fate [feɪt] fato *m*

'fat free privo di grassi

father ['fɑːðə(r)] padre *m*; **Father Christmas** Babbo *m* Natale; **fatherhood** paternità *f*; **father-in-law** suocero *m*; **fatherly** paterno

fatigue [fə'tiːg] stanchezza *f*

fatten ['fætn] *animal* ingrassare; **fatty 1** *adj* grasso **2** *n* F *person* ciccione *m*, -a *f* F

faucet ['fɔːsɪt] *Am* rubinetto *m*

fault [fɔːlt] *n* (*defect*) difetto *m*; **it's your / my** ~ è colpa tua / mia; **find** ~ **with** criticare; **faultless** impeccabile; **faulty** difettoso

favor *etc Am* ☞ **favour** *etc*

favour ['feɪvə(r)] **1** *n* favore *m*; **do s.o. a** ~ fare un favore a qu; **in** ~ **of** ... a favore di ... **2** *v/t* (*prefer*) preferire, prediligere; **favourable** favorevole; **favourite 1** *n* prediletto *m*, -a *f*; *food* piatto *m* preferito; *in race, competition* favorito *m*, -a *f* **2** *adj* preferito; **favouritism** favoritismo *m*

fax [fæks] **1** *n* fax *m inv* **2** *v/t document* inviare per fax

fear [fɪə(r)] **1** *n* paura *f* **2** *v/t*

avere paura di; **fearless** intrepido; **fearlessly** intrepidamente

feasibility study [fiːzəˈbɪlətɪ] studio *m* di fattibilità; **feasible** fattibile

feast [fiːst] banchetto *m*

feat [fiːt] prodezza *f*

feather [ˈfeðə(r)] piuma *f*

feature [ˈfiːtʃə(r)] **1** *n* on face tratto *m*; *of city, building, style* caratteristica *f*; *in newspaper* servizio *m*; *film* lungometraggio *m*; **make a ~ of ...** mettere l'accento su ... **2** *v/t of film* avere come protagonista; **feature film** lungometraggio *m*

February [ˈfebrʊərɪ] febbraio *m*

federal [ˈfedərəl] federale; **federation** federazione *f*

fed 'up F: **be ~ with ...** essere stufo di ... F

fee [fiː] tariffa *f*; *of lawyer, doctor etc* onorario *m*

feeble [ˈfiːbl] debole

feed [fiːd] nutrire; *family* mantenere; *baby* dare da mangiare a; **feedback** riscontro *m*, feedback *m*

feel [fiːl] **1** *v/t (touch)* toccare; *(sense)* sentire; *pain, pleasure* sentire; *(think)* pensare **2** *v/i* sentirsi; **it ~s like silk** sembra seta; **I ~ tired** sono stanco; **how are you ~ today?** come ti senti oggi?; **do you ~ like a drink?** hai voglia di bere qualcosa?; **I**

don't ~ like it non ne ho voglia

◆ **feel up to** sentirsi in grado di

feeler [ˈfiːlə(r)] *of insect* antenna *f*; **feeling** sentimento *m*; *(emotion)* sensazione *f*; *(sensation)* sensibilità *f*

feet [fiːt] *pl* ☞ **foot**

fellow 'citizen concittadino *m*, -a *f*

felony [ˈfelənɪ] delitto *m*

felt [felt] feltro *m*; **felt tip**, **felt-tip(ped) pen** pennarello *m*

female [ˈfiːmeɪl] **1** femmina *f*; *typical of women* femminile **2** *n* femmina *f*; F *(woman)* donna *f*

feminine [ˈfemɪnɪn] **1** *adj* femminile **2** *n* GRAM femminile *m*; **feminism** femminismo *m*; **feminist 1** *n* femminista *f* **2** *adj* femminista

fence [fens] *n* recinto *m*; **sit on the ~** non prendere partito

fender [ˈfendə(r)] *Am* parafango *m*

fermentation [fɜːmenˈteɪʃn] fermentazione *f*

ferocious [fəˈrəʊʃəs] feroce

ferry [ˈferɪ] traghetto *m*

fertile [ˈfɜːtaɪl] fertile; **fertility** fertilità *f*, **fertilize** *for soil* rendere fertile; **fertilizer** *for soil* fertilizzante *m*

fervent [ˈfɜːvənt] fervente

fester [ˈfestə(r)] *of wound* fare infezione

festival [ˈfestɪvl] festival *m*

385   **file**

inv; **festive** festivo; **the ~
season** le festività; **festivities** festeggiamenti *mpl*

fetal ['fiːtl] fetale

fetch [fetʃ] andare / venire a
prendere; *thing* prendere;
price rendere

fetus ['fiːtəs] feto *m*

feud [fjuːd] **1** *n* faida *f* **2** *v/i* litigare

fever ['fiːvə(r)] febbre *f*; **fe-
verish** *also fig* febbrile

few [fjuː] **1** *adj* pochi; **a ~ people** alcune persone, qualche
persona; **a ~ books** alcuni libri, qualche libro; **quite a ~,
a good ~** (*a lot*) parecchi **2**
pron (*not many*) pochi; **a ~**
(*some*) alcuni; **quite a ~,
a good ~** (*a lot*) parecchi; **few-
er** meno (**than** di)

fiancé [fɪˈɒnseɪ] fidanzato *m*;
fiancée fidanzata *f*

fiasco [fɪˈæskəʊ] fiasco *m*

fiber *Am* = **fibre**

fibre ['faɪbə(r)] fibra *f*; **fibre
optics** tecnologia *f* delle fibre ottiche; **fibreglass** fibra
f di vetro

fickle ['fɪkl] incostante

fiction ['fɪkʃn] narrativa *f*;
(*made-up story*) storia *f*; **fic-
tional** immaginario; **fic-
titious** fittizio

fiddle ['fɪdl] **1** *n* F (*violin*) violino *m*; **it's a ~** F (*cheat*) è una
fregatura F **2** *v/i*: **~ with ...**
giocherellare con ...; **~
around with ...** trafficare
con ... **3** *v/t accounts* truccare

fidget ['fɪdʒɪt] agitarsi; **fidg-
ety** in agitazione

field [fiːld] campo *m*; (*competitors in race*) formazione *f*;
fielder SP esterno *m*

fierce [fɪəs] *animal* feroce;
storm violento; **fiercely** fero-
cemente

fiery ['faɪərɪ] focoso

fifteen [fɪfˈtiːn] quindici; **fifteenth** quindicesimo; **fifth**
quinto; **fiftieth** cinquantesimo; **fifty** cinquanta; **fifty-fif-
ty** metà e metà

fig [fɪg] fico *m*

fight [faɪt] **1** *n* lotta *f*; *in war*
combattimento *m*; (*argu-
ment*) litigio *m*; *in boxing* incontro *m* **2** *v/t* combattere;
injustice, fire lottare contro;
in boxing battersi contro **3**
v/i in war combattere; *of
drunks, schoolkids* azzuffarsi; (*argue*) litigare; **fighter**
combattente *m/f*; *aeroplane*
caccia *m inv*; (*boxer*) pugile
m; **she's a ~** è combattiva;
fighting rissa *fpl*; MIL lotta *f*

figurative ['fɪgjərətɪv] *use of
word* figurato; *art* figurativo

figure ['fɪgə(r)] *n* (*digit*) cifra *f*;
of person linea *f*; (*form,
shape*) figura *f*

♦ **figure on** F (*plan*) contare
(di)

♦ **figure out** (*understand*) capire; *calculation* calcolare

file[1] [faɪl] **1** *n for papers* raccoglitore *m*; *contents* dossier *m
inv*; COMPUT file *m inv*; **on ~**

file

in archivio **2** *v/t documents* schedare

file² [faɪl] *n for wood, finger-nails* lima *f*

filing cabinet ['faɪlɪŋ], *Am* **file cabinet** schedario *m*

fill [fɪl] riempire; *tooth* otturare

◆ **fill in** *form* compilare; *hole* riempire; **fill s.o. in** mettere al corrente qu

◆ **fill out 1** *v/t form* compilare **2** *v/i (get fatter)* arrotondarsi

fillet ['fɪlɪt] filetto *m*

filling ['fɪlɪŋ] **1** *n in sandwich* ripieno *m; in tooth* otturazione *f* **2** *adj food* pesante; **filling station** stazione *f* di rifornimento

film [fɪlm] **1** *n in camera* pellicola *f; at cinema* film *m inv* **2** *v/t* filmare; *scene* girare; **film-maker** regista *m/f;* **film star** stella *f* del cinema

filter ['fɪltə(r)] **1** *n* filtro *m* **2** *v/t* filtrare

filth [fɪlθ] sporcizia *f;* **filthy** sporco; *language etc* volgare

final ['faɪnl] **1** *adj* finale **2** *n* SP finale *f;* **finale** finale *m;* **finalist** finalista *m/f;* **finalize** mettere a punto; **finally** infine; *(at last)* finalmente

finance ['faɪnæns] **1** *n* finanza *f* **2** *v/t* finanziare; **financial** finanziario; **financially** finanziariamente; **financial year** anno *m* fiscale; **financier** finanziatore *m,* -trice *f*

find [faɪnd] trovare

◆ **find out** scoprire

findings ['faɪndɪŋz] *of report* conclusioni *fpl*

fine¹ [faɪn] *day, weather, city* bello; *wine, performance* buono; *distinction, line* sottile; **how's that? – that's ~** com'è? – va benissimo; **that's ~ by me** a me sta bene

fine² [faɪn] **1** *n penalty* multa *f* **2** *v/t* multare

finger ['fɪŋgə(r)] **1** *n* dito *m* **2** *v/t* passare le dita su; **fingernail** unghia *f;* **fingerprint** impronta *f* digitale

finicky ['fɪnɪkɪ] *person* pignolo; *design* complicato

finish ['fɪnɪʃ] **1** *v/t* finire; **~ doing sth** finire di fare qc **2** *v/i* finire **3** *n of product* finitura *f*

◆ **finish up** *food* finire; **he finished up liking London** Londra ha finito per piacergli

◆ **finish with** *boyfriend etc* lasciare

'finishing line traguardo *m*

Finland ['fɪnlənd] Finlandia *f;* **Finn** finlandese *m/f;* **Finnish 1** *adj* finlandese, finnico **2** *n language* finlandese *m*

fir [fɜː(r)] abete *m*

fire ['faɪə(r)] **1** *n* fuoco *m; (blaze)* incendio *m; bonfire, campfire etc* falò *m inv;* **be on ~** essere in fiamme; **catch ~** prendere fuoco; **set sth on ~, set ~ to sth** dare fuoco a qc **2** *v/i (shoot)* sparare **3** *v/t* F *(dismiss)* li-

cenziare; **fire alarm** allarme
m antincendio; **firearm** arma *f* da fuoco; **fire brigade**
vigili *mpl* del fuoco; **firecracker** petardo *m*; **fire department** *Am* vigili *mpl* del
fuoco; **fire engine** autopompa *f*; **fire escape** scala *f* antincendio; **fire extinguisher**
estintore *m*; **fire fighter**
pompiere *m*; **fireman** pompiere *m*; **fireplace** camino
m; **fire station** caserma *f*
dei pompieri; **fire truck** autopompa *f*; **fireworks** fuochi
mpl d'artificio

firm[1] [fɜːm] *adj* grip, handshake energico; *muscles* sodo; *voice, parents* deciso; *decision* risoluto; *date, offer* definitivo; *control* rigido; *foundations* solido; *believer* convinto

firm[2] [fɜːm] *n* COM azienda *f*

first [fɜːst] **1** *adj* primo **2** *n* primo *m*, -a *f* **3** *adv* arrive, finish
per primo; (*beforehand*) prima; **~ of all** (*for one reason*)
innanzitutto; **at ~** in un primo tempo, al principio; **first
aid** pronto soccorso *m*; **first
class 1** *adj* di prima classe **2**
adv travel in prima classe;
first floor primo piano *m*;
piano *m* terra; **First Lady**
First Lady *f inv*; **firstly** in
primo luogo; **first name** nome
m di battesimo; **first
night** prima serata *f*; **first-rate** di prima qualità

fiscal ['fɪskl] fiscale; **fiscal
year** *Am* anno *m* fiscale

fish [fɪʃ] **1** *n* pesce *m* **2** *v/i* pescare; **fisherman** pescatore
m; **fish finger** bastoncino
m di pesce; **fishing** pesca
f; **fishing boat** peschereccio
m; **fishing rod** canna *f* da
pesca; **fishmonger** pescivendolo *m*; **fish stick** *Am*
bastoncino *m* di pesce; **fishy**
F (*suspicious*) sospetto

fist [fɪst] pugno *m*

fit[1] [fɪt] *n* MED attacco *m*; ***a ~
of jealousy*** un accesso di
gelosia

fit[2] [fɪt] *adj* physically in forma; morally adatto; ***keep ~***
tenersi in forma

fit[3] [fɪt] **1** *v/t of clothes* andare
bene a; (*attach*) installare **2**
v/i of clothes andare bene;
of piece of furniture etc starci

fitness ['fɪtnɪs] *physical* forma
f; **fitting** appropriato; **fittings** equipaggiamento *msg*

five [faɪv] cinque

fix [fɪks] **1** *n* (*solution*) soluzione *f* **2** *v/t* (*attach, arrange*) fissare; (*repair*) aggiustare;
lunch preparare; *dishonestly:
match etc* manipolare; **fixed**
in position fisso; *timescale,
exchange rate* stabilito

fizzy ['fɪzɪ] *drink* gassato

flab [flæb] *on body* ciccia *f*;
flabby *muscles* flaccido

flag[1] [flæg] *n* bandiera *f*

flag[2] [flæg] *v/i* (*tire*) soccombere

'flagpole asta f

flagrant ['fleigrənt] flagrante

flair [fleə(r)] (talent) talento m; (style) stile m

flake [fleik] of snow fiocco m; of paint, plaster scaglia f

flamboyant [flæm'bɔɪənt] personality esuberante; flamboyantly in modo vistoso

flame [fleim] n fiamma f; go up in ~s incendiarsi

flammable ['flæməbl] infiammabile

flank [flæŋk] 1 n fianco m 2 v/t: be ~ed by essere affiancato da

flannel ['flænl] guanto m di spugna

flap [flæp] 1 n of envelope, pocket falda f; of table ribalta f; be in a ~ F essere in fibrillazione F 2 v/t wings sbattere 3 v/i of flag etc sventolare

◆ flare up [fler] of violence, illness esplodere; of fire divampare

flash [flæʃ] 1 n of light lampo m; PHOT flash m inv; in a ~ F in un istante; ~ of lightning lampo m 2 v/i of light lampeggiare 3 v/t: ~ one's headlights lampeggiare; flashback in film flashback m inv; flashlight pila f; PHOT flash m inv; flashy pej appariscente

flask [flɑːsk] (vacuum ~) termos m inv

flat¹ [flæt] 1 adj piatto; beer sgassato; battery, tyre a terra;

shoes basso; A / B ~ MUS la / si bemolle; and that's ~ F punto e basta F 2 adv MUS sotto tonalità; ~ out work, run a tutto gas 3 n gomma f a terra

flat² [flæt] n (apartment) appartamento m

flatly ['flætli] refuse, deny risolutamente; flatmate compagno m, -a f di appartamento; flat rate tariffa f forfettaria; flat screen monitor schermo m piatto; flatten land, road livellare; by bombing, demolition radere al suolo

flatter ['flætə(r)] adulare; flatterer adulatore m, -trice f; flattering comments lusinghiero; Jane's dress is very ~ il vestito di Jane le dona molto; flattery adulazione f

flavor Am ◊ flavour

flavour ['fleɪvə(r)] 1 n gusto m 2 v/t food insaporire; flavouring aroma m

flaw [flɔː] difetto m; flawless perfetto

flea [fliː] pulce f

flee [fliː] scappare

fleet [fliːt] NAUT flotta f; of taxis, trucks parco m macchine

fleeting ['fliːtɪŋ] visit etc di sfuggita

flesh [fleʃ] carne f; of fruit polpa f

flex [fleks] 1 v/t muscles flettere 2 n ELEC cavo m; flex(i)-time orario m flessibile

flush

flexibility flessibilità *f*; **flexible** flessibile

flicker ['flɪkə(r)] *of light* tremolare

flier ['flaɪə(r)] *(circular)* volantino *m*

flight [flaɪt] volo *m*; *(fleeing)* fuga *f*; **~ (of stairs)** rampa *f* (di scale); **flight attendant** assistente *m/f* di volo; **flight deck** *in plane* cabina *f* di pilotaggio; *of aircraft carrier* ponte *m* di decollo; **flight number** numero *m* di volo; **flight path** rotta *f* (di volo); **flight recorder** registratore *m* (di volo); **flight time** *departure* orario *m* di volo; *duration* durata *f* di volo; **flighty** volubile

flimsy ['flɪmzɪ] *furniture* leggero; *dress, material* sottile; *excuse* debole

flinch [flɪntʃ] sobbalzare

flipper ['flɪpə(r)] *for swimming* pinna *f*

flirt [flɜːt] **1** *v/i* flirtare **2** *n* flirt *m inv*; **flirtatious** civettuolo

float [fləʊt] galleggiare; FIN fluttuare

flock [flɒk] **1** *n of sheep* gregge *m* **2** *v/i* accorrere in massa

flood [flʌd] **1** *n* inondazione *f* **2** *v/t of river* inondare; **flooding** inondazione *f*; **floodlight** riflettore *m*; **flood waters** acque *fpl* di inondazione

floor [flɔː(r)] pavimento *m*; *(story)* piano *m*; **floorboard**

asse *f* del pavimento; **floorlamp** *Am* lampada *f* a stelo

flop [flɒp] **1** *v/i* crollare; F *(fail)* fare fiasco **2** *n* F *(failure)* fiasco *m*; **floppy (disk)** floppy *m inv*, **floppy disk** *m inv*

Florence ['florəns] Firenze *f*; **Florentine 1** *adj* fiorentino **2** *n* fiorentino *m*, -a *f*

florist ['florɪst] fiorista *m/f*

flour ['flaʊə(r)] farina *f*

flourish ['flʌrɪʃ] fiorire; *of business, civilization* prosperare; **flourishing** *business, trade* prospero

flow [fləʊ] **1** *v/i of river, traffic, current* scorrere; *of work* procedere **2** *n of river, ideas* flusso *m*; **flowchart** diagramma *m* (di flusso)

flower ['flaʊə(r)] **1** *n* fiore *m* **2** *v/i* fiorire; **flowerpot** vaso *m* per fiori

flu [fluː] influenza *f*

fluctuate ['flʌktjʊeɪt] oscillare; **fluctuation** oscillazione *f*

fluency ['fluːənsɪ] *in a language* scioltezza *f*; **fluent** fluente; **he speaks ~ Spanish** parla correntemente lo spagnolo; **fluently** *speak, write* correntemente

fluid ['fluːɪd] fluido *m*

flunk [flʌŋk] *Am* F essere bocciato a

flush [flʌʃ] **1** *v/t toilet* tirare l'acqua di **2** *v/i (go red)* diventare rosso **3** *adj (level)* a filo; **~ with ...** a filo con ...

flute [flu:t] MUS flauto *m* traverso

flutter ['flʌtə(r)] *of wings* sbattere; *of flag* sventolare; *of heart* battere forte

fly[1] [flaɪ] *n insect* mosca *f*

fly[2] [flaɪ] *n on trousers* patta *f*

fly[3] [flaɪ] **1** *v/i* volare; *of flag* sventolare; (*rush*) precipitarsi; **~ into a rage** perdere le staffe **2** *v/t aeroplane* pilotare; *airline* volare con; (*transport by air*) spedire per via aerea

◆ **fly away** *of bird, plane* volare via

◆ **fly back** (*travel back*) ritornare (in aereo)

◆ **fly past** *of time* volare

flying ['flaɪɪŋ] volare *m*; **flyover** MOT cavalcavia *m inv*

foam [fəʊm] *on liquid* schiuma *f*; **foam rubber** gommapiuma® *f*

focus ['fəʊkəs] *of attention* centro *m*; PHOT fuoco *m*; **be in ~ / be out of ~** PHOT essere a fuoco / non essere a fuoco

◆ **focus on** *issue* focalizzare l'attenzione su; PHOT mettere a fuoco

fodder ['fɒdə(r)] foraggio *m*

fog [fɒg] nebbia *f*; **foggy** nebbioso

foil[1] [fɔɪl] *n* carta *f* stagnola

foil[2] [fɔɪl] *v/t* (*thwart*) sventare

fold [fəʊld] **1** *v/t paper etc* piegare; **~ one's arms** incrociare le braccia **2** *v/i of business*

chiudere i battenti **3** *n in cloth etc* piega *f*

◆ **fold up** *of chairs etc* chiudere; *clothes* piegare **2** *v/i of chair, table* chiudere

folder ['fəʊldə(r)] *for documents* cartellina *f*; COMPUT directory *f inv*; **folding** pieghevole

foliage ['fəʊlɪɪdʒ] fogliame *m*

folk [fəʊk] (*people*) gente *f*; **my ~** (*family*) i miei parenti; **come in, ~s** F entrate, gente F; **folk music** musica *f* folk; **folk singer** cantante *m/f* folk; **folk song** canzone *f* popolare

follow ['fɒləʊ] **1** *v/t* (*also understand*) seguire **2** *v/i* seguire; *logically* quadrare; **as ~s** quanto segue

◆ **follow up** *inquiry* dare seguito a

follower ['fɒləʊə(r)] *of politician etc* seguace *m/f*; *of football team* tifoso *m*, -a *f*; **following 1** *adj* seguente **2** *n people* seguito *m*; **the ~** quanto segue

fond [fɒnd] (*loving*) affezionato; *memory* caro; **he is ~ of travel** gli piace viaggiare; **I'm very ~ of him** gli voglio molto

fondle ['fɒndl] accarezzare

fondness ['fɒndnɪs] *for person* affetto *m*; *for wine, food* gusto *m*

font [fɒnt] *for printing* carattere *m*; *in church* fonte *f* batte-

simale
food [fuːd] cibo *m; Italian ~* la cucina italiana; *there's no ~ in the house* non c'è niente da mangiare in casa; **foodie** buongustaio *m,* -a *f;* **food poisoning** intossicazione *f* alimentare

fool [fuːl] **1** *n* pazzo *m,* -a *f; make a ~ of o.s.* rendersi ridicolo **2** *v/t* ingannare; **foolhardy** temerario; **foolish** sciocco; **foolproof** a prova di idiota

foot [fut] *(pl feet* [fiːt]) *also measurement* piede *m; on ~* a piedi; *at the ~ of the page* a piè di pagina; *put one's ~ in it* F fare una gaffe; **footage** pellicola *f* cinematografica; **football** *(soccer)* calcio *m; American football m* americano; *(ball)* pallone *m* da calcio; *for American football* pallone *m* da football americano; **footballer** calciatore *m,* -trice *f;* **football pitch** campo *m* da calcio; **football player** *soccer* calciatore *m,* -trice *f; American style* giocatore *m* di football americano; **foothills** colline *fpl* pedemontane; **footnote** nota *f* a piè di pagina; **footpath** sentiero *m;* **footprint** impronta *f* di piede; **footstep** passo *m*

for [fɔː(r)] per; *a train ~ ...* un treno per ...; *what is this ~?* a cosa serve?; *what ~?* a che

scopo?, perché?; *~ three days* per tre giorni; *I am ~ the idea* sono a favore dell'idea; *how much did you sell it ~?* a quanto l'hai venduto?

forbid [fə'bɪd] vietare, proibire *(to do* di fare); **forbidden** vietato, proibito; *smoking ~* vietato fumare; *parking ~* divieto di sosta; **forbidding** ostile

force [fɔːs] **1** *n* forza *f; come into ~* of *law* entrare in vigore; *the ~s* MIL le forze armate **2** *v/t door, lock* forzare; *~ s.o. to do sth* forzare *or* costringere qu a fare qc; **forced** forzato; **forced landing** atterraggio *m* d'emergenza; **forceful** *argument, speaker* convincente; *character* energico

forceps ['fɔːseps] MED forcipe *f*

forcibly ['fɔːsəblɪ] *restrain* con la forza

foreboding [fə'bəʊdɪŋ] presentimento *m;* **forecast 1** *n* previsione *f* **2** *v/t* prevedere; **forefathers** antenati *mpl;* **forefinger** indice *m;* **foregone**: *that's a ~ conclusion* è una conclusione scontata; **foreground** primo piano *m;* **forehand** *in tennis* diritto *m;* **forehead** fronte *f*

foreign ['fɒrən] straniero, *trade, policy* estero; **foreign affairs** affari *mpl* esteri; **foreign body** corpo *m* estra-

foreign currency 392

neo; **foreign currency** valuta *f* estera; **foreigner** straniero *m*, -a *f*; **foreign exchange** cambio *m* valutario; **Foreign Office** Ministero *m* degli esteri; **Foreign Secretary** *in UK* ministro *m* degli esteri

'foreman caposquadra *m*;

foremost 1 *adv* (*uppermost*) soprattutto **2** *adj* (*leading*) principale

forensic 'medicine [fə'renzık] medicina *f* legale; **forensic scientist** medico *m* legale

'forerunner precursore *m*;

fore'see prevedere; **foresight** lungimiranza *f*

forest ['fɒrɪst] foresta *f*; **forestry** scienze *fpl* forestali

fore'tell predire

forever [fə'revə(r)] per sempre

foreword ['fɔːwɜːd] prefazione *f*

forfeit ['fɔːfɪt] *right, privilege etc* perdere

forge [fɔːdʒ] (*counterfeit*) contraffare; *signature* falsificare; **forgery** (*banknote*) falsificazione *f*; (*document*) falso *m*

forget [fə'get] dimenticare; **forgetful** smemorato

forgive [fə'gɪv] perdonare; **forgiveness** perdono *m*

fork [fɔːk] *for eating* forchetta *f*; *for gardening* forca *f*; *in road* biforcazione *f*; **forklift truck** muletto *m*

form [fɔːm] **1** *n* (*shape*) forma

f; (*document*) modulo *m*; *in school* classe *f*; **be on / off** ~ essere in / fuori forma **2** *v/t in clay etc* modellare; *friendship* creare; (*constitute*) costituire **3** *v/i* (*take shape, develop*) formarsi; **formal** formale; **formality** formalità *f inv*; **formally** formalmente

format ['fɔːmæt] **1** *v/t diskette* formattare; *document* impaginare **2** *n* (*size: of magazine etc*) formato *m*; (*makeup: of programme*) formula *f*

formation [fɔː'meɪʃn] formazione *f*

former ['fɔːmə(r)] *wife, president* ex *inv*; *statement, arrangement* precedente; **the** ~ quest'ultimo; **formerly** precedentemente

formidable ['fɔːmɪdəbl] imponente

formula ['fɔːmjʊlə] formula *f*

fort [fɔːt] MIL forte *m*

forthcoming ['fɔːθkʌmɪŋ] (*future*) prossimo; *personality* comunicativo

'forthright schietto

fortieth ['fɔːtɪɪθ] quarantesimo, -a

fortnight ['fɔːtnaɪt] due settimane

fortress ['fɔːtrɪs] MIL fortezza *f*

fortunate ['fɔːtʃʊnət] fortunato; **fortunately** fortunatamente; **fortune** sorte *f*; (*lot* of money) fortuna f; **tell s.o.'s ~** predire il futuro a qu; **fortune-teller** chiromante m/f

forty ['fɔːtɪ] quaranta

Forum ['fɔːrəm] *Roman* foro m

forward ['fɔːwəd] **1** adv avanti **2** adj pej: person diretto **3** n SP attaccante m **4** v/t letter inoltrare; **forwarding agent** COM spedizioniere m; **forward-looking** progressista

fossil ['fɒsəl] fossile m

foster ['fɒstə(r)] child avere in affidamento; attitude, belief incoraggiare; **foster parents** genitori mpl con affidamento

foul [faʊl] **1** n SP fallo m **2** adj smell pessimo; weather orribile **3** v/t SP fare un fallo contro

found [faʊnd] school etc fondare; **foundation** of theory etc fondamenta fpl; (organization) fondazione f; make-up fondotinta m; **foundations** of building fondamenta fpl; **founder** fondatore m, -trice f

fountain ['faʊntɪn] fontana f

four [fɔː(r)] quattro; **four-star** hotel etc a quattro stelle; **fourteen** quattordici; **fourteenth** quattordicesimo; **fourth** quarto; **four-wheel drive** MOT quattro per quattro m inv

fox [fɒks] **1** n volpe f **2** v/t (puzzle) mettere in difficoltà

foyer ['fɔɪeɪ] atrio m

fraction ['frækʃn] frazione f; **fractionally** lievemente

fracture ['fræktʃə(r)] **1** n frattura f **2** v/t fratturare

fragile ['frædʒaɪl] fragile

fragment ['frægmənt] frammento m

fragrance ['freɪgrəns] fragranza f; **fragrant** profumato

frail [freɪl] gracile

frame [freɪm] **1** n of picture, window cornice f; of glasses montatura f; of bicycle telaio m; **~ of mind** stato m d'animo **2** v/t picture incorniciare; F person incastrare F; **framework** struttura f

France [frɑːns] Francia f

franchise ['fræntʃaɪz] for business concessione f

frank [fræŋk] franco; **frankly** francamente; **frankness** franchezza f

frantic ['fræntɪk] attempt frenetico; (worried) agitatissimo

fraternal [frə'tɜːnl] fraterno

fraud [frɔːd] frode f; person impostore m, -trice f; **fraudulent** fraudolento

frayed [freɪd] cuffs liso

freak [friːk] **1** n unusual event fenomeno m anomalo; two-headed person etc scherzo m di natura; F strange person tipo m, -a f strambo, -a; **movie ~** F (fanatic) fanatico

freckle 394

m, -a *f* del cinema **2** *adj* wind, storm violento

freckle ['frekl] lentiggine *f*

free [fri:] **1** *adj* libero; *(no cost)* gratuito; **for** ~ *travel, get sth* gratis **2** *v/t prisoners* liberare; **freedom** libertà *f*; **free enterprise** liberalismo *m* economico; **freefone number** numero *m* verde; **free kick** *in soccer* calcio *m* di punizione; **freelance** free lance *inv*; **freely** *admit* apertamente; **free sample** campione *m* gratuito; **free speech** libertà *f* di espressione; **freeway** *Am* autostrada *f*

freeze [fri:z] **1** *v/t* gelare; *wages, account* congelare; *video* bloccare **2** *v/i of water* gelare; **freeze-dried** liofilizzato; **freezer** freezer *m inv*, congelatore *m*; **freezing 1** *adj* gelato; **it's ~ (cold)** *of weather* si gela; *of water* è gelata; **I'm ~** sono congelato **2** *n*: **10 below ~** 10 gradi sotto zero

freight [freɪt] carico *m*; *costs* trasporto *m*; **freighter** *ship* nave *f* da carico; *plane* aereo *f* da carico

French [frentʃ] **1** *adj* francese **2** *n (language)* francese *m*; **the ~** i francesi; **French fries** patate *fpl* fritte; **Frenchman** francese *m*; **French windows** vetrata *f*; **Frenchwoman** francese *f*

frenzied ['frenzɪd] *attack, activity* frenetico; *mob* impaz-

zito; **frenzy** frenesia *f*

frequency ['fri:kwənsɪ] frequenza *f*

frequent[1] ['fri:kwənt] *adj* frequente

frequent[2] [frɪ'kwent] *v/t bar etc* frequentare

frequently ['fri:kwentlɪ] frequentemente

fresh [freʃ] fresco; *start* nuovo; *Am (impertinent)* sfacciato; **fresh air** aria *f* fresca

♦ **freshen up** ['freʃn] **1** *v/i* rinfrescarsi **2** *v/t room, paintwork* rinfrescare

freshly ['freʃlɪ] appena; **freshman** studente *m* del primo anno, matricola *f*; **freshwater** d'acqua dolce

friction ['frɪkʃn] PHYS frizione *f*; *between people* attrito *m*

Friday ['fraɪdeɪ] venerdì *m inv*

fridge [frɪdʒ] frigo *m*

fried egg [fraɪd] uovo *m* fritto

friend [frend] amico *m*, -a *f*; **make** ~**s** fare amicizia; **friendliness** amichevolezza *f*; **friendly 1** *adj* amichevole; *(easy to use)* facile da usare; **be** ~ **with s.o.** *(be friends)* essere amico di qu **2** *n* SP amichevole *f*; **friendship** amicizia *f*

fries [fraɪz] patate *fpl* fritte

fright [fraɪt] paura *f*; **frighten** spaventare; **be** ~**ed (of)** aver paura (di); **frightening** spaventoso

frill [frɪl] *on dress etc* volant *m inv*; ~**s** *(fancy extras)* fronzoli *mpl*

fringe ['frɪndʒ] frangia *f*; *(edge)* margini *mpl*; **fringe benefits** benefici *mpl* accessori

frisk [frɪsk] frugare F

♦ **fritter away** ['frɪtə(r)] *time, fortune* sprecare

frivolity [frɪ'vɒlɪtɪ] frivolezza *f*; **frivolous** frivolo

frizzy ['frɪzɪ] *hair* crespo

frog [frɒg] rana *f*; **frogman** sommozzatore *m*

from [from] ◇ *in time* da; **~ 9 to 5 (o'clock)** dalle 9 alle 5; **~ today on** da oggi in poi ◇ *in space* da; **~ here to there** da qui a lì ◇ *origin* di; **a letter ~ Jo** una lettera di Jo; **I am ~ Liverpool** sono di Liverpool ◇ *(because of)* di: **tired ~ the journey** stanco del viaggio; **it's ~ overeating** è a causa del troppo mangiare

front [frʌnt] **1** *n of building* lato *m* principale; *of car, statue* davanti *m inv*; *of book* copertina *f*; *(cover organization)* facciata *f*; MIL, *of weather* fronte *m*; **in ~** davanti; **in ~ of** davanti *f of* car *of* wheel, *seat* anteriore **3** *v/t* TV *programme* presentare; **front door** porta *f* principale

frontier ['frʌntɪə(r)] *also fig* frontiera *f*

'**front line** MIL fronte *m*; **front page** *of newspaper* prima pagina *f*; **front-wheel drive** trazione *f* anteriore

frost [frɒst] brina *f*; **frostbite**

congelamento *m*; **frosting** *Am on cake* glassatura *f*; **frosty** *also fig* gelido

froth [frɒθ] spuma *f*

frown [fraun] **1** *n* cipiglio *m* **2** *v/i* aggrottare le sopracciglia

frozen ['frəʊzn] gelato; *wastes* gelido; *food* surgelato; **I'm ~** F sono congelato F

fruit [fruːt] frutto *m*; *collective* frutta *f*; **fruitful** *discussions etc* fruttuoso; **fruit juice** succo *m* di frutta; **fruit machine** slot machine *f inv*; **fruit salad** macedonia *f*

frustrate [frʌ'streɪt] *person* frustrare; *plans* scombussolare; **frustrating** frustrante; **frustration** frustrazione *f*; **sexual ~** insoddisfazione *f* sessuale V

fry [fraɪ] friggere; **frying pan** padella *f*

fuck [fʌk] V scopare V; **~!** cazzo! V

fuel ['fjuːəl] **1** *n* carburante *m* **2** *v/t fig* alimentare

fugitive ['fjuːdʒətɪv] *n* fuggiasco *m*, -a *f*

fulfil, *Am* **fulfill** [fʊl'fɪl] *dreams* realizzare; *contract* eseguire; *requirements* corrispondere a; **feel ~led** *in job, life* sentirsi soddisfatto; **fulfilment**, *Am* **fulfillment** *of contract* esecuzione *f*; *of dreams* realizzazione *f*; *moral, spiritual* soddisfazione *f*

full [fʊl] pieno (**of** di); *account* esauriente; *life* intenso; **~ up**

hotel, with food pieno; **in ~** write per intero; **pay in ~** saldare il conto; **full moon** luna f piena; **full stop** punto m fermo; **full-time** a tempo pieno; **fully** booked, recovered completamente; understand, explain perfettamente; describe ampiamente

fumble ['fʌmbl] catch farsi sfuggire

fumes [fju:mz] esalazioni fpl

fun [fʌn] **1** n divertimento m; **it was great ~** era molto divertente; **have ~!** divertiti!; **for ~** per divertirsi; (joking) per scherzo; **make ~ of** prendere in giro **2** adj F divertente

function ['fʌŋkʃn] **1** n (purpose) funzione f; (reception etc) cerimonia f **2** v/i funzionare; **~ as** servire da; **functional** funzionale

fund [fʌnd] **1** n fondo m **2** v/t project etc finanziare

fundamental [fʌndə'mentl] fondamentale; **fundamentalist** fondamentalista m/f; **fundamentally** fondamentalmente

funding ['fʌndɪŋ] money fondi mpl

funeral ['fju:nərəl] funerale m; **funeral home**, **funeral parlour** obitorio m

fungus ['fʌŋɡəs] fungo m

funicular ('railway) [fju:'nɪkjʊlə(r)] funicolare f

funnily ['fʌnɪlɪ] (oddly) stra-

namente; (comically) in modo divertente; **~ enough** per quanto strano; **funny** (comical) divertente; (odd) strano

fur [fɜ:(r)] pelliccia f; on animal pelo m

furious ['fjʊərɪəs] (angry) furioso; (intense) spaventoso

furnace ['fɜ:nɪs] forno m

furnish ['fɜ:nɪʃ] room arredare; (supply) fornire; **furniture** mobili mpl; **a piece of ~** un mobile

further ['fɜ:ðə(r)] **1** adj (additional) ulteriore; (more distant) più lontano; **have you anything ~ to say?** ha qualcosa da aggiungere? **2** adv walk, drive oltre; **~, I want to say ...** inoltre, volevo dire ...; **two miles ~ (on)** due miglia più avanti **3** v/t cause etc favorire; **furthermore** inoltre; **furthest 1** adj più lontano **2** adv: **this is the ~ north** è il punto più a nord

furtive ['fɜ:tɪv] glance furtivo

fury ['fjʊrɪ] furore m

fuse [fju:z] ELEC **1** n fusibile m **2** v/i bruciarsi **3** v/t bruciare; **fusebox** scatola f dei fusibili

fusion ['fju:ʒn] fusione f

fuss [fʌs] agitazione f; about film, event scalpore m; **make a ~** complain fare storie; **make a ~ of** be very attentive to colmare qu di attenzioni; **fussy** person difficile; design *etc* complicato; **be a ~ eater** essere schizzinoso nel mangiare

futile ['fju:taɪl] futile; **futility** futilità *f*

future ['fju:tʃə(r)] **1** *n* futuro *m* **2** *adj* futuro; **futuristic** futuristico

fuzzy ['fʌzɪ] *hair* crespo; *(out of focus)* sfuocato

G

gadget ['gædʒɪt] congegno *m*

gag [gæg] **1** *n* bavaglio *m*; *(joke)* battuta *f* **2** *v/t person* imbavagliare; *the press* azzittire

gain [geɪn] *(acquire)* acquisire, acquistare; **~ 10 pounds** aumentare di 10 libbre

gala ['gɑ:lə] *concert etc* scrata *f* di gala

galaxy ['gæləksɪ] galassia *f*

gale [geɪl] bufera *f*

gallery ['gælərɪ] galleria *f*

gallon ['gælən] gallone *m*; *(0,546l, in USA 0,785l)*

gallop ['gæləp] galoppare

gamble ['gæmbl] giocare (d'azzardo); **gambler** giocatore *m*, -trice *f* (d'azzardo); **gambling** gioco *m* (d'azzardo)

game [geɪm] gioco *m*; *(match, in tennis)* partita *f*

gang [gæŋ] banda *f*; **gangster** malvivente *m*, gangster *m inv*; **gangway** passaggio *m*; *for ship* passerella *f*

gap [gæp] *in wall, for parking* buco *m*; *in conversation* vuoto *m*; *in time* intervallo *m*; *in story, education* lacuna *f*; *be-tween personalities* scarto *m*

gape [geɪp] *of person* rimanere a bocca aperta; **gaping** *hole* spalancato

'gap year anno tra la fine del liceo e l'inizio dell'università dedicato ad altre attività

garage ['gærɪdʒ] *for parking* garage *m inv*; *for repairs* officina *f*; *for petrol* stazione *f* di servizio

garbage ['gɑ:bɪdʒ] rifiuti *mpl*; *(fig: nonsense)* idiozie *fpl*; **garbage can** *Am* bidone *m* della spazzatura; **garbage truck** *Am* camion *m* della nettezza urbana

garbled ['gɑ:bld] *message* ingarbugliato

garden ['gɑ:dn] giardino *m*; *for vegetables* orto *m*; **gardening** giardinaggio *m*

garish ['geərɪʃ] sgargiante

garlic ['gɑ:lɪk] aglio *m*

garment ['gɑ:mənt] *fml* capo *m* d'abbigliamento

garnish ['gɑ:nɪʃ] guarnire

gas [gæs] gas *m inv*; *Am (gasoline)* benzina *f*

gash [gæʃ] taglio *m*

gasket ['gæskɪt] guarnizione f

gasoline ['gæsəli:n] Am benzina f

gasp [gɑ:sp] 1 n sussulto m 2 v/i rimanere senza fiato; ~ **for breath** essere senza fiato

'gas pedal Am acceleratore m; **gas pump** Am pompa f della benzina; **gas station** Am stazione f di rifornimento; **gas stove** cucina f a gas

gate [geɪt] cancello m; *of city, castle, at airport* porta f; **gateway** ingresso m, *fig* via f d'accesso

gather ['gæðə(r)] 1 v/t *facts* raccogliere; ~ **speed** acquistare velocità 2 v/i (*understand*) dedurre; **gathering** (*group of people*) raduno m

gaudy ['gɔ:dɪ] pacchiano

gauge [geɪdʒ] 1 n indicatore m 2 v/t *pressure* misurare; *opinion* valutare

gaunt [gɔ:nt] smunto

gawky ['gɔ:kɪ] impacciato

gawp [gɔ:p] F fissare come un ebete F

gay [geɪ] gay *inv*; **gay marriage** matrimonio m gay

gaze [geɪz] 1 n sguardo m 2 v/i fissare

gear [gɪə(r)] (*equipment*) equipaggiamento m; *in vehicles* marcia f; **gearbox** MOT scatola f del cambio; **gear lever**, **gear shift** MOT leva f del cambio

geese [gi:s] pl ☞ **goose**

gel [dʒel] *for hair, shower* gel m *inv*

gem [dʒem] gemma f; *fig: book etc* capolavoro m; *person* perla f rara

Gemini ['dʒemɪnaɪ] ASTR Gemelli *mpl*

gender ['dʒendə(r)] genere m

gene [dʒi:n] gene m

general ['dʒenrəl] 1 n MIL generale m 2 *adj* generale; **generalization** generalizzazione f; **generalize** generalizzare; **generally** generalmente; ~ **speaking** in generale

generate ['dʒenəreɪt] generare; *in linguistics* formare; **generation** generazione f; **generator** ELEC generatore m

generosity [dʒenə'rɒsɪtɪ] generosità f; **generous** generoso

genetic [dʒɪ'netɪk] genetico; **genetically** geneticamente; ~ **modified** transgenico; **genetic engineering** ingegneria f genetica; **genetic fingerprint** esame m del DNA; **genetics** genetica f

genial ['dʒi:nɪəl] gioviale

genitals ['dʒenɪtlz] genitali *mpl*

genius ['dʒi:nɪəs] genio m

Genoa ['dʒenəʊə] Genova f

genocide ['dʒenəsaɪd] genocidio m

gentle ['dʒentl] delicato; *breeze, slope* dolce; **gentle-**

399

get

man signore *m; he's a real ~*
è un vero gentleman; **gentleness** delicatezza *f; of breeze, slope* dolcezza *f;* **gently** delicatamente; *blow, slope* dolcemente

gents [dʒents] *toilet* bagno *m* degli uomini

genuine ['dʒenjuɪn] autentico; (*sincere*) sincero; **genuinely** sinceramente

geographical [dʒɪə'græfɪkl] geografico; **geography** geografia *f*

geological [dʒɪə'lɒdʒɪkl] geologico; **geologist** geologo *m, -a f;* **geology** geologia *f*

geometric, geometrical [dʒɪə'metrɪk(l)] geometrico; **geometry** geometria *f*

geriatric [dʒerɪ'etrɪk] **1** *adj* geriatrico **2** *n* anziano *m, -a f*

germ [dʒɜːm] *also fig* germe *m*

German ['dʒɜːmən] **1** *adj* tedesco **2** *n person* tedesco *m, -a f; language* tedesco *m;* **German measles** rosolia *f;* **German shepherd** pastore *m* tedesco; **Germany** Germania *f*

gesture ['dʒestʃə(r)] *also fig* gesto *m*

get [get] prendere; (*fetch*) andare a prendere; (*receive: letter*) ricevere; (*receive: knowledge, respect etc*) ottenere; (*become*) diventare; (*understand*) afferrare; *~ sth done causative* farsi fare qc; *~*

s.o. to do sth far fare qc a qu; *I'll ~ him to do it* glielo faccio fare; *~ to do sth* have opportunity avere occasione di fare qc; *~ one's hair cut* tagliarsi i capelli; *~ ready* preparare qc; *~ going (leave)* andare via; *have got* avere; *I have got to study* devo studiare

◆ **get at** (*criticize*) prendersela con; (*imply, mean*) volere arrivare a

◆ **get back 1** *v/i* (*return*) ritornare; *I'll get back to you on that* ti faccio sapere **2** *v/t* (*obtain again*) recuperare

◆ **get by** (*pass*) passare; *financially* tirare avanti

◆ **get down 1** *v/i from ladder etc* scendere; (*duck etc*) abbassarsi **2** *v/t* (*depress*) buttare giù

◆ **get in 1** *v/i of train, plane* arrivare; (*come home*) arrivare a casa; *to car* salire; *how did they get in?* of thieves, mice etc come sono entrati? **2** *v/t to suitcase etc* far entrare

◆ **get into** *house* entrare in; *car* salire in

◆ **get off 1** *v/i from bus etc* scendere; (*finish work*) finire; (*not be punished*) cavarsela **2** *v/t* (*remove*) togliere; *clothes* togliersi

◆ **get off with** F *sexually* amoreggiare F; *get off with a small fine* cavarsela con una piccola multa

◆ **get on 1** v/i to bike, bus, train salire; (be friendly) andare d'accordo; (advance: of time) farsi tardi; (become old) invecchiare; (make progress) procedere; **he's getting on well at school** se la sta cavando bene a scuola **2** v/t: **get on the bus** salire sull'autobus

◆ **get out 1** v/i of car etc scendere; of prison uscire; **get out! fuori!; let's get out of here** usciamo da qui **2** v/t nail, something jammed tirare fuori; stain mandare via; gun, pen tirare fuori

◆ **get over** fence, disappointment etc superare; lover etc dimenticare

◆ **get through** on telephone prendere la linea; (make self understood) farsi capire

◆ **get up 1** v/i of person, wind alzarsi **2** v/t (climb: hill) salire su

'getaway car macchina f per la fuga; **get-together** ritrovo m

ghastly ['gɑːstlɪ] orrendo

ghetto ['getəʊ] ghetto m

ghost [gəʊst] fantasma m, spettro m; **ghostly** spettrale

ghoul [guːl] persona f morbosa

giant ['dʒaɪənt] **1** n gigante m **2** adj gigante

gibberish ['dʒɪbərɪʃ] F bestialità fpl F

gibe [dʒaɪb] frecciatina f

giddiness ['gɪdɪnɪs] giramenti mpl di testa; **giddy: I feel~** mi gira la testa

gift [gɪft] regalo m; (talent) dono m; **gifted** dotato; **gift token**, **gift voucher** buono m d'acquisto; **giftwrap: ~ sth** fare un pacco regalo

gig [gɪg] F concerto m

gigabyte ['gɪgəbaɪt] COMPUT gigabyte m inv

gigantic [dʒaɪˈgæntɪk] gigante

giggle ['gɪgl] **1** v/i ridacchiare **2** n risatina f

gimmick ['gɪmɪk] trovata f

gin [dʒɪn] gin m inv; **~ and tonic** gin and tonic m inv

ginger ['dʒɪndʒə(r)] **1** n spice zenzero m **2** adj hair rosso carota; cat rosso

gipsy ['dʒɪpsɪ] zingaro m, -a f

giraffe [dʒɪˈrɑːf] giraffa f

girder ['gɜːdə(r)] n trave f

girl [gɜːl] ragazza f; **girlfriend** of boy ragazza f; of girl amica f; **girl guide** giovane esploratrice f; **girlish** tipicamente femminile

gist [dʒɪst] sostanza f

give [gɪv] dare; present fare; (supply: electricity etc) fornire; talk, groan fare; party dare; pain, appetite far venire

◆ **give away** as present regalare; (betray) tradire

◆ **give back** restituire

◆ **give in 1** v/i (surrender) arrendersi **2** v/t (hand in) consegnare

◆ **give onto** (*open onto*) dare
su

◆ **give out 1** *v/t leaflets etc* distribuire **2** *v/i of supplies, strength* esaurirsi

◆ **give up 1** *v/t smoking etc* rinunciare a; **give o.s. up to the police** consegnarsi alla polizia **2** *v/i* (*cease habit*) smettere; (*stop making effort*) lasciar perdere

◆ **give way** *of bridge etc* cedere; MOT dare la precedenza

give-and-take concessioni *fpl* reciproche

gizmo ['gɪzməʊ] *Am* aggeggio *m*

glad [glæd] contento; **gladly** volentieri

glamor ['glæmə(r)] *Am* ✓ **glamour**, **glamorize** esaltare; **glamorous** affascinante; **glamour** fascino *m*

glance [glɑːns] **1** *n* sguardo *m*; **at first ~** a prima vista **2** *v/i* dare un'occhiata *or* uno sguardo

gland [glænd] ghiandola *f*

glare [gleə(r)] **1** *n of sun, lights* luce *f* abbagliante **2** *v/i of sun, lights* splendere di luce abbagliante

◆ **glare at** guardare di storto

glaring ['gleərɪŋ] *mistake* lampante

glass [glɑːs] *material* vetro *m*; *for drink* bicchiere *m*; **glasses** occhiali *mpl*

glazed [gleɪzd] *expression* as-

sente

gleam [gliːm] **1** *n* luccichio *m* **2** *v/i* luccicare

glee [gliː] allegria *f*; **gleeful** allegro

glib [glɪb] poco convincente; **glibly** in modo poco convincente

glide [glaɪd] *of skier, boat* scivolare; *of bird, plane* planare; **glider** aliante *m*; **gliding** SP *n* volo *m* planato

glimpse [glɪmps] **1** *n* occhiata *f*; **catch a ~ of** intravedere **2** *v/t* intravedere

glint [glɪnt] **1** *n* luccichio *m* **2** *v/i of light, eyes* luccicare

glisten ['glɪsn] scintillare

glitter ['glɪtə(r)] brillare

gloat [gləʊt] gongolare

◆ **gloat over** compiacersi di

global ['gləʊbl] (*worldwide*) mondiale; *without exceptions* globale; **globalization** globalizzazione *f*; **globalize** globalizzare; **global warming** effetto *m* serra; **globe** globo *m*; *model of earth* mappamondo *m*

gloom [gluːm] (*darkness*) penombra *f*; *mood* tristezza *f*; **gloomy** *room* buio; *mood, person* triste; *day* grigio

glorious ['glɔːrɪəs] *weather, day* splendido; *victory* glorioso; **glory** gloria *f*; (*beauty*) splendore *m*

gloss [glɒs] (*shine*) lucido *m*; **glossary** glossario *m*; **gloss paint** vernice *f* lucida;

glossy 1 *adj paper* patinato **2** *n magazine* rivista *f* su carta patinata

glove [glʌv] guanto *m*; **glove compartment** cruscotto *m*

glow [gləʊ] **1** *n of light, fire* bagliore *m*; *in cheeks* colorito *m* vivo; *of candle* luce *f* fioca **2** *v/i of light* brillare; **her cheeks ~ed** è diventata rossa; **glowing** *description* entusiastico

glucose ['glu:kəʊs] glucosio *m*

glue [glu:] **1** *n* colla *f* **2** *v/t*: **~ sth to sth** incollare qc a qc

glum [glʌm] triste

glut [glʌt] eccesso *m*

glutton ['glʌtən] ghiottone *m*, -a *f*

gnaw [nɔː] *bone* rosicchiare

go [gəʊ] **1** *n* (*try*) tentativo *m*; **it's my ~** tocca a me; **have a ~ at sth** (*try*) fare un tentativo in qc; **be on the ~** essere indaffarato; **in one ~** *drink, write etc* tutto in una volta **2** *v/i* andare; (*leave: of train, plane*) partire; (*leave: of people*) andare via; (*work, function*) funzionare; (*become*) diventare; (*come out: of stain etc*) andare via; (*cease: of pain etc*) sparire; (*match: of colours etc*) stare bene insieme; **let's ~!** andiamo!; **how's the work ~ing?** come va il lavoro?; **be all gone** (*finished*) essere finito; **to ~** *Am food* da asporto

◆ **go along with** *suggestion* concordare con

◆ **go away** *of person, pain* andare via; *of rain* smettere

◆ **go back** (*return*) ritornare; (*date back*) rimontare; **go back to sleep** tornare a dormire

◆ **go by** *of car, people, time* passare

◆ **go down** scendere; *of sun, ship* tramontare; *of ship* affondare; *of swelling* diminuire

◆ **go in** *to room, house* entrare; *of sun* andare via; (*fit: of part etc*) andare

◆ **go off 1** *v/i* (*leave*) andarsene; *of bomb* esplodere; *of gun* sparare; *of alarm* scattare; *of light* spegnersi; *of milk etc* andare a male **2** *v/t* (*stop liking*) stufarsi di

◆ **go on** (*continue*) andare avanti; (*happen*) succedere

◆ **go out** *of person* uscire; *of light, fire* spegnersi

◆ **go out with** *romantically* uscire con

◆ **go over** (*check*) esaminare

◆ **go through** *hard times* passare; (*check*) controllare; (*read through*) leggere

◆ **go under** (*sink*) affondare; *of company* fallire

◆ **go up** salire

◆ **go without 1** *v/t food etc* fare a meno di **2** *v/i* farne a meno

'go-ahead 1 *n* via libera *m*;

get the ~ avere il via libera **2** *adj (enterprising, dynamic)* intraprendente

goal [gəʊl] *(sport: target)* rete *f; (sport: points)* gol *m* inv; *(objective)* obiettivo *m;* **goalie** F portiere *m;* **goalkeeper** portiere *m;* **goal kick** rimessa *f;* **goalpost** palo *m*

goat [gəʊt] capra *f*

gobble ['gɒbl] tranguiare

gobbledygook ['gɒbldɪgu:k] F linguaggio *m* incomprensibile

'go-between mediatore *m,* -trice *f*

god [gɒd] dio *m;* **thank God!** grazie a Dio!; **godchild** figlioccio *m,* -a *f;* **goddess** dea *f;* **godfather** *also in mafia* padrino *m;* **godmother** madrina *f*

gofer ['gəʊfə(r)] F galoppino *m,* -a *f* F

goggles ['gɒglz] occhialini *mpl*

goings-on [gəʊɪŋz'ɒn] vicende *fpl*

gold [gəʊld] **1** *n* oro *m* **2** *adj* d'oro; **golden** dorato; **golden wedding (anniversary)** nozze *fpl* d'oro; **goldfish** pesce *m* rosso; **gold mine** *fig* miniera *f* d'oro

golf [gɒlf] golf *m;* **golf ball** palla *f* da golf; **golf club** *organization* club *m* inv di golf; *stick* mazza *f* da golf; **golf course** campo *m* di golf; **golfer** giocatore *m,* -trice

di golf

gondola ['gɒndələ] gondola *f;* **gondolier** gondoliere *m*

good [gʊd] **1** *adj* buono; *weather, film* bello; *actor, child* bravo; *a ~ many* un bel po (di); *be ~ at* essere bravo in; *be ~ for s.o.* fare bene a qu; *be ~ for sth* andare bene per qc; *it's good of you!* bene!; *it's ~ to see you* è bello vederti **2** *n* bene *m; it did him no ~* non gli ha fatto bene; **goodbye** arrivederci; *say ~ to s.o.* salutare qu; **good-for-nothing** buono *m,* -a *f* a nulla; **Good Friday** venerdì *m* inv santo; **good-humoured**, *Am* **good-humored** di buon umore; **good-looking** attraente; **good-natured** di buon cuore; **goodness** bontà *f,* **thank ~!** grazie al cielo; **goods** COM merce *fsg;* **goodwill** buona volontà *f*

goof [gu:f] F fare una gaffe

goose [gu:s] *(pl* **geese** [gi:s]) oca *f;* **gooseberry** uva *f* spina; **goose bumps** pelle *f* d'oca

gorgeous ['gɔ:dʒəs] stupendo; *smell* ottimo

gorilla [gə'rɪlə] gorilla *m*

Gospel ['gɒspl] vangelo *m*

gossip ['gɒsɪp] **1** *n* pettegolezzo *m; person* pettegolo *m,* -a *f* **2** *v/i* spettegolare; **gossip column** cronaca *f* rosa

gourmet ['gʊəmeɪ] *n* buongu

staio m, -a f

govern ['gʌvn] governare; **government** governo m; **governor** governatore m

gown [gaʊn] long dress abito m lungo; wedding dress abito m da sposa; of academic, judge toga f; of surgeon camice m

grab [græb] afferrare; ~ **some sleep** farsi una dormita

grace [greɪs] of dancer etc grazia f; before meals preghiera f (prima di un pasto); **graceful** aggraziato; **gracious** person cortese; style elegante

grade [greɪd] **1** n (quality) qualità f inv; EDU voto m **2** v/t classificare; **grade crossing** Am passaggio m a livello; **grade school** Am scuola f elementare

gradient ['greɪdɪənt] pendenza f

gradual ['grædʒʊəl] graduale; **gradually** gradualmente

graduate ['grædʒʊət] **1** n laureato m, -a f **2** v/i from university laurearsi; **graduation** laurea f; ceremony cerimonia f di laurea

graffiti [grə'fiːtiː] graffiti mpl

graft [grɑːft] **1** n BOT innesto m; MED trapianto m, F (hard work) duro lavoro m; Am F corruzione f **2** v/t BOT innestare; MED trapiantare

grain [greɪn] cereali mpl; seed granello m; of rice, wheat chicco m; in wood venatura f

gram [græm] grammo m

grammar ['græmə(r)] grammatica f; **grammar school** liceo m; **grammatical** grammaticale

grand [grænd] **1** adj grandioso; F (very good) eccezionale **2** n F (£1000) mille sterline fpl; **grandchild** nipote m/f; **granddaughter** nipote f; **grandeur** grandiosità f; **grandfather** nonno m; **grand jury** Am gran giurì m; **grandmother** nonna f; **grandparents** nonni mpl; **grand piano** pianoforte m a coda; **grandson** nipote m

granite ['grænɪt] granito m

granny ['grænɪ] F nonna f

grant [grɑːnt] **1** n money sussidio m; for university borsa f di studio **2** v/t visa assegnare; permission concedere; wish esaudire; **take sth for ~ed** dare qc per scontato; **he takes his wife for ~ed** considera quello che fa sua moglie come dovuto

granule ['grænjuːl] granello m

grape [greɪp] acino m d'uva; ~s uva fsg; **grapefruit** pompelmo m; **grapefruit juice** succo m di pompelmo

graph [grɑːf] grafico m; **graphic 1** adj grafico; (vivid) vivido **2** n COMPUT grafico m; ~s grafica f

♦ **grapple with** ['græpl] attacker lottare con; problem

grill

etc essere alle prese con
grasp [grɑːsp] **1** *n physical*
presa *f; mental* comprensione *f* **2** *v/t* physically, mentally afferrare

grass [grɑːs] erba *f;* **grasshopper** cavalletta *f;* **grass roots** *people* massa *f* popolare; **grassy** erboso

grate[1] [greɪt] *n* metal grata *f*

grate[2] [greɪt] **1** *v/t in cooking* grattugiare **2** *v/i of sounds* stridere

grateful ['greɪtfʊl] grato (**to** a); **gratefully** con gratitudine

gratify ['grætɪfaɪ] soddisfare

grating ['greɪtɪŋ] **1** *n* grata *f* **2** *adj sound, voice* stridente

gratitude ['grætɪtjuːd] gratitudine *f*

grave[1] [greɪv] *n* tomba *f*

grave[2] [greɪv] *adj* grave

gravel ['grævl] ghiaia *f*

gravestone lapide *f;* **graveyard** cimitero *m*

gravity ['grævətɪ] PHYS forza *f* di gravità

gravy ['greɪvɪ] sugo *m* della carne

gray *Am* ☞ **grey**

graze[1] [greɪz] *v/i of cow, horse* brucare

graze[2] [greɪz] **1** *v/t arm etc* graffiare **2** *n* graffio *m*

grease [griːs] grasso *m;* **greasy** *food, hair* grasso; *hands, plate* unto

great [greɪt] grande; F (*very good*) fantastico; **Great Bri-**tain Gran Bretagna *f;* **greatly** molto; **greatness** grandezza *f*

Greece [griːs] Grecia *f*

greed [griːd] avidità *f; for food* ingordigia *f;* **greedily** con avidità; *eat* con ingordigia; **greedy** avido; *for food* ingordo

Greek [griːk] **1** *n* greco *m,* -a *f; language* greco *m* **2** *adj* greco

green [griːn] verde; *environmentally* ecologico; **the Greens** POL i verdi; **green beans** giardini *mpl;* **green belt** zona *f* verde tutt'intorno ad una città; **green card** *driving insurance* carta *f* verde; *Am* (*work permit*) permesso *m* di lavoro; **greenhouse** serra *f;* **greenhouse effect** effetto *m* serra; **greens** verdura *f*

greet [griːt] salutare; **greeting** saluto *m*

grenade [grɪ'neɪd] granata *f*

grey [greɪ] grigio; *hair* bianco; **grey-haired** con i capelli bianchi; **greyhound** levriero *m*

grid [grɪd] grata *f; on map* reticolato *m;* **gridiron** *Am* SP campo *m* da calcio; **gridlock** *in traffic* ingorgo *m*

grief [griːf] dolore *m;* **grief-stricken** addolorato; **grievance** rimostranza *f;* **grieve** essere addolorato (**for** per)

grill [grɪl] **1** *n for cooking* grill *m inv; metal frame* griglia *f;*

dish grigliata *f; on window* grata *f* **2** *v/t food* fare alla griglia; *(interrogate)* mettere sotto torchio

grille [grɪl] grata *f*

grim [grɪm] cupo; *(determination* accanito

grimace ['grɪməs] smorfia *f*

grime [graɪm] sporcizia *f*; **grimy** sudicio

grin [grɪn] **1** *n* sorriso *m* **2** *v/i* sorridere

grind [graɪnd] *coffee, meat* macinare; **~ one's teeth** digrignare i denti

grip [grɪp] **1** *n on rope etc* presa *f* **2** *v/t* afferrare; *of brakes* fare presa su; **be ~ped by sth** *by panic* essere preso da qc; **gripping** avvincente

gristle ['grɪsl] cartilagine *f*

grit [grɪt] **1** *n (dirt)* granelli *mpl; for roads* sabbia *f* **2** *v/t:* **~ one's teeth** stringere i denti; **gritty** F *book, film etc* realistico

groan [grəʊn] **1** *n* gemito *m* **2** *v/i* gemere

grocer ['grəʊsə(r)] droghiere *m; at the ~'s (shop)* dal droghiere; **groceries** generi *mpl* alimentari; **grocery store** *Am* drogheria *f*

groggy ['grɒgɪ] F intontito

groin [grɔɪn] ANAT inguine *m*

groom [gruːm] **1** *n for bride* sposo *m; for horse* stalliere *m* **2** *v/t horse* strigliare; *(train, prepare)* preparare; **well ~ed** *in appearance* ben curato

groove [gruːv] scanalatura *f*

grope [grəʊp] **1** *v/i in the dark* brancolare **2** *v/t sexually* palpeggiare

gross [grəʊs] *(coarse, vulgar)* volgare; *(exaggeration* madornale; FIN lordo

grotty ['grɒtɪ] F *street, flat* squallido; *I feel ~* sto da schifo F

ground [graʊnd] **1** *n* suolo *m; (area, for sport)* terreno *m; (reason)* motivo *m,* ragione *f; Am* ELEC terra *f; on the ~* per terra; **on the ~s of** a causa di **2** *v/t Am* ELEC mettere a terra; **ground floor** pianoterra *m inv;* **grounding** *in subject* basi *fpl;* **groundless** infondato; **ground meat** *Am* carne *f* tritata; **groundwork** lavoro *m* di preparazione

group [gruːp] **1** *n* gruppo *m* **2** *v/t* raggruppare; **groupie** *ragazza che segue un gruppo o cantante rock in tutti i concerti*

grouse [graʊs] F **1** *n* lamentela *f* **2** *v/i* brontolare

grovel ['grɒvl] *fig* umiliarsi

grow [grəʊ] **1** *v/i* crescere; *of number* aumentare; *of business* svilupparsi; **~ old / tired** invecchiare / stancarsi; **~ into sth** diventare qc **2** *v/t flowers* coltivare

◆ **grow up** *of person* crescere; *of city* svilupparsi

growl [graʊl] **1** *n* grugnito *m* **2** *v/i* ringhiare

'grown-up 1 *n* adulto *m*, -a *f* **2** *adj* adulto

growth [grəʊθ] *of person* crescita *f*; *of company* sviluppo *m*; (*increase*) aumento *m*; MED tumore *m*

grudge [grʌdʒ] **1** *n* rancore *m*; **bear s.o. a ~** portare rancore a qu **2** *v/t*: **~ s.o. sth** invidiare qc a qu; **grudging** riluttante; **grudgingly** a malincuore

gruelling, *Am* **grueling** ['gruːəlɪŋ] estenuante

gruff [grʌf] burbero

grumble ['grʌmbl] brontolare; **grumbler** brontolone *m*, -a *f*

grunt [grʌnt] **1** *n* grugnito *m* **2** *v/i* grugnire

guarantee [gærən'tiː] **1** *n* garanzia *f*; **~ period** periodo *m* di garanzia **2** *v/t* garantire; **guarantor** garante *m*

guard [gɑːd] **1** *n* guardia *m*; **be on one's ~ against** stare in guardia contro **2** *v/t* fare la guardia a; **guard dog** cane *m* da guardia; **guarded** *reply* cauto; **guardian** LAW tutore *m*, -trice *f*

guerrilla [gə'rɪlə] guerrigliero *m*, -a *f*; **guerrilla warfare** guerriglia *f*

guess [ges] **1** *n* supposizione *f* **2** *v/t the answer* indovinare; **I ~ so** suppongo di sì **3** *v/i* indovinare; **guesswork** congettura *f*

guest [gest] ospite *m/f*; **guesthouse** pensione *f*;

guestroom camera *f* degli ospiti

guidance ['gaɪdəns] consigli *mpl*; **guide 1** *n person, book* guida *f* **2** *v/t* guidare; **guide-book** guida *f* turistica; **guided missile** missile *m* guidato; **guide dog** cane *m* per ciechi; **guided tour** visita *f* guidata; **guidelines** direttive *fpl*

guilt [gɪlt] colpa *f*; LAW colpevolezza *f*; **guilty** *also* LAW colpevole; **have a ~ conscience** avere la coscienza sporca

guinea pig ['gɪnɪpɪg] porcellino *m* d'india; *for experiments, fig* cavia *f*

guitar [gɪ'tɑː(r)] chitarra *f*; **guitarist** chitarrista *m/f*

gulf [gʌlf] golfo *m*; *fig* divario *m*

gull [gʌl] *bird* gabbiano *m*

gullet ['gʌlɪt] ANAT esofago *m*

gullible ['gʌlɪbl] credulone *m*

gulp [gʌlp] **1** *n of water* sorso *m*; *of air* boccata *f* **2** *v/i in surprise* deglutire

◆ **gulp down** *drink* ingoiare; *food* tranguggiare

gum[1] [gʌm] *in mouth* gengiva *f*

gum[2] [gʌm] (*glue*) colla *f*; (*chewing gum*) gomma *f*

gun [gʌn] *pistol, revolver, rifle* arma *f* da fuoco; (*cannon*) cannone *m*

◆ **gun down** sparare a morte

'gunfire spari *mpl*; **gunman**

uomo *m* armato; *robber* rapinatore *m*; **gunshot** sparo *m*; **gunshot wound** ferita *f* da arma da fuoco
gurgle ['gɜːgl] *of baby, drain* gorgogliare
guru ['guru] *fig* guru *m inv*
gush [gʌʃ] *of liquid* sgorgare
gust [gʌst] raffica *f*
gusto ['gʌstəʊ]: **with** ~ con slancio
gusty ['gʌstɪ] *of weather* ventoso; ~ **wind** vento a raffiche
gut [gʌt] **1** *n* intestino *m*, F *(stomach)* pancia *f* **2** *v/t (destroy)* sventrare; **guts** F *(courage)* fegato *m* F; **gutsy**

F *person* che ha fegato; F *thing to do* che richiede fegato
gutter ['gʌtə(r)] *on pavement* canaletto *m* di scolo; *on roof* grondaia *f*
guy [gaɪ] F tipo *m* F; **hey, you** ~**s** ei, gente
guzzle ['gʌzl] ingozzarsi di
gym [dʒɪm] palestra *f*; *activity* ginnastica *f*; **gymnast** ginnasta *m/f*; **gymnastics** ginnastica *f*
gynaecologist [gaɪnɪ'kɒlədʒɪst] ginecologo *m*, -a *f*; **gynaecology**, *Am* **gynecology** ginecologia *f*
gypsy ['dʒɪpsɪ] zingaro *m*, -a *f*

H

habit ['hæbɪt] abitudine *f*
habitable ['hæbɪtəbl] abitabile; **habitat** habitat *m inv*
habitual [hə'bɪtjʊəl] solito; *smoker, drinker* incallito
hacker ['hækə(r)] COMPUT hacker *m/f inv*
hackneyed ['hæknɪd] trito
haemorrhage ['hemərɪdʒ] **1** *n* emorragia *f* **2** *v/i* avere un'emorragia
haggard ['hægəd] tirato
haggle ['hægl] contrattare
hail [heɪl] grandine *f*
hair [heə(r)] capelli *mpl*; *single* capello *m*; *on body, of animal* pelo *m*; **hairbrush** spazzola *f* per capelli; **haircut** taglio *m*

di capelli; **hairdo** pettinatura *f*; **hairdresser** parrucchiere *m*, -a *f*; **at the** ~**'s** dal parrucchiere; **hairdryer** fon *m inv*; **hairpin** forcina *f*; **hairpin bend** tornante *m*; **hair-raising** terrificante; **hair remover** crema *f* depilatoria; **hair-splitting** pedanteria *f*; **hairstyle** acconciatura *f*; **hairstylist** parrucchiere *m*, -a *f*; **hairy** *arm, animal* peloso; F *(frightening)* preoccupante
half [hɑːf] **1** *n* metà *f inv*, mezzo *m*; ~ **past ten** le dieci e mezza; ~ **an hour** mezz'ora **2** *adj* mezzo **3** *adv* a metà;

half-hearted poco convinto; **half time** SP intervallo *m*; **halfway 1** *adj* stage, point intermedio **2** *adv* also fig a metà strada; **~ finished** fatto a metà

hall [hɔːl] large room sala *f*; hallway in house ingresso *m*

Hallowe'en [hæləʊˈiːn] vigilia *f* d'Ognissanti

halo ['heɪləʊ] aureola *f*

halt [hɔːlt] **1** *v/i* fermarsi **2** *v/t* fermare

halve [hɑːv] dimezzare

ham [hæm] prosciutto *m*; **hamburger** hamburger *m inv*

hammer ['hæmə(r)] **1** *n* martello *m* **2** *v/i* martellare; **~ at the door** picchiare alla porta

hammock ['hæmək] amaca *f*

hamper¹ ['hæmpə(r)] *n for food* cestino *m*

hamper² ['hæmpə(r)] *v/t (obstruct)* ostacolare

hamster ['hæmstə(r)] criceto *m*

hand [hænd] *n* mano *m*; *of clock* lancetta *f*; *(worker)* operaio *m*; **at ~, to ~** a portata di mano; **by ~** a mano; **on the one ~ ..., on the other ~ ...** da un lato ..., dall'altro ...; **in ~** *(being done)* in corso; **on your right** sulla tua destra; **change ~s** cambiare di mano; **give s.o. a ~** dare una mano a qu

♦ **hand down** passare

♦ **hand out** distribuire

♦ **hand over** consegnare; *child to parent etc* dare

'handbag borsetta *f*; **hand baggage** bagaglio *m* a mano; **handbrake** freno *m* a mano; **handcuff** ammanettare; **handcuffs** manette *fpl*; **handheld** COMPUT palmare *m*, PDA *m inv*

handicap ['hændɪkæp] handicap *m inv*; **handicapped** handicappato

handkerchief ['hæŋkətʃɪf] fazzoletto *m*

handle ['hændl] **1** *n* maniglia *f* **2** *v/t goods* maneggiare; *case, deal* trattare; *difficult person* prendere, **let me ~ this** lascia fare a me; **handlebars** manubrio *msg*

'hand luggage bagaglio *m* a mano; **handmade** fatto a mano; **hands-free** vivavoce *m inv*; **handshake** stretta *f* di mano; **hands-off approach** teorico; **he has a ~ style of management** non partecipa direttamente agli aspetti pratici della gestione

handsome ['hænsəm] bello

hands-'on *experience* pratico; **he has a ~ style of management** partecipa direttamente agli aspetti pratici della gestione

'handwriting calligrafia *f*; **handwritten** scritto a mano; **handy** *tool, device* pratico; **it's ~ for the shops** è como-

hang 410

do per i negozi

hang [hæŋ] **1** v/t picture appendere; person impiccare **2** v/i of dress, hair cadere **3** n: **get the ~ of** F capire

◆ **hang on** (wait) aspettare

◆ **hang up** TELEC riattaccare

hangar ['hæŋə(r)] hangar m inv

hanger ['hæŋə(r)] for clothes gruccia f

hang glider ['hæŋglaɪdə(r)] deltaplano m; **hang gliding** deltaplano m; **hangover** postumi mpl della sbornia

hankie, hanky ['hæŋkɪ] F fazzoletto m

haphazard [hæp'hæzəd] a casaccio

happen ['hæpn] succedere

happily ['hæpɪlɪ] allegramente; (gladly) volentieri; (luckily) per fortuna; **happiness** felicità f; **happy** felice; **happy-go-lucky** spensierato

harass [hə'ræs] tormentare; sexually molestare; **harassed** stressato; **harassment** persecuzione f; **sexual ~** molestie fpl sessuali

harbour, Am **harbor** ['hɑːbə(r)] **1** n porto m **2** v/t criminal dar rifugio a; grudge covare

hard [hɑːd] **1** adj duro; (difficult) difficile; facts, evidence concreto; drug pesante; **~ of hearing** duro d'orecchio **2** adv work con impegno; rain, pull, push forte; **try ~**

impegnarsi; **hardback** libro m con copertina rigida; **hard-boiled** egg sodo; **hard copy** copia f stampata; **hard core** pornography pornografia f hard-core; **hard currency** valuta f forte; **hard disk** disco m rigido, hard disk m inv; **harden 1** v/t indurire **2** v/i of glue indurirsi; of attitude irrigidirsi; **hard hat** casco m; (construction worker) muratore m; **hardheaded** pratico; **hardhearted** dal cuore duro; **hard line** linea f dura; **hardliner** sostenitore m, -trice f della linea dura

hardly [ˈhɑːdlɪ] a malapena; **~ ever** quasi mai; **you can ~ expect him to ...** non puoi certo aspettarti che lui ...

hardness ['hɑːdnɪs] durezza f; (difficulty) difficoltà f; **hardship** difficoltà fpl economiche; **hard up** al verde; **hardware** ferramenta fpl, COMPUT hardware m; **hardware store** negozio m di ferramenta; **hard-working** che lavora duro; **hardy** resistente

harm [hɑːm] **1** n danno m **2** v/t danneggiare; **harmful** dannoso; **harmless** innocuo

harmonious [hɑːˈməʊnɪəs] armonioso; **harmonize** armonizzare; **harmony** armonia f

harp [hɑːp] arpa f

harsh [hɑːʃ] criticism, words

duro; *colour, light* troppo forte; *harshly* duramente

harvest ['hɑːvɪst] raccolto *m*

hashtag ['hæʃtæg] COMPUT
hashtag *m*, cancelletto *m*

haste [heɪst] fretta *f*; *hastily*
in fretta; **hasty** frettoloso

hat [hæt] cappello *m*

hatch [hætʃ] *for serving food*
passavivande *m inv*; *on ship*
boccaporto *m*

◆ **hatch out** *of eggs* schiuder-
si

hatchet ['hætʃɪt] ascia *f*; *bury
the ~* seppellire l'ascia di
guerra

hate [heɪt] **1** *n* odio *m* **2** *v/t*
odiare; **hatred** odio *m*

haughty ['hɔːtɪ] altezzoso

haul [hɔːl] **1** *n* *of fish* pescata *f*
2 *v/t* (*pull*) trascinare; **haul-
age** autotrasporto *m*

haunch [hɔːntʃ] anca *f*

haunt [hɔːnt] **1** *v/t*: *this place
is ~ed* qui c'è un fanta-
sma / ci sono i fantasmi **2** *n*
ritrovo *m*

have [hæv] **1** *v/t* ◇ avere;
breakfast, shower fare; *I'll ~
a coffee* prendo un caffè; *~
lunch / dinner* pranzare /
cenare ◇ *must*: ~ (*got*) *to*
dovere; *I ~ (got) to go* devo
andare ◇ *causative*: *I had
the printer fixed* ho fatto riparare la stampante **2** *v/aux*
avere; *with verbs of motion*
essere; *~ you seen her?*
l'hai vista?; *I ~ come* sono
venuto

◆ **have on** (*wear*) portare, indossare; *do you have anything on tonight?* (*have
planned*) hai programmi
per stasera?

haven ['heɪvn] *fig* oasi *f inv*

hawk [hɔːk] *also fig* falco *m*

hay [heɪ] fieno *m*; **hay fever**
raffreddore *m* da fieno

hazard ['hæzəd] *n* rischio *m*;
hazard lights MOT luci *fpl*
di emergenza; **hazardous**
rischioso

haze [heɪz] foschia *f*

hazelnut ['heɪzlnʌt] nocciola
f

hazy ['heɪzɪ] *view* indistinto;
memories vago

he [hiː] lui; *~'s French* è francese; *there ~ is* eccolo

head [hed] **1** *n* testa *f*; (*boss,
leader*) capo *m*; *of primary
school* direttore *m*, -trice *f*;
of secondary school preside
m/f; *on beer* schiuma *f*; *~s
or tails?* testa o croce?; *at
the ~ of the list* in cima alla
lista **2** *v/t* (*lead*) essere a capo
di; *ball* colpire di testa

◆ **head for** *place* dirigersi
verso; (*be destined for*) andare incontro a

'headache mal *m* di testa;
headband fascia *f* per i capelli; **header** *in soccer* colpo
m di testa; *in document* intestazione *f*; **headhunter** COM
cacciatore *m* di teste; **heading** *in list* titolo *m*; **head-
lamp** fanale *m*; **headline** *in*

newspaper titolo *m*; **make the ~s** fare titolo; **headmaster** *in primary school* direttore *m*; *in secondary school* preside *m*; **headmistress** *in primary school* direttrice *f*; *in secondary school* preside *f*; **head office** *of company* sede *f* centrale; **head-on 1** *adv* crash frontalmente **2** *adj* crash frontale; **headphones** cuffie *fpl*; **headquarters** sede *fsg*; MIL quartiere *msg* generale; **headrest** poggiatesta *m inv*; **headroom** *for vehicle under bridge* altezza *f* utile; *in car* altezza *f* dell'abitacolo; **headscarf** foulard *m inv*; **headstrong** testardo; **head waiter** capocameriere *m*; **heady** *wine etc* inebriante

heal [hiːl] guarire

health [helθ] salute *f*; (*public* ~) sanità *f*; **your ~!** (alla) salute!; **health care** assistenza *f* sanitaria; **health food** alimenti *mpl* naturali; **health food store** negozio *m* di alimenti naturali; **health insurance** assicurazione *f* contro le malattie; **health resort** stazione *f* termale; **healthy** *also fig* sano

heap [hiːp] *n* mucchio *m*

hear [hɪə(r)] sentire

◆ **hear from** (*have news from*) avere notizie di

hearing [ˈhɪərɪŋ] udito *m*; LAW udienza *f*; **be within / out of**

~ essere / non essere a portata di voce; **hearing aid** apparecchio *m* acustico

hearse [hɜːs] carro *m* funebre

heart [hɑːt] cuore *m*; *of problem etc* nocciolo *m*; **know sth by ~** sapere qc a memoria; **heart attack** infarto *m*; **heartbreaking** straziante; **heartbroken** affranto; **heartburn** bruciore *m* di stomaco; **heart failure** infarto *m*

hearth [hɑːθ] focolare *m*

heartless [ˈhɑːtlɪs] spietato; **heart throb** F idolo *m*; **hearty** *appetite* robusto; *meal* sostanzioso; *person* gioviale

heat [hiːt] calore *m*; (*hot weather*) caldo *m*

◆ **heat up** riscaldare

heated [ˈhiːtɪd] *pool* riscaldato; *discussion* animato; **heater** *radiator* termosifone *m*; *electric, gas* stufa *f*; *in car* riscaldamento *m*; **heating** riscaldamento *m*; **heatproof**, **heat-resistant** termoresistente; **heatwave** ondata *f* di caldo

heave [hiːv] (*lift*) sollevare

heaven [ˈhevn] paradiso *m*; **good ~s!** santo cielo!; **heavenly** F divino

heavy [ˈhevɪ] pesante; *cold, rain, accent* forte; *traffic* intenso; *food* pesante; *smoker* accanito; *drinker* forte; *loss, casualties* ingente; **heavy-duty** resistente; **heavy-**

weight SP di pesi massimi

hectic ['hektɪk] frenetico

hedge [hedʒ] siepe *f*; **hedge-hog** riccio *m*

heel [hiːl] *of foot* tallone *m*, calcagno *m*; *of shoe* tacco *m*; **heel bar** calzoleria *f* istantanea

hefty ['heftɪ] massiccio

height [haɪt] altezza *f*; *of aeroplane* altitudine *f*; **at the ~ of summer** nel pieno dell'estate; **heighten** *effect, tension* aumentare

heir [eə(r)] erede *m*; **heiress** ereditiera *f*

helicopter ['helɪkɒptə(r)] elicottero *m*

hell [hel] inferno *m*; **what the ~ are you doing** F che diavolo fai? F; **go to ~!** F va' all'inferno! F

hello [hə'ləʊ] *informal* ciao; *more formal* buongiorno; buona sera; TELEC pronto; **say ~ to s.o.** salutare qu

helmet ['helmɪt] *of motorcyclist* casco *m*; *of soldier* elmetto *m*

help [help] **1** *n* aiuto *m* **2** *v/t* aiutare; **~ o.s.** *to food* servirsi; **I can't ~ it** non ci posso far niente; **helper** aiutante *m/f*; **helpful** *person* di aiuto; *advice* utile; **he was very ~** mi è stato di grande aiuto; **helping** *of food* porzione *f*; **helpless** (*unable to cope*) indifeso; (*powerless*) impotente; **helplessness** impotenza

f; **help menu** COMPUT menu *m inv* della guida in linea

hem [hem] *of dress* orlo *m*

hemisphere ['hemɪsfɪə(r)] emisfero *m*

'hemline orlo *m*

hemorrhage Am ☞ **haemorrhage**

hen [hen] gallina *f*

'hen party equivalente al femminile della festa d'addio al celibato

hepatitis [hepə'taɪtɪs] epatite *f*

her [hɜː(r)] **1** *adj* il suo *m*, la sua *f*, i suoi *mpl*, le sue *fpl*; **~ sister / brother** sua sorella / suo fratello **2** *pron direct object* la; *indirect object* le; *after prep* lei; **I know ~** la conosco; **I gave ~ the keys** le ho dato le chiavi; **this is for ~** questo è per lei; **who? - ~** chi? - lei

herb [hɜːb] *for medicines* erba *f* medicinale; *for flavouring* erba *f* aromatica; **herb(al) tea** tisana *f*

herd [hɜːd] mandria *f*

here [hɪə(r)] qui, qua; **~'s to you!** *as toast* salute!; **~ you are** *giving sth* ecco qui

hereditary [hə'redɪtərɪ] ereditario; **heredity** ereditarietà *f inv*; **heritage** patrimonio *m*

hernia ['hɜːnɪə] MED ernia *f*

hero ['hɪərəʊ] eroe *m*; **heroic** eroico; **heroically** eroicamente

heroin ['herəʊɪn] eroina *f*

heroine ['herəʊɪn] eroina f

heroism ['herəʊɪzm] eroismo m

herpes ['hɜːpiːz] MED herpes m

hers [hɜːz] il suo m, la sua f, i suoi mpl, le sue fpl; *a friend of ~* un suo amico

herself [hɜː'self] *reflexive* si; *emphatic* se stessa; *after prep* sé, se stessa; *she hurt ~* si è fatta male

hesitant ['hezɪtənt] esitante; hesitantly con esitazione; hesitate esitare; hesitation esitazione f

heterosexual [hetərəʊ'seksjuəl] eterosessuale

hi [haɪ] ciao

hibernate ['haɪbəneɪt] andare in letargo

hiccup ['hɪkʌp] singhiozzo m; *(minor problem)* intoppo m

hidden ['hɪdn] nascosto

hide¹ [haɪd] 1 v/t nascondere 2 v/i nascondersi

hide² [haɪd] n *of animal* pelle f

hide-and-'seek nascondino m; hideaway rifugio m

hideous ['hɪdɪəs] orrendo; *crime* atroce

hiding ['haɪdɪŋ] *(beating)* batosta f; hiding place nascondiglio m

hierarchy ['haɪərɑːkɪ] gerarchia f

high [haɪ] 1 *adj* alto; *wind, speed* forte; *quality, hopes* buono; *(on drugs)* fatto F 2 *n in statistics* livello m record

3 *adv* in alto; highbrow intellettuale; highchair seggiolone m; highclass di (prima) classe; High Court Corte f Suprema; high-frequency ad alta frequenza; high-grade di buona qualità; high-handed autoritario; high-heeled col tacco alto; high jump salto m in alto; high-level ad alto livello; highlight 1 n *(main event)* clou m inv; *in hair* colpo m di sole 2 v/t *with pen* evidenziare; COMPUT selezionare; highlighter evidenziatore m; highly *desirable, likely* molto; *paid* profumatamente; *think ~ of s.o.* stimare molto qu; highly strung nervoso; high performance *drill, battery* ad alto rendimento; high-pitched acuto; high point clou m inv; high-powered *engine* potente; *intellectual* di prestigio; high-pressure TECH ad alta pressione; *salesman* aggressivo; high pressure *weather* alta pressione f; high school scuola f superiore; high street via f principale; high tech 1 n high-tech m 2 *adj* high tech; highway Am autostrada f

hijack ['haɪdʒæk] 1 v/t dirottare 2 n dirottamento m; hijacker dirottatore m, -trice f

hike¹ [haɪk] 1 n camminata f 2 v/i fare camminate

hike² [haɪk] *n in prices* aumento *m*

hiker ['haɪkə(r)] escursionista *m/f*; **hiking** escursionismo *m*

hilarious [hɪ'leərɪəs] divertentissimo

hill [hɪl] collina *f*; *(slope)* altura *f*; **hillside** pendio *m*; **hilltop** cima *f* della collina; **hilly** collinoso

hilt [hɪlt] impugnatura *f*

him [hɪm] *direct object* lo; *indirect object* gli; *after prep* lui; **I know ~** lo conosco; **I gave ~ the keys** gli ho dato le chiavi; **this is for ~** questo è per lui; **who? – ~** chi? – lui

himself [hɪm'self] *reflexive* si, se stesso; *after prep* sé, se stesso; **he hurt ~** si è fatto male

hinder ['hɪndə(r)] intralciare; **hindrance** intralcio *m*

hinge [hɪndʒ] cardine *m*

hint [hɪnt] *(clue)* accenno *m*; *(piece of advice)* consiglio *m*; *(implied suggestion)* allusione *f*; *of red, sadness etc* punta *f*

hip [hɪp] fianco *m*; **hip pocket** tasca *f* posteriore

hippopotamus [hɪpə'pɒtəməs] ippopotamo *m*

hire ['haɪə(r)] *room, hall* affittare; *workers, staff* assumere; *conjuror etc* ingaggiare; **hire car** macchina *f* a noleggio; **hire purchase** acquisto *m* rateale

his [hɪz] **1** *adj* il suo *m*, la sua *f*, i suoi *mpl*, le sue *fpl*; **~ sis-**

ter / brother sua sorella / suo fratello **2** *pron* il suo *m*, la sua *f*, i suoi *mpl*, le sue *fpl*; **a friend of ~** un suo amico

hiss [hɪs] sibilare

historian [hɪ'stɔːrɪən] storico *m*, -a *f*; **historic** storico; **historical** storico; **history** storia *f*

hit [hɪt] **1** *v/t* colpire; *(collide with)* sbattere contro; **I ~ my knee** ho battuto il ginocchio; **it suddenly ~ me** *(I realized)* improvvisamente ho realizzato **2** *n (blow)* colpo *m*; *(success)* successo *m*; **on website** visita *f*
◆ **hit out at** *(criticize)* attaccare

hitch [hɪtʃ] **1** *n (problem)* contrattempo *m* **2** *v/t*: **~ sth to sth** legare qc a qc; **~ a lift** chiedere un passaggio **3** *v/i* (*hitchhike*) fare l'autostop; **hitchhike** fare l'autostop; **hitchhiker** autostoppista *m/f*; **hitchhiking** autostop *m*

hi-'tech 1 *n* high-tech *m* **2** *adj* high tech

'hitlist libro *m* nero; **hitman** sicario *m*; **hit-or-miss: on a ~ basis** affidandosi al caso; **hit squad** commando *m*

HIV [eɪtʃaɪ'viː] (= **human immunodeficiency virus**) HIV *m*

hive [haɪv] *for bees* alveare *m*

HIV-'positive sieropositivo

hoard [hɔːd] **1** *n* provvista *f*; **~**

of money gruzzolo *m* **2** *v/t* accumulare; **hoarding** tabellone *m* per affissioni pubblicitarie

hoarse [hɔːs] rauco

hoax [həʊks] scherzo *m*; *malicious* falso allarme *m*

hobble ['hɒbl] zoppicare

hobby ['hɒbɪ] hobby *m inv*

hobo ['həʊbəʊ] *Am* barbone *m*, -a *f*

hockey ['hɒkɪ] hockey *m* (su prato); *Am* hockey *m* sul ghiaccio

hog [hɒg] *esp Am* maiale *m*

hoist [hɔɪst] **1** *n* montacarichi *m inv* **2** *v/t* (*lift*) sollevare; *flag* issare

hold [həʊld] **1** *v/t in hand* tenere; (*support, keep in place*) reggere; *passport* avere; *prisoner, suspect* trattenere; (*contain*) contenere; *job, post* occupare; **~ hands** tenersi per mano; **~ one's breath** trattenere il fiato; **~ that ...** (*believe, maintain*) sostenere che ...; **~ the line** TELEC resti in linea **2** *n in ship, plane* stiva *f*; **catch ~ of sth** afferrare qc; **lose one's ~ on sth** *on rope etc* perdere la presa su qc

◆ **hold back 1** *v/t crowds* contenere; *facts* nascondere **2** *v/i* (*hesitate*) esitare

◆ **hold out 1** *v/t hand* tendere; *prospect* offrire **2** *v/i of supplies* durare; (*survive*) resistere

◆ **hold up** *hand* alzare; *bank etc* rapinare; (*make late*) trattenere

holder ['həʊldə(r)] (*container*) contenitore *m*; *of passport* titolare *m*; *of ticket* possessore *m*; *of record* detentore *m*, -trice *f*; **holding company** holding *f inv*; **holdup** (*robbery*) rapina *f*; (*delay*) ritardo *m*

hole [həʊl] buco *m*

holiday ['hɒlədeɪ] vacanza *f*; *public* giorno *m* festivo; (*day off*) giorno *m* di ferie; **go on ~** andare in vacanza

Holland ['hɒlənd] Olanda *f*

hollow ['hɒləʊ] cavo, vuoto; *cheeks* infossato

holocaust ['hɒləkɔːst] olocausto *m*

hologram ['hɒləgræm] ologramma *m*

holster ['həʊlstə(r)] fondina *f*

holy ['həʊlɪ] santo; **Holy Spirit** Spirito *m* Santo; **Holy Week** settimana *f* santa

home [həʊm] **1** *n* casa *f*; (*native country*) patria *f*; *for old people* casa *f* di riposo; *for children* istituto *m*; **at ~** a casa; SP in casa; **make yourself at ~** fai come a casa tua; **work from ~** lavorare da casa **2** *adv* a casa; **go ~** andare a casa; **is she ~ yet?** è tornata?; **home address** indirizzo *m* di casa; **home banking** home-banking *m*; **homecoming** ritorno *m*; **home**

computer computer *m inv* (per casa); **home game** incontro *m*; **homeless** senza tetto; **the ~** i senzacasa; **homeloving** casalingo; **homely** semplice; (*welcoming*) accogliente; **homemade** fatto in casa, casalingo; **home match** incontro *m* casalingo; **Home Office** Ministero *m* degli Interni; **home page** home page *f*; **Home Secretary** Ministro *m* degli Interni; **homesick: be ~** avere nostalgia di casa; **home town** città *f inv* natale; **homeward** verso casa; **homework** EDU compiti *mpl* a casa

homicide ['hɒmɪsaɪd] *crime* omicidio *m*; *Am: police department* (squadra *f*) omicidi *f*

homophobia [hɒmə'fəʊbɪə] omofobia *f*

homosexual [hɒmə'seksjʊəl] **1** *adj* omosessuale **2** *n* omosessuale *m/f*

honest ['ɒnɪst] onesto; **honestly** onestamente; **~!** ma insomma!; **honesty** onestà *f*

honey ['hʌnɪ] miele *m*; F (*darling*) tesoro *m*; **honeymoon** luna *f* di miele

honk [hɒŋk] *horn* suonare

honor *Am* ☞ **honour**

honour ['ɒnə(r)] **1** *n* onore *m* **2** *v/t* onorare; **honourable** onorevole

hood [hʊd] *over head* cappuc-

cio *m*; *over cooker* cappa *f*; MOT *on convertible* capote *f inv*; *Am* MOT cofano *m*

hoodlum ['huːdləm] gangster *m inv*

hook [hʊk] gancio *m*; *for fishing* amo *m*; **off the ~** TELEC staccato; **hooked: be ~ on s.o. / sth** essere fanatico di qu / qc; **be ~ on sth drugs** essere assuefatto a qc; **hooker** F prostituta *f*; *in rugby* tallonatore *m*

hooligan ['huːlɪgən] teppista *m/f*; **hooliganism** teppismo *m*

hoot [huːt] **1** *v/t horn* suonare **2** *v/i of car* suonare il clacson; *of owl* gufare

hop [hɒp] saltare

hope [həʊp] **1** *n* speranza *f* **2** *v/i* sperare; **~ for sth** augurarsi qc; **I ~ so** spero di sì **3** *v/t*: **~ that ...** sperare che; **hopeful** ottimista; (*promising*) promettente; **hopefully** *say, wait* con ottimismo; (*I / we hope*) si spera; **hopeless** *position, prospect* senza speranza; (*useless: person*) negato F

horizon [hə'raɪzn] orizzonte *m*; **horizontal** orizzontale *m*

hormone ['hɔːməʊn] ormone *m*

horn [hɔːn] *of animal* corno *m*; MOT clacson *m inv*

hornet ['hɔːnɪt] calabrone *m*

horny ['hɔːnɪ] *Am* F *sexually* arrapato P

horrible ['hɒrɪbl] orribile; **horrify** inorridire; *I was horrified* ero scioccato; **horrifying** *experience* terrificante; *idea, prices* allucinante; **horror** orrore *m*; *the ~s of war* le atrocità della guerra

horse [hɔːs] cavallo *m*; **horse race** corsa *f* di cavalli; **horseshoe** ferro *m* di cavallo

horticulture ['hɔːtɪkʌltʃə(r)] orticoltura *f*

hose [həʊz] tubo *m* di gomma

hospitable [hɒ'spɪtəbl] ospitale

hospital ['hɒspɪtl] ospedale *m*; **hospitality** ospitalità *f*

host [həʊst] *at party, reception* padrone *m* di casa; *of TV programme* presentatore *m*, -trice *f*

hostage ['hɒstɪdʒ] ostaggio *m*; *be taken ~* essere preso in ostaggio; **hostage taker** sequestratore *m*

hostel ['hɒstl] *for students* pensionato *m*; *(youth ~)* ostello *m* (della gioventù)

hostess ['həʊstɪs] *at party, reception* padrona *f* di casa; *on aeroplane* hostess *f inv*

hostile ['hɒstaɪl] ostile; **hostility** ostilità *f inv*

hot [hɒt] *weather, water* caldo; *(spicy)* piccante; F *(good)* bravo *(at sth* in qc*)*; *it's ~* fa caldo; *I'm ~* ho caldo; **hot dog** hot dog *m inv*

hotel [həʊ'tel] albergo *m*

hour ['aʊə(r)] ora *f*

house 1 [haʊs] *n* casa *f*; POL camera *f*; THEA sala *f*; *at your ~* a casa tua, da te **2** [haʊz] *v/t* alloggiare; **housebreaking** furto *m* con scasso; **household** famiglia *f*; **household name** nome *m* conosciuto; **housekeeper** governante *f*; **House of Representatives** la camera *f* dei rappresentanti; **housewarming** (party) *festa per inaugurare la nuova casa*; **housewife** casalinga *f*; **housework** lavori *mpl* domestici; **housing** alloggi *mpl*; TECH alloggiamento *m*

hovel ['hɒvl] tugurio *m*

hover ['hɒvə(r)] librarsi

how [haʊ] come; *~ are you?* come stai?; *~ about ...?* che ne dici di ...?; *~ much?* quanto?; *~ much is it?* of cost quant'è?; *~ many?* quanti?; *~ odd / lovely!* che strano / bello!; *however* comunque; *~ big they are* per quanto grandi siano

howl [haʊl] of dog ululare; of person in pain urlare; *~ with laughter* sbellicarsi dalle risate; **howler** *mistake* strafalcione *m*

hub [hʌb] of wheel mozzo *m*; **hubcap** coprimozzo *m*

◆ **huddle together** ['hʌdl] stringersi l'un l'altro

hug [hʌg] **1** *v/t* abbracciare **2** abbraccio *m*

huge [hjuːdʒ] enorme
hull [hʌl] scafo *m*
hum [hʌm] canticchiare; *of machine* ronzare
human ['hjuːmən] **1** *n* essere *m* umano **2** *adj* umano; **human being** essere *m* umano
humane [hjuːˈmeɪn] umano
humanitarian [hjuːmænɪ-ˈteərɪən] umanitario
humanity [hjuːˈmænətɪ] umanità *f*; **human race** genere *m* umano; **human resources** risorse *fpl* umane
humble ['hʌmbl] umile; *house* modesto
humdrum ['hʌmdrʌm] monotono
humid ['hjuːmɪd] umido; **humidifier** umidificatore *m*; **humidity** umidità *f*
humiliate [hjuːˈmɪlɪeɪt] umiliare; **humiliating** umiliante; **humiliation** umiliazione *f*; **humility** umiltà *f*
humor *Am* → **humour**
humorous ['hjuːmərəs] *person* spiritoso; *story* umoristico; **humour** umorismo *m*; *(mood)* umore *m*; **sense of ~** senso dell'umorismo
hunch [hʌntʃ] *(idea)* impressione *f*; *of detective* intuizione *f*
hundred ['hʌndrəd] cento *m*; **a ~ ...** cento ...; **hundredth** centesimo
Hungarian [hʌŋˈgeərɪən] **1** *adj* ungherese **2** *n person* ungherese *m/f*; *language* un-

gherese *m*; **Hungary** Ungheria *f*
hunger ['hʌŋgə(r)] fame *f*
hung-'over: *feel ~* avere i postumi della sbornia
hungry ['hʌŋgrɪ] affamato; **I'm ~** ho fame
hunk [hʌŋk] *n* tocco *m*; F *(man)* fusto *m* F
hunt [hʌnt] **1** *n for animals* caccia *f*; *for job, house, missing child* ricerca *f* **2** *v/t animal* cacciare; **hunter** cacciatore *m*, -trice *f*; **hunting** caccia *f*
hurdle ['hɜːdl] *also fig* ostacolo *m*
hurl [hɜːl] scagliare
hurray [huˈreɪ] urrà!
hurricane ['hʌrɪkən] uragano *m*
hurried ['hʌrɪd] trettoloso;
hurry **1** *n* fretta *f*; *be in a ~* avere fretta **2** *v/i* sbrigarsi
♦ **hurry up** *v/i* sbrigarsi; *hurry up!* sbrigati! **2** *v/t* fare fretta a
hurt [hɜːt] **1** *v/i* far male; *does it ~?* ti fa male? **2** *v/t physically* far male a; *emotionally* ferire
husband ['hʌzbənd] marito *m*
hush [hʌʃ] silenzio *m*
♦ **hush up** *scandal etc* mettere a tacere
husky ['hʌskɪ] *voice* roco
hut [hʌt] capanno *m*
hybrid ['haɪbrɪd] ibrido *m*
hydrant ['haɪdrənt] idrante *m*

hydraulic [haɪˈdrɔːlɪk] idraulico

hydroelectric [haɪdrəʊˈlektrɪk] idroelettrico

hydrogen [ˈhaɪdrədʒən] idrogeno *m*

hygiene [ˈhaɪdʒiːn] igiene *f*; **hygienic** igienico

hymn [hɪm] inno *m* (sacro)

hype [haɪp] pubblicità *f*

hyperactive [haɪpərˈæktɪv] iperattivo; **hypermarket** ipermercato *m*; **hypersensitive** ipersensibile; **hypertext** COMPUT ipertesto *m*

hyphen [ˈhaɪfn] trattino *m*

hypnosis [hɪpˈnəʊsɪs] ipnosi

f; **hypnotize** ipnotizzare

hypocrisy [hɪˈpɒkrəsɪ] ipocrisia *f*; **hypocrite** ipocrita *m/f*; **hypocritical** ipocrita

hypothermia [haɪpəʊˈθɜːmɪə] ipotermia *f*

hypothesis [haɪˈpɒθəsɪs] ipotesi *f inv*; **hypothetical** ipotetico

hysterectomy [hɪstəˈrektəmɪ] isterectomia *f*

hysteria [hɪˈstɪərɪə] isteria *f*; **hysterical** isterico; F (*very funny*) buffissimo; **become** ~ avere una crisi isterica; **hysterics** *laughter* attacco *m* di risa; MED crisi *f* isterica

I

I [aɪ] io; ~ **am English** sono inglese; *here* ~ **am** eccomi

ice [aɪs] ghiaccio *m*; **iceberg** iceberg *m inv*; **icebox** *Am* frigo *m*; **ice cream** gelato *m*; **ice cube** cubetto *m* di ghiaccio; **iced** *drink* ghiacciato; *cake* glassato; **ice hockey** hockey *m* sul ghiaccio; **ice lolly** ghiacciolo *m*; **ice rink** pista *f* di pattinaggio; **ice skate** pattinare (sul ghiaccio); **ice skating** pattinaggio *m* (sul ghiaccio)

icicle [ˈaɪsɪkl] ghiacciolo *m*

icing [ˈaɪsɪŋ] glassa *f*

icon [ˈaɪkɒn] *cultural* mito *m*; COMPUT icona *f*

icy [ˈaɪsɪ] *road, surface* ghiac-

ciato; *welcome* glaciale

ID [aɪˈdiː] (= *identity*): *have you got any* ~ *on you?* ha un documento d'identità?

idea [aɪˈdɪə] idea *f*; *good* ~! ottima idea!; *I have no* ~ non ne ho la minima idea; **ideal** ideale; **idealistic** *person* idealista; **views** idealistico

identical [aɪˈdentɪkl] identico; ~ **twins** gemelli *mpl* monozigotici; **identification** identificazione *f*, riconoscimento *m*; *papers etc* documento *m* di riconoscimento *or* d'identità; **identify** (*recognize*) identificare, riconoscere; (*point out*) individuare;

identity identità f inv; ~ **card** carta f d'identità

ideological [aɪdɪə'lɒdʒɪkl] ideologico; **ideology** ideologia f

idiomatic [ɪdɪə'mætɪk] naturale

idiot ['ɪdɪət] idiota m/f; **idiotic** idiota

idle ['aɪdl] **1** adj person disoccupato; threat vuoto; machinery inattivo **2** v/i of engine girare al minimo

idol ['aɪdl] idolo m; **idolize** idolatrare

idyllic [ɪ'dɪlɪk] idilli(a)co

if [ɪf] se

ignite [ɪg'naɪt] dar fuoco a; **ignition** in car accensione f; **~ key** chiave f dell'accensione

ignorance ['ɪgnərəns] ignoranza f; **ignorant** (rude) cafone; **be ~ of sth** ignorare qc; **ignore** ignorare

ill [ɪl] ammalato; **fall ~, be taken ~** ammalarsi; **feel ~** sentirsi male

illegal [ɪ'liːgl] illegale

illegible [ɪ'ledʒəbl] illeggibile

illegitimate [ɪlɪ'dʒɪtɪmət] child illegittimo

illicit [ɪ'lɪsɪt] copy, imports illegale; pleasure, relationship illecito

illiterate [ɪ'lɪtərət] analfabeta

illness ['ɪlnɪs] malattia f

illogical [ɪ'lɒdʒɪkl] illogico

ill-treat maltrattare

illuminating [ɪ'luːmɪneɪtɪŋ] remarks etc chiarificatore

illusion [ɪ'luːʒn] illusione f

illustrate ['ɪləstreɪt] illustrare; **illustration** illustrazione f; with examples esemplificazione f; **illustrator** illustratore m, -trice f

image ['ɪmɪdʒ] immagine f; (exact likeness) ritratto; **image-conscious** attento all'immagine

imaginary [ɪ'mædʒɪnərɪ] immaginario; **imagination** immaginazione f, fantasia f; **imaginative** fantasioso; **imagine** immaginare; **you're imagining things** è frutto della tua immaginazione

IMF [aɪem'ef] (= International Monetary Fund) FMI m (= Fondo m Monetario Internazionale)

imitate ['ɪmɪteɪt] imitare; **imitation** imitazione f

immaculate [ɪ'mækjʊlət] immacolato

immature [ɪmə'tʃʊə(r)] immaturo

immediate [ɪ'miːdɪət] immediato; **the ~ family** i familiari più stretti; **immediately** immediatamente; **~ after the bank** subito dopo la banca

immense [ɪ'mens] immenso

immerse [ɪ'mɜːs] immergere

immigrant ['ɪmɪgrənt] immigrato m, -a f; **immigrate** immigrare; **immigration** immigrazione f

imminent ['ɪmɪnənt] imminente

immobilize [ɪˈməʊbɪlaɪz] immobilizzare; **immobilizer** on car immobilizzatore m

immoderate [ɪˈmɒdərət] smodato

immoral [ɪˈmɒrəl] immorale; **immorality** immoralità f inv

immortal [ɪˈmɔːtl] immortale; **immortality** immortalità f

immune [ɪˈmjuːn] to illness, infection immune; from ruling, requirement esente; **immune system** MED sistema m immunitario; **immunity** immunità f inv; from ruling esenzione f

impact [ˈɪmpækt] of meteorite, vehicle urto m; of new manager etc impatto m; (effect) effetto m

impair [ɪmˈpeə(r)] danneggiare

impartial [ɪmˈpɑːʃl] imparziale

impassable [ɪmˈpɑːsəbl] road impraticabile

impassioned [ɪmˈpæʃnd] speech, plea appassionato

impatience [ɪmˈpeɪʃəns] impazienza f; **impatient** impaziente; **impatiently** con impazienza

impeach [ɪmˈpiːtʃ] President mettere in stato d'accusa

impeccable [ɪmˈpekəbl] impeccabile

impede [ɪmˈpiːd] ostacolare; **impediment** in speech difetto m

impending [ɪmˈpendɪŋ] imminente

imperative [ɪmˈperətɪv] **1** adj essenziale **2** n GRAM imperativo m

imperfect [ɪmˈpɜːfekt] **1** adj imperfetto **2** n GRAM imperfetto m

impersonal [ɪmˈpɜːsənl] impersonale; **impersonate** as a joke imitare; illegally fingersi

impertinence [ɪmˈpɜːtɪnəns] impertinenza f; **impertinent** impertinente

impervious [ɪmˈpɜːvɪəs]: ~ to indifferente a

impetuous [ɪmˈpetjʊəs] impetuoso

impetus [ˈɪmpɪtəs] of campaign etc impeto m

implement [ˈɪmplɪmənt] **1** n utensile m **2** v/t implementare

implicate [ˈɪmplɪkeɪt] implicare; **implication** conseguenza f possibile; **by ~** implicitamente

implicit [ɪmˈplɪsɪt] implicito; trust assoluto

implore [ɪmˈplɔː(r)] implorare

imply [ɪmˈplaɪ] implicare; (suggest) insinuare

impolite [ɪmpəˈlaɪt] maleducato

import [ˈɪmpɔːt] **1** n importazione f; item articolo m d'importazione **2** v/t importare

importance [ɪmˈpɔːtəns] importanza f; **important** importante

importer [ɪmˈpɔːtə(r)] importatore *m*, -trice *f*

impose [ɪmˈpəʊz] *tax* imporre; ~ *o.s.* *on s.o.* disturbare qu; **imposing** imponente

impossibility [ɪmpɒsɪˈbɪlɪtɪ] impossibilità *f inv*; **impossible** impossibile

impotence [ˈɪmpətəns] impotenza *f*; **impotent** impotente

impractical [ɪmˈpræktɪkəl] *person* senza senso pratico; *suggestion* poco pratico

impress [ɪmˈpres] fare colpo su; **be ~ed by s.o.** / **sth** essere colpito da qu / qc; **impression** impressione *f*; (*impersonation*) imitazione *f*; **impressionable** impressionabile; **impressive** notevole

imprint [ˈɪmprɪnt] *of credit card* impressione *f*

imprison [ɪmˈprɪzn] incarcerare; **imprisonment** carcerazione *f*

improbable [ɪmˈprɒbəbl] improbabile

improve [ɪmˈpruːv] migliorare; **improvement** miglioramento *m*

improvise [ˈɪmprəvaɪz] improvvisare

impudent [ˈɪmpjʊdənt] impudente

impulse [ˈɪmpʌls] impulso *m*; **do sth on an ~** fare qc d'impulso; **impulsive** impulsivo

in [ɪn] **1** *prep* ◇ *place*: ~ **Milan** a Milano; ~ **the street** per strada; ~ **the box** nella scato-la; **wounded**; ~ **the leg** ferito alla gamba ◇ *time*: ~ **1999** nel 1999; ~ **two hours** *from now* tra due ore; *over period of* in due ore; ~ **the morning** la mattina; ~ **the summer** d'estate; ~ **September** a *or* in settembre ◇ *language*: ~ **English** in inglese; ~ **a loud voice** a voce alta; ~ **yellow** di giallo ◇ (*while*): ~ **crossing the road** mentre attraversava la strada ◇: **one** ~ **ten** uno su dieci **2** *adv*: **be** ~ *at home* essere a casa; *in the building etc* esserci; *arrived*: *of train* essere arrivato; *in its position* essere dentro; **is she** ~? c'è?; ~ **here / there** qui / lì (dentro) **3** *adj* (*fashionable, popular*) in, di moda

inability [ɪnəˈbɪlɪtɪ] incapacità *f inv*

inaccurate [ɪnˈækjʊrət] inaccurato

inactive [ɪnˈæktɪv] inattivo

inadequate [ɪnˈædɪkwət] inadeguato

inadvisable [ɪnədˈvaɪzəbl] sconsigliabile

inanimate [ɪnˈænɪmət] inanimato

inappropriate [ɪnəˈprəʊprɪət] inappropriato

inaudible [ɪnˈɔːdɪbl] impercettibile

inaugural [ɪˈnɔːgjʊrəl] *speech* inaugurale; **inaugurate** inaugurare

inborn [ˈɪnbɔːn] innato

Inc. [ɪŋk] (= *incorporated*)
Inc.

incalculable [ɪn'kælkjʊləbl]
incalcolabile

incapable [ɪn'keɪpəbl] incapace (*of doing* di fare)

incense ['ɪnsens] *in church* incenso *m*

incentive [ɪn'sentɪv] incentivo *m*

incessant [ɪn'sesnt] incessante; **incessantly** incessan-
temente

incest ['ɪnsest] incesto *m*

inch [ɪntʃ] pollice *m*

incident ['ɪnsɪdənt] incidente
m; **incidental** casuale; ~ *expenses* spese accessorie; **incidentally** a proposito

incision [ɪn'sɪʒn] incisione *f*;
incisive acuto

incite [ɪn'saɪt] incitare; ~ *s.o.
to do sth* istigare qu a fare
qc

inclination [ɪnklɪ'neɪʃn] inclinazione *f*

inclose, inclosure ☞ *enclose, enclosure*

include [ɪn'kluːd] includere,
comprendere; **including**
compreso, incluso; **inclusive** 1 *adj price* tutto compreso 2 *prep*: ~ *of VAT* IVA
compresa 3 *adv*: *from Monday to Thursday* ~ dal lunedì al giovedì compreso

incoherent [ɪnkəʊ'hɪrənt] incoerente

income ['ɪnkəm] reddito *m*;
income tax imposta *f* sul

reddito

incoming ['ɪnkʌmɪŋ] *adj
flight, phonecall, mail* in arrivo; *tide* montante; *president*
entrante

incomparable [ɪn'kɒmprəbl]
incomparabile

incompatibility [ɪnkəmpætɪ'-
bɪlɪtɪ] incompatibilità *f inv*;
incompatible incompatibile

incompetence [ɪn'-
kɒmpɪtəns] incompetenza *f*;
incompetent incompetente

incomplete [ɪnkəm'pliːt] incompleto

incomprehensible [ɪnkɒm-
prɪ'hensɪbl] incomprensibile

inconceivable [ɪnkən'siːvəbl]
inconcepibile

inconsiderate [ɪnkən'sɪd-
ərət] poco gentile

inconsistent [ɪnkən'sɪstənt]
incoerente

inconsolable [ɪnkən'səʊləbl]
adj inconsolabile

inconspicuous [ɪnkən'spɪk-
jʊəs] poco visibile; *make
o.s. ~* passare inosservato

inconvenience [ɪnkən'viː-
nɪəns] inconveniente *m*; **inconvenient** scomodo; *time*
poco opportuno

incorporate [ɪn'kɔːpəreɪt] includere

incorrect [ɪnkə'rekt] *answer*
errato; *behaviour* scorretto;
am I ~ in thinking …? sbaglio a pensare che …?

increase 1 [ɪn'kriːs] *v/t & v/i*
aumentare **2** ['ɪnkriːs] *n* au-

mento *m*; **on the ~** in aumento; **increasing** crescente; increasingly sempre più
incredible [ɪnˈkredɪbl] incredibile
incur [ɪnˈkɜː(r)] *costs* affrontare; *debts* contrarre; *s.o.'s anger* esporsi a
incurable [ɪnˈkjʊrəbl] incurabile
indecent [ɪnˈdiːsnt] indecente
indecisive [ɪndɪˈsaɪsɪv] indeciso; **indecisiveness** indecisione *f*
indeed [ɪnˈdiːd] (*in fact*) in effetti; (*yes, agreeing*) esatto; **very much ~** moltissimo
indefinable [ɪndɪˈfaɪnəbl] indefinibile
indefinite [ɪnˈdefɪnɪt] indeterminato; **~ article** GRAM articolo *m* indeterminativo; **indefinitely** a tempo indeterminato
indelicate [ɪnˈdelɪkət] indelicato
independence [ɪndɪˈpendəns] indipendenza *f*; **Independence Day** *in USA* festa *f* dell'indipendenza americana (4 luglio); **independent** indipendente; **independently** indipendentemente; **~ of** indipendentemente da
indescribable [ɪndɪˈskraɪbəbl] indescrivibile
index [ˈɪndeks] indice *m*
India [ˈɪndɪə] India *f*; **Indian 1** *adj* indiano **2** *n person* india-

no *m*, -a *f*; *American* indiano *m*, -a *f* d'america
indicate [ˈɪndɪkeɪt] **1** *v/t* indicare **2** *v/i when driving* segnalare (il cambiamento di direzione); **indication** indicazione *f*; **indicator** MOT freccia *f*
indict [ɪnˈdaɪt] incriminare
indifference [ɪnˈdɪfrəns] indifferenza *f*; **indifferent** indifferente; (*mediocre*) mediocre
indigestion [ɪndɪˈdʒestʃn] indigestione *f*
indignant [ɪnˈdɪgnənt] indignato; **indignation** indignazione *f*
indirect [ɪndɪˈrekt] indiretto; **indirectly** indirettamente
indiscreet [ɪndɪˈskriːt] indiscreto
indiscriminate [ɪndɪˈskrɪmɪnət] indiscriminato
indispensable [ɪndɪˈspensəbl] indispensabile
indisposed [ɪndɪˈspəʊzd] (*not well*) indisposto
indisputable [ɪndɪˈspjuːtəbl] indiscutibile
indistinct [ɪndɪˈstɪŋkt] indistinto
indistinguishable [ɪndɪˈstɪŋgwɪʃəbl] indistinguibile
individual [ɪndɪˈvɪdʒʊəl] **1** *n* individuo *m* **2** *adj* (*separate*) singolo; (*personal*) individuale; **individually** individualmente
indoctrinate [ɪnˈdɒktrɪneɪt]

indottrinare

Indonesia [ɪndəˈniːʒə] Indonesia f; **Indonesian 1** *adj* indonesiano **2** *n person* indonesiano *m*, -a *f*

indoor [ˈɪndɔː(r)] *activities, games* al coperto; *arena, pool* coperto; **indoors** *in building* all'interno; *at home* in casa

indorse ➙ **endorse**

indulgent [ɪnˈdʌldʒənt] indulgente

industrial [ɪnˈdʌstrɪəl] industriale; **industrial dispute** vertenza *f* sindacale; **industrialist** industriale *m*; **industrious** diligente; **industry** industria *f*

ineffective [ɪnɪˈfektɪv] inefficace

inefficient [ɪnɪˈfɪʃənt] inefficiente

inept [ɪˈnept] inetto

inequality [ɪnɪˈkwɒlɪtɪ] disuguaglianza *f*

inescapable [ɪnɪˈskeɪpəbl] inevitabile

inevitable [ɪnˈevɪtəbl] inevitabile; **inevitably** inevitabilmente

inexcusable [ɪnɪkˈskjuːzəbl] imperdonabile

inexhaustible [ɪnɪgˈzɔːstəbl] *supply* inesauribile

inexpensive [ɪnɪkˈspensɪv] poco costoso, economico

inexperienced [ɪnɪkˈspɪərɪənst] inesperto

inexplicable [ɪnɪkˈsplɪkəbl] inspiegabile

infallible [ɪnˈfælɪbl] infallibile

infamous [ˈɪnfəməs] famigerato

infancy [ˈɪnfənsɪ] *of person* infanzia *f*; *of state, institution* stadio *m* iniziale; **infant** bambino *m* piccolo, bambina *f* piccola; **infantile** *pej* infantile

infantry [ˈɪnfəntrɪ] fanteria *f*

infatuated [ɪnˈfætʃʊeɪtɪd]: **be ~ with s.o.** essere infatuato di qu

infect [ɪnˈfekt] *of person* contagiare; *food, water* contaminare; **become ~ed** *of wound* infettarsi; *of person* contagiarsi; **infection** infezione *f*; **infectious** *disease* infettivo, contagioso; *laughter* contagioso

infer [ɪnˈfɜː(r)]: **~ sth from sth** dedurre qc da qc

inferior [ɪnˈfɪərɪə(r)] inferiore; **inferiority** inferiorità *f*; **inferiority complex** complesso *m* d'inferiorità

infertile [ɪnˈfɜːtaɪl] sterile; **infertility** sterilità *f*

infidelity [ɪnfɪˈdelɪtɪ] infedeltà *f inv*

infinite [ˈɪnfɪnət] infinito; **infinitive** infinito *m*

infinity [ɪnˈfɪnɪtɪ] infinito *m*

inflammable [ɪnˈflæməbl] infiammabile; **inflammation** MED infiammazione *f*

inflatable [ɪnˈfleɪtəbl] *dinghy* gonfiabile; **inflate** *tyre, dinghy* gonfiare; *economy* infla-

zionare; **inflation** inflazione
f; **inflationary** inflazionisti-
co

inflexible [ɪnˈfleksɪbl] inflessibile

inflict [ɪnˈflɪkt]: **~ sth on s.o.**
punishment infliggere qc a
qu; *suffering* procurare qc a
qu

'in-flight: ~ entertainment in-
trattenimento a bordo

influence [ˈɪnfluəns] **1** *n* influenza f **2** *v/t s.o.'s thinking*
esercitare un'influenza su;
decision influenzare; **influential** *writer, film-maker* autorevole; **she knows ~ people** conosce gente influente

inform [ɪnˈfɔːm] **1** *v/t* informare **2** *v/t*: **~ on s.o.** denunciare
qu

informal [ɪnˈfɔːml] informale; **informality** informalità f

informant [ɪnˈfɔːmənt] informatore *m*, -trice f; **information** informazione f; **a bit of**
~ un'informazione; **information science** informatica f;
information technology informatica f; **informative** *article etc* istruttivo; **he wasn't**
very ~ non è stato di grande
aiuto; **informer** informatore
m, -trice f

infra-red [ɪnfrəˈred] infrarosso; **infrastructure** [ˈɪnfrə-
strʌktʃə(r)] infrastruttura f

infrequent [ɪnˈfriːkwənt] raro

infuriate [ɪnˈfjʊərɪeɪt] far infuriare; **infuriating** esaspe-

rante

ingenious [ɪnˈdʒiːnɪəs] ingegnoso

ingot [ˈɪŋgət] lingotto *m*

ingratitude [ɪnˈgrætɪtjuːd] ingratitudine f

ingredient [ɪnˈgriːdɪənt] *for*
cooking ingrediente *m; for*
success elemento *m*

inhabit [ɪnˈhæbɪt] abitare; **inhabitant** abitante *m/f*

inhale [ɪnˈheɪl] **1** *v/t* inalare **2**
v/i when smoking aspirare;
inhaler MED aerosol *m*

inherit [ɪnˈherɪt] ereditare; **inheritance** eredità f inv

inhibited [ɪnˈhɪbɪtd] inibito;
inhibition inibizione f

inhospitable [ɪnhɒˈspɪtəbl]
inospitale

'in-house 1 *adj* aziendale **2**
adv work all'interno dell'a-
zienda

inhuman [ɪnˈhjuːmən] disumano

initial [ɪˈnɪʃl] **1** *adj* iniziale **2** *n*
iniziale f **3** *v/t (write initials*
on) siglare (con le iniziali);
initially inizialmente; **initiate** avviare; **initiation** avviamento *m*; **initiative** iniziativa f; **do sth on one's own**
~ fare qc di propria iniziativa; **take the ~** prendere l'iniziativa

inject [ɪnˈdʒekt] iniettare;
capital investire; **injection**
iniezione f; *of capital* investimento *m*

injure [ˈɪndʒə(r)] ferire; **in-

jured 1 *adj leg* ferito; *feelings* offeso **2** *npl* feriti *mpl*; **injury** ferita *f*

injustice [ɪn'dʒʌstɪs] ingiustizia *f*

ink [ɪŋk] inchiostro *m*; **inkjet (printer)** stampante *f* a getto d'inchiostro

inland ['ɪnlənd] *areas* dell'interno; *mail* nazionale; **Inland Revenue** fisco *m*

in-laws ['ɪnlɔːz] famiglia della moglie / del marito; *(wife's / husband's parents)* suoceri *mpl*

inmate ['ɪnmeɪt] *of prison* detenuto *m*, -a *f*; *of mental hospital* ricoverato *m*, -a *f*

inn [m] locanda *f*

innate [ɪ'neɪt] innato

inner ['ɪnə(r)] interno; **inner city** centro *m* degradato di una zona urbana; ~ **decay** degrado del centro urbano

innocence ['ɪnəsəns] innocenza *f*; **innocent** innocente

innocuous [ɪ'nɒkjʊəs] innocuo

innovation [ɪnə'veɪʃn] innovazione *f*; **innovative** innovativo; **innovator** innovatore *m*, -trice *f*

inoculate [ɪ'nɒkjʊleɪt] vaccinare; **inoculation** vaccinazione *f*

inoffensive [ɪnə'fensɪv] inoffensivo

'in-patient degente *m/f*

input ['ɪnput] **1** *n* contributo *m*; COMPUT input *m inv* **2**

v/t into project contribuire con; COMPUT inserire

inquest ['ɪnkwest] inchiesta *f* giudiziaria

inquire [ɪn'kwaɪə(r)] domandare; ~ **into sth** svolgere indagini su qc; **inquiry** richiesta *f* di informazioni; *(public* ~) indagine *f*

inquisitive [ɪn'kwɪzətɪv] curioso

insane [ɪn'seɪn] pazzo

insanitary [ɪn'sænɪtrɪ] antigienico

insanity [ɪn'sænɪtɪ] infermità *f* mentale

inscription [ɪn'skrɪpʃn] iscrizione *f*

insect ['ɪnsekt] insetto *m*; **insecticide** insetticida *m*

insecure [ɪnsɪ'kjuə(r)] insicuro; **insecurity** insicurezza *f*

insensitive [ɪn'sensɪtɪv] insensibile

insert 1 ['ɪnsɜːt] *n in magazine etc* inserto *m* **2** [ɪn'sɜːt] *v/t* inserire

inside [ɪn'saɪd] **1** *n* interno *m*; *of road* destra *f*; sinistra *f*; ~ **out** a rovescio; **turn sth** ~ **out** rivoltare qc; **know sth** ~ **out** sapere qc a menadito **2** *prep* dentro; ~ **of 2 hours** in meno di due ore **3** *adv* stay, go dentro **4** *adj* interno; ~ **information** informazioni riservate; ~ **lane** SP corsia *f* interna; *on road* corsia *f* di marcia

inside 'pocket tasca *f* interna; **insider**: *an ~ from the Department* un impiegato del Ministero; **insider trading**FIN insider trading *m*; **insides** pancia *fsg*; *intestines* budella *fpl*

insignificant [ɪnsɪg'nɪfɪkənt] insignificante

insincere [ɪnsɪn'sɪə(r)] falso; **insincerity** falsità *f*

insinuate [ɪn'sɪnjʊeɪt] (*imply*) insinuare

insist [ɪn'sɪst] insistere; *please keep it, I ~* tienilo, ci tengo!

◆ **insist on** esigere; *insist on doing sth* insistere per fare qc

insistent [ɪn'sɪstənt] insistente

insolent ['ɪnsələnt] insolente

insoluble [ɪn'sɒljʊbl] *problem* insolubile; *substance* insolubile

insolvent [ɪn'sɒlvənt] insolvente

insomnia [ɪn'sɒmnɪə] insonnia *f*

inspect [ɪn'spekt] *work, tickets, baggage* controllare; *factory, school* ispezionare; **inspection** *of work, tickets, baggage* controllo *m*; *of factory, school* ispezione *f*; **inspector** *in factory* ispettore *m*, -trice *f*; *on buses* controllore *m*; *of police* ispettore *m*

inspiration [ɪnspə'reɪʃn] ispirazione *f*; (*very good idea*) lampo *m* di genio; **inspire**

respect etc suscitare; *be ~d by s.o. / sth* essere ispirato da qu / qc

instability [ɪnstə'bɪlɪtɪ] instabilità *f inv*

install [ɪn'stɔːl] installare; **installation** installazione *f*; *military* ~ struttura *f* militare; **instalment**, *Am* **installment** *of story, TV drama etc* puntata *f*; (*payment*) rata *f*; **installment plan** *Am* acquisto *m* rateale

instance ['ɪnstəns] (*example*) esempio *m*; *for ~* per esempio

instant ['ɪnstənt] **1** *adj* immediato **2** *n* istante *m*; *in an ~* in un attimo; **instantaneous** immediato; **instant coffee** caffè *m inv* istantaneo *or* solubile; **instantly** istantaneamente

instead [ɪn'sted] invece; *~ of* invece di

instinct ['ɪnstɪŋkt] istinto *m*; **instinctive** istintivo

institute ['ɪnstɪtjuːt] **1** *n* istituto *m* **2** *v/t new law* introdurre; *enquiry* avviare; **institution** istituto *m*; *sth traditional* istituzione *f*; (*setting up*) avviamento *m*

instruct [ɪn'strʌkt] (*order*) dare istruzioni a; (*teach*) istruire; **instruction** istruzione *f*; *~s for use* istruzioni per l'uso; **instructive** istruttivo; **instructor** istruttore *m*, -trice *f*

instrument [ˈɪnstrʊmənt]
strumento *m*

insubordinate [ɪnsəˈbɔː-
dɪnət] insubordinato

insufficient [ɪnsəˈfɪʃnt] insufficiente

insulate [ˈɪnsjʊleɪt] ELEC
against cold isolare ter-
micamente; **insulation** ELEC
isolamento *m*; *against cold*
isolamento *m* termico

insulin [ˈɪnsjʊlɪn] insulina *f*

insult 1 [ˈɪnsʌlt] *n* insulto *m* **2**
[ɪnˈsʌlt] *v/t* insultare

insurance [ɪnˈʃʊərəns] assicurazione *f*; **insurance
company** compagnia *f* di as-
sicurazioni; **insurance policy** polizza *f* di assicurazione;
insurance premium premio
m assicurativo; **insure** assicurare

insurmountable [ɪnsə-
ˈmaʊntəbl] insormontabile

intact [ɪnˈtækt] intatto

integrate [ˈɪntɪɡreɪt] integrare; **integrity** integrità *f*

intellect [ˈɪntəlekt] intelletto
m; **intellectual 1** *adj* intellettuale **2** *n* intellettuale *m/f*

intelligence [ɪnˈtelɪdʒəns] intelligenza *f*; *(information)* informazioni *fpl*; **intelligent**
intelligente

intelligible [ɪnˈtelɪdʒəbl] in-
telligibile

intend [ɪnˈtend] *~ to do sth*
(do on purpose) volere fare
qc; *(plan to do)* avere intenzione di fare qc

intense [ɪnˈtens] intenso; *concentration* profondo; *personality* serio; **intensify 1** *v/t* effect, *pressure* intensificare **2**
v/i of pain acuirsi; *of fighting*
intensificarsi; **intensity** in-
tensità *f inv*; **intensive** intensivo; **intensive care
(unit)** MED (reparto *m* di) terapia *f* intensiva

intention [ɪnˈtenʃn] intenzione *f*; **intentional** intenzionale; **intentionally** intenzio-
nalmente

interaction [ɪntərˈækʃn] inte-
razione *f*; **interactive** interattivo

intercept [ɪntəˈsept] intercettare

interchange [ˈɪntətʃeɪndʒ]
MOT interscambio *m*; **interchangeable** interscambia-
bile

intercom [ˈɪntəkɒm] citofono
m

intercourse [ˈɪntəkɔːs] *sexual*
rapporto *m* sessuale

interdependent [ɪntədɪˈpen-
dənt] interdipendente

interest [ˈɪntrəst] **1** *n* interesse *m*; *money paid / received*
interessi *mpl*; **take an ~ in
sth** interessarsi di qc **2** *v/t* interessare; **interested** interessato; **be ~ in sth** interessarsi di qc; **interesting** interessante; **interest rate** FIN
tasso *m* d'interesse

interface [ˈɪntəfeɪs] **1** *n* interfaccia *f* **2** *v/i* interfacciarsi

interfere [ɪntə'fɪə(r)] interferire; **interference** interferenza f; *on radio* interferenze fpl

interior [ɪn'tɪərɪə(r)] **1** adj interno **2** n of house interno m; of country entroterra m; **interior decorator** arredatore m, -trice f; **interior design** architettura f d'interni; **interior designer** architetto m d'interni

interlude ['ɪntəluːd] at theatre, concert intervallo m; (period) parentesi f inv

intermediary [ɪntə'miːdɪərɪ] intermediario m, -a f; **intermediate** intermedio

intermission [ɪntə'mɪʃn] in theatre, cinema intervallo m

internal [ɪn'tɜːnl] interno; **internally**: he's bleeding ~ ha un'emorragia interna; **not to be taken ~** per uso esterno; **Internal Revenue (Service)** Am fisco m

international [ɪntə'næʃnl] **1** adj internazionale **2** n match partita f internazionale; player giocatore m, -trice f della nazionale; **internationally** a livello internazionale

Internet ['ɪntənet] Internet m; **on the ~** su Internet; **~ service provider** provider m inv di servizi Internet

interpret [ɪn'tɜːprɪt] **1** v/t tradurre; piece of music, comment etc interpretare **2** v/i fare da interprete; **interpretation** traduzione f; of piece of music, meaning interpretazione f; **interpreter** interprete m/f

interrogate [ɪn'terəgeɪt] interrogare; **interrogation** interrogatorio m; **interrogator** interrogante m/f

interrupt [ɪntə'rʌpt] interrompere; **interruption** interruzione f

intersect [ɪntə'sekt] **1** v/t intersecare **2** v/i intersecarsi; **intersection** of roads incrocio m

interstate ['ɪntəsteɪt] Am autostrada f interstatale

interval ['ɪntəvl] intervallo m; **sunny ~s** schiarite

intervene [ɪntə'viːn] of person, police etc intervenire, of time trascorrere; **intervention** intervento m

interview ['ɪntəvjuː] **1** n on TV, in paper intervista f; for job intervista f d'assunzione, colloquio m di lavoro **2** v/t on TV, for paper intervistare; for job sottoporre a intervista; **interviewer** on TV, for paper intervistatore m, -trice f; (for job) persona che conduce un'intervista d'assunzione

intimate ['ɪntɪmət] intimo; **be ~ with s.o.** sexually avere rapporti intimi con qu

intimidate [ɪn'tɪmɪdeɪt] intimidire; **intimidation** intimi-

dazione f
into ['ıntu] in; **be ~ sth** F (*like*) amare qc; (*be involved with*) interessarsi di qc; **be ~ drugs** fare uso di droga; **when you're ~ the job** quando sei pratico del lavoro
intolerable [ın'tɒlərəbl] intollerabile; **intolerant** intollerante
intoxicated [ın'tɒksıkeıtıd] ubriaco
intravenous [ıntrə'vi:nəs] endovenoso
intricate ['ıntrıkət] complicato
intrigue 1 ['ıntri:g] *n* intrigo *m* **2** [ın'tri:g] *v/t* intrigare; **I would be ~d to know ...** m'interesserebbe molto sapere ...; **intriguing** intrigante
introduce [ıntrə'dju:s] *person* presentare; *new technique etc* introdurre; **may I ~ ...?** permette che le presenti ...?; **introduction** *to person* presentazione f; *to new food, sport etc* approccio *m*; *in book, of new technique* introduzione f
introvert ['ıntrəvɜ:t] introverso *m*, -a f
intrude [ın'tru:d] importunare; **intruder** intruso *m*, -a f; **intrusion** intrusione f
intuition [ıntju:'ıʃn] intuito *m*
invade [ın'veıd] invadere
invalid[1] [ın'vælıd] *adj* non valido
invalid[2] ['ınvəlıd] *n* MED invalido *m*, -a f

invalidate [ın'vælıdeıt] invalidare
invaluable [ın'væljubl] prezioso
invariably [ın'veırıəblı] (*always*) invariabilmente
invasion [ın'veıʒn] invasione f
invent [ın'vent] inventare; **invention** invenzione f; **inventive** fantasioso; **inventor** inventore *m*, -trice f
inventory ['ınvəntrı] inventario *m*
invert [ın'vɜ:t] invertire; **inverted commas** virgolette fpl
invest [ın'vest] investire
investigate [ın'vestıgeıt] indagare su; **investigation** indagine f; **investigative journalism** giornalismo *m* investigativo
investment [ın'vestmənt] investimento *m*; **investor** investitore *m*, -trice
invigorating [ın'vıgəreıtıŋ] *climate* tonificante
invincible [ın'vınsəbl] invincibile
invisible [ın'vızıbl] invisibile
invitation [ınvı'teıʃn] invito *m*; **invite** invitare
invoice ['ınvɔıs] **1** *n* fattura f **2** *v/t customer* fatturare
involuntary [ın'vɒləntrı] involontario
involve [ın'vɒlv] *hard work, expense* comportare; (*con-*

cern) riguardare; **what does it ~?** che cosa comporta?; **get ~d with sth** entrare a far parte di qc; **get ~d with s.o.** *emotionally, romantically* legarsi a qu; *involved* (*complex*) complesso; *involvement in a project etc* partecipazione *f*; *in crime, accident* coinvolgimento *m*

invulnerable [ɪnˈvʌlnərəbl] invulnerabile

inward [ˈɪnwəd] **1** *adj feeling, thoughts* intimo **2** *adv* verso l'interno; **inwardly** dentro di sé

IQ [aɪˈkjuː] (= **intelligence quotient**) quoziente *m* d'intelligenza

Iran [ɪˈrɑːn] Iran *m*; **Iranian 1** *adj* iraniano **2** *n* iraniano *m*, -a *f*

Iraq [ɪˈræːk] Iraq *m*; **Iraqi 1** *adj* iracheno **2** *n* iracheno *m*, -a *f*

Ireland [ˈaɪələnd] Irlanda *f*; **Irish** irlandese; **Irishman** irlandese *m*; **Irishwoman** irlandese *f*

iron [ˈaɪən] **1** *n* ferro *m*; *for clothes* ferro *m* da stiro **2** *v/t shirts etc* stirare

ironic(al) [aɪˈrɒnɪk(l)] ironico

'ironing board asse *m* da stiro

irony [ˈaɪərənɪ] ironia *f*

irrational [ɪˈræʃənl] irrazionale

irreconcilable [ɪrekənˈsaɪləbl] inconciliabile

irregular [ɪˈregjʊlə(r)] irrego-

lare

irrelevant [ɪˈreləvənt] non pertinente

irreplaceable [ɪrɪˈpleɪsəbl] insostituibile

irrepressible [ɪrɪˈpresəbl] *sense of humour* incontenibile; *person* che non si lascia abbattere

irresistible [ɪrɪˈzɪstəbl] irresistibile

irresponsible [ɪrɪˈspɒnsəbl] irresponsabile

irreverent [ɪˈrevərənt] irriverente

irrevocable [ɪˈrevəkəbl] irrevocabile

irrigate [ˈɪrɪgeɪt] irrigare; **irrigation** irrigazione *f*

irritable [ˈɪrɪtəbl] irritabile; **irritate** irritare; **irritating** irritante; **irritation** irritazione *f*

Islam [ˈɪzlɑːm] Islam *m*; **Islamic** islamico

island [ˈaɪlənd] isola *f*; **islander** isolano *m*, -a *f*

isolate [ˈaɪsəleɪt] isolare; **isolated** isolato; **isolation** isolamento *m*; **in ~ taken etc** da solo

ISP [aɪesˈpiː] (= **Internet service provider**) provider *m inv* di servizi Internet

Israel [ˈɪzreɪl] Israele *m*; **Israeli 1** *adj* israeliano **2** *n person* israeliano *m*, -a *f*

issue [ˈɪʃuː] **1** *n* (*matter*) questione *f*; (*result*) risultato *m*; *of magazine* numero *m*; **take ~ with s.o. / sth** prendere

posizione contro qu / qc **2**
v/t passports rilasciare; *sup-*
plies distribuire; *coins* emettere; *warning* dare
IT [aɪˈtiː] (= *information tech-*
nology) IT f
it [ɪt] ◇ *as subject:* **what col-**
our is ~? – ~ **is red** di che
colore è? – è rosso; ~**'s rain-**
ing piove; ~**'s me / him** sono
io / è lui; ~**'s Charlie here**
TELEC sono Charlie; **that's**
~! (*that's right*) proprio così!;
(*finished*) finito! ◇ *as object*
lo *m*, la *f*; **I broke** ~ l'ho rotto,
-a
Italian [ɪˈtæljən] **1** *adj* italiano
2 *n person* italiano *m*, -a *f*;
language italiano *m*

italic [ɪˈtælɪk] in corsivo
Italy [ˈɪtəlɪ] Italia *f*
itch [ɪtʃ] **1** *n* prurito *m* **2** v/i
prudere
item [ˈaɪtəm] *on agenda* punto
m (all'ordine del giorno); *on*
shopping list articolo *m*; *in*
accounts voce *f*; *news* ~ notizia *f*; **itemize** *invoice* detta-
gliare
itinerary [aɪˈtɪnərərɪ] itinerario *m*
its [ɪts] il suo *m*, la sua *f*, i suoi
mpl, le sue *fpl*
it's [ɪts] ☞ *it is, it has*
itself [ɪtˈself] *reflexive* si;
emphatic di per sé; **by** ~
(*alone*) da solo; (*automatical-*
ly) da sé

J

jab [dʒæb] conficcare
jack [dʒæk] MOT cric *m inv*; *in*
cards fante *m*
jacket [ˈdʒækɪt] *n* giacca *f*; *of*
book copertina *f*
'jackpot primo premio *m*;
hit the ~ vincere il primo
premio; *fig* fare un terno al
lotto
jagged [ˈdʒægɪd] frastagliato
jail [dʒeɪl] prigione *f*
jam¹ [dʒæm] *for bread* marmellata *f*
jam² [dʒæm] **1** *n* MOT ingorgo
m; **be in a** ~ F (*difficulty*) essere in difficoltà **2** v/t (*ram*)
ficcare; (*cause to stick*) bloc-

care; **be** ~**med** *of roads* essere congestionato; *of door,*
window essere bloccato **3**
v/i (*stick*) bloccarsi
janitor [ˈdʒænɪtə(r)] custode
m
January [ˈdʒænjʊərɪ] gennaio
m
Japan [dʒəˈpæn] Giappone
m; **Japanese 1** *adj* giappo-
nese **2** *n person* giapponese
m/*f*; *language* giapponese *m*
jar¹ [dʒɑː(r)] *container* barattolo *m*
jargon [ˈdʒɑːgən] gergo *m*
javelin [ˈdʒævlɪn] giavellotto
m

435   **joint venture**

jaw [dʒɔː] mascella *m*
jaywalker ['dʒeɪwɔːkə(r)] pedone *m* indisciplinato
jazz [dʒæz] jazz *m*
jealous ['dʒeləs] geloso; **jealousy** gelosia *f*
jeans [dʒiːnz] jeans *mpl*
jeep [dʒiːp] jeep *f inv*
jeer [dʒɪə(r)] **1** *n* scherno *m* **2** *v/i* schernire; **~ at** schernire
Jello® ['dʒeləʊ] *Am* gelatina *f*
jelly ['dʒelɪ] *Br* gelatina *f; Am* marmellata *f;* **jellyfish** medusa *f*
jeopardize ['dʒepədaɪz] mettere in pericolo
jerk¹ [dʒɜːk] **1** *n* scossone *m* **2** *v/t* dare uno strattone
jerk² [dʒɜːk] *n* F idiota *m/f*
jerky ['dʒɜːkɪ] *movements* a scatti
Jesus ['dʒiːzəs] Gesù *m*
jet [dʒet] **1** *n of water* zampillo *m; (nozzle)* becco *m; airplane* jet *m inv* **2** *v/i travel* volare;
jetlag jet-lag *m*
jettison ['dʒetɪsn] gettare; *fig* abbandonare
jetty ['dʒetɪ] molo *m*
Jew [dʒuː] ebreo *m, -a f*
jewel ['dʒuːəl] gioiello *m; fig: person* perla *f;* **jeweller,** *Am* **jeweler** gioielliere *m*
Jewish ['dʒuːɪʃ] ebraico; *people* ebreo
jigsaw (puzzle) ['dʒɪgsɔː] puzzle *m inv*
jilt [dʒɪlt] piantare F
jingle ['dʒɪŋgl] **1** *n song* jingle *m inv* **2** *v/i of keys, coins* tin-

tinnare
jinx [dʒɪŋks] *person* iettatore *m, -trice f;* **there's a ~ on this project** questo progetto è iellato
jittery ['dʒɪtərɪ] F nervoso
job [dʒɒb] *(employment)* lavoro *m; (task)* compito *m;* **it's a good ~ you ...** meno male che tu ...; **job description** elenco *m* delle mansioni; **jobless** disoccupato
jockey ['dʒɒkɪ] fantino *m*
jog [dʒɒg] **1** *n* corsa *f;* **go for a ~** andare a fare footing **2** *v/i as exercise* fare footing **3** *v/t elbow etc* urtare; **~ s.o.'s memory** rinfrescare la memoria a qu; **jogger** *person* persona *f che ...* fa footing; *Am shoe* scarpa *f* da ginnastica; **jogging** footing *m;* **go ~** fare footing
john [dʒɒn] *Am* F gabinetto *m*
join [dʒɔɪn] **1** *n* giuntura *f* **2** *v/i of roads, rivers* unirsi; *(become a member)* iscriversi **3** *v/t (connect)* unire; *person* unirsi a; *club* iscriversi a; *(go to work for)* entrare in; *of road* congiungersi a
◆ **join in** partecipare
joint [dʒɔɪnt] **1** *n* ANAT articolazione *f; in woodwork* giunto *m; of meat* arrosto *m; of cannabis* spinello *m* **2** *adj (shared)* comune; **joint account** conto *m* comune; **joint venture** joint venture *f inv*

joke

joke [dʒəʊk] **1** *n* story barzelletta *f*; (*practical* ~) scherzo *m* **2** *v/i* (*pretend*) scherzare; **joker** *in cards* jolly *m inv*; F burlone *m*, -a *f*; **jokingly** scherzosamente

jostle ['dʒɒsl] spintonare

journal ['dʒɜːnl] *magazine* rivista *f*; *diary* diario *m*; **journalism** giornalismo *m*; **journalist** giornalista *m/f*

journey ['dʒɜːnɪ] viaggio *m*

joy [dʒɔɪ] gioia *f*

jubilant ['dʒuːbɪlənt] esultante; **jubilation** giubilo *m*

judge [dʒʌdʒ] **1** *n* giudice *m* **2** *v/t* giudicare; *competition* fare da giudice a **3** *v/i* giudicare; **judg(e)ment** giudizio *m*; **an error of** ~ un errore di valutazione; **Judg(e)ment Day** il giorno *m* del giudizio

judicial [dʒuːˈdɪʃl] giudiziario

jug [dʒʌg] brocca *f*

juggle [dʒʌgl] fare giochi di destrezza con; *fig: conflicting demands* destreggiarsi fra; *figures* manipolare; **juggler** giocoliere *m*

juice [dʒuːs] succo *m*; juicy succoso; *news, gossip* piccante

July [dʒʊˈlaɪ] luglio *m*

jumbo (jet) ['dʒʌmbəʊ] jumbo *m* (jet); **jumbo-sized** gigante

jump [dʒʌmp] **1** *n* salto *m*; (*increase*) impennata *f* **2** *v/i* saltare; (*increase*) aumentare rapidamente, avere un'impennata; *in surprise* sobbalzare; ~ **to conclusions** arrivare a conclusioni affrettate **3** *v/t fence etc* saltare; F (*attack*) aggredire; ~ **the queue** non rispettare la fila; ~ **the lights** passare col rosso

◆ **jump at** *opportunity* prendere al balzo

jumper ['dʒʌmpə(r)] *Br* golf *m inv*; *Am dress* scamiciato *m*; **jumpy** nervoso

junction ['dʒʌŋkʃn] *of roads* incrocio *m*

June [dʒuːn] giugno *m*

jungle ['dʒʌŋgl] giungla *f*

junior ['dʒuːnɪə(r)] **1** *adj* (*subordinate*) subalterno; (*younger*) giovane **2** *n in rank* subalterno *m*, -a *f*; **she is ten years my** ~ ha dieci anni meno di me; **junior high** *Am scuola per ragazzi dai 12 ai 15 anni*

junk [dʒʌŋk] robaccia *f*; **junk food** alimenti *mpl* poco sani, porcherie *fpl*; **junkie** F tossico *m*, -a *f*; **junk mail** posta *f* spazzatura

jurisdiction [dʒʊərɪsˈdɪkʃn] LAW giurisdizione *f*

juror ['dʒʊərə(r)] giurato *m*, -a *f*; **jury** giuria *f*

just [dʒʌst] **1** *adj* giusto **2** *adv* (*barely*) appena; (*exactly*) proprio; (*only*) solo; **I've** ~ **seen her** l'ho appena vista; ~ **about** (*almost*) quasi; **I was** ~ **about to leave when** ... stavo proprio per andarmene quando ...; ~ *now* (*a few moments ago*) proprio ora; (*at the moment*) al momento; ~ *you wait!* aspetta un po'!; ~ *be quiet!* fai silenzio!; ~ *as rich* altrettanto ricco

justice ['dʒʌstɪs] giustizia *f*
justifiable [dʒʌstɪ'faɪəbl] giustificabile; **justifiably** a ragione; **justification** giustificazione *f*; **justify** *also text* giustificare

justly ['dʒʌstlɪ] giustamente
◆ **jut out** [dʒʌt] sporgere
juvenile ['dʒuːvənaɪl] **1** *adj* minorile; *pej* puerile **2** *n fml* minore *m/f*; **juvenile delinquent** delinquente *m/f* minorile

K

k [keɪ] (= *kilobyte*) k (= kilobyte *m inv*) (= *thousand*) mille
kangaroo [kæŋɡə'ruː] canguro *m*
keel [kiːl] NAUT chiglia *f*
keen [kiːn] *person* entusiasta; *interest, competition* vivo; **be ~ on sth** essere appassionato di qc; **be ~ to do sth** aver molta voglia di fare qc
keep [kiːp] **1** *v/t* tenere; (*not lose*) mantenere; (*detain*) trattenere; *family* mantenere; *animals* allevare; ~ *a promise* mantenere una promessa; ~ *s.o. company* tenere compagnia a qu; ~ *s.o. waiting* far aspettare qu; ~ *sth to o.s.* (*not tell*) tenere qc per sé; ~ *sth from s.o.* nascondere qc a qu; ~ *s.o. from doing sth* impedire a qu di fare qc; ~ *trying!* continua a provare! **2** *v/i* (*remain*) rimanere; *of food, milk* conservarsi; ~ *left* tenere la sinistra; ~ *straight on* vai sempre dritto; ~ *still* stare fermo

◆ **keep away 1** *v/i* stare alla larga; *keep away from* ... stai alla larga da ... **2** *v/t* tenere lontano; **keep s.o. away from sth** tenere qu lontano da qc
◆ **keep back** *v/t* (*hold in check*) trattenere; *information* nascondere
◆ **keep down** *voice* abbassare; *costs, inflation* contenere; *food* trattenere
◆ **keep off 1** *v/t* (*avoid*) evitare; *keep off the grass* non calpestare l'erba **2** *v/i: if the rain keeps off* se non piove
◆ **keep on 1** *v/i* continuare; **keep on doing sth** continuare a fare qc **2** *v/t employee, coat* tenere
◆ **keep out 1** *v/t the cold* pro-

teggere da; *person* escludere **2** v/i *of room* non entrare (*of in*); *of argument etc* non immischiarsi (*of in*); **keep out** *as sign* vietato l'ingresso

◆ **keep to** *path, rules* seguire; **keep to the point** non divagare

◆ **keep up 1** v/i *when running etc* tener dietro **2** v/t *pace, payments* stare dietro a; *bridge, pants* reggere

◆ **keep up with** stare al passo con; (*stay in touch with*) mantenere i rapporti con

keeping ['ki:pɪŋ]: **be in ~ with** essere in armonia con; **keepsake** ricordo *m*

kennel ['kenl] canile *m*; **kennels** canile *m*

kerb [kɜ:b] orlo *m* del marciapiede

ketchup ['ketʃʌp] ketchup *m inv*

kettle ['ketl] bollitore *m*

key [ki:] **1** *n to door, drawer*, MUS chiave *f*; *on keyboard* tasto *m* **2** *adj* (*vital*) chiave **3** v/t COMPUT battere

◆ **key in** data immettere

'keyboard COMPUT, MUS tastiera *f*; **keyboarder** COMPUT, MUS tastierista *m/f*; **keycard** tessera *f* magnetica; **keyed-up** agitato; **keyhole** buco *m* della serratura; **keyring** portachiavi *m inv*; **keyword** parola *f* chiave

khaki ['kɑ:kɪ] cachi *inv*

kick [kɪk] **1** *n* calcio *m*; (*just*)

for ~s F (solo) per il gusto di farlo **2** v/t dare un calcio a; F *habit* liberarsi da **3** v/i dare calci; SP calciare; *of horse* scalciare

◆ **kick around** (*treat harshly*) maltrattare; F (*discuss*) discutere di; **kick a ball around** giocare a pallone

◆ **kick off** *of player* dare il calcio d'inizio; F (*start*) iniziare;

◆ **kick out** buttar fuori

'kickback F (*bribe*) tangente *f*; **kickoff** SP calcio *m* d'inizio

kid [kɪd] **1** *n* F (*child*) bambino *m*, -a *f*; F (*young person*) ragazzo *m*, -a *f*; ◆ **brother** fratello minore **2** v/t F prendere in giro **3** v/i F scherzare

kidnap ['kɪdnæp] rapire, sequestrare; **kidnapper** rapitore *m*, -trice *f*, sequestratore *m*, -trice *f*; **kidnapping** rapimento *m*, sequestro *m* (di persona)

kidney ['kɪdnɪ] ANAT rene *m*; *in cooking* rognone *m*

kill [kɪl] uccidere; *plant, time* ammazzare; **be ~ed in an accident** morire in un incidente; **~ o.s.** suicidarsi; **killer** (*murderer*) assassino *m*, -a *f*; (*hired* ~) killer *m/f inv*; **killing** omicidio *m*; **make a** ~ F (*lots of money*) fare un pacco di soldi F

kiln [kɪln] fornace *f*

kilo ['ki:ləʊ] chilo *m*; **kilobyte**

kilobyte m inv; kilogram chilogrammo m; kilometre, Am kilometer chilometro m

kind¹ [kaɪnd] adj gentile

kind² [kaɪnd] n (sort) tipo m; (make, brand) marca f; **nothing of the ~!** niente affatto!; **~ of sad / strange** F un po' triste / strano

kind-hearted [kaɪnd'hɑːtɪd] di buon cuore; kindly gentile; kindness gentilezza f

king [kɪŋ] re m inv; kingdom regno m

kinky ['kɪŋkɪ] F particolare F

kiosk ['kiːɒsk] edicola f

kiss [kɪs] 1 n bacio m 2 v/t baciare 3 v/i baciarsi

kit [kɪt] kit m inv; (equipment) attrezzatura f

kitchen ['kɪtʃn] cucina f

kite [kaɪt] aquilone m

kitten ['kɪtn] gattino m

kitty ['kɪtɪ] money cassa f comune

knack [næk] capacità f; **there's a ~ to it** bisogna saperlo fare

knee [niː] ginocchio m; kneecap rotula f

kneel [niːl] inginocchiarsi

'knee-length al ginocchio

knife [naɪf] 1 n coltello m 2 v/t accoltellare

knight [naɪt] n cavaliere m

knit [nɪt] 1 v/t fare a maglia 2 v/i lavorare a maglia; knitwear maglieria f

knob [nɒb] on door pomello m; of butter noce f

knock [nɒk] 1 n on door colpo m; (blow) botta f 2 v/t (hit) colpire; head, knee battere; F (criticize) criticare 3 v/i at the door bussare (**at** a); **I ~ed my head** ho battuto la testa

◆ knock down of car investire; object, building etc buttar giù; F (reduce the price of) scontare

◆ knock out (make unconscious) mettere K.O. F; power lines etc mettere fuori uso; (eliminate) eliminare

◆ knock over far cadere; of car investire

'knockout in boxing K.O. m inv

knot [nɒt] 1 n nodo m 2 v/t annodare

know [nəʊ] 1 v/t sapere; person, place conoscere; (recognize) riconoscere; 2 v/i sapere; **I don't ~** non so 3 n: **be in the ~** F essere beninformato; know-all F sapientone m, -a f; knowhow know-how m; knowing d'intesa; knowingly (wittingly) deliberatamente; smile etc con aria d'intesa; know-it-all Am F sapientone m, -a f; knowledge conoscenza f; **to the best of my ~** per quanto ne sappia

knuckle ['nʌkl] nocca f

Koran [kəˈrɑːn] Corano m

Korea [kə'riːə] Corea f; **Korean 1** adj coreano **2** n coreano m, -a f; language coreano m

kosher ['kəʊʃə(r)] REL kasher; F a posto

kudos ['kjuːdɒs] gloria f

L

lab [læb] laboratorio m

label ['leɪbl] **1** n etichetta f **2** v/t baggage mettere l'etichetta su

labor Am ☞ **labour**

laboratory [lə'bɒrətrɪ] laboratorio m

laborious [lə'bɔːrɪəs] laborioso

'**labor union** Am sindacato m

labour ['leɪbə(r)] n lavoro m; in pregnancy travaglio m; **be in ~** avere le doglie fpl; **laboured** style, speech pesante; **labourer** manovale m

lace [leɪs] material pizzo m; for shoe laccio m

lack [læk] **1** n mancanza f **2** v/t mancare di **3** v/i: **be ~ing** mancare

lacquer ['lækə(r)] lacca f

lactose ['læktəʊs] lattosio m

ladder ['lædə(r)] scala f (a pioli); in tights sfilatura f

ladies room ['leɪdiːz] bagno m per donne

lady ['leɪdɪ] signora f; **ladybird**, Am **ladybug** coccinella f; **ladylike** da signora; **she's not very ~** non è certo una signora

lager ['lɑːgə(r)] birra f (bionda)

laidback [leɪd'bæk] rilassato

lake [leɪk] lago m

lamb [læm] agnello m

lame [leɪm] person zoppo; excuse zoppicante

laminated ['læmɪneɪtɪd] surface laminato; paper plastificato

lamp [læmp] lampada f; **lamppost** lampione m; **lampshade** paralume m

land [lænd] **1** n terreno m; (shore) terra f; (country) paese m; **by~** per via di terra; **on ~** sulla terraferma **2** v/t aeroplane far atterrare; job accapararsi **3** v/i of aeroplane atterrare; of ball, sth thrown cadere; **landing** of aeroplane atterraggio m; top of staircase pianerottolo m; **landing strip** pista f d'atterraggio; **landlady** of bar proprietaria f; of rented room padrona f di casa; **landlord** of bar proprietario m; of rented room padrone m di casa; **landmark** punto m di riferimento; fig pietra f miliare; **land owner** proprietario m, -a f terriero, -a; **landscape 1** n paesaggio m **2** adv print landscape, orizzontale;

landslide frana f; **landslide victory** vittoria f schiacciante

lane [leɪn] *in country* viottolo m; *(alley)* vicolo m; MOT corsia f

language ['læŋgwɪdʒ] lingua f; *(speech, style)* linguaggio m; **language lab** laboratorio m linguistico

lap[1] [læp] *of track* giro m (di pista)

lap[2] [læp] *of water* sciabordio m

lap[3] [læp] *of person* grembo m

lapel [lə'pel] bavero m

lapse [læps] **1** n *(mistake, slip)* mancanza f, *of time* intervallo m; **~ of memory** vuoto m di memoria **2** v/i scadere; **~ into** cadere in

laptop COMPUT laptop m inv

larceny ['lɑːsənɪ] furto m

larder ['lɑːdə(r)] dispensa f

large [lɑːdʒ] grande; **at ~** *in liberta*; **largely** *(mainly)* in gran parte

laryngitis [lærɪn'dʒaɪtɪs] laringite f

laser ['leɪzə(r)] laser m inv; **laser printer** stampante f laser

lash[1] [læʃ] *with whip* frustare

lash[2] [læʃ] *(eyelash)* ciglio m

last[1] [lɑːst] **1** adj *in series* ultimo; *(preceding)* precedente; **~ night** ieri sera; **~ year** l'anno scorso **2** adv **he finished ~** ha finito per ultimo; *in race* è arrivato ultimo; **when I ~ saw him** l'ultima volta che

l'ho visto; **at ~** finalmente

last[2] [lɑːst] v/i durare

lasting ['lɑːstɪŋ] duraturo; **lastly** per finire

late [leɪt] **1** adj *(behind time)* in ritardo; *in day* tardi; **it's getting ~** si sta facendo tardi; **the ~ 19th century** il tardo XIX secolo **2** adv tardi; **lately** recentemente; **later** più tardi; **see you ~!** a più tardi; **~ on** più tardi; **latest**1 adj ultimo, più recente **2** n: **at the ~** al più tardi

Latin ['lætɪn] **1** adj latino **2** n latino m; **Latin America** America f Latina; **Latin American 1** n latino-americano m, -a f **2** adj latino-americano

latitude ['lætɪtjuːd] latitudine f; *(freedom to act)* libertà f d'azione

latter ['lætə(r)]: **the ~** quest'ultimo

laugh [lɑːf] **1** n risata f; **it was a ~** F ci siamo divertiti **2** v/i ridere

◆ **laugh at** ridere di

laughter ['lɑːftə(r)] risata f

launch [lɔːntʃ] **1** n *boat* lancia f; *of rocket, product* lancio m; *of ship* varo m **2** v/t *rocket, product* lanciare; *ship* varare

launder ['lɔːndə(r)] lavare e stirare; **~ money** riciclare denaro sporco; **laundrette** lavanderia f automatica; **laundromat**® Am lavanderia f automatica; **laundry**

place lavanderia *f; clothes* bucato *m*

lavatory ['lævətrɪ] gabinetto *m*

lavish ['lævɪʃ] *meal* lauto; *reception, lifestyle* sontuoso

law [lɔ:] legge *f; criminal / civil* ~ diritto *m* penale / civile; **against the** ~ contro la legge; **forbidden by** ~ vietato dalla legge; **law-abiding** che rispetta la legge; **law court** tribunale *m; lawful* legale; **lawless** senza legge

lawn [lɔ:n] prato *m* (all'inglese); **lawn mower** tagliaerba *m inv*

lawsuit azione *f* legale; **lawyer** avvocato *m*

lax [læks] permissivo

laxative ['læksətɪv] lassativo *m*

lay [leɪ] (*put down*) posare; *eggs* deporre; V (*sexually*) scopare V

◆ **lay off** *workers* licenziare; *temporarily* mettere in cassa integrazione

◆ **lay out** *objects* disporre; *page* impaginare

layer ['leɪə(r)] strato *m*

'layman laico *m*

'lay-out *of page* impaginazione *f; of garden, room* disposizione *f*

lazy ['leɪzɪ] *person* pigro; *day* passato a oziare

lb (= *pound*) libbra *f*

lead¹ [li:d] **1** *v/t procession, race* essere in testa a; *compa-*

ny, team essere a capo di; (*guide, take*) condurre **2** *v/i in race, competition* essere in testa; (*provide leadership*) dirigere; **a street ~ing off the square** una strada che parte dalla piazza; **a street ~ing into the square** una strada che sbocca sulla piazza **3** *n in race* posizione *f* di testa; **be in the** ~ essere in testa; **take the** ~ passare in testa

lead² [li:d] *for dog* guinzaglio *m*

lead³ [led] *substance* piombo *m*

leaded ['ledɪd] *petrol* con piombo

leader ['li:də(r)] capo *m; in race, on market* leader *m/f inv; in newspaper* editoriale *m;* **leadership** *of party etc* direzione *f,* leadership *f;* ~ **contest** lotta *f* per la direzione

lead-free ['ledfri:] *petrol* senza piombo

leading ['li:dɪŋ] *runner* in testa; *company, product* leader *inv;* **leading-edge** *company, technology* all'avanguardia

leaf [li:f] foglia *f*

◆ **leaf through** sfogliare

leaflet ['li:flət] dépliant *m inv*

league [li:g] lega *f;* SP campionato *m*

leak [li:k] **1** *n of water* perdita *f; of gas* fuga *f;* **there's been a** ~ *of information* c'è stata

una fuga di notizie **2** v/i of
pipe perdere; of boat far acqua

lean[1] [li:n] **1** v/i be at an angle
pendere; **~ against** sth appoggiarsi a qc **2** v/t appoggiare

lean[2] [li:n] adj meat magro

leap [li:p] **1** n salto **2** v/i saltare; **leap year** anno m bisestile

learn [lɜ:n] imparare; (hear)
apprendere; **learner** principiante m/f; **learning** (knowledge) sapere m; act apprendi-
mento m

lease [li:s] **1** n (contratto m
di) affitto m **2** v/t flat, equip
ment affittare

◆ **lease out** dare in affitto

leash [li:ʃ] for dog guinzaglio
m

least [li:st] **1** adj (slightest) minimo **2** adv meno **3** n mini-
mo m; **not in the ~ suprised**
per niente sorpreso; **at ~** almeno

leather [ˈleðə(r)] **1** n pelle f,
cuoio m **2** adj di pelle, di
cuoio

leave [li:v] **1** n (holiday) congedo m; MIL licenza f **2** v/t lasciare; room, house, office
uscire da; station, airport partire da; (forget) dimenticare;
~ school finire gli studi;
~ s.o. / sth alone lasciare stare qu / qc; **be left** rimanere **3**
v/i of person, plane, bus partire

◆ **leave behind** intentionally
lasciare; (forget) dimenticare

◆ **leave out** omettere; (not
put away) lasciare in giro;
leave me out of this non
mi immischiare in questa
faccenda

'leaving party festa f d'addio

lecture [ˈlektʃə(r)] **1** n lezione
f **2** v/i at university insegnare;
lecture hall aula f magna;
lecturer professore m, -essa
universitario, -a

ledge [ledʒ] of window davanzale m; on rock face sporgenza f; **ledger** COM libro m ma-
stro

left[1] [left] **1** adj sinistro; POL di
sinistra **2** n sinistra f; **on / to
the ~** a sinistra **3** adv a sinistra; **left-hand** sinistro; **left-
-handed** mancino; **left luggage (office)** deposito m bagagli; **left-overs** food avanzi
mpl; **left-wing** POL di sinistra

leg [leg] of person, table gamba f; of animal zampa f; of
turkey, chicken coscia f; of
lamb cosciotto m; **pull
s.o.'s ~** prendere in giro qu

legacy [ˈlegəsɪ] eredità f inv

legal [ˈliːgl] legale; **legal adviser** consulente m/f legale;
legality legalità f inv; **legalize** legalizzare

legend [ˈledʒənd] leggenda f;
legendary leggendario

legible [ˈledʒəbl] leggibile

legislate [ˈledʒɪsleɪt] legifera-
re; **legislation** legislazione f;

legislative legislativo; **legis-lature** POL legislatura *f*

legitimate [lɪ'dʒɪtɪmət] legit-timo

'**leg room** spazio *m* per le gambe

leisure ['leʒə(r)] svago *m*; **at your ~** con comodo; **leisure-ly** tranquillo

lemon ['lemən] limone *m*; **le-monade** *fizzy* gazzosa *f*; *made from lemon juice* limo-nata *f*

lend [lend] prestare; **~ s.o. sth** prestare qc a qu

length [leŋθ] lunghezza *f*; *piece: of material* taglio *m*; **at ~** *explain* a lungo; *(eventu-ally)* alla fine; **lengthen** al-lungare; **lengthy** lungo

lenient ['li:nɪənt] indulgente

lens [lenz] *of camera* obiettivo *m*; *of spectacles* lente *f*; *of eye* cristallino *m*

Lent [lent] REL Quaresima *f*

Leo ['li:əʊ] ASTR Leone *m*

leopard ['lepəd] leopardo *m*

leotard ['li:ətɑːd] body *m* *inv*

lesbian ['lezbɪən] **1** *n* lesbica *f* **2** *adj* di / per lesbiche

less [les] (di) meno; **~ inter-esting** meno interessante; **~ than £200** meno di £200; **lessen** diminuire

lesson ['lesn] lezione *f*

let [let] *(allow)* lasciare; *(rent)* affittare; **~ s.o. do sth** la-sciar fare qc a qu; **~ me go!** lasciami andare!; **~'s go / stay** andiamo / restia-

mo; **~ alone** tanto meno; **~ go of sth** *of rope, handle* mollare qc

◆ **let down** *hair* sciogliersi; *blinds* abbassare; *(disap-point)* deludere; *dress, trou-sers* allungare

◆ **let in** *to house* far entrare

◆ **let out** *from room* far usci-re; *jacket etc* allargare; *groan, yell* emettere

◆ **let up** *(stop)* smettere

lethal ['li:θl] mortale

lethargic [lɪ'θɑːdʒɪk] fiacco; **lethargy** fiacchezza *f*

letter ['letə(r)] lettera *f*; **letter-box** *on street* buca *f* delle let-tere; *in door* cassetta *f* della posta; **letterhead** *heading* in-testazione *f*; *(headed paper)* carta *f* intestata

lettuce ['letɪs] lattuga *f*

leukemia [lu:'ki:mɪə] leuce-mia *f*

level ['levl] **1** *adj surface* pia-no; *in competition, scores* pa-ri; **draw ~ with s.o.** *in match* pareggiare **2** *n* livello *m*; **on the ~** F *(honest)* onesto; **level crossing** passaggio *m* a li-vello; **level-headed** posato

lever ['li:və(r), *Am* 'levər] **1** *n* leva *f* **2** *v/t*: **~ sth open** aprire qc facendo leva; **leverage** forza *f*; *(influence)* influenza *f*

levy ['levɪ] *taxes* imporre

liability [laɪə'bɪlətɪ] *(responsi-bility)* responsabilità *f inv*; **li-able** responsabile; **it's ~ to**

break (*likely*) è probabile
che si rompa
◆ **liaise with** [lɪ'eɪz] tenere i
contatti con
liaison [lɪ'eɪzɒn] (*contacts*)
contatti *mpl*
liar ['laɪə(r)] bugiardo *m*, -a *f*
libel ['laɪbl] **1** *n* diffamazione *f*
2 *v/t* diffamare
liberal ['lɪbrəl] (*broad-mind-
ed*), POL liberale; *portion
etc* abbondante
liberate ['lɪbəreɪt] liberare;
liberated emancipato; **liberation** liberazione *f*; **liberty**
libertà *f inv*; **at ~** *of prisoner
etc* in libertà; **be at ~ to do
sth** poter fare qc
Libra ['liːbrə] ASTR Bilancia *f*
librarian [laɪ'breərɪən] bibliotecario *m*, -a *f*; **library** biblioteca *f*
Libya ['lɪbɪə] Libia *f*; **Libyan 1**
adj libico **2** *n person* libico *m*,
-a *f*
lice [laɪs] *pl* ☞ **louse**
licence ['laɪsns] (*driving ~*)
patente *f*; (*road tax ~*) bollo
m (auto); *for TV* canone *m*
(televisivo); *for imports / ex-
ports* licenza *f*; *for dog* tassa *f*
license ['laɪsns] **1** *v/t* (*issue ~
to*) rilasciare la licenza a;
the car isn't ~d la macchina
non ha il bollo **2** *n Am* ☞ **licence**; **license number** *Am*
numero *m* di targa; **license
plate** *Am* targa *f*
lick [lɪk] **1** *n* leccata *f* **2** *v/t* leccare; *~ one's lips* leccarsi i

baffi
lid [lɪd] coperchio *m*
lie¹ [laɪ] **1** *n* bugia *f*; **tell ~s** dire bugie **2** *v/i* mentire
lie² [laɪ] *v/i of person* sdraiarsi;
of object stare; (*be situated*)
trovarsi
◆ **lie down** sdraiarsi
lieutenant [lef'tenənt, *Am* luː-
'tenənt] tenente *m*
life [laɪf] vita *f*; *of machine* durata *f*; *of battery* autonomia
f; *that's ~!* così è la vita!; **life
belt** salvagente *m inv*; **lifeboat** lancia *f* di salvataggio;
life expectancy aspettativa *f*
di vita; **lifeguard** bagnino *m*,
-a *f*; **life imprisonment** ergastolo *m*; **life insurance** assicurazione *f* sulla vita; **life
jacket** giubbotto *m* di salvataggio; **lifeless** senza vita;
lifelike fedele; **lifelong** di
vecchia data; **lifesized** a
grandezza naturale; **life-
-threatening** mortale; **lifetime**: *in my ~* in vita mia
lift [lɪft] **1** *v/t* sollevare **2** *v/i of
fog* diradarsi **3** *n in building*
ascensore *m*; *in car* passaggio *m*; *give s.o. a ~* dare
un passaggio a qu; *lift-off
of rocket* decollo *m*
ligament ['lɪɡəmənt] legamento *m*
light¹ [laɪt] **1** *n* luce *f*; *have
you got a ~?* hai da accende-
re? **2** *v/t* accendere; (*illuminate*) illuminare **3** *adj not
dark* chiaro

◆ **light up 1** v/t (*illuminate*) illuminare **2** v/i (*start to smoke*) accendersi una sigaretta

light² [laɪt] **1** *adj not heavy* leggero **2** *adv:* *travel ~* viaggiare leggero

'**light bulb** lampadina f

lighten¹ ['laɪtn] *colour* schiarire

lighten² ['laɪtn] *load* alleggerire

lighter ['laɪtə(r)] *for cigarettes* accendino m; **light-headed** stordito; **lighting** illuminazione f; **lightness** leggerezza f; **lightning** fulmine m; **lightweight** *in boxing* peso m leggero; **light year** anno m luce

like¹ [laɪk] **1** prep come; ~ **this / that** così; **what is she ~?** *in looks, character* com'è?; **it's not ~ him** non è da lui; **look ~ s.o.** assomigliare a qu **2** conj (*as*) come; ~ **I said** come ho già detto

like² [laɪk] v/t: **I ~ it / her** mi piace; **I would ~ ...** vorrei ...; **I would ~ to ...** vorrei ...; **would you ~ ...?** ti va ...?; **would you ~ to ...?** ti va di ...?; **he ~s swimming** gli piace nuotare; **if you ~** se vuoi

likeable ['laɪkəbl] simpatico; **likelihood** probabilità f; **likely** probabile; **not ~!** difficile!; **likeness** (*resemblance*) somiglianza f; **likewise** altrettanto; **liking** predilizione f; **take a ~ to s.o.** prendere qu in simpatia

lily ['lɪlɪ] giglio m

limb [lɪm] arto m

lime¹ [laɪm] *fruit* limetta f

lime² [laɪm] *substance* calce f

limit ['lɪmɪt] **1** n limite m; **that's the ~!** F è il colmo! **2** v/t limitare; **limitation** limite m; **limited company** società f inv a responsabilità limitata

limousine ['lɪməziːn] limousine f inv

limp¹ [lɪmp] *adj* floscio

limp² [lɪmp] **1** n: **he has a ~** zoppica **2** v/i zoppicare

line¹ [laɪn] n linea f; *of people, trees* fila f; *of text* riga f; *of business* settore m; **the ~ is busy** è occupato; **hold the ~** rimanga in linea; **draw the ~ at sth** non tollerare qc; ~ *of inquiry* pista f; ~ *of reasoning* filo m del ragionamento; **stand in ~** *Am* fare la fila; **in ~ with ...** (*conforming with*) in linea con ...

line² [laɪn] v/t foderare

linear ['lɪnɪə(r)] lineare

linen ['lɪnɪn] *material* lino m; *sheets etc* biancheria f

liner ['laɪnə(r)] *ship* transatlantico m

linesman ['laɪnzmən] SP guardalinee m inv

linger ['lɪŋɡə(r)] *of person* attardarsi; *of smell, pain* persistere

lingerie ['lænʒərɪ] lingerie f

linguist ['lɪŋgwɪst] linguista m/f; *person good at languages* poliglotta m/f; **linguistic** linguistico

lining ['laɪnɪŋ] *of clothes* fodera f; *of brakes* guarnizione f

link [lɪŋk] **1** n legame m; *in chain* anello m **2** v/t collegare

lion ['laɪən] leone m

lip [lɪp] labbro m; **~s** labbra

liposuction ['lɪpəʊsʌkʃən] liposuzione f

'lipread leggere le labbra; **lipstick** rossetto m

liqueur [lɪ'kjʊə(r)] liquore m

liquid ['lɪkwɪd] **1** n liquido m **2** adj liquido; **liquidate** liquidare; **liquidation** liquidazione f; **go into ~** andare in liquidazione; **liquidity** FIN liquidità f; **liquidize** frullare; **liquidizer** frullatore m

liquor ['lɪkə(r)] superalcolici mpl; **liquor store** Am negozio m di alcolici

lisp [lɪsp] **1** n lisca f **2** v/i parlare con la lisca

list [lɪst] **1** n elenco m, lista f **2** v/t elencare

listen ['lɪsn] ascoltare

◆ **listen to** ascoltare

listener ['lɪsnə(r)] *to radio* ascoltatore m, -trice f; **he's a good ~** sa ascoltare

listless ['lɪstlɪs] apatico

liter Am → **litre**

literal ['lɪtərəl] letterale; **literally** letteralmente

literary ['lɪtərərɪ] letterario; **literature** letteratura f; (*leaflets*) opuscoli mpl

litre ['liːtə(r)] litro m

litter ['lɪtə(r)] rifiuti mpl; *of animal* cucciolata f; **litter bin** bidone m dei rifiuti

little ['lɪtl] **1** adj piccolo **2** n: **the ~ I know** il poco che so; **a ~** un po'; **a ~ wine** un po' di vino **3** adv **~ by** (a) poco a poco; **a ~ bigger** un po' più grande

live[1] [lɪv] v/i (*reside*) abitare; (*be alive*) vivere

◆ **live up: live it up** fare la bella vita

◆ **live up to** essere all'altezza di

live[2] [laɪv] **1** adj *broadcast* dal vivo; *ammunition* carico **2** adv *broadcast* in diretta; *record* dal vivo

livelihood ['laɪvlɪhʊd] mezzi mpl di sostentamento; **earn one's ~** guadagnarsi da vivere; **liveliness** vivacità f; **lively** vivace

liver ['lɪvə(r)] fegato m

livestream ['laɪvstriːm] diretta f streaming

livestock ['laɪvstɒk] bestiame m

livid ['lɪvɪd] (*angry*) furibondo

living ['lɪvɪŋ] **1** adj in vita **2** n: **earn one's ~** guadagnarsi da vivere; **what do you do for a ~?** che lavoro fai?; **living room** salotto m, soggiorno m

lizard ['lɪzəd] lucertola f
load [ləʊd] **1** n carico m; **~s of**
F un sacco di **2** v/t caricare
loaf [ləʊf]: **a ~ of bread** una
pagnotta

◆ **loaf around** F oziare
loafer ['ləʊfə(r)] shoe mocassino m
loan [ləʊn] **1** n prestito m; **on
~** in prestito **2** v/t: **~ s.o. sth**
prestare qc a qu
loathe [ləʊð] detestare; **loathing** disgusto m
lobby ['lɒbɪ] in hotel, theatre
atrio m; POL lobby f inv
lobe [ləʊb] of ear lobo m
lobster ['lɒbstə(r)] aragosta f
local ['ləʊkl] **1** adj people, bar
del posto; produce locale **2** n
persona f del posto; local
call TELEC telefonata f urbana; **local elections** elezioni
fpl amministrative; **local
government** amministrazione f locale
locality località f inv; **localize**
localizzare; **locally** live,
work nella zona; **local time**
ora f locale
locate [ləʊ'keɪt] new factory
etc situare; identify position
of localizzare; **be ~d** essere
situato; **location** (siting) ubicazione f; identifying position
of localizzazione f; **on ~** film
in esterni
lock[1] [lɒk] of hair ciocca f
lock[2] [lɒk] **1** n on door serratura f **2** v/t door chiudere a
chiave

◆ **lock up** in prison mettere
dentro
locker ['lɒkə(r)] armadietto
m; **locker room** spogliatoio
m
locust ['ləʊkəst] locusta f
lodge [lɒdʒ] **1** v/t complaint
presentare **2** v/i of bullet conficcarsi
lofty ['lɒftɪ] peak alto; ideals
nobile
log [lɒg] wood ceppo m; written record giornale m

◆ **log in** fare il log in
◆ **log off** disconnettersi
(**from** da)
◆ **log on** fare il log on, connettersi (**to** a)
◆ **log out** fare il log out
log 'cabin casetta f di legno
logic ['lɒdʒɪk] logica f; **logical**
logico; **logically** a rigor di
logica; arrange in modo logico
logistics [lə'dʒɪstɪks] npl logistica f
logo ['ləʊgəʊ] logo m inv
loiter ['lɔɪtə(r)] gironzolare
lollipop ['lɒlɪpɒp] lecca lecca
m inv
London ['lʌndən] Londra f
loneliness ['ləʊnlɪnɪs] solitudine f; **lonely** person solo;
place isolato; **loner** persona
f solitaria
long[1] [lɒŋ] **1** adj lungo; **it's a ~
way** è lontano **2** adv: **don't
be ~** torna presto **5 weeks
is too ~** 5 settimane è troppo; **will it take ~?** ci vorrà

tanto?; *that was ~ ago* è stato tanto tempo fa; *~ before then* molto prima di allora; *before ~* poco tempo dopo; *we can't wait any ~er* non possiamo attendere oltre; *he no ~er works here* non lavora più qui; *so ~ as* (*provided*) sempre che; *so ~!* arrivederci!

long² [lɒŋ] *v/i*: *~ for sth* desiderare ardentemente qc; *be ~ing to do sth* desiderare ardentemente fare qc; **long-distance** *phonecall* interurbano; *race* di fondo; *flight* intercontinentale; **longevity** longevità *f*; **longing** desiderio *m*; **longitude** longitudine *f*; **long jump** salto *m* in lungo; **long-range** *missile* a lunga gittata; *forecast* a lungo termine; **long-sleeved** a maniche lunghe; **long-standing** di vecchia data; **long-term** *plans, investment* a lunga scadenza; *relationship* stabile; **long wave** RAD onde *fpl* lunghe

loo [luː] F gabinetto *m*

look [lʊk] **1** *n* (*appearance*) aspetto *m*; (*glance*) sguardo *m*; *have a ~ at sth* examine dare un'occhiata a qc; *can I have a ~ around?* in shop etc posso dare un'occhiata?; *~s* (*beauty*) bellezza *f* **2** *v/i* (*look*) guardare; (*search*) cercare; (*seem*) sembrare

◆ **look after** badare a

◆ **look ahead** *fig* pensare al futuro

◆ **look around** *in shop etc* dare un'occhiata in giro; (*look back*) guardarsi indietro

◆ **look at** guardare; (*consider*) considerare

◆ **look back** guardare indietro

◆ **look down on** disprezzare

◆ **look for** cercare

◆ **look forward to**: *I'm looking forward to the holidays* non vedo l'ora che arrivino le vacanze

◆ **look into** (*investigate*) esaminare

◆ **look onto** *garden, street* dare su su

◆ **look out** *of window etc* guardare fuori; (*pay attention*) fare attenzione; *look out!* attento!

◆ **look over** *house, translation* esaminare

◆ **look through** *magazine, notes* scorrere

◆ **look to** (*rely on*) contare su

◆ **look up 1** *v/i* from paper etc sollevare lo sguardo; (*improve*) migliorare **2** *v/t word, phone number* cercare; (*visit*) andare a trovare

◆ **look up to** (*respect*) avere rispetto per

'lookout *person* sentinella *f*; *be on the ~ for accommodation etc* cercare di trovare; *new staff etc* essere alla ricerca di

loop [luːp] cappio m; **loophole** in law etc scappatoia f

loose [luːs] wire, button allentato; clothes ampio; tooth che tentenna; morals dissoluto; wording vago; **~ change** spiccioli mpl; **loosely** tied senza stringere; worded vagamente; **loosen** allentare

loot [luːt] **1** n bottino m **2** v/t & v/i saccheggiare; **looter** saccheggiatore m, -trice f

lop-sided [lɒpˈsaɪdɪd] sbilenco

Lord [lɔːd] (God) Signore m; **the (House of) ~s** la camera dei Lord

lorry [ˈlɒrɪ] camion m inv; **lorry driver** camionista m

lose [luːz] **1** v/t object perdere **2** v/i SP perdere; of clock andare indietro; **I'm lost** mi sono perso; **get lost!** F sparisci!; **loser** in contest perdente m/f; F in life sfigato m, -a f F

loss [lɒs] perdita f; **make a ~** subire una perdita; **be at a ~** essere perplesso

lost [lɒst] perso; **lost property office**, Am **lost and found** ufficio m oggetti smarriti

lot [lɒt] **a ~ (of)**, **~s (of)** molto; **~s of ice creams** molti gelati; **the ~** tutto

lotion [ˈləʊʃn] lozione f

lottery [ˈlɒtərɪ] lotteria f

loud [laʊd] music, voice, noise forte; colour sgargiante; **loudspeaker** altoparlante m; for stereo cassa f dello stereo

lounge [laʊndʒ] in house soggiorno m; in hotel salone m; at airport sala f partenze

louse [laʊs] (pl **lice** [laɪs]) pidocchio m; **lousy** F schifoso F

lout [laʊt] teppista m/f

lovable [ˈlʌvəbl] adorabile; **love 1** n amore m; in tennis zero m; **be in ~** essere innamorato; **fall in ~** innamorarsi; **make ~** fare l'amore (**to** con) **2** v/t amare; **~ doing sth** amare fare qc; **love affair** relazione f; **lovely** face, colour, holiday bello; meal, smell buono; **we had a ~ time** siamo stati benissimo; **lover** amante m/f; **loving** affettuoso; **lovingly** amorosamente

low [ləʊ] **1** adj basso; quality scarso; **be feeling ~** sentirsi giù; **be ~ on petrol** avere poca benzina **2** n in weather depressione f; in sales, statistics minimo m; **lowbrow** di scarso spessore culturale; **low-calorie** ipocalorico; **low-cut** dress scollato; **lower** boat, sth to the ground calare; flag, hemline ammainare; pressure, price abbassare; **low-fat** a basso contenuto lipidico; **lowkey** discreto

loyal [ˈlɔɪəl] leale; **loyally** leal

mente; **loyalty** lealtà *f inv*

lozenge ['lɒzɪndʒ] rombo *m*; *tablet* pastiglia *f*

Ltd (= **limited**) s.r.l. (= società a responsabilità limitata)

lubricant ['lu:brɪkənt] lubrificante *m*; **lubricate** lubrificare; **lubrication** lubrificazione *f*

lucid ['lu:sɪd] (*clear*) chiaro; (*sane*) lucido

luck [lʌk] fortuna *f*; *bad* ~ sfortuna!; *good* ~ fortuna *f*; *good* ~! buona fortuna!; **luckily** fortunatamente; **lucky** fortunato; *you were* ~ hai avuto fortuna; *that's* ~! che fortuna!

lucrative ['lu:krətɪv] redditizio

ludicrous ['lu:dɪkrəs] ridicolo

lug [lʌg] F trascinare

luggage ['lʌgɪdʒ] bagagli *mpl*

lukewarm ['lu:kwɔ:m] tiepido

lull [lʌl] *in fighting* momento *m* di calma; *in conversation* pausa *f*

lumber ['lʌmbə(r)] (*timber*) legname *m*

luminous ['lu:mɪnəs] luminoso

lump [lʌmp] *of sugar* zolletta *f*; (*swelling*) nodulo *m*; **lump sum** pagamento *m* unico; **lumpy** *sauce* grumoso; *mattress* pieno di buchi

lunacy ['lu:nəsɪ] pazzia *f*

lunar ['lu:nə(r)] lunare

lunatic ['lu:nətɪk] pazzo *m*, -a *f*

lunch [lʌntʃ] pranzo *m*; *have* ~ pranzare; **lunch box** cestino *m* del pranzo; **lunch break** pausa *f* pranzo; **lunch hour** pausa *f* pranzo; **lunchtime** ora *f* di pranzo

lung [lʌŋ] polmone *m*

lurch [lɜ:tʃ] barcollare

lure [lʊə(r)] **1** *n* attrattiva *f* **2** *v/t* attirare

lurid ['lʊərɪd] *colour* sgargiante; *details* scandaloso

lurk [lɜ:k] *of person* appostarsi; *of doubt* persistere

lush [lʌʃ] *vegetation* lussureggiante

lust [lʌst] libidine *f*

luxurious [lʌg'ʒʊərɪəs] lussuoso; **luxuriously** lussuosamente; **luxury 1** *n* lusso *m* **2** *adj* di lusso

lynch [lɪntʃ] linciare

lyrics ['lɪrɪks] parole *fpl*, testi *mpl*

M

MA [em'eɪ] (= *Master of Arts*) master *m inv*

ma'am [mæm] *Am* signora *f*

machine [mə'ʃiːn] macchina *f*; **machine gun** mitragliatrice *f*; **machinery** macchinario *m*

machismo [mə'kɪzməʊ] machismo *m*

macho ['mætʃəʊ] macho *m*

macro ['mækrəʊ] COMPUT macro *f*

mad [mæd] pazzo *m*; F (*angry*) furioso; **be ~ about** F (*keen on*) andar matto per; **drive s.o. ~** far impazzire qu; **madden** (*infuriate*) esasperare; **maddening** esasperante

made-to-measure su misura

'madhouse *fig* manicomio *m*; **madly** come un matto; **~ in love** pazzamente innamorato; **madman** pazzo *m*; **madness** pazzia *f*

Madonna [mə'dɒnə] Madonna *f*

Mafia ['mæfɪə] Mafia *f*

magazine [mægə'ziːn] *printed* rivista *f*

Magi ['meɪdʒaɪ] REL Re Magi *mpl*

magic ['mædʒɪk] **1** *n* magia *f*; *tricks* giochi *mpl* di prestigio **2** *adj* magico; **magical** magico; **magician** *performer* mago *m*, -a *f*; **magic spell** incantesimo *m*

magnanimous [mæg'nænɪməs] magnanimo

magnet ['mægnɪt] calamita *f*, magnete *m*; **magnetic** calamitato; *also fig* magnetico; **magnetism** *of person* magnetismo *m*

magnificence [mæg'nɪfɪsns] magnificenza *f*; **magnificent** magnifico

magnify ['mægnɪfaɪ] ingrandire; *difficulties* ingigantire; **magnifying glass** lente *f* d'ingrandimento

magnitude ['mægnɪtjuːd] *of problem* portata *f*

maid [meɪd] *servant* domestica *f*; *in hotel* cameriera *f*

maiden name ['meɪdn] nome *m* da ragazza; **maiden voyage** viaggio *m* inaugurale

mail [meɪl] **1** *n* posta *f* **2** *v/t letter* spedire; *person* spedire a; **mailbox** *Am* buca *f* delle lettere; *of house* cassetta *f* delle lettere; COMPUT (*not Am*) casella *f* postale; **mailing list** mailing list *m inv*; **mailman** *Am* postino *m*; **mail-order firm** ditta *f* di vendita per corrispondenza; **mailshot** mailing *m inv*

maim [meɪm] mutilare

main [meɪn] principale; **main course** piatto *m* principale;

mainframe mainframe *m inv*; **mainland** terraferma *f*, continente *m*; **on the ~** sul continente; **mainly** principalmente; **main road** strada *f* principale; **main street** corso *m*

maintain [meɪnˈteɪn] *pace, speed, relationship* mantenere; *innocence, guilt* sostenere; **~ that** sostenere che; **maintenance** *of machine, house* manutenzione *f*; *money* alimenti *mpl*; *of law and order* mantenimento *m*

majestic [məˈdʒestɪk] maestoso

major [ˈmeɪdʒə(r)] **1** *adj* (*significant*) importante, principale; *in C ~* MUS in Do maggiore **2** *n* MIL maggiore *m*

◆ **major in** *Am* specializzarsi in

majority [məˈdʒɒrətɪ] *also* POL maggioranza *f*; **be in the ~** essere in maggioranza

make [meɪk] **1** *n* (*brand*) marca *f* **2** *v/t* fare; *decision* prendere; (*earn*) guadagnare; MATH fare; **~** *it catch bus, train, come, succeed* farcela; **what time do you ~ it?** che ore fai?; **~ believe** far finta; **~** *s.o.* **do sth** (*force to*) far fare qc a qu; (*cause to*) spingere qu a fare qc; **~** *s.o.* **happy** far felice qu, rendere felice qu

◆ **make off with** (*steal*) svignarsela con

◆ **make out** *list* fare; *cheque* compilare; (*see*) distinguere; (*imply*) far capire

◆ **make up 1** *v/i of woman, actor* truccarsi; *after quarrel* fare la pace **2** *v/t story, excuse* inventare; *face* truccare; (*constitute*) costituire; **be made up of** essere composto da; **make it up** *after quarrel* fare la pace

◆ **make up for** compensare

'make-believe finta *f*

maker [ˈmeɪkə(r)] *manufacturer* fabbricante *m/f*; **makeshift** improvvisato; **make-up** (*cosmetics*) trucco *m*

maladjusted [mæləˈdʒʌstɪd] disadattato

male [meɪl] **1** *adj* maschile, *animal* maschio **2** *n man* uomo *m*; *animal, bird* maschio *m*; **male chauvinism** maschilismo *m*; **male chauvinist pig** maschilista *m*

malevolent [məˈlevələnt] malevolo

malfunction [mælˈfʌŋkʃn] **1** *n* cattivo *m* funzionamento **2** *v/i* funzionare male

malice [ˈmælɪs] cattiveria *f*, malvagità *f*; **malicious** cattivo, malvagio

malignant [məˈlɪɡnənt] *tumour* maligno

mall [mæl] (*shopping ~*) centro *m* commerciale

malnutrition [mælnjuːˈtrɪʃn]

maltreat

denutrizione f

maltreat [mælˈtriːt] maltrattare; **maltreatment** maltrattamento m

mammal [ˈmæml] mammifero m

man [mæn] **1** n (pl **men** [men]) uomo m; humanity umanità f; in draughts pedina f **2** v/t telephones, front desk essere di servizio a; *it was ~ned by a crew of three* aveva un equipaggio di tre persone

manage [ˈmænɪdʒ] **1** v/t business, money gestire; *can you ~ the suitcase?* ce la fai a portare la valigia?; *~ to ...* riuscire a ... **2** v/i cope, financially tirare avanti; (financially): *can you ~?* ce la fai?; **manageable** suitcase etc maneggevole; hair docile; able to be done fattibile; **management** (managing) gestione f; (managers) direzione f; **management consultant** consulente m/f di gestione aziendale; **manager** manager m/f inv, direttore m, -trice f; **managerial** manageriale; **managing director** direttore m generale

mandate [ˈmændeɪt] (authority, task) mandato m; **mandatory** obbligatorio

maneuver Am ☞ **manoeuvre**

mangle [ˈmæŋgl] (crush) stritolare

manhandle [ˈmænhændl] person malmenare; object caricare

manhood [ˈmænhʊd] maturity età f adulta; (virility) virilità f; **manhunt** caccia f all'uomo

mania [ˈmeɪnɪə] (craze) mania f; **maniac** F pazzo m, -a f

manicure [ˈmænɪkjʊə(r)] manicure f inv

manifest [ˈmænɪfest] **1** adj palese **2** v/t manifestare

manipulate [məˈnɪpjʊleɪt] manipolare; **manipulation** manipolazione f; **manipulative** manipolatore

man'kind umanità f; **manly** virile; **man-made** sintetico

manner [ˈmænə(r)] of doing sth maniera f, modo m; (attitude) modo m di fare; **manners**: *good / bad ~* buone / cattive maniere fpl; *have no ~* essere maleducato

manoeuvre [məˈnuːvə(r)] **1** n manovra f **2** v/t manovrare

'manpower manodopera f, personale m; **manslaughter** omicidio m colposo

manual [ˈmænjʊəl] **1** adj manuale **2** n manuale m; **manually** manualmente

manufacture [mænjʊˈfæktʃə(r)] **1** n manifattura f **2** v/t equipment fabbricare; **manufacturer** fabbricante m/f; **manufacturing** industry manifatturiero

manure [məˈnjʊə(r)] letame

married

m

manuscript ['mænjʊskrɪpt]
manoscritto *m*; *typed* dattiloscritto *m*

many ['menɪ] **1** *adj* molti; ~
times molte volte; *not ~
people / taxis* poche persone / pochi taxi; *too ~ problems / beers* troppi problemi / troppe birre **2** *pron*
molti *m*, molte *f*; *a great ~,
a good ~* moltissimi; *how
~ do you need?* quanti te
ne servono?; *as ~ as 200*
ben 200

map [mæp] cartina *f*; *(street ~)*
pianta *f*, piantina *f*

maple ['meɪpl] acero *m*

mar [mɑː(r)] guastare

marathon ['mærəθən] *race*
maratona *f*

marble ['mɑːbl] *material* marmo *m*

March [mɑːtʃ] marzo *m*

march [mɑːtʃ] **1** *n* marcia *f*;
(demonstration) dimostrazione *f*, manifestazione *f* **2** *v/i*
marciare; *in protest* dimostrare, manifestare; **march**er dimostrante *m/f*, manifestante *m/f*

Mardi Gras ['mɑːdɪgrɑː] *Am*
martedì *m* grasso

margin ['mɑːdʒɪn] *of page*
margine *m*; COM margine
m di guadagno; *by a narrow
~* di stretta misura; **marginal**
(slight) leggero; **marginally**
(slightly) leggermente

marihuana, marijuana

[mærɪ'hwɑːnə] marijuana *f*

marina [mə'riːnə] porticciolo
m

marine [mə'riːn] **1** *adj* marino
2 *n* MIL marina *f* militare

marital ['mærɪtl] coniugale;
marital status stato *m* civile

maritime ['mærɪtaɪm] marittimo

mark [mɑːk] **1** *n (stain)* macchia *f*; *(sign, token)* segno
m; *(trace)* EDU voto *m* **2** *v/t
(stain)* macchiare; EDU correggere; *(indicate)* indicare;
(commemorate) celebrare **3**
v/i of fabric macchiarsi;
marked *(definite)* spiccato;
marker *(highlighter)* evidenziatore *m*

market ['mɑːkɪt] **1** *n* mercato
m **2** *v/t* vendere; **marketable**
commerciabile; **market
economy** economia *f* di
mercato; **marketing** marketing *m*; **market leader** leader
m inv del mercato; **market-place** *in town* piazza *f* del
mercato; *for commodities*
piazza *f*, mercato *m*; **market
research** ricerca *f* di mercato; **market share** quota *f* di
mercato

'mark-up ricarico *m*

marmalade ['mɑːməleɪd]
marmellata *f* d'arance

marriage ['mærɪdʒ] matrimonio *m*; *event* nozze *fpl*; **marriage certificate** certificato
m di matrimonio; **married**
sposato; *be ~ to ...* essere

sposato con ...; **married life** vita *f* coniugale; **marry** sposare; *of priest* unire in matrimonio; **get married** sposarsi

marsh [mɑːʃ] palude *f*

marshal ['mɑːʃl] *official* membro *m* del servizio d'ordine

martial arts [mɑːʃ'ɑːts] arti *fpl* marziali; **martial law** legge *f* marziale

martyr ['mɑːtə(r)] martire *m/f*

marvel ['mɑːvl] meraviglia *f*; **marvellous**, *Am* **marvelous** meraviglioso

Marxism ['mɑːksɪzm] marxismo *m*; **Marxist 1** *adj* marxista **2** *n* marxista *m/f*

mascara [mæ'skɑːrə] mascara *m inv*

mascot ['mæskət] mascotte *f inv*

masculine ['mæskjʊlɪn] maschile; **masculinity** (*virility*) virilità *f*

mash [mæʃ] passare, schiacciare; **mashed potatoes** purè *m* di patate

mask [mɑːsk] **1** *n* maschera *f* **2** *v/t feelings* mascherare

masochism ['mæsəkɪzm] masochismo *m*; **masochist** masochista *m/f*

mass¹ [mæs] **1** *n great amount* massa *f*; **~es of** *F* un sacco di F **2** *v/i* radunarsi

mass² [mæs] REL messa *f*

massacre ['mæsəkə(r)] **1** *n also fig* massacro *m* **2** *v/t also fig* massacrare

massage ['mæsɑːʒ] **1** *n* massaggio *m* **2** *v/t* massaggiare; **figures** manipolare

massive ['mæsɪv] enorme; **heart attack** grave

mass 'media mass media *mpl*; **mass-produce** produrre in serie; **mass production** produzione *f* in serie; **mass transit** *Am* i trasporti pubblici

mast [mɑːst] *of ship* albero *m*; *for radio signal* palo *m* dell'antenna

master ['mɑːstə(r)] **1** *n of dog* padrone *m*; *of ship* capitano *m* **2** *v/t skill, language* avere completa padronanza di; *situation* dominare; **master bedroom** camera *f* da letto principale; **master key** passe-partout *m inv*; **masterly** magistrale; **mastermind 1** *n fig* cervello *m* **2** *v/t* ideare; **masterpiece** capolavoro *m*; **master's (degree)** master *m inv*; laurea *f* magistrale; **mastery** padronanza *f*

mat [mæt] *for floor* tappetino *m*; *for table* tovaglietta *f* all'americana

match¹ [mætʃ] *for cigarette* fiammifero *m*; *made of wax* cerino *m*

match² [mætʃ] **1** *n* (*competition*) partita *f*; **be no ~ for s.o.** non poter competere con qu **2** *v/t* (*be the same as*) abbinare; (*equal*) uguagliare **3** *v/i of colours*, pat-

terns intonarsi

matching ['mætʃɪŋ] abbinato

mate [meɪt] **1** *n of animal* compagno *m*, -a *f*; NAUT secondo *m*; F *friend* amico *m*, -a *f* **2** *v/i* accoppiarsi

material [mə'tɪərɪəl] **1** *n fabric* stoffa *f*, tessuto *m*; *substance* materia *f*; *~s* occorrente *m* **2** *adj* materiale; **materialism** materialismo *m*; **materialist** materialista *m/f*; **materialistic** materialistico; **materialize** materializzarsi

maternal [mə'tɜːnl] materno; **maternity** maternità *f*; **maternity leave** congedo *m* per maternità; **maternity ward** reparto *m* maternità

math [mæθ] *Am* = **maths**; **mathematical** matematico; **mathematician** matematico *m*, -a *f*; **mathematics** matematica *f*; **maths** matematica *f*

matinée ['mætɪneɪ] matinée *f inv*

matriarch ['meɪtrɪɑːk] matriarca *f*

matrimony ['mætrɪmənɪ] matrimonio *m*

matt [mæt] opaco

matter ['mætə(r)] **1** *n (affair)* questione *f*, faccenda *f*; PHYS materia *f*; *as a ~ of fact* a dir la verità; *what's the ~?* cosa c'è?; *no ~ what she says* qualsiasi cosa dica **2** *v/i* importare; *it doesn't ~* non importa; **matter-of-fact**

distaccato

mattress ['mætrɪs] materasso *m*

mature [mə'tjʊə(r)] **1** *adj* maturo **2** *v/i of person, insurance policy etc* maturare; *of wine* invecchiare; **maturity** maturità *f*

maximize ['mæksɪmaɪz] massimizzare; **maximum 1** *adj* massimo **2** *n* massimo *m*

May [meɪ] maggio *m*

may [meɪ] ◊ *(possibility)*: *it ~ rain* potrebbe piovere, può darsi che piova; *it ~ not happen* può darsi che non succeda ◊ *(permission)*: *~ I help?* posso aiutare?

maybe ['meɪbiː] forse

mayonnaise [meɪə'neɪz] maionese *f*

mayor ['meə(r)] sindaco *m*

maze [meɪz] *also fig* dedalo *m*, labirinto *m*

MB (= **megabyte**) MB *m* (= megabyte *m inv*)

MBA [embiː'eɪ] (= **master of business administration**) master in amministrazione aziendale

MD [em'diː] (= **Doctor of Medicine**) dottore in medicina

me [miː] mi; *after prep, stressed* me; *she knows ~* mi conosce; *she spoke to ~* mi ha parlato; *it's ~* sono io; *who? ~ ~?* chi? - io?

meadow ['medəʊ] prato *m*

meagre, *Am* **meager** ['miːgə(r)] scarso

meal [miːl] pranzo *m*, pasto *m*;
enjoy your ~! buon appetito!

mean[1] [miːn] *adj with money*
avaro; *(nasty)* cattivo

mean[2] [miːn] 1 *v/t (signify)* significare, voler dire; ***do you
~ it?*** dici sul serio?; ***~ to do
sth*** avere l'intenzione di fare qc; ***be ~t for*** essere destinato a; *of remark* essere diretto a 2 *v/i*: **~ well** avere
buone intenzioni

meaning [ˈmiːnɪŋ] *of word* significato *m*; **meaningful**
(comprehensible) comprensibile; *(constructive)* costruttivo; *glance* eloquente; **mean-
ingless** *sentence etc* senza
senso; *gesture* vuoto

means [miːnz] *financial* mezzi
mpl; *(nsg: way)* modo *m*; **~ of
transport** mezzo *m* di trasporto; ***by all ~*** *(certainly)*
certamente; ***by no ~*** **rich**
lungi dall'essere ricco; ***by ~
of*** per mezzo di

meantime [ˈmiːntaɪm] intanto

measles [ˈmiːzlz] morbillo *m*

measure [ˈmeʒə(r)] 1 *n (step)*
misura *f* 2 *v/t* prendere le misure di 3 *v/i* misurare

◆ **measure up to** dimostrarsi all'altezza di

measurement [ˈmeʒəmənt]
action misurazione *f*; *(dimension)* misura *f*; **measuring
tape** metro *m* a nastro

meat [miːt] carne *f*; **meatball**

polpetta *f*

mechanic [mɪˈkænɪk] meccanico *m*; **mechanical** *also elg*
meccanico; **mechanical engineer** ingegnere *m* meccanico; **mechanically** *also elg*
meccanicamente; **mecha-
nism** meccanismo *m*; **mech-
anize** meccanizzare

medal [ˈmedl] medaglia *f*;
medallist, *Am* **medalist** vincitore *m*, -trice *f* di una medaglia

meddle [ˈmedl] *(interfere)* immischiarsi; **~ with** *(tinker)*
mettere le mani a

media [ˈmiːdɪə]: ***the ~*** i mass
media *mpl*; **media cover-
age:** ***it was given a lot of
~*** gli è stato dato molto spazio in TV e sui giornali

mediaeval ☞ **medieval**

median strip [miːdɪənˈstrɪp]
Am banchina *f* spartitraffico

'media studies scienze *fpl*
delle comunicazioni

mediate [ˈmiːdɪeɪt] fare da
mediatore *m*, -trice *f*; **mediation** mediazione *f*; **mediator** mediatore *m*, -trice *f*

medical [ˈmedɪkl] 1 *adj* medico 2 *n* visita *f* medica; **medi-
cated** medicato; **medica-
tion** medicina *f*; **medicinal**
medicinale; **medicine** medicina *f*

medieval [medɪˈiːvl] medievale

mediocre [miːdɪˈəʊkə(r)] mediocre; **mediocrity** medio-

crità f

meditate ['medɪteɪt] meditare; **meditation** meditazione f

Mediterranean [medɪtə'reɪnɪən] **1** *adj* mediterraneo **2** *n: the ~* il Mar Mediterraneo; *area* i paesi mediterranei

medium ['miːdɪəm] **1** *adj* (*average*) medio; *steak* cotto al punto giusto **2** *n in size* media f; (*vehicle*) strumento m; (*spiritualist*) medium m/f inv; **medium-sized** di grandezza media; **medium wave** RAD onde fpl medie

medley ['medlɪ] (*assortment*) misto m

meet [miːt] **1** *v/t* incontrare; (*get to know*) conoscere; (*collect*) andare *or* venire a prendere; *in competition* affrontare; *of eyes* incrociare; (*satisfy*) soddisfare; *I'll ~ you there* ci vediamo lì **2** *v/i* incontrarsi; *in competition* affrontarsi; *of eyes* incrociarsi; *of committee etc* riunirsi; *have you two met?* (*do you know each other?*) vi conoscete? **3** *n* SP raduno m sportivo
♦ **meet with** *person* avere un incontro con; *opposition, approval etc* incontrare; *it met with success / failure* ha avuto successo / è fallito

meeting ['miːtɪŋ] incontro m; *of committee, in business* riu-

nione f; *he's in a ~* è in riunione

megabyte ['megəbaɪt] COMPUT megabyte m inv

mellow ['meləʊ] **1** *adj* maturo **2** *v/i of person* addolcirsi

melodious [mɪ'ləʊdɪəs] melodioso

melodramatic [melədrə'mætɪk] melodrammatico

melody ['melədɪ] melodia f

melon ['melən] melone m

melt [melt] **1** *v/i* sciogliersi **2** *v/t* sciogliere; **melting pot** *fig* crogiolo m di culture

member ['membə(r)] *of family* componente m/f; *of club* socio m; *of organization* membro m; **Member of Congress** membro m del Congresso; **Member of Parliament** membro m del Parlamento, deputato m; **membership** iscrizione f; *number of members* numero m dei soci

membrane ['membreɪn] membrana f

memento [me'mentəʊ] souvenir m inv

memo ['meməʊ] circolare f

memoirs ['memwɑːz] memorie fpl

memorable ['memərəbl] memorabile

memorial [mɪ'mɔːrɪəl] **1** *adj* commemorativo **2** *n also fig* memorial m inv

memorize ['meməraɪz] memorizzare; **memory** (*recol-*

lection) ricordo *m; power of recollection* memoria *f;* COMPUT memoria *f;* **memory stick** memory stick *f inv*

men [men] *pl* ☞ **man**

menace ['menɪs] **1** *n (threat)* minaccia *f; person* pericolo *m* pubblico; *(nuisance)* peste *f* **2** *v/t* minacciare; **menacing** minaccioso

mend [mend] riparare

menial ['miːnɪəl] umile

menopause ['menəpɔːz] menopausa *f*

'men's room bagno *m* (degli uomini)

menstruate ['menstrʊeɪt] avere le mestruazioni; **menstruation** mestruazione *f*

mental ['mentl] mentale; F *(crazy)* pazzo; **mental hospital** ospedale *m* psichiatrico; **mental illness** malattia *f* mentale; **mentality** mentalità *f inv;* **mentally** *inwardly* mentalmente; *calculate etc* a mente; **mentally ill** malato di mente

mention ['menʃn] **1** *n* cenno *m* **2** *v/t* accennare a; **don't ~ it** *(you're welcome)* non c'è di che

mentor ['mentɔː(r)] guida *f* spirituale

menu ['menjuː] *also* COMPUT menu *m inv*

mercenary ['mɜːsɪnərɪ] **1** *adj* mercenario **2** *n* MIL mercenario *m*

merchandise ['mɜːtʃəndaɪz]

merce *f*

merchant ['mɜːtʃənt] commerciante *m/f;* **merchant bank** banca *f* d'affari

merciful ['mɜːsɪfʊl] misericordioso; **mercifully** *(thankfully)* per fortuna; **merciless** spietato; **mercy** misericordia *f;* **be at s.o.'s ~** essere alla mercé di qu

mere [mɪə(r)] semplice; **merely** soltanto

merge [mɜːdʒ] *of two lines etc* unirsi; *of companies* fondersi; **merger** COM fusione *f*

merit ['merɪt] **1** *n (worth)* merito *m; (advantage)* vantaggio *m* **2** *v/t* meritare

mesh [meʃ] *in net* maglia *f*

mess [mes] *(untidiness)* disordine *m; (trouble)* pasticcio *m; be a ~* *of room, desk, hair* essere in disordine; *of situation, s.o.'s life* essere un pasticcio

message ['mesɪdʒ] *also fig* messaggio *m*

messenger ['mesɪndʒə(r)] *(courier)* fattorino *m,* -a *f*

messy ['mesɪ] *room* in disordine; *person* disordinato; *job* sporco; *divorce, situation* antipatico

metabolism [mətæˈbəlɪzm] metabolismo *m*

metal ['metl] **1** *adj* in *or* di metallo **2** *n* metallo *m;* **metallic** metallico

metaphor ['metəfə(r)] metafora *f*

meteor ['miːtɪə(r)] meteora *f*; **meteoric** *fig* fulmineo; **meteorite** meteorite *m* or *f*

meteorological [miːtɪərə'lɒdʒɪkl] meteorologico; **meteorologist** meteorologo *m*, -a *f*; **meteorology** meteorologia *f*

meter[1] ['miːtə(r)] *for gas etc* contatore *m*; (*parking* ~) parchimetro *m*

meter[2] *Am* ☞ **metre**

method ['meθəd] metodo *m*; **methodical** metodico

meticulous [mɪ'tɪkjʊləs] meticoloso

metre ['miːtə(r)] metro *m*

metropolis [mɪ'trɒpəlɪs] metropoli *f inv*; **metropolitan** metropolitano

mew [mjuː] ☞ **miaow**

Mexican ['meksɪkən] **1** *adj* messicano **2** *n* messicano *m*, -a *f*; **Mexico** Messico *m*

miaow [mɪaʊ] **1** *n* miao *m* **2** *v/i* miagolare

mice [maɪs] *pl* ☞ **mouse**

'microchip microchip *m inv*; **microclimate** microclima *m*; **microcosm** microcosmo *m*; **microorganism** microrganismo *m*; **microphone** microfono *m*; **microprocessor** microprocessore *m*; **microscope** microscopio *m*; **microscopic** microscopico; **microwave** *oven* forno *m* a microonde

midday [mɪd'deɪ] mezzogiorno *m*

middle ['mɪdl] **1** *adj* di mezzo **2** *n* mezzo *m*; **in the ~ of** *of floor, room* nel centro di, in mezzo a; *of period of time* a metà di; **be in the ~ of doing sth** stare facendo qc; **middle-aged** di mezz'età; **Middle Ages** Medioevo *m*; **middle class** borghese; **middle class(es)** la borghesia *f*; **Middle East** Medio Oriente *m*; **middleman** intermediario *m*; **middle name** secondo nome *m*; **middleweight** *boxer* peso *m* medio

midfielder [mɪd'fiːldə(r)] centrocampista *m*

midnight ['mɪdnaɪt] mezzanotte *f*; **midsummer** piena estate *f*; **midweek** a metà settimana; **Midwest** *regione f medio-occidentale degli USA*; **midwife** ostetrica *f*; **midwinter** pieno inverno *m*

might[1] [maɪt]: *I ~ be late* potrei far tardi; *it ~ rain* magari piove; *you ~ have told me!* potevi dirmelo!

might[2] [maɪt] (*power*) forze *fpl*

mighty ['maɪtɪ] **1** *adj* potente **2** *adv* F (*extremely*) molto

migraine ['miːɡreɪn] emicrania *f*

migrant worker ['maɪɡrənt] emigrante *m*/*f*; **migrate** emigrare; *of birds* migrare; **migration** emigrazione *f*; *of birds* migrazione *f*

mike   462

mike [maɪk] F microfono *m*
Milan [mɪˈlæn] Milano *f*
mild [maɪld] *weather* mite;
cheese, person dolce; *curry*
poco piccante; *punishment,
sedative* leggero; **mildly** gen-
tilmente; *(slightly)* modera-
tamente; **to put it ~** a dir poco; **mildness** *of weather* mi-
tezza *f*; *of person, voice* dolcezza *f*
mile [maɪl] miglio *m*; **~s better** F molto meglio; **mileage**
chilometraggio *m*; **mileometer** contachilometri *m*;
milestone *also fig* pietra *f*
miliare
militant [ˈmɪlɪtənt] **1** *adj* militante **2** *n* militante *m/f*
military [ˈmɪlɪtrɪ] **1** *adj* militare **2** *n*: **the ~** l'esercito *m*; **military service** servizio *m* militare
militia [mɪˈlɪʃə] milizia *f*
milk [mɪlk] **1** *n* latte *m* **2** *v/t*
mungere; **milk chocolate**
cioccolato *m* al latte; **milk-
man** lattaio *m*; **milkshake**
frappé *m inv*
mill [mɪl] *for grain* mulino *m*;
for textiles fabbrica *f*
millennium [mɪˈlenɪəm] millennio *m*
milligram [ˈmɪlɪɡræm] milligrammo *m*
millimetre, *Am* **millimeter**
[ˈmɪlɪmiːtə(r)] millimetro *m*
million [ˈmɪljən] milione *m*;
millionaire miliardario *m*,
-a *f*

mime [maɪm] mimare
mimic [ˈmɪmɪk] **1** *n* imitatore
m, -trice *f* **2** *v/t* imitare
mince [mɪns] *meat* carne *f* tritata
mind [maɪnd] **1** *n* mente *f*; *it's
all in your ~* è solo la tua immaginazione; *be out of
one's ~* essere matto; *keep
sth in ~* tenere presente qc;
change one's ~ cambiare
idea; *it didn't enter my ~*
non mi è passato per la testa;
make up one's ~ decidersi;
have sth on one's ~ essere
preoccupato per qc; *keep
one's ~ on sth* concentrarsi
su qc; *speak one's ~* dire
quello che si pensa **2** *v/t
(look after)* tenere d'occhio;
children badare a; *(heed)* fare
attenzione a; *I don't ~ what
we do* non importa cosa facciamo; *do you ~ if I smoke?*
le dispiace se fumo?; *~ the
step!* attento al gradino!; *~
your own business!* fatti
gli affari tuoi! **3** *v/i*: *~!* (be
careful)* attenzione!; *never
~!* non farci caso!; *I don't ~*
è uguale o indifferente;
mind-boggling incredibile;
mindless *violence* insensato
mine[1] [maɪn] *pron* il mio *m*, la
mia *f*, i miei *mpl*, le mie *fpl*; *a
cousin of ~* un mio cugino
mine[2] [maɪn] *n for coal etc* miniera *f*
mine[3] [maɪn] **1** *n explosive* mina *f* **2** *v/t* minare

'minefield *also fig* campo *m* minato; 'miner minatore *m*

mineral ['mɪnərəl] minerale *m*; mineral water acqua *f* minerale

'minesweeper NAUT dragamine *m inv*

mingle ['mɪŋgl] *of sounds* mischiarsi, *at party* mescolarsi

mini ['mɪnɪ] *skirt* mini *f* inv

miniature ['mɪnɪtʃə(r)] in miniatura

minimal ['mɪnɪməl] minimo; minimalism minimalismo *m*; minimize minimizzare; minimum 1 *adj* minimo 2 *n* minimo *m*; minimum wage salario *m* minimo garantito

mining ['maɪnɪŋ] industria *f* mineraria

'miniskirt minigonna *f*

minister ['mɪnɪstə(r)] POL ministro *m*; REL pastore *m*; ministerial ministeriale; Minister of Defence ministro *m* della difesa; ministry POL ministero *m*

mink [mɪŋk] visone *m*

minor ['maɪnə(r)] 1 *adj* piccolo; *in D* ∼ MUS in Re minore 2 *n* LAW minorenne *m/f*; minority minoranza *f*

mint [mɪnt] *herb* menta *f*; *chocolate* cioccolato *m* alla menta; *sweet* mentina *f*

minus ['maɪnəs] 1 *n* (∼ *sign*) meno *m* 2 *prep* meno; ∼ **10 degrees** 10 gradi sotto zero

minuscule ['mɪnəskjuːl] minuscolo

minute[1] ['mɪnɪt] *n of time* minuto *m*; *in a* ∼ (*soon*) in un attimo; *just a* ∼ un attimo

minute[2] [maɪ'njuːt] *adj* (*tiny*) piccolissimo; (*detailed*) minuzioso; *in* ∼ *detail* minuziosamente

minute hand ['mɪnɪt] lancetta *f* dei minuti

minutely [maɪ'njuːtlɪ] (*in detail*) minuziosamente; (*very slightly*) appena

minutes ['mɪnɪts] *of meeting* verbale *m*

miracle ['mɪrəkl] miracolo *m*; miraculous miracoloso; miraculously miracolosamente

mirror ['mɪrə(r)] 1 *n* specchio *m*; MOT specchietto *m* 2 *v/t* riflettere

misanthropist [mɪ'zænθrəpɪst] misantropo *m*

misbehave [mɪsbə'heɪv] comportarsi male; misbehaviour, *Am* misbehavior comportamento *m* scorretto

miscalculate [mɪs'kælkjuleɪt] calcolare male; miscalculation errore *m* di calcolo

miscarriage ['mɪskærɪdʒ] MED aborto *m* spontaneo; ∼ *of justice* errore *m* giudiziario

miscellaneous [mɪsə'leɪnɪəs] eterogeneo

mischief ['mɪstʃɪf] (*naughtiness*) birichinate fpl; mischievous (*naughty*) birichino; (*malicious*) perfido

misconception [mɪskən-'sepʃn] idea *f* sbagliata

misconduct [mɪs'kɒndʌkt] reato *m* professionale

misconstrue [mɪskən'struː] interpretare male

misdemeanour, *Am* **misdemeanor** [mɪsdə'miːnə(r)] infrazione *f*

miser ['maɪzə(r)] avaro *m*, -a *f*

miserable ['mɪzrəbl] (*unhappy*) infelice; *weather, performance* deprimente

miserly ['maɪzəlɪ] *person* avaro; *amount* misero

misery ['mɪzərɪ] (*unhappiness*) tristezza *f*; (*wretchedness*) miseria *f*

misfire [mɪs'faɪə(r)] *of scheme* far cilecca; *of engine* perdere colpi

misfit ['mɪsfɪt] *in society* disadattato *m*, -a *f*

misfortune [mɪs'fɔːtʃən] sfortuna *f*

misgivings [mɪs'gɪvɪŋz] dubbi *mpl*

misguided [mɪs'gaɪdɪd] *attempts, theory* sbagliato

mishandle [mɪs'hændl] *situation* gestire male

misinform [mɪsɪn'fɔːm] informare male

misinterpret [mɪsɪn'tɜːprɪt] interpretare male; **misinterpretation** interpretazione *f* errata

misjudge [mɪs'dʒʌdʒ] giudicare male

mislay [mɪs'leɪ] smarrire

mislead [mɪs'liːd] trarre in inganno; **misleading** fuorviante

mismanage [mɪs'mænɪdʒ] gestire male; **mismanagement** cattiva gestione *f*

misprint ['mɪsprɪnt] refuso *m*

mispronounce [mɪs-prə'naʊns] pronunciare male; **mispronunciation** errore *m* di pronuncia

misread [mɪs'riːd] *word, figures* leggere male; *situation* interpretare male

misrepresent [mɪsreprɪ'zent] *facts, truth* travisare

miss¹ [mɪs]: *Miss Smith* signorina Smith; *~!* signorina!

miss² [mɪs] **1** *n*: *give the meeting a~* non andare alla riunione **2** *v/t* (*not hit*) mancare; *emotionally* sentire la mancanza di; *bus, train, plane* perdere; (*not be present at*) mancare a; *I ~ you* mi manchi **3** *v/i* fallire

misshapen [mɪs'ʃeɪpən] deforme

missile ['mɪsaɪl] (*rocket*) missile *m*

missing ['mɪsɪŋ] scomparso; *be ~ of person, plane* essere disperso; *there's a piece ~* manca un pezzo

mission ['mɪʃn] (*task, people*) missione *f*

misspell [mɪs'spel] scrivere male

mist [mɪst] foschia *f*

mistake [mɪ'steɪk] **1** *n* errore *m*, sbaglio *m*; **make a ~** fare un errore, sbagliarsi; **by ~** per errore **2** *v/t* sbagliare; **~ sth for sth** scambiare qc per qc; **mistaken** sbagliato; **be ~** sbagliarsi

mister ['mɪstə(r)] ☞ **Mr**

mistress ['mɪstrɪs] *lover* amante *f*; *of dog* padrona *f*

mistrust [mɪs'trʌst] **1** *n* diffidenza *f* **2** *v/t* diffidare di

misty ['mɪstɪ] *weather* nebbioso; *eyes* velato

misunderstand [mɪsʌndə-'stænd] fraintendere; **misunderstanding** *mistake* malinteso *m*, equivoco *m*; *argument* dissapore *m*

misuse **1** [mɪs'juːs] *n* uso *m* improprio **2** [mɪs'juːz] *v/t* usare impropriamente

mitigating circumstances ['mɪtɪgeɪtɪŋ] circostanze *fpl* attenuanti

mitt [mɪt] *in baseball* guantone *m*; **mitten** muffola *f*

mix [mɪks] **1** *n* (*mixture*) mescolanza *f*; *in cooking: ready to use* preparato *m* **2** *v/t* mescolare **3** *v/i socially* socializzare

◆ **mix up** confondere; **mix sth up with sth** scambiare qc per qc; **be mixed up** *emotionally* avere disturbi emotivi; *of figures, papers* essere in disordine; **be mixed up in** essere coinvolto in

mixed [mɪkst] misto; *reac-*

tions, reviews contrastante; **I've got ~ feelings** sono combattuto; **mixer** *for food* mixer *m inv*; *drink* bibita da mischiare a un superalcolico; **mixture** miscuglio *m*; *medicine* sciroppo *m*; **mix-up** confusione *f*

moan [məʊn] **1** *n of pain* lamento *m*, gemito *m*; (*complaint*) lamentela *f* **2** *v/i in pain* lamentarsi, gemere; (*complain*) lamentarsi

mob [mɒb] **1** *n* folla *f* **2** *v/t* prendere d'assalto

mobile ['məʊbaɪl] **1** *adj that can be moved* mobile; **she's less ~ now** non si può muovere tanto, ora **2** *n for decoration* mobile *m inv*; *phone* telefonino *m*; **mobile home** casamobile *f*; **mobile phone** telefono *m* cellulare; **mobility** mobilità *f*

mobster ['mɒbstə(r)] gangster *m inv*

mock [mɒk] **1** *adj exam, election* simulato **2** *v/t* deridere; **mockery** (*derision*) scherno *m*; (*travesty*) farsa *f*

mode [məʊd] *form* mezzo *m*; COMPUT modalità *f inv*

model ['mɒdl] **1** *adj employee, husband* modello; *boat, plane in miniatura* **2** *n* (*miniature*) modellino *m*; (*pattern*) modello *m*; (*fashion* ~) indossatrice *f*; **male ~** indossatore *m* **3** *v/t* indossare **4** *v/i for designer* fare l'indossatore /

-trice; *for artist* posare
modem ['məʊdem] modem *m*
inv
moderate 1 ['mɒdərət] *adj*
moderato **2** ['mɒdərət] *n*
POL moderato *m*, -a *f* **3**
['mɒdəreit] *v/t* moderare;
moderately abbastanza;
moderation (*restraint*) mo-
derazione *f*
modern ['mɒdn] moderno;
modernization modernizz-
azione *f*; **modernize 1** *v/t*
modernizzare **2** *v/i* moder-
nizzarsi
modest ['mɒdist] modesto;
modesty modestia *f*
modification [mɒdɪfɪ'keɪʃn]
modifica *f*; **modify** modificare
module ['mɒdjuːl] modulo *m*
moist [mɔɪst] umido;
moisten inumidire; **mois-
ture** umidità *f*; **moisturizer**
for skin idratante *m*
molasses [mə'læsɪz] melassa
f
mold *etc Am* ☞ **mould** *etc*
molecule [mə'lekjʊlə(r)] molecola *f*
molest [mə'lest] *child*, *woman*
molestare
mollycoddle ['mɒlɪkɒdl] F
coccolare
molten ['məʊltən] fuso
mom [mɒm] F mamma *f*
moment ['məʊmənt] attimo
m, istante *m*; **at the ~** al momento; **for the ~** per il momento; **momentarily** (*for a*

moment) per un momento;
Am (*in a moment*) da un momento all'altro; **momentary**
momentaneo; **momentous**
importante
momentum [mə'mentəm] impeto *m*
monarch ['mɒnək] monarca
m
monastery ['mɒnəstrɪ] monastero *m*; **monastic** mona-
stico
Monday ['mʌndeɪ] lunedì *m*
inv
monetary ['mʌnɪtrɪ] monetario
money ['mʌnɪ] denaro *m*, soldi *mpl*; **money belt** marsu-
pio *m*; **money market** mercato *m* monetario; **money
order** vaglia *m*
mongrel ['mʌŋgrəl] cane *m*
bastardo
monitor ['mɒnɪtə(r)] **1** *n* COM-
PUT monitor *m inv* **2** *v/t* osservare
monk [mʌŋk] frate *m*, monaco *m*
monkey ['mʌŋkɪ] scimmia *f*; F
(*child*) diavoletto *m*; **monkey wrench** chiave *f* a rullino
monologue, *Am* **monolog**
['mɒnəlɒg] monologo *m*
monopolize [mə'nɒpəlaɪz] *also fig* monopolizzare; **monopoly** monopolio *m*
monotonous [mə'nɒtənəs]
monotono; **monotony** monotonia *f*

monster ['mɒnstə(r)] mostro m; **monstrosity** obbrobio m

month [mʌnθ] mese m; **monthly** 1 adj mensile 2 adv mensilmente 3 n magazine mensile m

monument ['mɒnjʊmənt] monumento m

mood [muːd] (frame of mind) umore m; (bad ~) malumore m; of meeting, country clima m; **be in a good / bad ~** essere di cattivo / buon umore; **moody** lunatico; (bad-tempered) di cattivo umore

moon [muːn] luna f; **moonlight** 1 n chiaro m di luna 2 v/i F lavorare in nero; **moonlit** night di luna piena

moor [mʊə(r)] boat ormeggiare

moose [muːs] alce m

mop [mɒp] 1 n for floor mocio® m; for dishes spazzolino per i piatti 2 v/t floor lavare; eyes, face asciugare

♦ **mop up** raccogliere; MIL eliminare

moped ['məʊped] motorino m

moral ['mɒrəl] 1 adj morale; person di saldi principi morali 2 n of story morale f; **~s** principi mpl morali

morale [mə'rɑːl] morale m

morality [mə'rælətɪ] moralità f inv

morbid ['mɔːbɪd] morboso

more [mɔː(r)] 1 adj più, altro; **some ~ tea?** dell'altro tè?; **a few ~ sandwiches** qualche

altro tramezzino; **for ~ information** per maggiori informazioni; **~ and ~ students / time** sempre più students / tempo; **there's no ~ ...** non c'è più ...; 2 adv più; with verbs di più; **~ important** più importante; **~ and ~** sempre di più; **~ or less** più o meno; **once ~** ancora una volta; **~ than** oltre 100; **I don't live there any~** non abito più lì; 3 pron: **do you want some ~?** ne vuoi ancora?, ne vuoi dell'altro?; **a little ~** un altro po'; **moreover** inoltre

morgue [mɔːɡ] obitorio m

morning ['mɔːnɪŋ] mattino m, mattina f; **in the ~** di mattina; (tomorrow) domattina; **this ~** stamattina; **tomorrow ~** domani mattina; **good ~** buongiorno

moron ['mɔːrɒn] F idiota m/f

morphine ['mɔːfiːn] morfina f

mortal ['mɔːtl] 1 adj mortale 2 n mortale m/f; **mortality** mortalità f

mortar ['mɔːtə(r)] MIL mortaio m; cement malta f

mortgage ['mɔːɡɪdʒ] 1 n mutuo m ipotecario 2 v/t ipotecare

mortuary ['mɔːtjʊərɪ] camera f mortuaria

mosaic [məʊ'zeɪɪk] mosaico m

Moscow ['mɒskəʊ] Mosca f

Moslem ☞ **Muslim**

mosque [mɒsk] moschea f
mosquito [mɒsˈkiːtəʊ] zanzara f
moss [mɒs] muschio m
most [məʊst] **1** adj la maggior parte di; ~ **Saturdays** quasi tutti i sabati **2** adv (very) estremamente; the ~ **beautiful** il più bello; **the one I like** ~ quello che mi piace di più; ~ **of all** soprattutto **3** pron la maggior parte (**of** di); **at (the)** ~ al massimo; **make the** ~ **of** approfittare (al massimo) di; **mostly** per lo più
MOT [eməʊˈtiː] revisione annuale obbligatoria dei veicoli
motel [məʊˈtel] motel m inv
moth [mɒθ] falena f; (clothes ~) tarma f
mother [ˈmʌðə(r)] **1** n madre f **2** v/t fare da mamma a; **motherhood** maternità f; **Mothering Sunday**, **Mother's Day** mother-in-law suocera f; **motherly** materno; **Mother's Day** Festa f della mamma; **mother tongue** madrelingua f
motif [məʊˈtiːf] motivo m
motion [ˈməʊʃn] (movement) moto m; (proposal) mozione f; **motionless** immobile
motivate [ˈməʊtɪveɪt] person motivare; **motivation** motivazione f; **motive** motivo m
motor [ˈməʊtə(r)] motore m; F car macchina f; **motorbike** moto f; **motorboat** motoscafo m; **motorcycle** motoci-

cletta f; **motorcyclist** motociclista m/f; **motor home** casamobile f; **motorist** automobilista m/f; **motor mechanic** meccanico m; **motor racing** automobilismo m; **motor vehicle** autoveicolo m; **motorway** autostrada f
motto [ˈmɒtəʊ] motto m
mould[1] [məʊld] n on food muffa f
mould[2] [məʊld] **1** n stampo m **2** v/t also fig plasmare
mouldy [ˈməʊldɪ] food ammuffito
mound [maʊnd] (hillock) collinetta f; (pile) mucchio m; Am: in baseball pedana f del lanciatore
mount [maʊnt] **1** n (horse) cavalcatura f; **Mount McKinlay** il Monte McKinlay **2** v/t steps salire; horse montare a; bicycle montare in; campaign organizzare; jewel montare **3** v/i (increase) aumentare
♦ **mount up** accumularsi
mountain [ˈmaʊntɪn] montagna f; **mountain bike** mountain bike f inv; **mountaineer** alpinista m/f; **mountaineering** alpinismo m f; **mountainous** montuoso
mourn [mɔːn] **1** v/t piangere **2** v/i: ~ **for** piangere la morte di; **mourner** persona che partecipa a un corteo funebre; **mournful** triste; **mourning** lutto m; **be in** ~ essere in lut-

mug

to; **wear ~** portare il lutto
mouse [maʊs] (*pl* **mice**
[maɪs]) topo *m*; COMPUT
mouse *m inv*; **mouse mat**
COMPUT tappetino *m* del
mouse
moustache [məˈstɑːʃ] baffi
mpl
mouth [maʊθ] bocca *f*; *of river*
foce *f*; **mouthful** *of food* boccone *m*; *of drink* sorsata *f*;
mouthorgan armonica *f* a
bocca; **mouthpiece** *of instrument* bocchino *m*;
(*spokesperson*) portavoce
m/f; **mouthwash** collutorio
m; **mouthwatering** che fa
venire l'acquolina
move [muːv] **1** *n* (*step, action,
in game*) mossa *f*; *change of
house* trasloco *m*; **get a ~
on!** F spicciati! **2** *v/t object*
spostare, muovere; (*transfer*)
trasferire; *emotionally* commuovere; **~ house** portavoce
3 *v/i* muoversi, spostarsi;
(*transfer*) trasferirsi
◆ **move around** *in room*
muoversi; *from place to place*
spostarsi
◆ **move in** trasferirsi
movement [ˈmuːvmənt] movimento *m*; **movers** *Am firm*
ditta *f* di traslochi
movie [ˈmuːvɪ] film *m inv*; **go
to a ~ / the ~s** andare al cinema; **moviegoer** frequentatore *m*, **-trice** *f* di cinema;
movie theater *Am* cinema
m inv

moving [ˈmuːvɪŋ] *which can
move* mobile; *emotionally*
commovente
mow [məʊ] *grass* tagliare, fal-
ciare; **mower** tosaerba *m inv*
MP [emˈpiː] (= *Member of
Parliament*) deputato *m*;
(= *Military Policeman*) polizia *f* militare
mph [empiːˈeɪtʃ] (= *miles per
hour*) miglia orarie
Mr [ˈmɪstə(r)] signor
Mrs [ˈmɪsɪz] signora
Ms [mɪz] signora *appellativo
usato sia per donne sposate
che nubili*
much [mʌtʃ] **1** *adj* molto; **so ~
money** tanti soldi; **so ~
sugar?** quanto zucchero?;
as ~ ... as ... tanto ... quanto
... **2** *adv* molto; **very ~** moltissimo; **too ~** troppo; **as ~
as ...** tanto quanto ... **3** *pron*
molto; **nothing ~** niente di
particolare
mud [mʌd] fango *m*
muddle [ˈmʌdl] **1** *n* disordine
m; **I'm in a ~** sono confuso **2**
v/t confondere
muddy [ˈmʌdɪ] fangoso;
hands, boots sporco di fango
muesli [ˈmjuːzlɪ] müsli *m*
muffin [ˈmʌfɪn] pasticcino *m*
muffle [ˈmʌfl] *sound* attutire;
voice camuffare; **muffler**
Am MOT marmitta *f*
mug[1] [mʌg] *for tea, coffee*
tazzone *m*; F (*face*) faccia *f*
mug[2] [mʌg] *v/t attack* aggredire

mugger ['mʌgə(r)] aggressore *m*; **mugging** aggressione *f*; **muggy** afoso

mule [mju:l] *animal* mulo *m*; *Am (slipper)* mule *f inv*

multicultural [mʌltɪ'kʌltʃərəl] multiculturale

multilateral [mʌltɪ'lætərəl] POL multilaterale

multimedia [mʌltɪ'mi:dɪə] **1** *adj* multimediale **2** *n* multimedialità *f*

multinational [mʌltɪ'næʃnl] **1** *adj* multinazionale **2** *n* COM multinazionale *f*

multiple ['mʌltɪpl] multiplo; **multiple sclerosis** sclerosi *f* multipla

multiplex (cinema) ['mʌltɪpleks] cinema *m inv* multisale

multiplication [mʌltɪplɪ'keɪʃn] moltiplicazione *f*; **multiply** **1** *v/t* moltiplicare **2** *v/i* moltiplicarsi

multi-storey (car park) [mʌltɪ'stɔːrɪ] parcheggio *m* a più piani

mum [mʌm] mamma *f*

mumble ['mʌmbl] **1** *n* borbottio *m* **2** *v/t* & *v/i* borbottare

mummy ['mʌmɪ] mamma *f*

mumps [mʌmps] orecchioni *mpl*

munch [mʌntʃ] sgranocchiare

municipal [mju:'nɪsɪpl] municipale

mural ['mjʊərəl] murale *m*

murder ['mɜːdə(r)] **1** *n* omicidio *m* **2** *v/t* uccidere; *song* ro-

vinare; **murderer** omicida *m/f*

murky ['mɜːkɪ] *also fig* torbido

murmur ['mɜːmə(r)] **1** *n* mormorio *m* **2** *v/t* mormorare

muscle ['mʌsl] muscolo *m*; **muscular** *pain, strain* muscolare; *person* muscoloso

museum [mju:'zɪəm] museo *m*

mushroom ['mʌʃrʊm] **1** *n* fungo *m* **2** *v/i* crescere rapidamente

music ['mju:zɪk] musica *f*; in *written form* spartito *m*; **musical** **1** *adj* musicale; *person* portato per la musica; *voice* melodioso **2** *n* musical *m inv*; **musical instrument** strumento *m* musicale; **musician** musicista *m/f*

Muslim ['mʊzlɪm] **1** *adj* islamico **2** *n* musulmano *m*, -a *f*

mussel ['mʌsl] cozza *f*

must [mʌst] ◇ *(necessity)*: **I ~ be on time** devo arrivare in orario; **I ~n't be late** non devo far tardi ◇ *(probability)*: **it ~ be about 6 o'clock** devono essere circa le sei

mustache *Am* → **moustache**

mustard ['mʌstəd] senape *f*

musty ['mʌstɪ] *smell* di stantio; *room* che sa di stantio

mutilate ['mju:tɪleɪt] mutilare

mutiny ['mju:tɪnɪ] **1** *n* ammutinamento *m* **2** *v/i* ammutinarsi

mutter ['mʌtə(r)] farfugliare

mutual ['mjuːtjʊəl] *admiration* reciproco; *friend* in comune

muzzle ['mʌzl] **1** *n of animal* muso *m*; *for dog* museruola *f* **2** *v/t*: ~ **the press** imbavagliare la stampa

my [maɪ] il mio *m*, la mia *f*, i miei *mpl*, le mie *fpl*; ~ **sister / brother** mia sorella / mio fratello

myself [maɪ'self] mi; *emphatic* io stesso; *after prep* me stesso; **I've hurt** ~ mi sono fatto male

mysterious [mɪ'stɪərɪəs] misterioso; **mysteriously** misteriosamente; **mystery** mistero *m*; **mystify** lasciare perplesso

myth [mɪθ] *also fig* mito *m*; **mythical** mitico

N

nag [næg] **1** *v/i of person* brontolare di continuo **2** *v/t* assillare; **nagging** *person* brontolone; *doubt, pain* assillante

nail [neɪl] *for wood* chiodo *m*; *on finger, toe* unghia *f*; **nail clippers** *npl* tagliaunghie *m inv*; **nail file** limetta *f* per unghie; **nail polish** smalto *m* per unghie; **nail polish remover** solvente *m* per unghie

naive [naɪ'iːv] ingenuo

naked ['neɪkɪd] nudo

name [neɪm] **1** *n* nome *m*; **what's your** ~? come ti chiami? **2** *v/t* chiamare; **namely** cioè; **namesake** omonimo *m*, -a *f*

nanny ['næni] bambinaia *f*

nap [næp] sonnellino *m*; **have a** ~ farsi un sonnellino

napkin ['næpkɪn] *(table ~)* tovagliolo *m*; *(sanitary ~)* assorbente *m*

Naples ['neɪplz] Napoli *f*

nappy ['næpɪ] pannolino *m*

narcotic [nɑː'kɒtɪk] narcotico *m*

narrate [nə'reɪt] raccontare, narrare; **narrative 1** *n story* racconto **2** *adj poem, style* narrativo; **narrator** narratore *m*, -trice *f*

narrow ['nærəʊ] stretto; *views, mind* ristretto; *victory* di stretta misura; **narrowly** *win* di stretta misura; ~ **escape sth** scampare a qc per un pelo F; **narrow-minded** di idee ristrette

nasty ['nɑːstɪ] *person, remark, smell, weather* cattivo; *cut, wound, disease* brutto

nation ['neɪʃn] nazione *f*; **national 1** *adj* nazionale **2** *n* cittadino *m*, -a *f*; **national anthem** inno *m* nazionale; **national debt** debito *m* pubblico; **nationalism** nazionalismo *m*; **nationality** nazionalità *f inv*; **nationalize** *industry etc* nazionalizzare

native ['neɪtɪv] **1** *adj* indigeno; **~ language** madrelingua *f* **2** *n* (*tribesman*) indigeno *m*, -a *f*; **she's a ~ of New York** è originaria di New York; **Native American** indiano *m*, -a *f* d'america; **native speaker: English ~** persona *f* di madrelingua inglese

NATO ['neɪtəʊ] (= **North Atlantic Treaty Organization**) NATO *f*

natural ['nætʃrəl] naturale; **naturalist** naturalista *m/f*; **naturalize: become ~d** naturalizzarsi; **naturally** (*of course*) naturalmente; *behave, speak* con naturalezza; (*by nature*) per natura; **nature** natura *f*; **nature reserve** riserva *f* naturale

naughty ['nɔːtɪ] cattivo; *photograph, word etc* spinto

nausea ['nɔːzɪə] nausea *f*; **nauseate** ['nɔːzɪeɪt] (*fig: disgust*) disgustare; **nauseating** *smell, taste* nauseante; *person* disgustoso; **nauseous: feel ~** avere la nausea

nautical ['nɔːtɪkl] nautico

naval ['neɪvl] navale; *officer, uniform* della marina

navel ['neɪvl] ombelico *m*

navigate ['nævɪgeɪt] *also* COMPUT navigare; *in car* fare da navigatore / -trice; **navigation** navigazione *f*; **navi-**

gator *on ship, in aeroplane* ufficiale *m* di rotta; *in car* navigatore *m*, -trice *f*

navy ['neɪvɪ] marina *f* militare; **navy blue 1** *n* blu *m inv* scuro **2** *adj* blu scuro

near [nɪə(r)] **1** *adv* vicino **2** *prep* vicino a; **do you go ~ the bank?** va dalle parti della banca? **3** *adj* vicino; **in the ~ future** nel prossimo futuro; **nearby** *live* vicino; **nearly** quasi; **near-sighted** miope

neat [niːt] *room, desk, person* ordinato; *whisky* liscio; *solution* efficace; F (*terrific*) fantastico

necessarily ['nesəserɪlɪ] necessariamente; **necessary** necessario; **it is ~ to ...** è necessario ..., bisogna ...; **necessity** necessità *f inv*

neck [nek] collo *m*; **necklace** collana *f*; **neckline** *of dress* scollo *m*; **necktie** cravatta *f*

née [neɪ] nata *f*

need [niːd] **1** *n* bisogno *m*; **if ~ be** se necessario; **be in ~** (*be needy*) essere bisognoso; **be in ~ of sth** aver bisogno di qc; **you don't ~ to wait** non c'è bisogno che aspetti; **I ~ to talk to you** ti devo parlare

needle ['niːdl] *for sewing, on dial* ago *m*; **needlework** cucito *m*

needy ['niːdɪ] bisognoso

negative ['negətɪv] negativo

neglect [nɪ'glekt] **1** *n* trascuratezza *f* **2** *v/t* trascurare; **ne-**

glected *gardens*, *author* trascurato

negligence ['neglɪdʒəns] negligenza f; **negligent** negligente; **negligible** *quantity* trascurabile

negotiable [nɪ'gəʊʃəbl] negoziabile; **negotiate 1** v/i trattare **2** v/t *deal*, *settlement* negoziare; *obstacles* superare; *bend in road* affrontare; **negotiation** negoziato m; **negotiator** negoziatore m, -trice f

neighbor etc Am → **neighbour** etc

neighbour ['neɪbə(r)] vicino m, -a f; **neighbourhood** *in town* quartiere m; **in the ~ of** fig intorno a; **neighbouring** *house*, *state* confinante; **neighbourly** amichevole

neither ['naɪðə(r)] **1** *adj*: **~ player** nessuno dei due giocatori **2** *pron* nessuno dei due, nessuna f delle due **3** *adv*: **~ ... nor ...** né ... né ... **4** *conj* neanche; **~ do I** neanch'io

neon light ['niːɒn] luce f al neon

nephew ['nevjuː] nipote m (di zii)

nerve [nɜːv] nervo m; (*courage*) coraggio m; (*impudence*) faccia f tosta; **get on s.o.'s ~s** dare sui nervi a qu; **nerve-racking** snervante; **nervous** nervoso; **be ~ about doing sth** essere an-

sioso all'idea di fare qc; **nervous breakdown** esaurimento m nervoso; **nervousness** nervosismo m; **nervous wreck**: **be a ~** avere i nervi a pezzi

nest [nest] nido m

net¹ [net] n *for fishing* retino m; *for tennis* rete f; COMPUT Internet f; **on the ~** su Internet

net² [net] *adj* COM netto

nettle ['netl] ortica f

network *of contacts*, *cells*, COMPUT rete f; **social ~** rete f sociale; **networking** *presa di contatti professionali in situazioni informali*

neurologist [njʊ'rɒlədʒɪst] neurologo m, -a f

neurosis [njʊ'rəʊsɪs] nevrosi f inv

neurotic nevrotico

neuter ['njuːtə(r)] *animal* sterilizzare

neutral ['njuːtrəl] **1** *adj* *country* neutrale; *colour* neutro **2** n *gear* folle m; **neutrality** neutralità f; **neutralize** neutralizzare

never ['nevə(r)] mai; **~!** *in disbelief* ma va'!; **you're ~ going to believe this** non ci crederesti mai; **nevertheless** comunque, tuttavia

new [njuː] nuovo; **that's nothing ~** non è una novità; **newborn** neonato; **newcomer** nuovo arrivato m, nuova arrivata f; **newly** (*recently*) recentemente; **newly weds** sposini *mpl*

news [njuːz] notizia *f*; *on TV, radio* notiziario *m*; novità *f inv*; *any ~?* ci sono novità?; *that's ~ to me* mi giunge nuovo; **newsagent** giornalaio *m*; **newscast** telegiornale *m*; **newscaster** giornalista *m/f* televisivo, -a; **news flash** notizia *f* flash; **newspaper** giornale *m*; **newsreader** giornalista *m/f* radiotelevisivo, -a; **news report** notiziario *m*; **newsstand** edicola *f*; **newsvendor** edicolante *m/f*

New 'Year anno *m* nuovo; *Happy New Year!* buon anno!; **New Year's Day** capodanno *m*; **New Year's Eve** San Silvestro *m*

next [nekst] **1** *adj in time* prossimo; *in space* vicino; *the ~ month* il mese dopo; *who's ~?* a chi tocca? **2** *adv* dopo; *~ to (beside)* accanto a; *(in comparison with)* a paragone di; **next door 1** *adj*: *~ neighbour* vicino *m*, -a *f* di casa **2** *adv live* nella casa accanto; **next of kin** parente *m/f* prossimo

nibble ['nɪbl] mordicchiare

nice [naɪs] *person* carino, gentile; *day, weather, party* bello; *meal, food* buono; *that's very ~ of you* molto gentile da parte tua!; **nicely** *written, presented* bene

niche [niːʃ] nicchia *f*

nick [nɪk] *cut* taglietto *m*; *in the ~ of time* appena in tempo

nickel ['nɪkl] *material* nichel *m*; *Am coin* moneta *f* da 5 centesimi di dollaro

'nickname soprannome *m*

niece [niːs] nipote *f* (di zii)

night [naɪt] notte *f*; *(evening)* sera *f*; *at ~* di notte / di sera; *last ~* ieri notte / ieri sera; *stay the ~* rimanere a dormire; *work ~s* fare il turno di notte; *good ~* buona notte; **nightcap** *(drink)* bicchierino bevuto prima di andare a letto; **nightclub** night(-club) *m inv*; **nightdress** camicia *f* da notte; **night flight** volo *m* notturno; **nightlife** vita *f* notturna; **nightly** ogni sera; *late at night* ogni notte; **nightmare** *also fig* incubo *m*; **night porter** portiere *m* notturno; **night school** scuola *f* serale; **night shift** turno *m* di notte; **nightshirt** camicia *f* da notte *(da uomo)*; **nightspot** locale *m* notturno; **nighttime**: *at ~* di notte, la notte

nimble ['nɪmbl] agile

nine [naɪn] nove; **nineteen** diciannove; **nineteenth** diciannovesimo; **ninetieth** novantesimo; **ninety** novanta; **ninth** nono

nip [nɪp] *(pinch)* pizzico *m*; *(bite)* morso *m*

nipple ['nɪpl] capezzolo *m*

nitrogen ['naɪtrədʒn] azoto *m*

no [nəʊ] **1** *adv* no **2** *adj* nessuno; **there's** ~ **coffee left** non c'è più caffè; **I have** ~ **money** non ho soldi; ~ **smoking** vietato fumare

noble ['nəʊbl] nobile

nobody ['nəʊbədɪ] nessuno; ~ **knows** nessuno lo sa; **there was** ~ **at home** non c'era nessuno in casa

no-brainer [nəʊ'breɪnə(r)] F cretinata *f*; **a real** ~ **of a decision** una decisione semplicissima

nod [nɒd] **1** *n* cenno *m* del capo **2** *v/i* fare un cenno col capo; ~ **in agreement** annuire

◆ **nod off** (*fall asleep*) appisolarsi

noise [nɔɪz] (*sound*) rumore *m*; *loud, unpleasant* chiasso *m*; **noisy** rumoroso; *children, party* chiassoso; **don't be so** ~ non fate tanto rumore

nominal ['nɒmɪnl] *amount* simbolico

nominate ['nɒmɪneɪt] (*appoint*) designare; **nomination** (*appointing*) nomina *f*; *person proposed* candidato *m*, -a *f*; **nominee** candidato *m*, -a *f*

nonalco'holic analcolico

nonchalant ['nɒnʃələnt] noncurante

noncommissioned 'officer ['nɒnkəmɪʃnd] sottufficiale *m*

noncommittal [nɒnkə'mɪtl] *person, response* evasivo

nondescript ['nɒndɪskrɪpt] ordinario

none [nʌn] nessuno *m*, -a *f*; **there are** ~ **left** non ne sono rimasti; **there is** ~ **left** non ne è rimasto, non è rimasto niente

nonentity [nɒn'entətɪ] nullità *f inv*

nonetheless [nʌnðə'les] nondimeno

none'xistent inesistente

non'fiction opere *fpl* non di narrativa

noninter'ference, noninter'vention non intervento *m*

no-'nonsense *approach* pragmatico

non'payment mancato pagamento *m*

nonpol'luting non inquinante

non'resident *in country* non residente *m/f*; (*in hotel*) persona chi non è cliente di un albergo

nonre'turnable a fondo perduto

nonsense ['nɒnsəns] sciocchezze *fpl*; **don't talk** ~ non dire sciocchezze

non'smoker non fumatore *m*, -trice *f*

non'standard fuori standard, non di serie; *use of a word* che fa eccezione

non'stick *pans* antiaderente

non'stop 1 *adj flight, train* di-

retto; *chatter* continuo **2** *adv*
fly, travel senza scalo; *chatter,*
argue di continuo

non'union non appartenente
al sindacato

non'violence non violenza *f*;
nonviolent non violento

noodles ['nuːdlz] spaghetti
mpl cinesi

noon [nuːn] mezzogiorno *m*

'no-one ⇒ **nobody**

noose [nuːs] cappio *m*

nor [nɔː(r)] né; **~ do I** neanch'io, neanche a me

norm [nɔːm] norma *f*; **normal**
normale; **normality** normalità *f*; **normally** (*usually*) di solito; *in a normal way* normalmente

north [nɔːθ] **1** *n* nord *m* **2** *adj*
settentrionale, nord *inv* **3**
adv travel verso nord; **~ of**
a nord di; **North America**
America *f* del Nord; **North
American 1** *n* nordamericano *m*, -a *f* **2** *adj* nordamericano; **northeast** nordest
m; **northerly** *wind* settentrionale; *direction* nord *inv*; **northern** settentrionale; **northerner** settentrionale *m/f*;
North Korea Corea *f* del
Nord; **North Korean 1** *adj*
nordcoreano **2** *n* nordcoreano *m*, -a *f*; **North Pole** polo
m nord; **northward** *travel*
verso nord; **northwest** nordovest *m*

Norway ['nɔːweɪ] Norvegia *f*;
Norwegian 1 *adj* norvegese

2 *n person* norvegese *m/f*;
language norvegese *m*

nose [nəʊz] naso *m*; *right under my ~!* proprio sotto il naso!
♦ **nose around** F curiosare

nostalgia [nɒˈstældʒɪə] nostalgia *f*; **nostalgic** nostalgico

nostril ['nɒstrəl] narice *f*

nosy ['nəʊzɪ] F curioso

not [nɒt] non; *I hope ~* spero
di no; *I don't know* non so;
he didn't help non ha aiutato; **~ me** io no

notable ['nəʊtəbl] notevole

notch [nɒtʃ] tacca *f*

note [nəʊt] MUS, *comment on
text* nota *f*; *short letter* biglietto *m*; *memo to self* appunto
m; *money* banconota *f*; *take
~s* prendere appunti; *take ~
of sth* prendere nota di; **notebook** taccuino *m*; COMPUT notebook *m inv*; **noted**
noto; **notepad** bloc-notes
m inv; **notepaper** carta *f*
da lettere

nothing ['nʌθɪŋ] niente; **~ but**
nient'altro che; **~ much**
niente di speciale; **for ~**
(*for free*) gratis; (*for no reason*) per un nonnulla

notice ['nəʊtɪs] **1** *n on notice
board, in street* avviso *m*; (*advance warning*) preavviso *m*;
in newspaper annuncio *m*; *to
leave job* preavviso *m*; *to
leave house* disdetta *f*; *at
short ~* con un breve preav-

viso; **until further ~** fino a nuovo avviso; **hand in one's ~** *to employer* presentare le dimissioni; **take no ~ of s.o. / sth** non fare caso a qu / qc **2** v/t notare; **notice board** bacheca *f*; **noticeable** sensibile

notify ['nəʊtɪfaɪ] informare

notion ['nəʊʃn] idea *f*

notorious [nəʊ'tɔːrɪəs] famigerato

nought [nɔːt] zero *m*

noun [naʊn] nome *m*, sostantivo *m*

nourishing ['nʌrɪʃɪŋ] nutriente; **nourishment** nutrimento *m*

novel ['nɒvl] romanzo *m*; **novelist** romanziere *m*, -a *f*

novelty ['nɒvltɪ] novità *f inv*

November [nəʊ'vembə(r)] novembre *m*

novice ['nɒvɪs] principiante *m/f*

now [naʊ] ora, adesso; **~ and again, ~ and then** ogni tanto; **by ~** ormai; **from ~ on** d'ora in poi; **right ~** subito; **just ~** (proprio) adesso; **~, ~!** su, su!; **nowadays** oggigiorno

nowhere ['nəʊweə(r)] da nessuna parte; **it's ~ near finished** è ben lontano dall'essere terminato

nuclear ['njuːklɪə(r)] nucleare; **nuclear energy** energia *f* nucleare; **nuclear physics** fisica *f* nucleare; **nuclear**

power energia *f* nucleare; POL potenza *f* nucleare; **nuclear power station** centrale *f* nucleare; **nuclear reactor** reattore *m* nucleare; **nuclear waste** scorie *fpl* radioattive; **nuclear weapon** arma *f* nucleare

nude [njuːd] **1** *adj* nudo **2** *n painting* nudo *m*; **in the ~** nudo

nudge [nʌdʒ] dare un colpetto di gomito a; **parked car** spostare leggermente

nudist ['njuːdɪst] nudista *m/f*

nuisance ['njuːsns] seccatura *f*; **make a ~ of o.s.** dare fastidio

null and 'void [nʌl] nullo

numb [nʌm] intirizzito; *emotionally* impietrito

number ['nʌmbə(r)] **1** *n* numero *m*; *(quantity)* quantità *f inv* **2** v/t put a number on numerare; **number plate** *of vehicle* targa *f*

numeral ['njuːmərəl] numero *m*

numerate ['njuːmərət] *adj*: **be ~** avere buone basi in matematica; *of children* saper contare

numerous ['njuːmərəs] numeroso

nun [nʌn] suora *f*

nurse [nɜːs] infermiere *m*, -a *f*; **nursery school** asilo *m*; *in house* stanza *f* dei bambini; *for plants* vivaio *m*; **nursery rhyme** filastrocca *f*;

nursery school scuola f materna; **nursing** professione f d'infermiere; **nursing home** *for old people* casa f di riposo
nut [nʌt] noce f; *for bolt* dado m; **nutcrackers** schiaccianoci m inv
nutrient ['njuːtrɪənt] sostanza f nutritiva; **nutrition** alimen-

tazione f; **nutritious** nutriente
nuts [nʌts] F (*crazy*) svitato; **be ~ about s.o.** essere pazzo di qu
'nutshell: in a ~ in poche parole
nutty ['nʌtɪ] *taste* di noce; F (*crazy*) pazzo

O

oak [əʊk] *tree* quercia f; *wood* rovere m
oar [ɔː(r)] remo m
oasis [əʊ'eɪsɪs] *also fig* oasi f inv
oath [əʊθ] LAW giuramento m; (*swearword*) imprecazione f
'oatmeal farina f d'avena
obedience [ə'biːdɪəns] ubbidienza f; **obedient** ubbidiente; **obediently** docilmente
obese [əʊ'biːs] obeso; **obesity** obesità f
obey [ə'beɪ] *parents* ubbidire a; *law* osservare
obituary [ə'bɪtjʊərɪ] necrologio m
object¹ ['ɒbdʒɪkt] n (*thing*) oggetto m; (*aim*) scopo m; GRAM complemento m
object² [əb'dʒekt] v/i avere da obiettare
objection [əb'dʒekʃn] obiezione f; **objectionable** (*unpleasant*) antipatico; **objective 1** adj obiettivo **2** n obiet-

tivo m; **objectively** obiettivamente; **objectivity** obiettività f
obligation [ɒblɪ'geɪʃn] obbligo m; **obligatory** obbligatorio; **obliging** servizievole
oblique [ə'bliːk] **1** adj *reference* indiretto **2** n in punctuation barra f
obliterate [ə'blɪtəreɪt] city annientare; *memory* cancellare
oblivion [ə'blɪvɪən] oblio m; **fall into ~** cadere in oblio
oblong ['ɒblɒŋ] **1** adj rettangolare **2** n rettangolo m
obnoxious [əb'nɒkʃəs] offensivo; *smell* sgradevole; *person* odioso; *dog, child* insopportabile
obscene [əb'siːn] osceno; *salary, poverty* vergognoso; **obscenity** oscenità f inv
obscure [əb'skjʊə(r)] oscuro; **obscurity** oscurità f inv
observant [əb'zɜːvnt] osservante; **observation** osservazione f; **observatory** osser-

vatorio *m*; **observe** osservare; **observer** osservatore *m*, -trice *f*

obsess [əb'ses]: **be ~ed with** essere fissato con; **obsession** fissazione *f*; **obsessive** ossessivo

obsolete ['ɒbsəliːt] *model* obsoleto; *word* disusato

obstacle ['ɒbstəkl] *also fig* ostacolo

obstetrician [ɒbstə'trɪʃn] ostetrico *m*, -a *f*; **obstetrics** ostetricia *f*

obstinacy ['ɒbstɪnəsɪ] ostinazione *f*; **obstinate** ostinato

obstruct [əb'strʌkt] *road* ostruire; *investigation, police* ostacolare; **obstruction** *on road etc* ostruzione *f*; **obstructive** *behaviour, tactics* ostruzionista

obtain [əb'teɪn] ottenere; **obtainable** *products* reperibile

obtuse [əb'tjuːs] *fig* ottuso

obvious ['ɒbvɪəs] ovvio, evidente; **obviously** ovviamente, evidentemente

occasion [ə'keɪʒn] occasione *f*; **occasional** sporadico; **I like the ~ whisky** bevo un whisky ogni tanto; **occasionally** ogni tanto

occupant ['ɒkjupənt] *of vehicle* occupante *m/f*; *of building* abitante *m/f*; **occupation** (*job*) professione *f*; *of country* occupazione *f*; **occupy** occupare

occur [ə'kɜː(r)] accadere; *it*

~red to me that ... mi è venuto in mente che ...; **occurrence** evento *m*

ocean ['əuʃn] oceano *m*

o'clock [ə'klɒk]: **at five ~** alle cinque; **it's one ~** è l'una; **it's three ~** sono le tre

October [ɒk'təubə(r)] ottobre *m*

octopus ['ɒktəpəs] polpo *m*

odd [ɒd] (*strange*) strano; (*not even*) dispari; **the ~ one out** l'eccezione *f*; **50 ~** 50 e rotti; **oddball** F persona *f* stramba; **odds and ends** *objects* cianfrusaglie *fpl*; *things to do* cose *fpl*; **odds-on: the ~ favourite** il favorito; **it's ~ that ...** è praticamente scontato che ...

odometer [əu'dɒmətə(r)] *Am* contachilometri *m*

odour, *Am* **odor** ['əudə(r)] odore *m*

of [ɒv] di; **the name ~ the street / hotel** il nome della strada / dell'albergo; **it's made ~ steel** è di acciaio; **die ~ cancer** morire di cancro; **a friend ~ mine** un mio amico; **very nice ~ him** molto gentile da parte sua

off [ɒf] **1** *prep*: **a lane ~ the main road** *not far from* un sentiero poco lontano dalla strada principale; **leading off** un sentiero che parte dalla strada principale; **£20 ~ the price** 20 sterline di sconto **2** *adv*: **be ~ of light,**

TV etc essere spento; *of gas, tap* essere chiuso; *(cancelled)* essere annullato; *of food* essere finito; **she was ~ today not at work** oggi non era al lavoro; **we're ~ tomorrow leaving** partiamo domani; **take a day ~** prendere un giorno libero; **it's 3 miles ~** dista 3 miglia; **it's a long way ~** è molto lontano **3** *adj food* andato a male; **~ switch** interruttore *m* di spegnimento

offence [əˈfens] LAW reato *m*; **take ~ at sth** offendersi per qc; **offend** *(insult)* offendere; **offender** LAW delinquente *m/f*; **offense** *Am* ☞ **offence**

offensive 1 *adj behaviour, remark,* offensivo; *smell* sgradevole **2** *n* (MIL: *attack*) offensiva *f*

offer [ˈɒfə(r)] **1** *n* offerta *f* **2** *v/t* offrire; **~ s.o. sth** offrire qc a qu

off·hand *attitude* disinvolto

office [ˈɒfɪs] ufficio *m*; *(position)* carica *f*; **~ hours** orario *m* d'ufficio; **officer** MIL ufficiale *m*; *in police* agente *m/f*; **official 1** *adj* ufficiale **2** *n* funzionario *m*, -a *f*; **officially** ufficialmente; **officious** invadente

off-licence negozio *m* di alcolici

off-line disconnesso, off-line *inv*; **go ~** disconnettersi

off-peak *rates* ridotto; **~ elec-**

-tricity elettricità *f* a tariffa ridotta

off-season bassa stagione *f*

offset *losses* compensare

offshore *drilling rig, investment* off-shore *inv*

offside 1 *adj wheel etc* destro; *on the left* sinistro **2** *adv* SP in fuorigioco

offspring figli *mpl; of animal* piccoli *mpl*

off-the-record ufficioso

often [ˈɒfn] spesso; **how ~ do you go there?** ogni quanto tempo ci vai?

oil [ɔɪl] **1** *n* olio *m; petroleum* petrolio *m; for central heating* nafta *f* **2** *v/t* oliare; **oil change** cambio *m* dell'olio; **oil company** compagnia *f* petrolifera; **oilfield** giacimento *m* petrolifero; **oil painting** quadro *m* a olio; **oil refinery** raffineria *f* di petrolio; **oil rig** piattaforma *f* petrolifera; **oil slick** chiazza *f* di petrolio; **oil tanker** petroliera *f;* **oil well** pozzo *m* petrolifero; **oily** unto

ointment [ˈɔɪntmənt] pomata *f*

ok [əʊˈkeɪ]: **can I? - ~** posso? - va bene!; **it's ~ with you if ...?** ti va bene se ...?; **does that look ~?** ti sembra che vada bene?; **that's ~ by me** per me va bene; **are you ~?** *well, not hurt* stai bene?; **he's ~** *(is a good guy)* è in gamba

481   **one-parent family**

old [əʊld] vecchio; (*previous*)
precedente; **how ~ is he?**
quanti anni ha?; **old age**
vecchiaia *f*; **old-age pen-**
sioner pensionato *m*, *-a f*;
old-fashioned antiquato

olive ['ɒlɪv] oliva *f*; **olive oil**
olio *m* d'oliva

Olympic 'Games [ə'lɪmpɪk]
Olimpiadi *fpl*, giochi *mpl*
olimpici

omelette, *Am* omelet ['ɒmlɪt]
frittata *f*

ominous ['ɒmɪnəs] sinistro

omission [ə'mɪʃn] omissione
f; **on purpose** esclusione *f*;
omit omettere; **on purpose**
escludere; **~ to do sth** tralasciare di fare qc

on [ɒn] **1** *prep* su; **~ the table**
sul tavolo; **~ the bus** in autobus; **~ TV** alla TV; **~ Sunday**
domenica; **~ Sundays** di domenica; **~ the 1st of June** il
primo (di) giugno; **I'm ~**
antibiotics sto prendendo
antibiotici; **this is ~ me**
(*I'm paying*) offro io; **have**
you any money ~ you?
hai dei soldi con te?; **~ his**
arrival al suo arrivo; **~ hear-**
ing this al sentire queste
parole **2** *adv*: **be ~** *of light, TV*
etc essere acceso; *of gas, vt,*
tap essere aperto; *of machine*
essere in funzione; *of hand-*
brake essere inserito; **it's ~**
after the news *of pro-*
gramme è dopo il notiziario;
the meeting is ~ scheduled

to happen la riunione si fa;
with his jacket ~ con la giacca; **what's ~ tonight?** on TV
etc cosa c'è stasera?; **I've got**
something ~ tonight
planned stasera ho un impegno; **you're ~** I accept your
offer *etc* d'accordo; **that's**
not ~ (*not allowed, not fair*)
non è giusto; **~ you go** (*go*
ahead) fai pure; **~ talk ~** continuare a parlare; **and so ~** e
così via; **and ~ talk** *etc* senza sosta **3** *adj*: **the ~ switch**
l'interruttore *m* d'accensione

once [wʌns] **1** *adv* (*one time*)
una volta; (*formerly*) un tempo; **~ again**, **~ more** ancora
una volta; **at ~** (*immediately*)
subito; **all at ~** (*suddenly*) improvvisamente; **(all) at ~** (*to-*
gether) contemporaneamen-
te; **~ upon a time there was**
... c'era una volta ... **2** *conj*
non appena; **~ you have fin-**
ished non appena hai finito

one [wʌn] **1** *n number* uno *m* **2**
adj uno, *-a*; **~ day** un giorno
3 *pron* uno *m*, *-a f*; **which ~?**
quale?; **that ~** quello *m*, *-a f*;
this ~ questo *m*, *-a f*; **~ by ~**
enter, deal with uno alla volta;
~ another l'un l'altro, a vicenda; **what can ~ say?** cosa
si può dire?; **the little ~s** i
piccoli; **one-off** *n* fatto *m*
eccezionale; *person* persona
f eccezionale **2** *adj* unico;
one-parent family famiglia

f monogenitore; **oneself** si;
after prep se stesso *m*, -a *f*,
sé; *cut ~* tagliarsi; *do sth ~*
fare qc da sé; **one-way
street** strada *f* a senso unico;
one-way ticket biglietto *m*
di sola andata

onion ['ʌnjən] cipolla *f*

'on-line connesso, on-line
inv; **go ~** connettersi; **on-line
banking** telebanking *m*; **on-
-line shopping** shopping *m*
in Rete

onlooker ['ɒnlʊkə(r)] astante
m

only ['əʊnlɪ] **1** *adv* solo; *not ~
X but also Y* non solo X ma
anche Y; **~ just** a malapena **2**
adj unico; **~ son** unico figlio
maschio

'onset inizio *m*

'onside SP non in fuorigioco

on-the-job 'training training
m inv sul lavoro

onto ['ɒntu]: **put sth ~ sth**
mettere qc sopra qc

onwards ['ɒnwədz] in avanti;
from ... ~ da ... in poi

opaque [əʊ'peɪk] *glass* opaco

open ['əʊpən] **1** *adj* aperto; *in
the ~ air* all'aria aperta **2** *v/t*
aprire **3** *v/i* of door, shop
aprirsi; *of flower* sbocciare;
open-air *meeting, concert* al-
l'aperto; *pool* scoperto;
open day giornata *f* di apertura al pubblico; **open-ended**
contract etc aperto; **opening** *in wall etc* apertura *f*; *of
film, novel etc* inizio *m*; (*job*

going) posto *m* vacante;
openly (*honestly, frankly*)
apertamente; **open-minded**
aperto; **open ticket** biglietto
m aperto

opera ['ɒpərə] lirica *f*, opera *f*;
opera house teatro *m* del-
l'opera; **opera singer** cantante lirico *m*, -a *f*

operate ['ɒpəreɪt] **1** *v/i of
company* operare; *of airline,
bus service* essere in servizio;
of machine funzionare; MED
operare, intervenire **2** *v/t
machine* far funzionare

◆ **operate on** MED operare

'operating room *Am* MED sala *f* operatoria; **operating
system** COMPUT sistema *m*
operativo; **operation** operazione *f*; MED intervento *m*
(chirurgico), operazione *f*;
of machine funzionamento
m; *have an ~* MED subire
un intervento (chirurgico);
operator TELEC centralinista *m/f*; *of machine* operatore
m, -trice *f*; (*tour ~*) operatore
m turistico

opinion [ə'pɪnjən] opinione *f*,
parere *m*; *in my ~* a mio parere; **opinion poll** sondaggio
m d'opinione

opponent [ə'pəʊnənt] avversario *m*, -a *f*

opportunist [ɒpə'tjuːnɪst]
opportunista *m/f*; **opportunity** opportunità *f inv*

oppose [ə'pəʊz] opporsi a; *be
~d to ...* essere contrario a

...; **as ~d to ...** piuttosto che ...

opposite ['ɒpəzɪt] **1** adj direction opposto; meaning, views contrario; house di fronte; **the ~ side of the road** l'altro lato della strada **2** n contrario m; **opposite number** omologo m

opposition [ɒpə'zɪʃn] opposizione f

oppress [ə'pres] people opprimere; **oppressive** rule oppressivo; weather opprimente

optical illusion ['ɒptɪkl] illusione f ottica

optician [ɒp'tɪʃn] dispensing ottico m, -a f; ophthalmic optometrista m/f

optimism ['ɒptɪmɪzm] ottimismo m; **optimist** ottimista m/f; **optimistic** view ottimistico; person ottimista; **optimistically** ottimisticamente

optimum ['ɒptɪməm] **1** adj ottimale **2** n optimum m inv

option ['ɒpʃn] possibilità f inv, opzione f; **he had no other ~** non ha avuto scelta; **optional** facoltativo

or [ɔː(r)] o; **he can't hear ~ see** non può né sentire né vedere; **~ else!** o guai a te!

oral ['ɔːrəl] orale

orange ['ɒrɪndʒ] **1** adj colour arancione **2** n fruit arancia f; colour arancione m; **orange juice** succo m d'arancia

orator ['ɒrətə(r)] oratore m, -trice f

orbit ['ɔːbɪt] **1** n of earth orbita f **2** v/t the earth orbitare intorno a

orchard ['ɔːtʃəd] frutteto m

orchestra ['ɔːkɪstrə] orchestra f

orchid ['ɔːkɪd] orchidea f

ordain [ɔː'deɪn] priest ordinare

ordeal [ɔː'diːl] esperienza f traumatizzante

order ['ɔːdə(r)] **1** n ordine m; for goods, in restaurant ordinazione f; **in ~ to do sth** così da fare qc; **out of ~** (not functioning) fuori servizio; (not in sequence) fuori posto **2** v/t ordinare; **~ s.o. to do sth** ordinare a qu di fare qc **3** v/i ordinare

orderly ['ɔːdəlɪ] **1** adj room, mind ordinato; crowd disciplinato **2** n in hospital inserviente m/f

ordinarily [ɔːdɪ'neərɪlɪ] (as a rule) normalmente; **ordinary** normale; pej ordinario

ore [ɔː(r)] minerale m grezzo

organ ['ɔːgən] ANAT, MUS organo m; **organic** food, fertilizer biologico; organically grown biologicamente; **organism** organismo m

organization [ɔːgənaɪ'zeɪʃn] organizzazione f; **organize** organizzare; **organizer** person organizzatore m, -trice f

orgasm ['ɔːgæzm] orgasmo m

orient [ˈɔːrɪənt] *Am* orientare;
Oriental 1 *adj* orientale **2** *n*
orientale *m/f*; **orientate**
orientare

origin [ˈɒrɪdʒɪn] origine *f*;
original 1 *adj* originale **2** *n*
painting etc originale *m*;
originality originalità *f*;
originally (*at first*) in origine;
~ he comes from France è
di origini francesi; **originate**
1 *v/t scheme, idea* dare origine a **2** *v/i of idea, belief* avere
origine

ornamental [ɔːnəˈmentl] ornamentale

ornate [ɔːˈneɪt] *style* ornato

orphan [ˈɔːfn] orfano *m*, -a *f*

orthodox [ˈɔːθədɒks] *also fig*
ortodosso

orthopedic [ɔːθəˈpiːdɪk] ortopedico

ostensibly [ɒˈstensəblɪ] apparentemente

ostentatious [ɒstenˈteɪʃəs]
ostentato

ostracize [ˈɒstrəsaɪz] ostra-
cizzare

other [ˈʌðə(r)] **1** *adj* altro; **the**
~ day l'altro giorno; **every ~**
day a giorni alterni; **every ~**
person una persona su due
2 *n* l'altro *m*, -a *f*; **the ~s**
gli altri; **otherwise** altrimenti; (*differently*) diversamente

ought [ɔːt] **I / you ~ to know**
dovrei / dovresti saperlo;
you ~ to have done it avresti
dovuto farlo

ounce [aʊns] oncia *f*

our [ˈaʊə(r)] il nostro *m*, la nostra *f*, i nostri *mpl*, le nostre
fpl; **~ brother / sister** nostro
fratello / nostra sorella;
ours il nostro *m*, la nostra
f, i nostri *mpl*, le nostre *fpl*;
ourselves ci; *emphatic* noi
stessi / noi stesse; *after prep*
noi

oust [aʊst] *from office* esauto-
rare

out [aʊt]: **be ~** *of light, fire* essere spento; *of flower* essere
sbocciato; *of sun* splendere;
not at home, not in building
essere fuori; *of calculations*
essere sbagliato; (*be pub-
lished*) essere uscito; *of secret*
essere svelato; *no longer in
competition* essere elimina-
to; (*no longer in fashion*) essere out; **he's ~ in the garden** è in giardino; (**get**) **~!**
fuori!; **that's ~!** (*out of the
question*) è fuori discussione!; **he's ~ to win** fully in-
tends to è deciso a vincere

outboard 'motor motore *m*
fuoribordo

'outbreak scoppio *m*

'outcast emarginato *m*, -a *f*

'outcome risultato *m*

'outcry protesta *f*

out'dated sorpassato

out'do superare

out'door *toilet, activities, life*
all'aperto; *pool* scoperto;
outdoors all'aperto

outer [ˈaʊtə(r)] *wall etc*

esterno

'outfit (*clothes*) completo *m*; (*company, organization*) organizzazione *f*

'outgoing *flight, mail* in partenza; *personality* estroverso

out'grow *habits, interests* perdere

outing ['autɪŋ] (*trip*) gita *f*

out'last durare più di

'outlet *of pipe* scarico *m*; *for sales* punto *m* di vendita; *Am* ELEC presa *f* (di corrente)

'outline 1 *n of person, building etc* profilo *m*; *of plan, novel* abbozzo *m* **2** *v/t plans etc* abbozzare

out'live sopravvivere a

'outlook (*prospects*) prospettiva *f*

out'number superare numericamente

out of ◇ *motion* fuori; **fall ~ the window** cadere fuori dalla finestra ◇ *position* da **20 miles ~ Newcastle** 20 miglia da Newcastle ◇ *cause* per; **~ jealousy** per gelosia ◇ (*without*) senza; **we're ~ petrol** siamo senza benzina ◇ *from a group* su **5 ~ 10** 5 su 10

out-of-'date *passport* scaduto; *values* superato

'output 1 *n of factory* produzione *f*; COMPUT output *m inv* **2** *v/t* (*produce*) produrre

'outrage 1 *n feeling* sdegno *m*; *act* atrocità *f inv* **2** *v/t* indi-

gnare; **outrageous** *acts* scioccante; *prices* scandaloso

'outright 1 *adj winner* assoluto **2** *adv win* nettamente; *kill* sul colpo

'outset: *at / from the ~* all' / -dall'inizio

out'shine eclissare

'outside 1 *adj* esterno **2** *adv sit, go* fuori **3** *prep* fuori da; (*apart from*) al di fuori di **4** *n of building, case etc* esterno *m*; *at the ~* al massimo; **outsider** estraneo *m*, -a *f*; *in election, race* outsider *m inv*

'outsize *clothing* di taglia forte

'outskirts periferia *f*

out'smart ◇ *outwit*

out'source dare in appalto a terzi

out'standing eccezionale; FIN da saldare

outstretched ['autstretʃt] *hands* teso

'outward ['autwəd] *appearance* esteriore; *~ journey* viaggio *m* d'andata; **outwardly** esteriormente

out'weigh contare più di

out'wit riuscire a gabbare

oval ['əʊvl] ovale

oven ['ʌvn] forno *m*

over ['əʊvə(r)] **1** *prep* (*above*) sopra, su; (*across*) dall'altra parte di; (*more than*) oltre; (*during*) nel corso di; *travel all ~ Brazil* girare tutto il Brasile; *you find them*

all ~ Brazil si trovano dappertutto in Brasile; **we're ~ the worst** il peggio è passato; **~ and above** oltre a **2** *adv*: **be ~** *(finished)* essere finito; *(left)* essere rimasto; *~* **to you** *(your turn)* tocca a te; **~ here / there** qui / lì; **it hurts all ~** mi fa male dappertutto; **painted white all ~** tutto dipinto di bianco; **I've told you ~ and ~ again** te l'ho detto mille volte; **do sth ~ again** rifare qc
'**overall** *length* totale; **overalls** tuta *f* da lavoro
over'**awe** intimidire
over'**balance** perdere l'equilibrio
over'**bearing** autoritario
'**overcast** *sky* nuvoloso
over'**charge** *customer* far pagare più del dovuto a
'**overcoat** cappotto *m*
over'**come** *difficulties* superare; **be ~ by emotion** essere sopraffatto dall'emozione
over'**crowded** sovraffollato
over'**do** *(exaggerate)* esagerare; *in cooking* stracuocere; **overdone** *meat* stracotto
'**overdose** overdose *f inv*
'**overdraft** scoperto *m* (di conto); **have an ~** avere il conto scoperto; **overdraw**: **be £800 ~n** essere (allo) scoperto di 800 sterline
over'**dressed** troppo elegante
'**overdrive** MOT overdrive *m*

inv
over'**estimate** sovrastimare
over'**expose** sovraesporre
'**overflow**[1] *n pipe* troppopieno *m*
over'**flow**[2] *v/i of water* traboccare; *of river* straripare
over'**haul** *engine* revisionare; *plans* rivedere
'**overhead** *lights, cables* in alto, aereo; *railway* sopraelevato; **overheads** FIN costi *mpl* di gestione
over'**hear** sentire per caso
over'**heated** *room, engine* surriscaldato
over'**joyed** [əʊvə'dʒɔɪd] felicissimo
'**overland** via terra
over'**lap** *(partly cover)* sovrapporsi; *(partly coincide)* coincidere
over'**load** sovraccaricare
over'**look** *of tall building etc* dominare, dare su; *deliberately* chiudere un occhio su; *accidentally* non notare
'**overly** ['əʊvlɪ] troppo; **not ~ ...** non particolarmente ...
over'**night** *travel* di notte; **stay ~** per la notte; *fig change etc* da un giorno all'altro
'**overpass** cavalcavia *m inv*
over'**power** *physically* sopraffare
over'**priced** [əʊvə'praɪst] troppo caro
over'**rated** [əʊvə'reɪtɪd] sopravvalutato
over'**ride** *decision etc* annulla-

re; (*be more important than*) prevalere su; **overriding** *concern* principale

over'rule *decision* annullare

over'seas all'estero

over'see sorvegliare

over'shadow *fig* eclissare

'oversight svista *f*

oversimplifi'cation semplificazione *f* eccessiva

over'sleep non svegliarsi in tempo

over'state esagerare; **overstatement** esagerazione *f*

over'take *in work, development* superare; MOT sorpassare

over'throw¹ *v/t government* rovesciare

'overthrow² *n of government* rovesciamento *m*

'overtime 1 *n* straordinario *m* **2** *adv*: **work ~** fare lo straordinario

over'turn 1 *v/t vehicle, object* ribaltare; *government* rovesciare **2** *v/i of vehicle* ribaltar-

si

'overview visione *f* d'insieme

overwhelming [əʊvə'welmɪŋ] *feeling* profondo; *majority* schiacciante

over'work 1 *n* lavoro *m* eccessivo **2** *v/i* lavorare troppo

owe [əʊ] dovere **(s.o. a qu)**; **owing to** a causa di

owl [aʊl] gufo *m*

own¹ [əʊn] *v/t* possedere

own² [əʊn] **1** *adj* proprio; **my ~ car** la mia macchina; **my very ~ mother** proprio mia madre **2** *pron*: **a car of my ~** un'auto tutta mia; **on my / his ~** da solo

♦ **own up** confessare

owner ['əʊnə(r)] proprietario *m*, -a *f*; **ownership** proprietà *f*

oxygen ['ɒksɪdʒən] ossigeno *m*

oyster ['ɔɪstə(r)] ostrica *f*

ozone ['əʊzəʊn] ozono *m*; **ozone layer** fascia *f* or strato *m* d'ozono

P

PA [piː'eɪ] (= *personal assistant*) assistente personale

pace [peɪs] *(step)* passo *m*; *(speed)* ritmo *m*; **pacemaker** MED pacemaker *m inv*; SP battistrada *m inv*

Pacific [pə'sɪfɪk]: **the ~ (Ocean)** il Pacifico

pacifier ['pæsɪfaɪə(r)] *Am for*

baby succhiotto *m*; **pacifism** pacifismo *m*; **pacifist** pacifista *m/f*; **pacify** placare

pack [pæk] **1** *n* (*back~*) zaino *m*; *of cereal, food* confezione *f*; *of cigarettes* pacchetto *m*; *of peas etc* confezione *f*; *of cards* mazzo *m* **2** *v/t bag* fare; *item of clothing etc* mettere in

package

package 488

valigia; *goods* imballare; *groceries* imbustare **3** *v/i* fare la valigia / le valigie; **package 1** *n* (*parcel*) pacco *m*; *of offers etc* pacchetto *m* **2** *v/t* confezionare; **packaging** *also fig* confezione *f*; **packed** (*crowded*) affollato; *for writing* blocchetto *m* **2** *v/t with material* imbottire; *speech, report* farcire

pad² [pæd] *v/i* (*move quietly*) camminare a passi felpati

padding ['pædɪŋ] *material* imbottitura *f*; *in speech etc* riempitivo *m*

paddle ['pædl] **1** *n for canoe* pagaia *f* **2** *v/i in canoe* pagaiare

paddock ['pædək] paddock *m inv*

padlock ['pædlɒk] lucchetto *m*

page¹ [peɪdʒ] *n of book etc* pagina *f*

page² [peɪdʒ] *v/t* (*call*) chiamare con l'altoparlante

pager ['peɪdʒə(r)] cercapersone *m inv*

paid em'ployment occupazione *f* rimunerata

pain [peɪn] dolore *m*; **be in ~** soffrire; **a ~ in the neck** F una rottura *f* di scatole; **painful** (*distressing*) doloro-

so; (*laborious*) difficile; **painfully** (*extremely, acutely*) estremamente; **painkiller** analgesico *m*; **painstaking** accurato

paint [peɪnt] **1** *n for wall, car* vernice *f*; *for artist* colore *m* **2** *v/t wall etc* pitturare; *picture* dipingere; **paintbrush** pennello *m*; **painter** *decorator* imbianchino *m*; *artist* pittore *m*, -trice *f*; **painting** *activity* pittura *f*; (*picture*) quadro *m*; **paintwork** vernice *f*

pair [peə(r)] *of objects* paio *m*; *of animals, people* coppia *f*; **a ~ of shoes** un paio di scarpe

pajamas *Am* ☞ **pyjamas**

Pakistan [pɑːkɪˈstɑːn] Pakistan *m*; **Pakistani 1** *n* pakistano *m*, -a *f* **2** *adj* pakistano

pal [pæl] F (*friend*) amico *m*, -a *f*

palace ['pælɪs] palazzo *m* signorile

palate ['pælət] palato *m*

palatial [pə'leɪʃl] sfarzoso

pale [peɪl] pallido

Palestine ['pæləstaɪn] Palestina *f*; **Palestinian 1** *n* palestinese *m/f* **2** *adj* palestinese

pallet ['pælɪt] pallet *m inv*

pallor ['pælə(r)] pallore *m*

palm [pɑːm] *of hand* palma *f*; **palm tree** palma *f*

paltry ['pɔːltrɪ] irrisorio

pamper ['pæmpə(r)] viziare

pamphlet ['pæmflɪt] volantino *m*

pan [pæn] *for cooking* pentola

f; for frying padella *f;* **pan-cake** crêpe *f inv*
pandemonium [pændɪ'məʊnɪəm] pandemonio *m*
pane [peɪn]: ~ **(of glass)** vetro *m*
panel ['pænl] pannello *m; of experts* gruppo *m; of judges* giuria *f;* **panelling,** *Am* **paneling** rivestimento *m* a pannelli
panic ['pænɪk] **1** *n* panico *m* **2** *v/i:* **don't~** non farti prendere dal panico; **panic-stricken** in preda al panico
panorama [pænə'rɑːmə] panorama *m;* **panoramic** panoramico
pant [pænt] ansimare
panties ['pæntɪz] mutandine *fpl*
pantihose = **pantyhose**
pants [pænts] pantaloni *mpl*
pantyhose ['pæntɪhəʊz] collant *mpl*
papal ['peɪpl] pontificio
paper ['peɪpə(r)] **1** *n material* carta *f; (news~)* giornale *m; (wall~)* carta *f* da parati; *academic* relazione *f; (examination ~)* esame *m;* **~s** *(identity ~s, documents)* documenti *mpl* **2** *adj* di carta **3** *v/t room, walls* tappezzare; **paperback** tascabile *m;* **paper clip** graffetta *f;* **paperwork** disbrigo delle pratiche
parachute ['pærəʃuːt] **1** *n* paracadute *m inv* **2** *v/i* paracadutarsi **3** *v/t troops, supplies*

parachutare
parade [pə'reɪd] **1** *n (procession)* sfilata *f* **2** *v/i* sfilare
paradise ['pærədaɪs] paradiso *m*
paradox ['pærədɒks] paradosso *m;* **paradoxical** paradossale; **paradoxically** paradossalmente
paragraph ['pærəgrɑːf] paragrafo *m*
parallel ['pærəlel] **1** *n (in geometry)* parallela *f;* GEOG, *fig* parallelo *m;* **do two things in** ~ fare due cose in parallelo **2** *adj also fig* parallelo **3** *v/t (match)* uguagliare
paralysis [pə'ræləsɪs] *also fig* paralisi *f inv;* **paralyze** *also fig* paralizzare
paramedic [pærə'medɪk] paramedico *m,* -a *f*
parameter [pə'ræmɪtə(r)] parametro *m*
paramilitary [pærə'mɪlɪtrɪ] **1** *adj* paramilitare **2** *n appartenente ad un'organizzazione paramilitare*
paranoia [pærə'nɔɪə] paranoia *f;* **paranoid** paranoico
paraphrase ['pærəfreɪz] parafrasare
parasite ['pærəsaɪt] *also fig* parassita *m*
parasol ['pærəsɒl] parasole *m*
paratrooper ['pærətruːpə(r)] MIL paracadutista *m*
parcel ['pɑːsl] pacco *m*
pardon ['pɑːdn] **1** *n* LAW gra-

zia f; **I beg your~?** (*what did you say*) prego?; **I beg your~** (*I'm sorry*) scusi **2** *v/t* scusare; LAW graziare

parent ['peərənt] genitore *m*; **parental** dei genitori; **parent company** società *f inv* madre; **parent-teacher association** *organizzazione composta da genitori e insegnanti*

parish ['pærɪʃ] parrocchia *f*

park¹ [pɑːk] *n* parco *m*

park² [pɑːk] *v/t & v/i* MOT parcheggiare

parking ['pɑːkɪŋ] MOT parcheggio *m*; **no ~** sosta *f* vietata; **parking brake** *Am* freno *m* a mano; **parking garage** *Am* parcheggio *m* coperto; **parking lot** *Am* parcheggio *m*; **parking meter** parchimetro *m*; **parking ticket** multa *f* per sosta vietata

parliament ['pɑːləmənt] parlamento *m*

parole [pə'rəʊl] **1** *n* libertà *f* vigilata **2** *v/t* concedere la libertà vigilata a

parrot ['pærət] pappagallo *m*

part [pɑːt] **1** *n* parte *f*; *of machine* pezzo *m*; *Am: in hair* riga *f*; **take~in** prendere parte in **2** *adv* (*partly*) in parte **3** *v/i* separarsi **4** *v/t:* **~ one's hair** farsi la riga; **partial** (*incomplete*) parziale; **be ~ to** avere un debole per; **partially** parzialmente

participant [pɑː'tɪsɪpənt] partecipante *m/f*; **participate** partecipare (*in a*); **participation** partecipazione *f*

particular [pə'tɪkjʊlə(r)] (*specific*) particolare; (*fussy*) pignolo; **in ~** in particolare; **particularly** particolarmente

parting ['pɑːtɪŋ] *of people* separazione *f*; *in hair* riga *f*

partition [pɑː'tɪʃn] (*screen*) tramezzo *m*; (*of country*) suddivisione *f*

partly ['pɑːtlɪ] in parte

partner ['pɑːtnə(r)] COM socio *m*, -a *f*; *in relationship* partner *m/f inv*; *in particular activity* compagno *m*, -a *f*; **partnership** COM società *f inv*; *in particular activity* sodalizio *m*

'part-time part-time

party ['pɑːtɪ] **1** *n* (*celebration*) festa *f*; POL partito *m*; (*group*) gruppo *m* **2** *v/i* F far baldoria; **party-pooper** F guastafeste *m/f inv*

pass [pɑːs] **1** *n for entry* passi *m inv*; SP passaggio *m*; *in mountains* passo *m*; **make a ~ at** fare avances a **2** *v/t* (*hand*) passare; (*go past*) passare davanti a; (*overtake*) sorpassare; (*go beyond*) superare; (*approve*) approvare; SP passare; **~ an exam** superare un esame; **~ sentence** LAW emanare la sentenza; **~ the time** passare il tempo **3** *v/i* passare; *in exam* essere pro-

mosso
◆ **pass away** *euph* spegnersi
◆ **pass on 1** *v/t information,
book, savings* passare (**to** a)
2 *v/i* (*euph: die*) mancare
◆ **pass out** (*faint*) svenire
◆ **pass up** *opportunity* lasciarsi sfuggire

passable ['pɑːsəbl] *road* transitabile; (*acceptable*) passabi-
le

passage ['pæsɪdʒ] (*corridor*)
passaggio *m*; *from book* passo *m*; **the ~ of time** il passare
del tempo

passenger   ['pæsɪndʒə(r)]
passeggero *m*, -a *f*

passer-by [pɑːsə'baɪ] passante *m/f*

passion ['pæʃn] passione *f*;
passionate appassionato

passive ['pæsɪv] **1** *adj* passivo
2 *n* GRAM passivo *m*; **passive smoking** fumo *m* passivo

'**passport**   passaporto   *m*;
passport control controllo
m passaporti; **password** parola *f* d'ordine; COMPUT
password *f* *inv*

past [pɑːst] **1** *adj* (*former*) precedente; **in the ~ few days**
nei giorni scorsi **2** *n* passato
m; **in the ~** nel passato **3** *prep
in position* oltre; *it's half ~
two* sono le due e mezza;
it's ~ seven o'clock sono
le sette passate **4** *adv*: *run
~* passare di corsa

pasta ['pæstə] pasta *f*

paste [peɪst] **1** *n* (*adhesive*)
colla *f* **2** *v/t* (*stick*) incollare

pastime ['pɑːstaɪm] passatempo *m*

pastry ['peɪstrɪ] *for pie* pasta *f*
(sfoglia); (*small cake*) pasticcino *m*

'**past tense** GRAM passato *m*

pasty ['peɪstɪ] *complexion*
smorto

pat [pæt] **1** *n* colpetto *m*; *affectionate* buffetto *m* **2** *v/t* dare
un colpetto a; *affectionately*
dare un buffetto a

patch [pætʃ] **1** *n on clothing*
pezza *f*; (*period of time*) periodo *m*; (*area*) zona *f*; *go
through a bad ~* attraversare un brutto periodo, *be not
a ~ on fig* non essere niente a
paragone di **2** *v/t clothing*
rattoppare

◆ **patch up** (*repair*) riparare
alla meglio; *quarrel* risolvere

patchy ['pætʃɪ] *quality* irregolare; *work* discontinuo, disuguale

patent ['peɪtnt] **1** *adj* palese **2**
n for invention brevetto *m* **3**
v/t invention brevettare

paternal [pə'tɜːnl] paterno;
paternalism paternalismo
m; **paternalistic** paternali-
stico; **paternity** paternità *f
inv*; **paternity leave** congedo
m di paternità

path [pɑːθ] sentiero *m*; *fig*
strada *f*

pathetic [pə'θetɪk] patetico; F
(*very bad*) penoso

pathological [pæθə'lɒdʒɪkl]
patologico

patience ['peɪʃns] pazienza *f*;
card game solitario *m*; **patient 1** *n* paziente *m/f* **2** *adj*
paziente; *be ~!* abbi pazien-
za!; **patiently** pazientemen-
te

patio ['pætɪəʊ] terrazza *f*

patriot ['peɪtrɪət] patriota
m/f; **patriotic** patriottico;
patriotism patriottismo *m*

patrol [pə'trəʊl] **1** *n* pattuglia *f*
2 *v/t streets, border* pattuglia-
re; **patrol car** autopattuglia
f; **patrolman** agente *m/f* di
pattuglia; **patrol wagon**
Am furgone *m* cellulare

patron ['peɪtrən] *of artist* pa-
trocinatore *m*, -trice *f*; *of
charity* patrono *m*, -essa *f*;
of shop, cinema cliente *m/f*;
patronize *person* trattare
con condiscendenza; **pa-
tronizing** condiscendente;
patron saint patrono *m*, -a *f*

pattern ['pætn] *on fabric* motivo *m*, disegno *m*; *for sewing*
(carta) modello *m*; *in behaviour, events* schema *m*

paunch [pɔːntʃ] pancia *f*

pause [pɔːz] **1** *n* pausa *f* **2** *v/i*
fermarsi **3** *v/t tape* fermare

pave [peɪv] pavimentare; *~
the way for* fig aprire la strada a; **pavement** *Br* marciapiede *m*; *Am* manto *m* stradale

paw [pɔː] **1** *n of animal*, F
(hand) zampa *f* **2** *v/t* F palpa-

re

pawn [pɔːn] *in chess* pedone
m; *fig* pedina *f*

pay [peɪ] **1** *n* paga *f* **2** *v/t* pagare; *~ s.o. a compliment* fare
un complimento a qu **3** *v/i*
pagare; *(be profitable)* rendere; *it doesn't ~ ...* non
conviene ...; *~ for purchase*
pagare

◆ **pay back** *person* restituire i
soldi a; *loan* restituire; *(get
revenge on)* farla pagare a

◆ **pay off** *v/t debt* estinguere; *workers* liquidare; *corrupt
official* comprare **2** *v/i (be
profitable)* dare frutti

◆ **pay up** pagare

payable ['peɪəbl] pagabile;
pay cheque, *Am* **pay check**
assegno *m* paga; **payday**
giorno *m* di paga; **payee** be-
neficiario *m*, -a *f*; **payment**
pagamento *m*; **pay phone**
telefono *m* pubblico

PC [piː'siː] (= *personal computer*) PC *m inv*; (= *politically correct*) politicamente
corretto; (= *police consta-
ble*) agente *m/f* di polizia

PDA [piːdiː'eɪ] (= *personal
digital assistant*) PDA *m
inv*

pea [piː] pisello *m*

peace [piːs] pace *f*; **peaceful**
tranquillo; *demonstration* pacifico; **peacefully** tranquillamente; *demonstrate* pacifi-
camente

peach [piːtʃ] pesca *f*; *tree* pe-

sco m
peak [piːk] **1** n vetta f; fig apice m **2** v/i raggiungere il livello massimo; **peak hours** ore fpl di punta
peanut ['piːnʌt] arachide f; **get paid ~s** F essere pagati una miseria F; **peanut butter** burro m d'arachidi
pear [peə(r)] pera f; tree pero m
pearl [pɜːl] perla f
pebble ['pebl] ciottolo m
pecan ['piːkən] noce f pecan
peck [pek] **1** n (bite) beccata f; (kiss) bacetto m **2** v/t (bite) beccare; (kiss) dare un bacetto a
peculiar [pɪ'kjuːliə(r)] (strange) strano; **~ to** (special) caratteristico di; **peculiarity** [pɪkjuːli'ærətɪ] (strangeness) stranezza f; (special feature) caratteristica f
pedal ['pedl] **1** n of bike pedale m **2** v/i pedalare; (cycle) andare in bicicletta
pedantic [pɪ'dæntɪk] pedante
peddle ['pedl] drugs spacciare
pedestrian [pɪ'destrɪən] pedone m; **pedestrian crossing** passaggio m pedonale; **pedestrian precinct** zona f pedonale
pediatric [piːdɪ'ætrɪk] pediatrico; **pediatrician** pediatra m/f; **pediatrics** pediatria f
pedicure ['pedɪkjuə(r)] pedicure f inv
pedigree ['pedɪgriː] **1** n pedi-

gree m inv **2** adj di razza pura
pee [piː] F fare pipì m
peek [piːk] **1** n sbirciata F **2** v/i sbirciare
peel [piːl] **1** n buccia f; of citrus fruit scorza f **2** v/t fruit, vegetables sbucciare **3** v/i of nose, shoulders spellarsi; of paint scrostarsi
peep [piːp] v/t ☞ **peek**; **peephole** spioncino m
peer[1] [pɪə(r)] n (equal) pari m/f inv
peer[2] [pɪə(r)] v/i guardare; **~ at** scrutare
peg [peg] for coat attaccapanni m inv; for tent picchetto m; **off the ~** prêt-à-porter
pejorative [pɪ'dʒɒrətɪv] peggiorativo
pellet ['pelɪt] pallina f; (bullet) pallino m
pen[1] [pen] penna f
pen[2] [pen] (enclosure) recinto m
pen[3] [pen] Am ☞ **penitentiary**
penalize ['piːnəlaɪz] penalizzare
penalty ['penltɪ] ammenda f; in soccer rigore m; in rugby punizione f; **take the ~** battere il rigore / la punizione; **penalty area** SP area f di rigore; **penalty clause** LAW penale f; **penalty kick** in soccer calcio m di rigore; in rugby calcio m di punizione; **penalty shoot-out** rigori

mpl; **penalty spot** dischetto
m di rigore
pencil ['pensɪl] matita *f;* **pencil sharpener** temperamati-
te *m inv*
pendant ['pendənt] *necklace*
pendaglio *m*
penetrate ['penɪtreɪt] penetrare in; **penetration** penetra-
zione *f*
penguin ['peŋgwɪn] pinguino
m
penicillin [penɪ'sɪlɪn] penicil-
lina *f*
peninsula [pə'nɪnsjʊlə] penisola *f*
penis ['piːnɪs] pene *m*
penitence ['penɪtəns] penitenza *f;* **penitentiary** *Am*
prigione *f*
'pen name pseudonimo *m*
pennant ['penənt] gagliardet-
to *m*
penniless ['penɪlɪs] al verde
'pen pal amico *m,* -a *f* di penna
pension ['penʃn] pensione *f*
♦ **pension off** mandare in
pensione
'pension scheme schema *m*
pensionistico
pensive ['pensɪv] pensieroso
Pentagon ['pentəgɒn]: **the ~**
il Pentagono
pentathlon [pen'tæθlən] pentathlon *m inv*
penthouse ['penthaʊs] attico
m
pent-up ['pentʌp] represso
penultimate [pe'nʌltɪmət]

penultimo
people ['piːpl] gente *f,* persone *fpl; (nsg: race, tribe)* popolazione *f;* **the ~** *(the citizens)*
il popolo; **the American~** gli
americani; **~ say ...** si dice
che ...
pepper ['pepə(r)] *spice* pepe
m; vegetable peperone *m;*
peppermint *sweet* mentina
f; flavouring menta *f*
per [pɜː(r)] a **100 km ~ hour**
100 km all'ora; **£50 ~ night**
50 sterline a notte; **~ annum**
all'anno
perceive [pə'siːv] percepire;
(view, interpret) interpretare
percent [pə'sent] per cento;
percentage percentuale *f*
perceptible [pə'septəbl] per-
cettibile; **perceptibly** per-
cettibilmente; **perception**
percezione *f; (insightfulness)*
sensibilità *f;* **perceptive** perspicace
percolate ['pɜːkəleɪt] *of coffee* filtrare; **percolator** caffettiera *f* a filtro
perfect 1 ['pɜːfɪkt] *adj* perfetto **2** ['pɜːfɪkt] *n* GRAM passato *m* prossimo **3** [pə'fekt] *v/t*
perfezionare; **perfection**
perfezione *f;* **perfectionist**
perfezionista *m/f;* **perfectly**
perfettamente
perforated ['pɜːfəreɪtɪd] *line*
perforato
perform [pə'fɔːm] **1** *v/t (carry
out)* eseguire; *of actors* interpretare **2** *v/i of actor, musi-*

cian, dancer esibirsi; **the car ~s well** la macchina dà ottime prestazioni; **performance** *by actor* interpretazione *f; by musician* esecuzione *f;* (*show*) spettacolo *m; of employee, company etc* rendimento *m; of machine* prestazioni *fpl;* **performer** artista *m/f*

perfume ['pɜːfjuːm] profumo *m*

perfunctory [pə'fʌŋktəri] superficiale

perhaps [pə'hæps] forse

peril ['perəl] pericolo *m*

perimeter [pə'rɪmɪtə(r)] perimetro *m*

period ['pɪərɪəd] *time* periodo *m;* (*menstruation*) mestruazioni *fpl; Am punctuation mark* punto *m* fermo; **I don't want to, ~!** *Am* non voglio, punto e basta!; **periodic** periodico; **periodical** periodico *m*

peripheral [pə'rɪfərəl] **1** *adj not crucial* marginale **2** *n* COMPUT periferica *f;* **periphery** periferia *f*

perish ['perɪʃ] *of rubber* deteriorarsi; *of person* perire; **perishable** *food* deteriorabile

perjure ['pɜːdʒə(r)]: **~ o.s.** spergiurare; **perjury** falso giuramento *m*

perk [pɜːk] *of job* vantaggio *m*

perm [pɜːm] **1** *n* permanente *f* **2** *v/t:* **have one's hair ~ed**

farsi fare la permanente; **permanent** permanente; *job, address* fisso; **permanently** permanentemente

permeate ['pɜːmɪeɪt] permeare

permissible [pə'mɪsəbl] permesso, ammissibile; **permission** permesso *m;* **permissive** permissivo

permit 1 [pə'mɪt] *n* permesso *m* **2** [pə'mɪt] *v/t* permettere (**s.o. to do** a qu di fare)

perpendicular [pɜːpən'dɪkjʊlə(r)] perpendicolare

perpetual [pər'petʊəl] perenne; **perpetually** perennemente

perplex [pə'pleks] lasciare perplesso; **perplexity** perplessità *f inv*

persecute ['pɜːsɪkjuːt] perseguitare; **persecution** persecuzione *f;* **persecutor** persecutore *m,* -trice *f*

perseverance [pɜːsɪ'vɪərəns] perseveranza *f;* **persevere** perseverare

persist [pə'sɪst] persistere; **persistent** *person, questions* insistente; *rain, unemployment etc* continuo; **persistently** (*continually*) continuamente

person ['pɜːsn] persona *f;* **in ~** di persona; **personal** personale; **personal computer** personal computer *m inv;* **personality** personalità *f inv;* **personally** personalmente; **don't take it** ~ non offenderti; **personal organizer** agenda *f* elettronica; **personal stereo** Walkman® *m inv*; **personify** *of person* personificare

personnel [pɜːsəˈnel] *employees* personale *m*; *department* ufficio *m* del personale

perspective [pəˈspektɪv] *in art* prospettiva *f*; **get sth into** ~ vedere qc nella giusta prospettiva

perspiration [pɜːspɪˈreɪʃn] traspirazione *f*; **perspire** sudare

persuade [pəˈsweɪd] persuadere; ~ **s.o. to do sth** persuadere qu a fare qc; **persuasion** persuasione *f*; **persuasive** persuasivo

perturb [pəˈtɜːb] inquietare; **perturbing** inquietante

pervasive [pəˈveɪsɪv] *influence, ideas* diffuso

perversion [pəˈvɜːʃn] *sexual* perversione *f*; **pervert** *sexual* pervertito *m*, -a *f*

pessimism ['pesɪmɪzm] pessimismo *m*; **pessimist** pessimista *m/f*; **pessimistic** *view* pessimistico; *person* pessimista

pest [pest] *animale / insetto m* nocivo; *F person* peste *f*

pester ['pestə(r)] assillare; ~ **s.o. to do sth** assillare qu perché faccia qc

pesticide ['pestɪsaɪd] pesticida *m*

pet [pet] **1** *n animal* animale *m* domestico; *(favourite)* favorito *m*, -a *f* **2** *adj* preferito **3** *v/t animal* accarezzare **4** *v/i of couple* pomiciare F

petite [pəˈtiːt] minuta

petition [pəˈtɪʃn] petizione *f*

petrify ['petrɪfaɪ] terrorizzare

petrochemical [petrəʊˈkemɪkl] petrolchimico

petrol ['petrl] benzina *f*

petroleum [pɪˈtrəʊlɪəm] petrolio *m*

'petrol pump pompa *f* della benzina; **petrol station** stazione *f* di rifornimento

petting ['petɪŋ] petting *m*

petty ['petɪ] *person, behaviour* meschino; *details* insignificante; **petty cash** piccola cassa *f*

pew [pjuː] banco *m* (di chiesa)

pharmaceutical [fɑːməˈsjuːtɪkl] farmaceutico; **pharmaceuticals** farmaceutici *mpl*

pharmacist ['fɑːməsɪst] farmacista *m/f*; **pharmacy** *shop* farmacia *f*

phase [feɪz] fase *f*
◆ **phase in** introdurre gradualmente
◆ **phase out** eliminare gradualmente

PhD [piːeɪtʃˈdiː] (= *Doctor of Philosophy*) dottorato *m* di ricerca

phenomenal [fɪˈnɒmɪnl] fenomenale; **phenomenon** fenomeno *m*

philanthropic [fɪlən'θrɒpɪk] filantropico; **philanthropist** filantropo *m*, -a *f*; **philanthropy** filantropia *f*

Philippines ['fɪlɪpiːnz]: *the ~* le Filippine *fpl*

philosopher [fɪ'lɒsəfə(r)] filosofo *m*, -a *f*; **philosophical** filosofico; **philosophy** filosofia *f*

phobia ['fəʊbɪə] fobia *f*

phon(e)y ['fəʊnɪ] F falso

phone [fəʊn] **1** *n* telefono *m*; *be on the ~* be talking essere al telefono **2** *v/t* telefonare a **3** *v/i* telefonare; **phone book** guida *f* telefonica, elenco telefonico *m*; **phone booth** cabina *f* telefonica; **phone call** telefonata *f*; **phone card** scheda *f* telefonica; **phone number** numero *m* di telefono

photo ['fəʊtəʊ] foto *f*; **photocopier** fotocopiatrice *f*; **photocopy 1** *n* fotocopia *f* **2** *v/t* fotocopiare; **photogenic** fotogenico; **photograph 1** *n* fotografia *f* **2** *v/t* fotografare; **photographer** fotografo *m*, -a *f*; **photography** fotografia *f*

phrase [freɪz] **1** *n* frase *f* **2** *v/t* esprimere

physical ['fɪzɪkl] **1** *adj* fisico **2** *n* MED visita *f* medica; **physically** fisicamente

physician [fɪ'zɪʃn] medico *m*

physicist ['fɪzɪsɪst] fisico *m*, -a *f*; **physics** fisica *f*

physiotherapist [fɪzɪəʊ'θerəpɪst] fisioterapeuta *m/f*; **physiotherapy** fisioterapia *f*

physique [fɪ'ziːk] fisico *m*

pianist ['pɪənɪst] pianista *m/f*; **piano** piano *m*

pick [pɪk] (*choose*) scegliere; *flowers, fruit* raccogliere; *one's nose* mettersi le dita nel naso

◆ **pick up 1** *v/t* prendere; *phone* sollevare; *baby* prendere in braccio; *from ground* raccogliere; (*collect*) andare / venire a prendere; *information* raccogliere; *in car* far salire; *man, woman* rimorchiare F; *language, skill* imparare; *habit, illness* prendere; (*buy*) trovare **2** *v/i* (*improve*) migliorare

picket ['pɪkɪt] **1** *n of strikers* picchetto *m* **2** *v/t* picchettare

'pickpocket borseggiatore *m*, -trice *f*; **pick-up** (truck) furgone *m* (aperto), pick up *m* *inv*; **picky** F difficile (da accontentare)

picnic ['pɪknɪk] **1** *n* picnic *m* *inv* **2** *v/i* fare un picnic

picture ['pɪktʃə(r)] **1** *n photo* foto *f*; *painting* quadro *m*; *illustration* figura *f*; *film* film *m* *inv*; *put* / *keep s.o. in the ~* mettere / tenere al corrente qu **2** *v/t* immaginare; **pictures** cinema *m*; **picturesque** pittoresco

pie [paɪ] *sweet* torta *f*; *savoury* pasticcio *m*

piece [piːs] pezzo *m*; **a ~ of pie / bread** una fetta di torta / pane; **a ~ of advice** un consiglio; **take to ~s** smontare

◆ **piece together** *broken plate* rimettere insieme; *evidence* ricostruire

piecemeal ['piːsmiːl] poco alla volta

pier [pɪə(r)] *at seaside* pontile *m*

pierce [pɪəs] (*penetrate*) trapassare; *ears* farsi i buchi in; **piercing** *noise* lacerante; *eyes* penetranti; *wind* pungente

pig [pɪg] *also fig* maiale *m*

pigeon ['pɪdʒɪn] piccione *m*; **pigeonhole** casella *f*

pigheaded [pɪg'hedɪd] testardo; **pigsty** *also fig* porcile *m*

pile [paɪl] mucchio *m*; F **a ~ of work** un sacco di lavoro F

◆ **pile up 1** *v/i of work, bills* accumularsi **2** *v/t* ammucchiare

pile-up [paɪlʌp] MOT tamponamento *m* a catena

pilfering ['pɪlfərɪŋ] piccoli furti *mpl*

pilgrim ['pɪlgrɪm] pellegrino *m*, -a *f*

pill [pɪl] pastiglia *f*; **be on the ~** prendere la pillola

pillar ['pɪlə(r)] colonna *f*; **pillarbox** buca *f* delle lettere

pillow ['pɪləʊ] guanciale *m*; **pillowcase, pillowslip** federa *f*

pilot ['paɪlət] **1** *n of plane* pilota *m/f* **2** *v/t plane* pilotare

pimp [pɪmp] ruffiano *m*

pimple ['pɪmpl] brufolo *m*

PIN [pɪn] (= **personal identification number**) numero *m* di codice segreto

pin [pɪn] *for sewing* spillo *m*; *in bowling* birillo *m*; (*badge*) spilla *f*; ELEC spinotto *m* **2** *v/t* (*hold down*) immobilizzare; (*attach*) attaccare; *on lapel* appuntare

◆ **pin up** *notice* appuntare

pinafore dress ['pɪnəfɔː] scamiciato *m*

pincers ['pɪnsəz] *tool* tenaglie *fpl*; *of crab* chele *fpl*

pinch [pɪntʃ] **1** *n* pizzico *m* **2** *v/t* pizzicare **3** *v/i of shoes* stringere

pine [paɪn] pino *m*; **~ furniture** mobili *mpl* di pino; **pineapple** ananas *m inv*

pink [pɪŋk] rosa *inv*

pinnacle ['pɪnəkl] *fig* apice *m*

pinpoint indicare con esattezza; **pins and needles** formicolio *m*

pint [paɪnt] pinta *f*

pin-up (girl) pin-up *f inv*

pioneer [paɪə'nɪə(r)] **1** *n fig* pioniere *m*, -a *f* **2** *v/t* essere il / la pioniere di; **pioneering** *work* pionieristico

pious ['paɪəs] pio

pip [pɪp] *of fruit* seme *m*

pipe [paɪp] **1** *n* tubo *m*; *for smoking* pipa *f* **2** *v/t* trasportare con condutture; **pipe-**

line conduttura *f*; *in the ~ fig* in arrivo

pirate ['paɪərət] **1** *n* pirata *m* **2** *v/t software* piratare

Pisces ['paɪsiːz] ASTR Pesci *m/f inv*

piss [pɪs] **1** *v/i* P (*urinate*) pisciare P **2** *n* (*urine*) piscio *m* P; **take the ~out of s.o.** P prendere qu per il culo P ♦ **piss off** P **1** *v/i* sparire; **piss off!** levati dalle palle! P **2** *v/t*: **it pisses me off** mi fa incazzare

pissed [pɪst] P (*drunk*) sbronzo F; *Am* (*annoyed*) seccato F

pistol ['pɪstl] pistola *f*

piston ['pɪstən] pistone *m*

pit [pɪt] (*hole*) buca *f*; (*coal mine*) miniera *f*

pitch¹ [pɪtʃ] *n* MUS intonazione *f*

pitch² [pɪtʃ] *v/t tent* piantare; *ball* lanciare

pitcher¹ ['pɪtʃə(r)] *in baseball* lanciatore *m*

pitcher² ['pɪtʃə(r)] *container* brocca *f*

pitfall ['pɪtfɔːl] tranello *m*

pitiful ['pɪtɪfʊl] *sight* pietoso; *excuse, attempt* penoso; *pitiless* spietato

pittance ['pɪtns] miseria *f*

pity ['pɪtɪ] **1** *n* pietà *f*; *it's a ~ that* è un peccato che; *what a ~!* che peccato! *take ~ on* avere pietà di **2** *v/t person* avere pietà di

pizza ['piːtsə] pizza *f*

placard ['plækɑːd] cartello *m*

place [pleɪs] **1** *n* posto *m*; *flat, house* casa *f*; *at my / his ~* a casa mia / sua; *in ~ of* invece di; *feel out of ~* sentirsi fuori posto; *take ~* aver luogo; *in the first ~* (*firstly*) in primo luogo **2** *v/t* (*put*) piazzare; *I can't quite ~ you* non mi ricordo dove ci siamo conosciuti; *~ an order* fare un'ordinazione

placid ['plæsɪd] placido

plagiarism ['pleɪdʒərɪzm] plagio *m*; **plagiarize** plagiare

plague [pleɪg] **1** *n* peste *f* **2** *v/t* (*bother*) tormentare

plain¹ [pleɪn] *n* pianura *f*

plain² [pleɪn] **1** *adj* (*clear, obvious*) chiaro; *not fancy* semplice; *not pretty* scialbo; *not patterned* in tinta unita; (*blunt*) franco; *~ chocolate* cioccolato *m* fondente **2** *adv* semplicemente; **plainly** (*clearly*) chiaramente; (*bluntly*) francamente; (*simply*) semplicemente; **plain-spoken** franco

plaintive ['pleɪntɪv] lamentoso

plait [plæt] treccia *f*

plan [plæn] **1** *n* (*project, intention*) piano *m*; (*drawing*) progetto *m* **2** *v/t* (*prepare*) organizzare; (*design*) progettare; *~ to do* avere in programma di **3** *v/i* pianificare

plane¹ [pleɪn] (*aeroplane*) aereo *m*

plane² [pleɪn] *tool* pialla *f*
planet ['plænɪt] pianeta *m*
plank [plæŋk] *of wood* asse *f*; *fig: of policy* punto *m*
planning ['plænɪŋ] pianificazione *f*
plant¹ [plɑːnt] **1** *n* pianta *f* **2** *v/t* piantare
plant² [plɑːnt] *(factory)* stabilimento *m*; *(equipment)* impianto *m*
plantation [plæn'teɪʃn] piantagione *f*
plaque [plæk] *on wall, teeth* placca *f*
plaster ['plɑːstə(r)] **1** *n on wall* intonaco *m*; *sticking* cerotto *m* **2** *v/t wall* intonacare
plastic ['plæstɪk] **1** *n* plastica *f* **2** *adj* di plastica; **plastic money** carte *fpl* di credito; **plastic surgeon** chirurgo *m* plastico; **plastic surgery** chirurgia *f* plastica
plate [pleɪt] *for food* piatto *m*; *sheet of metal* lastra *f*
plateau ['plætəʊ] altopiano *m*
platform ['plætfɔːm] *(stage)* palco *m*; *of railway station* binario *m*; *fig: political* piattaforma *f*
platinum ['plætɪnəm] **1** *n* platino *m* **2** *adj* di platino
platonic [plə'tɒnɪk] platonico *m*
platoon [plə'tuːn] *of soldiers* plotone *m*
plausible ['plɔːzəbl] plausibile
play [pleɪ] **1** *n* gioco *m*; *in theatre, on TV* commedia *f* **2** *v/i*

of children, SP giocare; *of musician* suonare **3** *v/t* MUS suonare; *game* giocare a; *opponent* giocare contro; *(perform: Macbeth etc)* rappresentare; *particular role* interpretare; **~ a joke on** fare uno scherzo a

♦ **play around** F *(be unfaithful)*: **his wife's been playing around** sua moglie lo ha tradito
♦ **play down** minimizzare
♦ **play up** *of machine* dare noie; *of child* fare i capricci; *of tooth, bad back etc* fare male

player ['pleɪə(r)] SP giocatore *m*, -trice *f*; *musician* musicista *m/f*; *actor* attore *m*, -trice *f*; **playful** *punch, mood* scherzoso; *puppy* giocherellone; **playground** *in school* cortile *m* per la ricreazione; *in park* parco *m* giochi; **playing card** carta *f* da gioco; **playwright** commediografo *m*, -a *f*
plaza ['plɑːzə] *for shopping* centro *m* commerciale
plc [piːel'siː] (= **public limited company**) società *f inv* a responsabilità limitata quotata in borsa
plea [pliː] appello *m*
plead [pliːd]: **~ guilty / not guilty** dichiararsi colpevole / innocente; **~ with** supplicare
pleasant ['pleznt] piacevole

please [pli:z] **1** *adv* per favore; *more tea? – yes,* ~ ancora tè? – sì, grazie; ~ *do* fai pure, prego **2** *v/t* far piacere a; ~ *yourself* fai come ti pare; **pleased** contento; ~ *to meet you* piacere!; **pleasing** piacevole; **pleasure** (*happiness, satisfaction*) contentezza *f*; (*as opposed to work*) piacere *m*; (*delight*) gioia *f*; *it's a* ~ (*you're welcome*) è un piacere; *with* ~ con vero piacere

pleat [pli:t] *in skirt* piega *f*

pledge [pledʒ] **1** *n* (*promise*) promessa *f* **2** *v/t* (*promise*) promettere

plentiful ['plentɪfʊl] abbondante; **plenty** abbondanza *f*; ~ *of* molto; *that's* ~ basta così; *there's* ~ *for everyone* ce n'è per tutti

pliable ['plaɪəbl] flessibile

pliers ['plaɪəz] pinze *fpl*

plight [plaɪt] situazione *f* critica

plod [plɒd] *walk* trascinarsi

plook [plu:k] brufolo *m*

plot[1] [plɒt] *n land* appezzamento *m*

plot[2] [plɒt] **1** *n* (*conspiracy*) complotto *m*; *of novel* trama *f* **2** *v/t* & *v/i* complottare

plotter ['plɒtə(r)] cospiratore *m*, -trice *f*; COMPUT plotter *m inv*

plough, *Am* **plow** [plaʊ] **1** *n* aratro *m* **2** *v/t* & *v/i* arare

♦ **plough back** *profits* reinvestire

pluck [plʌk] *eyebrows* pinzare; *chicken* spennare

plug [plʌg] **1** *n for sink, bath* tappo *m*; *electrical* spina *f*; (*spark* ~) candela *f*; *for new book etc* pubblicità *f inv* **2** *v/t hole* tappare; *new book etc* fare pubblicità a

♦ **plug in** attaccare (alla presa)

plumage ['plu:mɪdʒ] piumaggio *m*

plumber ['plʌmə(r)] idraulico *m*; **plumbing** *pipes* impianto *m* idraulico

plummet ['plʌmɪt] *of aeroplane* precipitare; *of share prices* crollare

plump [plʌmp] *person, chicken* in carne; *hands, feet, face* paffuto

plunge [plʌndʒ] **1** *n* caduta *f*; *in prices* crollo *m*; *take the* ~ fare il gran passo **2** *v/i* precipitare; *of prices* crollare **3** *v/t knife* conficcare; **plunging** *neckline* profondo

plural ['plʊərəl] plurale *m*

plus [plʌs] **1** *prep* più **2** *adj*: *£500* ~ oltre 500 sterline **3** *n symbol* più *m inv*; (*advantage*) vantaggio *m* **4** *conj* (*moreover, in addition*) per di più

plush [plʌʃ] di lusso

plywood ['plaɪwʊd] compensato *m*

PM [pi:'em] (= *Prime Minister*) primo ministro *m*

p.m. [pi:'em] (= *post meridi-*

em): ***at 2 ~*** alle 2 del pomeriggio; ***at 10.30 ~*** alle 10.30 di sera

pneumonia [nju:'məʊnɪə] polmonite *f*

poach¹ [pəʊʧ] *cook* bollire; *egg* fare in camicia

poach² [pəʊʧ] *game* cacciare di frodo; *fish* pescare di frodo

poached egg [pəʊʧt'eg] uovo *m* in camicia

P.O. Box [pi:'əʊbɒks] casella *f* postale

pocket ['pɒkɪt] **1** *n* tasca *f* **2** *adj* (*miniature*) in miniatura **3** *v/t* intascare; **pocket book** *Am* (*wallet*) portafoglio *m*; (*purse*) borsetta *f*; **pocket calculator** calcolatrice *f* tascabile

podium ['pəʊdɪəm] podio *m*

poem ['pəʊɪm] poesia *f*; **poet** poeta *m*, -essa *f*; **poetic** poetico; **poetic justice** giustizia *f* divina; **poetry** poesia *f*

poignant ['pɔɪnjənt] commovente

point [pɔɪnt] **1** *n of pencil, knife* punta *f*; *in competition* punto *m*; (*purpose*) senso *m*; (*moment*) punto *m*; *in argument, discussion* punto *m*; *in decimals* virgola *f*; ***that's beside the ~*** non c'entra; ***be on the ~ of*** stare giusto per; ***get to the ~*** venire al dunque; ***that's a ~*** questo, in effetti, è vero; ***the ~ is ...*** il fatto è che ...; ***there's no ~ in waiting*** non ha senso aspettare **2** *v/i* indicare **3** *v/t gun* puntare (***at*** contro)

◆ **point out** *sights, advantages* indicare

◆ **point to** *with finger* additare; (*fig: indicate*) far presupporre

pointed ['pɔɪntɪd] *remark* significativo; **pointer** *for teacher* bacchetta *f*; (*hint*) consiglio *m*; (*sign, indication*) indizio *m*; **pointless** inutile; **point of view** punto *m* di vista

poise [pɔɪz] padronanza *f* di sé; **poised** *person* posato

poison ['pɔɪzn] **1** *n* veleno *m* **2** *v/t* avvelenare; **poisonous** velenoso

poke [pəʊk] **1** *n* colpetto *m* **2** *v/t* (*prod*) dare un colpetto a; (*stick*) ficcare

◆ **poke around** F curiosare

poker ['pəʊkə(r)] *card game* poker *m*

Poland ['pəʊlənd] Polonia *f*

polar ['pəʊlə(r)] polare

Pole [pəʊl] polacco *m*, -a *f*

pole¹ [pəʊl] *of wood, metal* paletto *m*

pole² [pəʊl] *of earth* polo *m*

'polevault salto *m* con l'asta

police [pə'li:s] polizia *f*; **police car** auto *f* della polizia; **policeman** poliziotto *m*; **police state** stato *m* di polizia; **police station** commissariato *m* di polizia; **policewoman** donna *f* poliziotto

policy¹ ['pɒlɪsɪ] politica *f*

policy² ['pɒlɪsɪ] (*insurance ~*) polizza *f*

polio ['pəʊlɪəʊ] polio *f*

Polish ['pəʊlɪʃ] **1** *adj* polacco **2** *n language* polacco *m*

polish ['pɒlɪʃ] **1** *n product* lucido *m*; (*nail ~*) smalto *m* **2** *v/t* lucidare; *speech* rifinire; **polished** *performance* impeccabile

polite [pə'laɪt] cortese; **politely** cortesemente; **politeness** cortesia *f*

political [pə'lɪtɪkl] politico; **politically correct** politicamente corretto; **politician** uomo *m* politico, donna *f* politica; **politics** politica *f*

poll [pəʊl] **1** *n* (*survey*) sondaggio *m*, **go to the ~s** (*vote*) andare alle urne **2** *v/t people* fare un sondaggio tra; *votes* guadagnare

pollen ['pɒlən] polline *m*

'polling station seggio *m* elettorale

pollster ['pɒlstə(r)] esperto *m*, -a *f* di sondaggi

pollutant [pə'luːtənt] sostanza *f* inquinante; **pollute** inquinare; **pollution** inquinamento *m*

'polo shirt polo *f inv*

polyester [pɒlɪ'estə(r)] poliestere *m*

polystyrene [pɒlɪ'staɪriːn] polistirolo *m*

polyunsaturated [pɒlɪʌn'sætjəreɪtɪd] polinsa-

turo

pompous ['pɒmpəs] pomposo

pond [pɒnd] stagno *m*

pontiff ['pɒntɪf] pontefice *m*

pony ['pəʊnɪ] pony *m inv*; **ponytail** coda *f* (di cavallo)

poo(h) [puː] F (*faeces*) popò *f inv*

poodle ['puːdl] barboncino *m*

pool¹ [puːl] *n* (*swimming ~*) piscina *f*; *of water, blood* pozza *f*

pool² [puːl] *n game* biliardo *m*

pool³ [puːl] **1** *n common fund* cassa *f* comune **2** *v/t resources* mettere insieme

'pool hall sala *f* da biliardo; **pool table** tavolo *m* da biliardo

poop [puːp] *Am* F (*faeces*) popò *f inv*

pooped [puːpt] F stanco morto

poor [pʊə(r)] **1** *adj* povero; *not good* misero; **be in ~ health** essere in cattiva salute **2** *n*: **the ~** i poveri; **poorly 1** *adv* male **2** *adj* (*unwell*) indisposto

pop¹ [pɒp] **1** *n noise* schiocco *m* **2** *v/i of balloon etc* scoppiare **3** *v/t cork* stappare; *balloon* far scoppiare

pop² [pɒp] *n* MUS pop *m* **2** *adj* pop *inv*

pop³ [pɒp] *Am* F papà *m inv*

◆ **pop out** F (*go out for a short time*) fare un salto fuori

◆ **pop up** F (*appear suddenly*)

saltare fuori

'popcorn popcorn *m*

pope [pəʊp] papa *m*

Popsicle® ['pɒpsɪkl] *Am* ghiacciolo *m*

popular ['pɒpjʊlə(r)] popolare; *belief, support* diffuso; **popularity** popolarità *f*

populate ['pɒpjʊleɪt] popolare; **population** popolazione *f*

porch [pɔːtʃ] porticato *m*; *Am: outside house* veranda *f*

◆ **pore over** studiare attentamente

pork [pɔːk] maiale *m*

porn [pɔːn] F porno *m* F; **pornographic** pornografico; **pornography** pornografia *f*

port¹ [pɔːt] *n* (*harbour, drink*) porto *m*

port² [pɔːt] *adj* (*left-hand*) babordo

portable ['pɔːtəbl] **1** *adj* portatile **2** *n* portatile *m*

porter ['pɔːtə(r)] portiere *m*

porthole ['pɔːthəʊl] NAUT oblò *m inv*

portion ['pɔːʃn] parte *f*; *of food* porzione *f*

portrait ['pɔːtreɪt] **1** *n* ritratto *m* **2** *adv print* verticale; **portray** *of artist* ritrarre; *of actor* interpretare; *of author* descrivere

Portugal ['pɔːtjʊgl] Portogallo *m*; **Portuguese 1** *adj* portoghese **2** *person* portoghese *m/f*; *language* portoghese *m*

pose [pəʊz] **1** *n* (*pretence*) posa *f* **2** *v/i for artist* posare; **~ as** farsi passare per **3** *v/t problem, threat* creare

posh [pɒʃ] F elegante; *pej* snob

position [pə'zɪʃn] **1** *n* posizione *f*; **what would you do in my ~?** cosa faresti al mio posto? **2** *v/t* sistemare, piazzare

positive ['pɒzətɪv] positivo; **be ~** (*sure*) essere certo; **positively** (*downright*) decisamente; (*definitely*) assolutamente; *think* in modo positivo

possess [pə'zes] possedere; **possession** (*ownership*) possesso *m*; *thing owned* bene *m*; **~s** averi *mpl*; **possessive** *also* GRAM possessivo

possibility [pɒsə'bɪlətɪ] possibilità *f*; *the best* ~ ... la miglior ... possibile; **possibly** (*perhaps*) forse; *that can't* ~ *be right* non è possibile che sia giusto

post¹ [pəʊst] **1** *n of wood, metal* palo *m* **2** *v/t notice* affiggere; *profits* annunciare; *keep s.o.* **~ed** tenere informato qu

post² [pəʊst] **1** *n* (*place of duty*) posto *m* **2** *v/t soldier, employee* assegnare; *guards* piazzare

post³ [pəʊst] **1** *n* (*mail*) posta *f* **2** *v/t letter* spedire (per posta); (*put in the mail*) imbucare

postage ['pəustɪdʒ] affrancatura f; **postage stamp** fml francobollo m; **postal** postale; **postbox** buca f delle lettere; **postcard** cartolina f; **postcode** codice m di avviamento postale; **postdate** postdatare

poster ['pəustə(r)] manifesto m; for decoration poster m inv

postgraduate ['pəustgrædjut] **1** n studente m / studentessa f di un corso post-universitario **2** adj post-universitario

posthumous ['pɒstjuməs] postumo

posting ['pəustɪŋ] (assignment) incarico m

'postman postino m; **postmark** timbro m postale

postmortem [pəust'mɔːtəm] autopsia f

'post office ufficio m postale

postpone [pəust'pəun] rinviare; **postponement** rinvio m

pot[1] [pɒt] for cooking pentola f; for coffee caffettiera f; for tea teiera f; for plant vaso m

pot[2] [pɒt] F (marijuana) erba f F

potato [pə'teɪtəu] patata f; **potato crisps,** Am **potato chips** patatine fpl

potent ['pəutənt] potente

potential [pə'tenʃl] **1** adj potenziale **2** n potenziale m;

potentially adv potenzialmente

pothole ['pɒthəul] in road buca f

potter ['pɒtə(r)] vasaio m, -a f; **pottery** ceramica f; items vasellame m; place laboratorio m di ceramica

potty ['pɒtɪ] for baby vasino m

pouch [pautʃ] (bag) borsa f

poultry ['pəultrɪ] birds volatili mpl; meat pollame m

pound[1] [paund] n weight libbra f; FIN sterlina f

pound[2] [paund] n for strays canile m municipale; for cars deposito m auto

pound[3] [paund] v/i of heart battere forte; ~ **on** (hammer on) picchiare su

pour [pɔː(r)] **1** v/t liquid versare **2** v/i: **it's ~ing (with rain)** sta diluviando

◆ **pour out** liquid versare; troubles sfogarsi raccontando

pout [paut] fare il broncio

poverty ['pɒvətɪ] povertà f

powder ['paudə(r)] **1** n polvere f; for face cipria f **2** v/t: ~ **one's face** mettersi la cipria

power ['pauə(r)] **1** n (strength) forza f; of engine potenza f; (authority) potere m; (energy) energia f; (electricity) elettricità f; **in** ~ POL al potere **2** v/t: **~ed by atomic energy** a propulsione atomica; **power cut** interruzione f di corrente; **power failure** guasto m

powerful 506

alla linea elettrica; **powerful**
potente; **powerless** impotente; **be ~ to ...** non poter
far niente per ...; **power line**
linea f elettrica; **power out-
age** Am interruzione f di
corrente; **power station**
centrale f elettrica; **power
steering** servosterzo m
PR [piː'ɑː(r)] (= *public relations*) relazioni fpl pubbli-
che
practical ['præktɪkl] pratico;
practically *behave, think* in
modo pratico; (*almost*) praticamente
practice ['præktɪs] **1** n pratica
f; (*training*) esercizio m; (*rehearsal*) prove fpl; (*custom*)
consuetudine f; **in ~** (*in reality*) in pratica; **be out of ~** essere fuori allenamento **2** v/t
& v/i Am ⊳ **practise**
practise ['præktɪs] **1** v/t esercitarsi in; *law, medicine* esercitare **2** v/i esercitarsi
pragmatic [præg'mætɪk]
pragmatico
prairie ['preərɪ] prateria f
praise [preɪz] **1** n lode f **2** v/t
lodare; **praiseworthy** lode-
vole
prawn [prɔːn] gamberetto m
pray [preɪ] pregare; **prayer**
preghiera f
preach [priːtʃ] predicare;
preacher predicatore m,
-trice f
precarious [prɪ'keərɪəs] precario

precaution [prɪ'kɔːʃn] precauzione f; **precautionary**
measure di precauzione
precede [prɪ'siːd] precedere;
precedent precedente m;
preceding precedente
precious ['preʃəs] prezioso
precise [prɪ'saɪs] preciso;
precisely precisamente; **precision** precisione f
precocious [prɪ'kəʊʃəs] *child*
precoce
preconceived [priːkən'siːvd]
idea preconcetto
precondition [priːkən'dɪʃn]
condizione f indispensabile
predator ['predətə(r)] *animal*
predatore m, -trice f; **predatory** rapace
predecessor ['priːdɪsesə(r)]
predecessore m
predicament [prɪ'dɪkəmənt]
situazione f difficile
predict [prɪ'dɪkt] predire;
predictable prevedibile;
prediction predizione f
predominant [prɪ'dɒmɪnənt]
predominante; **predomi-
nantly** prevalentemente
prefabricated [priː'fæbrɪkeɪ-
tɪd] prefabbricato
preface ['prefɪs] prefazione f
prefer [prɪ'fɜː(r)] preferire (**to**
a); **preferable** preferibile;
preferably preferibilmente;
preference preferenza f;
preferential preferenziale
pregnancy ['pregnənsɪ] gravidanza f; **pregnant** incinta;
get ~ restare incinta

press conference

prehistoric [priːhɪsˈtɒrɪk]
preistorico
prejudice [ˈpredʒʊdɪs] **1** *n*
pregiudizio *m* **2** *v/t person* influenzare; *chances* pregiudi-
care; **prejudiced** prevenuto
preliminary [prɪˈlɪmɪnərɪ]
preliminare
premarital [priːˈmærɪtl] pre-
matrimoniale
premature [ˈpremətjʊə(r)]
prematuro
premeditated [priːˈmedɪteɪ-
tɪd] premeditato
premier [ˈpremɪə(r)] (*Prime
Minister*) premier *m inv*
première [ˈpremɪeə(r)] pre-
miere *f inv*, prima *f*
premises [ˈpremɪsɪz] locali
mpl
premium [ˈpriːmɪəm] *in insurance* premio *m*
prenatal [priːˈneɪtl] prenatale
preoccupied [prɪˈɒkjʊpaɪd]
preoccupato
preparation [prepəˈreɪʃn]
preparazione *f*; **in ~ for** in vista di; **~s** preparativi *mpl*;
prepare 1 *v/t* preparare; **be
~d to do sth** (*willing*) essere
preparato a fare qc; **be ~d
for sth** (*be expecting*) essere
preparato per qc **2** *v/i* prepararsi
preposition [prepəˈzɪʃn] preposizione *f*
preposterous [prɪˈpɒstərəs]
ridicolo
prerequisite [priːˈrekwɪzɪt]
condizione *f* indispensabile

prescribe [prɪˈskraɪb] *of doctor* prescrivere; **prescription**
MED ricetta *f* medica
presence [ˈprezns] presenza
f; **in the ~ of** in presenza di
present¹ [ˈpreznt] **1** *adj* (*current*) attuale; **be ~** essere presente **2** *n*: **the ~** *also* GRAM il
presente; **at ~** al momento
present² [ˈpreznt] *n* (*gift*) regalo *m*
present³ [prɪˈzent] *v/t award*
consegnare; *bouquet* offrire;
programme presentare; **~
s.o. with sth**, **~ sth to s.o.**
offrire qc a qu
presentation [preznˈteɪʃn]
presentazione *f*; **present-
-day** di oggi; **presenter** presentatore *m*, -trice *f*; **pres-
ently** (*at the moment*) attual-
mente; (*soon*) tra breve
preservative [prɪˈzɜːvətɪv]
conservante *m*; **preserve 1**
n (*domain*) dominio *m* **2** *v/t
standards, peace etc* mantenere; *wood etc* proteggere;
food conservare
preside [prɪˈzaɪd] *at meeting*
presiedere; **presidency** presidenza *f*; **president** presidente *m*; **presidential** presi-
denziale
press [pres] **1** *n*: **the ~** la stampa **2** *v/t button* premere;
(*urge*) far pressione su;
(*squeeze*) stringere; *clothes*
stirare; *grapes, olives* spremere **3** *v/i*: **~ for** fare pressioni per ottenere; **press con-**

pressing 508

ference conferenza f stampa; **pressing** urgente; **press-up** flessione f sulle braccia

pressure ['preʃə(r)] **1** n pressione f **2** v/t fare delle pressioni su

prestige [pre'sti:ʒ] prestigio m; **prestigious** prestigioso

presumably [prɪ'zju:məblɪ] presumibilmente; **presume** presumere; **presumption** *of innocence, guilt* presunzione f

presuppose [pri:sə'pəʊs] presupporre

pre-tax ['pri:tæks] al lordo d'imposta

pretence [prɪ'tens] finta f; **pretend 1** v/t fingere **2** v/i fare finta; **pretense** *Am* → **pretence**; **pretentious** pretenzioso

pretext ['pri:tekst] pretesto m

pretty ['prɪtɪ] **1** adj carino **2** adv (quite) piuttosto

prevail [prɪ'veɪl] (triumph) prevalere; **prevailing** prevalente

prevent [prɪ'vent] prevenire; **∼ s.o. (from) doing sth** impedire a qu di fare qc; **prevention** prevenzione f; **preventive** preventivo

preview ['pri:vju:] *of film, exhibition* anteprima f

previous ['pri:vɪəs] precedente; **∼ to** prima di; **previously** precedentemente

prey [preɪ] preda f

price [praɪs] **1** n prezzo m **2** v/t COM fissare il prezzo di; **priceless** di valore inestimabile; **price war** guerra f dei prezzi; **pricey** F caro

prick¹ [prɪk] **1** n pain puntura f **2** v/t (jab) pungere

prick² [prɪk] n V (penis) cazzo m V; person testa f di cazzo V

prickle ['prɪkl] *on plant* spina f; **prickly** plant spinoso; beard ispido; (irritable) permaloso

pride [praɪd] **1** n in person, achievement orgoglio m; (self-respect) amor m proprio **2** v/t: **∼ o.s. on** vantarsi di

priest [pri:st] prete m

primarily [praɪ'meərɪlɪ] principalmente; **primary 1** adj principale **2** n Am POL (elezione f) primaria f; **primary school** scuola f elementare

prime 'minister primo ministro m

primitive ['prɪmɪtɪv] primitivo

prince [prɪns] principe m; **princess** principessa f

principal ['prɪnsəpl] **1** adj principale **2** n of school preside m/f; **principally** principalmente

principle ['prɪnsəpl] principio m; **on ∼** per principio; **in ∼** in linea di principio

print [prɪnt] **1** n in book etc caratteri mpl; photograph stampa f; mark impronta f; **out of ∼** esaurito **2** v/t stampare; (*use block capitals*) scrivere in stampatello; **printer** *person* tipografo *m; machine* stampante *f;* **printout** stampato *m*

prior ['praɪə(r)] **1** *adj* precedente **2** *prep:* ~ **to** prima di

prioritize [praɪ'ɒrətaɪz] (*put in order of priority*) classificare in ordine d'importanza; (*give priority to*) dare precedenza a; **priority** priorità *f inv;* **have** ~ avere la precedenza

prison ['prɪzn] prigione *f;* **prisoner** prigioniero *m,* -a *f;* **take s.o.** ~ fare prigioniero qu; **prisoner of war** prigioniero *m* di guerra

privacy ['prɪvəsɪ] privacy *f;* **private 1** *adj* privato *f,* MIL soldato *m* semplice; **in** ~ in privato; **privately** (*in private*) in privato; (*inwardly*) dentro di sé; ~ **owned** privato; **private sector** settore *m* privato; **privatize** privatizzare

privilege ['prɪvəlɪdʒ] privilegio *m;* (*honour*) onore *m;* **privileged** privilegiato; (*honoured*) onorato

prize [praɪz] **1** *n* premio *m* **2** *v/t* dare molto valore a; **prizewinner** vincitore *m,* -trice *f;* **prizewinning** vincente

pro¹ [prəʊ] *n:* **the ~s and cons** i pro e i contro

pro² [prəʊ] ☞ **professional**

pro³ [prəʊ] *prep:* **be** ~ ... (*in favour of*) essere a favore di ...

probability [prɒbə'bɪlətɪ] probabilità *f inv;* **probable** probabile; **probably** probabilmente

probation [prə'beɪʃn] *in job* periodo *m* di prova; LAW libertà *f* vigilata; **on** ~ *in job* in prova

probe [prəʊb] **1** *n* (*investigation*) indagine *f; scientific* sonda *f* **2** *v/t* esplorare; (*investigate*) investigare

problem ['prɒbləm] problema *m;* **no** ~ non c'è problema

procedure [prə'siːdʒə(r)] procedura *f*

proceed [prə'siːd] *of people* proseguire; *of work etc* procedere; **proceedings** (*events*) avvenimenti *mpl;* **proceeds** ricavato *m*

process ['prəʊses] **1** *n* processo *m* **2** *v/t food, raw materials* trattare; *data* elaborare; *application etc* sbrigare; **~ed cheese** formaggio *m* fuso; **procession** processione *f;* **processor** processore *m*

prod [prɒd] **1** *n* colpetto *m* **2** *v/t* dare un colpetto a

prodigy ['prɒdɪdʒɪ]: (*infant*) ~ bambino *m,* -a *f* prodigio

produce¹ ['prɒdjuːs] *n* prodotti *mpl*

produce² [prə'djuːs] *v/t* produrre; (*bring about*) dare origine a; (*bring out*) tirar fuori; *play* mettere in scena

producer [prə'dju:sə(r)] produttore *m*, -trice *f*; *of play* regista *m/f*; **product** prodotto *m*; (*result*) risultato *m*; **production** produzione *f*; *of play* regia *f*; **a new** ~ **of ...** una nuova messa in scena di ...; **productive** produttivo; **productivity** produttività *f*

profess [prə'fes] dichiarare; **profession** professione *f*; **professional 1** *adj* professionale; *advice, help* di un esperto; *piece of work* da professionista; **turn** ~ passare al professionismo **2** *n* professionista *m/f*; **professionally** *play sport* a livello professionistico; (*well, skilfully*) in modo professionale

professor [prə'fesə(r)] professore *m* (universitario)

proficiency [prə'fɪʃnsɪ] competenza *f*; **proficient** competente

profile ['prəʊfaɪl] profilo *m*

profit ['prɒfɪt] **1** *n* profitto *m* **2** *v/i*: ~ **from** trarre profitto da; **profitability** redditività *f*; **profitable** redditizio

profound [prə'faʊnd] profondo

prognosis [prɒg'nəʊsɪs] prognosi *f inv*

programme. *Am and Br* COMPUT **program** ['prəʊgræm] **1** *n* programma *m* **2** *v/t* programmare; **programmer** COMPUT programmato-

re *m*, -trice *f*

progress 1 ['prəʊgres] *n* progresso *m*; **in** ~ in corso **2** [prə'gres] *v/i* (*advance in time*) procedere; (*move on*) avanzare; (*make progress*) fare progressi; **progressive** (*enlightened*) progressista; *which progresses* progressivo; **progressively** progressivamente

prohibit [prə'hɪbɪt] proibire; **prohibitive** *prices* proibitivo

project[1] ['prɒdʒekt] *n* (*plan*) piano *m*; (*undertaking*) progetto *m*; EDU ricerca *f*

project[2] [prə'dʒekt] **1** *v/t figures, sales* fare una proiezione di; *film* proiettare **2** *v/i* (*stick out*) sporgere in fuori

projection [prə'dʒekʃn] (*forecast*) proiezione *f*; **projector** *for slides* proiettore *m*

prologue, *Am* **prolog** ['prəʊlɒg] prologo *m*

prolong [prə'lɒŋ] prolungare

prominent ['prɒmɪnənt] *nose, chin* sporgente; (*significant*) prominente

promiscuity [prɒmɪ'skju:ətɪ] promiscuità *f*; **promiscuous** promiscuo

promise ['prɒmɪs] **1** *n* promessa *f* **2** *v/t & v/i* promettere; **promising** promettente

promote [prə'məʊt] promuovere; *of event* promoter *m/f inv*; **promotion** promozione *f*; **get** ~ *in job* essere promosso

prompt [promt] **1** adj (on time) puntuale; (speedy) tempestivo **2** adv: **at two o'clock ~** alle due in punto **3** v/t (cause) causare; actor dare l'imbeccata a; **promptly** (on time) puntualmente; (immediately) prontamente

prone [prəʊn]: **be ~ to** essere soggetto a

pronoun ['prəʊnaʊn] pronome m

pronounce [prə'naʊns] pronunciare; (declare) dichiarare

pronto ['prontəʊ] F immediatamente

pronunciation [prənʌnsɪ'eɪʃn] pronuncia f

proof [pruːf] prova f; of book bozza f

prop [prop] **1** v/t appoggiare **2** n THEA materiale m di scena

♦ **prop up** also fig sostenere

propaganda [propə'gændə] propaganda f

propel [prə'pel] spingere; of engine, fuel azionare; **propeller** elica f

proper ['propə(r)] (real) vero e proprio; (correct) giusto; (fitting) appropriato; **properly** (correctly) correttamente; (fittingly) in modo appropriato

property ['propətɪ] proprietà f inv; **property developer** impresario m edile

proportion [prə'pɔːʃn] proporzione f; **proportional**

proporzionale; **proportional representation** POL rappresentanza f proporzionale

proposal [prə'pəʊzl] proposta f; **propose 1** v/t (suggest) proporre; **~ to do sth** (plan) proporsi di fare qc **2** v/i make offer of marriage fare una proposta di matrimonio; **proposition 1** n proposta f **2** v/t woman fare proposte sessuali a

proprietor [prə'praɪətə(r)] proprietario m, -a f

prose [prəʊz] prosa f

prosecute ['prosɪkjuːt] LAW intentare azione legale contro; of lawyer sostenere l'accusa contro; **prosecution** LAW azione f giudiziaria; (lawyers) accusa f

prospect ['prospekt] (chance, likelihood) probabilità f inv; thought of something in the future prospettiva f; **~s** prospettive fpl; **prospective** potenziale

prosper ['prospə(r)] prosperare; **prosperity** prosperità f; **prosperous** prospero

prostitute ['prostɪtjuːt] prostituta f; **male ~** prostituto m; **prostitution** prostituzione f

protect [prə'tekt] proteggere; **protection** protezione f; **protective** protettivo; **protector** protettore m, -trice f

protein ['prəʊtiːn] proteina f

protest 1 [prəʊtest] n protesta *f* 2 [prəˈtest] *v/t* protestare 3 [prəˈtest] *v/i* protestare; POL manifestare, protestare

Protestant [ˈprɒtɪstənt] 1 *n* protestante *m/f* 2 *adj* protestante

protester [prəˈtestə(r)] dimostrante *m/f*, manifestante *m/f*

prototype [ˈprəʊtətaɪp] prototipo *m*

protrude [prəˈtruːd] sporgere; **protruding** sporgente

proud [praʊd] orgoglioso, fiero; **be ~ of** essere fiero di; **proudly** con orgoglio

prove [pruːv] dimostrare

proverb [ˈprɒvɜːb] proverbio *m*

provide [prəˈvaɪd] *money, food* fornire; *opportunity* offrire; **~ s.o. with sth** fornire qu di qc; **~d that** (*on condition that*) a condizione che

province [ˈprɒvɪns] provincia *f*; **provincial** *also pej* provinciale

provision [prəˈvɪʒn] (*supply*) fornitura *f*; *of law, contract* disposizione *f*; **provisional** provvisorio

provocation [prɒvəˈkeɪʃn] provocazione *f*; **provocative** provocatorio; *sexually* provocante; **provoke** (*cause*) causare; (*annoy*) provocare

prowl [praʊl] aggirarsi; **prowler** tipo *m* sospetto

proximity [prɒkˈsɪmɪtɪ] prossimità *f*

proxy [ˈprɒksɪ] (*authority*) procura *f*; *person* procuratore *m*, -trice *f*, mandatario *m*, -a *f*

prudence [ˈpruːdns] prudenza *f*; **prudent** prudente

prudish [ˈpruːdɪʃ] che si scandalizza facilmente

pry [praɪ] essere indiscreto

PS [ˈpiːes] (= *postscript*) P.S. (= *post scriptum m*)

pseudonym [ˈsjuːdənɪm] pseudonimo *m*

psychiatric [saɪkɪˈætrɪk] psichiatrico; **psychiatrist** psichiatra *m/f*; **psychiatry** psichiatria *f*

psychoanalysis [saɪkəʊənˈæləsɪs] psicanalisi *f*; **psychoanalyst** psicanalista *m/f*; **psychoanalyze** psicanalizzare

psychological [saɪkəˈlɒdʒɪkl] psicologico; **psychologically** psicologicamente; **psychologist** psicologo *m*, -a *f*; **psychology** psicologia *f*

psychopath [ˈsaɪkəpæθ] psicopatico *m*, -a *f*

psychosomatic [saɪkəʊsəˈmætɪk] psicosomatico

pub [pʌb] pub *m inv*

pubic hair [pjuːˈbɪkˈheə(r)] peli *mpl* del pube

public [ˈpʌblɪk] 1 *adj* pubblico 2 *n*: **the ~** il pubblico; **in ~** in pubblico; **public transport** mezzi *mpl* pubblici

publication [pʌblɪˈkeɪʃn]

pubblicazione *f*

public 'holiday giorno *m* festivo

publicity [pʌb'lɪsətɪ] pubblicità *f*; **publicize** make known far sapere in giro; COM reclamizzare

publicly ['pʌblɪklɪ] pubblicamente

'public school Br scuola *f* privata; Am scuola pubblica

publish ['pʌblɪʃ] pubblicare; **publisher** editore *m*; **publishing** editoria *f*; **publishing company** casa *f* editrice

pudding ['pʊdɪŋ] dish budino *m*; part of meal dolce *m*

puddle ['pʌdl] *n* pozzanghera *f*

puff [pʌf] **1** *n* of wind, smoke soffio *m* **2** *v/i* (pant) ansimare; **puffy** eyes, face gonfio

puke [pjuːk] F vomitare

pull [pʊl] **1** *n* on rope tirata *f*; F (appeal) attrattiva *f*; F (influence) influenza *f* **2** *v/t* (drag) tirare; tooth togliere; **~ a muscle** farsi uno strappo muscolare **3** *v/i* tirare

◆ **pull ahead** in race, competition portarsi in testa

◆ **pull down** (lower) tirar giù; (demolish) demolire

◆ **pull in** of bus, train arrivare

◆ **pull out 1** *v/t* tirar fuori; troops (far) ritirare **2** *v/i* of agreement, competition, MIL ritirarsi; of ship partire

◆ **pull over** of driver accostarsi

◆ **pull through** from an illness farcela F

◆ **pull up 1** *v/t* (raise) tirar su; plant, weeds strappare **2** *v/i* of car etc fermarsi

pulley ['pʊlɪ] puleggia *f*

pulsate [pʌl'seɪt] of heart, blood pulsare; of rhythm vibrare

pulse [pʌls] polso *m*

pulverize ['pʌlvəraɪz] polverizzare

pump [pʌmp] **1** *n* pompa *f* **2** *v/t* pompare

pumpkin ['pʌmpkɪn] zucca *f*

pun [pʌn] gioco *m* di parole

punch [pʌntʃ] **1** *n* blow pugno *m*; implement punzonatrice *f* **2** *v/t* with fist dare un pugno a; hole perforare; ticket forare

punctual ['pʌŋktjʊəl] puntuale; **punctuality** puntualità *f*

punctuation [pʌŋktjʊ'eɪʃn] punteggiatura *f*

puncture ['pʌŋktʃə(r)] **1** *n* foratura *f* **2** *v/t* forare

punish ['pʌnɪʃ] punire; **punishing** pace, schedule estenuante; **punishment** punizione *f*

puny ['pjuːnɪ] person gracile

pup [pʌp] cucciolo *m*

pupil[1] ['pjuːpl] of eye pupilla *f*

pupil[2] ['pjuːpl] (student) allievo *m*, -a *f*

puppet ['pʌpɪt] burattino *m*; with strings marionetta *f*

puppy ['pʌpɪ] cucciolo *m*

purchase

514

purchase¹ ['pɜːtʃəs] **1** *n* acquisto *m* **2** *v/t* acquistare

purchase² ['pɜːtʃəs] *n* (*grip*) presa *f*

purchaser ['pɜːtʃəsə(r)] *n* acquirente *m/f*

pure [pjʊə(r)] puro; ~ *new wool* pura lana *f* vergine; **purely** puramente

purge [pɜːdʒ] **1** *n of political party* epurazione *f* **2** *v/t* epurare

purify ['pjʊərɪfaɪ] purificare

puritan ['pjʊərɪtən] puritano *m*, -a *f*

purity ['pjʊərɪtɪ] purezza *f*

purple ['pɜːpl] viola *inv*

purpose ['pɜːpəs] (*aim, object*) scopo *m*; **on ~** di proposito; **purposely** di proposito

purr [pɜː(r)] *of cat* fare le fusa

purse [pɜːs] *for money* borsellino *m*; *Am handbag* borsetta *f*

pursue [pə'sjuː] *person* inseguire; *career* intraprendere; *course of action* proseguire; **pursuer** inseguitore *m*, -trice *f*; **pursuit** (*chase*) inseguimento *m*; *of happiness etc* ricerca *f*; *activity* occupazione *f*

push [pʊʃ] **1** *n* (*shove*) spinta *f* **2** *v/t* (*shove*) spingere; *button* premere; (*pressurize*) fare pressioni su; F *drugs* spacciare; **be ~ed for** F essere a corto di **3** *v/i* spingere

◆ **push on** (*continue*) continuare

'pushchair passeggino *m*; **pusher** F *of drugs* spacciatore *m*, -trice *f*; **push-up** flessione *f* sulle braccia; **pushy** F troppo intraprendente

puss, pussy (cat) [pʊs, 'pʊsɪ (kæt)] F micio *m*, -a *f*

put [pʊt] mettere; *question* porre; ~ *the cost at* stimare il costo intorno a

◆ **put across** *ideas etc* trasmettere

◆ **put aside** mettere da parte

◆ **put away** *in cupboard etc* mettere via; *in institution* rinchiudere; (*consume*) far fuori; *money* mettere da parte; *Am animal* abbattere

◆ **put back** (*replace*) rimettere a posto

◆ **put down** mettere giù; *deposit* versare; *rebellion* reprimere; *animal* abbattere; (*belittle*) sminuire; *in writing* scrivere; *put X down to Y* (*attribute*) attribuire X a Y

◆ **put forward** *idea etc* avanzare

◆ **put in** inserire; *overtime* fare; *time, effort* dedicare; *request, claim* presentare

◆ **put off** *light, TV* spegnere; (*postpone*) rimandare; (*deter*) scoraggiare; (*repel*) disgustare

◆ **put on** *light, TV* accendere; *music* mettere su; *jacket, shoes, glasses* mettersi; *makeup* mettere; (*perform*) mettere in scena; (*assume*) affetta-

re; *she's just putting it on*
sta solo fingendo
◆ **put out** *hand* allungare; *fire
light* spegnere
◆ **put together** (*assemble*)
montare; (*organize*) organizzare
◆ **put up** ospitare; (*erect*) costruire;
prices aumentare; *poster* affiggere; *money* fornire; *put
up for sale* mettere in vendita

◆ **put up with** sopportare
putty ['pʌtɪ] mastice *m*
puzzle ['pʌzl] **1** *n* (*mystery*)
mistero *m*; *game* rebus *m
inv*; *jigsaw* puzzle *m inv* **2**
v/t lasciar perplesso; **puz-
zling** inspiegabile
PVC [piːviːˈsiː] (= *polyvinyl
chloride*) PVC *m* (= polivi-
nilcloruro *m*)
pyjamas [pəˈdʒɑːməz] pigiama *m*
pylon ['paɪlən] pilone *m*

Q

quack [kwæk] *of duck* fare
qua qua
quadrangle ['kwɒdræŋgl] *figure* quadrilatero *m*; *court
yard* cortile *m*
quadruped ['kwɒdruped]
quadrupede *m*
quail [kweɪl] perdersi d'animo
quaint [kweɪnt] *pretty* pittoresco; *eccentric: ideas etc* curioso
quake [kweɪk] **1** *n* (*earthquake*) terremoto *m* **2** *v/i also
fig* tremare
qualification [kwɒlɪfɪˈkeɪʃn]
from university etc titolo *m*
di studio; (*qualified doctor,
engineer etc* abilitato; (*restricted*) con riserva; **qualify
1** *v/t of degree, course etc* abi-
litare; *remark etc* precisare **2**
v/i (*get certificate etc*) ottene-

re la qualifica (*as* di); *in
competition* qualificarsi
quality ['kwɒlətɪ] qualità *f
inv*; **quality control** controllo *m* (di) qualità; **quality
time** tempo *m* di qualità
qualm [kwɑːm]: *have no ~s
about ...* non aver scrupoli
a ...
quandary ['kwɒndərɪ] dilemma *m*; *be in a ~* avere un dilemma
quantify ['kwɒntɪfaɪ] quanti-
ficare
quantity ['kwɒntətɪ] quantità
f inv
quarantine ['kwɒrəntiːn]
quarantena *f*
quarrel ['kwɒrəl] **1** *n* litigio *m*
2 *v/i* litigare
quarry[1] ['kwɒrɪ] *in hunt* preda
f
quarry[2] ['kwɒrɪ] *for mining*

cava f

quart [kwɔːt] quarto m di gallone (*Br 1,136 l, Am 0.946 l*)

quarter ['kwɔːtə(r)] quarto m; *part of town* quartiere m; **a ~ of an hour** un quarto d'ora; (**a**) **~ to 5** le cinque meno un quarto; (**a**) **~ past 5** le cinque e un quarto; **quarter-final** partita f dei quarti mpl di finale; **quarter-finalist** concorrente m/f dei quarti di finale; **quarterly 1** adj trimestrale **2** adv trimestralmente; **quarters** MIL quartieri mpl; **quartet** MUS quartetto m

quartz [kwɔːts] quarzo m

quash [kwɒʃ] *rebellion* reprimere; *court decision* annullare

quaver ['kweɪvə(r)] **1** n *in voice* tremolio m; MUS croma f **2** v/i *of voice* tremolare

quay [kiː] banchina f

queasy ['kwiːzɪ] nauseato

queen [kwiːn] regina f

queer [kwɪə(r)] (*peculiar*) strano

quell [kwel] soffocare

quench [kwentʃ] *also fig* spegnere

query ['kwɪərɪ] **1** n interrogativo m **2** v/t *express doubt about* contestare; *check* controllare

quest [kwest] ricerca f

question ['kwestʃn] **1** n domanda f; *matter* questione f; **it's a ~ of money** è questione di soldi; **that's out**

of the ~ è fuori discussione **2** v/t *person* interrogare; (*doubt*) dubitare di; **questionable** discutibile; (*dubious*) dubbio; **questioning 1** adj *look, tone* interrogativo **2** n interrogatorio m; **question mark** punto m interrogativo; **questionnaire** questionario m

queue [kjuː] **1** n coda f, fila f **2** v/i fare la fila or la coda

quibble ['kwɪbl] cavillare

quick [kwɪk] *person* svelto; *reply, change* veloce; **be ~!** fai presto!, fai in fretta!; **let's have a ~ drink** beviamo qualcosina?; **quickly** rapidamente, in fretta; **quick-witted** sveglio

quid [kwɪd] F sterlina f; **50 ~** 50 sterline

quiet ['kwaɪət] *voice, music* basso; *engine* silenzioso; *street, life, town* tranquillo; **keep ~ about sth** tenere segreto qc; **~!** silenzio!; (*without fuss*) semplicemente; (*peacefully*) tranquillamente; **quietness** *of night, street* tranquillità f, calma f; *of voice* dolcezza f

quilt [kwɪlt] *on bed* piumino m

quinine ['kwɪniːn] chinino m

quip [kwɪp] **1** n battuta f (di spirito) **2** v/i scherzare

quirk [kwɜːk] bizzarria f; **quirky** bizzarro

quit [kwɪt] **1** v/t job mollare F **2** v/i (leave job) licenziarsi; COMPUT uscire

quite [kwaɪt] (fairly) abbastanza; (completely) completamente; **is that right? – not ~ giusto?** – non esattamente; **~!** esatto!; **~ a lot** drink, change parecchio; **~ a lot better** molto meglio; **~ a few** un bel po'; **it was ~ a surprise** è stata una bella sorpresa

quiver ['kwɪvə(r)] tremare

quiz [kwɪz] **1** n quiz m inv **2** v/t interrogare

quota ['kwəʊtə] quota f

quotation [kwəʊ'teɪʃn] from author citazione f; price preventivo m; **quotation marks** virgolette fpl; **quote 1** n from author citazione f; price preventivo m; (quotation mark) virgoletta f; **in ~s** tra virgolette **2** v/t text citare; price stimare

R

rabbit ['ræbɪt] coniglio m

rabble ['ræbl] marmaglia f; **rabble-rouser** agitatore m, -trice f

rabies ['reɪbiːz] rabbia f, idrofobia f

raccoon [rə'kuːn] procione m

race[1] [reɪs] n of people razza f

race[2] [reɪs] **1** n SP gara f; **the ~s** (horse races) le corse **2** v/i (run fast) correre **3** v/t: **I'll ~ you** facciamo una gara

'racecourse ippodromo m; **racehorse** cavallo m da corsa; **race riot** scontri mpl razziali; **racetrack** pista f; for horses ippodromo m

racial ['reɪʃl] razziale

racing ['reɪsɪŋ] corse fpl; **racing car** auto f inv da corsa; **racing driver** pilota m automobilistico

racism ['reɪsɪzm] razzismo m;

racist **1** n razzista m/f **2** adj razzista

rack [ræk] **1** n for parking bikes rastrelliera f; for bags on train portabagagli m inv; for CDs porta-CD m inv **2** v/t: **~ one's brains** scervellarsi

racket[1] ['rækɪt] SP racchetta f

racket[2] ['rækɪt] (noise) baccano m; criminal activity racket m inv

radar ['reɪdɑː(r)] radar m inv

radiance ['reɪdɪəns] splendore m; **radiant** smile splendente; appearance raggiante; **radiate** of heat, light diffondersi; **radiation** PHYS radiazione f; **radiator** in room termosifone m; in car radiatore m

radical ['rædɪkl] **1** adj radicale **2** n radicale m/f; **radicalism**

POL radicalismo *m*; **radical-ly** radicalmente

radio ['reɪdɪəʊ] radio *f inv*; **on the ~** alla radio; **radioactive** radioattivo; **radioactivity** radioattività *f*; **radio alarm** radiosveglia *f*; **radiographer** radiologo *m*, -a *f*; **radiography** radiografia *f*; **radio station** stazione *f* radiofonica, radio *f inv*

radius ['reɪdɪəs] raggio *m*

raft [rɑːft] zattera *f*

rafter ['rɑːftə(r)] travicello *m*

rag [ræg] *for cleaning etc* straccio *m*

rage [reɪdʒ] **1** *n* rabbia *f*, collera *f*; **be all the ~** F essere di moda **2** *v/i of person* infierire; *of storm* infuriare

ragged ['rægɪd] stracciato

raid [reɪd] **1** *n* raid *m inv* **2** *v/t of police, robbers* fare un raid in; *fridge, orchard* fare razzia in; **raider** *on bank etc* rapinatore *m*, -trice *f*

rail [reɪl] *on track* rotaia *f*; *(hand~)* corrimano *m*; *(barrier)* parapetto *m*; **towel ~** portasciugamano *m inv*; **by ~** in treno; **railings** *around park etc* inferriata *f*; **railroad** *Am* ferrovia *f*; **railway** ferrovia *f*; **railway station** stazione *f* ferroviaria

rain [reɪn] **1** *n* pioggia *f*; **in the ~** sotto la pioggia **2** *v/i* piovere; **it's ~ing** sta piovendo; **rainbow** arcobaleno *m*; **raincheck: can I take a ~**

on that? *Am* F posso riservarmi di farlo in seguito?; **raincoat** impermeabile *m*; **raindrop** goccia *f* di pioggia; **rainfall** piovosità *f*; **rain forest** foresta *f* pluviale; **rainproof** *fabric* impermeabile; **rainstorm** temporale *m*; **rainy** *day* di pioggia; *weather* piovoso; **it's ~** piove molto

raise [reɪz] **1** *n in salary* aumento *m* **2** *v/t shelf, question* sollevare; *offer* aumentare; *children* allevare; *money* raccogliere

raisin ['reɪzn] uva *f* passa

rake [reɪk] *for garden* rastrello *m*

rally ['rælɪ] *meeting* raduno *m*; MOT rally *m inv*; *in tennis* scambio *m*

RAM [ræm] COMPUT (= *random access memory*) RAM *f inv*

ram [ræm] **1** *n* montone *m* **2** *v/t ship, car* sbattere contro

ramble ['ræmbl] **1** *n walk* escursione *f* **2** *v/i walk* fare passeggiate; *in speaking* divagare; *talk incoherently* vaneggiare; **rambling** *speech* sconnesso

ramp [ræmp] rampa *f*; *for raising vehicle* ponte *m* idraulico

rampant ['ræmpənt] *inflation* dilagante

rampart ['ræmpɑːt] bastione *m*

ramshackle ['ræmʃækl] sgangherato

ranch [rɑːntʃ] ranch *m inv*; **rancher** (*owner*) proprietario *m* di un ranch; **ranchhand** lavoratore *m*, -trice *f* di un ranch

rancid ['rænsɪd] rancido

rancour, *Am* **rancor** ['ræŋkə(r)] rancore *m*

R&D [ɑːr əndiː] (= *research and development*) ricerca *f* e sviluppo *m*

random ['rændəm] **1** *adj* casuale; **~ sample** campione *m* casuale **2** *n*: **at ~** a caso

randy ['rændɪ] F arrapato P

range [reɪndʒ] **1** *n of products* gamma *f*; *of missile, gun* gittata *f*; *of salary* scala *f*; *of voice* estensione *f*; *of mountains* catena *f*; **at close ~** a distanza ravvicinata **2** *v/i*: **~ from X to Y** variare da X a Y; **ranger** *Am* guardia *f* forestale

rank [ræŋk] **1** *n* MIL grado *m*; *in society* rango *m*; **the ~s** MIL la truppa **2** *v/t* classificare

♦ **rank among** classificarsi tra

ransack ['rænsæk] saccheggiare

ransom ['rænsəm] riscatto *m*; **ransom money** ((soldi *mpl* del) riscatto *m*

rap [ræp] **1** *n at door etc* colpo *m*; MUS rap *m* **2** *v/t table etc* battere

rape¹ [reɪp] **1** *n* stupro *m* **2** *v/t* violentare

rape² [reɪp] *n* BOT colza *f*

rapid ['ræpɪd] rapido; **rapidity** rapidità *f*; **rapidly** rapidamente; **rapids** rapide *fpl*

rapist ['reɪpɪst] violentatore *m*

rare [reə(r)] raro; *steak* al sangue; **rarely** raramente; **rarity** rarità *f inv*

rascal ['rɑːskl] birbante *m/f*

rash¹ [ræʃ] *n* MED orticaria *f*

rash² [ræʃ] *adj action* avventato

rashly ['ræʃlɪ] avventatamente

raspberry ['rɑːzbərɪ] lampone *m*

rat [ræt] ratto *m*

rate [reɪt] *of exchange* tasso *m*; *of pay, charge* tariffa *f*; (*speed*) ritmo *m*; **at this ~** (*at this speed, carrying on like this*) di questo passo; **at any ~** in ogni modo

rather ['rɑːðə(r)] piuttosto; **I would ~ stay here** preferirei stare qui

ratification [rætɪfɪ'keɪʃn] ratifica *f*; **ratify** ratificare

ratings ['reɪtɪŋz] indice *m* d'ascolto

ratio ['reɪʃɪəʊ] proporzione *f*

ration ['ræʃn] **1** *n* razione *f* **2** *v/t supplies* razionare

rational ['ræʃnl] razionale; **rationality** razionalità *f*; **rationalization** razionalizzazione *f*; **rationalize** razionalizzare; **rationally** razionalmente

rattle ['ræt] **1** *n* noise rumore *m*; *toy* sonaglio *m* **2** *v/t* scuotere **3** *v/i* far rumore; **rattle-snake** serpente *m* a sonagli

raucous ['rɔːkəs] sguaiato

rave [reɪv] **1** *v/i* delirare; ~ *about sth* be very enthusiastic entusiasmarsi per qc **2** *v/t party* rave *m inv*

ravenous ['rævənəs] famelico

'rave review recensione *f* entusiastica

ravine [rə'viːn] burrone *m*

ravishing ['rævɪʃɪŋ] incantevole

raw [rɔː] *meat, vegetable* crudo; *sugar, iron* grezzo; **raw materials** materia *f* prima

ray [reɪ] raggio *m*

razor ['reɪzə(r)] rasoio *m*; **razor blade** lametta *f* da barba

re [riː] COM con riferimento a

reach [riːtʃ] **1** *n*: *within* ~ vicino (*of* a); *within arm's reach* a portata (di mano); *out of* ~ non a portata (*of* di); *keep out of* ~ *of children* tenere lontano dalla portata dei bambini **2** *v/t city* arrivare a; *decision, agreement* raggiungere; *can you* ~ *it?* ci arrivi?

react [rɪ'ækt] reagire; **reaction** reazione *f*; **reactionary 1** *n* POL reazionario *m*, -a *f* **2** *adj* POL reazionario; **reactor nuclear** reattore *m*

read [riːd] leggere
◆ **read out** *aloud* leggere a voce alta
◆ **read up on** documentarsi su

readable ['riːdəbl] leggibile; **reader** *person* lettore *m*, -trice *f*

readily ['redɪlɪ] (*willingly*) volentieri; (*easily*) facilmente

reading ['riːdɪŋ] *also from meter* lettura *f*

readjust [riːə'dʒʌst] **1** *v/t* regolare **2** *v/i to conditions* riadattarsi

ready ['redɪ] pronto; *get (o.s.)* ~ prepararsi; *get sth* ~ preparare qc; **ready cash** contanti *mpl*; **ready-made** *stew etc* precotto; *solution* bell'e pronto; **ready-to-wear** confezionato

real [riːl] vero; **real estate** proprietà *fpl* immobiliari; **real estate agent** agente *m/f* immobiliare; **realism** realismo *m*; **realist** realista *m/f*; **realistic** realistico; **realistically** realisticamente; **reality** realtà *f inv*; **reality show** TV reality show *m inv*; **realize** rendersi conto di, realizzare; FIN realizzare; *I ~ now that ...* ora capisco che ...; **really** veramente; ~? davvero?; *not* ~ (*not much*) non proprio; **real-time** COMPUT in tempo reale; **real time** COMPUT tempo *m* reale

realtor ['riːltə(r)] *Am* agente *m/f* immobiliare; **realty** *Am*

521   **reciprocal**

proprietà *fpl* immobiliari
reappear [riːəˈpɪə(r)] riapparire; **reappearance** ricomparsa *f*
rear [rɪə(r)] **1** *n* of building retro *m*; of train parte *f* posteriore **2** *adj* posteriore
rearm [riːˈɑːm] **1** *v/t* riarmare **2** *v/i* riarmarsi
rearrange [riːəˈreɪndʒ] *furniture* spostare; *schedule, meetings* cambiare
rear-view 'mirror specchietto *m* retrovisore
reason [ˈriːzn] **1** *n* faculty ragione *f*; (cause) motivo *m*; **listen to** ~ ascoltare ragione **2** *v/i*: ~ **with s.o.** far ragionare con qu; **reasonable** *person, price* ragionevole; *weather, health* discreto; **a** ~ **number of people** un discreto numero di persone; **reasonably** *act, behave* ragionevolmente; (quite) abbastanza; **reasoning** ragionamento *m*
reassure [riːəˈʃuə(r)] rassicurare; **reassuring** rassicurante
rebate [ˈriːbeɪt] *money back* rimborso *m*
rebel 1 [ˈrebl] *n* ribelle *m/f* **2** [rɪˈbel] *v/i* ribellarsi; **rebellion** ribellione *f*; **rebellious** ribelle; **rebelliousness** spirito *m* di ribellione
rebound [rɪˈbaʊnd] of ball etc rimbalzare
rebuild [riːˈbɪld] ricostruire

recall [rɪˈkɔːl] richiamare; (remember) ricordare
recap [ˈriːkæp] F ricapitolare
recapture [riːˈkæptʃə(r)] criminal ricatturare; *town* riconquistare
recede [rɪˈsiːd] of flood waters abbassarsi; **receding** forehead, chin sfuggente; **have a ~ hairline** essere stempiato
receipt [rɪˈsiːt] for purchase ricevuta *f*, scontrino *m*; **~s** FIN introiti *mpl*; **receive** ricevere; **receiver** TELEC ricevitore *m*; for radio apparecchio *m* ricevente; **receivership**: **be in** ~ essere in amministrazione controllata
recent [ˈriːsnt] recente; **recently** recentemente
reception [rɪˈsepʃn] reception *f inv*; formal party ricevimento *m*; (welcome) accoglienza *f*; on radio, mobile ricezione *f*; **reception desk** banco *m* della reception; **receptionist** receptionist *m/f inv*; **receptive**: **be ~ to sth** essere ricettivo verso qc
recess [ˈriːses] in wall etc rientranza *f*; of parliament vacanza *f*; Am EDU intervallo *m*; **recession** economic recessione *f*
recharge [riːˈtʃɑːdʒ] battery ricaricare
recipe [ˈresəpɪ] ricetta *f*
recipient [rɪˈsɪpɪənt] destinatario *m*, -a *f*
reciprocal [rɪˈsɪprəkl] reci-

proco

recite [rɪ'saɪt] *poem* recitare; *details*, *facts* enumerare

reckless ['reklɪs] spericolato; **recklessly** in modo spericolato; *spend* avventatamente

reckon ['rekən] (*think*, *consider*) pensare

◆ **reckon on** contare su

reclaim [rɪ'kleɪm] *land* bonificare; *lost property* recuperare

recline [rɪ'klaɪn] sdraiarsi; **recliner** *chair* poltrona *f* reclinabile

recluse [rɪ'kluːs] eremita *m/f*

recognition [rekəg'nɪʃn] *of state*, *s.o.'s achievements* riconoscimento *m*; **recognizable** riconoscibile; **recognize** riconoscere

recoil [rɪ'kɔɪl] indietreggiare

recollect [rekə'lekt] rammentare; **recollection** ricordo *m*

recommend [rekə'mend] consigliare; **recommendation** consiglio *m*

recompense ['rekəmpens] ricompensa *f*; LAW risarcimento *m*

reconcile ['rekənsaɪl] *people*, *differences* riconciliare; *facts* conciliare; **~ o.s. to ...** rassegnarsi a ...; **reconciliation** *of people*, *differences* riconciliazione *f*; *of facts* conciliazione *f*

recondition [riːkən'dɪʃn] ricondizionare

reconnaissance [rɪ'kɒnɪsns] MIL ricognizione *f*

reconsider [riːkən'sɪdə(r)] **1** *v/t offer* riconsiderare **2** *v/i* ripensare

reconstruct [riːkən'strʌkt] *city*, *crime*, *life* ricostruire

record[1] ['rekɔːd] *n* MUS disco *m*; SP etc record *m inv*, primato *m*; *written document etc* nota *f*; *in database* record *m inv*; **~s** archivio *m*; **say sth off the ~** dire qc ufficiosamente; **have a criminal ~** avere precedenti penali

record[2] [rɪ'kɔːd] *v/t electronically* registrare; *in writing* annotare

'record-breaking da record; **recorder** [rɪ'kɔːdə(r)] MUS flauto *m* dolce

'record holder primatista *m/f*

recording [rɪ'kɔːdɪŋ] registrazione *f*; **recording studio** sala *f* di registrazione

'record player giradischi *m inv*

re-count ['riːkaʊnt] **1** *n of votes* nuovo conteggio *m* **2** *v/t* (*count again*) ricontare

recount [rɪ'kaʊnt] (*tell*) raccontare

recoup [rɪ'kuːp] *financial losses* rifarsi di

recover [rɪ'kʌvə(r)] **1** *v/t stolen goods* recuperare **2** *v/i from illness* rimettersi; *of business* riprendersi; **recovery** *of stolen goods* recupero *m*; *from illness* guarigione *f*

recreation [rekrɪ'eɪʃn] ricreazione *f*; **recreational** *done* *for pleasure* ricreativo

recruit [rɪ'kruːt] **1** *n* MIL recluta *f*; *to company* neoassunto *m*, -a *f* **2** *v/t new staff* assumere; *members* arruolare; **recruitment** assunzione *f*; MIL, POL reclutamento *m*

rectangle ['rektæŋgl] rettangolo *m*; **rectangular** rettangolare

rectify ['rektɪfaɪ] rettificare

recuperate [rɪ'kjuːpəreɪt] recuperare

recur [rɪ'kɜː(r)] *of error, event* ripetersi; *of symptoms* ripresentarsi; **recurrent** ricorrente

recyclable [riː'saɪkləbl] riciclabile; **recycle** riciclare; **recycling** riciclo *m*

red [red] rosso; **in the ~** FIN in rosso; **Red Cross** Croce *f* Rossa

redecorate [riː'dekəreɪt] ritinteggiare; *change wallpaper* ritapezzare

redeem [rɪ'diːm] *debt* estinguere; *sinners* redimere; **redeeming feature** aspetto *m* positivo

redevelop [riːdɪ'veləp] *part of town* risanare

red-handed [red'hændɪd]: **catch s.o. ~** cogliere qu in flagrante; **redhead** rosso *m*, -a *f*; **red light** *at traffic lights* rosso *m*; **red light district** quartiere *m* a luci rosse; **red meat** carni *fpl* rosse; **redneck** *Am* F reazionario

m, -a *f*; **red tape** F burocrazia *f*

reduce [rɪ'djuːs] ridurre; **reduction** riduzione *f*

redundancy [rɪ'dʌndənsɪ] *at work* licenziamento *m*; **redundant** (*unnecessary*) superfluo; **be made ~** *at work* essere licenziato

reef [riːf] *in sea* scogliera *f*; **reef knot** nodo *m* piano

reek [riːk] puzzare (**of** *di*)

reel [riːl] *of film* rullino *m*; *of thread* rocchetto *m*; *of tape* bobina *f*; *of fishing line* mulinello *m*

re-e'lect rieleggere; **re-election** rielezione *f*

re-'entry *of spacecraft* rientro *m*

ref [ref] F arbitro *m*

◆ **refer to** [rɪ'fɜː(r)] riferirsi a; *dictionary etc* consultare

referee [refə'riː] SP arbitro *m*; *for job* referenza *f*; **reference** (*allusion*) allusione *f*; *for job* referenza *f*; (**~ number**) (numero *m* di) riferimento *m*; **reference book** opera *f* di consultazione; **reference number** numero *m* di riferimento

referendum [refə'rendəm] referendum *m inv*

refill ['riːfɪl] riempire

refine [rɪ'faɪn] raffinare; **refinement** *to process, machine* miglioramento *m*; **refinery** raffineria *f*

reflect [rɪ'flekt] **1** *v/t light* riflettere; **be ~ed in** riflettersi in 2 *v/i* (*think*) riflettere; **reflection** *in water, glass etc* riflesso *m*; (*consideration*) riflessione *f*; **on ~** dopo aver riflettuto

reflex ['ri:fleks] *in body* riflesso *m*

reform [rɪ'fɔːm] **1** *n* riforma *f* **2** *v/t* riformare; **reformer** riformatore *m*, -trice *f*

refrain [rɪ'freɪn] *fml:* **please ~ from smoking** si prega di non fumare

refresh [rɪ'freʃ] *person* ristorare; **feel ~ed** sentirsi ristorato; **refreshing** *drink* rinfrescante; *experience* piacevole; **refreshments** rinfreschi *mpl*

refrigerate [rɪ'frɪdʒəreɪt]: **keep ~d** conservare in frigo; **refrigerator** frigorifero *m*

refuel [riː'fjuːəl] **1** *v/t aeroplane* rifornire di carburante **2** *v/i of aeroplane, car* fare rifornimento

refuge ['refjuːdʒ] rifugio *m*; **take ~ from** *storm etc* ripararsi; **refugee** rifugiato *m*, -a *f*, profugo *m*, -a *f*

refund 1 ['riːfʌnd] *n* rimborso *m* **2** [rɪ'fʌnd] *v/t* rimborsare

refusal [rɪ'fjuːzl] rifiuto *m*

refuse¹ [rɪ'fjuːz] rifiutare; **~ to do sth** rifiutare di fare qc

refuse² ['refjuːs] *n* rifiuti *mpl*

regain [rɪ'geɪn] *control, lost territory, the lead* riconquistare

regard [rɪ'gɑːd] **1** *n:* **have great ~ for s.o.** avere molta stima di qu; **with ~ to** riguardo a; (**kind**) **~s** cordiali saluti; **with no ~ for** senza alcun riguardo per 2 *v/t:* **~ as** considerare come qc; **regarding** riguardo a; **regardless** lo stesso; **~ of** senza tener conto di

regime [reɪ'ʒiːm] (*government*) regime *m*

regiment ['redʒɪmənt] reggimento *m*

region ['riːdʒən] regione *f*; **in the ~ of** intorno a; **regional** regionale

register ['redʒɪstə(r)] **1** *n* registro *m* **2** *v/t birth, death: by individual* denunciare; *by authorities* registrare; *vehicle* iscrivere; *letter* assicurare; *emotion* mostrare **3** *v/i at university* iscriversi; **registered letter** (lettera *f*) assicurata *f*; **registration** *at university* iscrizione *f*; **registration number** MOT numero *m* di targa; **registry office** ufficio *m* di stato civile

regret [rɪ'gret] **1** *v/t* rammaricarsi di; *missed opportunity* rimpiangere **2** *n* rammarico *m*; **regretful** di rammarico; **regrettable** deplorevole; **regrettably** purtroppo

regular ['regjʊlə(r)] **1** *adj* regolare; (*ordinary*) normale **2** *n at bar etc* cliente *m/f* abituale; **regularity** regolarità *f* *inv*; **regularly** regolarmente

regulate ['regjʊleɪt] regolare; **regulation** (*rule*) regolamento *m*; **control** controllo *m*

rehabilitate [riːhəˈbɪlɪteɪt] *ex--criminal* riabilitare; *disabled person* rieducare

rehearsal [rɪˈhɜːsl] prova *f*; **rehearse** provare

reign [reɪn] **1** *n* regno *m* **2** *v/i* regnare

reimburse [riːɪmˈbɜːs] rimborsare

reinforce [riːɪnˈfɔːs] rinforzare; **reinforced concrete** cemento *m* armato; **reinforcements** MIL rinforzi *mpl*

reinstate [riːɪnˈsteɪt] reintegrare

reiterate [riːˈɪtəreɪt] *fml* ripetere

reject [rɪˈdʒekt] respingere; **rejection** rifiuto *m*

relapse [rɪˈlæps] MED ricaduta *f*

relate [rɪˈleɪt] **1** *v/t story* raccontare **2** *v/i*: **~ to ...** *be connected with* riferirsi a ...; **he doesn't ~ to people** non sa stabilire un rapporto con gli altri; **related** *by family* imparentato; *events, ideas etc* collegato; **relation** *in family* parente *m/f*; *(connection)* rapporto *m*; **business ~s** rapporti d'affari; **relationship** rapporto *m*; **relative 1** *n* parente *m/f* **2** *adj* relativo; **relatively** relativamente

relax [rɪˈlæks] **1** *v/i* rilassarsi; **~!** rilassati! **2** *v/t* rilassare; **relaxation** relax *m inv*; *of rules etc* rilassamento *m*; **relaxed** rilassato; **relaxing** rilassante

relay [riːˈleɪ] **1** *v/t* trasmettere **2** *n*: **~ (race)** (corsa *f* a) staffetta *f*

release [rɪˈliːs] **1** *n from prison* rilascio *m*; *of CD etc* uscita *f*; *of software* versione *f* **2** *v/t prisoner* rilasciare; *handbrake* togliere; *film, record* far uscire; *information* rendere noto

relegate ['relɪgeɪt] relegare; **be ~d** SP essere retrocesso; **relegation** SP retrocessione *f*

relent [rɪˈlent] cedere; **relentless** incessante, implacabile

relevance ['reləvəns] pertinenza *f*

relevant ['reləvənt] pertinente

reliability [rɪlaɪəˈbɪlɪtɪ] affidabilità *f*; **reliable** affidabile; **reliance** dipendenza *f* (**on** da); **reliant**: **be ~ on** dipendere da

relic ['relɪk] reliquia *f*

relief [rɪˈliːf] sollievo *m*; **relieve** *pressure, pain* alleviare; *(take over from)* dare il cambio a; **be ~d** *at news etc* essere sollevato

religion [rɪˈlɪdʒən] religione *f*; **religious** religioso; **religiously** religiosamente

relinquish [rɪˈlɪŋkwɪʃ] rinun-

ciare a
relish ['relɪʃ] **1** *n sauce* salsa *f*; *(enjoyment)* gusto *m* **2** *v/t idea, prospect* gradire
relive [riː'lɪv] rivivere
relocate [riːlə'keɪt] *of business, employee* trasferirsi
reluctance [rɪ'lʌktəns] riluttanza *f*; **reluctant** riluttante; **be ~ to do sth** essere restio a fare qc; **reluctantly** a malincuore
♦ **rely on** [rɪ'laɪ] contare su; **rely on s.o. to do sth** contare su qu perché faccia qc
remain [rɪ'meɪn] rimanere; **remainder** *also* MATH resto *m*; **remaining** restante; **remains** *of body* resti *mpl*
remake ['riːmeɪk] *of film* remake *m inv*
remand [rɪ'mɑːnd] **1** *v/t:* **~ s.o. in custody** ordinare la custodia cautelare di qu **2** *n:* **be on ~** essere in attesa di giudizio
remark [rɪ'mɑːk] **1** *n* commento *m* **2** *v/t* osservare; **remarkable** notevole; **remarkably** notevolmente
remarry [riː'mærɪ] risposarsi
remedy ['remədɪ] rimedio *m*
remember [rɪ'membə(r)] **1** *v/t* ricordare **2** *v/i* ricordare, ricordarsi
remind [rɪ'maɪnd]: **~ s.o. of s.o. / sth** ricordare qu / qc a qu; **~ s.o. to do sth** ricordare a qu di fare qc; **reminder** promemoria *m*; COM for

payment sollecito *m*
reminisce [remɪ'nɪs] rievocare il passato
remission [rɪ'mɪʃn] REL MED remissione *f*
remnant ['remnənt] resto *m*; *of fabric* scampolo *m*
remorse [rɪ'mɔːs] rimorso *m*; **remorseless** spietato
remote [rɪ'məʊt] *village* isolato; *possibility* remoto; *(aloof)* distante; *ancestor* lontano; **remote control** *for TV* telecomando *m*; **remotely** *related, connected* lontanamente; **just ~ possible** vagamente possibile
removable [rɪ'muːvəbl] staccabile; **removal** rimozione *f*; *from home* trasloco; **removal firm** ditta *f* di traslochi; **remove** togliere; MED asportare; *doubt, suspicion* eliminare
remuneration [rɪmjuːnə'reɪʃn] rimunerazione *f*
Renaissance [rɪ'neɪsəns] Rinascimento *m*
rename [riː'neɪm] ribattezzare; *file* rinominare
rendez-vous ['rɒndeɪvuː] *(meeting)* incontro *m*
renew [rɪ'njuː] *contract* rinnovare; **feel ~ed** sentirsi rinato; **renewal** *of contract etc* rinnovo *m*
renounce [rɪ'naʊns] rinunciare a
renovate ['renəveɪt] ristrutturare; **renovation** ristruttura-

527

reprieve

zione f

rent [rent] **1** n affitto m; **for ~** affittasi **2** v/t apartment affittare; car, equipment, noleggiare; (~ out) affittare; **rental for apartment** affitto m; **for car** noleggio m; **for TV, phone** canone m; **rental car** macchina f a noleggio; **rent-free** gratis

reopen [riːˈəʊpn] riaprire

reorganization [riːɔːɡənaɪˈzeɪʃn] riorganizzazione f; **reorganize** riorganizzare

repaint [riːˈpeɪnt] ridipingere

repair [rɪˈpeə(r)] **1** v/t riparare **2** n: **in a bad state of ~** in cattivo stato; **~s** riparazioni fpl; **repairman** tecnico m

repatriate [riːˈpætrɪeɪt] rimpatriare; **repatriation** rimpatrio m

repay [riːˈpeɪ] money restituire; person ripagare; **repayment** pagamento m

repeal [rɪˈpiːl] law abrogare

repeat [rɪˈpiːt] **1** v/t ripetere **2** n programme replica f; **repeatedly** ripetutamente

repel [rɪˈpel] invaders, attack respingere; (disgust) ripugnare; **repellent 1** n (insect ~) insettifugo m **2** adj ripugnante

repercussions [riːpəˈkʌʃnz] ripercussioni fpl

repertoire [ˈrepətwɑː(r)] repertorio m

repetition [repɪˈtɪʃn] ripetizione f; **repetitive** ripetitivo

replace [rɪˈpleɪs] (put back) mettere a posto; (take the place of) sostituire; **replacement person** sostituto m, -a f; act sostituzione f; **replacement part** pezzo m di ricambio

replay [ˈriːpleɪ] **1** n recording replay m inv; match spareggio m **2** v/t match rigiocare

replenish [rɪˈplenɪʃ] container riempire; supplies rifornire

replica [ˈreplɪkə] copia f

reply [rɪˈplaɪ] **1** n risposta f **2** v/t & v/i rispondere

report [rɪˈpɔːt] **1** n (account) resoconto m; by journalist servizio m; EDU pagella f **2** v/t facts fare un servizio su; to authorities denunciare **3** v/i of journalist fare un reportage; (present o.s.) presentarsi

♦ **report to** in business rendere conto a

reporter [rɪˈpɔːtə(r)] giornalista m/f

repossess [riːpəˈzes] COM riprendere possesso di

represent [reprɪˈzent] rappresentare; **representative 1** n rappresentante m/f **2** adj (typical) rappresentativo

repress [rɪˈpres] reprimere; **repression** POL repressione f; **repressive** POL repressivo

reprieve [rɪˈpriːv] **1** n LAW sospensione f della pena capitale; fig proroga f **2** v/t prisoner sospendere l'esecuzione di

reprimand ['reprɪmɑːnd] ammonire

reprint ['riːprɪnt] **1** *n* ristampa *f* **2** *v/t* ristampare

reprisal [rɪ'praɪzl] rappresaglia *f*; **take ~s** fare delle rappresaglie

reproach [rɪ'prəʊtʃ] **1** *n* rimprovero *m*; **be beyond ~** essere irreprensibile **2** *v/t* rimproverare; **reproachful** di rimprovero

reproduce [riːprə'djuːs] **1** *v/t* riprodurre **2** *v/i* riprodursi; **reproduction** riproduzione *f*; **reproductive** riproduttivo

reptile ['reptaɪl] rettile *m*

republic [rɪ'pʌblɪk] repubblica *f*; **republican 1** *n* repubblicano *m*, -a *f* **2** *adj* repubblicano

repulsive [rɪ'pʌlsɪv] ripugnante

reputable ['repjʊtəbl] rispettabile; **reputation** reputazione *f*; **reputedly** a quanto si dice

request [rɪ'kwest] **1** *n* richiesta *f*; **on ~** su richiesta **2** *v/t* richiedere

require [rɪ'kwaɪə(r)] (*need*) aver bisogno di; **it ~s great care** richiede molta cura; **as ~d by law** come prescritto dalla legge; **required** (*necessary*) necessario; **requirement** (*need*) esigenza *f*; (*condition*) requisito *m*

requisition [rekwɪ'zɪʃn] re-

quisire

reroute [riː'ruːt] *aeroplane etc* deviare

rerun ['riːrʌn] **1** *n* of *programme* replica *f* **2** *v/t* programme replicare

reschedule [riː'ʃedjuːl] stabilire di nuovo

rescue ['reskjuː] **1** *n* salvataggio *m*; **come to s.o.'s ~** andare in aiuto a qu **2** *v/t* salvare

research [rɪ'sɜːtʃ] ricerca *f*; **research and development** ricerca *f* e sviluppo *m*; **research assistant** assistente ricercatore *m*, -trice *f*; **researcher** ricercatore *m*, -trice *f*

resemblance [rɪ'zembləns] somiglianza *f*; **resemble** (as)somigliare a

resent [rɪ'zent] risentirsi per; **resentful** pieno di risentimento; **resentfully** con risentimento; **resentment** risentimento *m*

reservation [rezə'veɪʃn] of *room, table* prenotazione *f*; *mental, special area* riserva *f*; **I have a ~** in *hotel, restaurant* ho prenotato; **reserve 1** *n* (*store*) riserva *f*; (*aloofness*) riserbo *m*; SP riserva *f*; **~s** FIN riserve *fpl*; **keep sth in ~** tenere qc di riserva **2** *v/t seat, table* prenotare; *judgment* riservarsi; **reserved** *person, manner* riservato; *table, seat* prenotato

restful

reservoir ['rezəvwɑː(r)] *for water* bacino *m* idrico

residence ['rezɪdəns] *fml: house etc* residenza *f; (stay)* permanenza *f;* **residence permit** permesso *m* di residenza; **resident** residente *m/f;* **residential** residenziale

residue ['rezɪdjuː] residuo *m*

resign [rɪ'zaɪn] **1** *v/t* position dimettersi da; **~ o.s. to** rassegnarsi a **2** *v/i from job* dimettersi; **resignation** *from job* dimissioni *fpl; mental* rassegnazione *f*

resilient [rɪ'zɪliənt] *personality* che ha molte risorse; *material* resistente

resist [rɪ'zɪst] **1** *v/t* resistere a **2** *v/i* resistere; **resistance** *o* sistenza *f;* **resistant** *material* resistente

resolute ['rezəluːt] risoluto; **resolution** *(decision)* risoluzione *f; made at New Year etc* proposito *m; (determination)* risolutezza *f; of problem* soluzione *f; of image* risoluzione *f*

resort [rɪ'zɔːt] *place* località *f inv; holiday* ~ luogo *m* di villeggiatura; **ski** ~ stazione *f* sciistica; **as a last** ~ come ultima risorsa

♦ **resort to** far ricorso a

♦ **resound with** [rɪ'zaʊnd] risuonare di

resounding [rɪ'zaʊndɪŋ] *success, victory* clamoroso

resource [rɪ'sɔːs] risorsa *f; fi-*

nancial ~s mezzi *mpl* economici; **leave s.o. to his own** ~**s** lasciare qu in balia di se stesso; **resourceful** pieno di risorse

respect [rɪ'spekt] **1** *n* rispetto *m;* **with** ~ **to** riguardo a; **in this / that** ~ quanto a questo; **in many** ~**s** sotto molti aspetti; **pay one's last** ~**s to s.o.** rendere omaggio a qu **2** *v/t* rispettare; **respectability** rispettabilità *f;* **respectable** rispettabile; **respectful** rispettoso; **respectively** rispettivamente

respiration [respɪ'reɪʃn] respirazione *f;* **respirator** MED respiratore *m*

respite ['respaɪt] tregua *f;* **without** ~ senza tregua

respond [rɪ'spɒnd] rispondere; **response** risposta *f*

responsibility [rɪspɒnsɪ'bɪlətɪ] responsabilità *f inv;* **responsible** responsabile **(for** di); *job, position* di responsabilità

rest[1] [rest] **1** *n* riposo *m;* **set s.o.'s mind at** ~ tranquillizzare qu **2** *v/i* riposare; ~ **on** ... *(be based on)* basarsi su ...; *(lean against)* poggiare su ... **3** *v/t (lean, balance)* appoggiare

rest[2] [rest]: **the** ~ il resto *m*

restaurant ['restrɒnt] ristorante *m*

restful ['restful] riposante;

rest home 530

rest home casa *f* di riposo;
restless irrequieto; *have a
~ night* passare una notte
agitata; **restlessly** nervosamente

restoration [restə'reɪʃn] restauro *m*; **restore** *building
etc* restaurare; *(bring back)*
restituire

restrain [rɪ'streɪn] *dog, troops*
frenare; *emotions* reprimere;
~ o.s. trattenersi; **restraint**
(self-control) autocontrollo
m

restrict [rɪ'strɪkt] limitare; **restricted** *view* limitato; **restriction** restrizione *f*

'rest room *Am* gabinetto *m*

result [rɪ'zʌlt] risultato *m*; *as
a ~ of this* in conseguenza di
ciò

◆ **result from** risultare da,
derivare da

◆ **result in** dare luogo a

résumé ['rezumeɪ] *Am* curriculum vitae *m inv*

resume [rɪ'zjuːm] riprendere

resumption [rɪ'zʌmpʃn] ripresa *f*

resurface [riː'sɜːfɪs] **1** *v/t
roads* asfaltare **2** *v/i (reappear)* riaffiorare

Resurrection [rezə'rekʃn]
REL resurrezione *f*

retail ['riːteɪl] **1** *adv* al dettaglio **2** *v/i*: *~ at* essere in vendita a; **retailer** dettagliante
m/f; **retail price** prezzo *m*
al dettaglio

retain [rɪ'teɪn] conservare; re-

tainer FIN onorario *m*

retaliate [rɪ'tælɪeɪt] vendicarsi; **retaliation** rappresaglia *f*

rethink [riː'θɪŋk] riconsiderare

reticence ['retɪsns] riservatezza *f*; **reticent** riservato

retire [rɪ'taɪə(r)] *from work*
andare in pensione; **retired**
in pensione; **retirement** pensione *f*; *act* pensionamento
m; **retirement age** età *f inv*
pensionabile; **retiring** riservato

retort [rɪ'tɔːt] **1** *n* replica *f* **2** *v/t*
replicare

retract [rɪ'trækt] *claws* ritrarre; *undercarriage* far rientrare; *statement* ritrattare

re-'train riqualificarsi

retreat [rɪ'triːt] **1** *v/i* ritirarsi **2**
n MIL ritirata *f*; *place* rifugio
m

retrieve [rɪ'triːv] recuperare;
retriever *dog* cane *m* da riporto

retroactive [retrəʊ'æktɪv] retroattivo; **retroactively** retroattivamente

retrograde ['retrəgreɪd] retrogrado

retrospective [retrə'spekt ɪv]
retrospettiva *f*

return [rɪ'tɜːn] **1** *n* ritorno *m*;
(giving back) restituzione *f*;
COMPUT *(tasto m)* invio *m*;
in tennis risposta *f* al servizio; *(~ ticket)* andata e ritorno *m inv*; *by ~ (of post)* a
stretto giro di posta; *~s*

(*profit*) rendimento *m*; **many happy ~s** (*of the day*) cento di questi giorni; **in ~ for** in cambio di 2 *v/t* (*give back*) restituire; (*put back*) rimettere; *favour, invitation* ricambiare 3 *v/i* (*go back, come back*) ritornare; *of symptoms, doubts etc* ricomparire; **return flight** volo *m* di ritorno; **return ticket** biglietto *m* (di) andata e ritorno

reunification [riːjuːnɪfɪ'keɪ-ʃn] riunificazione *f*

reunion [riː'juːnɪən] riunione *f*; **reunite** riunire

reusable [riː'juːzəbl] riutilizzabile; **reuse** riutilizzare

◆ **rev up** [rev] *engine* far andare su di giri

revaluation [riːvæljʊ'eɪʃn] rivalutazione *f*

reveal [rɪ'viːl] *v/t* (*make visible*) mostrare; (*make known*) rivelare; **revealing** *remark* rivelatore; *dress* scollato; **revelation** rivelazione *f*

revenge [rɪ'vendʒ] vendetta *f*; **take one's ~** vendicarsi

revenue ['revənjuː] reddito *m*

reverberate [rɪ'vɜːbəreɪt] *v/i of sound* rimbombare

revere [rɪ'vɪə(r)] riverire; **reverence** rispetto *m*; **Reverend** REL reverendo *m*; **reverent** riverente

reverse [rɪ'vɜːs] 1 *adj sequence* opposto; **in ~ order** in ordine inverso 2 *n* (*opposite*) contrario *m*; (*back*) ro-

vescio *m*; MOT retromarcia *f* 3 *v/t sequence* invertire; **~ the charges** TELEC telefonare a carico del destinatario 4 *v/i* MOT fare marcia indietro

review [rɪ'vjuː] 1 *n of book, film* recensione *f*, *of troops* rivista *f*, *of situation etc* revisione *f* 2 *v/t book, film* recensire; *troops* passare in rivista; *situation etc* riesaminare

reviewer *of book, film* critico *m*, -a *f*

revise [rɪ'vaɪz] 1 *v/t opinion, text* rivedere; EDU ripassare 2 *v/i* EDU ripassare; **revision** *of opinion, text* revisione *f*; *for exam* ripasso *m*

revival [rɪ'vaɪvl] *of custom, style etc* revival *m inv*; *of patient* ripresa *f*; **revive** 1 *v/t custom, style etc* riportare alla moda; *patient* rianimare 2 *v/i of business etc* riprendersi

revoke [rɪ'vəʊk] *licence* revocare

revolt [rɪ'vəʊlt] 1 *n* rivolta *f* 2 *v/i* ribellarsi; **revolting** schifoso; **revolution** rivoluzione *f*; **revolutionary** 1 *n* POL rivoluzionario *m*, -a *f* 2 *adj* rivoluzionario; **revolutionize** rivoluzionare

revolve [rɪ'vɒlv] ruotare; **revolver** revolver *m inv*

revulsion [rɪ'vʌlʃn] ribrezzo *m*

reward [rɪ'wɔːd] 1 *n financial* ricompensa *f*; *benefit derived* vantaggio *m* **2** *v/t financially* ricompensare; **rewarding** *experience* gratificante

rewind [riːˈwaɪnd] *film, tape* riavvolgere

rewrite [riːˈraɪt] riscrivere

rhetoric [ˈretərɪk] retorica *f*

rheumatism [ˈruːmətɪzm] reumatismo *m*

rhinoceros [raɪˈnɒsərəs] rinoceronte *m*

rhubarb [ˈruːbɑːb] rabarbaro *m*

rhyme [raɪm] **1** *n* rima *f* **2** *v/i* rimare; **~ with** fare rima con

rhythm [ˈrɪðm] ritmo *m*

rib [rɪb] ANAT costola *f*

ribbon [ˈrɪbən] nastro *m*

rice [raɪs] riso *m*

rich [rɪtʃ] **1** *adj* ricco; *food* pesante **2** *n:* **the ~** i ricchi *mpl*; **richly** *deserved* pienamente

ricochet [ˈrɪkəʃeɪ] rimbalzare

rid [rɪd]: **get ~ of** sbarazzarsi di; **riddance!** **good ~!** che liberazione!

ride [raɪd] **1** *n on horse* cavalcata *f*; *in vehicle* giro *m*; *(journey)* viaggio *m*; **do you want a ~ into town?** vuoi uno strappo in città? **2** *v/t* **~ a horse** andare a cavallo; **~ a bike** andare in bicicletta **3** *v/i on horse* andare a cavallo; *on bike* andare; *in vehicle* viaggiare; **rider** *on horse* cavallerizzo *m*, -a *f*; *on bike* ciclista *m/f*

ridge [rɪdʒ] *raised strip* sporgenza *f*; *of mountain* cresta

f; *of roof* punta *f*

ridicule [ˈrɪdɪkjuːl] **1** *n* ridicolo *m* **2** *v/t* ridicolizzare; **ridiculous** ridicolo; **ridiculously** incredibilmente

riding [ˈraɪdɪŋ] *on horseback* equitazione *f*

rifle [ˈraɪfl] fucile *m*

rift [rɪft] *in earth* crepa *f*; *in party etc* spaccatura *f*

rig [rɪg] **1** *n (oil ~)* piattaforma *f* petrolifera **2** *v/t elections* manipolare

right [raɪt] **1** *adj (correct)* esatto; *(proper, just)* giusto; *(suitable)* adatto; *not left* destro; **be ~** *of answer* essere esatto; *of person* avere ragione; *of clock* essere giusto; **put things ~** sistemare le cose **2** *adv (directly)* proprio; *(correctly)* bene; *(completely)* completamente; *not left* a destra; **~ now** *(immediately)* subito; *(at the moment)* adesso **3** *n civil, legal etc* diritto *m*; *not left,* POL destra *f*; **on the ~** *turn to the* ~, **take a ~** girare a destra; **be in the ~** avere ragione; **know ~ from wrong** saper distinguere il bene dal male; **right-angle** angolo *m* retto; **rightful** *owner etc* legittimo; **right-hand drive** MOT guida *f* a destra; *car* auto *f inv* con guida a destra; **righthanded:** **be ~** usare la (mano) destra; **righthand man** braccio *m* destro; **right of way** *in traffic* (diritto *m* di) precedenza *f*; *across land* diritto *m* di accesso; **right wing** POL destra *f*; SP esterno *m* destro; **right-wing** POL di destra; **right winger** POL persona *f* di destra; **right-wing extremism** POL estremismo *m* di destra

rigid ['rɪdʒɪd] *material, principles* rigido; *attitude* inflessibile

rigor *Am* ☞ **rigour**

rigorous ['rɪgərəs] rigoroso; **rigorously** *check* rigorosamente; **rigour** rigore *m*

rile [raɪl] F irritare

rim [rɪm] *of wheel* cerchione *m*; *of cup* orlo *m*; *of spectacles* montatura *f*

ring¹ [rɪŋ] *(circle)* cerchio *m*; *on finger* anello *m*; *in boxing* ring *m inv*, quadrato *m*; *at circus* pista *f*

ring² [rɪŋ] **1** *n of bell* trillo *m*; *of voice* suono *m* **2** *v/t bell* suonare; TELEC chiamare **3** *v/i of bell* suonare

'ringleader capobanda *m inv*; **ring-pull** linguetta *f*

rink [rɪŋk] pista *f* di pattinaggio su ghiaccio

rinse [rɪns] **1** *n for hair colour* cachet *m inv* **2** *v/t* sciacquare

riot ['raɪət] **1** *n* sommossa *f* **2** *v/i* causare disordini; **rioter** dimostrante *m/f*; **riot police** reparti *mpl* (di polizia) antisommossa

rip [rɪp] **1** *n in cloth etc* strappo

m **2** *v/t cloth etc* strappare
♦ **rip off** F *customers* fregare F

ripe [raɪp] *fruit* maturo; **ripen** *of fruit* maturare; **ripeness** *of fruit* maturazione *f*

'rip-off F fregatura *f* F

ripple ['rɪpl] *on water* increspatura *f*

rise [raɪz] **1** *v/i from chair etc* alzarsi; *of sun* sorgere; *of price, temperature* aumentare; *of water level* salire **2** *n aumento m*; *give* **~** *to* dare origine a; *riser: be an early / be a late* **~** essere mattiniero / alzarsi sempre tardi

risk [rɪsk] **1** *n take a* **~** correre un rischio **2** *v/t* rischiare; **risky** rischioso

ritual ['rɪtjuəl] **1** *n* rituale *m* **2** *adj* rituale

rival ['raɪvl] **1** *n* rivale *m/f*, *in business* concorrente *m/f* **2** *v/t* competere con; **rivalry** rivalità *f inv*

river ['rɪvə(r)] fiume *m*; **riverbank** sponda *f* del fiume; **riverbed** letto *m* del fiume; **riverside 1** *adj* sul fiume **2** *n* riva *f* del fiume

riveting ['rɪvɪtɪŋ] avvincente

Riviera [rɪvɪ'eərə]: *the Italian* **~** la riviera (ligure)

road [rəʊd] strada *f*; *it's just down the* **~** è qui vicino; **roadblock** posto *m* di blocco; **road hog** pirata *m* della strada; **road holding** *of vehicle* tenuta *f* di strada; **road**

map carta *f* automobilistica;
road rage *comportamento di estrema aggressività da parte di automobilisti*; **road safety** sicurezza *f* sulle strade; **roadsign** cartello *m* stradale; **roadway** carreggiata *f*; **road works** *npl* lavori *mpl* stradali; **roadworthy** in buono stato di marcia

roam [rəʊm] vagabondare

roar [rɔː(r)] **1** *n of engine* rombo *m*; *of lion* ruggito *m*; *of traffic* fragore *m* **2** *v/i of engine* rombare; *of lion* ruggire; *of person* gridare; **~ with laughter** ridere fragorosamente

roast [rəʊst] **1** *n beef etc* arrosto *m* **2** *v/t arrostire; coffee beans, peanuts* tostare **3** *v/i of food* arrostire; *in hot room, climate* scoppiare di caldo; **roast beef** arrosto *m* di manzo; **roast pork** arrosto *m* di maiale

rob [rɒb] *person, bank* rapinare; **robber** rapinatore *m*, -trice *f*; **robbery** rapina *f*

robe [rəʊb] *of judge* toga *f*; *of priest* tonaca *f*; *Am (dressing gown)* vestaglia *f*

robin [ˈrɒbɪn] pettirosso *m*

robot [ˈrəʊbɒt] robot *m inv*

robust [rəʊˈbʌst] robusto

rock [rɒk] **1** *n* roccia *f*; *MUS* rock *m*; **on the ~s** *drink* con ghiaccio; *marriage* in crisi **2** *v/t baby* cullare; *cradle* far dondolare; *(surprise)* scon-

volgere **3** *v/i on chair* dondolarsi; **rock and roll** rock and roll *m*; **rock band** gruppo *m* rock; **rock-bottom** *prices* bassissimo; **rock bottom: reach ~** toccare il fondo; **rock climber** rocciatore *m*, -trice *f*; **rock climbing** roccia *f*

rocket [ˈrɒkɪt] **1** *n* razzo *m* **2** *v/i of prices etc* salire alle stelle

rocking chair [ˈrɒkɪŋ] sedia *f* a dondolo; **rocking horse** cavallo *m* a dondolo

'rock star rockstar *f inv*

rocky [ˈrɒkɪ] *shore* roccioso; *(shaky)* instabile

rod [rɒd] sbarra *f*; *for fishing* canna *f*

rodent [ˈrəʊdnt] roditore *m*

rogue [rəʊg] briccone *m*, -a *f*

role [rəʊl] ruolo *m*; **role model** modello *m* di comportamento

roll [rəʊl] **1** *n of bread* panino *m*; *of film* rullino *m*; *(list, register)* lista *f* **2** *v/i of ball etc* rotolare; *of boat* dondolare

◆ **roll over 1** *v/i* rigirarsi **2** *v/t person, object* girare; *loan, agreement* rinnovare

'roll call appello *m*; **roller** *for hair* bigodino *m*; **roller blade®** roller blade *m inv*; **roller coaster** montagne *fpl* russe; **roller skate** pattino *m* a rotelle

ROM [rɒm] COMPUT (= *read only memory*) ROM *f inv*

Roman ['rəυmən] **1** adj romano **2** n Romano m, -a f; **Roman Catholic** l n REL cattolico m, -a f **2** adj cattolico

romance [rə'mæns] (affair) storia f d'amore; novel romanzo m rosa; film film m inv d'amore; **romantic** romantico

Rome [rəυm] Roma f

roof [ru:f] tetto m; **roof box** MOT box portabagagli m inv; **roof rack** MOT portabagagli m inv

rookie ['rυki] Am F pivello m

room [ru:m] stanza f; (bedroom) camera f (da letto); (space) posto m; **room clerk** Am receptionist m/f inv; **room mate** Am compagno m, -a f di stanza; in apartment compagno m, -a f di appartamento; **room service** servizio m in camera; **room temperature** temperatura f ambiente; **roomy** house, car etc spazioso; clothes ampio

root [ru:t] radice f

rope [rəυp] corda f, fune f

rosary ['rəυzərɪ] REL rosario m

rose [rəυz] BOT rosa f

roster ['rɒstə(r)] turni mpl; actual document tabella f dei turni

rostrum ['rɒstrəm] podio m

rosy ['rəυzɪ] roseo

rot [rɒt] **1** n marciume m **2** v/i marcire

rotate [rəυ'teɪt] **1** v/i of blades,

earth ruotare **2** v/t girare; crops avvicendare; **rotation** rotazione f; in ~ a turno

rotten ['rɒtn] food, wood etc marcio; F (very bad) schifoso F

rough [rʌf] **1** adj hands, skin, surface ruvido; ground accidentato; (coarse) rozzo; (violent) violento; crossing movimentato; seas grosso; (approximate) approssimativo; ~ **draft** abbozzo m **2** adv: **sleep** ~ dormire all'addiaccio **3** n in golf erba f alta; **roughage** in food fibre fpl; **roughly** (approximately) circa; (harshly) bruscamente; ~ **speaking** grosso modo

roulette [ru:'let] roulette f inv

round [raυnd] **1** adj rotondo **2** n of postman, doctor giro m; of toast fetta f; of drinks giro m; of competition girone m; in boxing match round m inv **3** v/t corner girare **4** adv & prep ☞ **around**

◆ **round up** figure arrotondare; suspects, criminals radunare

roundabout ['raυndəbaυt] **1** adj indiretto **2** n on road rotatoria f; **round-the-world** intorno al mondo; **round trip ticket** Am biglietto m (di) andata e ritorno; **round-up** of cattle raduno m; of suspects, criminals retata f; of news riepilogo m

rouse [raυz] from sleep svegliare; *emotions* risvegliare; **rousing** entusiasmante

route [ru:t] *n of car* itinerario *m*; *of plane, ship* rotta *f*; *of bus* percorso *m*

routine [ru:'ti:n] **1** *adj* abituale **2** *n* routine *f*; **as a matter of ~** *q* abituale

row¹ [rəʊ] *n* (*line*) fila *f*; **5 days in a ~** 5 giorni di fila

row² [rəʊ] *v/t boat* remare

row³ [raʊ] *n* (*quarrel*) litigio *m*; (*noise*) baccano *m*

'rowboat *Am* barca *f* a remi

rowdy ['raʊdɪ] turbolento

'rowing boat barca *f* a remi

royal ['rɔɪəl] reale; **royalty** (*royal persons*) reali *mpl*; *on book, recording* royalty *f inv*

rub [rʌb] sfregare, strofinare

rubber ['rʌbə(r)] **1** *n* gomma *f* **2** *adj* di gomma; **rubber band** elastico *m*

rubbish ['rʌbɪʃ] immondizia *f*; (*poor quality*) porcheria *f*; (*nonsense*) sciocchezza *f*; **rubbish bin** pattumiera *f*

rubble ['rʌbl] macerie *fpl*

ruby ['ru:bɪ] *jewel* rubino *m*

rucksack ['rʌksæk] zaino *m*

rudder ['rʌdə(r)] timone *m*

ruddy ['rʌdɪ] *complexion* rubicondo

rude [ru:d] maleducato; *language* volgare; **it's ~ to ...** è cattiva educazione ...; **rudely** (*impolitely*) scortesemente; **rudeness** maleducazione *f*

rudimentary [ru:dɪ'mentərɪ]

rudimentale; **rudiments** rudimenti *mpl*

rueful ['ru:ful] rassegnato; **ruefully** con aria rassegnata

ruffian ['rʌfɪən] delinquente *m/f*

ruffle ['rʌfl] **1** *n* (*on dress*) gala *f* **2** *v/t hair* scompigliare; *person* turbare; **get ~d** agitarsi

rug [rʌg] tappeto *m*; (*blanket*) coperta *f* (da viaggio)

rugby ['rʌgbɪ] rugby *m*; **rugby league** rugby *m* a tredici; **rugby player** giocatore *m* di rugby; **rugby union** rugby *m* a quindici

rugged ['rʌgɪd] *coastline* frastagliato; *face, features* marcato

ruin ['ru:ɪn] **1** *n* rovina *f* **2** *v/t* rovinare

rule [ru:l] **1** *n of club, game* regola *f*; (*authority*) dominio *m*; *for measuring* metro *m* (a stecche); **as a ~** generalmente **2** *v/t country* governare; **the judge ~d that ...** il giudice ha stabilito che ... **3** *v/i of monarch* regnare

◆ **rule out** escludere

ruler ['ru:lə(r)] *for measuring* righello *m*; *of state* capo *m*; **ruling 1** *n* decisione *f* **2** *adj party* di governo

rum [rʌm] *drink* rum *m inv*

rumble ['rʌmbl] *of stomach* brontolare; *of thunder* rimbombare

rumour, *Am* **rumor** ['ru:-

rural

mə(r)] **1** *n* voce *f* **2** *v/t*: *it is
~ed that ...* corre voce che
...

rump [rʌmp] *of animal* groppa
f

rumple ['rʌmpl] *clothes, paper*
spiegazzare

'**rumpsteak** bistecca *f* di girello

run [rʌn] **1** *n on foot* corsa *f*;
Am in tights sfilatura *f*; *to
go for a ~* andare a correre;
go for a ~ in the car andare
a fare un giro in macchina;
make a ~ for it scappare; *a
criminal on the ~* un evaso,
un'evasa; *in the short ~ / in
the long ~* sulle prime / alla
lunga; *a ~ on the dollar* una
forte richiesta di dollari **2** *v/i
of person, animal* correre; *of
river* scorrere; *of trains, buses*
viaggiare; *of paint, makeup*
sbavare; *of nose* colare; *of
play* tenere il cartellone; *of
software* girare; *of engine,
machine* funzionare; *~ for
President in election* candidarsi alla presidenza **3** *v/t*
correre; *(take part in: race)*
partecipare a; *business, hotel,
project etc* gestire; *software*
lanciare; *car* usare; *risk* correre; *can I ~ you to the station?* ti porto alla stazione?

◆ **run across** *(meet)* imbattersi in

◆ **run away** scappare

◆ **run down 1** *v/t (knock
down)* investire; *(criticize)*

parlare male di; *stocks* ridurre **2** *v/i of battery* scaricarsi

◆ **run into** *(meet)* imbattersi
in; *difficulties* trovare

◆ **run off 1** *v/i* scappare **2** *v/t
(print off)* stampare

◆ **run out** *of contract, time*
scadere; *of supplies* esaurirsi
| I ran out of petrol ho finito
la benzina

◆ **run out of** *patience* perdere; *supplies* rimanere senza;

◆ **run over 1** *v/t (knock down)*
investire; *details* rivedere **2**
v/i of water etc traboccare

◆ **run up** *debts, bill* accumulare

'**runaway** ragazzo *m*, -a *f*
scappato di casa; **run-down**
person debilitato; *area, building* fatiscente

rung [rʌŋ] *of ladder* piolo *m*

runner ['rʌnə(r)] *athlete* velocista *m/f*; **runner beans** fagiolini *mpl*; **runner-up** secondo *m*, -a *f* classificato
(-a); **running 1** *n SP* corsa
f; *of business* gestione *f* **2**
adj: *for two days ~* per due
giorni di seguito; **running
water** acqua *f* corrente; **run-
ny** *substance* liquido; *nose*
che cola; **run-up** SP rincorsa
f; *in the ~ to* nel periodo che
precede; **runway** pista *f*

rupture ['rʌptʃə(r)] **1** *n* rottura
f; MED lacerazione *f*; *(hernia)*
ernia *f* **2** *v/i of pipe etc* scoppiare

rural ['rʊərəl] rurale

ruse [ruːz] stratagemma *m*
rush [rʌʃ] 1 *n* corsa *f*; **do sth in a ~** fare qc di corsa; **be in a ~** andare di fretta 2 *v/t person* mettere fretta a; *meal* mangiare in fretta; **~ s.o. to hospital** portare qu di corsa all'ospedale 3 *v/i* affrettarsi; **rush hour** ora *f* di punta
Russia ['rʌʃə] Russia *f*; **Russian** 1 *adj* russo 2 *n* russo *m*, -a *f*; *language* russo *m*

rust [rʌst] 1 *n* ruggine *f* 2 *v/i* arrugginirsi; **rust-proof** a prova di ruggine
rusty ['rʌstɪ] *also fig* arrugginito
rut [rʌt] *in road* solco *m*; **be in a ~** *fig* essersi fossilizzato
ruthless ['ruːθlɪs] spietato; **ruthlessly** spietatamente; **ruthlessness** spietatezza *f*
rye [raɪ] segale *f*; **rye bread** pane *m* di segale

S

sabotage ['sæbətɑːʒ] 1 *n* sabotaggio *m* 2 *v/t* sabotare; **saboteur** sabotatore *m*, -trice *f*
sachet ['sæʃeɪ] bustina *f*
sack [sæk] 1 *n bag* sacco *m* 2 *v/t* F licenziare
sacred ['seɪkrɪd] sacro
sacrifice ['sækrɪfaɪs] 1 *n also fig* sacrificio *m* 2 *v/t* sacrificare
sacrilege ['sækrɪlɪdʒ] sacrilegio *m*
sad [sæd] triste; *state of affairs* deplorevole
saddle ['sædl] 1 *n* sella *f* 2 *v/t horse* sellare; **~ s.o. with sth** *fig* affibbiare qc a qu
sadism ['seɪdɪzm] sadismo *m*; **sadist** sadista *m/f*; **sadistic** sadistico
sadly ['sædlɪ] tristemente; (*regrettably*) purtroppo; **sadness** tristezza *f*

safe [seɪf] 1 *adj not dangerous* sicuro; *not in danger* al sicuro; *driver* prudente 2 *n* cassaforte *f*; **safeguard** 1 *n* protezione *f*, salvaguardia *f*; **as a ~ against** per proteggersi contro 2 *v/t* proteggere; **safely** *arrive, complete test etc* senza problemi; *drive* prudentemente; *assume* tranquillamente; **safety** sicurezza *f*; **safety pin** spilla *f* di sicurezza
sag [sæg] *of ceiling* incurvarsi; *of rope* allentarsi
saga ['sɑːgə] saga *f*
sage [seɪdʒ] *herb* salvia *f*
Sagittarius [sædʒɪ'teərɪəs] ASTR Sagittario *m*
sail [seɪl] 1 *n of boat* vela *f*; *trip* veleggiata *f*; **go for a ~** fare un giro in barca (a vela) 2 *v/t yacht* pilotare 3 *v/i* fare vela; (*depart*) salpare; **sail-**

board 1 n windsurf m inv **2** v/i fare windsurf; **sailboarding** windsurf m; **sailboat** Am barca f a vela; **sailing** SP vela f; **sailing boat** barca f a vela; **sailor** marinaio m

saint [seɪnt] santo m, -a f

sake [seɪk]: **for my ~** per il mio bene; **for the ~ of** per

salad ['sæləd] insalata f; **salad dressing** condimento m per l'insalata

salary ['sælərɪ] stipendio m

sale [seɪl] vendita f; at reduced prices svendita f, saldi mpl; **for ~** sign in vendita; **be on ~** essere in vendita; **sales department** reparto m vendite; **sales clerk** Am in store commesso m, -a f; **sales figures** fatturato m; **salesman** venditore m; **sales manager** direttore m, -trice f delle vendite; **saleswoman** venditrice f

salient ['seɪlɪənt] saliente

saliva [sə'laɪvə] saliva f

salmon ['sæmən] salmone m

saloon [sə'luːn] (bar) bar m inv; MOT berlina f

salt [sɒlt] sale m; **salty** salato

salute [sə'luːt] **1** n MIL saluto m **2** v/t & v/i salutare

salvage ['sælvɪdʒ] from wreck ricuperare

salvation [sæl'veɪʃn] salvezza f

same [seɪm] **1** adj stesso **2** pron stesso; **the ~** lo stesso, la stessa; **Happy New Year** – **the ~ to you** Buon anno! – grazie e altrettanto!; **it's all the ~ to me** per me è uguale **3** adv: **the ~** allo stesso modo; **look / sound the ~** sembrare uguale

sample ['sɑːmpl] campione m

sanction ['sæŋkʃn] **1** n (approval) approvazione f; (penalty) sanzione f **2** v/t (approve) sancire

sanctity ['sæŋktətɪ] santità f

sand [sænd] **1** n sabbia f **2** v/t with sandpaper smerigliare

sandal ['sændl] sandalo m

sandbag sacchetto m di sabbia; **sand dune** duna f; **sander** tool smerigliatrice f; **sandpaper 1** n carta f smerigliata **2** v/t smerigliare

sandwich ['sænwɪdʒ] tramezzino m

sandy ['sændɪ] beach sabbioso; full of sand pieno di sabbia; hair rossiccio

sane [seɪn] sano di mente

sanitarium [sænɪ'terɪəm] casa f di cura

sanitary ['sænɪtərɪ] conditions igienico; installations assortario; **sanitary towel** assorbente m (igienico); **sanitation** impianti mpl igienici; (removal of waste) fognature fpl

sanity ['sænətɪ] sanità f mentale

Santa Claus ['sæntəklɔːz] Babbo m Natale

sap [sæp] **1** n in tree linfa f **2** v/t

s.o.'s energy indebolire

sapphire ['sæfaɪə(r)] zaffiro
m

sarcasm ['sɑːkæzm] sarcasmo *m*; **sarcastic** sarcastico; **sarcastically** sarcasticamente

sardine [sɑː'diːn] sardina *f*

Sardinia [sɑː'dɪnɪə] Sardegna *f*; **Sardinian 1** *adj* sardo **2** *n* sardo *m*, -a *f*

sardonic [sɑː'dɒnɪk] sardonico

Satan ['seɪtn] Satana *m*

satellite ['sætəlaɪt] satellite *m*; **satellite dish** antenna *f* parabolica; **satellite TV** TV *f inv* satellitare

satin ['sætɪn] satin *m*

satire ['sætaɪə(r)] satira *f*; **satirical** satirico; **satirize** satireggiare

satisfaction [sætɪs'fækʃn] soddisfazione *f*; **satisfactory** soddisfacente; *just good enough* sufficiente; **satisfy** soddisfare; *requirement* rispondere a; *I am satisfied that ...* (*convinced*) sono convinto che ...

Saturday ['sætədeɪ] sabato *m*

sauce [sɔːs] salsa *f*, sugo *m*; **saucepan** pentola *f*; **saucer** piattino *m*

Saudi Arabia [saʊdɪə'reɪbɪə] Arabia *f* Saudita; **Saudi Arabian 1** *adj* saudita **2** *n person* saudita *m/f*

sauna ['sɔːnə] sauna *f*

sausage ['sɒsɪdʒ] salsiccia *f*

savage ['sævɪdʒ] **1** *adj animal* selvaggio; *criticism* feroce **2** *n* selvaggio *m*, -a *f*; **savagery** ferocia *f*

save [seɪv] **1** *v/t* (*rescue*) salvare; *money, time, effort* risparmiare; (*collect*) raccogliere; COMPUT salvare; *goal* parare **2** *v/i* (*put money aside*) risparmiare; SP parare **3** *n* SP parata *f*; **saver** *person* risparmiatore *m*, -trice *f*; **savings** risparmi *mpl*; **savings account** libretto *m* di risparmio; **savings and loan** *Am* istituto *m* di credito immobiliare; **savings bank** cassa *f* di risparmio

saviour, *Am* **savior** ['seɪvjə(r)] REL salvatore *m*

savor *etc Am* ☞ **savour** *etc*

savour ['seɪvə(r)] assaporare; **savoury** *not sweet* salato (*non dolce*)

saw [sɔː] **1** *n tool* sega *f* **2** *v/t* segare; **sawdust** segatura *f*

saxophone ['sæksəfəʊn] sassofono *m*

say [seɪ] dire; *that is to ~* sarebbe a dire; **saying** detto *m*

scab [skæb] *on skin* crosta *f*

scaffolding ['skæfəldɪŋ] impalcature *fpl*

scald [skɔːld] scottare; *~ o.s.* scottarsi

scale¹ [skeɪl] *on fish* scaglia *f*

scale² [skeɪl] **1** *n of map*, MUS scala *f*; *of project* portata *f* **2** *v/t cliffs etc* scalare

scales [skeɪlz] *for weighing*

bilancia *fsg*

scallop ['skɒləp] capasanta *f*

scalp [skælp] cuoio *m* capelluto

scalpel ['skælpl] bisturi *m*

scam [skæm] F truffa *f*

scampi ['skæmpi] gamberoni *mpl* in pastella fritti

scan [skæn] **1** *v/t horizon* scrutare; *page* scorrere; *foetus* fare l'ecografia di; *brain* fare la TAC di; COMPUT scannerizzare **2** *n* (*brain* ~) TAC *f inv*; *of foetus* ecografia *f*

◆ **scan in** COMPUT scannerizzare

scandal ['skændl] scandalo *m*; **scandalize** scandalizzare; **scandalous** scandaloso

scanner ['skænə(r)] scanner *m inv*

scanty ['skænti] *clothes* succinto

scapegoat ['skeipgəut] capro *m* espiatorio

scar [skɑː(r)] **1** *n* cicatrice *f* **2** *v/t face* lasciare cicatrici su; *fig* segnare

scarce [skeəs] *in short supply* scarso; **scarcely** appena; **there was ~ anything left** non rimaneva quasi più niente; **scarcity** scarsità *f inv*

scare [skeə(r)] **1** *v/t* spaventare; **be ~d of** avere paura di **2** *n* (*panic, alarm*) panico *m*; **scaremonger** allarmista *m/f*

scarf [skɑːf] *around neck*

sciarpa *f*; *over head* foulard *m inv*

scarlet ['skɑːlət] scarlatto

scary ['skeəri] che fa paura

scathing ['skeiðiŋ] caustico

scatter ['skætə(r)] **1** *v/t leaflets, seeds* spargere; *crowd* disperdere **2** *v/i of people* disperdersi; **scatterbrained** sventato; **scattered** *family, villages* sparpagliato; **~ showers** precipitazioni sparse

scavenge ['skævindʒ] frugare tra i rifiuti; **scavenger** *animale m* necrofago; *person* persona che fruga tra i rifiuti

scenario [si'nɑːriəu] scenario *m*

scene [siːn] scena *f*; (*argument*) scenata *f*; **make a ~** fare una scenata; **~s** THEA scenografia *f*; **behind the ~s** dietro le quinte; **scenery** paesaggio *m*; THEA scenario *m*

scent [sent] profumo *m*; *of animal* odore *m*

sceptic ['skeptik] scettico *m*, -a *f*; **sceptical** scettico *m*; **scepticism** scetticismo *m*

schedule ['ʃedjuːl] **1** *n of events, work* programma *m*; *for trains* orario *m*; **be on ~** *of work, of train etc* essere in orario; **be behind ~** *of work, of train etc* essere in ritardo **2** *v/t* put on schedule programmare; **scheduled flight** volo *m* di linea

scheme [skiːm] **1** *n* (*plan*) pia-

no *m*; (*plot*) complotto *m* **2**
v/i (*plot*) complottare, tramare; **scheming** intrigante
schizophrenia [skɪtsə'fri:-
nɪə] schizofrenia *f*; **schizo-
phrenic 1** *n* schizofrenico
m, -a *f* **2** *adj* schizofrenico
scholar ['skɒlə(r)] studioso
m, -a *f*; **scholarly** dotto;
scholarship (*scholarly
work*) erudizione *f*; (*financial award*) borsa *f* di studio
school [sku:l] scuola *f*; *Am*
(*university*) università *f inv*;
school bag cartella *f*;
schoolboy scolaro *m*;
schoolchildren scolari
mpl; **school days** tempi
mpl della scuola; **schoolgirl**
scolara *f*; **schoolteacher** insegnante *m/f*
science ['saɪəns] scienza *f*;
science fiction fantascienza
f; **scientific** scientifico; **scientist** scienziato *m*, -a *f*
scissors ['sɪzəz] forbici *fpl*
scoff[1] [skɒf] *v/t food* sbafare
scoff[2] [skɒf] *v/i* (*mock*) canzonare
scold [skəʊld] sgridare
scoop [sku:p] *for grain, flour*
paletta *f*; *for ice cream* cucchiaio *m* dosatore; *of ice
cream* pallina *f*; (*story*) scoop
m inv
scooter ['sku:tə(r)] *with motor* scooter *m inv*; *child's* monopattino *m*
scope [skəʊp] portata *f*; (*freedom, opportunity*) possibilità

f
scorch [skɔ:tʃ] bruciare;
scorching scottante
score [skɔ:(r)] **1** *n* SP punteggio *m*; (*written music*) spartito *m*; *of film etc* colonna *f* sonora; *what's the ~?* SP a
quanto sono / siamo? **2** *v/t
goal, point* segnare; (*cut*) incidere **3** *v/i* segnare; (*keep
the score*) tenere il punteggio; **scoreboard** segnapunti
m inv; **scorer** *of goal, point*
marcatore *m*, -trice *f*
scorn [skɔ:n] **1** *n* disprezzo *m*
2 *v/t idea* disprezzare; **scornful** sprezzante; **scornfully**
sprezzantemente
Scorpio ['skɔ:pɪəʊ] ASTR
Scorpione *m*
Scot [skɒt] scozzese *m/f*;
Scotch (whisky) scotch *m
inv*; **Scotch tape**® *Am*
scotch® *m*; **Scotland** Scozia
f; **Scotsman** scozzese *m*;
Scotswoman scozzese *f*;
Scottish scozzese
scoundrel ['skaʊndrəl] birbante *m/f*
scour ['skaʊə(r)] (*search*) setacciare
scowl [skaʊl] **1** *n* sguardo *m*
torvo **2** *v/i* guardare storto
scramble ['skræmbl] **1** *n*
(*rush*) corsa *f* **2** *v/t message*
rendere indecifrabile **3** *v/i*:
he ~d to his feet si rialzò
in fretta; **scrambled eggs**
uova *fpl* strapazzate
scrap [skræp] **1** *n metal* rotta-

sculpture

me *m*; *(fight)* zuffa *f*; *(little bit)* briciolo *m* **2** *v/t* plan, project abbandonare

scrape [skreip] **1** *n* on paintwork graffio *m* **2** *v/t* paintwork, arm etc graffiare; **~ a living** sbarcare il lunario

'scrap metal rottami *mpl*

scrappy ['skræpi] *work, writing* senza capo né coda

scratch [skrætʃ] **1** *n* mark graffio *m*; **start from ~** ricominciare da zero; **not up to ~** non all'altezza **2** *v/t (mark)* graffiare; *because of itch* grattare **3** *v/i* of cat, nails graffiare

scrawl [skrɔːl] **1** *n* scarabocchio *m* **2** *v/t* scarabocchiare

scrawny ['skrɔːnɪ] scheletrico

scream [skriːm] **1** *n* urlo *m* **2** *v/i* urlare

screech [skriːtʃ] **1** *n* of tyres stridio *m*; *(scream)* strillo *m* **2** *v/i* of tyres stridere; *(scream)* strillare

screen [skriːn] **1** *n* in room, hospital paravento *m*; of smoke cortina *f*; cinema, COMPUT, of television schermo *m* **2** *v/t (protect, hide)* riparare; *film* proiettare; *for security reasons* vagliare; **screenplay** sceneggiatura *f*; **screen saver** COMPUT salvaschermo *m inv*; **screen test** *for movie* provino *m*

screw [skruː] **1** *n* vite *f* (metallica) **2** *v/t* avvitare *(to* a); V scopare V; F *(cheat)* fregare

F; **screwdriver** cacciavite *m*; **screwed up** F *psychologically* complessato; **screw top** *on bottle* tappo *m* a vite; **screwy** F svitato

scribble ['skrɪbl] **1** *n* scarabocchio *m* **2** *v/t & v/i (write quickly)* scarabocchiare

script [skrɪpt] *for film, play* copione *m*; *(form of writing)* scrittura *f*; **scripture: the (Holy) Scriptures** le Sacre Scritture *fpl*; **scriptwriter** sceneggiatore *m*, -trice *f*

◆ **scroll down** [skrəʊl] COMPUT far scorrere il testo in avanti

◆ **scroll up** COMPUT far scorrere il testo indietro

scrounge [skraʊndʒ] scroccare; **scrounger** scroccone *m*, -a *f*

scrub [skrʌb] *floors, hands* sfregare (con spazzola)

scrum [skrʌm] *in rugby* mischia *f*

scruples ['skruːplz] scrupoli *mpl*; **scrupulous** scrupoloso; **scrupulously** *(meticulously)* scrupolosamente

scrutinize ['skruːtɪnaɪz] *text* esaminare attentamente; *face* scrutare; **scrutiny** attento esame *m*

scuba diving ['skuːbə] immersione *f* subacquea

scuffle ['skʌfl] tafferuglio *m*

sculptor ['skʌlptə(r)] scultore *m*, -trice *f*; **sculpture** scultura *f*

scum [skʌm] *on liquid* schiuma *f*; (*pej: people*) feccia *f*

sea [siː] *n* mare *m*; **by the ~** al mare; **seabird** uccello *m* marino; **seafood** frutti *mpl* di mare; **seafront** lungomare *m inv*; **seagull** gabbiano *m*

seal[1] [siːl] *n animal* foca *f*

seal[2] [siːl] **1** *n on document* sigillo *m*; TECH chiusura *f* ermetica **2** *v/t container* chiudere ermeticamente

'sea level: **above / below ~** sopra / sotto il livello del mare

seam [siːm] *on garment* cucitura *f*; *of ore* filone *m*

'seaman marinaio *m*; **seaport** porto *m* marittimo

search [sɜːtʃ] **1** *n for s.o. / sth* ricerca *f*; *of person, building* perquisizione *f* **2** *v/t person, building, baggage* perquisire; *area* perlustrare

◆ **search for** cercare

searching ['sɜːtʃɪŋ] *look* penetrante; **searchlight** riflettore *m*

'seashore riva *f* (del mare); **seasick**: **be ~** avere il mal di mare; **get ~** soffrire il mal di mare; **seaside**: **at the ~** al mare; **~ resort** località *f inv* balneare

season ['siːzn] stagione *f*; **in / out of ~** in / fuori stagione; **seasonal** stagionale; **seasoned** *wood* stagionato; *traveller, campaigner etc*

esperto; **seasoning** condimento *m*; **season ticket** abbonamento *m*

seat [siːt] **1** *n* posto *m*; *of trousers* fondo *m*; POL seggio *m*; **please take a ~** si accomodi **2** *v/t* (*have seating for*) avere posti a sedere per; **seat belt** cintura *f* di sicurezza

'sea urchin riccio *m* di mare; **seaweed** alga *f*

secluded [sɪ'kluːdɪd] appartato

second ['sekənd] **1** *n of time* secondo *m*; **just a ~** un attimo **2** *adj* secondo **3** *adv* come in secondo **4** *v/t motion* appoggiare; **secondary** secondario; **second floor** secondo piano; *Am* primo piano *m*; **second hand** *on clock* lancetta *f* dei secondi; **second-hand** di seconda mano; **secondly** in secondo luogo; **second-rate** di second'ordine; **second thoughts**: **I've had ~ thoughts** ci ho ripensato

secrecy ['siːkrəsɪ] segretezza *f*; **secret 1** *n* segreto *m* **2** *adj* segreto; **secret agent** agente *m* segreto

secretarial [sekrə'teərɪəl] *tasks, job* di segretaria; **secretary** segretario *m*, -a *f*; POL ministro *m*; **Secretary of State** *in USA* Segretario *m* di Stato

secretive ['siːkrətɪv] riservato; **secretly** segretamente;

secret service servizio *m* segreto

sect [sekt] setta *f*

section ['sekʃn] sezione *f*

sector ['sektə(r)] settore *m*

secular ['sekjʊlə(r)] laico

secure [sɪ'kjʊə(r)] **1** *adj shelf etc* saldo *feeling* sicuro; *job* stabile **2** *v/t shelf etc* assicurare; *s.o.'s help, finances* assicurarsi; **securities market** FIN mercato *m* dei titoli; **security** sicurezza *f*; *in relationship* stabilità *f*; *for investment* garanzia *f*; **security alert** stato *m* di allarme; **security-conscious** attento alla sicurezza; **security forces** forze *fpl* di sicurezza; **security guard** guardia *f* giurata; **security risk** minaccia *f* per la sicurezza

sedan [sɪ'dæn] *Am* MOT berlina *f*

sedate [sɪ'deɪt] *patient* somministrare sedativi a; **sedation: be under ~** essere sotto l'effetto di sedativi; **sedative** sedativo *m*

sedentary ['sedəntərɪ] *job* sedentario

sediment ['sedɪmənt] sedimento *m*

seduce [sɪ'djuːs] sedurre; **seduction** seduzione *f*; **seductive** *smile, look* seducente; *offer* allettante

see [siː] vedere; (*understand*) capire; **I'll ~ you to the door** t'accompagno alla porta; **~**

you! F ciao! F

◆ **see off** *at airport etc* salutare; (*chase away*) scacciare

seed [siːd] *single* seme *m*; *collective* semi *mpl*; *in tennis* testa *f* di serie; **seedy** *bar, district* squallido

seeing (that) ['siːɪŋ] visto che

'seeing eye dog® *Am* cane *m* per ciechi

seek [siːk] cercare

seem [siːm] sembrare; **seemingly** apparentemente

seesaw ['siːsɔː] altalena *f* (a bilico)

'see-through trasparente

segment ['segmənt] segmento *m*; *of orange* spicchio *m*

segregate ['segrɪgeɪt] separare; **segregation** segregazione *f*

seismology [saɪz'mɒlədʒɪ] sismologia *f*

seize [siːz] *s.o., s.o.'s arm* afferrare; *power* prendere; *opportunity* cogliere; *of police etc* sequestrare

◆ **seize up** *of engine* grippare

seizure ['siːʒə(r)] MED attacco *m*; *of drugs etc* sequestro *m*

seldom ['seldəm] raramente

select [sɪ'lekt] **1** *v/t* selezionare **2** *adj* (*exclusive*) scelto; **selection** scelta *f*; *that / those chosen* selezione *f*; **selective** selettivo

self [self] io *m*; **self-assurance** sicurezza *f* di sé; **self--assured** sicuro di sé; **self-**

-**catering apartment** appartamento *m* indipendente con cucina; **self-centred**, *Am* **self-centered** egocentrico; **self-confessed** dichiarato; **self-confidence** fiducia *f* in se stessi; **self-confident** sicuro di sé; **self-conscious** insicuro; *smile* imbarazzato; *feel ~* sentirsi a disagio; **self-consciousness** disagio *m*; **self-control** autocontrollo *m*; **self-defence**, *Am* **self-defense** *personal* legittima difesa *f*, *of state* autodifesa *f*; **self-doubt** dubbi *mpl* personali; **self-employed** autonomo; **self-evident** evidente; **self-government** autogoverno *m*

selfie ['selfi] selfie *m*

self-interest interesse *m* personale

selfish egoista; **selfless** *person* altruista; *attitude* altruistico; **self-made man** self-made man *m inv*; **self-pity** autocommiserazione *f*; **self-portrait** autoritratto *m*; **self-reliant** indipendente; **self-respect** dignità *f*; **self-satisfied** *pej* soddisfatto di sé; **self-service** self-service; **self-service restaurant** self-service *m inv*; **self-taught** autodidatta

sell [sel] **1** *v/t* vendere **2** *v/i of products* vendere; **sell-by date** data *f* di scadenza; *be past its ~* essere scaduto;

seller venditore *m*, -trice *f*; **selling** COM vendita *f*; **selling point** COM punto *m* forte (che fa vendere il prodotto)

Sellotape® ['seləteɪp] scotch® *m*

semester [sɪ'mestə(r)] semestre *m*

semi ['semɪ, *Am* 'semaɪ] *Br villa f* bifamiliare; *Am truck* autoarticolato *m*; **semicircle** semicerchio *m*; **semi-colon** punto e virgola *m*; **semiconductor** ELEC semiconduttore *m*; **semidetached (house)** villa *f* bifamiliare; **semifinal** semifinale *f*; **semifinalist** semifinalista *m/f*

seminar ['semɪnɑː(r)] seminario *m*

semi'skilled parzialmente qualificato

senate ['senət] senato *m*; **senator** senatore *m*, -trice *f*

send [send] mandare (*to* a)

♦ **send back** mandare indietro

♦ **send for** *doctor, help* (mandare a) chiamare

♦ **send off** *letter, fax etc* spedire; *footballer* espellere

♦ **send up** (*mock*) prendere in giro

sender ['sendə(r)] *of letter* mittente *m/f*

senile ['siːnaɪl] *pej* rimbambito; **senility** *pej* rimbambimento *m*

senior ['siːnɪə(r)] (*older*) più

anziano; *in rank* di grado superiore; **senior citizen** anziano *m*, -a *f*; **seniority** *in job* anzianità *f*

sensation [sen'seɪʃn] *(feeling)* sensazione *f*; *(surprise event)* scalpore *m*; **be a ~** essere sensazionale; **sensational** sensazionale

sense [sens] **1** *n (meaning)* significato *m*; *(purpose, point, sight, smell etc)* senso *m*; *(common sense)* buonsenso *m*; *(feeling)* sensazione *f*; **come to one's ~s** tornare in sé; **it doesn't make ~** non ha senso; **there's no ~ in trying** non ha senso provare **2** *v/t* sentire; **senseless** *(pointless)* assurdo

sensible ['sensəbl] *person, decision* assennato; *advice* sensato; *clothes, shoes* pratico; **sensibly** assennatamente

sensitive ['sensətɪv] sensibile; **sensitivity** sensibilità *f inv*

sensor ['sensə(r)] sensore *m*

sensual ['sensjʊəl] sensuale; **sensuality** sensualità *f*

sensuous ['sensjʊəs] sensuale

sentence ['sentəns] **1** *n* GRAM frase *f*; LAW condanna *f* **2** *v/t* LAW condannare

sentiment ['sentɪmənt] *(sentimentality)* sentimentalismo *m*; *(opinion)* opinione *f*; **sentimental** sentimentale; **sentimentality** sentimentalismo

m

sentry ['sentrɪ] sentinella *f*

separate 1 ['sepərət] *adj* separato **2** ['sepəreɪt] *v/t* separare **(from** da) **3** ['sepəreɪt] *v/i* of couple separarsi; **separated couple** separato; **separately** separatamente; **separation** separazione *f*

September [sep'tembə(r)] settembre *m*

septic ['septɪk] infetto; **go ~** of wound infettarsi

sequel ['siːkwəl] seguito *m*

sequence ['siːkwəns] sequenza *f*; **in ~** di seguito

Serbia ['sɜːbɪə] Serbia *f*; **Serbian 1** *adj* serbo **2** *n* serbo *m*, -a *f*; *language* serbo *m*

serene [sɪ'riːn] sereno

sergeant ['sɑːdʒənt] sergente *m*

serial ['sɪərɪəl] serial *m inv*; **serialize** *novel on TV* trasmettere a puntate; **serial killer** serial killer *m/f inv*; **serial number** *of product* numero *m* di serie

series ['sɪəriːz] serie *f inv*

serious ['sɪərɪəs] *illness, situation* grave; *person, company* serio; **I'm ~** dico sul serio; **seriously injured** gravemente; *(extremely)* estremamente; **take s.o. ~** prendere sul serio qu; **seriousness** *of situation, illness etc* gravità *f*; *of person* serietà *f*

sermon ['sɜːmən] predica *f*

servant ['sɜːvənt] domestico

m, -a *f*

serve [sɜːv] **1** *n* in tennis servizio *m* **2** *v/t food, customer, one's country* servire; *it ~s you right* ti sta bene **3** *v/i* servire; *as politician etc* prestare servizio; **server** COMPUT server *m inv*; **service 1** *n also in tennis* servizio *m*; *for machine* manutenzione *f*; *for vehicle* revisione *f*; *the ~s* MIL le forze armate **2** *v/t vehicle* revisionare; *machine* fare la manutenzione di; **service charge** servizio *m*; **serviceman** MIL militare *m*; **service provider** COMPUT fornitore *m* di servizi; **service sector** settore *m* terziario; **service station** stazione *f* di servizio; **serving** *of food* porzione *f*

session ['seʃn] *of parliament* sessione *f*; *with consultant etc* seduta *f*

set [set] **1** *n* *of tools* set *m inv*; *of dishes, knives* servizio *m*; *of books* raccolta *f*; *group of people* cerchia *f*; MATH insieme *m*; (THEA: *scenery*) scenografia *f*; *where a film is made, in tennis* set *m inv* **2** *v/t* (*place*) mettere; *film, novel etc* ambientare; *date, time, limit* fissare; *alarm clock* mettere; *broken limb* ingessare; *jewel* montare; ~ *the table* apparecchiare (la tavola); ~ *a task for s.o.* assegnare un compito a qu **3**

v/i of sun tramontare; *of glue* indurirsi **4** *adj ideas* rigido; (*ready*) pronto; *be very ~ in one's ways* essere abitudinario; *~ meal* menù *m inv* fisso

◆ **set off 1** *v/i on journey* partire **2** *v/t explosion* causare; *alarm* far scattare

◆ **set out 1** *v/i on journey* partire **2** *v/t ideas, goods* esporre; *set out to do sth* (*intend*) proporsi di fare qc

◆ **set up 1** *v/t company* fondare; *system* mettere in opera; *equipment, machine* piazzare; F (*frame*) incastrare F **2** *v/i in business* mettersi in affari

'setback contrattempo *m*

settee [se'tiː] divano *m*

setting ['setɪŋ] *of novel etc* ambientazione *f*; *of house* posizione *f*

settle ['setl] **1** *v/i of bird, dust, beer* posarsi; *of building* assestarsi; *to live* stabilirsi **2** *v/t dispute* comporre; *issue, uncertainty* risolvere; *debts, bill* saldare; *nerves, stomach* calmare; *that ~s it!* è deciso!

◆ **settle down** (*stop being noisy*) calmarsi; (*stop wild living*) mettere la testa a posto; *in an area* stabilirsi

◆ **settle for** (*accept*) accontentarsi di

◆ **settle up** (*pay*) regolare i conti; *in hotel etc* pagare il conto

settled ['setld] *weather* stabile; **settlement** *of dispute* composizione *f*; (*payment*) pagamento *m*; **settler** *in new country* colonizzatore *m*, -trice *f*

'set-up (*structure*) organizzazione *f*; (*relationship*) relazione *f*; F (*frameup*) montatura *f*

seven ['sevn] sette; **seventeen** diciassette; **seventeenth** diciassettesimo; **seventh** settimo; **seventieth** settantesimo; **seventy** settanta

sever ['sevə(r)] *arm, cable etc* recidere; *relations* troncare

several ['sevrl] **1** *adj* parecchi **2** *pron* parecchi *m*, -ie *f*

severe [sɪ'vɪə(r)] *illness* grave; *penalty, teacher, face* severo; *winter, weather* rigido; **severely** *punish* severamente; *speak* duramente; *injured, disrupted* gravemente; **severity** *of illness* gravità *f*; *of look etc* durezza *f*; *of penalty* severità *f*; *of winter* rigidità *f*

sew [səʊ] cucire

sewage ['su:ɪdʒ] acque *fpl* di scolo; **sewer** fogna *f*

sewing ['səʊɪŋ] cucito *m*

sex [seks] sesso *m*; **have ~ with** avere rapporti sessuali con; **sexist 1** *adj* sessista **2** *n* sessista *m/f*; **sexual** sessuale; **sexual intercourse** rapporti *mpl* sessuali; **sexuality** sessualità *f*; **sexually** ses-

sualmente; **sexually transmitted disease** malattia *f* venerea; **sexy** sexy *inv*

shabbily ['ʃæbɪlɪ] *dressed* in modo trasandato; *treat* in modo meschino; **shabby** *coat etc* trasandato; *treatment* meschino

shack [ʃæk] baracca *f*

shade [ʃeɪd] **1** *n for lamp* paralume *m*; *of colour* tonalità *f inv*; **in the ~** all'ombra **2** *v/t from sun, light* riparare

shadow ['ʃædəʊ] ombra *f*

shady ['ʃeɪdɪ] *spot* all'ombra; *character* losco

shaft [ʃɑːft] *of axle* albero *m*; *of mine* pozzo *m*

shake [ʃeɪk] **1** *n*: **give sth a good ~** dare una scrollata a qc **2** *v/t* scuotere; *emotionally* sconvolgere; **~ one's head** *in refusal* scuotere la testa; **~ hands with s.o.** stringere la mano a qu **3** *v/i of hands, voice, building* tremare; **shaken** *emotionally* scosso; **shake-up** rimpasto *m*; **shaky** *table etc* traballante; *after illness, shock* debole; *grasp of sth, grammar etc* incerto; *voice, hand* tremante

shall [ʃæl] ◇ *future*: **I ~ do my best** farò del mio meglio ◇ *suggesting*: **~ we go now?** andiamo?

shallow ['ʃæləʊ] *water* poco profondo; *person* superficiale

shambles [ˈʃæmblz] casino *m* F

shame [ʃeɪm] **1** *n* vergogna *f*; *what a ~!* che peccato!; *~ on you!* vergognati! **2** *v/t family etc* svergognare; **shameful** vergognoso; **shameless** svergognato

shampoo [ʃæmˈpuː] shampoo *m inv*

shape [ʃeɪp] **1** *n* forma *f* **2** *v/t clay* dar forma a; *character* forgiare; *the future* determinare; **shapeless** *dress etc* informe; **shapely** *figure* ben fatto

share [ʃeə(r)] **1** *n* parte *f*; FIN azione *f* **2** *v/t* dividere; *s.o.'s feelings* condividere **3** *v/i* dividere; **shareholder** azionista *m/f*

shark [ʃɑːk] squalo *m*

sharp [ʃɑːp] **1** *adj knife* affilato; *mind, pain* acuto; *taste* aspro **2** *adv* MUS in diesis; *at 3 o'clock ~* alle 3 precise; **sharpen** *knife* affilare; *skills* raffinare; **sharp practice** pratiche *fpl* poco oneste

shatter [ˈʃætə(r)] **1** *v/t glass* frantumare; *illusions* distruggere **2** *v/i of glass* frantumarsi; **shattered** F (*exhausted*) esausto; (*very upset*) sconvolto; **shattering** *news, experience* sconvolgente

shave [ʃeɪv] **1** *v/t* radere **2** *v/i* farsi la barba **3** *n*: *have a ~* farsi la barba; *that was a close ~* ce l'abbiamo fatta

per un pelo; **shaven** *head* rasato; **shaver** *electric* rasoio *m*

shawl [ʃɔːl] scialle *m*

she [ʃiː] lei; *~ has three children* ha tre figli; *there ~ is* eccola

shears [ʃɪəz] *for gardening* cesoie *fpl*; *for sewing* forbici *fpl*

sheath [ʃiːθ] *for knife* guaina *f*; *contraceptive* preservativo *m*

shed¹ [ʃed] *v/t blood* spargere; *tears* versare; *leaves* perdere

shed² [ʃed] *n* baracca *f*

sheep [ʃiːp] pecora *f*; **sheepdog** cane *m* pastore; **sheepish** imbarazzato

sheer [ʃɪə(r)] *madness, luxury* puro; *cliffs* lastra *f*

sheet [ʃiːt] *for bed* lenzuolo *m*; *of paper* foglio *m*; *of metal, glass* lastra *f*

shelf [ʃelf] mensola *f*; *shelves* scaffale *msg*, ripiani *mpl*

shell [ʃel] **1** *n of mussel etc* conchiglia *f*; *of egg* guscio *m*; *of tortoise* corazza *f*; MIL granata *f* **2** *v/t peas* sbucciare; MIL bombardare; **shellfire** bombardamento *m*; **shellfish** crostacei *mpl*

shelter [ˈʃeltə(r)] **1** *n* (*refuge*) riparo *m*; *construction* rifugio *m* **2** *v/i* ripararsi **3** *v/t* (*protect*) proteggere; **sheltered** *place* riparato; *lead a ~ life* vivere nella bambagia

shelve [ʃelv] *fig plans* accan-

551 **shopkeeper**

tonare

shepherd ['ʃepəd] pastore *m*
sherry ['ʃeri] sherry *m inv*
shield [ʃiːld] **1** *n* scudo *m*; *sports trophy* scudetto *m*; TECH schermo *m* di protezione *f*; *Am badge of policeman* distintivo *m* **2** *v/t* (*protect*) proteggere
shift [ʃift] **1** *n* (*change*) cambiamento *m*; *period of work* turno *m* **2** *v/t* (*move*) spostare; *stains etc* togliere **3** *v/i* (*move*) spostarsi; *of wind* cambiare direzione; **shift key** COMPUT tasto *m* shift; **shifty** *pej* losco
shimmer ['ʃimə(r)] luccicare
shin [ʃin] stinco *m*
shine [ʃain] **1** *v/i* splendere; *fig: of student etc* brillare **2** *n on shoes etc* lucentezza *f*
shingle ['ʃingl] *on beach* ciottoli *mpl*
shiny ['ʃaini] lucido
ship [ʃip] **1** *n* nave *f* **2** *v/t* (*send*) spedire; (*send by sea*) spedire via mare **3** *v/i of new product* essere spedito; **shipment** carico *m*; **shipowner** armatore *m*; **shipping** (*sea traffic*) navigazione *f*; (*sending*) trasporto *m*; **shipping company** compagnia *f* di navigazione; **shipshape** in perfetto ordine; **shipwreck 1** *n* naufragio *m* **2** *v/t*: **be ~ed** naufragare; **shipyard** cantiere *m* navale
shirker ['ʃɜːkə(r)] scansafatiche *m/f inv*

shirt [ʃɜːt] camicia *f*
shit [ʃit] **1** *n* P merda *f* P; *bad quality goods, work* stronzata *f* P **2** *v/i* cagare P **3** *int* merda P; **shitty** F di merda P
shiver ['ʃivə(r)] rabbrividire
shock [ʃɒk] **1** *n* shock *m inv*; ELEC scossa *f*; *be in* ~ MED essere in stato di shock **2** *v/t* scioccare; **shock absorber** MOT ammortizzatore *m*; **shocking** scandaloso; F (*very bad*) allucinante F
shoddy ['ʃɒdi] *goods* scadente; *behaviour* meschino
shoe [ʃuː] scarpa *f*; **shoe-lace** laccio *m* di scarpa; **shoemaker** calzolaio *m*; **shoe mender** calzolaio *m*; **shoeshop**, *Am* **shoestore** negozio *m* di scarpe
shoot [ʃuːt] **1** *n* BOT germoglio *m* **2** *v/t* sparare; *film* girare; ~ *s.o. in the leg* colpire qu alla gamba
♦ **shoot down** *plane* abbattere
♦ **shoot up** *of prices* salire alle stelle; *of children* crescere molto; *of new buildings etc* spuntare
shooting star ['ʃuːtiŋ] stella *f* cadente
shop [ʃɒp] **1** *n* negozio *m*; *talk* ~ parlare di lavoro **2** *v/i* fare acquisti; *go* ~*ping* andare a fare spese; **shop assistant** commesso *m*, -a *f*; **shopkeeper** negoziante *m/f*;

shoplifter taccheggiatore m, -trice f; **shoplifting** taccheggio m; **shopper** acquirente m/f; **shopping** items spesa f; **go ~** andare a fare spese; **do one's ~** fare la spesa; **shopping bag** borsa f per la spesa; **shopping list** lista f della spesa; **shopping mall** centro m commerciale; **shop window** vetrina f

shore [ʃɔː(r)] riva f; **on ~** not at sea a terra

short [ʃɔːt] **1** adj corto; in height basso; in time breve; **be ~ of** essere a corto di **2** adv: **cut ~** interrompere; **go ~ of** fare a meno di; **in ~** in breve; **shortage** mancanza f; **shortcoming** difetto m; **shortcut** scorciatoia f; **shorten 1** v/t accorciare **2** v/i accorciarsi; **shortfall** deficit m inv; in hours etc mancanza f; **shortlist** of candidates rosa f dei candidati; **short-lived** di breve durata; **shortly** (soon) tra breve; **~ before / after** poco prima / dopo; **shortness** of visit brevità f; in height bassa statura f; **shorts** calzoncini mpl; **shortsighted** also fig miope; **short-sleeved** a maniche corte; **short-staffed** a corto di personale; **short-tempered** irascibile; **short-term** a breve termine; **short wave** RAD onde fpl corte

shot [ʃɒt] from gun sparo m; (photograph) foto f; (injection) puntura f; **like a ~** accept, run off come un razzo; **shotgun** fucile m da caccia

should [ʃʊd]: **what ~ I do?** cosa devo fare?; **you ~n't do that** non dovresti farlo; **you ~ have heard him!** avresti dovuto sentirlo!

shoulder ['ʃəʊldə(r)] ANAT spalla f

shout [ʃaʊt] **1** n grido m, urlo m **2** v/t & v/i gridare, urlare; **shouting** urla fpl

shove [ʃʌv] **1** n spinta f **2** v/t & v/i spingere

shovel ['ʃʌvl] **1** n pala f **2** v/t spalare

show [ʃəʊ] **1** n THEA, TV spettacolo m; (display) manifestazione f; **on ~** at exhibition esposto; **it's all done for ~** pej è tutta una scena **2** v/t passport etc mostrare; interest, emotion dimostrare; at exhibition esporre; film proiettare **3** v/i (be visible) vedersi; **does it ~?** si vede?; **what's ~ing at the cinema?** cosa danno al cinema?

◆ **show in** far entrare

◆ **show off 1** v/t skills mettere in risalto **2** v/i pej mettersi in mostra

◆ **show up 1** v/t shortcomings etc far risaltare **2** v/i F (arrive, turn up) farsi vedere F; (be visible) notarsi

'**show business** il mondo dello spettacolo; **showcase**

vetrinetta *f*; *fig* vetrina *f*;
showdown regolamento *m*
di conti
shower ['ʃaʊə(r)] **1** *n of rain*
acquazzone *m*; *to wash* doccia *f*; ***take a ~*** fare una doccia
2 *v/i* fare la doccia; **shower-
proof** impermeabile
'**showjumping** concorso *m*
ippico; **show-off** *pej* esibizionista *m/f*; **showroom**
show-room *m inv*; **showy**
appariscente
shred [ʃred] **1** *n of paper* stri-
sciolina *f*; *of cloth* brandello
m; *of evidence etc* briciolo *m*
2 *v/t paper* stracciare; *in
cooking* sminuzzare; **shred-
der** *for documents* distrutto-
re *m* di documenti
shrewd [ʃruːd] scaltro; *investment* oculato; **shrewdness**
oculatezza *f*
shriek [ʃriːk] **1** *n* strillo *m* **2** *v/i*
strillare
shrill [ʃrɪl] stridulo
shrimp [ʃrɪmp] gamberetto *m*
shrine [ʃraɪn] santuario *m*
shrink[1] [ʃrɪŋk] *v/i of material*
restringersi; *of support etc* diminuire
shrink[2] [ʃrɪŋk] *n* F (*psychiatrist*) strizzacervelli *m/f inv*
'**shrink-wrapping** *process*
cellofanatura *f*; *material* cel-
lophane® *m*
shrivel ['ʃrɪvl] avvizzire
Shrove 'Tuesday [ʃrəʊv]
martedì *m* grasso
shrub [ʃrʌb] arbusto *m*;

shrubbery arboreto *m*
shrug [ʃrʌg]: **~ *one's
shoulders*** alzare le spalle
shudder ['ʃʌdə(r)] **1** *n of fear,
disgust* brivido *m*; *of earth etc*
tremore *m* **2** *v/i with fear, disgust* rabbrividire; *of earth,
building* tremere; *I ~ to think*
non oso immaginare
shuffle ['ʃʌfl] **1** *v/t cards* mescolare **2** *v/i in walking* stra-
scicare i piedi
shun [ʃʌn] evitare
shut [ʃʌt] **1** *v/t* chiudere **2** *v/i
of door, box* chiudersi; *of
shop, bank* chiudere; *they
were ~* era chiuso
◆ **shut down 1** *v/t business*
chiudere; *computer* spegnere
2 *v/i of business* chiudere i
battenti; *of computer* spegnersi
◆ **shut up** F (*be quiet*) star
zitto; *shut up!* zitto!
shutter ['ʃʌtə(r)] *on window*
battente *m*; PHOT otturatore
m
'**shuttlebus** bus *m inv* navetta
shy [ʃaɪ] timido; **shyness** timidezza *f*
Sicilian [sɪ'sɪlɪən] **1** *adj* siciliano **2** *n* siciliano *m*, -a *f*; **Sicily**
Sicilia *f*
sick [sɪk] malato; *sense of humour* crudele; *I feel ~ about
to vomit* ho la nausea; *be ~*
(*vomit*) vomitare; *be ~ of*
(*fed up with*) essere stufo di
sicken ['sɪkn] **1** *v/t* (*disgust*) disgustare; *Am* (*make ill*) fare

ammalare **2** v/i: *be ~ing for sth* covare qc; **sickening** disgustoso; **sick leave:** *be on ~* essere in (congedo per) malattia; **sickness** malattia *f*; (*vomiting*) nausea *f*

side [saɪd] *of box, house* lato *m*; *of person, mountain* fianco *m*; *of page, record* facciata *f*; SP squadra *f*; *take ~s* (*favour one side*) prendere posizione; *I'm on your ~* sono dalla tua (parte); *~ by ~* fianco a fianco; *at the ~ of the road* sul ciglio della strada; *on the small ~* piuttosto piccolo; **sideboard** *furniture* credenza *f*; **side effect** effetto *m* collaterale; **sideline 1** *n* attività *f inv* collaterale **2** v/t: *feel ~d* sentirsi sminuito; **sidestep** scansare; *fig* schivare; **side street** via *f* laterale; **sidewalk** *Am* marciapiede *m*; **sideways** di lato

siege [siːdʒ] assedio *m*; *lay ~ to* assediare

sieve [sɪv] setaccio *m*

sift [sɪft] setacciare

sigh [saɪ] **1** *n* sospiro *m* **2** v/i sospirare

sight [saɪt] vista *f*; *~s of city* luoghi *mpl* da visitare; *catch ~ of* intravedere; *know by ~* conoscere di vista; *be within ~ of* essere visibile da; *out of ~* non visibile; *lose ~ of* main objective etc perdere di vista; **sightseeing** visita *f* turistica; *go ~* fare un giro turisti-

co; **sightseer** turista *m/f*

sign [saɪn] **1** *n* (*indication*) segno *m*; (*road* ~) segnale *m*; *outside shop* insegna *f* **2** v/t & v/i *document* firmare

signal ['sɪɡnl] **1** *n* segnale *m* **2** v/i *of driver* segnalare

signatory ['sɪɡnətrɪ] firmatario *m*, -a *f*

signature ['sɪɡnətʃə(r)] firma *f*

significance [sɪɡ'nɪfɪkəns] importanza *f*; (*meaning*) significato *m*; **significant** *event etc* significativo; (*quite large*) notevole; **significantly** *larger, more expensive* notevolmente

signify ['sɪɡnɪfaɪ] significare

'**sign language** linguaggio *m* dei segni; **signpost** cartello *m* stradale

silence ['saɪləns] **1** *n* silenzio *m* **2** v/t mettere a tacere; **silencer** MOT marmitta *f*; **silent** silenzioso; *film* muto; *stay ~ not comment* tacere

silhouette [sɪluː'et] sagoma *f*

silicon ['sɪlɪkən] silicio *m*

silicone ['sɪlɪkəʊn] silicone *m*

silk [sɪlk] **1** *n* seta *f* **2** *adj shirt etc* di seta; **silky** setoso

silliness ['sɪlɪnɪs] stupidità *f*; **silly** stupido

silo ['saɪləʊ] silo *m*

silver ['sɪlvə(r)] **1** *n* argento *m*; *objects* argenteria *f* **2** *adj ring* d'argento; *colour* argentato; **silverware** argenteria *f*

similar ['sɪmɪlə(r)] simile (*to*

a); **similarity** rassomiglianza *f*; **similarly** allo stesso modo

simple ['sɪmpl] semplice; *person* sempliciotto; **simple-minded** *pej* sempliciotto; **simplicity** semplicità *f*; **simplify** semplificare; **simplistic** semplicistico; **simply** (*absolutely*) assolutamente; *in a simple way* semplicemente

simultaneous [sɪml'teɪnɪəs] simultaneo; **simultaneously** simultaneamente

sin [sɪn] **1** *n* peccato *m* **2** *v/i* peccare

since [sɪns] **1** *prep* da; **~ last week** dalla scorsa settimana **2** *adv* da allora; *I haven't seen him ~* non lo vedo da allora **3** *conj* in expressions of time da quando; (*seeing that*) visto che

sincere [sɪn'sɪə(r)] sincero; **sincerely** con sincerità; *hope* sinceramente; *Yours ~* Distinti saluti; **sincerity** sincerità *f*

sinful ['sɪnfʊl] peccaminoso

sing [sɪŋ] cantare

singe [sɪndʒ] bruciacchiare

singer ['sɪŋə(r)] cantante *m/f*

single ['sɪŋgl] **1** *adj* (*sole*) solo; (*not double*) singolo; *bed, sheet* a una piazza; (*not married*) single; *with reference to Europe* unico; *there wasn't a ~ ...* non c'era nemmeno un ...; *in ~ file* in fila indiana **2** *n* MUS singolo *m*; (*~ room*) (camera *f*) singola *f*; *ticket*

biglietto *m* di sola andata; *person* single *m/f inv*; **~s** *in tennis* singolo; **single-handed** da solo; **single-minded** determinato; **single mother** ragazza *f* madre; **single parent** genitore *m* single; **single parent family** famiglia *f* monoparentale; **single room** (camera *f*) singola *f*

singular ['sɪŋgjʊlə(r)] GRAM **1** *adj* singolare **2** *n* singolare *m*

sinister ['sɪnɪstə(r)] sinistro

sink [sɪŋk] **1** *n* lavandino *m* **2** *v/i of ship* affondare; *of object* andare a fondo; *of sun* calare; *of interest rates etc* scendere **3** *v/t ship* (far) affondare; *funds* investire

♦ **sink in** *of liquid* penetrare; *it still hasn't really sunk in of realization* ancora non mi rendo conto

sinner ['sɪnə(r)] peccatore *m*, -trice *f*

sinusitis [saɪnə'saɪtɪs] MED sinusite *f*

sip [sɪp] **1** *n* sorso *m* **2** *v/t* sorseggiare

sir [sɜː(r)] signore *m*; *Sir Charles* Sir Charles

siren ['saɪrən] sirena *f*

sirloin ['sɜːlɔɪn] controfiletto *m*

sister ['sɪstə(r)] sorella *f*; *in hospital* (infermiera *f*) caposala *f*; **sister-in-law** cognata *f*

sit [sɪt] **1** *v/i* sedere; (*sit down*)

sedersi **2** *v/t exam* dare
◆ **sit down** sedersi
sitcom ['sɪtkɒm] sitcom *f inv*
site [saɪt] **1** *n* luogo *m* **2** *v/t
new offices etc* situare
sitting ['sɪtɪŋ] *of committee,
court* sessione *f; for artist* seduta *f; for meals* turno *m*; **sitting room** salotto *m*
situated ['sɪtjʋeɪtɪd] situato;
be ~ trovarsi; **situation** situazione *f; of building etc* posizione *f*
six [sɪks] sei; **sixteen** sedici;
sixteenth sedicesimo; **sixth**
sesto; **sixtieth** sessantesimo;
sixty sessanta
size [saɪz] dimensioni *fpl; of
clothes* taglia *f,* misura *f; of
shoes* numero *m*; **sizeable**
considerevole
skate [skeɪt] **1** *n* pattino *m* **2**
v/i pattinare; **skateboard**
skateboard *m inv;* **skate-
boarding** skateboard *m;*
skater pattinatore *m,* -trice
f; **skating** pattinaggio *m;*
skating rink pista *f* di pattinaggio
skeleton ['skelɪtn] scheletro
m
skeptic *Am* ☞ **sceptic**
sketch [sketʃ] **1** *n* abbozzo *m;*
THEA sketch *m inv* **2** *v/t* abbozzare; **sketchy** *knowledge
etc* lacunoso
ski [skiː] **1** *n* sci *m inv* **2** *v/i* sciare
skid [skɪd] **1** *n* sbandata *f* **2** *v/i*
sbandare

skier ['skiːə(r)] sciatore *m,*
-trice *f;* **skiing** sci *m;* **go ~**
andare a sciare; **ski instructor** maestro *m,* -a *f* di sci
skilful, *Am* **skillful** ['skɪlfʊl]
abile; **skilfully,** *Am* **skillfully**
abilmente
'ski lift impianto *m* di risalita
skill [skɪl] abilità *f inv;* **what
~s do you have?** quali capacità possiede?; **skilled** abile;
skillful *Am* ☞ **skilful**
skim [skɪm] *surface* sfiorare;
milk scremare
skimpy ['skɪmpɪ] *account etc*
scarso; *dress* succinto
skin [skɪn] **1** *n* pelle *f; of
fruit* buccia *f* **2** *v/t* scoiare;
skin diving immersioni *fpl*
subacquee
skinny ['skɪnɪ] magro; **skin-
tight** aderente
skip [skɪp] **1** *n little jump* salto
m **2** *v/i* saltellare; *with skip-
ping rope* saltare **3** *v/t (omit)*
saltare
'ski pole racchetta *f* da sci
skipper ['skɪpə(r)] NAUT skipper *m inv; of team* capitano
m
'ski resort stazione *f* sciistica
skirt [skɜːt] gonna *f;* **skirting
board** battiscopa *m inv*
'ski run pista *f* da sci; **ski tow**
sciovia *f*
skull [skʌl] cranio *m*
skunk [skʌŋk] moffetta *f*
sky [skaɪ] cielo *m;* **skylight** lu-
cernario *m;* **skyline** profilo
m (contro il cielo); **sky-**

slide

scraper grattacielo *m*
slab [slæb] *of stone* lastra *f; of cake etc* fetta *f*
slack [slæk] *rope* allentato; *person, work* negligente; *period* lento; **slacken** *rope* allentare; *pace* rallentare; **slacks** pantaloni *mpl* casual
◆ **slag off** [slæg] P parlare male di
slam [slæm] *door* sbattere
slander ['slɑːndə(r)] **1** *n* diffamazione *f* **2** *v/t* diffamare; **slanderous** diffamatorio
slang [slæŋ] slang *m inv; of a specific group* gergo *m*
slant [slɑːnt] **1** *v/i* pendere **2** *n* pendenza *f; given to a story* angolazione *f;* **slanting** *roof* spiovente
slap [slæp] **1** *n blow* schiaffo *m* **2** *v/t* schiaffeggiare; **slap-dash** *work* frettoloso; *person* pressappochista; **slap-up** *meal* F pranzo *m* coi fiocchi
slash [slæʃ] **1** *n cut* taglio *m; in punctuation* barra *f* **2** *v/t skin, painting* squarciare; *prices* abbattere
slaughter ['slɔːtə(r)] **1** *n of animals* macellazione *f; of people, troops* massacro *m* **2** *v/t animals* macellare; *people, troops* massacrare; **slaughterhouse** macello *m*
slave [sleɪv] schiavo *m*, -a *f*
slay [sleɪ] ammazzare; **slaying** *Am (murder)* omicidio *m*
sleaze [sliːz] POL corruzione *f*; **sleazy** *bar, characters* sordido

sleep [sliːp] **1** *n* sonno *m;* **go to** ~ addormentarsi; *I couldn't get to* ~ non sono riuscito a dormire **2** *v/i* dormire
◆ **sleep in** *(have a long lie)* dormire fino a tardi
◆ **sleep on** *proposal, decision* dormire su; *sleep on it* dormirci su
◆ **sleep with** *(have sex with)* andare a letto con
sleeping bag ['sliːpɪŋ] sacco *m* a pelo; **sleeping car** RAIL vagone *m* letto; **sleeping pill** sonnifero *m;* **sleepless night** in bianco; **sleep walker** sonnambulo *m*, -a *f;* **sleep walking** sonnambulismo *m;* **sleepy** *child* assonnato; *town* addormentato; *I'm* ~ ho sonno
◆ **sleet** [sliːt] nevischio *m*
sleeve [sliːv] *of jacket etc* manica *f;* **sleeveless** senza maniche
sleight of 'hand [slaɪt] gioco *m* di prestigio
slender ['slendə(r)] snello; *chance, margin* piccolo
slice [slaɪs] **1** *n also fig* fetta *f* **2** *v/t loaf etc* affettare
slick [slɪk] **1** *adj performance* brillante; *(pej: cunning)* scaltro **2** *n of oil* chiazza *f* di petrolio
slide [slaɪd] **1** *n for kids* scivolo *m;* PHOT diapositiva *f* **2** *v/i* scivolare; *of exchange rate etc*

calare **3** v/t far scivolare

slight [slaɪt] **1** adj person, figure gracile; (small) leggero; **no, not in the ~est** no, per nulla **2** n (insult) offesa f; **slightly** leggermente

slim [slɪm] **1** adj slanciato; chance gracile **2** v/i dimagrire; **I'm ~ming** sono a dieta

slime [slaɪm] melma f; **slimy** liquid melmoso; person viscido

sling [slɪŋ] **1** n for arm fascia f a tracolla **2** v/t (throw) lanciare

slip [slɪp] **1** n (mistake) errore m **2** v/i on ice etc scivolare; of quality etc peggiorare; **he ~ped out of the room** è sgattaiolato fuori dalla stanza **3** v/t (put) far scivolare; **it ~ped my mind** mi è passato di mente

♦ **slip up** (make a mistake) sbagliarsi

slipped 'disc [slɪpt] ernia f del disco

slipper ['slɪpə(r)] pantofola f

slippery ['slɪpərɪ] scivoloso

'slip road rampa f di accesso; **slip-up** (mistake) errore m

slit [slɪt] **1** n (tear) strappo m; (hole) fessura f; in skirt spacco m **2** v/t envelope, packet aprire (tagliando); throat tagliare

sliver ['slɪvə(r)] scheggia f

slob [slɒb] pej sudicione m, -a f

slog [slɒg] faticata f

slogan ['sləʊgən] slogan m inv

slop [slɒp] rovesciare, versare

slope [sləʊp] **1** n pendenza f; of mountain pendio m **2** v/i essere inclinato; **the road ~s down to the sea** la strada scende fino al mare

sloppy ['slɒpɪ] work, editing trascurato; in dressing sciatto; (too sentimental) sdolcinato

slot [slɒt] fessura f; in schedule spazio m; **slot machine** for vending distributore m automatico; for gambling slot-machine f inv

Slovak ['sləʊvæk] **1** adj slovacco **2** n slovacco m, -a f; language slovacco m; **Slovakia** Slovacchia f

Slovene ['sləʊviːn] **1** adj sloveno **2** n sloveno m, -a f; language sloveno m; **Slovenia** Slovenia f

slovenly ['slʌvnlɪ] sciatto

slow [sləʊ] lento; **be ~** of clock essere indietro

♦ **slow down** rallentare

'slowcoach F lumaca f F; **slowdown** in production rallentamento m; **slowly** lentamente; **slow motion: in ~** al rallentatore; **slowness** lentezza f

sluggish ['slʌgɪʃ] lento

slum [slʌm] slum m inv

slump [slʌmp] **1** n in trade crollo m **2** v/i economically crollare; of person accasciar-

si
slur [slɜː(r)] **1** n calunnia f **2** v/t words biascicare

slush [slʌʃ] fanghiglia f; (pej: sentimental stuff) smancerie fpl; **slush fund** fondi mpl neri

slut [slʌt] pej sgualdrina f

sly [slaɪ] scaltro

smack [smæk] **1** n on the bottom sculacciata f; in the face schiaffo m **2** v/t child picchiare; bottom sculacciare

small [smɔːl] **1** adj piccolo **2** n: **the ~ of the back** le reni; **small change** spiccioli mpl; **small hours: the ~** le ore fpl piccole; **small talk** conversazione f di circostanza

smart¹ [smɑːt] adj (elegant) elegante; (intelligent) intelligente; pace svelto; **get ~ with** fare il furbo con F

smart² [smɑːt] v/i (hurt) bruciare

'smart card smart card f inv; **smartly** dressed elegantemente; **smartphone** ['smɑːtfəʊn] smartphone m

smash [smæʃ] **1** n noise fracasso m; (car crash) scontro m; in tennis schiacciata f **2** v/t break spaccare; hit hard sbattere; **~ sth to pieces** mandare in frantumi qc **3** v/i break frantumarsi

smattering ['smætərɪŋ] of a language infarinatura f

smear [smɪə(r)] **1** n of ink etc

macchia f; MED striscio m; on character calunnia f **2** v/t character calunniare

smell [smel] **1** n odore m; **sense of ~** olfatto m, odorato m **2** v/t sentire odore di; test by smelling sentire **3** v/i unpleasantly puzzare; (sniff) odorare; **what does it ~ of?** che odore ha?; **you ~ of beer** puzzi di birra; **smelly** puzzolente

smile [smaɪl] **1** n sorriso m **2** v/i sorridere

smirk [smɜːk] sorriso m compiaciuto

smoke [sməʊk] **1** n fumo m; **have a ~** fumare **2** v/t cigarettes etc fumare; bacon affumicare **3** v/i fumare; **smoke-free** totalmente non smoking; **smoker** fumatore m, -trice f; **smoking** fumo m; **no ~** vietato fumare; **smoky** room, air pieno di fumo

smolder Am → **smoulder**

smooth [smuːð] **1** adj surface, skin, sea liscio; sea calmo; transition senza problemi; pej: person mellifluo **2** v/t hair lisciare; **smoothly** without problems senza problemi

smother ['smʌðə(r)] flames, person soffocare

smoulder ['sməʊldə(r)] cova re sotto la cenere

smudge [smʌdʒ] **1** n sbavatura f **2** v/t sbavare

smug [smʌɡ] compiaciuto

smuggle ['smʌgl] contrabbandare; **smuggler** contrabbandiere *m*, -a *f*; **smuggling**
contrabbando *m*

smutty ['smʌtɪ] *joke* sconcio

snack [snæk] spuntino *m*

snag [snæg] (*problem*) problema *m*

snail [sneɪl] chiocciola *f*, *in
cooking* lumaca *f*; **snail mail**
F posta *f* lumaca

snake [sneɪk] serpente *m*

snap [snæp] **1** *n* sound botto
m; PHOT foto *f* **2** *v/t break*
spezzare; (*say sharply*) dire
bruscamente **3** *v/i break*
spezzarsi **4** *adj decision* immediato; **snappy** *person,
mood* irritabile; F (*quick*) rapido; (*elegant*) elegante;
snapshot istantanea *f*

snarl [snɑːl] **1** *n of dog* ringhio
m **2** *v/i* ringhiare

snatch [snætʃ] afferrare;
(*steal*) scippare; (*kidnap*) rapire

snazzy ['snæzɪ] F chic *inv*

sneakers ['sniːkəz] *Am* scarpe *fpl* da ginnastica

sneaky ['sniːkɪ] F (*crafty*)
scaltro

sneer [snɪə(r)] **1** *n* sogghigno
m **2** *v/i* sogghignare

sneeze [sniːz] **1** *n* starnuto *m*
2 *v/i* starnutire

snicker ['snɪkə(r)] ridacchiare

sniff [snɪf] **1** *v/i to clear nose*
tirare su col naso; *of dog* fiutare **2** *v/t smell* annusare

sniper ['snaɪpə(r)] cecchino *m*

snivel ['snɪvl] *pej* frignare

snob [snɒb] snob *m/f inv*;
snobbery snobismo *m*;
snobbish snob *inv*

♦ **snoop around** [snuːp] fic-
canasare

snooty [snuːtɪ] snob *inv*

snooze [snuːz] **1** *n* sonnellino
m; **have a ~** fare un sonnellino **2** *v/i* sonnecchiare

snore [snɔː(r)] russare; **snor-
ing** russare *m*

snorkel ['snɔːkl] boccaglio *m*

snort [snɔːt] sbuffare

snow [snəʊ] **1** *n* neve *f* **2** *v/i*
nevicare

♦ **snow under**: **be snowed
under with ...** essere sommerso di ...

snowball palla *f* di neve;
snow chains *npl* MOT cate-
ne *fpl* da neve; **snowdrift** cumulo *m* di neve; **snowflake**
fiocco *m* di neve; **snowman**
pupazzo *m* di neve; **snow-
plough**, *Am* **snowplow**
spazzaneve *m inv*; **snowstorm** tormenta *f*; **snowy**
weather nevoso; *roofs, hills*
innevato

snub [snʌb] **1** *n* affronto *m*
2 *v/t* snobbare; **snub-nosed**
col naso all'insù

snug [snʌg] al calduccio;
(*tight-fitting*) attillato

so [səʊ] **1** *adv* cosi; **~ hot** cosi
caldo; **not ~ much** non cosi
tanto; **~ much easier** molto
più facile; **I miss you ~** mi

manchi tanto; **~ am / do I** anch'io; **and ~ on** e così via **2** *pron*: **I hope ~** spero di sì; **I don't think ~** non credo, credo di no **50 or ~** circa 50 **3** *conj (for that reason)* così; *(in order that)* così che; **~ (that) I could come too** così che potessi venire anch'io; **~ what?** E e allora?

soak [səʊk] *(steep)* mettere a bagno; *of water* inzuppare; **soaked** fradicio; **soaking (wet)** bagnato fradicio

soap [səʊp] *for washing* sapone *m*; **soap (opera)** soap (opera) *f inv*, telenovela *f*; **soapy** *water* saponato

soar [sɔː(r)] *of rocket etc* innalzarsi; *of prices* aumentare vertiginosamente

sob [sɒb] **1** *n* singhiozzo *m* **2** *v/i* singhiozzare

sober ['səʊbə(r)] sobrio; *(serious)* serio

♦ **sober up** smaltire la sbornia

so-'called cosiddetto

soccer ['sɒkə(r)] calcio *m*

sociable ['səʊʃəbl] socievole

social ['səʊʃl] sociale; **social democrat** socialdemocratico *m*, *-a f*; **socialism** socialismo *m*; **socialist 1** *adj* socialista **2** *n* socialista *m/f*; **socialize** socializzare; **social life** vita *f* sociale; **social science** scienza *f* sociale; **social security** sussidio *m* della previdenza sociale; **social**

work assistenza *f* sociale; **social worker** assistente *m/f* sociale

society [sə'saɪətɪ] società *f inv*; *(organization)* associazione *f*

sociologist [səʊsɪ'ɒlədʒɪst] sociologo *m*, *-a f*; **sociology** sociologia *f*

sock[1] [sɒk] *n* calzino *m*

sock[2] [sɒk] *v/t* F *(punch)* dare un pugno a

socket ['sɒkɪt] *for light bulb* portalampada *m inv*; *in wall* presa *f* (di corrente); *of eye* orbita *f*

soda ['səʊdə] *(~ water)* seltz *m inv*; *Am* bibita *f* analcolica

sofa ['səʊfə] divano *m*

soft [sɒft] *pillow* soffice; *chair, skin* morbido; *light, colour* tenue; *music* soft *inv*; *voice* sommesso; *(lenient)* indulgente; **soft drink** bibita *f*; **soft drug** droga *f* leggera; **soften** *butter etc* ammorbidire; *position* attenuare; *impact, blow* attutire; **softly** *speak* sommessamente; **software** software *m*

soggy ['sɒgɪ] molle e pesante

soil [sɔɪl] **1** *n (earth)* terra *f* **2** *v/t* sporcare

solar energy ['səʊlə(r)] energia *f* solare; **solar panel** pannello *m* solare

soldier ['səʊldʒə(r)] soldato *m*

sole[1] [səʊl] *n of foot* pianta *f* (del piede); *of shoe* suola *f*

sole² ['səʊl] *adj* unico; (*exclusive*) esclusivo

solely ['səʊlɪ] solamente

solemn ['sɒləm] solenne; **solemnity** solennità *f inv*; **solemnly** solennemente

solicit [sə'lɪsɪt] *of prostitute* adescare; **solicitor** avvocato *m*

solid ['sɒlɪd] (*hard*) solido; (*without holes*) compatto; *gold, silver* massiccio; (*sturdy*) robusto; *evidence* concreto; *support* forte; **solidarity** solidarietà *f*

solitaire ['sɒlɪteə(r)] *card game* solitario *m*

solitary ['sɒlɪtərɪ] *life, activity* solitario; (*single*) solo; **solitude** solitudine *f*

solo ['səʊləʊ] **1** *n* MUS assolo *m* **2** *adj performance* solista; **soloist** solista *m/f*

soluble ['sɒljʊbl] *substance* solubile; *problem* risolvibile; **solution** soluzione *f*

solve [sɒlv] risolvere; **solvent** *financially* solvibile

sombre, *Am* **somber** ['sɒmbə(r)] (*dark*) scuro; (*serious*) tetro

some [sʌm] **1** *adj* (*amount*) un po' di, del; (*number*) qualche, dei *m*, delle *f*; ~ **people say that** ... alcuni dicono che ... **2** *pron* (*amount*) un po'; (*number*) alcuni *m*, -e *f*; **would you like** ~? ne vuoi un po'?; ~ **of the students** alcuni studenti; **somebody**

qualcuno; **someday** un giorno; **somehow** (*by one means or another*) in qualche modo; (*for some unknown reason*) per qualche motivo; **someone** ☞ **somebody**; **someplace** ☞ **somewhere**

somersault ['sʌməsɔːlt] **1** *n* capriola *f* **2** *v/i* fare una capriola

'something qualcosa; **sometime** (*one of these days*) uno di questi giorni; ~ **last year** l'anno scorso; **sometimes** a volte; **somewhat** piuttosto; **somewhere 1** *adv* da qualche parte **2** *pron* un posto; **let's go** ~ **quiet** andiamo in un posto tranquillo

son [sʌn] figlio *m*

song [sɒŋ] canzone *f*; *of birds* canto *m*

'son-in-law genero *m*; **son of a bitch** V figlio *m* di puttana P

soon [suːn] presto; **as** ~ **as** non appena; **as** ~ **as possible** prima possibile; ~**er or later** presto o tardi; **the** ~**er the better** prima è, meglio è; **how** ~ **can you be ready?** fra quanto sei pronto?

soothe [suːð] calmare

sophisticated [sə'fɪstɪkeɪtɪd] sofisticato; **sophistication** *of person* raffinatezza *f*; *of machine* complessità *f*

sophomore ['sɒfəmɔːr] *Am* studente *m/f* del secondo anno

soprano [sə'prɑːnəʊ] soprano *m/f*

sordid ['sɔːdɪd] sordido

sore [sɔː(r)] **1** *adj* (*painful*) dolorante; *is it ~?* fa male? **2** *n* piaga *f*; **sore throat** mal *m* di gola

sorrow ['sɒrəʊ] dispiacere *m*, dolore *m*

sorry ['sɒrɪ] *day, sight* triste; (*I'm*) *~!* apologizing scusa!; *polite form* scusi!; *I'm ~ regretting* mi dispiace; *I feel ~ for her* mi dispiace per lei

sort [sɔːt] **1** *n* tipo *m*; *~ of ...* un po' ...; *is it finished? - ~ of* F è terminato? quasi **2** *v/t* separare; COMPUT ordinare

SOS [esəʊ'es] SOS *m inv*

so-'so F così così

soul [səʊl] anima *f*; *the poor ~* il poverino, la poverina

sound[1] [saʊnd] **1** *adj* (*sensible*) valido; (*healthy*) sano; *sleep* profondo; *structure* solido **2** *adv*: *be ~ asleep* dormire profondamente

sound[2] [saʊnd] **1** *n* suono *m*; (*noise*) rumore *m* **2** *v/i*: *~s interesting* sembra interessante

'soundbite slogan *m inv*; **soundly** *sleep* profondamente; *beaten* duramente; **soundproof** insonorizzato; **soundtrack** colonna *f* sonora

soup [suːp] minestra *f*

sour ['saʊə(r)] *apple, orange*

aspro; *milk, expression, comment* acido

source [sɔːs] fonte *f*; *of river* sorgente *f*

south [saʊθ] **1** *adj* meridionale, del sud **2** *n* sud *m* **3** *adv travel* verso sud; *~ of* a sud di; **South Africa** Repubblica *f* Sudafricana; **South African 1** *adj* sudafricano **2** *n* sudafricano *m*, -a *f*; **South America** Sudamerica *m*; **South American 1** *adj* sudamericano **2** *n* sudamericano *m*, -a *f*; **southeast 1** *n* sud-est *m* **2** *adj* sud-orientale **3** *adv* verso sud-est; **southeastern** sud-orientale; **southerly** meridionale; **southern** del sud; **southerner** abitante *m/f* del sud; **southernmost** più a sud; **South Pole** polo *m* sud; **southwards** verso sud; **southwest 1** *n* sud-ovest *m* **2** *adj* sud-occidentale **3** *adv* verso sud-ovest; **southwestern** sud-occidentale

souvenir [suːvə'nɪə(r)] souvenir *m inv*

sovereign ['sɒvrɪn] *state* sovrano; **sovereignty** *of state* sovranità *f*

sow[1] [saʊ] *n pig* scrofa *f*

sow[2] [saʊ] *v/t seeds* seminare

soya ['sɔɪə], *US* **soy** [sɔɪ] soia *f*; **soy(a) milk** latte *m* di soia; **soya sauce** ['sɔɪə] salsa *f* di soia

spa [spɑː] *resort m* spa; (*hotel*)

hotel *m* spa
space [speɪs] spazio *m*; *in car park* posto *m*; **space-bar** COMPUT barra *f* spaziatrice; **spacecraft** veicolo *m* spaziale; **spaceship** astronave *f*; **space shuttle** shuttle *m inv*; **space station** stazione *f* spaziale; **spacious** spazioso

spade [speɪd] *for digging* vanga *f*; **~s** *in card game* picche
spaghetti [spə'getɪ] spaghetti *mpl*
Spain [speɪn] Spagna *f*
spam [spæm] spam *f*
span [spæn] coprire; *of bridge* attraversare
Spaniard ['spænjəd] spagnolo *m*, -a *f*; **Spanish** 1 *adj* spagnolo 2 *n language* spagnolo *m*
spanner ['spænə(r)] chiave *f* inglese
spare [speə(r)] 1 *v/t* (*do without*) fare a meno di; *can you* **~ £50?** mi puoi prestare 50 sterline?; *can you* **~ the time?** hai tempo?; *have money* / *time to* **~** avere soldi / tempo d'avanzo 2 *adj* in più 3 *n ricambio m*; **spare part** pezzo *m* di ricambio; **spare ribs** costine *fpl* di maiale; **spare room** stanza *f* degli ospiti; **spare time** tempo *m* libero; **spare wheel** MOT ruota *f* di scorta; **sparing**: *be* **~ with** andarci piano con; **sparingly** con modera-

zione
spark [spɑːk] scintilla *f*
sparkle ['spɑːkl] brillare; **sparkling wine** vino *m* frizzante
'spark plug candela *f*
sparrow ['spærəʊ] passero *m*
sparse [spɑːs] *vegetation* rado; **sparsely**: **~ populated** scarsamente popolato
spartan ['spɑːtn] spartano
spasmodic [spæz'mɒdɪk] irregolare
spate [speɪt] *fig* ondata *f*
spatial ['speɪʃl] spaziale
speak [spiːk] 1 *v/i* parlare; **~ing** TELEC sono io 2 *v/t foreign language* parlare; *the truth* dire
♦ **speak up** (*speak louder*) parlare ad alta voce
speaker ['spiːkə(r)] oratore *m*, -trice *f*; *of sound system* cassa *f*; *Italian* **~** italofono *m*, -a *f*; **speaker phone** telefono *m* con vivavoce
spear [spɪə(r)] lancia *f*
special ['speʃl] speciale; (*particular*) particolare; **special effects** effetti *mpl* speciali; **specialist** specialista *m/f*; **speciality** specialità *f inv*; **specialize** specializzarsi (*in* in); **specially** ☞ **especially**; **specialty** specialità *f inv*
species ['spiːʃiːz] specie *f inv*
specific [spə'sɪfɪk] specifico; **specifically** specificamente; **specifications** *of machine etc* caratteristiche *fpl* tecni-

che; **specify** specificare

specimen ['spesɪmən] campione *m*

spectacle ['spektəkl] (*impressive sight*) spettacolo *m*; (**a pair of**) **~s** (un paio di) occhiali *mpl*; **spectacular** spettacolare

spectator [spek'teɪtə(r)] spettatore *m*, -trice *f*

spectrum ['spektrəm] *fig* gamma *f*

speculate ['spekjʊleɪt] fare congetture (**on** su); FIN speculare, **speculation** congetture *fpl*; FIN speculazione *f*; **speculator** FIN speculatore *m*, -trice *f*

speech [spiːtʃ] discorso *m*; *in play* monologo *m*; (*ability to speak*) parola *f*; (*way of speaking*) linguaggio *m*; **speechless** with shock, surprise senza parole

speed [spiːd] **1** *n* velocità *f inv*; (*quickness*) rapidità *f inv* **2** *v/i* (*go quickly*) andare a tutta velocità; (*drive too quickly*) superare il limite di velocità

◆ **speed up 1** *v/i* andare più veloce **2** *v/t* accelerare

'**speedboat** motoscafo *m*; **speed bump** dosso *m* di rallentamento; **speedily** rapidamente; **speeding** *when driving* eccesso *m* di velocità; **speed limit** limite *m* di velocità; **speedometer** tachimetro *m*; **speedy** rapido

spell[1] [spel] **1** *v/t:* **how do you ~ ...?** come si scrive ...?; **could you ~ that please?** me lo può dettare lettera per lettera? **2** *v/i* sapere come si scrivono le parole

spell[2] [spel] *n* (*period of time*) periodo *m*

'**spellchecker** COMPUT correttore *m* ortografico; **spelling** ortografia *f*

spend [spend] *money* spendere; *time* passare; **spendthrift** *pej* spendaccione *m*, -a *f*

sperm [spɜːm] spermatozoo *m*; (*semen*) sperma *m*

sphere [sfɪə(r)] *also fig* sfera *f*

spice [spaɪs] (*seasoning*) spezia *f*; **spicy** *food* piccante

spider ['spaɪdə(r)] ragno *m*; **spider's web** ragnatela *f*

spike [spaɪk] *on railings* spunzone *m*; *on plant* spina *f*; *on animal* aculeo *m*; *on running shoes* chiodo *m*

spill [spɪl] **1** *v/t* versare **2** *v/i* versarsi **3** *n of oil etc* fuoriuscita *f*

spin[1] [spɪn] **1** *n* giro *m*; *on ball* effetto *m* **2** *v/t ball* imprimere l'effetto a **3** *v/i of wheel* girare

spin[2] [spɪn] *v/t wool, cotton* filare; *web* tessere

spinach ['spɪnɪdʒ] spinaci *mpl*

spinal ['spaɪnl] spinale; **spinal column** colonna *f* vertebrale, spina *f* dorsale; **spinal cord** midollo *m* spinale 'spin doctor *esperto che ha il compito di presentare ai media le decisioni di un partito o personaggio politico sotto la luce migliore*

spine [spaɪn] *of person, animal* spina f dorsale; *of book* dorso m; *on plant, hedgehog* spina f; spineless (*cowardly*) smidollato

'spin-off applicazione f secondaria

spinster ['spɪnstə(r)] zitella f

spiny ['spaɪnɪ] spinoso

spiral ['spaɪrəl] 1 n spirale f 2 v/i (*rise quickly*) salire vertiginosamente; spiral staircase scala f a chiocciola

spire ['spaɪə(r)] spira f, guglia f

spirit ['spɪrɪt] spirito m; spirited *debate* animato; *defence* energico; *performance* brioso; spirits (*morale*) morale msg; be in good / poor – essere su / giù di morale; spiritual spirituale

spit [spɪt] *of person* sputare

spite [spaɪt] dispetto m; in ~ of malgrado; spiteful dispettoso; spitefully dispettosamente

spitting image ['spɪtɪŋ] be the ~ of s.o. essere il ritratto sputato di qu

splash [splæʃ] 1 n (*noise*) tonfo m; (*small amount of liquid*) schizzo m; *of colour* macchia f 2 v/t *person* schizzare; *water, mud* spruzzare 3 v/i schizza-

re; *of waves* infrangersi

'splashdown ammaraggio m

splendid ['splendɪd] magnifico; splendour, Am splendor magnificenza f

splint [splɪnt] MED stecca f

splinter ['splɪntə(r)] 1 n scheggia f 2 v/i scheggiarsi

split [splɪt] 1 n *in leather* strappo m; *in wood* crepa f; (*disagreement*) spaccatura f; (*division, share*) divisione f 2 v/t *leather* strappare; *wood, logs* spaccare; (*cause disagreement in*) spaccare; (*divide*) dividere 3 v/i *of leather* strapparsi; *of wood* spaccarsi; (*disagree*) spaccarsi

♦ split up *of couple* separarsi

splitting ['splɪtɪŋ]: ~ headache feroce mal m inv di testa

spoil [spɔɪl] *child* viziare; *surprise, party* rovinare; spoilsport F guastafeste m/f; spoilt *child* viziato; be ~ for choice avere (solo) l'imbarazzo della scelta

spoke [spəʊk] *of wheel* raggio m

spokesperson ['spəʊkspɜːsən] portavoce m/f

sponge [spʌndʒ] spugna f; sponger F scroccone m, -a f

sponsor ['spɒnsə(r)] 1 n *for immigration etc* garante m/f inv; *of TV programme, sports event, for fundraising* sponsor m inv 2 v/t *for immigra-*

sprint

tion, membership garantire per; *TV programme, sports event* sponsorizzare; **sponsorship** sponsorizzazione *f*

spontaneous [spɒn'teɪnɪəs] spontaneo; **spontaneously** spontaneamente

spool [spuːl] bobina *f*

spoon [spuːn] cucchiaio *m*; **spoonful** cucchiaio *f*

sporadic [spə'rædɪk] sporadico

sport [spɔːt] sport *m inv*; **sporting** sportivo; **sports jacket** giacca *f* sportiva; **sports car** auto *f inv* sportiva; **sportsman** sportivo *m*; **sportswear** abbigliamento *m* sportivo; **sportswoman** sportiva *f*; **sporty** sportivo

spot[1] [spɒt] *n (pimple)* brufolo *m; caused by measles etc* foruncolo *m; part of pattern* pois *m inv*

spot[2] [spɒt] *n (place)* posticino *m;* **on the ~** *(in the place in question)* sul posto; *(immediately)* immediatamente

spot[3] [spɒt] *v/t (notice)* notare; *(identify)* trovare

'spot check controllo *m* casuale; **spotless** pulitissimo; **spotlight** faretto *m*; **spotty** *with pimples* brufoloso

spouse [spaʊs] *fml* coniuge *m/f*

spout [spaʊt] **1** *n* beccuccio *m* **2** *v/i of liquid* sgorgare **3** *v/t* F: **~ nonsense** ciarlare

sprain [spreɪn] **1** *n* slogatura *f*

2 *v/t* slogarsi

sprawl [sprɔːl] stravaccarsi; *of city* estendersi; **send s.o. ~ing** *of punch* mandare qu a gambe all'aria; **sprawling** *city* tentacolare

spray [spreɪ] **1** *n of sea water* spruzzi *mpl; for hair* lacca *f; (container)* spray *m inv* **2** *v/t* spruzzare; **spraygun** pistola *f* a spruzzo

spread [spred] **1** *n of disease, religion etc* diffusione *f;* F *big meal* banchetto *m* **2** *v/t (lay)* stendere; *butter, jam* spalmare; *news, rumour, disease* diffondere; *arms, legs* allargare **3** *v/i* diffondersi; **spreadsheet** COMPUT spreadsheet *m inv*

sprightly ['spraɪtlɪ] arzillo

spring[1] *n* [sprɪŋ] *season* primavera *f*

spring[2] [sprɪŋ] *n device* molla *f*

spring[3] [sprɪŋ] **1** *n (jump)* balzo *m; (stream)* sorgente *f* **2** *v/i (jump)* balzare; **~ from** derivare da

'springboard trampolino *m*; **spring onion** cipollotto *m*; **springtime** primavera *f*

sprinkle ['sprɪŋkl] spruzzare; **~ sth with** cospargere qc di; **sprinkler** *for garden* irrigatore *m; in ceiling* sprinkler *m inv*

sprint [sprɪnt] **1** *n:* scatto *m*; **the 100 metres ~** i cento metri piani **2** *v/i* fare uno scatto;

sprinter SP velocista *m/f*
spud [spʌd] F patata *f*
spy [spaɪ] **1** *n* spia *f* **2** *v/i* fare la
  spia **3** *v/t* (*see*) scorgere
◆ **spy on** spiare
squabble ['skwɒbl] **1** *n* bisticcio *m* **2** *v/i* bisticciare
squalid ['skwɒlɪd] squallido;
  squalor squallore *m*
squander ['skwɒndə(r)] *money* dilapidare
square [skweə(r)] **1** *adj in
  shape* quadrato; **~ mile** miglio quadrato **2** *n shape* quadrato *m*; *in town* piazza *f*; *in
  board game* casella *f*; MATH
  quadrato *m*; **we're back to
  ~ one** siamo punto e a capo;
  square root radice *f* quadrata
squash[1] [skwɒʃ] *n vegetable*
  zucca *f*
squash[2] [skwɒʃ] *n game*
  squash *m*
squash[3] [skwɒʃ] *v/t* (*crush*)
  schiacciare
squat [skwɒt] **1** *adj in shape*
  tozzo **2** *v/i* (*sit*) accovacciarsi;
  illegally occupare abusiva-
  mente
squeak [skwi:k] **1** *n of mouse*
  squittio *m*; *of hinge* cigolio *m*
  2 *v/i of mouse* squittire; *of
  hinge* cigolare; *of shoes* scricchiolare; **squeaky** *hinge* ci-
  golante; *shoes* scricchiolan-
  te; *voice* stridulo; **squeaky
  clean** F pulito
squeal [skwi:l] **1** *n of pain,
  laughter* strillo *m*; *of brakes*

stridore *m* **2** *v/i* strillare; *of
brakes* stridere
squeamish ['skwiːmɪʃ]: **be ~**
  avere lo stomaco delicato
squeeze [skwiːz] **1** *n of hand,
  shoulder* stretta *f* **2** *v/t hand*
  stringere; *orange, lemon*
  spremere; *sponge* strizzare
squid [skwɪd] calamaro *m*
squint [skwɪnt] strabismo *m*
squirm [skwɜːm] (*wriggle*)
  contorcersi; **~ (with embarrassment)** morire di vergogna
squirrel ['skwɪrəl] scoiattolo
  m
squirt [skwɜːt] **1** *v/t* spruzzare
  2 *n* F *pej* microbo *m* F
St *abbr* (= *saint*) S. (= santo
  m, santa *f*); (= *street*) v. (=
  via *f*)
stab [stæb] accoltellare
stability [stə'bɪlətɪ] stabilità *f*;
  stabilize 1 *v/t* stabilizzare **2**
  v/i stabilizzarsi; **stable 1**
  adj stabile; **2** *n for horses* stalla *f*; *establishment* scuderia *f*
stack [stæk] **1** *n* (*pile*) pila *f*;
  ~s of F un sacco di F **2** *v/t*
  mettere in pila
stadium ['steɪdɪəm] stadio *m*
staff [stɑːf] (*employees*) personale *msg*; (*teachers*) corpo *m*
  insegnante; **staffroom** *in
  school* sala *f* professori
stage[1] [steɪdʒ] *n in life, project
  etc* fase *f*; *of journey* tappa *f*
stage[2] [steɪdʒ] **1** *n* THEA palcoscenico *m* **2** *v/t play* mettere in scena; *demonstration*

organizzare

stagger ['stægə(r)] **1** v/i barcollare *f; (amaze)* sbalordire; *holidays, breaks etc* scaglionare; **staggering** sbalorditivo

stagnant ['stægnənt] *also fig* stagnante; **stagnate** *of person, mind* vegetare

'stag party (festa *f* di) addio *m* al celibato

stain [steɪn] **1** n *(dirty mark)* macchia *f; for wood* mordente *m* **2** v/t *(dirty)* macchiare; *wood* dare il mordente a **3** v/i *of wine etc* macchiarsi; *of fabric* macchiarsi; **stained-glass window** vetrata *f* colorata; **stainless steel** acciaio *m* inossidabile

stair [steə(r)] scalino *m;* **the ~s** le scale; **staircase** scala *f*

stake [steɪk] **1** n *of wood* paletto *m; when gambling* puntata *f; (investment)* partecipazione *f;* **be at ~** essere in gioco **2** v/t *tree* puntellare; *money* puntare

stale [steɪl] *bread* raffermo; *air* viziato; *fig: news* vecchio; *fig* punto *m* morto

stalemate in chess stallo *m; fig* punto *m* morto

stalk¹ [stɔːk] n *of fruit* picciolo *m; of plant* gambo *m*

stalk² [stɔːk] v/t *animal* seguire; *person* perseguitare (con telefonate, lettere ecc)

stall¹ [stɔːl] n *at market* bancarella *f; for cow, horse* box *m inv*

stall² [stɔːl] **1** v/i *of vehicle* fermarsi; *(play for time)* temporeggiare **2** v/t *engine* far spegnere; *people* trattenere

stalls [stɔːlz] platea *f*

stalwart ['stɔːlwət] *supporter* fedele

stamina ['stæmɪnə] resistenza *f*

stammer ['stæmə(r)] **1** n balbuzie *f* **2** v/i balbettare

stamp¹ [stæmp] **1** n *for letter* francobollo *m; (date ~ etc)* timbro *m* **2** v/t *letter* affrancare; *document, passport* timbrare; **~ed addressed envelope** busta *f* affrancata per la risposta

stamp² [stæmp] v/t: **~ one's foot** pestare i piedi

stance [stɑːns] *(position)* presa *f* di posizione

stand [stænd] **1** n *at exhibition* stand *m inv; (witness ~)* banco *m* dei testimoni; *(support, base)* base *f;* **take the ~** LAW testimoniare **2** v/i *(be situated: of person)* stare; *of object, building* trovarsi; *as opposed to sit* stare in piedi; *(rise)* alzarsi in piedi **3** v/t *(tolerate)* sopportare; *(put)* mettere; **you don't ~ a chance** non hai alcuna probabilità; **~ s.o. a drink** offrire da bere a qu

♦ **stand by 1** v/i *(not take action)* stare a guardare; *(be ready)* tenersi pronto **2** v/t *person* stare al fianco di; *de-*

cision mantenere

◆ **stand down** (*withdraw*) ritirarsi

◆ **stand for** (*tolerate*) tollerare; (*mean*) significare; *freedom etc* rappresentare

◆ **stand out** spiccare; *of person, building* distinguersi

◆ **stand up 1** *v/i* alzarsi in piedi **2** *v/t* F *on date* dare buca a F

◆ **stand up for** difendere

◆ **stand up to** far fronte a

standard ['stændəd] **1** *adj* (*usual*) comune; *model* standard *inv* **2** *n* (*level*) livello *m*; (*expectation*) aspettativa *f*; TECH standard *m inv*; **be up to ~** essere di buona qualità; **standardize** standardizzare; **standard of living** tenore *m* di vita

'**standby** *ticket* biglietto *m* stand-by; **on ~** *at airport* in lista d'attesa; **on ~** *of troops etc* pronto; **standing** *in society etc* posizione *f*; (*repute*) reputazione *f*; **of long ~** di lunga durata; **standoffish** scostante; **standpoint** punto *m* di vista; **standstill**: **be at a ~** essere fermo; **bring to a ~** fermare

staple¹ ['steɪpl] *n* (*foodstuff*) alimento *m* base

staple² ['steɪpl] **1** *n* (*fastener*) graffa *f* **2** *v/t* pinzare

stapler ['steɪplə(r)] pinzatrice *f*

star [stɑː(r)] **1** *n in sky* stella *f*;

fig star f inv **2** *v/t*: *a film ~ring Julia Roberts* un film interpretato da Julia Roberts; **starboard** a tribordo

stare [steə(r)] fissare; **~ at** fissare

stark [stɑːk] **1** *adj landscape* desolato; *colour scheme* austero; *reminder, contrast etc* brusco **2** *adv*: **~ naked** completamente nudo

starling ['stɑːlɪŋ] storno *m*

starry ['stɑːrɪ] *night* stellato

start [stɑːt] **1** *n* inizio *m*; **get off to a good~** cominciare bene **2** *v/i* iniziare, cominciare; *of engine, car* partire; **~ing from tomorrow** a partire da domani **3** *v/t* cominciare; *engine, car* mettere in moto; *business* mettere su; **~ to do sth, ~ doing sth** cominciare a fare qc; **starter** *of meal* antipasto *m*; *of car* motorino *m* d'avviamento; *in race* starter *m inv*; **starting point** punto *m* di partenza; **starting salary** stipendio *m* iniziale

startle ['stɑːtl] far trasalire; **startling** sorprendente

'**start-up** COM nuova azienda *f*

starvation [stɑː'veɪʃn] fame *f*; **starve** soffrire la fame; *I'm starving* F sto morendo di fame

state¹ [steɪt] **1** *n of car, house, part of country* stato *m*; **the States** gli Stati Uniti **2** *adj* di stato; *school* statale; *banquet etc* ufficiale

state² [steɪt] *v/t* dichiarare

'**State Department** Ministero *m* degli Esteri; **statement** *to police* deposizione *f*; *(announcement)* dichiarazione *f*; *(bank ~)* estratto *m* conto, **state of emergency** stato *m* d'emergenza; **state-of-the-art** allo stato dell'arte; **statesman** statista *m*

static (elec'tricity) [ˈstætɪk] elettricità *f* statica

station [ˈsteɪʃn] **1** *n* stazione *f* **2** *v/t guard etc* disporre; **stationary** fermo

stationery [ˈsteɪʃənərɪ] articoli *mpl* di cancelleria

'**station wagon** giardiniera *f*

statistical [stəˈtɪstɪkl] statistico; **statistically** statisticamente; **statistician** esperto *m*, -a *f* di statistica; **statistics** *science* statistica *f*; *npl figures* statistiche *fpl*

statue [ˈstætjuː] statua *f*

status [ˈsteɪtəs] posizione *f*; **status symbol** status symbol *m inv*

statute [ˈstætjuːt] statuto *m*

staunch [stɔːntʃ] leale

stay [steɪ] **1** *n* soggiorno *m* **2** *v/i in a place* stare; *in a condition* restare; ~ *in a hotel* stare in albergo; ~ *right there!* non ti muovere!

◆ **stay behind** rimanere

◆ **stay up** *(not go to bed)* rimanere alzato

steadily [ˈstedɪlɪ] *improve etc* costantemente; *look* fisso; **steady 1** *adj voice, hands* fermo; *job, boyfriend* fisso; *beat* regolare; *improvement, decline* costante **2** *adv*: *be going ~* fare coppia fissa; ~ *on!* calma! **3** *v/t bookcase etc* rendere saldo

steak [steɪk] bistecca *f*, carne *f* (di manzo)

steal [stiːl] **1** *v/t* rubare **2** *v/i (be a thief)* rubare; ~ *in / out* entrare / uscire furtivamente

stealthy [ˈstelθɪ] furtivo

steam [stiːm] **1** *n* vapore *m* **2** *v/t food* cuocere al vapore; **steamed up** F *angry* furibondo; **steamer** *for cooking* vaporiera *f*

steel [stiːl] **1** *n* acciaio *m* **2** *adj* d'acciaio; **steelworker** operaio *m* di acciaieria

steep¹ [stiːp] *adj hill etc* ripido; F *prices* alto

steep² [stiːp] *v/t (soak)* lasciare a bagno

steer¹ [stɪr] *n animal* manzo *m*

steer² [stɪə(r)] *v/t* manovrare; *person* guidare; *conversation* spostare; **steering** MOT sterzo *m*; **steering wheel** volante *m*

stem¹ [stem] *n of plant, glass* stelo *m*; *of word* radice *f*

stem² [stem] *v/t (block)* arginare

'**stem cell** cellula *f* staminale

stench [stentʃ] puzzo *m*

stencil ['stensɪl] 1 *n* stencil *m inv* 2 *v/t pattern* disegnare con lo stencil

step [step] 1 *n* (*pace*) passo *m*; (*stair*) gradino *m*; (*measure*) provvedimento *m*; ~ *by* ~ poco a poco 2 *v/i*: ~ *into* / *out of* salire in / scendere da

◆ step down *from post etc* dimettersi

◆ step up (*increase*) aumentare

'stepbrother fratellastro *m*; stepdaughter figliastra *f*; stepfather patrigno *m*; stepladder scala *f* a libretto; stepmother matrigna *f*; stepsister sorellastra *f*; stepson figliastro *m*

stereo ['sterɪəʊ] (*sound system*) stereo *m inv*; stereotype stereotipo *m*

sterile ['sterail] sterile; sterilize sterilizzare

sterling ['stɜːlɪŋ] FIN sterlina *f*

stern¹ [stɜːn] *adj* severo

stern² [stɜːn] *n* NAUT poppa *f*

sternly ['stɜːnlɪ] severamente

steroids ['sterɔɪdz] anabolizzanti *mpl*

stethoscope ['steθəskəʊp] fonendoscopio *m*

stew [stjuː] spezzatino *m*

steward ['stjuːəd] *on plane, ship* steward *m inv*; *at demonstration, meeting* membro *m* del servizio d'ordine; stewardess *on plane, ship* hostess *f inv*

stick¹ [stɪk] *n wood* rametto *m*; (*walking* ~) bastone *m*; out in the ~s F a casa del diavolo F

stick² [stɪk] 1 *v/t with adhesive* attaccare; *needle, knife* conficcare; F (*put*) mettere 2 *v/i* (*jam*) bloccarsi; (*adhere*) attaccarsi

◆ stick by F *person* rimanere al fianco di

◆ stick to F (*keep to*) attenersi a; F (*follow*) seguire

◆ stick up for F difendere

sticker ['stɪkə(r)] adesivo *m*; sticking plaster cerotto *m*; stick-in-the-mud F abitudinario *m*, -a *f*; sticky appiccicoso; *label* adesivo

stiff [stɪf] 1 *adj brush, cardboard, leather* rigido; *muscle, body* anchilosato; *paste* sodo; *in manner* freddo; *drink, competition* forte; *fine* salato 2 *adv*: be bored ~ F essere annoiato a morte F; stiffness *of muscles* indolenzimento *m*; *of material* rigidità *f*; *of manner* freddezza *f*

stifle ['staɪfl] *also fig* soffocare; stifling soffocante

stigma ['stɪgmə] vergogna *f*

stilettos [stɪ'letəʊz] *npl* (*shoes*) scarpe *fpl* con tacco a spillo

still¹ [stɪl] 1 *adj* (*motionless*) immobile; *without wind* senza vento; *drink* non gas(s)ato 2 *adv*: keep / stand ~! stai fermo!

still² [stɪl] *adv* (*yet*) ancora; (*nevertheless*) comunque; *she ~ hasn't finished* non ha ancora finito; *~ more* ancora più

'stillborn nato morto; *life* natura *f* morta

stilted ['stɪltɪd] poco naturale

stimulant ['stɪmjʊlənt] stimolante *m*; **stimulate** stimolare; **stimulating** stimolante; **stimulation** stimolazione *f*; **stimulus** (*incentive*) stimolo *m*

sting [stɪŋ] **1** *n from bee* puntura *f*; *from jellyfish* pizzico *m* **2** *v/t of bee* pungere; *of jellyfish* pizzicare **3** *v/i of eyes, scratch* bruciare; **stinging** *criticism* pungente

stingy ['stɪndʒɪ] F tirchio F

stink [stɪŋk] **1** *n* (*bad smell*) puzza *f* F (*fuss*) putiferio *m* F; *kick up a ~* F fare un casino F **2** *v/i* (*smell bad*) puzzare; F (*be very bad*) fare schifo F

stipulate ['stɪpjʊleɪt] stabilire; **stipulation** condizione *f*

stir [stɜː(r)] **1** *v/t* mescolare **2** *v/i of sleeping person* muoversi; **stirring** *music, speech* commovente

stitch [stɪtʃ] **1** *n in sewing* punto *m*; *in knitting* maglia *f*; *~es* MED punti *mpl* (di sutura); *be in ~es laughing* ridere a crepapelle **2** *v/t sew* cucire; **stitching** (*stitches*) cucitura *f*

stock [stɒk] **1** *n* (*reserves*)

provvista *f*; COM *of store* stock *m inv*; *animals* bestiame *m*; FIN titoli *mpl*; *for soup etc* brodo *m*; *in ~* / *out of ~* disponibile / esaurito; *take ~ fare il punto* **2** *v/t* COM vendere; **stockbroker** agente *m/f* di cambio; **stock exchange** borsa *f* valori; **stockholder** azionista *m/f*; **stockist** rivenditore *m*; **stock market** mercato *m* azionario; **stockpile 1** *n of food, weapons* scorta *f* **2** *v/t* fare scorta di

stocky ['stɒkɪ] tarchiato

stodgy ['stɒdʒɪ] *food* pesante

stoical ['stəʊɪkl] stoico; **stoicism** stoicismo *m*

stomach ['stʌmək] **1** *n* stomaco *m*; (*abdomen*) pancia *f* **2** *v/t* (*tolerate*) sopportare; **stomach-ache** mal *m* di stomaco

stone [stəʊn] pietra *f*; (*pebble*) sasso *m*; *in fruit* nocciolo *m*; **stoned** F *on drugs* fatto F; **stone-deaf** sordo (come una campana)

stool [stuːl] *seat* sgabello *m*

stoop¹ [stuːp] *v/i* (*bend down*) chinarsi; (*have bent back*) essere curvo

stoop² [stuːp] *n Am* (*porch*) porticato *m*

stop [stɒp] **1** *n for train, bus* fermata *f*; *put a ~ to* mettere fine a **2** *v/t* (*put an end to*) mettere fine a; (*prevent*) fermare; (*cease*) smettere; *per-*

son, car, bus fermare; _cheque_ bloccare; **~ doing sth** smettere di fare qc **3** _v/i_ (_come to a halt_) fermarsi; _of rain, noise_ smettere

◆ **stop over** fare sosta

'stopgap _person_ tappabuchi _m/f inv_; _thing_ soluzione _f_ temporanea; **stoplight** (_traffic light_) rosso _m_; (_brake light_) fanalino _m_ d'arresto; **stopover** sosta _f_; _in air travel_ scalo _m_ intermedio; **stopper** tappo _m_; **stop sign** (segnale _m_ di) stop _m inv_; **stopwatch** cronometro _m_

storage ['stɔːrɪdʒ]: **put sth in ~** mettere qc in magazzino; **store 1** _n large shop_ negozio _m_; (_stock_) riserva _f_; (_storehouse_) deposito _m_ **2** _v/t_ tenere; COMPUT memorizzare; **storekeeper** _Am_ negoziante _m/f_; **store window** _Am_ vetrina _f_

storey ['stɔːrɪ] _of building_ piano _m_

storm [stɔːm] tempesta _f_; **stormy** tempestoso

story[1] ['stɔːrɪ] (_tale_) racconto _m_; (_account_) storia _f_; (_newspaper article_) articolo _m_; F (_lie_) bugia _f_

story[2] ['stɔːrɪ] _of building_ piano _m_

stout [staʊt] _person_ robusto

stove [stəʊv] _for cooking_ cucina _f_; _for heating_ stufa _f_

stow [stəʊ] riporre

◆ **stow away** imbarcarsi clandestinamente

'stowaway passeggero _m_, -a _f_ clandestino, -a

straight [streɪt] **1** _adj line_ retto; _hair, whisky_ liscio; _back, knees_ dritto; (_honest, direct_) onesto; (_tidy_) in ordine; (_conservative_) convenzionale; (_not homosexual_) etero; **keep a ~ face** non ridere **2** _adv_ dritto; _think_ con chiarezza; **go ~** F _of criminal_ rigare dritto; **give it to me ~** F dimmi francamente; **~ ahead** avanti dritto; **carry ~ on** proseguire dritto; **~away, ~ off** immediatamente; **~ out** _say sth_ chiaro e tondo; **straighten** raddrizzare; **straightforward** (_honest, direct_) franco; (_simple_) semplice

strain[1] [streɪn] **1** _n physical_ sforzo _m_; _mental_ tensione _f_ **2** _v/t_ (_injure_) affaticare; _finances_, gravare su

strain[2] [streɪn] _v/t vegetables_ scolare; _oil, fat etc_ filtrare

strained [streɪnd] teso; **strainer** _for vegetables etc_ colino _m_

strait [streɪt] GEOG stretto _m_; **straitlaced** puritano

strand [strænd] piantare in asso F; **be ~ed** essere bloccato

strange [streɪndʒ] (_odd, curious_) strano; (_unknown, foreign_) sconosciuto; **strangely** (_oddly_) stranamente; **~ enough** strano ma vero;

stranger *person you don't know* sconosciuto *m*, -a *f*; **I'm a ~ here myself** non sono di queste parti

strangle ['stræŋgl] strangolare

strap [stræp] *of bag* tracolla *f*; *of bra, dress* bretellina *f*, spallina *f*; *of watch* cinturino *m*; *of shoe* listino *m*; **strapless** senza spalline

strategic [strə'ti:dʒik] strategico; **strategy** strategia *f*

straw [strɔː] paglia *f*; *for drink* cannuccia *f*; **strawberry** fragola *f*

stray [strei] **1** *adj animal* randagio; *bullet* vagante **2** *n dog, cat* randagio *m* **3** *v/i of animal* smarrirsi; *of child* allontanarsi; *fig: of eyes, thoughts* vagare

streak [striːk] **1** *n of dirt, paint* striscia *f*; *in hair* mèche *f inv*; *fig: of nastiness etc* vena *f* **2** *v/i move quickly* sfrecciare

stream [striːm] **1** *n* ruscello *m*; *fig: of people, complaints* fiume *m*; **come on ~** *of plant* entrare in attività; *of oil* arrivare **2** *v/i* riversarsi; **streamline** *fig* snellire; **streamlined** *car, plane* aerodinamico; *organization* snellito

street [striːt] strada *f*; *in address* via *f*; **streetcar** *Am* tram *m inv*; **streetlight** lampione *m*; **street value** *of drugs* valore *m* di mercato; **streetwise** scafato F

strength [streŋθ] forza *f*; *(strong point)* punto *m* forte; **strengthen 1** *v/t* rinforzare **2** *v/i* consolidarsi

strenuous ['strenjʊəs] faticoso; **strenuously** *deny* recisamente

stress [stres] **1** *n (emphasis)* accento *m*; *(tension)* stress *m inv* **2** *v/t syllable* accentare; *importance etc* sottolineare; **stressed out** stressato; **stressful** stressante

stretch [stretʃ] **1** *n of land, water* tratto *m*; **at a ~** *(non-stop)* di fila **2** *adj fabric* elasticizzato **3** *v/t material* tendere; *small income* far bastare; **the rules** F fare uno strappo (alla regola); **he ~ed out his hand** allungò la mano **4** *v/i to relax muscles* stirarsi; *to reach sth* allungarsi; *(spread)* estendersi; **stretcher** barella *f*

strict [strikt] *person* severo; *instructions* tassativo; **strictly**: **be brought up ~** ricevere un'educazione rigida; **it is ~ forbidden** è severamente proibito

stride [straid] **1** *n* falcata *f*; **take sth in one's ~** affrontare qc senza drammi; **make great ~s** *fig* far passi da gigante **2** *v/i* procedere a grandi passi; **he strode up to me** avanzò verso di me

strident ['straidnt] stridulo; *demands* veemente

strike [straɪk] **1** *n of workers* sciopero *m*; *of oil* scoperta *f*; **be on ~** essere in sciopero **2** *v/i of workers* scioperare; (*attack*) aggredire; *of disaster* colpire; *of clock* suonare **3** *v/t* (*hit*) colpire; *match* accendere (*sfregando*); *of idea, thought* venire in mente *a*; *oil* trovare; **she struck me as being ...** mi ha dato l'impressione di essere ...
◆ **strike out** (*delete*) depennare

'strikebreaker crumiro *m*, -a *f*; **striker** *person on strike* scioperante *m/f*; *in football* bomber *m inv*, cannoniere *m*; **striking** (*marked*) marcato; (*eye-catching*) impressionante; (*attractive*) attraente; *colour* forte

string [strɪŋ] (*cord*) spago *m*; *of violin, tennis racket* corda *f*; **the ~s** MUS gli archi; **a ~ of** (*series*) una serie di; **stringed instrument** strumento *m* ad arco

stringent ['strɪndʒnt] rigoroso

strip [strɪp] **1** *n* striscia *f*; (*comic ~*) fumetto *m*; *of soccer player* divisa *f* **2** *v/t* (*remove*) staccare; *bed* disfare; (*undress*) spogliare; **~ s.o. of sth** (*undress*) spogliarsi; *of stripper* fare lo spogliarello; **strip club** locale *m* di spogliarelli

stripe [straɪp] striscia *f*; MIL gallone *m*; **striped** a strisce

stripper ['strɪpə(r)] spogliarellista *f*; **male ~** spogliarellista *m*; **striptease** spogliarello *m*

strive [straɪv]: **~ to do sth** sforzarsi di fare qc; **~ for sth** lottare per (ottenere) qc

stroke [strəʊk] **1** *n* MED ictus *m inv*; *when painting* pennellata *f*; *style of swimming* stile *m* di nuoto; **~ of luck** colpo di fortuna **2** *v/t* accarezzare

stroll [strəʊl] **1** *n* passeggiata *f*; **go for a ~** fare una passeggiata **2** *v/i* fare due passi; **she ~ed back to the office** tornò in ufficio in tutta calma; **stroller** *Am for baby* passeggino *m*

strong [strɒŋ] forte; *structure* resistente; *candidate* valido; *taste, smell* intenso; *views, beliefs* fermo; *arguments* convincente; *objections* energici; **~ support** largo consenso; **strongly** believe, object fermamente; *built* solidamente; **feel ~ about sth** avere molto a cuore qc; **strong-minded** risoluto; **strong point** (punto *m*) forte *m*; **strongroom** camera *f* blindata; **strong-willed** deciso

structural ['strʌktʃərəl] strutturale; **structure 1** *n something built* costruzione *f*; *of novel, society etc* struttura *f* **2** *v/t* strutturare

subdue

struggle ['strʌgl] **1** n (fight)
colluttazione f; fig lotta f;
(hard time) fatica f **2** v/i with
a person lottare; (have a hard
time) faticare; **~ to do sth** faticare a fare qc

strut [strʌt] camminare im-
pettito

stub [stʌb] **1** n of cigarette
mozzicone m; of cheque,
ticket matrice f **2** v/t: **~ one's
toe** urtare il dito del piede
♦ **stub out** spegnere

stubble ['stʌbl] on man's face
barba f ispida

stubborn ['stʌbən] person testardo; defence, refusal ostinato

stubby ['stʌbɪ] tozzo

stuck [stʌk] F: **be~ on s.o.** essere cotto di qu F; **stuck-up**
F presuntuoso

student ['stju:dnt] studente
m, -essa f

studio ['stju:dɪəu] studio m;
(recording ~) sala f di registrazione

studious ['stju:dɪəs] studioso; **study 1** n studio m **2**
v/t & v/i studiare

stuff [stʌf] **1** n roba f **2** v/t turkey farcire; **~ sth into sth** ficcare qc in qc; **stuffing** for
turkey farcia f; in chair, teddy
bear imbottitura f; **stuffy**
room mal ventilato; person
inquadrato

stumble ['stʌmbl] inciampare; **stumbling-block** fig scoglio m

stump [stʌmp] **1** n of tree ceppo m **2** v/t of question, ques-
tioner sconcertare

stun [stʌn] of blow stordire; of
news sbalordire; **stunning**
(amazing) sbalorditivo; (very
beautiful) splendido

stunt [stʌnt] for publicity trovata f pubblicitaria; in film
acrobazia f; **stuntman** in
movie cascatore m

stupefy ['stju:pɪfaɪ] sbalordire

stupendous [stju:'pendəs]
(marvellous) fantastico; mistake enorme

stupid ['stju:pɪd] stupido;
stupidity stupidità f

sturdy ['stɜ:dɪ] robusto

stutter ['stʌtə(r)] balbettare

style [staɪl] stile m; (fashion)
moda f; (fashionable ele-
gance) classe f; (hair~) pettinatura f; **stylish** elegante;
stylist (hair ~) parrucchiere
m, -a f

subcommittee ['sʌbkəmɪtɪ]
sottocommissione f

subconscious [sʌb'kɒnʃəs]
subconscio; **the ~ (mind)** il
subconscio; **subcon-
sciously** inconsciamente

subcontract [sʌbkən'trækt]
subappaltare; **subcontrac-
tor** subappaltatore m, -trice
f

subdivide [sʌbdɪ'vaɪd] suddividere

subdue [səb'dju:] sottomettere

subheading ['sʌbhedɪŋ] sottotitolo *m*

subhuman [sʌb'hju:mən] subumano

subject 1 ['sʌbdʒɪkt] *n of monarch* suddito *m*, -a *f*; *(topic)* argomento *m*; EDU materia *f*; GRAM soggetto *m*; **change the** ~ cambiare argomento **2** ['sʌbdʒɪkt] *adj*: **be** ~ **to** essere soggetto a; ~ **to availability** nei limiti della disponibilità **3** [səb'dʒekt] *v/t* sottoporre; **subjective** soggettivo *m*

sublet ['sʌblet] subaffittare

subma'chine gun mitra *m*

submarine [sʌbmə'ri:n] sottomarino *m*, sommergibile *m*

submerge [səb'mɜ:dʒ] **1** *v/t* sommergere **2** *v/i of submarine* immergersi

submission [səb'mɪʃn] *(surrender)* sottomissione *f*; *request to committee etc* richiesta *f*; **submissive** sottomesso; **submit 1** *v/t plan, proposal* presentare **2** *v/i* sottomettersi

subordinate [sə'bɔ:dɪnət] *adj employee, position* subalterno **2** *n* subalterno *m*, -a *f*

subpoena [sə'pi:nə] **1** *n* citazione *f* **2** *v/t person* citare in giudizio

♦ **subscribe to** [səb'skraɪb] *magazine etc* abbonarsi a; *theory* condividere

subscriber [səb'skraɪbə(r)] *to*

magazine abbonato *m*, -a *f*; **subscription** abbonamento *m*

subsequent ['sʌbsɪkwənt] successivo; **subsequently** successivamente

subside [səb'saɪd] *of waters, winds* calare; *of building* sprofondare; *of fears* calmarsi

subsidiary [səb'sɪdɪərɪ] filiale *f*

subsidize ['sʌbsɪdaɪz] sovvenzionare; **subsidy** sovvenzione *f*

substance ['sʌbstəns] sostanza *f*

substandard [sʌb'stændəd] scadente

substantial [səb'stænʃl] considerevole; *meal* sostanzioso; **substantially** *(considerably)* considerevolmente; *(in essence)* sostanzialmente; **substantive** [səb'stæntɪv] sostanziale

substitute ['sʌbstɪtju:t] **1** *n for person* sostituto *m*, -a *f*; *for commodity* alternativa *f*; SP riserva *f* **2** *v/t*: ~ **X for Y** sostituire Y con X **3** *v/i*: ~ **for s.o.** sostituire qu; **substitution** *(act)* sostituzione *f*

subtitle ['sʌbtaɪtl] sottotitolo *m*

subtle ['sʌtl] sottile; *flavour* delicato

subtract [səb'trækt] sottrarre

suburb ['sʌbɜ:b] sobborgo *m*; **the** ~**s** la periferia; **subur-**

ban di periferia

subversive [səb'vɜːsɪv] **1** adj
sovversivo **2** n sovversivo m,
-a f

subway ['sʌbweɪ] Br sottopassaggio m; Am metropolitana f

sub'zero: ~ **temperatures**
temperature sottozero

succeed [sək'siːd] **1** v/i avere
successo; to throne succede-
re; ~ **in doing sth** riuscire
a fare qc **2** v/t (come after)
succedere a; **success** successo m; **be a** ~ avere successo; **successful** person affer-
mato; marriage, party riusci-
to; **be** ~ riuscire; **he's very** ~
è arrivato; **successfully** con
successo; **we** ~ **completed**
... siamo riusciti a portare
a termine ...; **successive**
successivo; **three** ~ **days**
tre giorni di seguito; **successor** successore m

succinct [sək'sɪŋkt] succinto

succumb [sə'kʌm] (give in)
cedere

such [sʌtʃ] **1** adj (of that kind)
del genere; ~ **a** (so much of a)
un / una tale; ~ **as** come; **he
made** ~ **a fuss** ha fatto una
tale scenata; **there is no** ~
word as ... la parola ...
non esiste **2** adv così; ~ **nice
people** gente così simpatica

suck [sʌk] **1** v/t lollipop etc
succhiare **2** v/i: **it** ~**s** P fa
schifo P

◆ **suck up to** F leccare i pie-

di a F

sucker ['sʌkə(r)] F person
pollo F; **suction** aspirazione
f

sudden ['sʌdn] improvviso;
all of a ~ all'improvviso;
suddenly improvvisamente

sue [suː] v/t fare causa a **2** v/i
fare causa

suede [sweɪd] pelle f scamo-
sciata

suffer ['sʌfə(r)] **1** v/i (be in
pain) soffrire; **be** ~**ing from**
avere; ~ **from** soffrire di **2**
v/t loss, setback subire; **suffering** sofferenza f

sufficient [sə'fɪʃnt] sufficiente; **sufficiently** abbastanza

suffocate ['sʌfəkeɪt] soffocare; **suffocation** soffocamen-
to m

sugar ['ʃʊɡə(r)] **1** n zucchero
m **2** v/t zuccherare

suggest [sə'dʒest] proporre,
suggerire; **suggestion** proposta f, suggerimento m

suicide ['suːɪsaɪd] suicidio m;
commit ~ suicidarsi; **suicide
bomber** kamikaze m inv

suit [suːt] **1** n for man vestito
m, completo m; for woman
tailleur m inv; in cards seme
m **2** v/t of clothes, colour stare
bene a; ~ **yourself!** F fai come ti pare!; **be** ~**ed for sth**
essere fatto per qc; **suitable**
adatto; **suitably** adeguatamente; **suitcase** valigia f

suite [swiːt] of rooms suite f
inv; of furniture divano m e

poltrone *fpl* coordinati; MUS
suite *f inv*
sulk [sʌlk] fare il broncio;
sulky imbronciato
sullen ['sʌlən] crucciato
sultry ['sʌltrɪ] *climate* afoso;
sexually sensuale
sum [sʌm] somma *f*; *in arithmetic* addizione *f*
◆ **sum up 1** *v/t* (*summarize*)
riassumere; (*assess*) valutare
2 *v/i* LAW riepilogare
summarize ['sʌməraɪz] riassumere; **summary** riassunto
m
summer ['sʌmə(r)] estate *f*
summit ['sʌmɪt] *of mountain*
vetta *f*; POL summit *m inv*
summon ['sʌmən] convocare;
summons LAW citazione *f*
sun [sʌn] sole *m*; **in the ~** al
sole; **out of the ~** all'ombra;
sunbathe prendere il sole;
sunbed lettino *m* solare;
sunblock protezione *f* solare totale; **sunburn** scottatu-
ra *f*; **sunburnt** scottato;
Sunday domenica *f*; **sunglasses** occhiali *mpl* da sole; **sunny** *day* di sole; *spot*
soleggiato; *disposition* allegro; **it's ~** c'è il sole; **sunrise**
alba *f*; **sunset** tramonto *m*;
sunshade ombrellone *m*;
sunshine (luce *f* del) sole
m; **sunstroke** colpo *m* di sole; **suntan** abbronzatura *f*;
get a ~ abbronzarsi
super ['suːpə(r)] F fantastico
superb [suˈpɜːb] magnifico

superficial [suːpəˈfɪʃl] superficiale
superfluous [suˈpɜːfluəs] superfluo
super'human sovrumano
superintendent [suːpərɪn-
ˈtendənt] *Br of police* commissario *m*; *Am of apartment
block* custode *m/f*
superior [suːˈpɪərɪə(r)] **1** *adj*
(*better*) superiore **2** *n in organization* superiore *m*
superlative [suːˈpɜːlətɪv] **1**
adj (*superb*) eccellente **2** *n*
GRAM superlativo *m*
'**supermarket** supermarket
m inv, supermercato *m*
super'natural 1 *adj powers*
soprannaturale **2** *n*: **the ~** il
soprannaturale
'**superpower** POL superpo-
tenza *f*
supersonic [suːpəˈsɒnɪk] su-
personico
superstition [suːpəˈstɪʃn] superstizione *f*; **superstitious**
superstizioso
supervise ['suːpəvaɪz] super-
visionare; **supervisor** *at
work* supervisore *m*
supper ['sʌpə(r)] cena *f*
supple ['sʌpl] *person, limbs*
snodato; *material* flessibile
supplement ['sʌplɪmənt]
supplemento *m*
supplier [səˈplaɪə(r)] COM fornitore *m*; **supply 1** *n* fornitura *f*; **~ and demand** domanda e offerta; **supplies** rifor-
nimenti **2** *v/t goods* fornire; **~**

s.o. with sth fornire qc a qu
support [səˈpɔːt] **1** *n for structure* supporto *m*; (*backing*) sostegno *m* **2** *v/t structure*, (*back*) sostenere; *financially* mantenere; *football team* fare il tifo per; **supporter** sostenitore *m*, -trice *f*; *of football team* etc tifoso *m*, -a *f*; **supportive**: *be ~ towards s.o.* dare il proprio appoggio a qu

suppose [səˈpəʊz] (*imagine*) supporre; *it is ~d to ...* (*is meant to*) dovrebbe ...; (*is said to*) dicono che ...; *you are not ~d to ...* (*not allowed to*) non dovresti ...; **supposedly** presumibilmente

suppress [səˈpres] reprimere; **suppression** repressione *f*

supremacy [suːˈpreməsɪ] supremazia *f*; **supreme** supremo; **Supreme Court** Corte *f* Suprema

surcharge [ˈsɜːtʃɑːdʒ] *for travel* sovrapprezzo *m*; *for mail* soprattassa *f*

sure [ʃʊə(r)] **1** *adj* sicuro; *make ~ that ...* assicurarsi che ... **2** *adv* certamente; *~ enough* infatti; *~!* F certo!; **surely** certamente; (*gladly*) volentieri; *~ that's not right!* non può essere!; **surety** *for loan* cauzione *f*

surf [sɜːf] **1** *n on sea* spuma *f* **2** *v/t the Net* navigare in
surface [ˈsɜːfɪs] **1** *n* superficie

f; *on the ~* *fig* superficialmente **2** *v/i from water* risalire in superficie; (*appear*) farsi vivo; **surface mail** posta *f* ordinaria
'surfboard tavola *f* da surf; **surfer** surfista *m/f*; **surfing** surf *m*; *go ~* fare surf

surge [sɜːdʒ] *in electric current* sovratensione *f* transitoria; *in demand* impennata *f*

surgeon [ˈsɜːdʒən] chirurgo *m*; **surgery** intervento *m* chirurgico; *place of work* ambulatorio *m*; *~ hours* orario *m* d'ambulatorio; **surgical** chirurgico; **surgically** chirurgicamente

surly [ˈsɜːlɪ] scontroso
surmount [səˈmaʊnt] *difficulties* sormontare
surname [ˈsɜːneɪm] cognome *m*
surpass [səˈpɑːs] superare
surplus [ˈsɜːpləs] **1** *n* surplus *m inv* **2** *adj* eccedente
surprise [səˈpraɪz] **1** *n* sorpresa *f* **2** *v/t* sorprendere; *be ~d* essere sorpreso; *look ~d* avere l'aria sorpresa; **surprising** sorprendente; **surprisingly** sorprendentemente
surrender [səˈrendə(r)] **1** *v/i of army* arrendersi **2** *v/t weapons* etc consegnare **3** *n* resa *f*
surrogate 'mother [ˈsʌrəgət] madre *f* biologica
surround [səˈraʊnd] **1** *v/t* circondare **2** *n of picture* etc

bordo *m*; **surrounding** circostante; **surroundings** dintorni *mpl*; *fig* ambiente *m*

survey 1 [ˈsɜːveɪ] *n of modern literature etc* quadro *m* generale; *of building* perizia *f*; *poll* indagine *f* **2** [səˈveɪ] *v/t* (*look at*) osservare; *building* periziare; **surveyor** perito *m*

survival [səˈvaɪvl] sopravvivenza *f*; **survive 1** *v/i* sopravvivere; *his two surviving daughters* le due figlie ancora in vita **2** *v/t* sopravvivere a; **survivor** superstite *m/f*; *he's a ~ fig* se la cava sempre

suspect 1 [ˈsʌspekt] *n* indiziato *m*, -a *f* **2** [səˈspekt] *v/t person* sospettare; (*suppose*) supporre; **suspected** *murderer* presunto; *cause, heart attack etc* sospetto

suspend [səˈspend] (*hang*), *from office* sospendere; **suspenders** *Br* giarrettiere *fpl*; *Am for pants* bretelle *fpl*

suspense [səˈspens] suspense *f*; **suspension** MOT, *from duty* sospensione *f*

suspicion [səˈspɪʃn] sospetto *m*; **suspicious** *causing suspicion* sospetto; *feeling suspicion* sospettoso; *be ~ of* sospettare di; **suspiciously** *behave* in modo sospetto; *examine* sospettosamente

sustain [səˈsteɪn] sostenere; **sustainable** sostenibile

SUV [esjuːˈviː] (= *sports utility vehicle*) Suv *m inv*, gip-

pone *m*

swab [swɒb] tampone *m*

swallow[1] [ˈswɒləʊ] *v/t & v/i* inghiottire

swallow[2] [ˈswɒləʊ] *n bird* rondine *f*

swamp [swɒmp] **1** *n* palude *f* **2** *v/t*: *be ~ped with* essere sommerso da; **swampy** paludoso

swan [swɒn] cigno *m*

swap [swɒp] **1** *v/t*: *~ sth for sth* scambiare qc con qc **2** *v/i* fare scambio

swarm [swɔːm] **1** *n of bees* sciame *m* **2** *v/i*: *the town was ~ing with ...* la città brulicava di ...

swarthy [ˈswɔːðɪ] scuro

swat [swɒt] *fly* schiacciare

sway [sweɪ] **1** *n* (*power*) influenza *f* **2** *v/i* barcollare

swear [sweə(r)] **1** *v/i* (*use swearword*) imprecare; *~ at s.o.* dire parolacce a qu **2** *v/t* (*promise*) giurare; LAW, *on oath* giurare

♦ **swear in**: *the witness was sworn in* il testimone ha prestato giuramento

'swearword parolaccia *f*

sweat [swet] **1** *n* sudore *m* **2** *v/i* sudare; **sweat band** fascia *f* asciugasudore; **sweater** maglione *m*; **sweats** *Am* tuta *f* (da ginnastica); **sweatshirt** felpa *f* **2** **sweaty** *hands* sudato; *smell* di sudore

Swede [swiːd] svedese *m/f*; **Sweden** Svezia *f*; **Swedish**

1 *adj* svedese **2** *n* svedese *m*

sweep [swiːp] **1** *v/t floor, leaves* spazzare **2** *n* (*long curve*) curva *f*; **sweeping** *changes* radicale; **a ~ statement** una generalizzazione

sweet [swiːt] **1** *adj* dolce; F (*kind*) gentile; F (*cute*) carino **2** *n* caramella *f*; (*dessert*) dolce *m*; **sweet and sour** agrodolce; **sweetcorn** mais *m*; **sweetheart** innamorato *m*, -a *f*

swell [swel] **1** *v/i of wound, limb* gonfiarsi **2** *n of the sea* mare *m* lungo; **swelling** MED gonfiore *m*

sweltering ['sweltəriŋ] *heat* afoso, soffocante

swerve [swɜːv] *of driver, car* sterzare (bruscamente)

swift [swift] rapido

swim [swim] **1** *v/i* nuotare **2** *n* nuotata *f*; **go for a ~** andare a nuotare; **swimmer** nuotatore *m*, -trice *f*; **swimming** nuoto *m*; **swimming costume** costume *m* da bagno; **swimming pool** piscina *f*; **swimsuit** *esp Am* costume *m* da bagno

swindle ['swindl] **1** *n* truffa *f* **2** *v/t* truffare; **~ s.o. out of sth** estorcere qc a qu (con l'inganno)

swing [swiŋ] **1** *n of pendulum etc* oscillazione *f*; *for child* altalena *f*; **a ~ to the left** una svolta verso la sinistra **2** *v/t* far dondolare **3** *v/i* dondola-

re; (*turn*) girare; *of public opinion etc* indirizzarsi

Swiss [swis] **1** *adj* svizzero **2** *n person* svizzero *m*, -a *f*; **the ~** gli svizzeri

switch [swit͡ʃ] **1** *n for light* interruttore *m*; (*change*) cambiamento *m* **2** *v/t* (*change*) cambiare **3** *v/i* (*change*) cambiare; **~ to** passare a

◆ **switch off** spegnere

◆ **switch on** accendere

Switzerland ['switsələnd] Svizzera *f*

swivel ['swivl] girarsi

swollen ['swəʊlən] gonfio

sword [sɔːd] spada *f*; **swordfish** pesce *m* spada *inv*

syllable ['siləbl] sillaba *f*

syllabus ['siləbəs] programma *m*

symbol ['simbəl] simbolo *m*; **symbolic** simbolico; **symbolism** simbolismo *m*; **symbolist** simbolista *m/f*; **symbolize** simboleggiare

symmetrical [si'metrikl] simmetrico; **symmetry** simmetria *f*

sympathetic [simpə'θetik] (*showing pity*) compassionevole; (*understanding*) comprensivo; **be ~ towards an idea** simpatizzare per un'idea

◆ **sympathize with** ['simpəθaiz] *person, views* capire

sympathizer ['simpəθaizə(r)] POL simpatizzante *m/f*; **sympathy** (*pity*) compassione *f*;

(*understanding*) comprensione f

symphony ['sɪmfənɪ] sinfonia f

symptom ['sɪmptəm] *also fig* sintomo m; **symptomatic**; **be ~ of** essere sintomatico di

synchronize ['sɪŋkrənaɪz] sincronizzare

synonym ['sɪnənɪm] sinonimo m; **synonymous** sinonimo

synthesizer ['sɪnθəsaɪzə(r)] MUS sintetizzatore m; **syn-**

thetic sintetico

syphilis ['sɪfɪlɪs] sifilide f

Syria ['sɪrɪə] Siria f; **Syrian 1** *adj* siriano **2** n siriano m, -a f

syringe [sɪ'rɪndʒ] siringa f

syrup ['sɪrəp] sciroppo m

system ['sɪstəm] *also* computer sistema m; (*orderliness*) ordine m; **systematic** sistematico; **systematically** sistematicamente; **systems analyst** COMPUT analista m/f di sistemi

T

table ['teɪbl] tavolo m; *of figures* tabella f, tavola f; **tablecloth** tovaglia f; **table lamp** lampada f da tavolo; **table of contents** indice m; **tablespoon** cucchiaio m da tavola

tablet ['tæblɪt] MED compressa f

'table tennis tennis m da tavolo, ping pong m

tabloid ['tæblɔɪd] *newspaper* quotidiano m formato tabloid; *pej* quotidiano m scandalistico

taboo [tə'buː] tabù m inv

tacit ['tæsɪt] tacito

tack [tæk] **1** n (*nail*) chiodino m **2** v/t (*sew*) imbastire **3** v/i *of yacht* virare di bordo

tackle ['tækl] **1** n (*equipment*) attrezzatura f; SP *in football*,

hockey contrasto m; *in rugby* placcaggio m **2** v/t *in football*, *hockey* contrastare; *in rugby* placcare; *problem*, *intruder* affrontare

tacky ['tækɪ] *paint* fresco; *glue* appiccicoso; F (*cheap*, *poor quality*) di cattivo gusto

tact [tækt] tatto m; **tactful** pieno di tatto; **tactfully** con grande tatto

tactical ['tæktɪkl] tattico; **tactics** tattica f

tactless ['tæktlɪs] privo di tatto

tadpole ['tædpəʊl] girino m

tag [tæg] (*label*) etichetta f

tail [teɪl] coda f; **tailback** coda f; **tail light** luce f posteriore

tailor ['teɪlə(r)] sarto m, -a f; **tailor-made** *also fig* (fatto) su misura

talk

'**tailpipe** tubo *m* di scappamento

take [teɪk] prendere; (*transport*) portare; (*accompany*) accompagnare; (*accept: money, gift*) accettare; *maths, French, photograph, exam, shower, stroll* fare; (*endure*) sopportare; (*require*) richiedere; *how long does it ~?* quanto ci vuole?

◆ **take after** aver preso da

◆ **take away** *pain* far sparire; *object* togliere; MATH sottrarre; *take sth away from s.o.* togliere qc a qu; *to take away food* da asporto

◆ **take back** (*return: object*) riportare; (*receive back*) riprendere; *person* riaccompagnare; (*accept back: husband etc*) rimettersi insieme a; *sth said* ritirare; *that takes me back* mi riporta al passato

◆ **take down** *from shelf* tirare giù; *scaffolding* smontare; (*write down*) annotare

◆ **take in** (*take indoors*) portare dentro; (*give accommodation*) ospitare; (*make narrower*) stringere; (*deceive*) imbrogliare; (*include*) includere

◆ **take off** 1 *v/t clothes, 10%* togliere; (*mimic*) imitare; *take a day off* prendere un giorno di ferie 2 *v/i of aeroplane* decollare; (*become popular*) far presa

◆ **take on** *job* intraprendere;

staff assumere

◆ **take out** *from bag, pocket* tirare fuori; *stain, appendix, tooth, word* togliere; *money from bank* prelevare; *to dinner etc* portar fuori; *insurance policy* stipulare, fare; *take it out on s.o.* prendersela con qu

◆ **take over** 1 *v/t company etc* assumere il controllo di 2 *v/i of new management etc* assumere il controllo; (*do sth in s.o.'s place*) dare il cambio

◆ **take to** (*like*) prendere in simpatia; (*form habit of*) prendere l'abitudine di; *he immediately took to the new idea* la nuova idea gli è piaciuta subito

◆ **take up** *carpet etc* togliere; (*carry up*) portare sopra; *dress etc* accorciare; *judo, Spanish, new job* incominciare; *offer* accettare; *space, time* occupare; *I'll take you up on your offer* accetto la tua offerta

'**takeoff** *of airplane* decollo *m*; (*impersonation*) imitazione *f*; **takeover** COM rilevamento *m*; **takeover bid** offerta *f* pubblica di acquisto, OPA *f*; **takings** incassi *mpl*

tale [teɪl] storia *f*

talent ['tælənt] talento *m*; **talented** pieno di talento; **talent scout** talent scout *m/f inv*

talk [tɔːk] 1 *v/i* parlare 2 *v/t*

English etc parlare; *business, politics* parlare di; **~ s.o. into doing sth** convincere qu a fare qc **3** *n* (*conversation*) conversazione *f*; (*lecture*) conferenza *f*; **~s** (*negotiations*) trattative *fpl*
◆ **talk back** ribattere

talkative ['tɔːkətɪv] loquace;
talk show talk show *m inv*
tall [tɔːl] alto; **tall story** baggianata *f*
tally ['tælɪ] **1** *n* conto **2** *v/i* quadrare
tame [teɪm] *animal* addomesticato; *joke etc* blando
◆ **tamper with** ['tæmpə(r)] manomettere
tampon ['tæmpɒn] tampone *m*
tan [tæn] **1** *n from sun* abbronzatura *f*; *colour* marrone *m* rossiccio **2** *v/i in sun* abbronzarsi **3** *v/t leather* conciare
tangent ['tændʒənt] MATH tangente *f*
tangerine [tændʒə'riːn] tangerino *m*
tangible ['tændʒɪbl] tangibile
tangle ['tæŋgl] nodo *m*
tango ['tæŋgəʊ] tango *m*
tank [tæŋk] recipiente *m*; MOT serbatoio *m*; MIL carro *m* armato; *for skin diver* bombola *f* (d'ossigeno); **tanker ship** nave *f* cisterna; **truck** autocisterna *f*
tanned [tænd] abbronzato
tantalizing ['tæntəlaɪzɪŋ] allettante; *smell* stuzzicante

tantamount ['tæntəmaʊnt]: **be ~ to** essere equivalente a
tantrum ['tæntrəm] capricci *mpl*; **throw a ~** fare (i) capricci
tap [tæp] **1** *n* rubinetto *m* **2** *v/t* (*hit*) dare un colpetto a; *phone* mettere sotto controllo; **tap dance** *n* tip tap *m*
tape [teɪp] **1** *n magnetic* nastro *m* magnetico; *recorded* cassetta *f*; (*sticky*) nastro *m* adesivo; **on ~** registrato **2** *v/t conversation etc* registrare; **~ sth to sth** attaccare qc a qc col nastro adesivo; **tape deck** registratore *m*; **tape drive** COMPUT unità *f inv* di backup a nastro; **tape measure** metro *m* a nastro
taper ['teɪpə(r)] assottigliarsi
'**tape recorder** registratore *m* a cassette; **tape recording** registrazione *f* su cassetta
tar [tɑː(r)] catrame *m*
tardy ['tɑːdɪ] *Am* tardivo; *arrival* in ritardo
target ['tɑːgɪt] **1** *n* bersaglio *m*; *for sales etc* obiettivo *m* **2** *v/t market* rivolgersi a; **target audience** target *m inv* di pubblico; **target date** data *f* fissata; **target group** COM gruppo *m* target; **target market** mercato *m* target
tariff ['tærɪf] (*price*) tariffa *f*; (*tax*) tassa *f*
tarmac ['tɑːmæk] *at airport* pista *f*
tarnish ['tɑːnɪʃ] *metal* ossida-

tear

re; *reputation* macchiare

tarpaulin [tɑːˈpɔːlɪn] tela *f* cerata

tart [tɑːt] torta *f*

task [tɑːsk] compito *m*; **task force** task force *f inv*

taste [teɪst] **1** *n* gusto *m* **2** *v/t food* assaggiare; *(experience: freedom etc)* provare **3** *v/i*: **it ~s like ...** ha sapore di ...; **it ~s very nice** è molto buono; **tasteful** di gusto; **tastefully** con gusto; **tasteless** *food* insaporo; *remark, person* privo di gusto; **tasting** *of wine* degustazione *f*; **tasty** gustoso

tattered [ˈtætəd] malridotto

tattoo [təˈtuː] tatuaggio *m*

taunt [tɔːnt] **1** *n* scherno *m* **2** *v/t* schernire

Taurus [ˈtɔːrəs] ASTR Toro *m*

taut [tɔːt] teso

tax [tæks] **1** *n* tassa *f*; **before / after ~** al lordo / al netto di imposte **2** *v/t* tassare; **taxable income** reddito *m* imponibile; **taxation** tassazione *f*; **tax bracket** fascia *f* di reddito; **tax-deductible** deducibile dalle imposte; **tax disc** *for car* bollo *m* (di circolazione); **tax evasion** evasione *f* fiscale; **tax-free** esentasse *inv*; **tax haven** paradiso *m* fiscale

taxi [ˈtæksɪ] taxi *m inv*; **taxi driver** tassista *m/f*

taxing [ˈtæksɪŋ] estenuante

'taxi rank stazione *f* dei taxi

'taxpayer contribuente *m/f*; **tax return** *form* dichiarazione *f* dei redditi; **tax year** anno *m* fiscale

TB [tiːˈbiː] (= *tuberculosis*) tbc *f* (= tubercolosi *f*)

tea [tiː] *drink* tè *m inv*; *meal* cena *f*; **teabag** bustina *f* di tè

teach [tiːtʃ] *subject* insegnare; *person* insegnare a; **~ s.o. to do sth** insegnare a qu a fare qc; **teacher** insegnante *m/f*; **teaching** *profession* insegnamento *m*

'tea-cup tazza *f* da tè

teak [tiːk] tek *m*

team [tiːm] *in sport* squadra *f*; *at work* équipe *f inv*; **team mate** compagno *m*, -a *f* di squadra; **team spirit** spirito *m* d'équipe; **teamster** *Am* camionista *m*; **teamwork** lavoro *m* d'équipe

teapot [ˈtiːpɒt] teiera *f*

tear[1] [ter] **1** *n in cloth etc* strappo *m* **2** *v/t paper, cloth* strappare; **be torn between two alternatives** essere combattuto tra due alternative **3** *v/i (run fast, drive fast)* sfrecciare

◆ **tear down** *poster* strappare; *building* buttar giù

◆ **tear out** *page* strappare; *hair* strapparsi

◆ **tear up** *paper* distruggere; *agreement* rompere

tear[2] [tɪr] *n in eye* lacrima *f*; **burst into ~s** scoppiare a piangere; **be in ~s** essere in lacrime

tearful ['tɪrful] *look, voice* piangente; **tear gas** gàs *m* lacrimogeno

tease [ti:z] *person* prendere in giro; *animal* stuzzicare

teaspoon cucchiaino *m* da caffè

technical ['teknɪkl] tecnico; **technically** tecnicamente; **technician** tecnico *m*; **technique** tecnica *f*

technological [teknə'lɒdʒɪkl] tecnologico; **technology** tecnologia *f*; **technophobia** tecnofobia *f*

teddy bear ['tedɪbeə(r)] orsacchiotto *m*

tedious ['ti:dɪəs] noioso

tee [ti:] *in golf* tee *m inv*

teenage ['ti:neɪdʒ] *problems* degli adolescenti; ~ *fashions* moda giovane; **teenager** adolescente *m/f*

teens [ti:nz] adolescenza *f*; *be in one's* ~ essere adolescente

teeny ['ti:nɪ] F piccolissimo

teeth [ti:θ] *pl* ☞ **tooth**

teethe [ti:ð] mettere i denti; **teething problems** difficoltà *fpl* iniziali

teetotal [ti:'təʊtl] *person* astemio; *party* senza alcolici

telecommunications [telɪkəmju:nɪ'keɪʃnz] telecomunicazioni *fpl*

telegraph pole ['telɪgrɑ:fpəʊl] palo *m* del telegrafo

telepathic [telɪ'pæθɪk] telepa-

tico; **telepathy** telepatia *f*

telephone ['telɪfəʊn] **1** *n* telefono *m* **2** *v/t person* telefonare a **3** *v/i* telefonare; **telephone book** guida *f* telefonica; **telephone booth** cabina *f* telefonica; **telephone call** telefonata *f*; **telephone conversation** conversazione *f* telefonica; **telephone directory** elenco *m* telefonico; **telephone number** numero *m* telefonico

telephoto lens [telɪfəʊtəʊ'lenz] teleobiettivo *m*

telesales ['telɪseɪlz] vendita *f* telefonica

telescope ['telɪskəʊp] telescopio *m*

televise ['telɪvaɪz] trasmettere in televisione

television ['telɪvɪʒn] *also set* televisione *f*; *on* ~ alla televisione; **television programme**, *Am* **television program** programma *m* televisivo; **television studio** studio *m* televisivo

tell [tel] **1** *v/t* dire; *story* raccontare; ~ *s.o. sth* dire qc a qu; ~ *s.o. to do sth* dire a qu di fare qc; *it's hard to* ~ è difficile a dirsi; *you never can* ~ non si può mai dire; ~ *X from Y* distinguere X da Y; *I can't* ~ *the difference between* ... non vedo nessuna differenza tra ... **2** *v/i* (*have effect*) farsi sentire; *time will* ~ il tempo lo dirà;

teller *in bank* cassiere *m*, -a *f*; **telling off** rimprovero *m*; **give s.o. a ~** rimproverare qu; **telltale 1** *adj signs* rivelatore **2** *n* spione *m*, spiona *f*

temp [temp] **1** *n employee* impiegato *m*, -a interinale **2** *v/i* fare lavori interinali

temper ['tempə(r)] (*bad ~*): **have a terrible ~** essere irascibile; **be in a ~** essere arrabbiato; **keep one's ~** mantenere la calma; **lose one's ~** perdere le staffe

temperament ['temprəmənt] temperamento *m*; **temperamental** (*moody*) lunatico; *machine* imprevedibile

temperate ['tempərət] temperato

temperature ['temprətʃə(r)] temperatura *f*; (*fever*) febbre *f*

temple¹ ['templ] REL tempio *m*

temple² ['templ] ANAT tempia *f*

tempo ['tempəu] ritmo *m*; MUS tempo *m*

temporarily [tempə'reərɪlɪ] temporaneamente; **temporary** temporaneo, provvisorio

tempt [tempt] tentare; **temptation** tentazione *f*; **tempting** allettante; *meal* appetitoso

ten [ten] dieci

tenacious [tɪ'neɪʃəs] tenace; **tenacity** tenacità *f*

tenant ['tenənt] inquilino *m*, -a *f*, locatario *m*, -a *f*

tend¹ [tend] *v/t* (*look after*) prendersi cura di

tend² [tend] *v/i*: **~ to do sth** tendere a fare qc

tendency ['tendənsɪ] tendenza *f*

tender¹ ['tendə(r)] *adj* (*sore*) sensibile; (*affectionate*) tenero; *steak* tenero

tender² ['tendə(r)] *n* COM offerta *f* ufficiale

tenderness ['tendənɪs] (*soreness*) sensibilità *f*; *of kiss, steak* tenerezza *f*

tendon ['tendən] tendine *m*

tennis ['tenɪs] tennis *m*; **tennis ball** palla *f* da tennis; **tennis court** campo *m* da tennis; **tennis player** tennista *m/f*

tenor ['tenə(r)] MUS tenore *m*

tense¹ [tens] *n* GRAM tempo *m*

tense² [tens] *adj voice, person* teso; *atmosphere* carico di tensione

tension ['tenʃn] tensione *f*

tent [tent] tenda *f*

tentative ['tentətɪv] esitante

tenterhooks ['tentəhuks]: **be on ~** essere sulle spine

tenth [tenθ] decimo

tepid ['tepɪd] tiepido

term [tɜːm] periodo *m*; *of office* durata *f* in carica; EDU *three months* trimestre *m*; *two months* bimestre *m*; (*condition, word*) termine *m*; *be on good / bad ~s with s.o.* essere in buoni / cattivi rapporti con qu; *in the long / short ~* a lungo / breve termine; *come to ~s with sth* venire a patti con qc

terminal ['tɜ:mɪnl] **1** *n* at airport, for containers, COMPUT terminale *m*; for buses capolinea *m* inv; ELEC morsetto *m* **2** *adj illness* in fase terminale; **terminally:~ ill** malato (in fase) terminale; **terminate 1** *v/t contract, pregnancy* interrompere **2** *v/i* terminare; **termination** of contract, pregnancy interruzione *f*

terminology [tɜ:mɪ'nɒlədʒɪ] terminologia *f*

terminus ['tɜ:mɪnəs] for buses capolinea *m* inv; for trains stazione *f* di testa

terrace ['terəs] on hillside, at hotel terrazza *f*; of houses fila *f* di case a schiera

terracotta [terə'kɒtə] di terracotta

terrain [tə'reɪn] terreno *m*

terrestrial [tə'restrɪəl] **1** *n* terrestre *m/f* **2** *adj television* di terra

terrible ['terəbl] terribile; **terribly** *play* malissimo; *(very)* molto

terrific [tə'rɪfɪk] eccezionale; **~!** bene!; **terrifically** *(very)* eccezionalmente

terrify ['terɪfaɪ] terrificare; **terrifying** terrificante

territorial [terɪ'tɔːrɪəl] territoriale; **territory** also fig territorio *m*

terror ['terə(r)] terrore *m*; **terrorism** terrorismo *m*; **terrorist** terrorista *m/f*; **terrorist attack** attentato *m* terroristico; **terrorize** terrorizzare

terse [tɜːs] brusco

test [test] **1** *n* prova *f*, test *m* inv; for driving, medical esame *m*; **blood ~** analisi *f* inv del sangue **2** *v/t soup, bathwater* provare; *machine, theory* testare; *person, friendship* mettere alla prova

testament ['testəmənt]: **Old / New Testament** REL Vecchio / Nuovo Testamento *m*

'test-drive: go for a ~ fare un giro di prova

testicle ['testɪkl] testicolo *m*

testify ['testɪfaɪ] LAW testimoniare

testimony ['testɪmənɪ] LAW testimonianza *f*

'test tube provetta *f*

testy ['testɪ] suscettibile

tetanus ['tetənəs] tetano *m*

text [tekst] **1** *n* testo *m*; *(message)* SMS *m* inv, messaggino *m* **2** *v/t* mandare un SMS a; **textbook** libro *m* di testo

textile ['tekstaɪl] tessuto *m*

'text-message SMS *m* inv, messaggino *m*

texture ['tekstʃə(r)] consistenza *f*

Thai [taɪ] **1** *adj* tailandese **2** *n*

therapeutic

person tailandese *m/f*; *language* tailandese *m*; **Thailand** Tailandia *f*

than [ðæn] *che*; *with numbers, pronouns, names* di; *older ~ me* più vecchio di me; *more French ~ Italian* più francese che italiana

thank [θæŋk] ringraziare; *~ you* grazie; *no ~ you* no, grazie; **thankful** riconoscente; **thankfully** con riconoscenza; (*luckily*) fortunatamente; **thankless** ingrato; **thanks** ringraziamenti *mpl*; *~!* grazie!; *~ to* grazie a; **Thanksgiving (Day)** *in USA* giorno *m* del ringraziamento

that [ðæt] **1** *adj* quel; *with masculine nouns before s+consonant, gn, ps and z* quello; *~ one* quello **2** *pron* quello *m*, *-a f*; *what is ~?* cos'è?; *who is ~?* chi è?; *~'s mine* è mio; *~'s tea* quello è tè; *~'s very kind* è molto gentile **3** *relative pron* che; *the car ~ you saw* la macchina che hai visto; *the day ~ he was born* il giorno in cui è nato **4** *adv* (*so*) così; *~ expensive* così caro **5** *conj* che; *I think ~ ... credo che ...

thaw [θɔ:] *of snow* sciogliersi; *of frozen food* scongelare

the [ðə] il *m*, la *f*; i *mpl*, le *fpl*; *with masculine nouns before s+consonant, gn, ps and z* lo *m*, gli *mpl*; *before vowel* l' *m/f*, gli *mpl*; *to ~ bathroom*

al bagno; *~ sooner ~ better* prima è, meglio è

theatre, *Am* **theater** [ˈθɪətə(r)] teatro *m*; *MED* sala *f* operatoria

theatrical [θɪˈætrɪkl] *also fig* teatrale

theft [θeft] furto *m*

their [ðeə(r)] il loro *m*, la loro *f*; i loro *mpl*, le loro *fpl*; (*his or her*) il suo *m*, la sua *f*, i suoi *mpl*, le sue *fpl*; **theirs** il loro *m*, la loro *f*; i loro *mpl*, le loro *fpl*; *it was an idea of ~* è stata una loro idea

them [ðem] *direct object* li *m*, le *f*; *referring to things* essi *m*, esse *f*; *indirect object* loro, gli; *after preposition* loro; *referring to things* essi *m*, esse *f*; (*him or her*) lo *m*, la *f*; *I know ~* li / le conosco; *I sold it to ~* gliel'ho venduto, l'ho venduto a loro

theme [θi:m] tema *m*; **theme park** parco *m* a tema

themselves [ðemˈselvz] si; *emphatic* loro stessi *mpl*, loro stesse *fpl*; *after prep* se stessi / se stesse; *they enjoyed ~* si sono divertiti

then [ðen] (*at that time, deducing*) allora; (*after that*) poi; *by ~* allora

theology [θɪˈɒlədʒɪ] teologia *f*

theoretical [θɪəˈretɪkl] teorico; **theoretically** teoricamente; **theory** teoria *f*

therapeutic [θerəˈpju:tɪk] te-

therapist   592

rapeutico; **therapist** terapista *m/f*, terapeuta *m/f*; **therapy** terapia *f*

there [ðeə(r)] lì, là; **over ~** là;
down ~ laggiù; **~ is** ... c'è; **~
are** ... ci sono; **is ~ ...?** c'è
...?; **are ~ ...?** ci sono ...?;
isn't ~ ...? non c'è ...?;
aren't ~? non ci sono ...?; **~ you
are** giving sth ecco qui; *finding sth* ecco; *completing sth*
ecco fatto; **~ and back** andata e ritorno; **~ he is!** eccolo!;
~, ~! *comforting* su, dai!;
thereabouts giù di lì; **therefore** quindi, pertanto
thermometer [θə'mɒmɪtə(r)]
termometro *m*
thermos flask ['θɜ:məsflɑ:sk]
termos *m inv*
thermostat ['θɜ:məstæt] termostato *m*
these [ði:z] **1** *adj* questi **2** *pron*
questi *m*, -e *f*
thesis ['θi:sɪs] tesi *f inv*
they [ðeɪ] ◊ loro; **~'re going
to the theatre** vanno a teatro; **there ~ are** eccoli *mpl*,
eccole *fpl* ◊ **if anyone
looks at this, ~ will see that**
... se qualcuno lo guarda,
vedrà che ...; **~ say that** ...
si dice che ...; **~ are going
to change the law** cambieranno la legge
thick [θɪk] spesso *m*; *hair* folto,
fog, forest fitto; *liquid* denso;
F *(stupid)* ottuso; **thicken**
sauce ispessire; **thick-
skinned** *fig* insensibile

thief [θi:f] ladro *m*, -a *f*
thigh [θaɪ] coscia *f*
thin [θɪn] sottile; *person* magro; *hair* rado; *liquid* fluido
thing [θɪŋ] cosa *f*; **~s** *(belongings)* cose *fpl*; **it's a good ~
you told me** è un bene che
tu me l'abbia detto
thingumajig ['θɪŋəmədʒɪg] F
coso *m*, cosa *f* F
think [θɪŋk] pensare; **I ~ so**
penso *or* credo di sì; **I don't
~ so** non credo; **I'm ~ing
about emigrating** sto pensando di emigrare
◆ **think over** riflettere su
◆ **think through** analizzare a
fondo
◆ **think up** *plan* escogitare
'think tank comitato *m* di
esperti
thin-skinned [θɪn'skɪnd] *fig*
sensibile
third [θɜ:d] **1** *adj* terzo **2** *n* terzo *m*; thirdly in terzo luogo;
third-party terzi *mpl*; **third-
party insurance** assicurazione *f* sulla responsabilità
civile; **Third World** Terzo
Mondo *m*
thirst [θɜ:st] sete *f*; **thirsty** assetato; **be ~** avere sete
thirteen [θɜ:'ti:n] tredici; **thirteenth** tredicesimo; **thirtieth**
trentesimo; **thirty** trenta
this [ðɪs] **1** *adj* questo; **~ one**
questo (qui) **2** *pron* questo
m, -a *f*; **~ is easy** è facile; **~
is** ... *introducing s.o.* questo / questa è ... **3** *adv*:

high alto così

thorn [θɔːn] spina *f*; **thorny** *also fig* spinoso

thorough [ˈθʌrə] *search, knowledge* approfondito; *person* scrupoloso; **thoroughbred** *horse* purosangue *inv*; **thoroughly** *search for* accuratamente; *know, understand, clean* perfettamente; *agree, spoil* completamente; *stupid, rude* extremamente

those [ðəʊz] **1** *adj* quelli; *with masculine nouns before* s+consonant, gn, ps and z quegli **2** *pron* quelli *m*, -e *f*; *with masculine nouns before* s+consonant, gn, ps and z quegli

though [ðəʊ] **1** *conj* (*although*) benché (+*subj*); **as ~** come se **2** *adv* però

thought [θɔːt] pensiero *m*; **thoughtful** pensieroso; *reply* meditato; (*considerate*) gentile; **thoughtless** sconsiderato

thousand [ˈθaʊznd] mille; **~ of** migliaia di; **thousandth** millesimo

thrash [θræʃ] picchiare; SP battere

◆ **thrash out** *solution* mettere a punto

thrashing [ˈθræʃɪŋ] botte *fpl*; SP batosta *f*

thread [θred] **1** *n* filo *m*; *of screw* filettatura *f* **2** *v/t needle* infilare il filo in; *beads* infila-

re; **threadbare** liso

threat [θret] minaccia *f*; **threaten** minacciare; **threatening** minaccioso; **~ letter** lettera *f* minatoria

three [θriː] tre; **three quarters** tre quarti *mpl*

threshold [ˈθreʃhəʊld] *of house, new era* soglia *f*

thrifty [ˈθrɪftɪ] parsimonioso

thrill [θrɪl] **1** *n* emozione *f*; *physical feeling* brivido *m* **2** *v/t*: **be ~ed** essere emozionato; **thriller** giallo *m*; **thrilling** emozionante

thrive [θraɪv] *of plant* crescere rigoglioso; *of business* prosperare

throat [θrəʊt] gola *f*; **have a sore ~** avere mal di gola; **throat lozenge** pastiglia *f* per la gola

throb [θrɒb] pulsare; *of heart* battere; *of music* rimbombare

throne [θrəʊn] trono *m*

throttle [ˈθrɒtl] **1** *n on motorbike* manetta *f* di accelerazione; *on boat* leva *f* di accelerazione **2** *v/t* (*strangle*) strozzare

through [θruː] **1** *prep* (*across*) attraverso; (*during*) durante; (*by means of*) tramite; **go ~ the city** attraversare la città; **~ the winter** per tutto l'inverno; **arranged ~ him** organizzato tramite lui **2** *adv*: **wet ~** completamente bagnato **3** *adj*: **be ~ of couple** essersi lasciati; *have arrived: of news etc* essere arrivato; **I'm ~ with ...** *(finished with)* ho finito con ...; **~ the night** per tutta la notte **2** *adv (in all parts)* completamente

throw [θrəʊ] **1** *v/t* lanciare; *into bin etc* gettare; *of horse* disarcionare; *(disconcert)* sconcertare; *party* dare **2** *n* lancio *m*

◆ **throw away** buttare via, gettare

◆ **throw out** *old things* buttare via; *from bar, house etc* buttare fuori; *plan* scartare

◆ **throw up 1** *v/t ball* lanciare **2** *v/i (vomit)* vomitare

'throw-away *remark* buttato lì; *(disposable)* usa e getta *inv*; **throw-in** SP rimessa *f*

thru [θruː] *Am* ☞ **through**

thrust [θrʌst] *v/t (push hard)* spingere; *knife* conficcare; **~ one's way through the crowd** farsi largo tra la folla

thud [θʌd] tonfo *m*

thug [θʌɡ] *hooligan* teppista *m*; *tough guy* bullo *m*

thumb [θʌm] **1** *n* pollice *m* **2** *v/t*: **~ a lift** fare l'autostop; **thumbtack** *Am* puntina *f*

thunder [ˈθʌndə(r)] tuono *m*; **thunderous** *applause* fragoroso; **thunderstorm** temporale *m*; **thunderstruck** allibito; **thundery** *weather* temporalesco

Thursday [ˈθɜːzdeɪ] giovedì *m inv*

thus [ðʌs] *(in this way)* così

thwart [θwɔːt] *person, plans* ostacolare

Tiber [ˈtaɪbə(r)] Tevere *m*

tick [tɪk] **1** *n of clock* ticchettio *m*; *in text* segno *m* **2** *v/i of clock* ticchettare **3** *v/t with a ~* segnare

ticket [ˈtɪkɪt] biglietto *m*; *in cloakroom* scontrino *m*; **ticket machine** distributore *m* di biglietti; **ticket office** biglietteria *f*

ticking [ˈtɪkɪŋ] *noise* ticchettio *m*

tickle [ˈtɪkl] **1** *v/t person* fare il solletico a **2** *v/i of material* dare prurito; *of person* fare il solletico

tidal wave [ˈtaɪdlweɪv] onda *f* di marea

tide [taɪd] marea *f*; **the ~ is in / out** c'è l'alta / la bassa marea

tidiness [ˈtaɪdɪnɪs] ordine *m*; **tidy** ordinato

◆ **tidy up 1** *v/t room, shelves* mettere in ordine; **tidy o.s. up** darsi una sistemata **2** *v/i* mettere in ordine

tie [taɪ] **1** *n (necktie)* cravatta *f*; SP: *even result* pareggio *m*; **he doesn't have any ~s** non ha legami **2** *v/t knot, hands* legare **3** *v/i* SP pareggiare

◆ **tie down** *with rope* legare; *(restrict)* vincolare

◆ **tie up** *person, laces, hair* legare; *boat* ormeggiare; *I'm tied up tomorrow* sono impegnato domani
tier [tɪə(r)] *of hierarchy* livello *m*; *in stadium* anello *m*
tiger ['taɪɡə(r)] tigre *f*
tight [taɪt] **1** *adj clothes* stretto; *security* rigido; *rope* teso; *not leaving much time* giusto; *schedule* serrato; **F** *(drunk)* sbronzo **F 2** *adv*: *hold s.o. / sth* ~ tenere qu / qc stretto; *shut sth* ~ chiudere bene qc; **tighten** *screw* serrare; *belt* stringere; *rope* tendere; *security* intensificare; **tight-fisted** ~ taccagno; **tightly** ☞ **tight** *adv*; **tightrope** fune *f* (per funamboli); **tights** collant *mpl*
tile [taɪl] *on floor* mattonella *f*; *on wall* piastrella *f*; *on roof* tegola *f*
till¹ [tɪl] ☞ **until**
till² [tɪl] *(cash register)* cassa *f*
tilt [tɪlt] **1** *v/t* inclinare **2** *v/i* inclinarsi
timber ['tɪmbə(r)] legname *m*
time [taɪm] tempo *m*; *by the clock* ora *f*; *(occasion)* volta *f*; *for the* ~ *being* al momento; *have a good* ~! divertiti!; *what's the* ~? che ora è?, che ore sono?; *the first* ~ la prima volta; *take your* ~ fai con calma; *for a* ~ per un po'(di tempo); *at any* ~ in qualsiasi momento; *(and) about* ~! era ora!;

two at a ~ due alla volta; *at the same* ~ *speak, reply etc* contemporaneamente; *(however)* nel contempo; *in* ~ in tempo; *(eventually)* col tempo; *on* ~ in orario; *in no* ~ in un attimo; **time bomb** bomba *f* a orologeria; **time difference** fuso *m* orario; **time-lag** scarto *m* di tempo; **time limit** limite *m* temporale; **timely** tempestivo; **time out** SP time-out *m inv*; **timer** cronometro *m*; *on oven* timer *m inv*; **time-saving** risparmio *m* di tempo; **timescale** *of project* cronologia *f*; **time share** *(house, apartment)* multiproprietà *f inv*; **time switch** interruttore *m* a tempo; **timetable** orario *m*; **timewarp** trasposizione *f* temporale; **time zone** zona *f* di fuso orario
timid ['tɪmɪd] timido
tin [tɪn] *metal* stagno *m*; *container* barattolo *m*; **tinfoil** carta *f* stagnola
tinge [tɪndʒ] sfumatura *f*
tingle ['tɪŋɡl] pizzicare
tinkle ['tɪŋkl] *of bell* tintinnio *m*
'tin opener apriscatole *m inv*
tinsel ['tɪnsl] fili *mpl* d'argento
tint [tɪnt] **1** *n of colour* sfumatura *f*; *in hair* riflessante *m* **2** *v/t hair* fare dei riflessi a; **tinted** *glasses* fumé *inv*
tiny ['taɪnɪ] piccolissimo

tip¹ [tɪp] *n of stick, finger* punta *f; of cigarette* filtro *m*

tip² [tɪp] **1** *n advice* consiglio *m; money* mancia *f* **2** *v/t waiter etc* dare la mancia a

♦ **tip off** fare una soffiata a

'tip-off soffiata *f*

tipped [tɪpt] *cigarettes* col filtro

Tipp-Ex® ['tɪpeks] bianchetto *m*

tippy-toe ['tɪpɪtəʊ] *Am:* **on ~** sulla punta dei piedi

tipsy ['tɪpsɪ] alticcio

'tip-toe: on ~ sulla punta dei piedi

tire¹ [taɪr] *n Am* gomma *f*, pneumatico *m*

tire² [taɪr] **1** *v/t* stancare **2** *v/i* stancarsi

tired ['taɪəd] stanco; **be ~ of s.o. / sth** essere stanco di qu / sth; **tiredness** stanchezza *f*; **tireless** instancabile; **tiresome** (*annoying*) fastidioso; **tiring** stancante

tissue ['tɪʃuː] ANAT tessuto *m*; (*handkerchief*) fazzoletino *m* (di carta); **tissue paper** carta *f* velina

title ['taɪtl] titolo *m*; LAW diritto *m*; **titleholder** SP detentore *m*, -trice *f* del titolo

to [tuː] **1** *prep a:* **~** *Italy* in Italia; **~** *Rome* a Roma; **let's go ~ my place** andiamo a casa mia; **~ the north of ...** a nord di ...; **give sth ~ s.o.** dare qc a qu; **from 10 ~ 15 people** tra 10 e 15 persone; **it's 5 ~ 11**

sono le undici meno cinque **2** *with verbs:* **~ speak, ~ see** parlare, vedere; **learn ~ drive** imparare a guidare; **nice ~ eat** buono da mangiare; **~ learn Italian** *in order to* per imparare l'italiano **3** *adv:* **~ and fro** avanti e indietro

toast [təʊst] **1** *n* pane *m* tostato; (*drinking*) brindisi *m inv* **2** *v/t bread* tostare; *drinking* fare un brindisi a; **toaster** tostapane *m inv*

tobacco [tə'bækəʊ] tabacco *m*

today [tə'deɪ] oggi

toddler ['tɒdlə(r)] bambino *m*, -a *f* ai primi passi

to-'do F casino *m* F

toe [təʊ] dito *m* del piede; *of shoes, socks* punta *f*; **big ~** alluce *m*; **toenail** unghia *f* del piede

toffee ['tɒfɪ] caramella *f* al mou

together [tə'geðə(r)] insieme

toilet ['tɔɪlɪt] gabinetto *m*; **go to the ~** andare in bagno; **toilet paper** carta *f* igienica; **toiletries** prodotti *mpl* da toilette

token ['təʊkən] (*sign*) pegno *m*; *for gambling* gettone *m*; (*gift ~*) buono *m*

tolerable ['tɒlərəbl] *pain etc* tollerabile; (*quite good*) accettabile; **tolerance** tolleranza *f*; **tolerant** tollerante; **tolerate** tollerare

toll[1] [təʊl] *v/i of bell* suonare

toll[2] [təʊl] *n (deaths)* bilancio *m* delle vittime

toll[3] [təʊl] *n for bridge, road* pedaggio *m*

'**toll booth** casello *m*; **toll-free number** *Am* TELEC numero *m* verde; **toll road** strada *f* a pedaggio

tomato [təˈmɑːtəʊ] pomodoro *m*; **tomato ketchup** ketchup *m inv*; **tomato sauce** *for pasta etc* salsa *f* or sugo *m* di pomodoro; *(ketchup)* ketchup *m inv*

tomb [tuːm] tomba *f*; **tombstone** lapide *f*

tomcat ['tɒmkæt] gatto *m* (maschio)

tomorrow [təˈmɒrəʊ] domani; *the day after* ~ dopodomani; ~ *morning* domattina, domani mattina

ton [tʌn] tonnellata *f* (*Br* 1016kg, *Am* 907kg)

tone [təʊn] *of colour, musical instrument* tonalità *f inv*; *of conversation etc* tono *m*; *of neighbourhood* livello *m* sociale; ~ *of voice* tono di voce; **toner** toner *m inv*

tongue [tʌŋ] lingua *f*

tonic ['tɒnɪk] MED ricostituente *m*; **tonic (water)** acqua *f* tonica

tonight [təˈnaɪt] stanotte; *(this evening)* stasera

tonsillitis [tɒnsəˈlaɪtɪs] tonsillite *f*

too [tuː] *(also)* anche; *(exces-*sively)* troppo; *me* ~ anch'io; ~ *much rice* troppo riso; ~ *many mistakes* troppi errori; *eat* ~ *much* mangiare troppo

tool [tuːl] attrezzo *m*; *fig* strumento *m*

tooth [tuːθ] (*pl* **teeth** [tiːθ]) dente *m*; **toothache** mal *m* di denti; **toothbrush** spazzolino *m* da denti; **toothpaste** dentifricio *m*; **toothpick** stuzzicadenti *m inv*

top [tɒp] **1** *n of mountain, tree* cima *f*; *of wall, screen* parte *f* alta; *of page, list, street* inizio *m*; *(lid: of bottle etc, pen)* tappo *m*; *of the class, league* testa *f*; *(clothing)* maglia *f*; (MOT: *gear*) marcia *f* più alta; *on* ~ *of* in cima a; *at the* ~ *of* list, tree, mountain in cima a; league in testa a; *page, street* all'inizio di; *get to the* ~ *of company etc* arrivare in cima; *get to the* ~ *of mountain* arrivare alla vetta; *be over the* ~ *(exaggerated)* essere esagerato **2** *adj branches* più alto; *floor* ultimo; *management* di alto livello; *official* di alto rango; *player* migliore; *speed, note* massimo

topic ['tɒpɪk] argomento *m*; **topical** attuale

topless ['tɒplɪs] topless *inv*; **topmost** *branches, floor* più alto; **topping** *on pizza* guarnizione *f*

topple ['tɒpl] **1** *v/i* crollare **2**

v/t government far cadere

top 'secret top secret *inv*

topsy-turvy ['tɒpsɪ'tɜːvɪ] sottosopra *inv*

torch [tɔːtʃ] pila *f*; *with flame* torcia *f*

torment 1 ['tɔːment] *n* tormento *m* **2** [tɔː'ment] *v/t* tormentare

tornado [tɔː'neɪdəʊ] tornado *m*

torpedo [tɔː'piːdəʊ] **1** *n* siluro *m* **2** *v/t* silurare; *fig* far saltare

torrent ['tɒrənt] torrente *m*; *of lava* fiume *m*; *of abuse, words* valanga *f*; **torrential** *rain* torrenziale

tortoise ['tɔːtəs] tartaruga *f*

torture ['tɔːtʃə(r)] **1** *n* tortura *f* **2** *v/t* torturare

toss [tɒs] **1** *v/t ball* lanciare; *rider* disarcionare; *salad* mescolare; **~ a coin** fare testa o croce **2** *v/i:* **~ and turn** rigirarsi

total ['təʊtl] **1** *n* totale *m* **2** *adj amount, disaster* totale; *stranger* perfetto; **totalitarian** totalitario; **totally** totalmente, completamente

totter ['tɒtə(r)] barcollare

touch [tʌtʃ] **1** *n* tocco *m*; *sense* tatto *m*; *in rugby* touche *f*; **lose one's ~** perdere la mano; **kick the ball into ~** calciare la palla fuoricampo; **lose ~ with s.o.** perdere i contatti con qu; **keep in ~ with s.o.** rimanere in contatto con qu; **be out of ~** *with*

news non essere al corrente; *with people* non avere contatti **2** *v/t* toccare; *emotionally* commuovere **3** *v/i* toccare; *of two lines etc* toccarsi

◆ **touch down** *of plane* atterrare; *SP* fare meta

'touchdown *of plane* atterraggio *m*; *touching* commovente; **touchline** *SP* linea *f* laterale; **touch screen** schermo *m* tattile; **touchy** *person* suscettibile

tough [tʌf] *person* forte; *question, exam, meat, punishment* duro; *material* resistente

tour [tʊə(r)] **1** *n* giro *m*; *of tourist* giro *m* turistico; *of band* tournée *f inv* **2** *v/t area* girare **3** *v/i of tourist* andare in giro; *of band* andare in tournée; **tour guide** guida *f* turistica; **tourism** turismo *m*; **tourist** turista *m/f*; **tourist industry** industria *f* del turismo; **tourist (information) office** ufficio *m* informazioni turistiche

tournament ['tʊənəmənt] torneo *m*

'tour operator operatore *m* turistico

tow [təʊ] rimorchiare

◆ **tow away** *car* portare via col carro attrezzi

toward(s) [tɔːd(z)] verso; *rude ~* maleducato nei confronti di; *work~* (**achieving**) *sth* lavorare per (raggiungere) qc

towel ['tauəl] asciugamano *m*

tower ['tauə(r)] torre *f*; **tower block** condominio *m* a torre

town [taun] città *f inv; opposed to city* cittadina *f*; **town centre,** *Am* **town center** centro *m*; **town council** consiglio *m* comunale; **town hall** municipio *m*

toxic ['tɒksɪk] tossico *m*; **toxin** tossina *f*

toy [tɔɪ] giocattolo *m*

trace [treɪs] **1** *n of substance* traccia *f* **2** *v/t (find)* rintracciare; *(draw)* tracciare

track [træk] *(path)* sentiero *m*; *on race course* pista *f*; *(race course)* circuito *m*; RAIL binario *m*; *on CD* brano *m*; **keep ~ of sth** tenersi al passo con qc

♦ **track down** rintracciare

'tracksuit tuta *f* (da ginnastica)

tractor ['træktə(r)] trattore *m*

trade [treɪd] **1** *n* commercio *m*; *(profession, craft)* mestiere *m* **2** *v/i (do business)* essere in attività; **~ in sth** commerciare in qc **3** *v/t (exchange)* scambiare (**for** con); **trade fair** fiera *f* campionaria; **trademark** marchio *m* registrato; **trader** commerciante *m/f*; **trade union** sindacato *m*

tradition [trə'dɪʃn] tradizione *f*; **traditional** tradizionale; **traditionally** tradizionalmente

traffic ['træfɪk] *on roads, in drugs* traffico *m*

♦ **traffic in** *drugs* trafficare

'traffic circle *Am* rotatoria *f*; **traffic cop** F vigile *m* (urbano); **traffic jam** ingorgo *m*; **traffic island** isola *f* spartitraffico; **traffic light(s)** semaforo *m* sing; **traffic police** polizia *f* stradale; **traffic sign** segnale *m* stradale; **traffic warden** ausiliario *m* (del traffico)

tragedy ['trædʒədɪ] tragedia *f*; **tragic** tragico

trail [treɪl] **1** *n (path)* sentiero *m*; *of person, animal* tracce *fpl; of blood* scia *f* **2** *v/t (follow)* seguire; *(drag)* trascinare; *caravan etc* trainare **3** *v/i (lag behind)* trascinarsi; **they're ~ing 3-1** stanno perdendo 3 a 1; **trailer** *pulled by vehicle* rimorchio *m*; *of film* trailer *m inv*; *(mobile home)* roulotte *f inv*

train¹ [treɪn] *n* treno *m*; **go by ~** andare in treno

train² [treɪn] **1** *v/t team, athlete* allenare; *employee* formare; *dog* addestrare **2** *v/i of team, athlete* allenarsi; *of teacher etc* fare il tirocinio

trainee [treɪ'niː] apprendista *m/f*; **trainer** SP allenatore *m*, -trice *f; of dog* addestratore *m*, -trice *f*; **~s** *shoes* scarpe *fpl* da ginnastica; **trainers** *shoes* scarpe *fpl* da ginnastica; **training** *of new staff* for-

mazione *f*; SP allenamento
m; **be in ~** SP allenarsi; **be
out of ~** SP essere fuori allenamento

'train station stazione *f* ferroviaria

traitor ['treɪtə(r)] traditore *m*,
-trice *f*

tram [træm] tram *m inv*

tramp [træmp] barbone *m*, -a
f

◆ **trample on** calpestare

trampoline ['træmpəliːn]
trampolino *m*

tranquil ['træŋkwɪl] tranquillo; **tranquillity**, *Am* **tranquility** tranquillità *f*; **tranquilizer**, *Am* **tranquilizer**
tranquillante *m*

transaction [træn'zækʃn]
transazione *f*

transatlantic
[trænzət'læntɪk] transatlantico

transcript ['trænskrɪpt] trascrizione *f*

transfer 1 [træns'fɜː(r)] *v/t*
trasferire; LAW cedere **2**
[træns'fɜː(r)] *v/i* cambiare **3**
['trænsfɜː(r)] *n* trasferimento *m*; LAW cessione *f*; *of money* bonifico *m* bancario;
transferable *ticket* trasferibile; **transfer fee** *for football
player* prezzo *m* d'acquisto

transform [træns'fɔːm] trasformare; **transformation**
trasformazione *f*; **transformer** ELEC trasformatore
m

transfusion [træns'fjuːʒn]
trasfusione *f*

transit ['trænzɪt]: **in ~** in transito; **transition** transizione *f*;
transitional di transizione;
transit lounge *at airport* sala
f passeggeri in transito;
transit passenger passeggero *m*, -a *f* in transito

translate [træns'leɪt] tradurre; **translation** traduzione
f; **translator** traduttore *m*,
-trice *f*

transmission [trænz'mɪʃn]
trasmissione *f*; **transmit**
news, programme, disease
trasmettere; **transmitter**
RAD, TV trasmettitore *m*

transparency
[træns'pærənsɪ] PHOT diapositiva *f*; **transparent** trasparente

transplant 1 [træns'plɑːnt] *v/t*
MED trapiantare **2**
['trænsplɑːnt] *n* MED trapianto *m*

transport 1 [træn'spɔːt] *v/t*
trasportare **2** ['trænspɔːt] *n*
of trasporto *m*; *means of
transport* mezzo *m* di trasporto; **public ~** i trasporti
pubblici; **transportation**
trasporto *m*

transvestite [træns'vestaɪt]
travestito *m*

trap [træp] **1** *n* trappola *f*;
question tranello *m* **2** *v/t* intrappolare; **trappings** *of
power* segni *mpl* esteriori

trash [træʃ] *poor product* robaccia *f; despicable person* fetente *m/f; Am (garbage)* spazzatura *f;* **trashcan** *Am* bidone *m* della spazzatura; **trashy** *goods, novel* scadente

trauma ['trɔːmə] trauma *m;* **traumatic** traumatico; **traumatize** traumatizzare

travel ['trævl] **1** *n* viaggiare *m;* **~s** viaggi *mpl* **2** *v/i* viaggiare; **I ~ to work by train** vado a lavorare in treno **3** *v/t miles* percorrere; **travel agency** agenzia *f* di viaggio; **travel agent** agente *m/f* di viaggio; **traveller,** *Am* **traveler** viaggiatore *m,* -trice *f,* **traveller's cheque,** *Am* **traveler's check** traveller's cheque *m inv;* **travel expenses** spese *fpl* di viaggio; **travel insurance** assicurazione *f* di viaggio

trawler ['trɔːlə(r)] peschereccio *m*

tray [treɪ] *for food, photocopier* vassoio *m; to go in oven* teglia *f*

treacherous ['tretʃərəs] traditore; **treachery** tradimento *m*

tread [tred] **1** *n* passo *m; of staircase* gradino *m; of tyre* battistrada *m inv* **2** *v/i* camminare

treason ['triːzn] tradimento *m*

treasure ['treʒə(r)] **1** *n also person* tesoro *m* **2** *v/t gift etc* custodire gelosamente;

treasurer tesoriere *m,* -a *f;* **Treasury Department** *Am* tesoro *m*

treat [triːt] **1** *n* trattamento *m* speciale; **it's my ~** (*I'm paying*) offro io **2** *v/t* trattare; *illness* curare; **~ s.o. to sth** offrire qc a qu; **treatment** trattamento *m; of illness* cura *f*

treaty ['triːtɪ] trattato *m*

treble ['trebl] **1** *adv:* **~ the price** il triplo del prezzo **2** *v/i* triplicarsi

tree [triː] albero *m*

tremble ['trembl] tremare

tremendous [trɪ'mendəs] (*very good*) fantastico; (*enormous*) enorme; **tremendously** (*very*) incredibilmente; (*a lot*) moltissimo

tremor ['tremə(r)] *of earth* scossa *f*

trench [trentʃ] trincea *f*

trend [trend] tendenza *f;* **trendy** alla moda

trespass ['trespəs] invadere una proprietà privata; **no ~ing** divieto d'accesso; **trespasser** intruso *m,* -a *f*

trial ['traɪəl] LAW processo *m; of equipment* prova *f;* **on ~** LAW sotto processo; **stand ~ for sth** essere processato per qc; **have sth on ~** *equipment* avere qc in prova; **trial period** periodo *m* di prova

triangle ['traɪæŋɡl] triangolo *m;* **triangular** triangolare

tribe [traɪb] tribù *f inv*

tribunal [traɪ'bjuːnl] tribunale *m*

tributary ['trɪbjʊtərɪ] *of river* affluente *m*

trick [trɪk] **1** *n to deceive* stratagemma *m*; *(knack)* trucco *m*; *play a ~ on s.o.* fare uno scherzo a qu **2** *v/t* ingannare; *trickery* truffa *f*

trickle ['trɪkl] **1** *n* filo *m*; *a ~ of replies* poche risposte sporadiche **2** *v/i* gocciolare

tricky ['trɪkɪ] *(difficult)* complicato

trifle ['traɪfl] *n (triviality)* inezia *f*; *pudding* zuppa *f* inglese; *trifling* insignificante

trigger ['trɪgə(r)] *on gun* grilletto *m*

◆ **trigger off** scatenare

trim [trɪm] **1** *adj (neat)* ordinato; *figure* snello **2** *v/t hair, hedge* spuntare; *costs* tagliare; *(decorate: dress)* ornare **3** *n (light cut)* spuntata *f*; *in good ~* in buone condizioni

trinket ['trɪŋkɪt] ninnolo *m*

trio ['triːəʊ] MUS trio *m*

trip [trɪp] **1** *n (journey)* viaggio *m*, gita *f* **2** *v/i (stumble)* inciampare *(over* in) **3** *v/t (make fall)* fare inciampare

◆ **trip up** *v/t (make fall)* fare inciampare; *(cause to make a mistake)* confondere **2** *v/i (stumble)* inciampare; *(make a mistake)* sbagliarsi

triple ['trɪpl] → **treble**

trite [traɪt] trito

triumph ['traɪʌmf] trionfo *m*

trivial ['trɪvɪəl] banale; **trivial-**

ity banalità *f inv*

trolley ['trɒlɪ] *in supermarket, at airport* carrello *m*

trombone [trɒm'bəʊn] trombone *m*

troops [truːps] truppe *fpl*

trophy ['trəʊfɪ] trofeo *m*

tropic ['trɒpɪk] tropico *m*; **tropical** tropicale; **tropics** tropici *mpl*

trot [trɒt] trottare

trouble ['trʌbl] **1** *n (difficulties)* problemi *mpl*; *(inconvenience)* fastidio *m*; *(disturbance)* disordini *mpl*; **the ~ with you is …** il tuo problema è …; **get into ~** mettersi nei guai **2** *v/t (worry)* preoccupare; *(bother, disturb)* disturbare; *of back, liver etc* dare dei fastidi a; **troublemaker** attaccabrighe *m/f inv*; **troubleshooting** mediazione *f*; *in software manual* ricerca *f* problemi e soluzioni; **troublesome** fastidioso

trousers ['traʊzəz] pantaloni *mpl*, **a pair of ~** un paio di pantaloni

trout [traʊt] trota *f*

truant ['truːənt]: **play ~** marinare la scuola

truce [truːs] tregua *f*

truck [trʌk] camion *m inv*; **truck driver** camionista *m*; **truck stop** *Am* posto *m* di ristoro per camionisti

trudge [trʌdʒ] *v/i* arrancare; **~ around the shops** trascinarsi per i negozi **2** *n* camminata *f* stancante

true [truː] vero; ***come ~ of hopes***, *dream* realizzarsi; **truly** davvero; ***Yours ~*** distinti saluti

trumpet ['trʌmpɪt] tromba *f*

trunk [trʌŋk] *of tree, body* tronco *m*; *of elephant* proboscide *f*; (*large case*) baule *m*; MOT bagagliaio *m inv*

trust [trʌst] **1** *n* fiducia *f*; FIN fondo *m* fiduciario **2** *v/t* fidarsi di; **trusted** fidato; **trustee** amministratore *m*, -trice *f* fiduciario, -a; **trustful**, **trusting** fiducioso; **trustworthy** affidabile

truth [truːθ] verità *f inv*; **truthful** *account* veritiero; *person* sincero

try [traɪ] **1** *v/t* provare; LAW processare; ***~ to do sth*** provare a fare qc, cercare di fare qc **2** *v/i* provare, tentare; ***you must ~ harder*** devi provare con più impegno **3** *n* tentativo *m*; *in rugby* meta *f*; **trying** (*annoying*) difficile

T-shirt ['tiːʃɜːt] maglietta *f*

tub [tʌb] (*bath*) vasca *f* da bagno; *of liquid* tinozza *f*; *for yoghurt* barattolo *m*; **tubby** tozzo

tube [tjuːb] tubo *m*; *of toothpaste* tubetto *m*; **tubeless** *tyre* senza camera d'aria

Tuesday ['tjuːzdeɪ] martedì *m inv*

tuft [tʌft] ciuffo *m*

tug [tʌg] **1** *n* NAUT rimorchiatore *m* **2** *v/t* (*pull*) tirare

tuition [tjuːˈɪʃn] lezioni *fpl*

tulip ['tjuːlɪp] tulipano *m*

tumble ['tʌmbl] ruzzolare; *of wall, prices* crollare; **tumbledown** in rovina, fatiscente; **tumbler** *for drink* bicchiere *m* (senza stelo); *in circus* acrobata *m/f*

tummy ['tʌmɪ] F pancia *f*; **tummy ache** mal *m* di pancia

tumour, *Am* **tumor** ['tjuːmə(r)] tumore *m*

tumult ['tjuːmʌlt] tumulto *m*; **tumultuous** tumultuoso

tuna ['tjuːnə] tonno *m*

tune [tjuːn] **1** *n* motivo *m*; ***in ~*** *instrument* accordato **2** *v/t* *instrument* accordare; *engine* mettere a punto

◆ **tune up 1** *v/i* *of orchestra* accordare gli strumenti **2** *v/t* *engine* mettere a punto

tuneful ['tjuːnfl] melodioso; **tuner** (*hi-fi*) sintonizzatore *m*, tuner *m inv*; **tune-up** *of engine* messa *f* a punto

tunnel ['tʌnl] galleria *f*, tunnel *m inv*

turbine ['tɜːbaɪn] turbina *f*

turbulence ['tɜːbjʊləns] *in air travel* turbolenza *f*; **turbulent** turbolento

turf [tɜːf] tappeto *m* erboso; (*piece*) zolla *f*

Turin [tjʊˈrɪn] Torino *f*

Turk [tɜːk] turco *m*, -a *f*; **Turkey** Turchia *f*

turkey ['tɜːkɪ] tacchino *m*

Turkish ['tɜːkɪʃ] **1** *adj* turco **2** *n language* turco *m*

turmoil ['tɜːmɔɪl] agitazione *f*

turn [tɜːn] **1** *n* (*rotation*) giro *m*; *in road* curva *f*; *in variety show* numero *m*; **take ~ in doing sth** fare a turno a fare qc; **it's my ~** è il mio turno, tocca a me; **do s.o. a good ~** fare un favore a qu **2** *v/t wheel, corner* girare **3** *v/i of driver, car, wheel* girare; (*become*) diventare; **it has ~ed cold** è diventato freddo; **he has ~ed 40** ha compiuto 40 anni

◆ **turn around 1** *v/t object* girare; *company* dare una svolta positiva a; (COM *deal with*) eseguire; *order* evadere **2** *v/i of person* girarsi; *of driver* girare

◆ **turn away 1** *v/t* (*send away*) mandare via **2** *v/i* (*walk away*) andare via; (*look away*) girarsi dall'altra parte

◆ **turn back 1** *v/t edges, sheets* ripiegare **2** *v/i of walkers etc* tornare indietro; *in course of action* tirarsi indietro

◆ **turn down** *offer, invitation* rifiutare; *volume, heating* abbassare; *edge* ripiegare

◆ **turn in 1** *v/i* (*go to bed*) andare a letto **2** *v/t to police* denunciare

◆ **turn off 1** *v/t* TV, *engine* spegnere; *tap* chiudere; F (*sexually*) far passare la voglia a **2** *v/i of driver* svoltare

◆ **turn on 1** *v/t* TV, *engine* accendere; *tap* aprire; F (*sexually*) eccitare **2** *v/i of machine* accendersi

◆ **turn over 1** *v/i in bed* girarsi; *of vehicle* capottare **2** *v/t object, page* girare; FIN fatturare

◆ **turn up 1** *v/t collar, volume, heating* alzare **2** *v/i* (*arrive*) arrivare

turning ['tɜːnɪŋ] svolta *f*; **turning point** svolta *f* decisiva; **turnout** *of people* affluenza *f*; **turnover** FIN fatturato *m*; *of staff* ricambio *m*; **turnpike** *Am* strada *f* a pedaggio; **turn signal** *Am* MOT freccia *f*; **turn-up** *of trousers* risvolto *m*

turquoise ['tɜːkwɔɪz] turchese

turtle ['tɜːtl] tartaruga *f* marina; **turtleneck sweater** maglia *f* a lupetto

Tuscany ['tʌskəni] Toscana *f*

tusk [tʌsk] zanna *f*

tutor ['tjuːtə(r)] EDU *insegnante universitario che segue un piccolo gruppo di studenti*; (*private*) **~** insegnante *m/f* privato, -a

tuxedo [tʌk'siːdəʊ] *Am* smoking *m inv*

TV [tiː'viː] TV *f inv*; **on ~** alla TV; **TV dinner** piatto *m* pronto; **TV guide** guida *f* dei programmi TV; **TV programme**, *Am* **TV program** programma *m* televisivo

twang [twæŋ] **1** *n in voice* suono *m* nasale **2** *v/t guitar string* vibrare

tweezers ['twi:zəz] pinzette *fpl*

twelfth [twelfθ] dodicesimo; **twelve** dodici

twentieth ['twentiɪθ] ventesimo; **twenty** venti; **twenty--four-seven** ventiquattr'ore su ventiquattro, sette giorni su sette

twice [twaɪs] due volte; **~ as much** il doppio; **~ as fast** veloce due volte tanto

twig [twɪg] ramoscello *m*

twilight ['twaɪlaɪt] crepuscolo *m*

twin [twɪn] gemello *m*; **twin beds** due lettini *mpl*

twinge [twɪndʒ] *of pain* fitta *f*

twinkle ['twɪŋkl] *of stars, eyes* scintillare

'**twin room** camera *f* a due letti; **twin town** città *f inv* gemellata

twirl [twɜːl] **1** *v/t* fare roteare **2** *n of cream etc* ricciolo *m*

twist [twɪst] **1** *v/t* attorcigliare; **~ one's ankle** prendere una storta **2** *v/i of road* snodarsi;

of river serpeggiare **3** *n in rope* attorcigliata *f*; *in road* curva *f*; *in plot* svolta *f*; **twisty road** contorto

twit [twɪt] F scemo *m*, -a *f*

twitch [twɪtʃ] **1** *n nervous* spasmo *m* **2** *v/i (jerk)* contrarsi

twitter ['twɪtə(r)] cinguettare

two [tuː] due; **the ~ of them** loro due

tycoon [taɪ'kuːn] magnate *m*

type [taɪp] **1** *n (sort)* tipo *m* **2** *v/t & v/i (use a keyboard)* battere (a macchina)

typhoon [taɪ'fuːn] tifone *m*

typhus ['taɪfəs] tifo *m*

typical ['tɪpɪkl] tipico; *that's ~ of you / him!* tipico!; **typically** tipicamente

typist ['taɪpɪst] dattilografo *m*, -a *f*

tyrannical [tɪ'rænɪkl] tirannico; **tyrannize** tiranneggiare; **tyranny** tirannia *f*; **tyrant** tiranno *m*, -a *f*

tyre [taɪr] gomma *f*, pneumatico *m*

Tyrol [tɪ'rɒl] Tirolo *m*; **Tyrolean** tirolese

Tyrrhenian Sea [taɪˈriːnɪən] mar *m* Tirreno

U

ugly ['ʌglɪ] brutto

UK [juː'keɪ] (= *United Kingdom*) Regno *m* Unito

ulcer ['ʌlsə(r)] ulcera *f*

ultimate ['ʌltɪmət] (*best, de-*

finitive) definitivo; (*final*) ultimo; (*basic*) fondamentale; **ultimately** (*in the end*) in definitiva

ultimatum [ʌltɪ'meɪtəm] ulti-

matum *m inv*
ultrasound ['ʌltrəsaʊnd]
MED ecografia *f*
ultraviolet [ʌltrə'vaɪələt] ultravioletto
umbrella [ʌm'brelə] ombrello
m
umpire ['ʌmpaɪə(r)] arbitro *m*
umpteenth [ʌmp'tiːnθ] F ennesimo
UN [juː'en] (= *United Nations*) ONU *f* (= Organizzazione *f* delle Nazioni Unite)
unable [ʌn'eɪbl]: *be ~ to do
sth* not know how to non
saper fare qc; *not be in a
position to* non poter fare
qc
unacceptable [ʌnək'septəbl]
inaccettabile
unaccountable [ʌnə-
'kaʊntəbl] inspiegabile
unanimous [juː'nænɪməs]
verdict unanime; *unanimously* all'unanimità
unapproachable [ʌnə-
'prəʊtʃəbl] *person* inavvicina-
bile
unarmed [ʌn'ɑːmd] *person* disarmato; *~ combat* combattimento senz'armi
unassuming [ʌnə'sjuːmɪŋ]
senza pretese
unattached [ʌnə'tætʃt] (*without a partner*) libero
unattended [ʌnə'tendɪd] incustodito
unauthorized [ʌn'ɔːθəraɪzd]
non autorizzato
unavoidable [ʌnə'vɔɪdəbl]

inevitabile
unbalanced [ʌn'bælənst] non
equilibrato; PSYCH squilibrato
unbearable [ʌn'beərəbl] insopportabile
unbeatable [ʌn'biːtəbl] *team,
quality* imbattibile
unbeaten [ʌn'biːtn] *team* im-
battuto
unbelievable [ʌnbɪ'liːvəbl]
incredibile
unbias(s)ed [ʌn'baɪəst] imparziale
unblock [ʌn'blɒk] sbloccare
unbreakable [ʌn'breɪkəbl]
plates infrangibile; *world record* imbattibile
unbutton [ʌn'bʌtn] sbottonare
uncanny [ʌn'kænɪ] *resemblance, skill* sorprendente;
(*worrying: feeling*) inquietante
unceasing [ʌn'siːsɪŋ] incessante
uncertain [ʌn'sɜːtn] incerto;
origins dubbio; *be ~ about
sth* non essere certo su qc;
uncertainty *of the future* incertezza *f*; *there is still ~
about ...* ci sono ancora
dubbi su ...
uncle ['ʌŋkl] zio *m*
uncomfortable [ʌn'kʌmf-
təbl] scomodo; *I feel ~ with
him* mi sento a disagio con
lui
uncommon [ʌn'kɒmən] raro
uncompromising [ʌn'kɒm-

undervalue

prə'maizin] fermo; *in a negative way* intransigente

unconditional [ʌnkən'diʃnl] incondizionato

unconscious [ʌn'kɒnʃəs] MED svenuto; PSYCH inconscio; *knock s.o.* – stordire qu con un colpo; *be* ~ *of sth* (*not aware*) non rendersi conto di qc

uncontrollable [ʌnkən'trəʊləbl] incontrollabile

unconventional [ʌnkən'venʃnl] poco convenzionale

uncooperative [ʌnkəʊ'ɒprətɪv] poco cooperativo

uncover [ʌn'kʌvə(r)] scoprire

undamaged [ʌn'dæmɪdʒd] intatto

undecided [ʌndɪ'saɪdɪd] *question* irrisolto; *be* ~ *about sth* essere indeciso su qc

undeniable [ʌndɪ'naɪəbl] innegabile

under ['ʌndə(r)] sotto; (*less than*) meno di; *it is* ~ *investigation* viene indagato

'undercarriage carrello *m* d'atterraggio

'undercover *agent* segreto

under'cut COM vendere a minor prezzo di

under'done *meat* al sangue; (*not cooked enough*) non cotto abbastanza

under'estimate sottovalutare

under'fed malnutrito

under'go *treatment* sottoporsi a; *experiences* vivere

under'graduate studente *m*, -essa *f* universitario, -a

'underground 1 *adj passages etc* sotterraneo; POL clandestino **2** *adv work* sottoterra; *go* – POL entrare in clandestinità **3** *n* RAIL metropolitana *f*

'undergrowth sottobosco *m*

under'hand (*devious*) subdolo

under'line *text* sottolineare

under'lying di fondo

under'mine *s.o.'s position* minare

underneath [ʌndə'niːθ] sotto

'underpants mutande *fpl* da uomo

'underpass *for pedestrians* sottopassaggio *m*

underprivileged [ʌndə'prɪvɪlɪdʒd] svantaggiato

under'rate sottovalutare

'undershirt *Am* canottiera *f*

understaffed [ʌndə'stɑːft] a corto di personale

under'stand capire; *I* ~ *that you* ... mi risulta che tu ...;

understandable comprensibile; **understandably** comprensibilmente; **understanding 1** *adj person* comprensivo **2** *n* comprensione *f*; (*agreement*) intesa *f*

under'take *task* intraprendere; ~ *to do sth* impegnarsi a fare qc; **undertaking** (*enterprise*) impresa *f*; (*promise*) promessa *f*

under'value sottovalutare

'underwear biancheria *f* intima

'underworld *criminal* malavita *f*; *in mythology* inferi *mpl*

under'write FIN sottoscrivere

undeserved [ʌndɪ'zɜːvd] immeritato

undesirable [ʌndɪ'zaɪərəbl] **1** *adj* indesiderabile **2** *n* persona *f* indesiderata

undisputed [ʌndɪ'spjuːtɪd] *champion* indiscusso

undo [ʌn'duː] *parcel* disfare; *shirt* sbottonare; *shoes* slacciare; *s.o.'s work* annullare

undoubtedly [ʌn'dautɪdlɪ] indubbiamente

undress [ʌn'dres] **1** *v/t* spogliare; **get ~ed** spogliarsi **2** *v/i* spogliarsi

undue [ʌn'djuː] *(excessive)* eccessivo; **unduly** *(excessively)* eccessivamente

unearth [ʌn'ɜːθ] *remains* portare alla luce; *(fig: find)* scovare

uneasy [ʌn'iːzɪ] *relationship, peace* precario; **feel ~ about** non sentirsela di

uneatable [ʌn'iːtəbl] immangiabile

uneconomic [ʌniːkə'nɒmɪk] poco redditizio

uneducated [ʌn'edjukeɪtɪd] senza istruzione

unemployed [ʌnɪm'plɔɪd] **1** *adj* disoccupato **2** *npl*: **the ~** i disoccupati; **unemployment** disoccupazione *f*; **~ benefit** sussidio *m* di disoc-

cupazione

unending [ʌn'endɪŋ] interminabile

unequal [ʌn'iːkwəl] disuguale

unerring [ʌn'erɪŋ] *judgement, instinct* infallibile

uneven [ʌn'iːvn] *quality* irregolare; *ground* accidentato

uneventful [ʌnɪ'ventful] *day, journey* tranquillo

unexpected [ʌnɪk'spektɪd] inatteso; **unexpectedly** inaspettatamente

unfair [ʌn'feə(r)] ingiusto

unfaithful [ʌn'feɪθful] *husband, wife* infedele; **be ~ to s.o.** essere infedele a qu

unfamiliar [ʌnfə'mɪljə(r)] sconosciuto; **be ~ with sth** non conoscere qc

unfasten [ʌn'fɑːsn] *belt* slacciare

unfavourable, *Am* **unfavorable** [ʌn'feɪvərəbl] *report, review* negativo; *weather conditions* sfavorevole

unfinished [ʌn'fɪnɪʃt] non terminato; **leave sth ~** non terminare qc

unfit [ʌn'fɪt] *adj physically* fuori forma; **be ~ to ... morally** non essere degno di ...; **~ to eat / drink** non commestibile / non potabile

unfold [ʌn'fəuld] **1** *v/t letter* spiegare; *arms* aprire **2** *v/i of story etc* svolgersi; *of view* spiegarsi

unforeseen [ʌnfɔː'siːn] imprevisto

unforgettable [ʌnfə'getəbl] indimenticabile

unforgivable [ʌnfə'gɪvəbl] imperdonabile

unfortunate [ʌn'fɔːtʃənət] *people* sfortunato; *event, choice of words* infelice; *that's ~ for you* è spiacevole per lei; **unfortunately** sfortunatamente

unfounded [ʌn'faʊndɪd] infondato

unfriendly [ʌn'frendlɪ] poco amichevole

ungrateful [ʌn'greɪtfʊl] ingrato

unhappiness [ʌn'hæpɪnɪs] infelicità *f*; **unhappy** infelice; *customers etc* non soddisfatto (*with* di)

unharmed [ʌn'hɑːmd] illeso

unhealthy [ʌn'helθɪ] *person* malaticcio; *conditions* malsano; *food, atmosphere* poco sano; *economy* traballante

unheard-of [ʌn'hɜːdɒv] inaudito

unhygienic [ʌnhaɪ'dʒiːnɪk] non igienico

unification [juːnɪfɪ'keɪʃn] unificazione *f*

uniform ['juːnɪfɔːm] **1** *n* divisa *f*; MIL *also* uniforme *f* **2** *adj* uniforme

unify ['juːnɪfaɪ] unificare

unilateral [juːnɪ'lætrəl] unilaterale

unimaginable [ʌnɪ'mædʒɪnəbl] inimmaginabile

unimaginative [ʌnɪ'mædʒɪnətɪv] senza fantasia

unimportant [ʌnɪm'pɔːtənt] senza importanza

uninhabitable [ʌnɪn'hæbɪtəbl] inabitabile; **uninhabited** *building* disabitato; *region* deserto

unintentional [ʌnɪn'tenʃnl] involontario; **unintentionally** involontariamente

uninteresting [ʌn'ɪntrəstɪŋ] poco interessante

uninterrupted [ʌnɪntə'rʌptɪd] ininterrotto

union ['juːnɪən] POL unione *f*; (*trade ~*) sindacato *m*

unique [juː'niːk] unico

unit ['juːnɪt] unità *f inv*; (*department*) reparto *m*

unit 'cost COM costo *m* unitario

unite [juː'naɪt] **1** *v/t* unire **2** *v/i* unirsi; **united** unito; **United Kingdom** Regno *m* Unito; **United Nations** Nazioni *fpl* Unite; **United States (of America)** Stati *mpl* Uniti (d'America); **unity** unità *f inv*

universal [juːnɪ'vɜːsl] universale; **universe** universo *m*

university [juːnɪ'vɜːsətɪ] università *f inv*

unjust [ʌn'dʒʌst] ingiusto

unkind [ʌn'kaɪnd] cattivo

unknown [ʌn'nəʊn] **1** *adj* sconosciuto **2** *n*: *a journey into the ~* un viaggio nell'ignoto

unleaded [ʌn'ledɪd] senza

piombo

unless [ən'les] a meno che; ~ **he pays us tomorrow** a meno che non ci paghi domani; ~ **I am mistaken** se non mi sbaglio

unlikely [ʌn'laɪklɪ] improbabile

unlimited [ʌn'lɪmɪtɪd] illimitato

unload [ʌn'ləʊd] scaricare

unlock [ʌn'lɒk] aprire (con la chiave)

unluckily [ʌn'lʌkɪlɪ] sfortunatamente; **unlucky** *day, choice, person* sfortunato; *that was so ~ for you!* che sfortuna hai avuto!

unmanned [ʌn'mænd] *spacecraft* senza equipaggio

unmarried [ʌn'mærɪd] non sposato

unmistakable [ʌnmɪ'steɪkəbl] inconfondibile

unnatural [ʌn'nætʃrəl] non normale

unnecessary [ʌn'nesəsrɪ] non necessario; *comment, violence* gratuito

unnerving [ʌn'nɜːvɪŋ] inquietante

unobtainable [ʌnəb'teɪnəbl] *goods* introvabile; TELEC non ottenibile

unobtrusive [ʌnəb'truːsɪv] discreto

unoccupied [ʌn'ɒkjʊpaɪd] *building, house* vuoto; *post* vacante; *room* libero

unofficial [ʌnə'fɪʃl] non ufficiale; *announcement* ufficioso; **unofficially** non ufficialmente

unorthodox [ʌn'ɔːθədɒks] poco ortodosso

unpack [ʌn'pæk] **1** *v/t* disfare **2** *v/i* disfare le valige

unpaid [ʌn'peɪd] *work* non retribuito

unpleasant [ʌn'pleznt] *person, thing to say* antipatico; *smell, taste* sgradevole

unplug [ʌn'plʌg] *TV, computer* staccare (la spina di)

unpopular [ʌn'pɒpjʊlə(r)] *person* mal visto; *decision* impopolare

unprecedented [ʌn'presɪdentɪd] senza precedenti

unpredictable [ʌnprɪ'dɪktəbl] imprevedibile

unpretentious [ʌnprɪ'tenʃəs] senza pretese

unproductive [ʌnprə'dʌktɪv] *meeting* sterile; *soil* improduttivo

unprofessional [ʌnprə'feʃnl] *workmanship* poco professionale

unprofitable [ʌn'prɒfɪtəbl] non redditizio

unprovoked [ʌnprə'vəʊkt] *attack* non provocato

unqualified [ʌn'kwɒlɪfaɪd] *worker* non qualificato; *doctor, teacher* non abilitato

unquestionably [ʌn'kwestʃnəblɪ] indiscutibilmente; **unquestioning** *attitude* assoluto

unreadable [ʌnˈriːdəbl] *book* illeggibile

unrealistic [ʌnrɪəˈlɪstɪk] *person* poco realista; *expectations* poco realistico

unreasonable [ʌnˈriːznəbl] *person* irragionevole; *demand* eccessivo

unrelated [ʌnrɪˈleɪtɪd] *issues* senza (alcuna) attinenza; *people* non imparentati

unrelenting [ʌnrɪˈlentɪŋ] incessante

unreliable [ʌnrɪˈlaɪəbl] poco affidabile

unrest [ʌnˈrest] agitazione *f*

unrestrained [ʌnrɪˈstreɪnd] *emotions* incontrollato, sfrenato

unroll [ʌnˈrəʊl] srotolare

unruly [ʌnˈruːlɪ] indisciplinato

unsafe [ʌnˈseɪf] pericoloso; **~ to drink / eat** non potabile / non commestibile; **it is ~ to ...** è rischioso ...

unsanitary [ʌnˈsænɪtrɪ] antigienico

unsatisfactory [ʌnsætɪsˈfæktrɪ] poco soddisfacente

unscathed [ʌnˈskeɪðd] (*not injured*) incolume; (*not damaged*) intatto

unscrew [ʌnˈskruː] svitare

unscrupulous [ʌnˈskruːpjələs] senza scrupoli

unselfish [ʌnˈselfɪʃ] *person* altruista; *act* altruistico

unsettled [ʌnˈsetld] *issue* irrisolto; *weather* instabile; *life-*

style irrequieto; *bills* non pagato

unshaven [ʌnˈʃeɪvn] non rasato

unskilled [ʌnˈskɪld] non specializzato

unsophisticated [ʌnsəˈfɪstɪkeɪtɪd] *person, beliefs* semplice; *equipment* rudimentale

unstable [ʌnˈsteɪbl] instabile; *person* squilibrato

unsteady [ʌnˈstedɪ] *ladder* malsicuro; **be ~ on one's feet** non reggersi bene sulle gambe

unsuccessful [ʌnsəkˈsesful] *writer etc* di scarso successo; *candidate, party* sconfitto; *attempt* fallito; **he tried but was ~** ha provato ma non ha avuto fortuna; **unsuccessfully** senza successo

unsuitable [ʌnˈsuːtəbl] *partner, clothing* inadatto; *thing to say* inappropriato

unswerving [ʌnˈswɜːvɪŋ] *loyalty* incrollabile

unthinkable [ʌnˈθɪŋkəbl] impensabile

untidy [ʌnˈtaɪdɪ] in disordine

untie [ʌnˈtaɪ] *knot* disfare; *laces* slacciare; *prisoner* slegare

until [ənˈtɪl] **1** *prep* fino a; **from Monday ~ Friday** da lunedì a venerdì; **not ~ Friday** non prima di venerdì **2** *conj* finché (non); **can you wait ~ I'm ready?** puoi aspettare che sia pronta?

untiring [ʌnˈtaɪrɪŋ] *efforts* instancabile

untold [ʌnˈtəʊld] *riches* incalcolabile; *suffering* indescrivibile; *story* inedito

untrue [ʌnˈtruː] falso

unused [ʌnˈjuːzd] mai usato

unusual [ʌnˈjuːʒʊəl] insolito; *it's ~ for them not to write* non è da loro non scrivere; **unusually** insolitamente

unveil [ʌnˈveɪl] *statue etc* scoprire

unwell [ʌnˈwel]: *be / feel ~* stare / sentirsi male

unwilling [ʌnˈwɪlɪŋ]: *be ~ to do* non essere disposto a fare; **unwillingly** malvolentieri

unwind [ʌnˈwaɪnd] **1** *v/t tape* svolgere **2** *v/i of tape* svolgersi; *of story* dipanarsi; (*relax*) rilassarsi

unwise [ʌnˈwaɪz] avventato, imprudente

unwrap [ʌnˈræp] aprire, scartare

unzip [ʌnˈzɪp] *dress etc* aprire (la chiusura lampo di); COMPUT espandere

up [ʌp] **1** *adv*: *~ in the sky / on the roof* in alto nel cielo / sul tetto; *~ here / there* quassù / lassù; *be ~ (out of bed)* essere in piedi; *of sun* essere sorto; *of temperature* essere aumentato; (*have expired*) essere scaduto; *what's ~?* F che c'è?; *~ to the year 1989* fino al 1989;

he came ~ to me mi si è avvicinato; *what are you ~ to these days?* cosa fai di bello?; *what are those kids ~ to?* cosa stanno combinando i bambini?; *be ~ to something (bad)* stare architettando qualcosa; *I don't feel ~ to it* non me la sento; *it's ~ to you* dipende da te; *it is ~ to them to solve it their duty* sta a loro risolverlo; *be ~ and about after illness* essersi ristabilito **2** *prep*: *further ~ the mountain* più in alto sulla montagna; *they ran ~ the street* corsero per strada; *we travelled ~ to Milan* siamo andati a Milano **3** *n*: *~s and downs* alti e bassi *mpl*

'upbringing educazione *f*

'upcoming (*forthcoming*) prossimo

up'date *file, records* aggiornare; *~ s.o. on sth* mettere qu al corrente di qc

up'grade *equipment etc* aggiornare; *memory* potenziare; *passenger* promuovere a una classe superiore; *product* migliorare

upheaval [ʌpˈhiːvl] *emotional* sconvolgimento *m*; *physical* scombussolamento *m*; *political, social* sconvolgimento *m*

uphill [ˈʌphɪl] **1** *adv*: *go / walk ~* salire **2** *adj* *climb* in salita; *struggle* arduo

up'hold *traditions, rights* sostenere; (*vindicate*) confermare

'upkeep manutenzione *f*

'upload COMPUT caricare, fare l'upload di

up'market *restaurant, hotel* elegante; *product* di qualità

upon [ə'pɒn] ☞ **on**

upper ['ʌpə(r)] superiore; *deck, rooms* di sopra

upper 'class *adj accent* aristocratico; *family* dell'alta borghesia

'upright 1 *adj citizen* onesto **2** *adv sit* (bene) dritto; **upright** (**piano**) pianoforte *m* verticale

'uprising insurrezione *f*

'uproar trambusto *m*; (*protest*) protesta *f*

up'scale *Am restaurant, hotel* elegante; *product* di qualità

up'set 1 *v/t* drink, glass rovesciare; (*make sad*) fare stare male; (*distress*) sconvolgere; (*annoy*) seccare **2** *adj* (*sad*) triste; (*distressed*) sconvolto; (*annoyed*) seccato; **be** / **get ~** prendersela (**about** per); **have an ~ stomach** avere l'intestino in disordine; **upsetting**: **it's so ~** (*for me*) mi fa stare male, mi turba

upside 'down capovolto; **turn sth ~** capovolgere qc

up'stairs 1 *adv* di sopra **2** *adj room* al piano di sopra

up'stream a monte

up'tight F (*nervous*) nervoso; (*inhibited*) inibito

up-to-'date *information* aggiornato; *fashions* più attuale

'up turn *in economy* ripresa *f*

upward ['ʌpwəd] in su; **~ of 10,000** oltre 10.000

uranium [jʊ'reɪnɪəm] uranio *m*

urban ['ɜːbən] *areas, population* urbano; *redevelopment* urbanistico

urchin ['ɜːtʃɪn] monello *m*, -a *f*

urge [ɜːdʒ] **1** *n* (forte) desiderio *m* **2** *v/t*: **~ s.o. to do sth** raccomandare (caldamente) a qu di fare qc; **urgency** urgenza *f*; **the ~ of the situation** la gravità della situazione; **urgent** urgente

urinate ['jʊərɪneɪt] orinare; **urine** urina *f*

US [juː'es] (= **United States**) USA *mpl*

us [ʌs] ci; *when two pronouns are used* ce; *after prep* noi; **don't leave ~** non ci lasciare, non lasciarci; **she gave them to ~** ce le ha date; **that's for ~** quello è per noi; **who's that? - it's ~** chi è? - siamo noi

USA [juːes'eɪ] (= **United States of America**) USA *mpl*

usage ['juːzɪdʒ] uso *m*

use 1 [juːz] *v/t tool, skills, knowledge* usare, utilizzare; *word, s.o.'s car* usare; *a lot of petrol* consumare; *pej: person* usare **2** [juːs] *n* uso *m*; **be**

of no ~ to s.o. non essere d'aiuto a qu; *it's no ~ waiting* non serve a niente aspettare

◆ **use up** finire

used[1] ['juːzd] *adj car* etc usato

used[2] [juːst]: *be ~ to* essere abituato a; *get ~ to* abituarsi a

used[3] [juːst]: *I ~ to know him* lo conoscevo; *I ~ to like him* un tempo mi piaceva

useful ['juːsfʊl] utile; *person* di grande aiuto; **usefulness** utilità *f*; **useless** *information*, *advice* inutile; F *person* incapace; *machine* inservibile; *feel ~* sentirsi inutile; **us-**

er *of product* utente *m/f*; **userfriendly** di facile uso

usual ['juːʒʊəl] solito; *it's not ~ for this to happen* non succede quasi mai; *as ~* come al solito; **usually** di solito

utensil [juːˈtensl] utensile *m*

utility [juːˈtɪlɪtɪ] (*usefulness*) utilità *f*; **utility pole** *Am* palo *m* del telegrafo; **utilize** utilizzare

utmost ['ʌtməʊst] **1** *adj* massimo **2** *n*: *do one's ~* fare (tutto) il possibile

utter ['ʌtə(r)] **1** *adj* totale **2** *v/t sound* emettere; *word* proferire; **utterly** totalmente

V

vacancy ['veɪkənsɪ] *at work* posto *m* vacante; *in hotel* camera *f* libera; *~ for a driver as advert* autista cercasi; *"no vacancies"* "completo"; **vacant** *building* vuoto; *room* libero; *look*, *expression* assente; *position* vacante; **vacantly** con sguardo assente; **vacate** *room* lasciar libero; **vacation** vacanza *f*; *be on ~* essere in vacanza

vaccinate ['væksɪneɪt] vaccinare; **vaccination** vaccinazione *f*; **vaccine** vaccino *m*

vacuum ['vækjʊəm] **1** *n also fig* vuoto *m* **2** *v/t floors* passare l'aspirapolvere su

vagina [vəˈdʒaɪnə] vagina *f*

vague [veɪg] vago; *I'm still ~ about it* non ho ancora le idee chiare al riguardo; **vaguely** vagamente

vain [veɪn] **1** *adj person* vanitoso; *hope* vano **2** *n*: *in ~* invano

valiant ['vælɪənt] valoroso

valid ['vælɪd] valido; **validate** *with official stamp* convalidare; *alibi* confermare; **validity** *of reason*, *argument* validità *f*

valley ['vælɪ] valle *f*

valuable ['væljʊəbl] **1** *adj* prezioso **2** *n*: *~s* oggetti *mpl* di valore; **valuation** valutazione *f*; **value 1** *n* valore *m* **2**

615   venerable

v/t friendship, freedom tenere
a; **have an object ~d** far valutare un oggetto

valve [vælv] valvola *f*

van [væn] furgone *m*

vandal ['vændl] vandalo *m*;
vandalism vandalismo *m*;
vandalize vandalizzare

vanilla [vəˈnɪlə] **1** *n* vaniglia *f*
2 *adj ice cream* alla vaniglia;
flavour di vaniglia

vanish ['vænɪʃ] sparire

vanity ['vænətɪ] *of person* vanità *f inv*

vapor ['veɪpə(r)] *Am* ☞ **vapour; vaporize** vaporizzare;
vapour vapore *m*

variable ['veərɪəbl] **1** *adj* variabile **2** *n* MATH, COMPUT
variabile *f*; **variant** variante
f; **variation** variazione *f*; **varied** *range, diet* vario; *life* movimentato; **variety** varietà *f*
inv; *(type)* tipo *m*; **a ~ of
things to do** varie cose da
fare; **various** *(several)* vario;
(different) diverso

varnish ['vɑːnɪʃ] **1** *n for wood*
vernice *f*; *(nail ~)* smalto *m* **2**
v/t wood verniciare; *nails*
smaltare

vary ['veərɪ] variare

vase [vɑːz] vaso *m*

vast [vɑːst] vasto; *improvement* immenso; **vastly** im-
mensamente

VAT [viːeɪˈtiː, væt] *abbr (= value added tax)* IVA *f (= imposta f sul valore aggiunto)*

Vatican ['vætɪkən]: **the ~** il Va-

ticano

vault[1] [vɔːlt] *n in roof* volta *f*;
cellar cantina *f*; **~s of bank**
caveau *m inv*

vault[2] [vɔːlt] **1** *n* SP volteggio
m **2** *v/t* saltare

VCR [viːsiːˈɑː(r)] (= **video
cassette recorder**) videoregistratore *m*

veal [viːl] *(carne f di)* vitello *m*

veer [vɪə(r)] *of car* sterzare; *of
wind, party* cambiare dire-
zione

vegan ['viːgən] *food, person*
vegano

vegetable ['vedʒtəbl] verdura
f; **vegetarian 1** *n* vegetariano *m*, -a *f* **2** *adj* vegetariano;
vegetation vegetazione *f*

vehement ['viːəmənt] veemente

vehicle ['viːɪkl] veicolo *m*; *for
information etc* mezzo *m*

veil [veɪl] velo *m*

vein [veɪn] ANAT vena *f*; **in
this ~** *fig* su questo tono

Velcro® ['velkrəʊ] velcro *m*

velocity [vɪˈlɒsɪtɪ] velocità *f
inv*

velvet ['velvɪt] velluto *m*

vendetta [venˈdetə] vendetta
f

vending machine ['vendɪŋ]
distributore *m* automatico;
vendor LAW venditore *m*,
-trice *f*

veneer [vəˈnɪə(r)] impiallac-
ciatura *f*; *of politeness etc*
parvenza *f*

venerable ['venərəbl] venerabile; **veneration** venerazione *f*

venereal disease [vɪ'nɪərɪəl] malattia *f* venerea

Venetian [və'niːʃn] **1** *adj* veneziano **2** *n* veneziano *m*, -a *f*; **venetian blind** veneziana *f*; **Venice** Venezia *f*

venom ['venəm] veleno *m*

ventilate ['ventɪleɪt] ventilare; **ventilation** ventilazione *f*; **ventilator** ventilatore *m*; MED respiratore *m*

venture ['ventʃə(r)] **1** *n* impresa *f* **2** *v/i* avventurarsi

venue ['venjuː] *for meeting, concert etc* luogo *m*

veranda [və'rændə] veranda *f*

verb [vɜːb] verbo *m*; **verbal** *(spoken)* verbale; **verbally** verbalmente

verdict ['vɜːdɪkt] LAW verdetto *m*; *(opinion, judgment)* giudizio *m*

verge [vɜːdʒ] *of road* bordo *m*; *be on the ~ of ... ruin, collapse* essere sull'orlo di ...; *on the ~ of tears* sul punto di piangere

verification [verɪfɪ'keɪʃn] verifica *f*; **verify** verificare

vermin ['vɜːmɪn] animali *mpl* nocivi

vermouth ['vɜːməθ] vermut *m*

versatile ['vɜːsətaɪl] versatile; **versatility** versatilità *f*

verse [vɜːs] *poetry* poesia *f*; *part of poem, song* strofa *f*

version ['vɜːʃn] versione *f*

versus ['vɜːsəs] contro

vertical ['vɜːtɪkl] verticale

vertigo ['vɜːtɪɡəʊ] vertigini *fpl*

very ['verɪ] **1** *adv* molto; *~ fast* molto veloce, velocissimo; *the ~ best* il meglio **2** *adj*: *at that ~ moment* in quel preciso momento; *that's the ~ thing I need* è proprio quello che mi serve

vessel ['vesl] NAUT natante *m*

vest [vest] *Br* undershirt canottiera *f*; *Am* gilè *m inv*

vestige ['vestɪdʒ] vestigio *m*; *not a ~ of truth* un'ombra di verità

vet[1] [vet] *n (veterinary surgeon)* veterinario *m*, -a *f*

vet[2] [vet] *v/t applicants etc* passare al vaglio

vet[3] [vet] *n* MIL reduce *m/f*

veteran [vest] **1** *n* veterano *m*, -a *f*; MIL reduce *m/f* **2** *adj* veterano

veto ['viːtəʊ] **1** *n* veto *m* **2** *v/t* mettere il veto a

via ['vaɪə] attraverso

viable ['vaɪəbl] in grado di sopravvivere; *alternative, plan* fattibile

vibrate [vaɪ'breɪt] vibrare; **vibration** vibrazione *f*

vicar ['vɪkə(r)] parroco *m* anglicano

vice[1] [vaɪs] vizio *m*

vice[2] [vaɪs] *tool* morsa *f*

vice 'president vice-presidente *m*

vice versa [vaɪs'vɜːsə] vice-

versa
vicious ['vɪʃəs] *dog* feroce; *attack, criticism* brutale; **viciously** brutalmente
victim ['vɪktɪm] vittima *f*; **victimize** perseguitare
victorious [vɪk'tɔːrɪəs] *army* vittorioso; *team* vincente; **victory** vittoria *f*
video ['vɪdɪəʊ] **1** *n* video *m inv*; *tape* videocassetta *f*; *(VCR)* videoregistratore *m* **2** *v/t* registrare; **video camera** videocamera *f*; **video cassette** videocassetta *f*; **video conference** video-conferenza *f*; **video game** videogame *m inv*; **video recorder** videoregistratore *m*; **videotape** videocassetta *f*
vie [vaɪ] competere
Vietnam [vɪet'næm] Vietnam *m*; **Vietnamese 1** *adj* vietnamita **2** *n* vietnamita *m/f*; *language* vietnamita *m*
view [vjuː] **1** *n* veduta *f*; *of situation* parere *m*; **in ~ of** considerato; **be on ~** *of paintings* essere esposto; **with a ~ to** con l'intenzione di **2** *v/t* vedere; *TV programme* guardare **3** *v/i* *(watch TV)* guardare la TV; **viewer** *TV* telespettatore *m*, -trice *f*; **viewpoint** punto *m* di vista
vigor ['vɪgər] *Am* ☞ **vigour**
vigorous ['vɪgərəs] vigoroso; **vigorously** vigorosamente; **vigour** vigore *m*
village ['vɪlɪdʒ] paese *m*; vil-

lager abitante *m/f* (del paese)
villain ['vɪlən] cattivo *m*, -a *f*; *F criminal* delinquente *m/f*
vindicate ['vɪndɪkeɪt] *(prove correct)* confermare; *(prove innocent)* scagionare; **I feel ~d by the report** il resoconto mi dà ragione
vindictive [vɪn'dɪktɪv] vendicativo
vine [vaɪn] *(grape~)* vite *f*; *climber* rampicante *m*
vinegar ['vɪnɪgə(r)] aceto *m*
vineyard ['vɪnjɑːd] vigneto *m*
vintage ['vɪntɪdʒ] **1** *n* *of wine* annata *f* **2** *adj* *(classic)* d'annata
viola [vɪ'əʊlə] *MUS* viola *f*
violate ['vaɪəleɪt] violare; **violation** violazione *f*; *Am* *(traffic ~)* infrazione *f*
violence ['vaɪələns] violenza *f*; **violent** violento
violin [vaɪə'lɪn] violino *m*; **violinist** violinista *m/f*
VIP [viːaɪ'piː] *(= very important person)* VIP *m/f*
viral ['vaɪrəl] virale
virgin ['vɜːdʒɪn] vergine *m/f*; **virginity** verginità *f*
Virgo ['vɜːgəʊ] *ASTR* Vergine *f*
virile ['vɪraɪl] virile; **virility** virilità *f*
virtual ['vɜːtjʊəl] effettivo; *COMPUT* virtuale; **virtually** *(almost)* praticamente
virtue ['vɜːtjuː] virtù *f inv*
virtuoso [vɜːtʊ'əʊzəʊ] *MUS* virtuoso *m*, -a *f*

virtuous [ˈvɜːtjʊəs] virtuoso

virus [ˈvaɪrəs] MED, COMPUT virus *m inv*

visa [ˈviːzə] visto *m*

vise *Am* ☞ **vice²**

visibility [vɪzəˈbɪlətɪ] visibilità *f*; **visible** visibile; *anger etc* evidente

vision [ˈvɪʒn] (*eyesight*) vista *f*; REL *etc* visione *f*

visit [ˈvɪzɪt] **1** *n* visita *f*; **pay s.o. a ~** fare una visita a qu **2** *v/t person* andare a trovare; *place, country, city, website* visitare; *doctor, dentist* andare da; *visitor* (*guest*) ospite *m*; *to museum etc* visitatore *m*, -trice *f*; (*tourist*) turista *m/f*

visor [ˈvaɪzə(r)] visiera *f*

visual [ˈvɪzjʊəl] *organs, memory* visivo; *arts* figurativo; **visualize** immaginare; (*foresee*) prevedere; **visually** visivamente

vital [ˈvaɪtl] (*essential*) essenziale; **vitality** vitalità *f*; **vitally**: **~ important** di vitale importanza

vitamin [ˈvɪtəmɪn] vitamina *f*; **vitamin pill** (confetto *m* di) vitamina *f*

vivacious [vɪˈveɪʃəs] vivace; **vivacity** vivacità *f*

vivid [ˈvɪvɪd] vivido; **vividly** in modo vivido

V-neck [ˈviːnek] maglione *m* con scollo a V

vocabulary [vəˈkæbjʊlərɪ] vocabolario *m*; *list of words*

glossario *m*

vocal [ˈvəʊkl] *to do with the voice* vocale; *expressing opinions* eloquente; **become ~** cominciare a farsi sentire; **vocal group** MUS gruppo *m* vocale; **vocalist** MUS cantante *m/f*

vocation [vəˈkeɪʃn] (*calling*) vocazione *f* (**for** a); (*profession*) professione *f*; **vocational** *guidance* professionale

vodka [ˈvɒdkə] vodka *f inv*

vogue [vəʊɡ] moda *f*; **be in ~** essere in voga

voice [vɔɪs] **1** *n* voce *f* **2** *v/t opinions* esprimere; **voice-activated** attivato dalla voce; **voice mail** segreteria *f* telefonica; *message* messaggio *m* in segreteria

volatile [ˈvɒlətaɪl] *personality* volubile

volcano [vɒlˈkeɪnəʊ] vulcano *m*

volley [ˈvɒlɪ] *of shots* raffica *f*; *in tennis* volée *f*

volt [vəʊlt] volt *m inv*; **voltage** voltaggio *m*; **high ~** alta tensione *f*

volume [ˈvɒljuːm] volume *m*

voluntarily [vɒlənˈteərɪlɪ] spontaneamente; **voluntary** volontario; **~ work** volontariato; **volunteer 1** *n* volontario *m*, -a *f* **2** *v/i* offrirsi volontario

vomit [ˈvɒmɪt] **1** *n* vomito *m* **2** *v/i* vomitare

voracious [vəˈreɪʃəs] vorace
vote [vəʊt] **1** n voto m; **right to vote** diritto m di voto **2** v/i POL votare (**for** a favore di, **against** contro); **voter** POL elettore m, -trice f; **voting** POL votazione f
◆ **vouch for** [vaʊtʃ] truth garantire; person garantire per

vow [vaʊ] **1** n voto m **2** v/t: **~ to do** giurare di fare
vowel [vaʊl] vocale f
voyage [ˈvɔɪɪdʒ] viaggio m
vulgar [ˈvʌlɡə(r)] volgare
vulnerable [ˈvʌlnərəbl] vulnerabile
vulture [ˈvʌltʃə(r)] avvoltoio m

W

waddle [ˈwɒdl] camminare ondeggiando
wade [weɪd] guadare
wafer [ˈweɪfə(r)] cookie cialda f; REL ostia f
waffle [ˈwɒfl] (to eat) tipo di cialda
wag [wæɡ] finger scuotere; **the dog ~ged its tail** il cane scodinzolò
wages [ˈweɪdʒɪz] paga f
waggle [ˈwæɡl] far muovere
wail [weɪl] of person gemere; of siren ululare
waist [weɪst] vita f; **waistcoat** gilè m inv; **waistline** vita f
wait [weɪt] **1** n attesa f **2** v/i aspettare; **I can't ~ to ...** non vedo l'ora di ... **3** v/t meal ritardare
◆ **wait for** aspettare
◆ **wait on** (serve) servire
◆ **wait up** restare alzato ad aspettare
waiter [ˈweɪtə(r)] cameriere m; **waiting list** lista f d'attesa; **waiting room** sala f d'at-

tesa; **waitress** cameriera f
waive [weɪv] (renounce) rinunciare a; (dispense with) fare al meno di
wake [weɪk] **1** v/i: **~ (up)** svegliarsi **2** v/t svegliare; **wake-up call** sveglia f (telefonica)
Wales [weɪz] Galles m
walk [wɔːk] **1** n camminata f; **go for a ~** fare due passi **2** v/i camminare; as opposed to driving andare a piedi; (hike) passeggiare **3** v/t dog portare fuori; **~ the streets** (walk around) girare in lungo e in largo
◆ **walk out** of spouse etc, from theatre andarsene; (go on strike) scendere in sciopero
◆ **walk out on** spouse, family abbandonare
walker [ˈwɔːkə(r)] (hiker) escursionista m/f; for baby girello m; for old person deambulatore m; **be a slow / fast ~** avere il passo lento / spedito; **walking as**

opposed to driving camminare *m*; *(hiking)* escursionismo *m*; **it's within ~ distance** ci si arriva a piedi; **Walkman®** walkman *m inv*; **walkout** *strike* sciopero *m* selvaggio; **walkover** *(easy win)* vittoria *f* facile

wall [wɔːl] *also fig* muro *m*; *internal* parete *f*; **~s of a city** mura *f/pl*; **drive s.o. up the ~ F** far diventare matto qu

wallet ['wɒlɪt] portafoglio *m*

wallpaper 1 *n* tappezzeria *f*, carta *f* da parati **2** *v/t* tappezzare; **wall-to-wall carpet** moquette *f*

waltz [wɔːlts] valzer *m inv*

wan [wɒn] *face* pallido

wander ['wɒndə(r)] *(roam)* gironzolare; *(stray)* allontanarsi

wangle ['wæŋgl] F rimediare F

want [wɒnt] **1** *n*: **for ~ of** per mancanza di **2** *v/t* volere; *(need)* avere bisogno di; **~ to do sth** volere fare qc; **she ~s you to go back** vuole che torni indietro **3** *v/i*: **~ for nothing** non mancare di niente; **wanted** *by police* ricercato

war [wɔː(r)] guerra *f*; *fig* lotta *f*

ward [wɔːd] *in hospital* corsia *f*; *child* minore *m* sotto tutela

◆ **ward off** *blow* parare; *attacker* respingere; *cold* combattere

warden ['wɔːdn] *(traffic ~)* vi-

gile *m* urbano; *of hostel* direttore *m*, -trice *f*; *of nature reserve* guardiano *m*, -a *f*; *of prison* agente *m/f* di custodia; *Am* direttore *m*, -trice *f*

'wardrobe *for clothes* armadio *m*; *clothes* guardaroba *m*

warehouse ['weəhaʊs] magazzino *m*

'warfare guerra *f*; **warhead** testata *f*

warily ['weərɪlɪ] con aria guardinga

warm [wɔːm] caldo; *welcome, smile* caloroso; **it's ~** *of weather* fa caldo

◆ **warm up 1** *v/t* scaldare **2** *v/i* scaldarsi; *of athlete etc* fare riscaldamento

warmly ['wɔːmlɪ] *dressed* con abiti pesanti; *welcome, smile* calorosamente; **warmth** calore *m*; *of welcome, smile* calorosità *f*; **warm-up** SP riscaldamento *m*

warn [wɔːn] avvertire; **warning** avvertimento *m*; **without ~** senza preavviso

warp [wɔːp] *of wood* deformarsi; **warped** *fig* contorto

'warplane aereo *m* militare

warrant ['wɒrənt] **1** *n* mandato *m* **2** *v/t* giustificare; **warranty** *(guarantee)* garanzia *f*

warrior ['wɒrɪə(r)] guerriero *m*, -a *f*

'warship nave *f* da guerra

wart [wɔːt] verruca *f*

wary ['weərɪ] guardingo; **be ~ of** diffidare di

wash [wɒʃ] **1** *n*: **have a ~** darsi una lavata **2** *v/t* lavare; **~ one's hair** lavarsi i capelli **3** *v/i* lavarsi

◆ **wash up** *Br* lavare i piatti; *Am* (*wash one's hands and face*) lavarsi

washable ['wɒʃəbl] lavabile; **washbasin**, **washbowl** lavandino *m*; **washcloth** *Am* guanto *m* di spugna; **washed out** sfinito; **washer** *for tap etc* guarnizione *f*; **washing** washed clothes bucato *m*; *clothes to be washed* biancheria *f* da lavare; **do the ~** fare il bucato; **washing machine** lavatrice *f*; **washing-up liquid** detersivo *m* per i piatti; **washroom** *Am* servizi *mpl*

wasp [wɒsp] vespa *f*

waste [weɪst] **1** *n* spreco *m*; *from industrial process* rifiuti *mpl*; **it's a ~ of time / money** è tempo sprecato / sono soldi sprecati **2** *adj* material of scarto **3** *v/t* sprecare; **waste disposal (unit)** tritarifiuti *m inv*; **wasteful** *person* sprecone; *methods* dispendioso; **wasteland** distesa *f* desolata; **wastepaper** cartaccia *f*; **wastepaper basket**, *Am* **waste basket** cestino *m* della cartaccia

watch [wɒtʃ] **1** *n* timepiece orologio *m*; MIL guardia *f*; **keep ~** stare all'erta **2** *v/t* guardare; (*spy on*) sorvegliare; (*look after*) tenere d'occhio **3** *v/i* guardare; **watchful** vigile

water ['wɔːtə(r)] **1** *n* acqua *f* **2** *v/t plant* annaffiare **3** *v/i of eyes* lacrimare; **my mouth is ~ing** ho l'acquolina in bocca; **watercolour**, *Am* **watercolor** acquerello *m*; **watered down** *fig* edulcorato; **waterfall** cascata *f*; **waterline** linea *f* di galleggiamento; **waterlogged** allagato; **watermelon** anguria *f*, cocomero *m*; **waterproof** impermeabile; **waterside**: **at the ~** sulla riva; **waterskiing** sci *m* nautico; **watertight** *compartment* stagno; *fig* inattaccabile; **waterway** corso *m* d'acqua navigabile; **watery** acquoso

watt [wɒt] watt *m inv*

wave[1] [weɪv] *n in sea* onda *f* **wave**[2] [weɪv] **1** *n of hand* saluto *m* (con la mano) **2** *v/i with hand* salutare (con la mano) **3** *v/t flag etc* sventolare

'wavelength RAD lunghezza *f* d'onda; **be on the same ~** *fig* essere sulla stessa lunghezza d'onda

waver ['weɪvə(r)] vacillare

wavy ['weɪvɪ] ondulato

wax [wæks] *for furniture* cera *f*; *in ear* cerume *m*

way [weɪ] **1** *n* (*method, manner*) modo *m*; (*manner*) maniera *f*; (*route*) strada *f*; **this ~** (*like this*) così; (*in this direc-*

tion) da questa parte; **by the ~** (*incidentally*) a proposito; **in a ~** (*in certain respects*) in un certo senso; **be under ~** essere in corso; **give ~** MOT dare la precedenza; (*collapse*) crollare; **X has given ~ to** Y (*been replaced by*) Y ha preso il posto di X; **have one's (own) ~** averla vinta; **lead the ~** *also fig* fare strada; **lose one's ~** smarrirsi; **be in the ~** (*be an obstruction*) essere d'intralcio; **it's on the ~ to the station** è sulla strada della stazione; **I was on my ~ to the station** stavo andando alla stazione; **no ~!** neanche per sogno!; **there's no ~ he can do it** è impossibile che ce la faccia **2** *adv* F (*much*): **it's ~ too soon** è veramente troppo presto; **they are ~ behind with their work** sono molto indietro con il lavoro; **way in** entrata *f*; **way of life** stile *m* di vita; **way out** uscita *f*; *fig*: *from situation* via *f* d'uscita

we [wiː] *noi*; **~'re the best** siamo i migliori

weak [wiːk] debole; *tea, coffee* leggero; **weaken 1** *v/t* indebolire **2** *v/i* indebolirsi; **weakness** debolezza *f*; **have a ~ for sth** (*liking*) avere un debole per qc

wealth [welθ] ricchezza *f*; **a ~ of** una grande abbondanza di; **wealthy** ricco

weapon ['wepən] arma *f*

wear [weə(r)] **1** *n*: **~ (and tear)** usura *f* **2** *v/t* (*have on*) indossare; (*damage*) logorare **3** *v/i* (*wear out*) logorarsi; (*last*) durare

♦ **wear down** fiaccare
♦ **wear off** *of effect* svanire
♦ **wear out 1** *v/t* (*tire*) estenuare; *shoes* consumare **2** *v/i of shoes, carpet* consumarsi

wearily ['wɪərɪlɪ] stancamente; **weary** stanco

weather ['weðə(r)] **1** *n* tempo *m*; **be feeling under the ~** sentirsi poco bene **2** *v/t crisis* superare; **weather-beaten** segnato; **weather forecast** previsioni *fpl* del tempo; **weatherman** meteorologo *m*

weave [wiːv] **1** *v/t cloth* tessere; *basket* intrecciare **2** *v/i* (*move*) zigzagare

web [web] *of spider* ragnatela *f*; **the Web** COMPUT il web *m*; **web page** pagina *f* web; **web site** sito *m* web

wedding ['wedɪŋ] matrimonio *m*; **wedding anniversary** anniversario *m* di matrimonio; **wedding day** giorno *m* del matrimonio; **wedding dress** abito *m* or vestito *m* da sposa; **wedding ring** fede *f*

wedge [wedʒ] *to hold sth in place* zeppa *f*; *of cheese etc* fetta *f*

623

west

Wednesday ['wenzdeɪ] mercoledì *m inv*

weed [wi:d] **1** *n* erbaccia *f* **2** *v/t* diserbare; **weed-killer** diserbante *m*; **weedy** F mingherlino

week [wi:k] settimana *f*; *a ~ tomorrow* una settimana a domani; **weekday** giorno *m* feriale; **weekend** fine *m* settimana, weekend *m inv*; *on the ~* durante il fine settimana; **weekly 1** *adj* settimanale **2** *n magazine* settimanale *m* **3** *adv* settimanalmente

woep [wi:p] piangere

'wee-wee F pipì *f inv* F; *do a ~* fare la pipì

weigh [weɪ] pesare
◆ **weigh up** (*assess*) valutare

weight [weɪt] peso *m*; *put on / lose ~* ingrassare / dimagrire; **weightlessness** assenza *f* di peso; **weightlifter** pesista *m/f*; **weightlifting** sollevamento *m* pesi

weir [wɪə(r)] chiusa *f*

weird [wɪəd] strano; **weirdo** F pazzoide *m/f*

welcome ['welkəm] **1** *adj* benvenuto; *make s.o. ~* accogliere bene qu; *you're ~!* prego!; *you're ~ to try some* serviti pure **2** *n also fig* accoglienza *f* **3** *v/t guests etc* accogliere; *fig: decision etc* rallegrarsi di; *she ~s a challenge* apprezza le sfide

weld [weld] saldare

welfare ['welfeə(r)] bene *m*;

welfare check *Am* sussidio *m* di disoccupazione; **welfare state** stato *m* sociale; **welfare worker** assistente *m/f* sociale

well[1] [wel] *n for water, oil* pozzo *m*

well[2] [wel] **1** *adv* bene; *~ done!* bravo!; *as ~ (too)* anche; *as ~ as in addition to* oltre a; *it's just as ~ you told me* hai fatto bene a dirmelo; *very ~ acknowledging order* benissimo; *reluctantly agreeing* va bene; *~, ~! surprise* bene!; *~...! uncertainty, thinking* beh ... **2** *adj*: *be ~* stare bene; *feel ~* sentirsi bene; *get ~ soon!* guarisci presto!

well-'balanced equilibrato; **well-behaved** educato; **well-being** benessere *m*; **well-done** *meat* ben cotto; **well-dressed** ben vestito; **well-earned** meritato; **well-heeled** F danaroso; **well-informed** ben informato; **well-known** famoso; **well-meaning** spinto da buone intenzioni

wellness benessere *m*, wellness *m*

well-off benestante; **well-timed** tempestivo

Welsh [welʃ] **1** *adj* gallese **2** *n language* gallese *m*; *the ~* i gallesi

west [west] **1** *n* ovest *m*, occidente *m*; *the West* POL l'Occidente **2** *adj* occidentale **3** *adv travel* verso ovest; **~ of** a ovest di; **westerly** occidentale; **western 1** *adj* occidentale; **Western** occidentale **2** *n* (film) Western *m inv*; **Westerner** occidentale *m/f*; **westernized** occidentalizzato; **West Indian 1** *adj* delle Indie Occidentali **2** *n* nativo *m* delle Indie Occidentali; **West Indies:** *the* **~** le Indie Occidentali; **westward** verso ovest

wet [wet] bagnato; (rainy) piovoso; **~ paint** as sign vernice fresca; **wet suit** *for diving* muta *f*

whack [wæk] **1** *n* F (blow) colpo *m* **2** *v/t* F colpire; **whacked** F stanco morto

whale [weɪl] balena *f*

wharf [wɔːf] *n* banchina *f*

what [wɒt] **1** *pron* (che) cosa; **~ is that?** (che) cos'è?; **~ is it?** (what do you want) (che) cosa c'è?; **~?** cosa?; **it's not ~ I meant** non è ciò che volevo dire; **~ about some dinner?** e se mangiassimo qualcosa?; **~ for?** (why) perché? **2** *adj* che *inv*, quale; **~ colour is the car?** di che colore è la macchina? **3** *adv*: **~ a brilliant idea!** che bella idea!; **whatever: I'll do ~ you want** farò (tutto) quello che vuoi; **~ I do, it'll be a probem** qualsiasi cosa faccia, ci saranno problemi;

~ people say qualunque cosa dica la gente; **~ gave you that idea?** cosa mai te lo ha fatto pensare?; **ok, ~** F va bene, come vuoi / volete

wheat [wiːt] grano *m*, frumento *m*

wheel [wiːl] ruota *f*; (steering **~**) volante *m*

'wheelchair sedia *f* a rotelle; **wheel clamp** ceppo *m* bloccaruote

wheeze [wiːz] ansimare

when [wen] quando; **whenever** (each time) ogni volta che; *regardless of when* in qualunque momento

where [weə(r)] dove; **this is ~ I used to live** io abitavo qui; **whereabouts 1** *adv* dove **2** *npl:* **know s.o.'s ~** sapere dove si trova qu; **whereas 1** *conj* mentre; **wherever 1** *conj* ovunque; **~ you go** dovunque tu vada **2** *adv* dove; **~ can he be?** dove sarà mai?

whet [wet] *appetite* stuzzicare

whether ['weðə(r)] se

which [wɪtʃ] **1** *adj* quale; **~ one is yours?** qual è il tuo? **2** *pron interrogative* quale; *relative* che; **the car ~ ...** la macchina che ...; **on / in ~** su / in cui; **whichever 1** *adj* qualunque **2** *pron* quello che *m*, quella che *f*; **~ of the methods** qualunque metodo

whiff [wɪf]: **catch a ~ of** sentire

while [waɪl] **1** *conj* mentre; (*although*) benché (+ *subj*) **2** *n*: **a long ~ ago** molto tempo fa; **wait a long ~** aspettare molto *or* lungo; **for a ~** per un po'; **in a ~** fra poco

whim [wɪm] capriccio *m*

whimper ['wɪmpə(r)] gemere; *of animal* mugolare

whine [waɪn] *of dog* guaire; F (*complain*) piagnucolare

whip [wɪp] **1** *n* frusta *f* **2** *v/t* (*beat*) sbattere; *cream* montare; F (*defeat*) stracciare F

'whirlpool *in river* mulinello *m*; *for relaxation* vasca *f* per idromassaggio

whisk [wɪsk] **1** *n* frusta *f*; *mechanical* frullino *m* **2** *v/t eggs* frullare

whisky, *Am* **whiskey** ['wɪskɪ] whisky *m inv*

whisper ['wɪspə(r)] bisbigliare

whistle ['wɪsl] **1** *n sound* fischio *m*; *device* fischietto *m* **2** *v/i* fischiare **3** *v/t* fischiettare

white [waɪt] **1** *n* bianco *m*; *person* bianco *m*, -a *f* **2** *adj* bianco; **go ~** sbiancare (in viso); **white coffee** caffè *m inv* con latte *or* panna; **white-collar worker** impiegato *m*, -a *f*; **White House** Casa *f* Bianca; **white lie** bugia *f* innocente; **whitewash 1** *n* calce *f*; *fig* copertura *f* **2** *v/t* imbiancare(con calce); **white wine** vino *m* bianco

whittle ['wɪtl] *wood* intagliare
◆ **whittle down** ridurre

whizzkid ['wɪzkɪd] F mago *m*, -a *f*

who [huː] *interrogative* chi; *relative* che; **the man ~ I was talking to** l'uomo con cui parlavo; *whoever* chiunque; (*interrogative*) chi mai; **~ can that be?** chi sarà mai?

whole [həʊl] **1** *adj* intero; **the ~ town** tutta la città; **two hours / days** tutte due ore / giorni; **it's a ~ lot easier** è molto più facile **2** *n* tutto *m*; **the ~ of the United States** tutti gli Stati Uniti; **on the ~** nel complesso; **whole-hearted** senza riserve; **wholemeal bread** pane *m* integrale; **wholesale** all'ingrosso; *fig* in massa; **wholesaler** grossista *m/f*; **wholesome** sano; **wholly** completamente

whom [huːm] *fml* chi; **to / for ~** a cui

whore [hɔː(r)] puttana *f*

whose [huːz] *interrogative* di chi; *relative* il / la cui; **~ is this?** di chi è questo?; **a man ~ wife …** un uomo la cui moglie …

why [waɪ] perché; **the reason ~** il motivo per cui

wicked ['wɪkɪd] (*evil*) malvagio; (*mischievous*) malizioso; P (*great*) grande

wicker ['wɪkə(r)] di vimini

wicket ['wɪkɪt] *Br* SP porta *f*;

Am in station, bank etc porta
f

wide [waɪd] largo; *experience*
vasto; *range* ampio; **be 12
metres** ∼ essere largo 12 metri; **widely** used, known larga-
mente; **widen 1** *v/t* allargare **2** *v/i* allargarsi; **wide-
open** spalancato; **wide-
ranging** di largo respiro;
widespread diffuso

widow ['wɪdəʊ] vedova *f*;
widower vedovo *m*

width [wɪdθ] larghezza *f*; *of
fabric* altezza *f*

wield [wiːld] *weapon* brandire; *power* esercitare

wife [waɪf] moglie *f*

wig [wɪg] parrucca *f*

wiggle ['wɪgl] *loose screw etc*
muovere; ∼ **one's hips** an-
cheggiare

wild [waɪld] **1** *adj animal, flowers* selvatico; *teenager, party*
scatenato; *scheme* folle; *applause* fragoroso; **be** ∼ **about
...** (*keen on*) andare pazzo
per ...; **go** ∼ impazzire; (*become angry*) andare su tut-
te le furie **2** *n:* **the** ∼**s** le zone
sperdute

wilderness ['wɪldənɪs] deserto *m*; *fig: garden etc* giungla *f*

'wildlife fauna *f*

wilful ['wɪlfəl] *person* ostinato; *action* intenzionale

will[1] [wɪl] *n* LAW testamento
m

will[2] [wɪl] *n* (*willpower*) volontà *f inv*

will[3] [wɪl] *v/aux:* **I** ∼ **let you
know tomorrow** ti farò sa-
pere entro domani; **the car
won't start** la macchina
non parte; ∼ **you tell her that
...?** dille che ...; ∼ **you have
some more tea?** vuoi del-
l'altro tè?; ∼ **you stop that!**
smettila!

wilful *Am* ☞ **wilful**

willing ['wɪlɪŋ] disponibile;
are you ∼ **to pay more?**
sei disposto a pagare di
più?; **willingly** volentieri;
willingness disponibilità *f*;
willpower forza *f* di volontà

willy-nilly [wɪlɪ'nɪlɪ] (*at random*) a casaccio

wilt [wɪlt] *of plant* appassire

wily ['waɪlɪ] astuto

wimp [wɪmp] F pappamolle
m/f

win [wɪn] **1** *n* vittoria *f* **2** *v/t &
v/i* vincere

wince [wɪns] fare una smorfia

wind[1] [wɪnd] *n* vento *m*; (*flat-
ulence*) aria *f*

wind[2] [waɪnd] **1** *v/i of path,
stream* snodarsi; *of plant* av-
volgersi **2** *v/t* avvolgere

◆ **wind up 1** *v/t clock* caricare; *car window* tirar su;
speech concludere; *affairs,
company* chiudere **2** *v/i:*
wind up in hospital finire
in ospedale

'wind-bag F trombone *m*;
windfall *fig* colpo *m* di fortuna

winding ['waɪndɪŋ] tortuoso

627

with

window ['wɪndəʊ] *also* COM-
PUT finestra *f*; *of shop* vetrina *f*; *of car, train* finestrino
m; **in the ∼** *of shop* in vetrina;
∼-shop: go ∼ping guardare le
vetrine; **windowsill** davanzale *m*; **windscreen wiper**
tergicristallo *m*; **windscreen**, *Am* **windshield** parabrezza *m inv*; **windsurfer**
windsurfista *m/f*; *board*
windsurf *m inv*; **windsurfing**
windsurf *m*; **windy** ventoso;
it's getting ∼ si sta alzando il
vento

wine [waɪn] vino *m*; **wine
glass** bicchiere *m* da vino;
wine merchant *company*
azienda *f* vinicola; *individual*
vinaio *m*, -a *f*; **wine cellar**
cantina *f*; **wine list** lista *f*
dei vini; **winery** *Am* vigneto
m

wing [wɪŋ] *also* SP ala *f*; *of car*
parafango *m*; **wingspan**
apertura *f* alare

wink [wɪŋk] *of person* strizzare gli occhi; **∼ at s.o.** fare
l'occhiolino a qu

winner ['wɪnə(r)] vincitore *m*,
-trice *f*; **winning** vincente;
winning post traguardo *m*;
winnings vincita *fsg*

winter ['wɪntə(r)] inverno *m*;
winter sports sport *m* invernali; **wintry** invernale

wipe [waɪp] *(dry)* asciugare;

(clean) pulire; *tape* cancellare; **wiper** MOT tergicristallo
m

wire ['waɪə(r)] filo *m* di ferro;
ELEC filo *m* elettrico; **wiring**
ELEC impianto *m* elettrico; **wi-
ry** *person* dal fisico asciutto

wisdom ['wɪzdəm] saggezza
f; **wisdom tooth** dente *m*
del giudizio

wise [waɪz] saggio; **wisecrack** F spiritosaggine *f*;
wisely *act* saggiamente

wish [wɪʃ] **1** *n* desiderio *m*;
best ∼es for birthday etc tanti auguri; *as greetings* cordiali
saluti **2** *v/t* volere; **∼ s.o. well**
fare tanti auguri a qu
♦ **wish for** desiderare

wisp [wɪsp] *of hair* ciocca *f*; *of
smoke* filo *m*

wistful ['wɪstfʊl] malinconico; **wistfully** malinconica-
mente

wit [wɪt] *(humour)* spirito *m*;
person persona *f* di spirito;
be at one's ∼s' end non sapere più che fare; **keep
one's ∼s about one** non perdere la testa

witch [wɪtʃ] strega *f*; **witch-
hunt** *fig* caccia *f* alle stre-
ghe

with [wɪð] *con*; *(cause)* di;
shiver ∼ fear tremare di paura; **a girl ∼ blue eyes** una
ragazza dagli *o* con gli occhi
azzurri; **I'm staying with my
uncle** sto da mio zio; **are**

withdraw

you ~ me? (*do you understand*) mi segui?; **~ no money** senza soldi

with'draw 1 *v/t* ritirare; *money from bank* prelevare **2** *v/i* ritirarsi; **withdrawal** ritiro *m*; *of money* prelievo *m*; **withdrawal symptoms** sindrome *f* da astinenza; **withdrawn** *person* chiuso

wither ['wɪðə(r)] seccare

with'hold *information* nascondere; *consent* rifiutare; *payment* trattenere

with'in (*inside*) dentro; *in expressions of time* nel giro di, entro; *in expressions of distance* a meno di

with'out senza; **~ you / him** senza (di) te / lui; **~ looking** senza guardare

with'stand resistere a

witness ['wɪtnɪs] **1** *n* testimone *m/f* **2** *v/t* essere testimone di; *signature* attestare l'autenticità di

witticism ['wɪtɪsɪzm] arguzia *f*; **witty** arguto

wobble ['wɒbl] *of person* vacillare; *of object* traballare; **wobbly** *person* vacillante; *object* traballante; *voice, hand* tremante

wolf [wʊlf] **1** *n animal* lupo *m* **2** *v/t*: **~ (down)** divorare

woman ['wʊmən] donna *f*; **womanizer** donnaiolo *m*; **womanly** femminile

womb [wuːm] utero *m*

women [wɪmɪn] *pl* ☞ **woman**;

women's lib movimento *m* di liberazione della donna

wonder ['wʌndə(r)] **1** *n* (*amazement*), *of science etc* meraviglia *f*; **no ~!** non mi stupisce!; **it's a ~ that ...** è incredibile che ... **2** *v/i* domandarsi; **I ~ if you could help** mi chiedevo se potessi aiutarmi; **wonderful** stupendo; **wonderfully** (*extremely*) estremamente

won't [wəʊnt] ☞ **will not**

wood [wʊd] legno *m*; *for fire* legna *f*; (*forest*) bosco *m*; **wooded** boscoso; **wooden** *made of wood* di legno; **woodpecker** picchio *m*; **woodwork** *parts made of wood* strutture *fpl* in legno; *activity* lavorazione *f* del legno

wool [wʊl] lana *f*; **woollen**, *Am* **woolen 1** *adj* di lana **2** *n* indumento *m* di lana

word [wɜːd] **1** *n* parola *f*; (*news*) notizie *fpl*; **have ~s** (*argue*) litigare; **have a ~ with s.o.** parlare con qu **2** *v/t article, letter* formulare; **word processor** word processor *m inv*

work [wɜːk] **1** *n* lavoro *m*; **out of ~** disoccupato **2** *v/i of person* lavorare; *study* studiare; *of machine*, (*succeed*) funzionare

◆ **work out 1** *v/t problem* capire; *solution* trovare **2** *v/i at gym* fare ginnastica; *of rela-*

tionship etc funzionare

workable ['wɜːkəbl] *solution* realizzabile; **workaholic** F stacanovista *m/f*; **workday** *hours of work* giornata *f* lavorativa; *not a holiday* giorno *m* feriale; **worker** lavoratore *m*, -trice *f*; **workforce** forza *f* lavoro; **work hours** orario *m* di lavoro; **working class** classe *f* operaia; **working-class** operaio *m*; **working hours** → **workhours**; **workload** carico *m* di lavoro; **workman** operaio *m*; **workmanlike** professionale; **workmanship** fattura *f*; **work of art** opera *f* d'arte; **workout** allenamento *m*; **work permit** permesso *m* di lavoro; **workshop** laboratorio *m*; *for mechanic* officina *f*; *(seminar)* workshop *m inv*

world ['wɜːld] mondo *m*; *out of this ~* F fantastico; **world-class** di livello internazionale; **World Cup** mondiali *mpl* (di calcio); **world-famous** di fama mondiale; **worldly** *goods* materiale; *not spiritual* terreno; *power* temporale; *person* mondano; **world record** record *m inv* mondiale; **world war** guerra *f* mondiale; **worldwide 1** *adj* mondiale **2** *adv* a livello mondiale

worn-'out *shoes, carpet* logoro; *person* esausto

worried ['wʌrɪd] preoccupato; **worry 1** *n* preoccupazione *f* **2** *v/t* preoccupare; *(upset)* turbare **3** *v/i* proccuparsi; **worrying** preoccupante

worse [wɜːs] **1** *adj* peggiore; *things will get ~* le cose peggioreranno **2** *adv* peggio; **worsen** peggiorare

worship ['wɜːʃɪp] **1** *n* culto *m* **2** *v/t* venerare; *fig* adorare

worst [wɜːst] **1** *adj* peggiore **2** *adv* peggio **3** *n*: *the ~* il peggio; *if the ~ comes to the ~* nel peggiore dei casi; **worst-case scenario**: *the ~* la peggiore delle ipotesi

worth [wɜːθ] **1** *adj*: *be ~* valere; *it's ~ reading* vale la pena leggerlo; *be ~ it* valerne la pena **2** *n* valore *m*; **worthwhile** *cause* lodevole; *be ~ (worth the effort, worth doing)* valere la pena

worthy ['wɜːðɪ] degno; *cause* lodevole; *be ~ of (deserve)* meritare

would [wʊd]: *I ~ help if I could* ti aiuterei se potessi; *~ you like to go to the cinema?*; *~ you tell her that …?* le dica che …; *~ you close the door?* le dispiace chiudere la porta?

wound [wuːnd] **1** *n* ferita *f* **2** *v/t* ferire

wow [waʊ] wow

wrap [ræp] *gift* incartare; *(wind, cover)* avvolgere;

wrapper incarto *m*; **wrapping** involucro *m*; **wrapping paper** carta *f* da regalo

wrath [rɒθ] ira *f*

wreath [ri:θ] corona *f*

wreck [rek] **1** *n* of ship relitto *m*; *of car* carcassa *f*; **be a nervous ~** sentirsi un rottame **2** *v/t ship* far naufragare; *car* demolire; *plans, marriage* distruggere; **wreckage** of *car, plane* rottami *mpl*; *of marriage, career* brandelli *mpl*; **wrecker** *Am truck* carro *m* attrezzi

wrench [rentʃ] **1** *n tool* chiave *f* inglese **2** *v/t (pull)* strappare

wrestle [ˈresl] fare la lotta; **wrestler** lottatore *m*, -trice *f*; **wrestling** lotta *f* libera

wriggle [ˈrɪgl] *(squirm)* dimenarsi; *along the ground* strisciare

wrinkle [ˈrɪŋkl] *in skin* ruga *f*; *in clothes* grinza *f*

wrist [rɪst] polso *m*; **wristwatch** orologio *m* da polso

write [raɪt] scrivere; *cheque* fare

◆ **write down** annotare, scrivere

◆ **write off** *debt* cancellare; *car* distruggere

writer [ˈraɪtə(r)] autore *m*, -trice *f*; *professional* scrittore *m*, -trice *f*; **write-up** F recensione *f*

writhe [raɪð] contorcersi

writing [ˈraɪtɪŋ] *as career* scrivere *m*; *(hand-writing)* scrittura *f*; *(words)* scritta *f*; *(script)* scritto *m*; **in ~** per iscritto; **writing paper** carta *f* da lettere

wrong [rɒŋ] **1** *adj* sbagliato; **be ~** *of person* sbagliare, avere torto; *of answer, morally* essere sbagliato; **get the ~ train** sbagliare treno; **what's ~?** cosa c'è?; **there is something ~ with the car** la macchina ha qualcosa che non va **2** *adv* in modo sbagliato; **go ~** *of person* sbagliare; *of marriage, plan etc* fallire **3** *n immoral action* torto *m*; *immorality* male *m*; **be in the ~** avere torto; **wrongful** illegale; **wrongly** erroneamente; **wrong number** numero *m* sbagliato

wry [raɪ] beffardo

X

xenophobia [zenəʊˈfəʊbɪə] xenofobia *f*

X-ray [ˈeksreɪ] **1** *n* radiografia *f* **2** *v/t* radiografare

Y

yacht [jɒt] *for pleasure* yacht *m inv*; *for racing* imbarcazione *f* da diporto; **yachting** navigazione *f* da diporto

Yank [jæŋk] F yankee *m inv*

yank [jæŋk] dare uno strattone a

yard¹ [jɑːd] *of prison, institution etc* cortile *m*; *for storage* deposito *m* all'aperto; *Am behind house* giardino *m*; (*l')anno*

yard² [jɑːd] *measurement* iarda *f*

'yardstick *fig* metro *m*

yarn [jɑːn] (*thread*) filato *m*; F *story* racconto *m*

yawn [jɔːn] **1** *n* sbadiglio *m* **2** *v/i* sbadigliare

year [jɪə(r)] anno *m*; *be six ~s old* avere sei anni; **yearly 1** *adj* annuale **2** *adv* annualmente; *twice ~* due volte (al)l'anno

yeast [jiːst] lievito *m*

yell [jel] **1** *n* urlo *m* **2** *v/t & v/i* urlare

yellow ['jeləʊ] giallo; **yellow pages®** pagine *fpl* gialle

yelp [jelp] **1** *n* guaito *m* **2** *v/i* guaire

yes [jes] sì; *say ~* dire di sì; **yes-man** *pej* yes man *m inv*

yesterday ['jestədeɪ] ieri; *the day before ~* l'altro ieri

yet [jet] **1** *adv* finora; *the fast-*

est ~ il più veloce finora; *as ~ up to now* per ora; *have you finished ~?* (non) hai (ancora) finito?; *he hasn't arrived ~* non è ancora arrivato; *~ bigger* ancora più grande **2** *conj* eppure

yield [jiːld] **1** *n from fields etc* raccolto *m*; *from investment* rendita *f* **2** *v/t fruit, harvest* dare, produrre; *interest* fruttare **3** *v/i* (*give way*) cedere

yob [jɒb] P teppista *m/f*

yoga ['jəʊgə] yoga *m*

yoghurt ['jɒgət] yogurt *m inv*

yolk [jəʊk] tuorlo *m*

you [juː] ◇ *subject: familiar singular* tu; *familiar polite singular* lei; *do ~ know him?* lo conosci / conosce / conoscete? ◇ *direct object: familiar singular* ti; *familiar polite plural* vi; *polite singular* la; *he knows ~* ti / vi / la conosce ◇ *indirect object: familiar singular* ti; *when two pronouns are used* te; *familiar polite plural* vi; *when two pronouns are used* ve; *polite singular* le; *did he talk to ~?* ti / vi / le ha parlato?; *I told ~* te / ve l'ho detto, glielo ho detto ◇ *after prep: familiar singular* te; *familiar polite plural* voi; *polite singular* lei;

this is for* ~** questo è per te / voi / lei ◇ *impersonal:* **~ *have to pay si deve pagare; ***fruit is good for* ~** la frutta fa bene

young [jʌŋ] giovane; **youngster** ragazzo *m*, -a *f*

your [jɔː(r)], **yours** [jɔːz] *familiar singular* il tuo *m*, la tua *f*, i tuoi *mpl*, le tue *fpl*; *polite singular* il suo *m*, la sua *f*, i suoi *mpl*, le sue *fpl*; *familiar & polite plural* il vostro *m*, la vostra *f*, i vostri *mpl*, le vostre *fpl*; ***your brother*** tuo / suo / vostro fratello; ***a friend of yours*** un tuo / suo / vostro amico; ***yours ... at end of letter*** saluti ...; ***yours sincerely*** distinti saluti

your'self ti; *reflexive polite* si; *emphatic* tu stesso *m*, tu stessa *f*; *emphatic polite* lei stesso *m*, lei stessa *f*; ***did you hurt* ~?** ti sei / si è fatto male?

your'selves vi; *emphatic* voi stessi *mpl*, voi stesse *fpl*; ***did you hurt* ~?** vi siete fatti male?

youth [juːθ] gioventù *f*; (*young man*) ragazzo *m*; (*young people*) giovani *mpl*; **youth club** circolo *m* giovanile; **youthful** giovanile; *ideas* giovane

yo-yo ['jəʊjəʊ] yo-yo *m inv*; **yo-yo dieting** dieta *f* yo-yo

yuppie ['jʌpɪ] F yuppie *m/f inv*

Z

zap [zæp] F COMPUT (*delete*) cancellare; (*kill*) annientare; (*hit*) colpire; (*send*) mandare

zeal [ziːl] zelo *m*

zebra ['zebrə] zebra *f*; **zebra crossing** strisce *fpl* pedonali

zero ['zɪərəʊ] zero *m*

zest [zest] (*enthusiasm*) gusto *m*; (*peel*) scorza *f*

zigzag ['zɪgzæg] **1** *n* zigzag *m inv* **2** *v/i* zigzagare

zilch [zɪltʃ] F un bel niente

zip [zɪp] (*cerniera f*) lampo *f*

◆ **zip up** *dress, jacket* allacciare; COMPUT zippare

'zip code *Am* codice *m* di avviamento postale; **zipper** *Am* (cerniera *f*) lampo *f*

zit [zɪt] *Am* brufolo *m*

zone [zəʊn] zona *f*

zonked [zɒŋkt] P (*exhausted*) stanco morto

zoo [zuː] zoo *m inv*

zoology [zuːˈɒlədʒɪ] zoologia *f*

zoom lens [zuːm] zoom *m inv*

zucchini [zuːˈkiːnɪ] *Am* zucchino *m*

Verbi irregolari inglesi

Si riportano le tre forme principali di ciascun verbo: infinito, passato, participio passato.

arise – arose – arisen

awake – awoke – awoken, awaked

be (am, is, are) – was (were) – been

bear – bore – borne

beat – beat – beaten

become – became – become

begin – began – begun

bend – bent – bent

bet – bet, betted – bet, betted

bid – bid – bid

bind – bound – bound

bite – bit – bitten

bleed – bled – bled

blow – blew – blown

break – broke – broken

breed – bred – bred

bring – brought – brought

broadcast – broadcast – broadcast

build – built – built

burn – burnt, burned – burnt, burned

burst – burst – burst

buy – bought – bought

cast – cast – cast

catch – caught – caught

choose – chose – chosen

cling – clung – clung

come – came – come

cost (v/i) – cost – cost

creep – crept – crept

cut – cut – cut

deal – dealt – dealt

dig – dug – dug

dive – dived, dove [dəʊv] (1) – dived

do – did – done

draw – drew – drawn

dream – dreamt, dreamed – dreamt, dreamed

drink – drank – drunk

drive – drove – driven

eat – ate – eaten

fall – fell – fallen

feed – fed – fed

feel – felt – felt

fight – fought – fought

find – found – found

flee – fled – fled

fling – flung – flung

fly – flew – flown

forbid – forbad(e) – forbidden

forecast – forecast(ed) – forecast(ed)

forget – forgot – forgotten

forgive – forgave – forgiven

freeze – froze – frozen

get – got – got, gotten (2)

give – gave – given

go – went – gone

grind – ground – ground

grow – grew – grown

hang – hung, hanged – hung, hanged (3)

have – had – had

hear – heard – heard

hide – hid – hidden

hit – hit – hit

hold – held – held

hurt – hurt – hurt

keep – kept – kept

kneel – knelt, kneeled – knelt, kneeled

know – knew – known

lay – laid – laid

lead – led – led

lean – leaned, leant – leaned, leant (4)

leap – leaped, leapt – leaped, leapt (4)

learn – learned, learnt – learned, learnt (4)

leave – left – left

lend – lent – lent

let – let – let

lie – lay – lain

light – lighted, lit – lighted, lit

lose – lost – lost

make – made – made

mean – meant – meant

meet – met – met

mow – mowed – mowed, mown

pay – paid – paid

plead – pleaded, pled – pleaded, pled (5)

prove – proved – proved, proven

put – put – put

quit – quit(ted) – quit(ted)

read – read [red] – read [red]

ride – rode – ridden

ring – rang – rung

rise – rose – risen

run – ran – run

saw – sawed – sawn, sawed

say – said – said

see – saw – seen

seek – sought – sought

sell – sold – sold

send – sent – sent

set – set – set

sew – sewed – sewed, sewn

shake – shook – shaken

shed – shed – shed

shine – shone – shone

shit – shit(ted), shat – shit(ted), shat

shoot – shot – shot

show – showed – shown

shrink – shrank – shrunk

shut – shut – shut

sing – sang – sung

sink – sank – sunk

sit – sat – sat

slay – slew – slain

sleep – slept – slept

slide – slid – slid

sling – slung – slung

slit – slit – slit

smell – smelt, smelled – smelt, smelled (4)

sow – sowed – sown, sowed

speak – spoke – spoken

speed – sped, speeded – sped, speeded

spell – spelt, spelled – spelt, spelled (4)

spend – spent – spent

spill – spilt, spilled – spilt, spilled (4)

spin – spun – spun

spit – spat – spat

split – split – split

spoil – spoiled, spoilt – spoiled, spoilt (4)

spread – spread – spread

spring – sprang, sprung – sprung

stand – stood – stood

steal – stole – stolen

stick – stuck – stuck

sting – stung – stung

stink – stunk, stank – stunk

stride – strode – stridden

strike – struck – struck

swear – swore – sworn

sweep – swept – swept

swell – swelled – swollen

swim – swam – swum

swing – swung – swung

take – took – taken

teach – taught – taught

tear – tore – torn

636

tell – told – told

think – thought –
thought

thrive – throve – thriven,
thrived (6)

throw – threw – thrown

thrust – thrust – thrust

tread – trod – trodden

wake – woke, waked –
woken, waked

wear – wore – worn

weave – wove – woven (7)

weep – wept – wept

win – won – won

wind – wound – wound

write – wrote – written

1) **dove** non si usa nell'inglese britannico
2) **gotten** non si usa nell'inglese britannico
3) **hung** per i quadri, ma **hanged** per gli omicidi
4) l'inglese parlato in America ha di solito la forma
   in **-ed**
5) **pled** si usa nell'inglese parlato in America e in
   Scozia
6) **thrived** è la forma più comune
7) ma **weaved** quando significa *zigzagare*

Numbers / Numerali

Cardinal Numbers / Numerali cardinali

0	*zero*	zero
1	*one*	uno
2	*two*	due
3	*three*	tre
4	*four*	quattro
5	*five*	cinque
6	*six*	sei
7	*seven*	sette
8	*eight*	otto
9	*nine*	nove
10	*ten*	dieci
11	*eleven*	undici
12	*twelve*	dodici
13	*thirteen*	tredici
14	*fourteen*	quattordici
15	*fifteen*	quindici
16	*sixteen*	sedici
17	*seventeen*	diciassette
18	*eighteen*	diciotto
19	*nineteen*	diciannove
20	*twenty*	venti
21	*twenty-one*	ventuno
22	*twenty-two*	ventidue
23	*twenty-three*	ventitrè
28	*twenty-eight*	ventotto
29	*twenty-nine*	ventinove
30	*thirty*	trenta

40	*forty* quaranta
50	*fifty* cinquanta
60	*sixty* sessanta
70	*seventy* settanta
80	*eighty* ottanta
100	*one/a hundred* cento
101	*one/a hundred and one* centouno
102	*one/a hundred and two* centodue
200	*two hundred* duecento
201	*two hundred and one* duecentouno
300	*three hundred* trecento
400	*four hundred* quattrocento
500	*five hundred* cinquecento
600	*six hundred* seicento
700	*seven hundred* settecento
800	*eight hundred* ottocento
900	*nine hundred* novecento
1,000	*one/a thousand* mille
1,001	*one/a thousand and one* milleuno/mille e uno
2,000	*two thousand* duemila
3,000	*three thousand* tremila
4,000	*four thousand* quattromila
5,000	*five thousand* cinquemila
10,000	*ten thousand* diecimila
100,000	*one/a hundred thousand* centomila
1,000,000	*one/a million* un milione
2,000,000	*two million* due milioni
1,000,000,000	*one/a billion* un miliardo

Note: i) 1,000,000 (in inglese) = 1.000.000 (in Italian)

ii) 1.25 (one point two five) = 1,25 (uno virgola venticinque)

Ordinal numbers / Numerali ordinali

1st	*first*	1°	il primo, la prima
2nd	*second*	2°	secondo
3rd	*third*	3°	terzo
4th	*fourth*	4°	quarto
5th	*fifth*	5°	quinto
6th	*sixth*	6°	sesto
7th	*seventh*	7°	settimo
8th	*eighth*	8°	ottavo
9th	*ninth*	9°	nono
10th	*tenth*	10°	decimo
11th	*eleventh*	11°	undicesimo
12th	*twelfth*	12°	dodicesimo
13th	*thirteenth*	13°	tredicesimo
14th	*fourteenth*	14°	quattordicesimo
15th	*fifteenth*	15°	quindicesimo
16th	*sixteenth*	16°	sedicesimo
17th	*seventeenth*	17°	diciassettesimo
18th	*eighteenth*	18°	diciottesimo
19th	*nineteenth*	19°	diciannovesimo
20th	*twentieth*	20°	ventesimo
21st	*twenty-first*	21°	ventunesimo
22nd	*twenty-second*	22°	ventiduesimo
30th	*thirtieth*	30°	trentesimo
40th	*fortieth*	40°	quarantesimo
50th	*fiftieth*	50°	cinquantesimo
60th	*sixtieth*	60°	sessantesimo

70th	*seventieth*	70°	settantesimo
80th	*eightieth*	80°	ottantesimo
90th	*ninetieth*	90°	novantesimo
100th	*hundredth*	100°	centesimo
101st	*hundred and first*	101°	centunesimo
103rd	*hundred and third*	103°	centotreesimo
200th	*two hundredth*	200°	duecentesimo
1000th	*thousandth*	1000°	millesimo
1001st	*thousand and first*	1001°	millesimo primo
2000th	*two thousandth*	2000°	duemillesimo
1,000,000th	*millionth*	1.000.000°	milionesimo

Note: Italian ordinal numbers are ordinary adjectives and consequently must agree:

> **her 13th granddaughter**
> la sua tredicesima nipote

Dates / Date

1996	nineteen ninety-six	*millenovecentonovantasei*
2005	two thousand and five	*duemilacinque*

the 10/11th of November,
Am **November 10/11 (ten/eleven)**
il dieci/undici novembre

the first of March, *Am* **March 1 (first)**
il primo marzo